Blue & Gray
Diplomacy

The University of North Carolina Press
Chapel Hill

The Littlefield History of the Civil War Era

GARY W. GALLAGHER AND T. MICHAEL PARRISH, editors

Supported by the

LITTLEFIELD FUND FOR SOUTHERN HISTORY,

UNIVERSITY OF TEXAS LIBRARIES

HOWARD JONES

Blue & Gray
Diplomacy

A HISTORY OF

Union and Confederate Foreign Relations

Designed by Courtney Leigh Baker
Set in Minion Pro by Rebecca Evans
Manufactured in the United States of America

The paper in this book meets the guidelines for permanence
and durability of the Committee on Production Guidelines
for Book Longevity of the Council on Library Resources.

The University of North Carolina Press has been
a member of the Green Press Initiative since 2003.

Library of Congress Cataloging-in-Publication Data
Jones, Howard, 1940–
Blue and gray diplomacy : a history of Union and Confederate
foreign relations / Howard Jones. — 1st ed.
p. cm. — (Littlefield history of the Civil War era)
Includes bibliographical references and index.
ISBN 978-0-8078-3349-0 (cloth : alk. paper)
1. United States — Foreign relations — 1861–1865. 2. Confederate
States of America — Foreign relations. 3. United States — Foreign
relations — Great Britain. 4. Great Britain — Foreign relations —
United States. 5. United States — Foreign relations — France.
6. France — Foreign relations — United States. 7. Confederate States
of America — Foreign relations — Great Britain. 8. Great Britain —
Foreign relations — Confederate States of America. 9. Confederate
States of America — Foreign relations — France. 10. France —
Foreign relations — Confederate States of America. I. Title.
E469.J563 2010
973.7′2 — dc22   2009031564
14 13 12 11 10   5 4 3 2 1

FOR

Maurice, Bob, & Frank

Under the favor of Divine Providence, we hope to perpetuate the principles of our revolutionary fathers.—PRESIDENT JEFFERSON DAVIS, *Inaugural Address, February 18, 1861*

The Union of these States is perpetual. . . . Plainly,

the central idea of secession, is the essence

of anarchy.—PRESIDENT ABRAHAM LINCOLN,

Inaugural Address, March 4, 1861

Contents

Illustrations

Acknowledgments

I want to thank the many good people at the University of North Carolina Press for making this work possible. David Perry as editor-in-chief remained a paragon of patience, always providing warm, encouraging, and gracious support throughout the publication process. Ron Maner headed the editorial project with his usual friendly and accommodating manner. Zach Read made the final preparations for the manuscript to go to press.

How fortunate I am to have profited from a close association with all those who have facilitated this contribution to "The Littlefield History of the Civil War Era." Some years ago the series editors, Gary W. Gallagher and T. Michael Parrish, encouraged me to write a volume on the diplomacy of the war. Gary read the manuscript on its submission, applying his scholarly expertise to the work and improving its quality. Michael meanwhile regularly inquired about my progress when we met at conferences, offering to help in any way possible. Martin Crawford served as an outside reader for the manuscript, thankfully revealing his identity and thereby allowing me to express the deepest appreciation for his numerous superb suggestions since incorporated into the final product. Stevie Champion provided excellent copyediting, making many recommendations that improved the manuscript. Immensely helpful were the archivists and staffs of several research institutions, including the Library of Congress, National Archives, Massachusetts Historical Society, British Library, Public Record Office, University of Southampton, and Bodleian Library of Oxford University in England. Pat Causey in the Interlibrary Loan office at the University of Alabama was particularly adept at securing elusive materials. Dean Robert Olin approved a sabbatical at a critical juncture in my writing. Two colleagues here at the University of Alabama, George C. Rable and Lawrence F. Kohl, shared their rich knowledge of the Civil War and provided constant encouragement. My close friend Donald A. Rakestraw drew my attention to many key sources and clarified my thoughts by asking the right questions.

I am dedicating this volume to my two mentors at Indiana University, Maurice G. Baxter and Robert H. Ferrell, and to longtime friend Frank J. Merli, who has passed on but remains a constant influence on my thinking on the Civil War. Some years ago, I met Maurice and Bob in Kokomo, Indiana, where I interviewed for an Eli Lilly Fellowship in American History at Indiana University that launched my college teaching career. Maurice, too, is deceased but also had a lasting impact on my professional life. Bob stands as a model for all those fortunate to have worked with him. Author or editor of more than fifty books, he has always maintained a work regimen unmatched by anyone, high ethical standards that are unimpeachable, and a deep humility that is enviable. From Frank I first grasped the importance of the international dimension of the Civil War—that this tragic story of our divided nation involved diplomats and negotiations as well as generals and battles. Frank and I profited immeasurably from what became known among history graduate students at Indiana University as the "Ferrell treatment" in our writings, but more than that we learned the sacred responsibility of relating the nation's history to readers along with the importance of maintaining a gentle, kindly disposition both inside and outside the classroom.

My dedication would not be complete, however, without thanking Frank's loving wife Margaret for sharing the "Merli Archives" with me and thereby helping to strengthen this work.

And, finally, my family has again provided the chief reason for my spending so much time in solitude. My partner in life and dearest friend, Mary Ann, has never complained about my long hours glaring into a computer; nor have my daughters Debbie and Shari failed to express interest in the current project, whatever that one may be. My hope is that the grandchildren—Tim, Ashley, and Lauren—will come to appreciate history as much as the rest of the family, including my late mom and dad.

If this book has any value, it is primarily due to the inspiration, friendship, support, and guidance of those mentioned above; any problems still on these pages are of my own making.

Northport, Alabama
Summer 2009

Blue & Gray
Diplomacy

Prologue

This horrible war, this terrible war, this wholly unnecessary war—these words were not mere rhetoric to contemporary Europeans who avidly followed the American Civil War and roundly denounced what they perceived as a blind rage propelling the vicious conflict. The sectional struggle had spun out of control, ultimately leading to more than 600,000 deaths and threatening to disable not only North America but also Atlantic commerce and thereby do irreparable harm to Europe. Trench warfare, cannon, long-range artillery, and rifled muskets; massive armies engaged in fierce hand-to-hand combat with guns, knives, and sabers; ironclad warships that made the Union navy seemingly invincible and the once-dominant British and French wooden fleets virtually obsolete—these were some of the killing features of this internecine fighting that had gone beyond the pale of so-called civilized warfare to appall onlookers both inside and outside the divided American republic.[1]

And so needless from the European perspective: The outcome was a fait accompli, most sage observers in London, Paris, and other continental capitals had asserted from the war's beginning. How could a stumbling Union subjugate the Confederacy, an aggregate of eleven states composed of millions of primarily Anglicized people fervently pushing for independence against a mongrelized northern majority? Almost three years into the war, Union secretary of state William H. Seward bitterly complained that British and French policy toward America still rested on the original assumption that the Union could not reconcile the South and that its independence was unavoidable. President Abraham Lincoln's insistence on preserving the Union had led to a mindless waste of blood and treasure; Confederate president Jefferson Davis's support for secession as the pathway to a new nation seemed irreversible. The republican experiment, long ridiculed by the Old World, had finally imploded, exposing the myriad weaknesses of a popular government now collapsing in anarchy.

To many Europeans, the breakup of the large and unwieldy republic had starkly revealed the inherent strife in a democracy that had degenerated into mob rule, insurrection, rebellion, and chaos—only to reappear as two vastly weakened American republics. Had not the American crisis combined with the political upheavals of the 1840s in Europe to signal the danger to stability and order in supporting democratic reforms in both Britain and France? At the war's outset, many British and French observers took sides and continued to do so throughout, but as the conflict ground on, increasing numbers became repulsed by its human and material destruction and simply wanted the hostilities to end, regardless of who won. Self-interest, of course, guided much of the Anglo-French reaction to the war, but often overlooked was a growing moral concern that weighed heavily on their responsibilities as world leaders. In both practical and moral terms, the British and the French thought the Union engaged in an unrealistic attempt to restore southerners to a nation now permanently ripped apart by secession and whose fighting threatened to inflict external collateral damage.

A great economic and security issue was at stake in America, Europeans believed, one that affected the key question in diplomacy of whether to recognize the Confederacy as a nation. The North American economy was a vital cog in the ocean trade, and the longer the fighting continued, the more other nations suffered from the commercial disruption of what had become an integrated Atlantic network. By the mid-nineteenth century, America and Europe had become the economic basis of an Atlantic commercial world that meshed finance with Union and Confederate foreign affairs to help shape the Blue and Gray diplomacy of the Civil War. Both northern grain and southern cotton had framed this new Atlantic economy, creating a unique relationship between the United States and England (and with France and other European countries, though on a lesser scale) that helped to smooth over difficulties. Economic interests had not allied with the Washington government in determining policy, but they ran in parallel if uneven paths. Especially significant was the series of financial connections that Americans made with European investors during the Civil War as both Union and Confederate agents sought large foreign loans. The Union repeatedly failed, largely because of the prevailing belief overseas that it could not win the war. And, except for the modest Erlanger loan of 1863, the Confederacy likewise stumbled because of the war's uncertainties, along with its use of cotton as leverage for extracting recognition rather than as collateral for loans that might have facilitated the battlefield victories so essential to winning recognition.[2]

The rising atrocities in the war, many British observers argued as the fighting drummed on, made it their duty as civilized Victorians to resolve the conflict. Starkly realistic engravings appeared in *Harper's Weekly* and *Frank Leslie's Illustrated Newspaper*, bringing the war into the homes of numerous contemporaries. Mathew Brady's photographs even more graphically introduced civilians to the war's realities by displaying the bodies in the grisly aftermath of battle. Neither Union nor Confederacy could convince outsiders of the righteousness of one cause over the other, making the fighting incomprehensible and therefore pointless. Both antagonists had denied at the war's beginning that slavery was the central issue, which made it difficult for those on the outside to determine why brother fought brother and who was right and who was wrong. Yet the war proved morbidly fascinating to those insulated from its touch by distance and water. Whether the British, the French, and other Europeans grasped what some writers have called the "culture of death," it had cast a long shadow over American events. Northerners and southerners had seemingly accepted dying on the battlefield as a part of life—a bloody medium through which they passed before entering the "heavenly country" to meet loved ones as a reward for exemplifying duty, honor, and love of country. Many of those fighting in the Civil War had already lived half or more of their expected life span of forty-five, and to die in glory on the battlefield meant to live in glory in heaven. Europeans, however, failed to realize how the promise of a heavenly afterlife drove up the level of destruction as much as death was a product of that destruction. Many observers dismissed the fighting as insane and considered every means possible to bring it to an end.[3]

This study focuses on Union and Confederate foreign relations during the Civil War from a European as well as an American perspective. Its central thrust is statecraft at the highest levels, with references to public opinion as it appeared to have impact on policy. The events recounted here break into two basic time frames, both highlighting the issue of foreign intervention: from the outbreak of the war in April 1861 through the fall of 1862, when the British took the lead in considering a mediation pointing to recognition of the Confederacy; and from the close of 1862 to the end of the war in April 1865, when the French emerged as the chief proponent of intervention based on an armistice and tied the question of recognition to their military presence in Mexico.

This intricate four-year story highlights numerous themes: the international dimension of the war; the Union's attempts to block the Confederacy from winning foreign recognition; the role of slavery in determining Anglo-French considerations of intervention; the influence of international law on diplomacy; the perils of European neutrality; the shadowy impact of Russia on almost every interventionist venture; the French military intervention in Mexico as a threat to the Western Hemisphere and to the Old World's balance of power; the mixture of reasons for European interest in the American war that ranged from self-interest to the humanitarian obligations of neutral, civilized nations to stop a war hurting them as well as the principal antagonists; the relationship of the Constitution and the Declaration of Independence to slavery and the Union; the evolving belief by Lincoln and others that the death of slavery and the horrendous shedding of blood in battle would bring a new birth of freedom; and, finally, the inability of Europeans to understand the Lincoln administration's devotion to Union and emphasis on the integrated nature of slavery to that Union, which led them to interpret the war as a senseless struggle between a Confederacy too large and populous for anyone to deny its independence and a Union too stubborn to admit to the futility of returning to its prewar position. Most of all, this work explores the horrible nature of a war that attracted outside involvement as much as it repelled it.

International law confirmed the Lincoln administration's argument against intervention as a violation of domestic affairs but permitted a loophole that boded ill for the Union and, therefore, boded well for the Confederacy. Other nations affected by the fighting had the right to make their good offices available in encouraging peace talks. If such an offer did not appeal to either warring party, the nations could act out of self-interest in deciding the merits of the case and, if the party adjudged to have justice on its side asked for help or accepted the offer, they could intervene with the purpose of ending that war for the general good. Once the European nations took this interventionist approach—whether by a mediation proposal, a call for an armistice, or the use of military force—they were expected to suggest peace terms.[4]

Yet this stipulation promised all kinds of problems—not only the necessity of understanding the war's causes before devising its solution, but, most notably, the danger of joining the fighting and widening the war. Neither Union nor Confederacy had been able to reconcile their differences and therefore went to war. How could outside nations better comprehend its causes and formulate a settlement? Would they have to resort to military action to stop the American conflict? More ominous was the Union's pledge to resist any form of intervention in what it termed a domestic conflict, even to waging war on the intruder. And who could guarantee against the interventionist powers falling out among themselves over the drafting of peace terms and, after ending the war, demanding compensation for damages sustained?

Both Union and Confederacy regarded any form of outside involvement in their affairs as a major step toward a foreign recognition that could decide the outcome of the war. Any intervention, the Union argued, constituted meddling in domestic matters and bestowed legitimacy on traitors subverting the U.S. Constitution and the republic based on the central governing ideas set out by the Founding Fathers. The Confederacy countered that the Union had become oppressive, forcing southerners into secession as the initial step toward returning to the republic resting on the principles of self-government envisioned by the Founding Fathers. So serious was the threat of dissolution that Seward privately warned both England and France of war on the intruder; so serious was the Confederacy's attempt at nationhood that it was willing to fight for independence. Had not the resort to war showed irreconcilable differences between northerners and southerners? Did not both sides confront a heightened danger from the outside, particularly as the powers involved in the American contest grew in number and perhaps pondered the gains they might make after bringing the war to a close?

The Union rejected (just as the Confederacy welcomed) all types of intervention as an impetus to southern nationhood. Making good offices available for peace talks afforded the Confederacy a status it did not deserve—whether or not the outside nation participated in the discussions. Mediation, though on the surface an innocent move that imposed no binding decisions, implied the existence of two entities and therefore constituted a major step toward recognition. Arbitration posed an even greater danger, for it required the formulation of a plan of settlement between the American antagonists, its decisions *were* binding, and it left the way open for broader action if the war hurt neutrals. An armistice likewise was dangerous, for even though its purpose was to permit the opposing camps to consider the wisdom of restarting the war, it also provided time for both sides to refuel for renewed fighting. Neutrality seemed innocuous because it dictated equal treatment to both antagonists. Yet in addition to elevating the Confederacy's stature, the policy could lead to intervention. According to international law, a declaration of neutrality automatically classified both Union and Confederacy as belligerents entitled to negotiate foreign loans; purchase supplies, including arms; conduct searches and seize contraband at sea; enter foreign ports; license privateers; impose blockades; and command moral support and respect for its flag.[5] Furthermore, it was virtually impossible for outside nations to be truly neutral because any action beneficial to one belligerent was automatically detrimental to the other. Most important, however, the doctrine of neutrality included the right of interested nations to intervene when the ongoing war threatened them with collateral damage.

Recognition of the Confederacy had great potential for securing southern independence, particularly in the initial eighteen months of the war when the Union was reeling from poor military leadership and battlefield performance. The Confederacy could sign treaties—economic and military—with foreign governments and enjoy all the rights of a nation. Britain, France, and other nations realized there was a razor-thin line between Confederate status as a "traitor" and as an independent nation—much like the margin separating day from night. The rebellious people must demonstrate freedom from the parent state, maintain order at home, deal responsibly with other nations, and show promise of permanence and stability. Perhaps Secretary of State John Quincy Adams said it best in 1818 when writing President James Monroe that a people deserved recognition "when independence is established as a matter of fact so as to leave the chances of the opposite party to recover their dominion utterly desperate." Five years later, Adams warned the American minister to Colombia that Spain could declare war on the United States if it recognized Latin American independence before its time.[6] The principle seemed applicable to the 1860s or any other time period: Premature recognition of Confederate independence justified the Union's declaring war on the intervening nations. To act precipitously made them virtual allies and thus participants in a war determining Confederate independence. Thus the Confederacy's chief frustration became clear: how to achieve a recognition that depended on victory on the battlefield when that victory on the battlefield depended on foreign assistance stemming from recognition.[7]

There are numerous excellent studies of various aspects of Union and Confederate relations with the European powers, but no one has taken on the daunting task of integrating their diplomacy with that of both England and France—and to some extent Russia.[8] The closest attempt at this broad-scale synthesis of wartime diplomacy came some years ago, when David P. Crook published two books, the second a shortened version of the first: *The North, the South, and the Powers, 1861–1865* (1974) and *Diplomacy during the American Civil War* (1975). It would have been easier (and faster) for me to write an account of Union diplomacy that bookended with Frank L. Owsley's longtime standard work on Confederate diplomacy—*King Cotton*

Diplomacy: Foreign Relations of the Confederate States of America (1959). But the two stories would have run parallel to each other without intersecting and could not fully convey the complicated underpinnings of a transatlantic diplomacy that had a major impact on the war's outcome. The following history is therefore an analysis of Union-Confederate foreign relations with Britain and France and not an account of either the Union's or the Confederacy's diplomacy with the two major European powers. The reason is simple: Events of this period did not happen that way. They occurred in neither an orderly nor a predictable manner, but in a chaotic and concurrent fashion posing problems for diplomats that matched those confronting the generals and the politicians in speed and complexity.

Making sense of the intricacies of the international dimension of the Civil War has been a difficult and yet highly rewarding experience. To make this rendition as faithful as possible to the way it transpired, I have relied on a narrative style aimed at relating the story as its participants saw it play out around them. This approach therefore permitted a look at the intersection of events, both domestic and foreign, that do not become evident in a topical setting. Thus my challenge was to provide a clear summation of the major issues, events, and personalities without obscuring the disorderly and complicated manner in which these matters presented themselves to policy-makers in Richmond, Washington, London, and Paris. If the ensuing story is readable and understandable while maintaining its complexity, the book will have fulfilled my purpose.

The Civil War imperiled the Union as Lincoln thought it was in 1861 and soon wished it to be, whereas Davis believed it confirmed the Union formed in Philadelphia in 1787 but since undermined by Washington's tyrannical rule. Lincoln's determination to preserve the Union as he envisioned it was no idle charge; nor was Davis's resolve to restore the original Union that he perceived as created by the Founding Fathers. Lincoln regarded his task as a sacred trust bequeathed to later generations and now belonging to him; Davis thought his responsibility just as precious—to leave a Union that was beyond repair and start anew.

Both northerners and southerners believed themselves morally and legally correct—which left civil war as the only reconciler and thus a certain impetus to the worst kind of fighting and a predictable catalyst to foreign intervention.

CHAPTER 1

Republic in Peril

No, you dare not make war on cotton.
No power on earth dares make war upon it. Cotton is King!
—SENATOR JAMES H. HAMMOND of South Carolina, March 4, 1858

The firm and universal conviction here is, that Great Britain,
France, and Russia will acknowledge us at once in the family of nations.
—SENATOR THOMAS R. R. COBB of Georgia, February 21, 1861

What possible chance can the South have?
—CALEB CUSHING of New York, late April 1861

Supporters of the Confederate States of America regarded themselves as the true progenitors of the republic and their secession from the Union as a return to the world of limited national government envisioned by the Founding Fathers. In his Inaugural Address of February 1861 delivered in Montgomery, Alabama, President Jefferson Davis declared: "We have assembled to usher into existence the Permanent Government of the Confederate States. Through this instrumentality, under the favor of Divine Providence, we hope to perpetuate the principles of our revolutionary fathers. . . . Therefore we are in arms to renew such sacrifices as our fathers made to the holy cause of constitutional liberty." Thus from the southern perspective, the Union was in peril, but *not* from the secessionists; rather, the danger came from a big government in Washington that had subverted the original Union's emphasis on states' rights into a northern tyranny. Southerners sought to unseat the northern power brokers who had devised an oppressive central government that had for too long trampled on the minority South by violating its right to manage its own affairs, whether tariffs, internal improvements, or slavery. The Union, as southerners saw it, had become an overly centralized governing mechanism run by a repressive northern majority. The agreement underlying the Philadelphia compact of 1787 had been broken; secession was the only remedy.[1]

Shortly after the Civil War erupted in April 1861, President Abraham Lincoln asserted that his central objective was to preserve the Union based on a strong federal government created by the Founding Fathers. Secession therefore posed its most severe challenge because the South's attempt to stand on its own would destroy that Union. "The right of revolution," he wrote, "is never a legal right. The very term implies the breaking, and not the abiding by, organic law. At most, it is a moral right, when exercised for a morally justifiable cause." Otherwise, revolution is "simply a wicked exercise of physical power." In his Inaugural Address of March 1861, he declared: "I hold, that in contemplation of universal law, and of the Constitution, the Union of these States is perpetual." No government ever included "a provision in its organic law for its own termination." Secession was "the essence of anarchy."[2]

On many levels Davis and Lincoln waged a war for the very survival of the republic as each president defined the vision of the Founding Fathers. Well known were Davis's advantages in military leadership from the beginning of the war; also well known was Lincoln's frustrating search for a general who could rally a massive yet ineptly led war machine to victory. Lesser known were the two presidents' struggles on an international level—Davis's efforts to win diplomatic recognition of the Confederacy and hence the right to negotiate military and commercial treaties, and Lincoln's attempts to ward off a foreign intervention in the war that could have led to southern alliances undermining the Union. Whereas Davis sought to maintain the status quo—a southern civilization built on slavery and dependent on the Constitution's guarantees of property—Lincoln soon tried to construct an improved America based on ending slavery and adhering to the natural rights doctrine that underlay the Declaration of Independence. Davis considered the war a struggle for liberty, which he defined as the absence of governmental interference in state, local, and personal affairs—including the right to own slaves. In contrast, Lincoln came to regard the war as the chief means for forming a more perfect Union emanating from a new birth of freedom that fellow white northerners interpreted as the political and economic freedoms enjoyed under the Constitution but that he expanded to include the death of slavery and the Old South. Davis had such a legalistic mind that he thought the European powers relied on international law only when it served their self-interest; Lincoln was highly pragmatic, knowing he had to convince the foreign governments that it was not in their best interest to intervene in America's affairs. Davis appealed to Europe to acknowledge southern independence as a righteous cause and welcome the Confederacy into the community of nations; Lincoln insisted that the conflict in America was a purely domestic concern and warned that any outside interference meant war with the Union.[3]

Both sets of arguments were morally and legally defensible and thereby right, making the two opposing leaders' positions irreconcilable and, combined with the vendettalike infighting that often comes in a familial contest, ensuring a massive bloodletting that would stop only when both sides were exhausted.

From the outbreak of the Civil War, the Confederacy's chief objective in foreign affairs was to secure diplomatic recognition from England first and then other European powers. Loans, a morale boost, military and economic assistance, perhaps even an alliance—everything was possible once the Confederacy won recognition as a nation. Shortly after the creation of its government in Montgomery in February 1861, the South sent three commissioners abroad, assigned to Great Britain, France, Russia, and Belgium, but always looking first to London. By no means did they expect British sympathy for their cause; not only were the British cold practitioners of a foreign policy grounded in self-interest, but also they opposed slavery, having outlawed it within their empire in 1833 and then hosting World Antislavery Conventions in London during the early 1840s. Furthermore, strong ties had developed between antislavery advocates in England and the United States. True, the British were not as staunchly antislavery as earlier, but they still supported abolition. Some of the more radical abolitionists, in fact, argued that southern independence would bring an end to slavery by making the region vulnerable to the influence of adjoining free territories. Southerners assumed that British sympathies would initially go to the Union and prepared to argue that the sectional struggle did not focus on slavery but on their drive for independence against an oppressive northern majority.[4]

Confederate leaders appealed to British self-interest by reminding their Atlantic cousins that mutual economic needs based on cotton tied them together. Thus "King Cotton Diplomacy" held the key to Confederate recognition and hence victory in the war. In 1858 Senator James H. Hammond of South Carolina insisted that if the South withheld cotton, "England would topple headlong and carry the whole civilized world with her, save the South. No, you dare not make war on cotton. No power on earth dares make war upon it. Cotton is King!" On December 12, 1860, just eight days before South Carolina announced secession, Senator Louis T. Wigfall of Texas confidently asserted in that august chamber: "I say that cotton is King, and that he waves his scepter not only over these thirty-three States, but over the island of Great Britain and over continental Europe." A leading southerner assured a colleague that cotton was "the king who can shake the jewels in the crown of Queen Victoria."[5]

The South appeared correct in assuming the overweening importance of cotton at home and abroad. The 1850s had been a time of great profit for cotton growers. The North, many southerners believed, needed the product so badly (about a fifth of the South's cotton went to markets above the Mason-Dixon Line by 1860) that it had no choice but to accept secession. As for the British, they consumed three times that amount and must extend recognition to the Confederacy in an effort to maintain the flow. If the North resisted secession, the British would act out of self-interest and intervene on behalf of the South. Up to 85 percent of the product they imported came from the South. A great portion of Britain's economic base—the textile industry and its five million workers—depended on southern cotton.[6]

The South's only concern, which it quickly dismissed, was that the British might seek other sources of cotton. Their Cotton Supply Association had already engaged in a search around the globe. But secession's supporters argued persuasively that the British had failed to increase their draw from India, which had offered the greatest potential alternative source. The South's cotton was king and hence its chief means for attaining recognition. The *Richmond Whig* boasted that the Confederacy had "its hand on the mane of the British lion, and that beast, so formidable to all the rest of the world, must crouch at her bidding."[7]

By every economic measure, King Cotton Diplomacy should have won British recognition of southern independence. Cotton provided the breath of life for the Confederacy, and it surely was the lifeblood of the British textile industry. American cotton was purer and cheaper than that from India. In the two decades preceding the Civil War, British manufacturers turned to the South for most of their cotton supply. France and other nations in Europe were proportionately as reliant, although none of their production figures matched those in England. The British recognized the danger in becoming overly dependent on the South, but they also knew that Indian cotton lacked comparable quality. The latter, according to the *Economist* in April 1861, "yields more waste, that is, loses more in the process of spinning" because of the dirt and other particles gathered in the lint. "The Surat [Indian cotton] when cleaned, though of a richer color than the bulk of the American, is always much shorter in staple or fibre; the result of which is that in order to make it into equally strong yarn it requires to be harder twisted. . . . The consequence is that the same machinery will give out from 10 to 20% more American yarn than Surat yarn." American cotton "spins better, does not break so easily and cause delay in work." The cloth from Surat cotton "does not take the finish so well, and is apt, after washing, to look poor and thin. . . . In all respects (except color) the Indian cotton is an inferior article."[8]

By 1860, more than four million people of about twenty-one million in the British Isles owed their livelihood to the cotton mills. The *Times* of London later warned that "so nearly are our interests intertwined with America that civil war in the States means destitution in Lancashire." Soon afterward it proclaimed that "the destiny of the world hangs on a thread—never did so much depend on a mere flock of down!" A writer in *De Bow's Review* declared that a loss of southern cotton to England would lead to "the most disastrous political results—if not a revolution." President Davis and his advisers were so confident in the leverage of cotton, according to his wife, that "foreign recognition was looked forward to as an assured fact." They counted on "the stringency of the English cotton market, and the suspension of the manufactories, to send up a ground-swell from the English operatives, that would compel recognition." The mere threat of a cotton cutoff, the South concluded, would force England to intervene in the war.[9]

The Confederacy, however, had overestimated the importance of cotton to diplomacy. The implicit though heavy-handed threat of extortion by slaveholders almost immediately alienated the British. In mid-January 1861 the *Saturday Review* in London warned that "it will be national suicide if we do not strain every nerve to emancipate ourselves from moral servitude to a community of slaveowners." Later that month, the *Economist* likewise blasted King Cotton Diplomacy. How could southerners think that British merchants would want their government to "interfere in a struggle between the Federal Union and revolted states, and interfere on the side of those they deem willfully and fearfully in the wrong, simply for the sake of buying their cotton at a cheaper rate?" Furthermore, in a strange twist of fate, the region's economic successes hurt its drive for recognition. Southern farmers had produced bumper crops in the two seasons preceding secession winter, saddling both England and France with an enormous surplus of cotton. In early February 1861, the *Economist* issued a warning sign, denying the need for cotton and asserting that "the stock of cotton in our ports has never been so large as now." But no Confederate official carefully examined the King Cotton premise. Moreover, southern strategists had overlooked the concurrent surge in British reliance on northern grains and foodstuffs during the 1850s, which had received impetus from their repeal of the Corn Laws in 1846. Britain depended on wheat imports from the Union that would predictably increase because of lower costs than in Europe. The need for wheat joined with other concerns to severely weaken King Cotton Diplomacy.[10]

The Confederacy nonetheless counted on cotton to overcome all obstacles to recognition, including British antipathy toward slavery, and fell under the illusion that success would come as a matter of course. In reality, southerners had no other viable economic options than King Cotton Diplomacy. Their greatest assets lay in slaves and real estate, neither of which was easily convertible into money. Cotton as collateral for loans, of course, carried little weight in light of England and France's huge surplus that would probably last into the fall of 1862. In addition, the Confederacy never officially implemented a cotton embargo. Davis did not support such a measure, despite authorization by some states, and Confederate leaders put an export tax on cotton and tacitly approved holding back supplies. The Confederacy's almost total dependence on outside manufactures dictated a turn to Europe for war necessities and other goods—a need hampered by its small fleet of ten viable merchant vessels. It was no surprise that on numerous occasions southern spokesmen ignored these hard realities and referred to either justice or divine intervention in asserting the surety of diplomatic recognition. A young southern patriot proudly chided the *Times*'s military correspondent in the United States, William H. Russell: "The Yankees ain't such cussed fools as to think they can come here and whip us, let alone the British." "Why, what have the British got to do with it?" asked Russell. "They are bound to take our part," came the reply without hesitation and perhaps with a smirk. "If they don't we'll just give them a hint about cotton, and that will set matters right."[11]

To facilitate recognition, southerners tried to make slavery a nonissue. Louisiana secessionists told the British consul in New Orleans how much they wanted European support and, not by coincidence, took the occasion to offer assurances that their new government opposed reopening the African slave trade. Alabama and Georgia soon joined Louisiana in denouncing this "infamous traffic," as did southern leaders then gathered in Montgomery to form their new government. Indeed, the Montgomery convention opening in early February 1861 required the Confederate Congress to outlaw the practice.[12]

British contemporaries remained skeptical about the South's efforts to diminish the importance of the peculiar institution. The great majority of workers hated slavery and favored the Union because of its emphasis on democracy and free labor. The *Economist* accused the South of lacking "scruples" and "morality" in supporting a system "strangely warped by slavery." British Conservatives were torn by their opposition to the democracy associated with the Union and by their hesitation to support a southern struggle for nationalism that rested on a secession doctrine conducive to the same government disorder underlying the recent revolutions on the Continent. Despite the oft-argued claim that the so-called aristocratic South appealed to British Conservatives, they had found in their visits to the region that it was backward and based on slavery, whereas the North was industrialized, based on free labor, and more advanced. The highly heralded cities of Richmond and Charleston, in particular, were stricken by poverty and decay and greatly disappointed British travelers. Most of the British press considered slavery the root of America's troubles. *Punch* in London made its position clear when it sneered at the Confederacy as "Slaveownia."[13]

The French likewise thought slavery lay at the heart of the sectional division in America. Numerous French journals joined Liberals and the public in considering Harriet Beecher Stowe's best-selling novel *Uncle Tom's Cabin* an accurate portrayal of slavery's inhumanity in the South and a sure stimulus to servile war. The Liberal opposition party perhaps seized on the slavery issue for domestic political purposes, but these same domestic issues could have great impact on the French government's decision on recognizing the Confederacy. According to Paul Pecquet du Bellet, a New Orleans attorney who had lived in Paris for several years, "War meant Emancipation." Even the few "neutral" editors in France blasted the "*Southern Cannibals*" who feasted on young blacks for breakfast.[14]

The future of recognition rested largely in the hands of President Davis, of Mississippi, who appeared to personify everything the Old South romanticized itself to be. His administrative, political, and military background suggested wisdom in his choice as chief executive. After graduating from West Point, he fought heroically in the Mexican War, served creditably as secretary of war under President Franklin Pierce, and amassed an enviable record as a U.S. senator. But the image belied the reality. Davis was a distinguished and knowledgeable southern statesman, but beneath the admirable exterior ran an innate, cold aloofness that soon manifested itself in a stubborn, self-righteous attitude rarely tolerant of either criticism or advice. Furthermore, he was so provincial that his experience in foreign policy was limited to his regular reading of the *Times*. Like his colleagues, however, he firmly believed that cotton would win the allegiance of Britain and other commercial and manufacturing nations.[15]

Davis joined his cohorts in maintaining that Britain (and France) would recognize the Confederacy within a short time. In Stevenson, Alabama, he glowingly proclaimed his belief that the Border States of Missouri, Kentucky, Maryland, and Delaware (slave states that had not yet decided whether to secede) would soon join the Confederacy and that "England will recognize us." Consequently, he ignored those few southerners who understood the delicate nature of the recognition issue and cajoled him to appoint a commission of qualified diplomats. Instead, he agreed with those others who boastfully cited both public and private sources that certified the imminence of British and French recognition. In addition to encouraging remarks by the British press emerged other positive signs. John Slidell, former Louisiana senator, wrote a friend that the French minister in Washington, Henri Mercier, felt certain that Emperor Napoleon III would extend recognition and that if the Union government passed a protective tariff, England would surely follow. The most telling fact was that 93 percent of French cotton imports came from the South.[16]

Armed with these assurances, Davis failed to exercise sound judgment in selecting fiery secessionist William L. Yancey of Alabama to head the three-member commission to Europe. Indeed, the probability is that Davis's dislike for Yancey provided the impetus for sending him out of the country. Whatever the reasoning behind the decision, it was a mistake. Yancey had a history of violent behavior that included killing his wife's uncle over a point of honor. He had been instrumental in writing the Alabama platform in 1848 that fitted nicely with the *Dred Scott* decision of 1857 in asserting the right of Americans to take their property—that is, slaves—anywhere in the Union and that became the chief divisive element in the collapse of the Democratic Party in 1860. Yancey then capitalized his defense of slavery by ardently advocating a reopened Atlantic slave trade. As for secession, he proved so viscerally supportive of southern independence that moderates had distanced themselves from the man billed by the *New York Tribune* as the "most precipitate of precipitators." The British consul in Charleston, Robert Bunch, dismissed Yancey as "impulsive, erratic and hot-headed; a rabid Secessionist, a favourer of a revival of the Slave-Trade, and a 'filibuster' of the extremist type of 'manifest destiny.'"[17]

Yancey's volatile defense of slavery and unquestioned oratorical talents did not appeal to all southerners. Diarist Mary Chesnut recognized that even elegantly worded bombast did not guarantee success in diplomacy. "Who wants eloquence?" she indignantly demanded. "We want somebody who can hold his tongue. . . . No stump speeches will be possible, but only a little quiet conversation with slow, solid, commonsense people who begin to suspect as soon as any flourish of trumpets meet their ear." Yancey, she disdainfully concluded, was "a common creature" from a "shabby set" of men.[18]

Davis demonstrated a comparable lack of thought in appointing Pierre A. Rost of Louisiana and Ambrose D. Mann of Virginia to join Yancey. Rost, a former state congressman from Mississippi, had moved to Louisiana and later became a member of the state's supreme court. It quickly became clear that this elderly, soft-spoken gentleman's only qualifications in foreign affairs were his birth in France and his claim to speak the language. "Has the South no sons capable of representing your country?" indignantly asked one French noble of a Louisianan after hearing Rost struggle with his broken French. Mann, a native Virginian, had attended West Point before becoming disenchanted with the military. He then served as assistant secretary of state, only to resign during the mid-1850s to work for a stronger economic position for the South. His sole distinction, more than a few noted, lay in his mastery of platitudes. Bunch was not even that charitable. Mann was the "son of a bankrupt grocer in the Eastern part of Virginia" and had "no special merit of any description." Rost, Bunch concluded with fewer words, was a nobody.[19]

Thus Yancey was the dominant figure among three less-than-impressive commissioners, even though Mann had proven ability in commercial matters and was personally close to Davis. Indeed, the president of the Confederacy effusively praised Mann for "all the accomplishments of a trained diplomat" who had "united every Christian virtue" into a "perfect man." Rost, meanwhile, failed to make an impression except, perhaps, by his obscurity and weak French language skills.[20] Yancey's liabilities, however, far outweighed any assets possessed by his two colleagues. In the meantime, a small band of anxious Confederate spokesmen preferred not to wait for the work of a commission: They sought to force British recognition of the Confederacy by levying an export duty on cotton and creating a shortage overseas. Late in February 1861, Thomas R. R. Cobb from Georgia presented the proposal to the Confederate Congress. A cotton embargo, he argued, "could soon place, not only the United States, but many of the European powers, under the necessity of electing between such a recognition of our independence, as we may require, or domestic convulsions at home." But Cobb's efforts aroused little support among the majority of congressmen who considered it prudent to await a decision from London rather than alienate its leaders before they had had a chance to act. Even Cobb saw the wisdom in patience. To his wife, he wrote, "The firm and universal conviction here is, that Great Britain, France, and Russia will acknowledge us at once in the family of nations."[21]

Everything seemed to be falling into place for the Confederacy, capped on March 2, 1861, when the U.S. Congress raised import duties with the Morrill Tariff. Many northerners warned that the rise in costs would anger the British—and at precisely the time the Confederacy sought recognition. In the debate over the bill, New York congressman Daniel E. Sickles lashed out at his colleagues for provoking the mother country when "all eyes are turned upon the policy which will control European States—whether it is to be the policy of non-interference, or the policy of recognition."[22]

In actuality, the higher tariff did not help the Confederacy. When the British learned that Yancey headed the Confederate commission, they turned whatever negative thoughts they had about the tariff to indignation over having to receive what the *Times* termed three "American fanatics" who mistakenly thought that in Britain "the coarsest self-interest overrules every consideration." Confederate talk of an export tax on cotton further angered the British. The *Times* directed its ire at both Union and Confederate officials who, "agreeing on nothing else, are quite unanimous on two things: first, the avoidance of direct taxes on themselves, and secondly, the desire to fix upon England the expenses of their inglorious and unnatural combat."[23]

The Confederacy meanwhile experimented with other ways to achieve European recognition. Less than a week after Cobb's abortive call for a cotton embargo, the Confederacy opened its coastal trade and attempted to establish direct commercial and communication links with Europe. Shortly afterward, the Montgomery Congress followed Cobb's recommendation to direct its three commissioners to negotiate treaties with those nations interested in guaranteeing reciprocal copyright protection to all authors. Such an arrangement, Cobb confidently wrote his wife, would "operate strongly to bring the literary world, especially of Great Britain, to sympathize with us against the Yankee literary pirates."[24]

The Confederacy's unfounded optimism clouded the reality in its hopes for British recognition. As a veteran of the diplomatic wars, the London government would not take such an important step without considering its impact on the British national interest. Sentiment must never be the guiding principle in international relations; nor could the threat of copyright violations gear the nation into militant action. Cotton likewise failed to provide the leverage for forcing recognition: The British (and French) had such a

First Confederate cabinet. *Seated, left to right:* Attorney General Judah P. Benjamin, Secretary of the Navy Stephen R. Mallory, Vice President Alexander H. Stephens, President Jefferson Davis, Postmaster General John H. Reagan, Secretary of State Robert Toombs. *Standing, left to right:* Secretary of the Treasury Christopher G. Memminger, Secretary of War Leroy P. Walker. (Courtesy of the Library of Congress)

huge backlog on hand that a southern embargo posed no threat to either European nation's security. The only path to recognition lay in the Confederacy's proving itself a nation not subject to a forced restoration of the Union. Herein lay the Confederacy's central dilemma: Recognition had the potential of assuring independence, but the Confederacy had to convince the European governments of its independence before they would consider recognition. In other words, the Confederacy came to fear that it would get no help from abroad until it required none.

On March 16 Confederate secretary of state Robert Toombs formally provided the commissioners with instructions that further demonstrated the Confederacy's inability to find the leverage needed to extract recognition. They were to assure their host governments that southerners had not violated "obligations of allegiance" in withdrawing from the Union and now sought the "friendly recognition" due any people "capable of self-government" and possessing "the power to maintain their independence." They were also to negotiate treaties of amity and commerce. The commissioners carried with them, among other items, an essay on states' rights theory and a lecture on the importance of cotton. Inexplicably, they had no directives to seek either foreign assistance or other treaties beyond those assuring commerce and friendship. Toombs presumably considered recognition so much a matter of right that he saw no need to make a formal request. In a mild use of cotton as leverage with England, he instructed the commissioners to make a "delicate allusion" to "the condition to which the British realm would be reduced if the supply of our staple should suddenly fail or even be considerably diminished." Robert Barnwell Rhett, an outspoken proponent of reopening the international slave trade and highly influential in shaping the views of the *Charleston Mercury* (edited by his son), advocated a strong economic alliance with England. To Yancey he indignantly snorted: "Sir, you have no business in Europe. You carry no argument which Europe cares to hear. . . . My counsel to you as a friend is, if you value your reputation, to stay at home or to go prepared to conciliate Europe by irresistible proffers of trade."[25]

Rhett's advice, no matter how realistic, never guided the commission's work. Most southerners continued to believe that recognition by Britain and other European powers would automatically take place because of cotton's importance to the Old World's textile industry. Negotiations seemed unnecessary because they could lead only to bothersome obligations incurred by the Confederacy. Such an attitude provides a classic example of how overconfidence can breed naïveté.

The Confederacy raised more false hopes after Lincoln's inauguration as president in March 1861. Repeatedly compared in an unfavorable light to Davis, Lincoln emerged in southern imagery as seriously deficient in physical appearance, dress, intellect, and administrative experience when placed alongside those much heralded qualities of the stately looking president from Mississippi. But what Lincoln lacked in image, he amply possessed in humility, character, sincerity, warmth, wisdom, and sheer common sense. Furthermore, he had a realistic view of the sectional crisis. The tall and gangly Illinois lawyer and former state and national congressman fitted uncomfortably with most of his political colleagues who, throughout their public careers, had drifted behind the shifting winds of political change. Lincoln too had swayed from one side to the other on some issues, but never on the central principle now at stake—the sanctity of the Union. Its preservation became his guiding principle in all deliberations, both domestic and foreign.

Lincoln admitted to having no knowledge in foreign affairs but humbly expressed his willingness to take advice. Unlike his counterpart from the Confederacy, Lincoln did not subscribe to the *Times* of London, and he was the first to acknowledge that he was a novice in international matters. "I don't

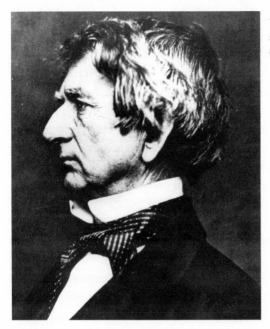

William H. Seward, U.S. secretary of state (Courtesy of the National Archives)

know anything about diplomacy," he confessed to a foreign emissary just before inauguration. "I will be apt to make blunders." Lincoln consequently relied heavily on his secretary of state, the cosmopolitan former governor of New York and recent rival for the Republican nomination for the presidency, the pugnacious and outspoken William H. Seward.[26]

Lincoln compensated for his inexperience in international relations by proving himself an innate and consummate diplomatist. What qualities he lacked in formal preparation, he possessed by his very nature. Lincoln was blessed with the essential virtues of a born diplomat: a calm and patient demeanor, a trusting yet careful and genteel temperament, unquestioned integrity, an interest in listening to advice and learning from those who disagreed with him, and a willingness to compromise on issues requiring no sacrifice of principles. Furthermore, he ingeniously related the role of foreign policy to his chief objective of preserving the Union. Stories are legend of his long hours into the night at the War Office, studying battle plans and maneuvers, agonizing over the human costs of both victory and defeat, and wondering what Providence had in store for a nation at war with itself. Not so well known were his many informal conversations with Seward about the dread of British recognition and how, given the precarious balance of the war on the battlefield, such a decision by London virtually assured calamity for the Union.

Lincoln's public focus on the domestic problems underlying the Civil War should not obscure his quiet, yet forceful role in foreign affairs. Most important, he grasped the intimate relationship between the two. Early in his administration, he underlined his intention to head the government in all matters. Seward's dispatches characteristically opened with his acknowledging the president's approval of their contents. Given Lincoln's reserved and nonassuming character, along with Seward's steadily growing respect for his superior, it should come as no surprise that the president became deeply involved in all subjects affecting the Union's welfare. He certainly remained abreast of the diplomatic issues that touched on British intervention in the war.

Seward's appointment as secretary of state testifies to Lincoln's capacity to rise above personal differences for the good of the larger cause. The New Yorker had been so bitter about losing the Republican Party's nomination to Lincoln that he had reconciled himself to a life of sullen political oblivion. But Lincoln recognized Seward's personal capabilities and highly respected position in the party and persuaded him to take the senior seat in the cabinet. Just two days before the inauguration, Seward accepted the appointment, immodestly muttering to his wife that the country needed him in these dire times because of the infinite ineptitude of the incoming president.

As a self-anointed prime minister of the new government, Seward intended to save the faltering country from its new leader by seizing control of both foreign and domestic affairs. He seemed capable. This short, thin man commanded attention in a crowd, even though his most noticeable physical features were his unkempt gray hair, floppy ears, big eyes rimmed by thick, bushy eyebrows, a pale and almost empty complexion, and a long beaked nose that cast a shadow over his recessed chin. But what he lacked in appearance, he made up in experience and, more often than not, a brash, intimidating behavior that he accented by sheer noise. Had he not served with distinction as a member of the Senate Foreign Relations Committee since 1857? Had he not twice traveled in Europe where, in 1859, he received a royal reception in Britain, albeit because of his expected ascendancy to the Executive Mansion? But he was outspoken and hot tempered, and, particularly after his aggressive role in the Alexander McLeod crisis of the 1840s, he gained the reputation in England of being an avowed Anglophobe who exploited anti-British feeling in America for his own political purposes. This reputation was not entirely undeserved. Britain, he once proclaimed in a calculated exaggeration, was "the greatest, the most grasping and the most rapacious" power in the world.[27]

Richard B. Lyons, British minister to the United States (Lord Newton, *Lord Lyons: A Record of British Diplomacy*, 2 vols. [London: Edward Arnold, 1913], 1:frontispiece)

The secretary of state soon took advantage of his fiery notoriety to pursue a dangerous strategy: warning the British and French that any form of interference in the American conflict meant war with the Union. Seward planted stories around Washington that he intended to *seek* a foreign war to cure the ills of secession by reuniting all Americans—northerners and southerners—under the flag.

The Confederacy found little support from the British minister to Washington, the calm and staid Richard B. Lyons, who had intended to wind down his career in peace but found himself thrust into the apex of a gathering storm in which his own country could play the decisive role. Lyons hated slavery as much as he respected the law and had therefore reacted unfavorably to secession. The British, he wrote his home office, must always oppose "intimate relations with a Confederacy formed on the avowed principle of perpetuating, if not extending, Slavery." Lyons had held this often-caricatured frontier post in Washington since 1858 without recording any mark of distinction more heralded than any upstanding Briton believed the obscure position deserved. Indeed, his appointment had drawn considerable criticism from Americans as further evidence of the British government's insulting refusal to send first-rate diplomats to the United States. Lyons, reserved almost to the point of reticence, acted well under pressure and, as matters became increasingly grim, rose to the occasion and won the respect of those around him. Privately, however, he dismissed most American leaders as petty politicians who continually shifted their positions according to the demands of the mob and did not have the vaguest understanding of right and wrong. But he proved remarkably adept in concealing these feelings. As Britain's chief official source of information in America, Lyons provided well-reasoned and thorough dispatches that carried special weight in London.[28]

At first, Lyons believed that Lincoln's secretary of state seemed determined to turn the British against the Union. Seward, Lyons declared with disgust, had made a career out of publicly displaying "insolence" toward the British. One contemporary ridiculed him as "an ogre fully resolved to eat all Englishmen raw."[29] But ever so gradually did Lyons realize that Seward was playing a game with the British (and French), a dangerous, high-stakes game to be sure in which foreign recognition of the Confederacy could mean the death of the Union.

Lyons's assessment of Seward was harsh but, in large part, purposely orchestrated by his American host. Admittedly, the secretary's lightning-rod demeanor did not fit the image of a studious and calm diplomatist, but he joined Lincoln in realizing that the central issue in this sectional conflict was the Union's safety and never wavered from its defense. His desperate type of diplomacy rested on war threats intended to convince the British that they should not even think about interfering in American affairs. He knew that the entire Union edifice could collapse if the British intervened and, in so doing, determine the outcome of the contest. Seward used his Anglophobic reputation to cultivate the image of a madman willing to go to war to prevent foreign recognition of the Confederacy. Whether he would follow through on his threats became a critical consideration for British policymakers. Such a provocative strategy seemed fitting in light of their refusal to offer assurances against recognizing the Confederacy and their decision to receive its commissioners, albeit on an unofficial basis.[30]

In actuality, European politics argued against British involvement in the American Civil War. The London ministry's endemic distrust of the French—in particular, the unpredictable and opportunistic Napoleon III—raised fear that its involvement in America or elsewhere would free him to engage in nefarious schemes wherever possible. Napoleon's interest in reestablishing French holdings on the Continent was legend; his ancestral loyalty drove him to restore a French Empire in the New World that would have the residual effect of enhancing his stature in the Old; his push for building a larger navy and broadening his involvement in the Mediterranean provided ample warning of an emerging challenge in maritime matters that England had long considered its special province. Then came reports in early 1861 of some form of private agreement between France and Russia that threatened to change the balance of power in Europe by healing the wounds of the Crimean War. British involvement in the American crisis could take place only at heavy risk to the empire.[31]

For both practical and legal reasons, then, the British ministry from the eve of southern secession exercised great care not to antagonize either side in the imminent conflict. As early as May 1860, Lyons had warned his superior in London, Foreign Secretary Lord John Russell, that among northerners "a Foreign war finds favour, as a remedy for intestine divisions." After Lincoln's election, Lyons emphasized that the ministry avoid "anything likely to give the Americans a pretext for quarreling with us." As for the Confederacy, Lyons declared, its leaders would probably "establish a low Tariff and throw themselves fraternally into our arms, if we let them." Still, it would be difficult to lay in the same bed with supporters of slavery who had arrogantly boasted of cotton's importance to Britain. Lyons admonished Russell to follow a policy of "caution and Watchfulness to avoid giving serious offence to either party."[32]

But there was a limit to the transgressions the British would bear before feeling compelled to act. They could not quietly accept the Union's recently announced intention to close Confederate ports because, Russell assured his minister in Washington, the move endangered British commerce and therefore had the potential of promoting recognition. Such port closures, insisted the White House, were municipal in jurisdiction and fell within the constitutional authority of the federal government in Washington. The British argued, however, that the action would be international in thrust and thus violate their maritime rights and insult their honor. Furthermore, a Union closure of southern ports would be illegal under international law—a move tantamount to a paper blockade. Port closures had no established procedural guidelines and were subject to abuse; they could force the British to recognize the Confederacy. Indeed, the Union's anticipated policy threatened to push the British and French together. Perhaps this was good, Lyons thought. Knowing that recognition could cause war with the United States, he considered Anglo-French cooperation a wise precautionary measure. He pointedly warned Seward that Union interference with British commerce would force a European involvement detrimental to northern interests.[33]

Lord John Russell,
British foreign secretary
(Courtesy of the Massachu-
setts Historical Society)

As Lyons had predicted, Seward's provocative policy soon drove the British and French together. At a dinner party in late March 1861, the secretary of state sternly advised his guests from the diplomatic corps that their countries' merchant vessels must not enter or leave a southern port without federal authorization. Lyons had earlier that same day alerted his home government to potential Union interference with British commerce, suggesting that "it certainly appeared that the most simple, if not the only way, would be to recognize the Southern Confederacy." That evening Seward engaged in a heated discussion of maritime rights with Lyons, Mercier, and Russian minister Edouard de Stoeckl, highlighted by the secretary's blunt challenge: "If one of your ships comes out of a Southern Port, without the Papers required by the laws of the United States, and is seized by one of our Cruisers and carried into New York and confiscated, we shall not make any compensation." Stoeckl, Lyons later reported, objected "good-humouredly" to this stance by contending that a blockade must be effective to be legal. But a port closure was not a blockade, Seward insisted. The Union's problems were domestic, meaning that its ships off the southern coast were following municipal law in collecting duties and enforcing customs laws. Lyons called this a thinly disguised paper blockade and warned that the United States's actions would leave other nations with the choice of either submitting to commercial violations or extending recognition to the Confederacy. If the United States interfered with British commerce, Lyons stressed, "I could not answer for what might happen." Such interference "placed Foreign Powers in the Dilemma of recognizing the Southern Confederation or of submitting to the interruption of this Commerce." Seward, by that time braced by whiskey and enveloped by his own cigar smoke, became "more and more violent and noisy," blasting such a policy with invectives that Lyons related would have been "more convenient not to have heard." For a moment Lyons lost his composure, just as provocatively apprising Seward that "we must have cotton and we shall have it!" To Russell in London, Lyons recommended that the ministry form a united front with France.[34]

The image of recklessness fostered by Seward became manifest less than a week later, when rumors of his war-making interest became fact, if only within the deepest recesses of the Lincoln government: On April 1 he handed the president a memorandum calling for war with Europe as a remedy for the threatening conflict in the United States. The administration, he wrote Lincoln, should demand explanations from both France and Spain for their recent interventionist activities in Mexico and Santo Domingo. If they failed to justify these acts, Seward asserted, Congress should declare war on both countries. "I neither seek to evade nor assume responsibility," he not so humbly noted.[35]

President Lincoln gave this memorandum the cold reception it deserved on this appropriately timed April Fool's Day. Already concerned about the threat of domestic conflict attracting external interference, he now saw his secretary of state actually *invite* outside trouble. A risky theory it was to expect Americans from both the Union and the Confederacy to rally around the flag against an alleged greater danger posed by the Old World. What if the Confederates stayed out of the ensuing foreign crisis and left the Union to fend on its own? Seward nonetheless believed Union sentiment so strong in the South that it only needed some cause to become active. Lincoln, however, refused to throw down the gauntlet to Europe and thereby have the Union fight two wars at once. Besides, he suspected Seward of using foreign interference in the New World as a ploy for his seizing control of the cabinet and the administration itself. The president ignored the memorandum, while making clear that if such action proved necessary, he would assume responsibility.[36]

That dangerous proposition aside, the Lincoln administration now confronted the serious challenge of convincing the British and others across the Atlantic that the conflagration threatening to break out over slavery did not concern slavery after all. This was the central political dilemma facing the president. Although personally detesting slavery, he had supported the Republican Party's platform during the presidential campaign of opposing only the expansion of slavery in the territories and focused instead on preserving the Union. Seward likewise disliked slavery without taking the abolitionist position and emphasized the Union above all. The Confederacy, he argued, needed a gradual emancipation program that afforded time for the region to convert from a slave economy to one based on free labor. Both he and the president also realized that few northerners would fight for black people and that even fewer had any interest in abolition. A crusade against slavery thus carried the triple liability of alienating fellow northerners as well as Unionists in the Confederacy while forcing the four Border States out of the Union.[37]

The concept of Union and both antagonists' appeals to liberty particularly baffled Europeans. Did freedom have different meanings? How could such an amorphous concept rule out compromise between northern and southern Americans? A range of nationalities had managed to live alongside each other on the European continent; surely so many Americans of similar ancestries could work out their differences. Yet neither the Confederates nor the Unionists could compromise, each side tracing its lineage directly to the Founding Fathers and believing the other had corrupted the republic—the Union with its Hamiltonian principles of centralized government masking its oppressive rule, and the Confederacy pursuing the Jeffersonian ideals of states' rights that clouded its real concern about maintaining slavery. Europeans never comprehended the depth of the differences between the Union and the Confederacy. Both sides considered themselves the true protectors of the American Revolutionary heritage—the Union in preserving the nation from dissolution, the Confederacy in fighting for independence from a tyranny that this time came from Washington, not London.[38] From thousands of miles away, Europeans found this conflict difficult to understand. To Americans on both sides, the issues were clear. The North-South differences were irreconcilable because they struck at the very essence of the republic and what it meant to its Constitution, states, and citizens.

The British and other European observers also never grasped the integral relationship between American internal politics and slavery, and when Lincoln pronounced Union rather than slavery as the core issue between the sections, he inadvertently opened the way for outsiders to judge the struggle based on commercial interests. The British no longer had to make the hard choice between upholding their moral commitment against slavery and their need to maintain connections with the Confederacy's cotton distributors. With morality set aside, the chief consideration became trade. Despite "all our virulent abuse of slavery and slave-owners," wrote one Englishman, "we are just as anxious for, and as much interested in, the prosperity of the slavery interest in the Southern States as the Carolinian and Georgian planters themselves, and all Lancashire would deplore a successful resurrection of the slaves, if such a thing were possible." This unexpected twist of circumstances replaced conscience with economics in British deliberations and thereby removed a major obstacle to their extending recognition to the Confederacy.[39]

The Lincoln administration nonetheless considered slavery the root of the Union-Confederate struggle and assumed the British astute enough to recognize the obvious. The new president appointed abolitionists to several foreign ministries, hoping to send a message to those outside the United States that he opposed slavery.[40] He believed that the Republican Party's resistance to the extension of slavery guaranteed its collapse. Was not slavery dependent on cotton which, in turn, drained the soil of nitrogen and necessitated a continual search for new fields that someday had to end? Slavery had threatened to tear apart the Union because the sanctity of that institution rested on the divisive doctrines of sectionalism and states' rights. In his Inaugural Address, Lincoln had exalted nationalism in a nearly mystical fashion, declaring his undying faith in the permanence of the Union and promising to destroy any issue threatening its survival. Yet he realized that the law protected slavery and that he could not disturb it wherever it already existed. Nonetheless, both he and southerners recognized that the Republican Party's stand against the spread of slavery meant its "ultimate extinction." With justification, southerners believed the only way to preserve their way of life was to leave the Union.

By the eve of a nearly certain war, the existence of slavery had forced

Charles Francis Adams, U.S. minister to England (Courtesy of the Massachusetts Historical Society)

the development of two sections of Americans, one slave and one free. The American republic, which had tried for years to join slavery and freedom under one banner, found itself too divided on the inside to remain united on the outside. Slavery permeated almost every debate between northerners and southerners, making their exchanges particularly embittered when more than a few observers predicted racial war once four million slaves became free. Such a terrible specter alarmed, among others, Seward, Attorney General Edward Bates, John Hay, Lincoln's secretary, and the president as well.[41]

The British and many Americans, however, did not understand how deeply embedded slavery had burrowed into the nation's consciousness. Russell in London was perplexed by events in America, lamenting in December 1860 that he could not understand why the northern antislavery majority did not simply outlaw slavery. Americans also failed to realize the depth of the problem. At a White House dinner the following March, several dignitaries almost casually remarked that the Union was about to embark on a war for emancipation and easily dismissed the possibility of England's supporting a southern people attempting to construct a nation on slavery.[42]

An integral part of Lincoln's attempt to stave off British recognition of the Confederacy was his appointment of Charles Francis Adams of Massachusetts to the pivotal ministerial post in London. Grandson of the famous Founding Father John Adams, the younger Adams was the son of former president John Quincy Adams and enjoyed a well-deserved reputation for his scholarly demeanor, rigid opposition to slavery, and air of genteel self-control that made him appear almost British in manner. "Diplomacy and statesmanship run in his blood," a Boston newspaper enthusiastically remarked. Both his forebears had served as minister to the Court of St. James's, and his mother's father had been a consul in London. "The first and greatest qualification of a statesman," Charles Francis Adams declared, was "the mastery of the whole theory of morals which makes the foundation of all human society." The second was "the application of the knowledge thus gained to the events of his time in a continuous and systematic way." In temperament, education, breeding, and opposition to slavery, Adams fitted comfortably in British political and social circles. As fate would have it, however, he did not depart for England until May 1, 1861, two days after his son John's wedding but several weeks after the Confederate commissioners had left on their mission abroad.[43]

By late March 1861 it appeared that British leaders had already made up their minds for recognition when a well-known southern sympathizer in Parliament, William H. Gregory, announced his intention to present a motion for recognizing the Confederacy. War in America, he feared, would hurt British industry. The Morrill Tariff, according to southerners, had convinced the British to act in their own economic interests by welcoming the Confederacy into the community of nations. Henry William Ravenel, a plantation owner and internationally known botanist from South Carolina, privately recorded: "Old prejudices against our misunderstood domestic institution of African servitude . . . are giving way before the urgent calls of Self Interest." Cotton was the key to freedom, he believed. Britain's only choice was recognition. Not only did southerners provide a product vital to British mills, but they also offered a market for England's manufactured goods and an invitation to its merchants to conduct the Confederacy's carrying trade in light of the few vessels it had after the estrangement from its northern cousins. The United States had enacted a tariff that would damage the European side of Atlantic commerce, and it now posed a formidable manufacturing and commercial rival to Britain. Self-interest, Ravenel repeated with confidence, was "the ruling power among nations, no less than among individuals."[44]

Gregory, however, postponed his motion after it drew little preliminary support. Parliamentary member William E. Forster responded to Gregory's notice with an amendment declaring that "the House does not at present desire to express any opinion in favour of such recognition, and trusts that the Government will at no time make it without obtaining due security against the renewal of the African Slave Trade." Forster's opposition to any involvement with the Confederacy was not surprising, given his Quaker and antislavery lineage—his father a missionary and his uncle, Thomas Fowell Buxton, a legendary proponent of abolition until his death in 1845. Gregory also encountered resistance from the prime minister, Lord Palmerston, who did not want to invite accusations from America that Parliament was meddling in its affairs.[45]

British belief in the Union's imminent collapse provided further evidence of their outspoken distaste for a democratic rule in the United States that might set an example for reformers in England. How could Washington hold so many Americans in the Union against their will? The democratic principles so cherished in America had led to its undoing. One hardened British observer virtually spat out the rhythmic charge that "the Yankees are a damned lot and republican institutions all rot." Adams later lamented that the British reaction to the Union's troubles rested on the "grim spectre of democracy, the ingrained jealousy of American power, and the natural pugnacity of John Bull." The breakup of the Union, smirked editor Walter Bageot of the *Economist*, would make Americans "less aggressive, less insolent, and less irritable." The *Times* declared with bitter satisfaction that democracy's failure would stand as a stern lesson for "unthinking and unprincipled demagogues" at home—particularly Radicals John Bright and Richard Cobden in Parliament—who demanded a broadened franchise in a move more exemplary of "tyranny than true liberty."[46]

American events spiraled into a crisis on April 12, 1861, when Confederate forces fired on the small federal garrison stationed at Fort Sumter in South Carolina's Charleston Harbor, sounding the death knell of peace and convincing many British observers of democracy's inherent failings. The *London Morning Post* joined the chorus of criticism by expressing wonder at American naïveté. "Equal citizenship, popular supremacy, vote by ballot and universal suffrage may do well for a while, but they invariably fail in the day of trial." Those ill-advised reformers who had set their sights on changing the

English constitution should study history to understand why the American republic was about to emulate the fate of Greece, Rome, Venice, and France. They had "all suffered and died from intestine disorders."[47]

Yet despite the indisputable advantages at home resulting from the coming American disaster abroad, the press in both Britain and France spoke for many observers both inside and outside of government in asserting that a civil war benefited no one. Admittedly, smugly declared one British magazine, such an internal upheaval justified the wisdom of British political institutions while undermining "the diplomatic influence and external power of the United States." But if disunion must come, many observers declared, let it come peacefully. Indeed, most of the British and French press soon considered southern independence a fait accompli. Let the South go, urged a British abolitionist. War would be total, which meant "extermination, or a fierce and horrible encounter of long duration." The Union should allow the South to "quietly secede" and escape complicity with slavery. A war itself would bring emancipation, insisted many abolitionists along with Forster, Bright, Cobden, and the Duke of Argyll from Parliament. By no stretch of the imagination could the Union subdue so many people and seize so much territory. The best the Lincoln administration could achieve was a prolonged occupation of the Confederacy at horrific cost in blood and treasure.[48]

In the meantime, argued many British spokesmen, the wisest policy was neutrality. A severe time of trial was coming, they darkly predicted. The British secretary for war, the scholarly and usually unruffled George Cornewall Lewis, had long feared a civil war in America that would lead to a servile war disrupting the cotton flow. The loss of southern cotton due to a lengthy war meant devastation of the British textile industry. Potential Union violations of British rights at sea would test their character and threaten national honor. Still, the *Times* declared, "All we can do is keep aloof." Calls for neutrality came also from *Punch*, which appealed directly to Palmerston as the longtime critic of Americans, and from his recognized mouthpiece, the *Morning Post*, which urged "strict and impartial neutrality."[49]

The Union's fate in England rested primarily in Palmerston's hands. Now seventy-six years of age, he had spent most of his public career in foreign affairs, and, although he had lost the spring in his step, he remained vibrant and very much alive. Palmerston's single most driving energy was British self-interest, which he particularly savored when vying against America in either political or commercial matters. During the McLeod crisis of the early 1840s, he as foreign secretary had threatened war with the United States because its laws had brought a British citizen to trial in a New York courtroom.

Lord Palmerston, British prime minister
(Courtesy of the Massachusetts
Historical Society)

America's democracy he despised as a catalyst to disorder both there and everywhere else—including his beloved hierarchical England. Furthermore, he regarded it as hypocrisy for a nation to espouse equality while opposing British attempts to destroy the African slave trade. Indeed, he more than once considered offering recognition to the Confederacy in exchange for assurances against reopening what he denounced as an ugly, immoral practice. Moreover, America's land-grabbing lust of the 1840s—pitifully disguised and weakly justified by the thinly veneered and self-serving label of "manifest destiny"—threatened British interests both in Canada and Central America. The United States, he had decided years earlier, was like other voracious and growing republics, "essentially and inherently aggressive." As he explained to Russell (who needed no convincing), when "the masses influence or direct the destinies" of a country, they adhere more to "Passion than Interest."[50]

British foreign policy officially fell under Russell's control, but its real direction came from Palmerston. As longtime rivals for the leadership of the Whig Party, they had more than once found that one could not rule without the other. In 1859 Palmerston, now head of the recently formed Liberal Party, could not form a government without giving Russell a position. Although differing over many issues in succeeding months, they agreed that British interests were the guiding principle in all matters. Palmerston's hair was thin and white, his walk stooped, and his eyesight fading, but he remained flamboyant, outspoken, and unquestionably in command. Russell was less impressive in demeanor and presence, more reserved, even small and weak in physical appearance. So regularly did he report to Palmerston that a contemporary derisively remarked that "John Russell has neither policy nor principles of his own, and is in the hands of Palmerston, who is an artful old dodger."[51]

Yet it is not entirely correct to say that Palmerston dominated foreign policy; his mixed breed of cabinet members dictated that he could not act independently. In addition to appointing Liberal stalwarts to key posts, the prime minister had found it politically necessary to invite Whigs, Radicals, and Peelites into his inner circle of advisers, and they demanded that their adventuresome chief of state keep them apprised of every foreign policy decision. Intervention in the American crisis, if Palmerston ever considered the idea, would take place behind a veritable looking glass held by his colleagues. Most notable among these cabinet members was the politically popular William E. Gladstone, who as chancellor of the exchequer found support not only among the Peelites but, in advocating free trade, a smaller tax load, and reduced government, drew the cheers of Cobden Radicals as well. As guardians of an idealized British order, these scions of a new era of balanced government control refused to permit Palmerston as the perennial sword rattler—now regarded as an anachronism in an age that had passed him by—to roam freely around the world, bullying all peoples in his path. Interference in the American crisis could not take place without his having to go through an inherently wary and highly reluctant cabinet.[52]

It is likewise clear that Russell was not always the prime minister's obedient servant in foreign affairs and that, as foreign secretary, he was capable of acting on his own. As the person having direct and regular contact with foreign emissaries in London, Russell exerted considerable influence on foreign policy. The Union had expected him to take a strong stand against southern separation and publicly guarantee against recognition. But even though he admitted to favoring the Union's restoration and expressed reluctance to help the Confederacy, he could not be sure of the outcome of the struggle and understandably adopted a safe middle ground. In doing so, he infuriated the Union by refusing to make promises against recognition and insisting that the conflict itself must determine British policy. To southerners looking for the slightest sign of British encouragement, this response furnished great cause for exultation. To northerners keenly sensitive about any indication of British favor for the Confederacy, this stance provided proof of dangerous designs.

Indeed, both Union and Confederacy were correct in their assessments of the foreign secretary. Russell was a Whig in philosophy and a Liberal in party, meshing these two into a position advocating the natural right of oppressed peoples to rebel against established authority. Such a stand had particular appeal once the Lincoln administration declared that the central issue was the Union. To northerners who believed that England saw great advantages in disunion, Russell's bland refusal to guarantee against recognition provided evidence for their worst suspicions. It did not seem coincidental that, less than a week later, Gregory announced his intention to present a motion in the House of Commons calling for recognition of the Confederacy.[53]

If Lincoln and Seward had devised a strategy of threatening war to prevent recognition, it seemed to be working. Palmerston and Russell had already decided to avoid the appearance of interference in American affairs, but the prime minister and others in high British governing circles could not resist their initial gut impulse to applaud the Union's trial. The battle-hardened prime minister had already grappled with the upstart Americans in numerous diplomatic encounters and now expressed ill-concealed satisfaction with the plight of the "disunited States of America."[54]

Especially surprising, though only on the surface, was Argyll's reaction to the possible outbreak of war in America. Fervently opposed to slavery, he considered secession anarchy but thought the breakup of the Union would remove U.S. protection from the evil institution and permit the world's progressive opinion to exert its remedial influence on the wayward Americans. For too long northerners had silently acquiesced in slavery by refusing to act on conscience and destroy the blight afflicting four million black people. *Both* Union and Confederacy were responsible for impeding the advance of civilization.[55]

Yet a major irritant in British thinking was the Confederacy's haughty attitude of expecting to prescribe British policy. From his firsthand position as consul in Charleston, Robert Bunch witnessed several southerners' openly expressed delight at seeing how dependent the crown was on their actions and how they wished to embarrass the British as recompense for their longtime criticism of slavery. But Lyons warned Russell that even the poor quality of the three Confederate commissioners must not lead him to turn them away. Such rash action might throw more power to the "violent party" in Washington "who maintained that any measures whatever may be taken by this Government against Foreign Commerce" without causing British recognition of the Confederacy.[56]

The other side of the argument was Russell's apparent willingness to meet with the southern commissioners, which threw Seward into a rage. "God damn them, I'll give them hell," he stormed to Senate Foreign Relations Committee chair and friend Charles Sumner of Massachusetts. Having just been privately rebuked by Lincoln over the threat-of-war strategy contained in his April 1 memorandum, the secretary of state was in no mood to countenance even the briefest British flirtation with the rebels. He drafted a strongly worded dispatch to Adams that Lincoln toned down before countermanding Seward's directive to give Russell a copy. The president instructed Adams to keep the dispatch for his eyes only, while using it to guide his discussions with Russell.[57]

Not to be denied, Seward found another way to get his sharp message to London by sharing his strong feelings with *Times* correspondent William H. Russell. Two weeks after Lincoln revised the dispatch to Adams, Seward invited Russell into his home. "The Secretary lit his cigar," Russell recorded in his diary, "gave one to me, and proceeded to read slowly and with marked emphasis a very long, strong, and able dispatch, which he told me was to be read by Mr. Adams, the American Minister in London, to Lord John Russell. It struck me that the tone of the paper was hostile, that there was an undercurrent of menace through it, and that it contained insinuations that Great Britain would interfere to split up the Republic, if she could, and was pleased at the prospect of the dangers which threatened it." Seward orchestrated his presentation by raising his voice while reading strongly worded passages and pausing after each one for full impact. Russell admitted that the dispatch, if publicly known, would find an appreciative audience among Americans. But, he darkly added, "It would not be quite so acceptable to the Government and people of Great Britain."[58] Seward knew that John Russell was second in importance only to Richard Lyons in shaping the Palmerston ministry's views toward America.

What was in the dispatch? Seward directed Adams that on his arrival in London he was to warn the British that any discussion with the southern commissioners would be tantamount to recognizing the Confederacy's authority to send them. In that event, Adams was to "desist from all intercourse whatever, official as well as unofficial, with the British government so long as it shall continue intercourse of either kind with the domestic enemies of this country." *Any* British dealings with the Confederacy would terminate the Union's friendship. British recognition of the Confederacy meant an endless struggle between the Union and the Confederacy over control of the North American continent. "Permanent dismemberment of the American Union in consequence of that intervention would be perpetual war—civil war." Not only that, Seward made clear, a break in diplomatic relations with England could lead to another Anglo-American war.[59]

Lincoln may have tempered the dispatch and prohibited its direct delivery to Russell, but he did nothing to stop Adams from sharing Seward's warning with the British. Seward was brash and outspoken; Lincoln was subtle and quietly persuasive. Yet even though their styles were as different as night and day, they worked in close harmony after the debacle over the April 1 war memorandum—both realizing that British intervention in the Civil War would lead France and other European nations to follow and virtually ensure southern independence.

The Confederate bombardment of Fort Sumter meanwhile pushed Americans closer to war. Two days after the opening barrage of April 12, 1861, Union forces evacuated the fort, leaving the Confederacy in control of a federal military facility. Within a week, President Davis took the first step toward building a Confederate navy by announcing the licensing of privateers.[60] President Lincoln, however, refused to consider the Confederacy a separate sovereignty and threatened to hang as pirates all those engaged in privateering. The showdown at Fort Sumter led four other states—Arkansas, Tennessee, North Carolina, and Virginia—to proclaim secession, raising the number of states in the Confederacy to eleven.

The prospect of the Union surviving this sectional assault struck British observers as inconceivable. As early as New Year's Day of 1861, Palmerston had told Queen Victoria that the Union's dissolution was inescapable. Russell soon thereafter decided that the Union could not be "cobbled together again" by some nebulous compromise and should accept secession: "One Republic to be constituted on the principle of freedom and personal liberty—the other on the principle of slavery and the mutual surrender of fugitives." Thus would southern independence seal the fate of slavery by isolating slaveowners in a Western world opposed to slavery and surrounded by nations promising freedom to escaping slaves. Contrary to the widespread perception that Europeans considered the United States as the last hope for emancipation, they did so only by default. The British foreign secretary concluded that the differences between northerners and southerners were irreconcilable but that "in a legal sense" the Confederacy was right. The breakup of the Union seemed assured—and not just to observers more than three thousand miles away. Journalist William H. Russell noted little Union sentiment in the Confederacy. A Georgian expressed his people's feelings of invincibility by proudly declaring to the *Times* correspondent, "They can't conquer us, Sir!"[61]

British exultation over the Union's troubles sent misleading signals that it supported the Confederacy. The recent southern decision to outlaw the African slave trade did not draw extensive European support; instead, the British spoke for others in denouncing this long-needed move as too conveniently timed—a calculated effort to placate the Border States while pandering to foreign opinion. After his first response, Palmerston soberly warned that a more assertive Confederacy would challenge British interests in Central America and Mexico.[62] Such were the underlying truths of the London ministry's position that got lost in the chaotic aftermath of Fort Sumter's collapse.

The Confederacy believed recognition forthcoming when, on April 16, Bunch informed Governor Francis Pickens of South Carolina that Adams in London had failed to secure Lord Russell's guarantee against southern recognition. That this response came just two days after the Confederate victory at Fort Sumter provided further reason to believe the foreign secretary's evasive stand to be a subtle signal of imminent recognition. Even more hopeful was Bunch's assurance to Pickens "that if the United States Government attempted a blockade of the Southern ports or if Congress at Washington declared the Southern ports were no longer ports of entry, . . . it would immediately lead to the recognition of the Independence of the South by Great Britain."[63]

Recognition seemed certain when on April 19 President Lincoln made public his intention to impose a blockade on the Confederacy. In the excitement of the time, hardly anyone read the president's declaration with care and assumed that a blockade instantly went into effect. "I have deemed it advisable to set on foot a blockade," he announced, signaling his objective of putting it into place. Seward likewise called the proclamation a "mere notice of an intention to carry it into effect." When established, the blockade would be "actual and effective."[64]

The Lincoln administration had taken a dangerous step in announcing a move toward a blockade. International law stipulated that the establishment of a blockade automatically elevated the status of antagonists to belligerents and permitted both sides to deal with neutral nations. But the president wanted the European powers to be aware that the American problems were domestic in nature and that foreign vessels could not enter rebel ports. Doubtless he and his advisers hoped to stall the Confederacy's receiving belligerent status by proclaiming their *intention* to install a blockade. In the meantime, they could add the cruisers necessary to implement a blockade that commanded the respect of other nations. They knew that the immediate imposition of a blockade made it a paper blockade, which was contrary to international law and sure to constitute a challenge to Britain and other maritime nations to ignore the Union's patrol vessels. More than anything, the Union needed time to expand its navy.

The British reacted in a mixed way to the president's proclamation. Lyons grasped the subtleties in the administration's move. He regarded Seward's notification as "an announcement of an intention to set on foot a blockade, not as a notification of the actual commencement of one." The London ministry, however, could not risk certain maritime confrontations over long-standing and sensitive questions of search that raised the issue of national honor. It decided to declare neutrality and, in an effort to avoid responsibility for its nationals' possible behavior, issued a warning that if they violated international law or British municipal law, they did so without either government approval or protection.[65]

The London ministry nonetheless regarded Lincoln's proclamation as the actual implementation of a blockade, thus placing the American struggle within the dictates of international law and thereby establishing the guidelines for a policy of neutrality. Lincoln's words indicated that the blockade process was under way and that the Palmerston government had to act quickly in implementing the British Foreign Enlistment Act of 1819, which prohibited its subjects from any conduct capable of drawing the nation into the American conflict. All nations affected by the fighting must declare neutrality and thereby put into play a whole system of rules governing a neutral's actions.

A civil war it was, but, in accordance with international law, the rules of war between nations applied to this American conflict between two antagonists. In his legal deliberations, Russell regularly consulted the writings of the Swiss theorist on international law, Emmerich de Vattel. As recently as the Italian crisis in October 1860, the foreign secretary had cited Vattel in arguing that the rebels in Naples and the Roman states should determine their own affairs. Vattel maintained that in a civil war, the opposing sides were "two separate bodies, two distinctive societies" that "stand therefore in precisely the same predicament as two nations, who engage in a contest, and, being unable to come to an agreement, have recourse to arms." The "common laws of war" applied to civil wars.[66]

In another matter that indirectly related to the blockade issue, the British expressed great concern over Lincoln's threat to hang privateers as pirates.

The Declaration of Paris of 1856 had outlawed privateering, but the United States was not a signatory to the pact. Now, however, the Lincoln administration thought this a propitious time to join the pact and hence take a stand against privateering. The move was ingenious but transparent in purpose. If the measure went into effect, the president's rejection of secession made privateers subject to charges of piracy and required all signatories of the Paris pact—Austria, England, France, Prussia, Russia, Sardinia, and Turkey—to help the Union navy capture privateers. Indeed, the British (and other signatory powers) would find themselves not only involved in the American war but also in the awkward position of pursuing privateers while leaving the Union to enforce its blockade. And the alternative was equally unattractive. Failure to support the provision against privateering would subject the British to the charge of approving such illegal action while condoning the Confederacy's right as a belligerent to join Union vessels in carrying prizes into British ports.[67]

Lyons considered Seward's maneuver to be "rather amusing" and advised the ministry in London to turn it down. "It no doubt would be very convenient," he sneered to Russell, "if the Navies of Europe would put down the Privateers, and thus leave the whole Navy of the United States free to blockade the Ports against European Merchant Vessels." Then, turning to Seward, Lyons asked whether the Union was capable of enforcing an antiprivateering policy against the Confederacy. Of course, Seward replied in a breezy manner. Southerners must comply with the Declaration of Paris because they were citizens of the United States. After Lyons collected his thoughts and perhaps only partially concealed his incredulous reaction, he exposed the inconsistencies in the Union's maritime policy toward the Confederates: "Very well. If they are not independent then the President's proclamation of blockade is not binding. A blockade, according to the definition of the convention, applies only to two nations at war."[68]

Despite the danger arising from the privateering controversy, it suddenly lost intensity. The Palmerston ministry took a big step toward averting a confrontation with the United States by barring privateers and their prizes from British ports. Also, the Confederacy soon altered its maritime strategy from privateering to *destroying* goods seized from Union vessels.[69] The narrow escape from this furor did not ease the Union's growing resentment over British policy toward the American conflict.

Seward, with the president's approval, took advantage of a maritime dispute to drive home the point to both the British and the French ministers that the Lincoln administration would not tolerate foreign involvement in the war. The secretary had learned from several sources that Confederates had purchased a Canadian steamer, the *Peerless*, presumably for use as a privateer. If evidence supported the charge, Seward sharply warned Lyons, Union commanders intended to seize the vessel. Even the usually placid British minister could not contain himself. Such an action, Lyons indignantly declared, constituted direct interference with British rights at sea. Although the reports of privateering proved groundless, Seward had convinced the British of his intentions. Lest doubt remain in France, he wrote his minister in Paris that the French foreign minister had intruded in American affairs by recently asking about troubles inside the president's cabinet. Seward used the occasion to warn that the United States would go to war to prevent European recognition of the Confederacy. As a final stroke, he authorized publication of this inflammatory dispatch in New York newspapers.[70]

As fate would have it, at about the same time Seward was attempting to ensure against recognition, the crown sent mixed signals about its intentions regarding the conflict. On May 1 Russell invited the outgoing U.S. minister in London, George Dallas, to his home and informed him that three Confederate commissioners had recently arrived in England, seeking an interview. Dallas was stunned when Russell stated that he intended to meet with them, albeit unofficially. Before Dallas could respond, Russell followed Lyons's recommendation to announce that England and France intended to pursue a joint wait-and-see attitude toward American events. Then, when British recognition seemed closer than ever before, Russell (perhaps pushed by Palmerston) took a seemingly contradictory position. In the House of Commons the following day, he promised that only an attack on British interests could justify interference. "We have not been involved in any way in that contest by any act or giving any advice in the matter, and," to cheers from parliamentary members, he declared that "for God's sake, let us if possible keep out of it."[71]

But even this strong public statement did little to allay Union fears. The British soon announced a policy of neutrality toward the American conflict that achieved their purpose of signaling no favor for the Union but, for that reason, offered encouragement to the Confederacy. The same day Russell made his pronouncement in the Commons, he sought counsel from the crown's law officers. The wisest approach, according to the lord chancellor, was "to determine that the war between the two Confederacies shall be carried on on the principle of *justum bellum* and shall be conducted according to the rules of the Treaty of Paris [of 1856]." Accordingly, the two warring parties must accept the principles that free ships make free goods, that privateering was forbidden, and that a blockade had to seal off access to a coast to be legal. Thus the conflict in America was an actual war and Britain deserved the rights guaranteed to neutrals. Although the United States had not been a signatory to the Declaration of Paris, it had long recognized the unlawful nature of a paper blockade. Surely the Union did not believe it possible to close more than three thousand miles of jagged coastline with fewer than a hundred vessels, less than half of them active and only forty steam-driven. The British expected the Union to abide by its own precedent.[72] If not, the prognosis was a virtual web of legal difficulties that would harden relations between Washington and London.

Russell continued his uncertain behavior by meeting with the southern commissioners twice—on May 3 and 9. At their initial interview, the representatives presented their credentials (which he could not accept), explained the background of the new Confederacy, defended secession as legal, and expressed their objective of establishing relations with the world community. Russell assured his visitors that he would present the matter to the ministry. In the second meeting, he expressed interest in both the Union's and the Confederacy's policies toward the Declaration of Paris regarding the issues of blockade, letters of marque (authorized privateering), neutral rights, and the presence of neutral goods in an enemy power's ships. The British government intended to discuss these matters and the question of Confederate independence with the European powers. The commissioners believed that the London government had not yet developed a policy regarding recognition and thus remained open to argument. British journals had meanwhile expressed favor for the Confederate cause. Most people, however, considered the Confederacy incapable of overcoming the combined force of a Union blockade and armies and believed the government would not extend recognition under these conditions.[73]

Russell now took further actions that, although unintentional, were bound to alienate the Union. His decision to meet with the southern emissaries had already infuriated the Lincoln administration. To safeguard British maritime rights, he asked the admiralty to strengthen the North American Squadron and soon afterward made clear that the crown intended to bolster its defense of Canada against a possible Union attack. Finally, he proclaimed that, as a natural consequence of declaring neutrality, his government was about to recognize southern belligerency. The latter step, although not equivalent to recognition of independence, proved chilling to the Union because it signified a state of war between entities and therefore constituted a major notch upward in establishing diplomatic relations with a fledgling country. The Lincoln administration concluded that the Palmerston ministry had adopted a sinister, self-serving policy aimed at recognizing the Confederacy.[74] Britain and the Union had taken irreconcilable positions.

Such was the tense international atmosphere when Adams arrived in England on May 13—the very day Queen Victoria issued a formal proclamation of neutrality and thereby extended British recognition to the Confederacy as a belligerent. The announcement appeared to be timed with Adams's arrival and thus a studied slap in the face of all northerners. The Confederacy gained instant credibility in international circles because its vessels could confiscate enemy goods on the basis of self-preservation; enter British ports with prizes resulting from lawful vessels engaged in privateering, not robbery or piracy (privateering being still acceptable under international law because the United States was not a party to the Paris Declaration of 1856); borrow money and buy matériel for an army and a navy legitimized as combatants, rather than regarded as bandits; enlist recruits for any activity not in violation of neutrality strictures; and, in accordance with British municipal law—the Foreign Enlistment Act of 1819—commission the construction of vessels in British shipyards, as long as they were *not* equipped or fitted for war while in England. British neutrality did *not* recognize Confederate independence and hence condone the negotiation of treaties, but it opened the way for the Confederacy as a belligerent to enhance its military strength by purchasing weapons and building a navy.[75]

Indeed, the Confederacy had already sent a special agent to England to buy arms and munitions. Caleb Huse, superintendent at the University of Alabama, had arrived in Liverpool just three days before the British announcement of neutrality, determined to prove New York lawyer and shipper Caleb Cushing wrong. As Huse departed for London, Cushing put it bluntly in declaring the Confederacy's cause futile: "The money is all in the North; the manufactures are all in the North; the ships are all in the North; the arms and arsenals are all in the North; the arsenals of Europe are within ten days of New York and they will be closed to the South; and the Southern ports will be blockaded. What possible chance can the South have?"[76]

The queen's proclamation meanwhile drew a bitter and not entirely justified response from the Union. According to one of Adams's sons, Charles Francis Adams Jr., the Confederacy had already "scored the apparently great success of a recognition of belligerency." The *Richmond Whig* called the neutrality proclamation "a long and firm [step] in exactly the direction which the people of the Southern States expected." The chair of the Senate Foreign Relations Committee in Washington, the irascible and embittered antisoutherner from Massachusetts, Charles Sumner, termed it "the most hateful act of English history since the time of Charles 2nd." Yet Lincoln himself had brought on this British action. According to international law (upheld by the U.S. Supreme Court in the *Prize Cases* of 1863), his blockade proclamation (whether or not it actually implemented the measure) constituted an act of war that automatically defined the antagonists as belligerents and necessitated British neutrality. The Palmerston ministry wanted to keep its citizenry out of the American conflict and to safeguard Canada from any transgressions in the course of these events. But neutrality came at the heavy price of alienating the Union. Seward denounced the queen's proclamation as a measure intended "to recognize . . . the insurgents as a belligerent national power." The Confederacy had done nothing to deserve nationhood status, he charged, and yet it urged the British "to intervene and give it body and independence by resisting our measures of suppression." When France likewise declared neutrality in June, Seward warned *both* nations of war.[77]

CHAPTER 2

British Neutrality on Trial

> If any European Power provokes a war, we shall not shrink from it.
> A contest between Great Britain and the United States would wrap the world in fire.
> —WILLIAM H. SEWARD, July 4, 1861

> I am not disposed to walk alone in the hornets' nest at Washington.
> —LORD JOHN RUSSELL, July 13, 1861

> [At stake was] nothing less than the life of the republic itself.
> —WILLIAM H. SEWARD, July 21, 1861

News of British neutrality drew venomous attacks from the Union and wild exultation from the Confederacy. From the British perspective, the policy provided the best means for averting involvement in the war, but it recognized the existence of two belligerents and thereby infuriated the Union by awarding the Confederacy a stature higher than rebel. Confederate ships could raid Union commerce and enter neutral ports with prizes, and they could seek ship repairs in those same ports along with foods and other materials necessary for survival. Furthermore, the Confederacy could float loans, purchase war materials, and contract the building of ships *not* fitted for war. On the other side, however, the Union could exercise all of its material and manpower advantages in waging war on the Confederacy.

But both the Lincoln administration and the Confederacy saw much more involved than war between belligerents. The Constitution itself lay at the center of their differences. The Union claimed to be the only legitimate government in the United States and interpreted any foreign action bestowing credibility onto the Confederacy as an unwarranted interference in a domestic dispute over the very heart of the republic. The Confederacy, however, regarded the British move as the proper reaction to its declaration of independence based on constitutional, legal, and moral principles.

The Lincoln administration failed to realize that British neutrality more directly benefited the Union. Without such restraints on the British populace, private citizens were free to become involved in the war and thereby increase the chances of pulling the government into the conflagration. Furthermore, the growing economic interdependence of the Atlantic world prohibited any possibility of the British isolating themselves from the American conflict. Southern cotton, northern wheat—these products and more forced the British to maintain economic connections with both American antagonists. For the time being, the British surplus in cotton left the Confederacy with little leverage, but this reality remained unknown—if irrelevant—to northerners who regarded the secessionists as traitors and looked upon anyone consorting with them as fellow conspirators.

The Palmerston ministry's decision for neutrality had come from a sincere desire to stay out of the American conflict, which, in turn, derived in part from its hasty and inaccurate reading of Lincoln's blockade proclamation. Under international law, the Union's imposition of a blockade automatically defined the ongoing conflict as a "war." Accordingly, the British government announced its recognition of both the Union and the Confederacy as belligerents and thereby claimed, as a neutral power, the right of free passage of its vessels through American waters as long as they carried *non*contraband goods. From three thousand miles away in London, the president's blockade proclamation seemed eminently logical, given the physical size of the Confederacy, its population of millions, and the magnitude of its success at Fort Sumter. Lincoln's declaration had substantiated Britain's conclusion that war had come to America.

Just as British neutrality was a natural result of the blockade proclamation, so was the Union's indignant reaction to a neutrality policy that raised Confederate hopes. Both the Union and the British had followed procedures well established in international law, but their actions inadvertently gave substance to southern efforts and generated an explosive Anglo-American relationship that neither Washington nor London wanted but the Confederacy welcomed.

From the southern perspective, the queen's proclamation had enacted a pro-Confederate neutrality that encouraged southerners to take bolder action. Not by coincidence did they intensify pressure on Europe for recognition through King Cotton Diplomacy. Shortly after the queen's announcement, the Confederate Congress (moved to Richmond after Virginia's secession) barred the exportation of cotton to Europe except through southern ports—which made their staying open all the more important. The implicit threat of an all-out cotton embargo became clear. "The cards are in our hands," the *Charleston Mercury* defiantly asserted, "and we intend to play them out to the bankruptcy of every cotton factory in Great Britain and France or the acknowledgment of our independence." Numerous southerners, according to *Times* journalist William H. Russell, boasted of certain British recognition and military aid as if England were "a sort of appanage to their cotton kingdom." Edmund Rhett from Charleston, a relative of fire-eater Robert Barnwell Rhett, smartly observed that England's "Lord Chancellor sits on a cotton bale."[1]

At this delicate juncture in international relations, the Confederacy's threatened cotton embargo proved ill advised, because the action infuriated the British and fostered an unfriendly neutrality. On the surface, the spring of 1861 seemed a good time to focus on King Cotton. Relations between the United States and Britain were raw. Even though the British had a year's back supply of cotton, their neutrality increased the likelihood of a protracted war that would eat into that surplus and perhaps, in a year's time, force England and other cotton-hungry nations to challenge the Union blockade. The wisest southern strategy lay in avoiding any action that irritated the British. But the Confederacy's resort to economic pressure clarified the precarious position now occupied by the British and made them increasingly wary of any contact with the Richmond government. The threat of a cotton embargo again underlined the wisdom of England's neutral course.

The United States, however, considered British neutrality mean-spirited and became livid over the turn of events. At the least, the queen's proclamation was precipitate in leaving the Lincoln administration only sixty days to devise a policy toward neutrality. More important, the British had injected life into the Confederacy before it had demonstrated its right to existence either by the maintenance of long-term relations with established nations or by a decisive victory on the battlefield. The British countered that the Confederacy had a de facto government in Richmond that entitled it to belligerent status and insisted that their refusal to recognize a de jure (legal) government provided proof of an honest neutrality.

Adams was not convinced of British sincerity. On May 18 he met with Foreign Secretary Russell at his lodging in Richmond, impatiently listening to his assurances against any British intention to interfere in the American contest. Russell missed the point, Adams believed. Actual interference was not *the* issue; the United States opposed *any* action that encouraged Confederate dreams of separation. The queen's neutrality proclamation, Adams charged, had "raised the insurgents to the level of a belligerent State." Regardless of purpose, that pronouncement had mobilized the Confederacy's friends in England. The lord chancellor's recent address had termed the rebels "a belligerent State" engaged in a "*justum bellum*." But, Russell replied, the crown's law officers had advised him that a large number of states were in "open resistance" in what could only be a war between two sides and that they had not meant to impute a moral judgment on right or wrong. The sole purpose of the neutrality proclamation was to implement "the rules of modern civilized warfare." British citizens must be aware of the risks in taking part in these American events. Adams nonetheless thought the action too hasty in that it had given the Lincoln administration barely two months to formulate a policy. Furthermore, the British government extended belligerent rights before the Confederates had demonstrated any capacity to wage war beyond their immediate areas. The American people, Adams warned, would denounce this action as a deliberate attempt to prolong the struggle. If the British pursued this policy, he solemnly asserted, "I had nothing further left to do in Great Britain."[2]

Adams had already felt compromised by Russell's decision to meet with the southern commissioners. When he inquired about that touchy matter, Russell had not been convincing in stating that his government "would not at any future time, no matter what the circumstances might be, recognize an existing State in America." In a dispatch that did not reach London until June 10, Seward angrily instructed Adams to refrain from any contact with the British government if it persisted in actions tantamount to recognizing the Confederacy. The Confederacy was not "*de facto* a self-sustaining power" and did not deserve nationhood status. "British recognition," he hotly maintained, "would be British intervention to create within our own territory a hostile state by overthrowing this Republic itself." The United States might have to go to war with any European nations that "fraternize with our domestic enemy." Lincoln had insisted that Seward delete some of the strong language in other parts of the dispatch and mark it private. But the president sought to reduce the intensity of the threat rather than eliminate it. Adams could use its contents to direct his conversations with Russell.[3]

The British feared that a confrontation with the United States over neutrality would drag them into the American conflict and as a matter of course help the Confederate cause. Toward averting that outcome, Parliament engaged in a lengthy debate on how to avoid trouble over the Union blockade, even leading a dubious Adams to believe that considerable British sentiment existed for the United States. A large majority of members in the House of Commons condemned Sir John Ramsden, who had gleefully declared that they "were now witnessing the bursting of the great republican bubble which had been so often held up to us as the model on which to recast our own English Constitution." America's problems, Russell heatedly countered in that chamber, had stemmed from slavery, "the poisoned garment" that the British crown had draped around its former colonies. It did not seem appropriate "that there should be among us anything like exultation at their discord, and still less that we should reproach them with an evil for the origin of which we are ourselves to blame."[4]

The British found it difficult to convince the United States that they were not guilty of malicious intent in supporting neutrality. Russell repeatedly insisted that his country refused to take sides in the conflict and that the proclamation "was designed . . . to explain to British subjects their liabilities in case they should engage in the war." But the United States remained bitterly skeptical in the face of the Confederacy's new belligerent status. It was little wonder that Adams blasted the queen's neutrality proclamation as an "admission of equality."[5]

But despite Union protests, the British had adhered to international law in equating a civil war with a war between nations and then assuming a position of neutrality intended to keep them out of the American contest. Other countries affected by the fighting likewise saw the wisdom in declaring neutrality and thus coming within the rules of international conduct. Russell emphasized that the Confederacy had a civil government and deserved belligerent standing. Vattel had defined rebellion as "open and unjust resistance" against lawful authority (the Union's position) and civil war as "a just insurrection of the subjects against their sovereign." A rebellion, the Swiss legal theorist continued, became a civil war when the rebels "acquired sufficient strength to give [the sovereign] effectual opposition, and to oblige him to carry on the war against them according to the established rules." Union leaders gave no credence to this broad edict and cherry-picked only those parts of the law that benefited their position. Rebellion, they insisted, best characterized the Confederacy's resistance, because its action was not just; they discarded the other part of the argument that spoke of a "just insurrection" and thereby awarded the Confederacy belligerent status.[6]

To encourage neutrality among its subjects, the Palmerston ministry tied the queen's proclamation to the British Foreign Enlistment Act of 1819. This municipal law was so far reaching in aim that it proved impossible to enforce. It barred British subjects from enlisting or participating in foreign service and from "fitting out or equipping" vessels in British possessions for warlike purposes without government approval. It also forbade them from enlisting in the military or naval services or transgressing the lawful blockade of any nation at peace with Britain. In reality, of course, the London government lacked the ability to govern all of its citizens' behavior and implemented the act to escape legal culpability for their predictable actions. The British emphasized that, as President George Washington had done in 1793 during the Anglo-French war, they were adhering to international law in declaring neutrality.[7]

The Union, however, refused to believe in the purity of British motives. It considered secession an act of treason and understandably interpreted British neutrality as a deceitful action in support of traitors who had found a foreign accomplice long interested in permanently damaging the United States. Both in the upper and lower parts of the Western Hemisphere the British would expand their holdings as the result of a vastly weakened American republic in the middle. And what more respectable way than an appeal to international law, which itself grew out of the natural law that Americans had exalted in their Declaration of Independence?

The Union complained that in bestowing status and credibility onto the Confederacy, British neutrality justified the rebels' destructive interpretation of the Constitution and sanctified the right of revolution. Furthermore, the Confederacy's new stature as belligerent meant that its raids on Union shipping did not fall into the category of piracy and were legitimate wartime actions by a fledgling navy engaged in privateering. Finally, the Confederacy's status as belligerent permitted private dealings with British merchants in military as well as commercial goods. Adams noted with disgust that most British observers thought America's division into two republics an incontrovertible fact. British neutrality provided the Confederacy with the stamp of legitimacy, constituting a provocative measure tantamount to outright interference in the war and part of a sweeping effort to eliminate the United States as a major player in the Western Hemisphere. The Confederacy, Adams bitterly argued, had committed treason in its futile attempt to leave the Union and had no legal or moral right to outside help. The British had unjustly raised southern expectations of assistance and thereby facilitated the destructive aims of secession.[8]

Adams met again with Russell on June 12, this time somewhat encouraged by the foreign secretary's assurances. Less than a week earlier, William H. Gregory had introduced his previously postponed motion in the House of Commons to recognize Confederate independence, but withdrew it at the request of Russell and the representatives from Manchester, Liverpool, and other cities and towns. To discuss the matter would sharply divide the lawmakers, Russell warned, and make it difficult for the government to act impartially. He told Adams there would be no more meetings with the southern commissioners and, much to the minister's relief, said that British naval officers were under instructions to respect the Union blockade. Adams now assured Seward that the queen's proclamation of neutrality did not suggest ill will toward the United States. British spokesmen expressed sympathy with the Lincoln administration—an attitude in marked contrast to what Adams had encountered on his arrival in London in May. British neutrality appeared sincere; the government's problem was to enforce that policy among its people.[9]

Actually, the British had been correct: Their neutrality benefited the Union far more than it did the Confederacy. Given the Union's enormous advantages in population, resources, and maritime vessels, its superiority over the Confederacy would continue if Britain treated the belligerents equally. In addition, British neutrality afforded respectability to a virtually nonexistent blockade by guaranteeing no challenge to its jurisdiction from the world's leading maritime power. Indeed, one of the Union's strongest supporters in the House of Commons, William E. Forster, favored neutrality as a measure capable of hurting the Confederacy. He was right. International law required neutral nations to accept the following ramifications of a civil war, all granting privileges particularly beneficial to the Union: alleviation of Union (as the parent government) responsibility for the insurgents' actions, the right of search by both belligerents (the Confederacy had no cruisers) of foreign merchant vessels for contraband and the submission of illegal goods to prize courts, the right of the parent state to impose a blockade that other nations must respect, and the prohibition of insurgents from hostile preparations in a neutral nation's territory. These were distinct advantages that the Union failed to comprehend, however, in lodging complaints against the British. The Lincoln administration actually sought the best of both worlds. While denying the existence of a war and therefore branding southerners as traitors, it nonetheless implied a state of war by insisting on the right to confiscate contraband headed for the Confederacy.[10]

Lincoln's views on international law and the American Civil War derived from his dual definition of the conflict. On the one side, he refused to call the fighting a war because that term elevated the Confederacy's status to a belligerent that had broken from the Union to take a major step toward becoming a nation. Hence he considered the conflict a domestic insurrection or armed uprising led by traitors who had failed in their quest to leave the United States and whose fate rested in the hands of patriotic Union supporters determined to defend the Constitution. On the other side, Lincoln labeled the conflict a rebellion, which suggested a wider and better organized effort to bring down the government and justified his use of all military powers at his disposal. His reasoning was clear. As president, Lincoln had a constitutional duty to guarantee a republican form of government throughout the country, and as commander in chief of the armed forces he could exercise military means to put down the rebellion. The problem in 1861 was that the Constitution nowhere enumerated the president's military powers as commander in chief, meaning that Lincoln would have to define them in accordance with constantly changing situations. But he had a compass to guide him through this novel experience. As he later declared, "As commander in chief of the army and navy, in time of war, I suppose I have a right to take any measure which may best subdue the enemy." He added, "I conceive that I may in an emergency do things on military grounds that cannot be done constitutionally by Congress."[11]

Neither definition of the Confederacy's actions proved satisfactory to the Union; even Lincoln's attempt to extract only the most favorable qualities of each stand caused all manner of difficulties. His reference to the conflict as an insurrection was not convincing, given the huge size of the area and the great number of people involved. That left two realistic avenues for defining the conflict—a rebellion or an actual war—both of which automatically bestowed belligerent status onto the Confederacy. Then, when Lincoln claimed military powers as commander in chief, he thoroughly confounded the situation. His exercise of these powers included the imposition of a blockade, which, under international law, denoted the existence of war and required other nations either to take sides in the matter or declare neutrality.

The more attractive option—adopted by both England and France—was neutrality, which they pursued in an effort to stay out of the war but necessarily bestowed belligerent status onto both antagonists and succeeded only in drawing the deepest hostilities from the Union and the greatest anticipation from the Confederacy. The Union minister to Paris, William Dayton, reported as early as mid-May 1861 that an Anglo-French concert regarding American affairs had already developed. French foreign minister Edouard Thouvenel soon took the British position on the war, whether or not coincidental, by remarking to Dayton that southern separation seemed certain in light of the Confederacy's command of so much territory and so many people. Consequently, Napoleon III found no support in Washington when making his offices available for promoting a reconciliation to prevent a war certain to harm everyone's commerce and insisting that his offer was "neither an overture nor even an intimation." Seward immediately warned the French against "giving any countenance to treason," declaring any communications with Confederate agents as "injurious to the dignity and honor of the United States" and granting them "a prestige" that "would only protract and aggravate the civil war." Both American antagonists regarded neutrality and its natural outgrowth of Confederate belligerent status as an important first step toward diplomatic recognition of southern independence.[12]

French opinion on the war was mixed and went through many of the same changes experienced in England. The semiofficial *Constitutionnel* (and hence the emperor) had initially expressed support for the Union's efforts to fulfill the revolutionary principles of the Founding Fathers of the republic over the resistance of the Confederacy, which had "turned its back upon the Revolution and deceived the hopes of 1776." If the doctrine of states' rights were acceptable, southerners had the right to rebellion, but they had gone too far in expecting to take slaves into the territories. At the risk of oversimplifying a highly complex matter that involved domestic as well as foreign considerations, one could argue that Liberals praised the Union for its democracy and freedom, and opposed the Confederacy for supporting aristocracy and slavery, whereas Conservatives favored the Confederacy because of their hope that a Union failure would undermine its argument for democracy and justify the authoritarian government in France. But the *Constitutionnel* (and the emperor) in early May 1861 led others in the Liberal press in switching sides when the Lincoln administration emphasized maintenance of the Union rather than the elimination of slavery, and news arrived that the Confederacy had taken Fort Sumter. A southern separation had already occurred, the paper declared, making the American conflict a "war without meaning" and potentially injurious to the French economy. "What difference does it make whether it be based upon a true or false interpretation of the federal compact?" If the American government rested on the consent of the governed, it had no right "to impose its government upon the South."[13]

At present, however, Britain's (and France's) safest stance lay in adhering to international law. The effectiveness of a blockade largely depended on other nations' willingness to respect its strictures, and the Palmerston ministry found it more expedient to interpret the measure as an actual rather than a paper blockade. The British did not want to resist a blockade and thus set a precedent that might work against them in future wars. More important, they realized that such a challenge dramatically increased the chances of a war that could benefit only the Confederacy. War with the Union would make Britain a virtual ally of the Confederacy and hence determine the outcome of the Civil War. But time was running out for the Union. By the spring of 1862, Britain's cotton supply (and that of France) would need replenishing, making the blockade a crucial issue in Anglo-American relations.[14]

While the British tried to quiet the blockade issue, the Lincoln administration followed through on a previously announced idea that aimed at defusing a potential problem but instead brought more trouble: It intended to close southern ports under municipal law. On the surface, such a simple-sounding step appeared practical because it offered an alternative to the hotly contested blockade approach. But in reality, the move—a poorly disguised effort to allow the Union time to enlarge its navy and implement an effective blockade—proved enormously complicated in its ramifications and demonstrated a remarkable lack of foresight by the administration.

Despite Lincoln's argument that port closures affirmed the domestic nature of the conflict, their implementation guaranteed both foreign and domestic problems. First, the measure promised all kinds of legal entanglements because it barred neutral vessels from belligerent ports on the basis of the United States's municipal law. In addition, the move did not fall within the parameters of international law and hence invoked no procedural guidelines. Most important, it posed a profound constitutional problem for the United States: Failure to close *all* ports signified U.S. recognition of southern independence for those states whose ports remained open. The U.S. Constitution barred Congress from enacting laws favoring one American port over another—which meant that the Lincoln administration either had to shut every port in the United States, or, in failing to do so, tacitly admit that those states with open ports were no longer part of the United States because secession had worked. Seward tried to avert this new imbroglio by arguing that the port closure idea constituted a lenient and more humane blockade to permit some trade in necessities for survival. Once the full blockade was in place, enforcement would be uniform.[15]

The United States's plan to close southern ports had unexpected effects: It encouraged the British to respect the blockade as a better choice, but it also drove the British and French closer together. The Palmerston ministry preferred a blockade over port closings because international law was clear on the former measure and thereby reduced the danger of confrontation if all parties played by the rules. Russell, in fact, thought that port closures enhanced the Confederacy's prospects of recognition by creating a fog of legal uncertainties. Consequently, he deemed it safer to concede the effectiveness of the Union blockade so that every party affected by it knew what procedures to follow. Convinced that France would agree, he instructed Richard Lyons to work closely with the French minister in Washington on resolving this potential problem. Lyons concurred. He feared that the port closings would force the recognition question more than would a blockade and was doubtless relieved to learn that the French thought so as well. For the moment at least, the blockade issue had eased, and with it, perhaps, the chances of a maritime confrontation conducive to recognition.[16]

By mid-June, the British had made clear their unwillingness to challenge the blockade. Their cotton surplus reduced the impact of any loss in trade until at least the end of the year. But they also knew that a maritime confrontation over the blockade would inject the British into American affairs and increase the chances of an Atlantic war. From his vantage point close to a potential line of fire, Lyons expressed fear of a conflict with the United States after its war with the Confederacy, one that would involve an invasion of British North America. It was in the British interest to help end the hostilities as quickly as possible. Palmerston, however, cautioned Russell: "They who in quarrels interpose, will often get a bloody nose." Russell heeded that advice. British naval commanders had orders to adhere to the Union's blockade unless it endangered British subjects or property. A recent admiralty court decision in Washington, Russell wrote Lyons, was relevant. The Union had seized the *Tropic Wind*, a British schooner, for violating the blockade in Richmond. In a remarkable if unintended concession, the admiralty court ruled on June 13, 1861, that a blockade became effective in either a public war or civil war upon notice of implementation, whether "actual or constructive."[17]

The port closings issue gradually subsided in intensity, even though Congress in mid-July authorized the president to shut those ports in which the Union proved unable to collect duties. Lyons predictably termed the intended action a paper blockade but acknowledged that the administration planned to use the interlude to make the blockade effective. Lincoln privately admitted as much. Following a dinner in the Executive Mansion later that same month, he assured friend and confidant Senator Orville Browning of Illinois that the chief means of averting war with the British lay in building a larger Union navy capable of blockading all southern ports. Adams had conceded to Russell in London that the president lacked the constitutional power to close southern ports (thereby evading the question of whether his navy was physically capable of doing so), but the foreign secretary recognized the expediency in accepting the Union's claim that a rebellion afforded an exception.[18]

Yet the Union remained suspicious of the British, particularly when Lyons played out Dayton's premonition by acting in concert with the French minister in Washington, Henri Mercier, on American matters. Less than a week earlier, Russell had expressed concern to his ambassador in Paris, Lord Cowley, that the Union wanted to divide the British and the French. But they must "act together in this critical business." Accordingly, France had joined Britain in declaring neutrality, and on June 15 Mercier and Lyons unexpectedly appeared at Seward's office to officially announce their governments' position on the war and recognition of the Confederacy as a belligerent. Their visit resulted in part from Seward's statement that he would ignore British and French recognition of Confederate belligerency until formally notified, but he read much more into their unannounced appearance. If this mission constituted a subtle warning of a joint Anglo-French intervention in the war, he would have none of it. He refused to meet with them jointly and would not formally acknowledge their instructions. After their departure, Seward hotly warned his emissaries in London and Paris about the European threat, stressing that he would not brook "any abridgment" of American sovereignty. In Paris ten years afterward, he still bristled when he indignantly told Lyons, then British ambassador to France, that "the three most impudent men in history . . . were Hernando Cortes, Lyons, and Mercier: Cortes for the way he treated Montezuma, Mercier and Lyons for the fifteenth of June, 1861."[19]

Seward remained alarmed about this incident and reemphasized less than a week later that foreign intervention meant war. "The fountains of discontent in any society are many," he wrote Adams, but outside meddling in a country's domestic affairs especially ensured trouble. If foreign nations had the right to intervene in another country's internal concerns, the result would be continual chaos and probable war. To British news correspondent William H. Russell on July 4, Seward delivered an ominous warning that he knew would make its way back to the London government: "If any European Power provokes a war, we shall not shrink from it. A contest between Great Britain and the United States would wrap the world in fire." Russell did not consider Seward's threat a bluff. In his diary that evening, the journalist

remarked with no small wonder: "I could not but admire the confidence—
may I say the coolness?—of the statesman who sat in his modest little room
within the sound of the evening's guns, in a capital menaced by their forces
who spoke so fearlessly of war with a power which could have blotted out
the paper blockade of the Southern forts and coast in a few hours, and, in
conjunction with the Southern armies, have repeated the occupation and
destruction of the capital." At stake, Seward wrote Adams, was "nothing less
than the life of the republic itself."[20]

Seward had correctly interpreted the Anglo-French visit as carrying more
meaning than its stated purpose. Lyons and Mercier were undoubtedly sincere in alleging their intention to keep all actions in the open and consistent
with established procedures. One could argue that because the two ministers
dealt with the U.S. State Department on a regular basis, they predictably
banded together after Seward's harsh warning against intervention. But in
the tense context of war, they were not persuasive in asserting that their sole
aim was to respond to Seward's declaration that the United States would
ignore their recognition of southern belligerency until formally notified.
Thouvenel raised Dayton's suspicions when informing him of receiving Rost
not as a commissioner from the Confederacy but only in seeking information from all sources. Any kind of exchange, official or not, did injury to the
United States, Dayton protested.[21]

If Thouvenel's intention was harmless, Russell in London had more in
mind. The foreign secretary had already decided to work with France in
seeking a resolution to the blockade issue. He also realized that the longer
the American war went on, the greater the chances for British involvement.
How long could the British merchant marine avert a confrontation with
Union cruisers, particularly when cotton stocks at home eventually ran out
and the resultant slowdown in the textile mills led to domestic pressure to
force open southern ports? Could he expect laid-off workers in Lancashire's
mill districts to remain patient while the two American antagonists fought
it out, leaving in their wake a dried-up cotton stream that translated into no
food on British family tables?

Slowly, almost imperceptibly at first, Russell was becoming a convert to
intervening in the American war with the primary purpose of bringing it
to a close. Although unsure about how to do so, he came to believe that the
best chance lay in a joint effort with France: "I am not disposed to walk alone
in the hornets' nest at Washington," he wrote his emissary in Paris. "These
Yankees will require watching." Russell had moved a step closer to some still-
undefined type of intervention that aimed at stopping the war. But if his chief

motive was peace, he failed to convince the Lincoln administration. Any form of peace short of a full restoration of the Union was as unacceptable to the Union as was any form of peace short of southern independence unacceptable to the Confederacy. Russell had still not fathomed the critical issue of "Union" that underlay both antagonists' view of the Civil War. Although a reasonable man who believed in the power of compromise, he failed to recognize that the burgeoning conflict in America had already gone beyond the pale of reason.[22]

Adams, of course, was not privy to the London ministry's intergovernmental communications, leaving him to discern from various public statements a growing British support for the Union that had nothing to do with sentiment and everything to do with the war's impact on England. Seward's sharp warnings were having their desired effect on Britain's sensibilities, Adams reported to Washington, as was the British realization that any action injurious to the Union automatically meant support for the Confederacy and slavery. Adams's perceptive son and private secretary in the London legation, Henry Adams, noted that ever since the Union's virulent reaction to the queen's neutrality proclamation, the British had taken advantage of every opportunity to demonstrate goodwill to the Lincoln administration. The problem, as the younger Adams saw it, was that even British friends believed the United States's breakup unavoidable and that "this would be best for us as well as for themselves." The elder Adams worried, however, that few Englishmen grasped the integral relationship between the Union and slavery. One group denied that slavery was the issue in the war because the Union had not supported emancipation; the other side thought the breakup of the United States would promote abolition by isolating slavery in the Confederacy. Growing numbers of British observers believed the *Economist* correct in thinking southern independence certain and the Union's "forcible re-incorporation of the seceding states . . . about as hopeless a scheme as it is unwise an aim." The *Saturday Review* was angry with both American antagonists: "Neither of the belligerents has any reason to count on English assistance or sympathy, for the slave-owners are as loud in their childish threats of withholding their cotton from its principal market as the Republicans of the North in their blustering denunciations of [British] neutrality." In this regard, Russell and his contemporaries remained in harmony: The Union's continued resistance to southern separation would lead to a pointless waste of lives.[23]

These issues meshed with numerous others to show that international law did not guarantee security for everyone involved in a conflict even if they followed the prescribed rules of conduct. The vast body of law did not encompass every principle governing the behavior of all parties affected by the American Civil War. As in all wars, no antagonist will comply with rules that endanger its existence. And it follows that compliance by either side on any issue rested on advantages gained at the expense of the other. British neutrality fell within the dictates of international law, yet it caused bitter resentment in the North because of the prevailing belief that the Union had everything to lose while the Confederacy had everything to gain. At the same time, British neutrality offered the Confederacy unintended and false hopes of recognition and assured a prolongation of the war. Seward therefore concluded that the best strategy lay in his heated warnings that any form of foreign intervention meant war with the United States. It slowly became clear that the only solution to the diplomatic problems caused by the Civil War lay in the very antithesis of diplomacy: the battlefield.

On July 21, 1861, Confederate forces routed the Union army at Bull Run (Manassas Junction) in Virginia, further solidifying the British view that southern independence was a fait accompli. In all circles, recognition seemed closer than ever before. From his perch above the road leading from the battlefield, *Times* correspondent William H. Russell gazed at the huge dust clouds swirling upward in the wake of a once-proud but now panic-stricken Union army, scurrying piecemeal back to Washington a bare thirty miles away while frantically warning in that day's stifling summer heat of an imminent southern invasion of the capital. How ironic, he perhaps thought, that President Davis had moved to Richmond not two months earlier, creating an embarrassing challenge for the Union by putting the Confederate capital much closer to Washington and tempting an attack that now would more likely come on Washington itself rather than on Richmond. Russell's letters printed in the *New York Herald* and the *Times* of London vividly described the chaotic aftermath in a manner having a profound impact on both sides of the Atlantic. His graphic accounts of Union forces in full disarray earned him the contempt of northerners as "Bull-Run Russell" while giving the lie to the official claim that the Army of the Potomac had merely beat a strategic retreat. Palmerston snidely referred to the "Bull's Run Races" and "Yankee's Run" in declaring with undisguised relief that the Confederacy had confirmed its separation with a single stroke and the stubborn Union must accept the obvious conclusion. The end of the war was nigh.[24]

Bull Run further undercut an ongoing but stumbling Union project: New York banker August Belmont's efforts on behalf of the Lincoln administration to negotiate a European loan. The previous June, Belmont, American agent of the Rothschilds' banking firm in London, conducted a mission at the request of Secretary of the Treasury Salmon P. Chase that had not achieved any success primarily because of the military and financial uncertainty of the time. More than a month before Bull Run, the London bank turned down the monetary request, maintaining that "if the war should continue, it can only be carried on at a monumental expense, and loan would have to follow loan in order to provide the means." Applications to other London banks met the same response.[25]

If Belmont could not negotiate a loan for the Union, he appeared successful in helping to undermine one for his wartime enemy. He had earlier advised British financiers against granting loans to the Confederacy, insisting that such action could cause a war with the United States that would "entail ruin . . . upon the material interests of the commerce of the world." Such fears shook the *Economist*, which warned that "a war with either of the belligerents would be a terrible calamity, but a war between England and the *Northern* states of America would be the most affecting misfortune which could happen to civilization." It would wreck British shipping and investments in the Union, while destroying England's most lucrative commercial market.[26]

The Union army's defeat at Bull Run proved devastating to Belmont's loan efforts. Recognition of the Confederacy seemed certain as growing numbers of British observers considered southern independence a fait accompli. When Belmont tried to ease these thoughts and to remind Palmerston of southern slavery, the prime minister shot back: "We do not like slavery, but we want cotton and we dislike your Morrill tariff." Belmont, an ardent free trader himself, urged Seward to seek repeal of the law because it alienated British capitalists and Liberals who leaned toward the Union. Even John Bright, no supporter of the Confederacy, denounced the measure as "stupid and unpatriotic," and the *Times* bitterly dubbed it the "immoral tariff." The Republican Congress, however, refused to repeal the tariff and, in fact, raised its rates a number of times during the war. The Union's rout in the first pitched battle of the Civil War confirmed European doubts about investing in such a risky cause.[27]

Another outcome of Bull Run was increased British interest in intervening in the war for humanitarian reasons. Slavery was not the stated issue; nor was a pro-Union feeling. In late April, the Paris Rothschilds had called for an end to the hostilities in the name of humanitarianism. The London Rothschilds told Belmont that they had thought for some time that the South would not rejoin the Union by force, that the federal government must "see the evil of prosecuting so destructive a war" for no attainable purpose, and that a foreign mediation seemed wise.[28]

The image of Bull Run consumed the reality as the Confederacy sought to exploit this first—and surely the last—major battle of the war. Lyons thought that "cooler heads" in the North would realize there was no big silent pocket of loyalists in the South and that the chances for a Union victory had disappeared after this fiasco. The Union seemed thoroughly demoralized by the defeat, leading southerners to overlook their inability to amass an assault on Washington and boast that the war was over. But Russell and other careful observers soon noted that northern resilience was stronger than anyone had expected even if based on a reckless stubbornness. Russell wrote in his diary that "this prick in the great Northern balloon will let out a quantity of poisonous gas, and rouse the people to a sense of the nature of the conflict on which they have entered."[29] Angry northerners gained some consolation from blasting William Russell's lurid (but accurate) accounts of the battle, even though their reaction was a transparent attempt to avoid admitting that the enemy was much stronger than presumed. President Davis already had a secret service operation under way in Europe, and its leader, the enormously talented businessman James D. Bulloch, suddenly found mercantile doors swing open when he sought contracts with private firms for constructing so-called commercial vessels that in reality became the warships of a Confederate navy.

The prognosis for Confederate recognition appeared to be the greatest benefactor of the Union's humiliation at Bull Run. The three southern commissioners had agreed that the British and French governments would remain neutral until they realized that the Union could not subdue the Confederacy. Antislavery feeling had no bearing on the issue; the Confederacy must prove itself a nation by winning a major battle in Virginia. Now, elated by the news from Bull Run, the commissioners sent Lord John Russell a note requesting a treaty of friendship, commerce, and navigation. They informed the foreign secretary of their decision to hold off making a formal request for recognition until the full impact of Bull Run had set in and removed all doubt of their right to independence. They reminded Russell that Lincoln had made no move to free the slaves and that even if he did so now, his action would only be a frantic attempt to win British sympathies. Indeed, they darkly warned, he was not above inciting slave insurrections to undermine the Confederacy. Restoration of the Union had proved impossible, the commissioners argued. Recognition of the Confederacy must follow.[30]

Even though Russell remained unconvinced that the time had come for recognition, the Union could not have known this and angrily believed the worst. The British foreign secretary responded to the Confederate commissioners with a note affirming his nation's neutrality and declaring that any treaty with the Confederacy was out of the question because it was tantamount to extending recognition. The decisive consideration had become clear to Russell. Only a resolution by arms or a negotiated settlement, he wrote the southern commissioners, would lead to British recognition of Confederate independence. Russell refused to take any action that might determine the war's verdict. Adams, however, concluded that the British regarded southern independence as a fait accompli after the battle of Bull Run. Since they already thought Union subjugation of the Confederacy impossible, they now believed "the only thing to do is to recognize the necessity of a new government."[31]

The Union's concern over the outcome at Bull Run encouraged the Lincoln administration to assuage British fears regarding the port closing measure. Seward suddenly emphasized that Lincoln would consider the interests of other nations before implementing what the secretary now carefully referred to as "enabling" legislation. Its enactment, Seward explained, did not mean that the president *would* close the ports but that he *should* have the power to do so. Furthermore, he apologized to Lyons for failing to keep Adams abreast of the administration's views so that he might inform the ministry in London; increasing work demands were responsible for the delay. But Lyons was not fooled by Seward's new coat of sheepskin and recommended that his superiors in London "disabuse both [the U.S.] Government and [its] people of the delusion that they can carry their points with us by bluster and violence, and that we are more afraid of a war than they are."[32]

The ephemeral truce in Anglo-American relations came to an abrupt end in mid-August, when news reached Seward that a private citizen from Charleston, Robert Mure, was preparing to leave New York for London, carrying dispatches from Richmond to the British Foreign Office that suggested imminent recognition of the Confederacy. Regardless of the content of the papers, Seward realized, their acceptance in London meant the establishment of Anglo-Confederate relations and the surety of war between the United States and Britain.[33]

As in so many earlier incidents, the British found that no matter how noble their intentions, their claim to neutrality convinced neither the Union nor the Confederacy. In an effort to establish commercial guidelines that reduced the likelihood of British involvement, Russell had taken it upon himself to urge the Confederacy (as he had the Union) to adhere to all terms in the Declaration of Paris except the ban on privateering. But this seemingly innocent overture carried the seeds of recognition—or so believed both American antagonists.

If Russell's intentions were laudatory, his judgment was not. He should have realized that *any* British contact with the Richmond government elevated it to a level above that of rebel. Had not the harsh Union reaction to his reception of the southern commissioners provided ample warning of the danger in communicating with the Confederacy? Furthermore, the Union thought the plot thickened when learning that Mure held the position of colonel in the Confederacy's military forces in South Carolina and was a cousin of the British consul in New Orleans. Moreover, he carried dispatches for the southern commissioners in London and had secured his passport from the British consul in Charleston, Robert Bunch—the latter action a violation of a State Department directive barring foreign consuls from issuing passports without the countersignatures of the secretary of state and the U.S. Army's commanding general. The web of conspiracy proved too tightly woven for Seward to dismiss as a coincidence. Nor could he believe that Russell was so lacking in common sense as to stray innocently into this mindless jumble. Seward ordered New York police to seize Mure and his papers. Among the confiscated items were a sealed pouch, numerous private letters (only four of which were unsealed), a letter of introduction by Bunch, and, most exasperating, several copies of a pamphlet praising the Confederate army's performance at Bull Run.[34]

Impressions again spoke louder than truth, and in the feverish aftermath of Bull Run threatened to cause a major Anglo-American confrontation over intervention. Seward was infuriated that a British consul, whose authority was commercial and not diplomatic, had placed a diplomatic seal on dispatches to Confederate emissaries in England and had the audacity to include inflammatory anti-Union materials in those diplomatic pouches. If not a violation of neutrality, what further action was necessary to make it so? If not proof of southern treason, how far must the rebels go before the Lincoln government could take action? That the papers had not gone through Lyons's hands in Washington provided further proof of malicious intent. Indeed, Bunch's letter of introduction emphasized the importance of *hiding* the papers from Union officials. Without breaking the diplomatic seal protecting the bulk of the package, Seward read the few letters that were open and became incensed over Britain's sinister behavior and the Confederacy's traitorous actions. Particularly galling was the revelation that Bunch had worked with the French consul in Charleston in sending an intermediary to Richmond to discuss diplomatic issues. One letter addressed to a Confederate agent overseas boasted, "This is the first step of direct treating with our government." Seward sent the entire bag to Adams in London, angrily calling Bunch a "conspirator" against the Union and declaring that the British had taken "the *first step* to recognition."[35]

A testy exchange ensued between Adams and Russell, during which the Union minister bitterly assailed the transparent effort at negotiations and the British foreign secretary vehemently denied any designs on granting recognition to the Confederacy. Adams charged that the British and French consuls, whether or not by home directives, had collaborated with the Confederacy against the Union. Russell must recall Bunch, Adams insisted. Now under fire, the foreign secretary reluctantly admitted that Bunch had acted under "secret instructions" but quickly assured Adams that they had nothing to do with recognition. Russell initially explained that since the Washington government had suspended postal communications of British subjects across Union-Confederate lines, Bunch had merely facilitated their contact by authorizing the inclusion of private correspondence in consular bags. This argument proved reckless and foolish behavior even if true, because anyone in Bunch's position should have seen the danger in such a rash act. Worse, Russell should have prohibited such action as provocative to the extreme. Seeing Adams's skeptical reaction to this remarkably lame defense, Russell decided to reveal the whole truth and in doing so acknowledged that he had not been straightforward from the beginning. The British and French, he explained, had earlier agreed to cooperate in maintaining the right of neutral commercial traffic with America and, to promote this objective, decided that the Confederacy must adhere to all provisions in the Declaration of Paris, save that on privateering. Russell had been willing to negotiate with the Confederacy, somehow reasoning that to do so did *not* constitute recognition. He refused to recall Bunch and emphatically declared that his government had "not recognized, and [was] not prepared to recognize the so-called Confederate States as a separate and independent State."[36]

Palmerston could not have been pleased at his foreign secretary's monumental indiscretion, but he predictably closed ranks in supporting his colleague and hoped the two Atlantic nations could escape the situation short of war. The prime minister doubted that Lincoln would "draw the sword," though he could not be sure. Americans had proved themselves "so wild" about other seemingly inconsequential matters that they were capable of barbaric behavior at any time. The Bunch affair appeared to be another effort by the Lincoln administration to instigate war with the British. Both Palmerston and Russell sought to build up Canada's defenses and enlarge Britain's Atlantic squadron. Careful not to provoke Gladstone and others who resisted the buildup on economic grounds, Palmerston exclaimed that no one "with half an Eye in his Head, or half an Idea in his Brain could fail to perceive what a lowering of the Position of England in the world would follow the Conquest of our North American provinces by the north americans, especially after the Bulls Run Races." At the worst, Palmerston believed, the United States would act on emotions and order Lyons out of the country. In that event, the prime minister declared, Lyons should relocate in Canada until Seward's hotheadedness had passed.[37]

Despite Russell's last-second candor, he had again demonstrated his inability to grasp the magnitude of the conflict in North America. He had repeatedly experienced how sensitive the United States was to every action he took in the name of neutrality. Had not Lyons made clear that a mere conversation with Confederate officials would raise a cry of outrage in the Union? Ignoring repeated warning signs, Russell had secretly authorized a consul having no diplomatic status to negotiate with a belligerent. Surely bilateral discussions extended tacit recognition to the Confederacy. Furthermore, he had accepted Bunch's assurance that Mure told the truth in asserting that the diplomatic pouch contained only private letters of a business nature. Indeed, Bunch had added, the so-called passport given to Mure was a simple certificate authorizing him to transport British dispatches to London. This last statement angered Russell, for Bunch had violated Lyons's directives against entrusting British dispatches to anyone carrying private correspondence. Russell nonetheless continued to insist that the British had *not* taken a step toward recognition, still failing to see a connection between negotiations and recognition. This is incomprehensible, given this touchy period in which every action he took was subject to intense scrutiny about whether it related to recognition. He knew the danger, once remarking that recognition was the "only step which the US have any pretence to take ill."[38]

The Confederacy meanwhile saw the potential gains derived from Russell's invitation and welcomed negotiations with the British. To foster its image as a nation and to exploit the raw relationship between Britain and the Union, the Richmond Congress immediately approved Russell's request. Despite his disclaimers, the foreign secretary had initiated talks with the Confederacy and thereby signified its status as a nation.[39]

Russell had gotten involved in an imprudent effort that directly interfered in American affairs and yet lacked the support of his colleagues primarily because of the *way* he had proceeded rather than because he had taken the British government one step closer to recognition. Gladstone saw the danger that somehow escaped the head of the Foreign Office. A consul, he wrote Secretary for War George Cornewall Lewis, must not act as an "instrument in making any necessary arrangement with the Southern States." Lyons allowed that Russell's motives were defensible but his methods were not. Russell had tried to achieve something that did not fall within his power. Under the Paris Declaration, no signatory had the right to negotiate a separate agreement on any of its terms with a nonsignatory. Then, in a statement demonstrating that Lyons, too, failed to understand the intensity of the American war, he blandly observed that there was a better way. By "conciliatory words, by avoiding as far as possible abstract assertions of principle, and especially by never yielding an iota in practice, we shall by degrees accustom the government and the People here to see us treat the Confederate States as *de facto* independent." Indeed, Lyons rethought his remarks about the Paris pact by musing that Russell's attempt to secure Confederate compliance with its provisions might have succeeded if Mure had not carried "foolish private letters."[40]

The Lincoln administration reacted to Russell's actions in predictable fashion: It revoked the British consul's exequatur (the U.S. government's written recognition of his authority as consul), accusing him of seeking British recognition of the Confederacy. Russell's clandestine attempt to initiate diplomatic contact with the Confederacy left an image of backhandedness that substantiated Seward's direst premonitions about British self-interest. The "proceeding in which [Bunch] was engaged," the secretary furiously charged, "was in the nature of a treaty with the insurgents, and the first step towards a recognition by Great Britain of their sovereignty."[41]

Ill feelings over the Bunch affair gradually receded, only to resume over a host of other issues that more often than not related to intervention. The British continued their military buildup in Canada, increasing northern apprehension about an attack rather than a defensive measure. In London, Mobile journalist and now Confederate agent Henry Hotze hurriedly prepared to publish the *Index*, a newly created weekly journal that sought to build pro-Confederate support throughout Britain. From the British capital came disturbing news: Rebel agents had purchased the sleek and fast *Bermuda*, which soon ran the Union blockade and arrived safely in Savannah, Georgia. Furthermore, these same agents had contracted with British shipbuilders in

Liverpool for the construction of two huge cruisers that, under their eventual names of *Alabama* and *Florida*, would serve as blockade-runners and Union raiders and thus become the heart of a fledgling Confederate navy. The Union, however, confronted its most immediate problem in Mexico, where the War of the Reform had ended in December 1860 but left a legacy of violence that, like the Civil War raging above the Rio Grande, virtually invited foreign intervention and threatened hemispheric peace. Especially striking, outside involvement in Mexico could set a precedent for similar actions in the American Civil War.[42]

Russell realized that the American situation was fast slipping out of control. To his friend and former U.S. minister in London, Edward Everett, the foreign secretary revealed his deepest concerns. The Union's continual harping about his policies had worn his patience to the point that he must have questioned the wisdom of adhering to principle. Did not his own hatred of slavery make clear that only this emotional issue combined with its racial underpinnings could underlay the ferocity of the American contest? Russell attributed England's problems to Lincoln's refusal to admit that the war was over slavery. The London ministry would surely have leaned toward the antislavery Union if it had focused on the moral differences dividing the two sides in the war. Instead, Lincoln had talked fuzzily of preserving the Union and succeeded only in confusing everyone who struggled to understand the basis of the fighting. In accordance with international law, the Palmerston government had declared neutrality, confident that the White House would recognize the advantages falling in its favor. The United States's best interest, Russell fervently believed, lay in accepting southern separation as a fait accompli. Two American republics—one free, the other slave—offered the only feasible way to halt a war that almost daily reached new levels of atrocity. But all Russell gained from his many anxious hours of dealing with the conflict as an honest neutral was the bitter Union accusation that he was pro-Confederate and the Confederacy's continual entreaties for recognition.[43]

Russell was both angry and hurt by the Union's scurrilous attacks on his character. Why should a strict adherent to the rules come under vicious assault? How could the Union fail to understand that its blockade had implied a state of war that, based on international law, necessitated British neutrality and recognition of southern belligerency? The British government would never ponder the question of recognizing southern independence until the Confederacy, in fact, had won its independence. The conflict must render its own verdict on the battlefield.

Perhaps, Russell began to suspect, the only solution lay in an intervention to end the fighting. How ironic and yet satisfying that such action fell within the confines of international law. Nonbelligerent nations, he knew, had the right—even the duty—to urge those peoples at war to stop fighting and resolve their differences nonviolently. As a civilized nation, England bore a moral responsibility to devise a peaceful solution. Both antagonists had proved their point: The Union had given all it had and would suffer no loss of honor in acknowledging southern independence; the Confederacy had demonstrated sufficient determination to entitle it to a place in the community of nations. The Union had found it impossible to subjugate an area so large and a people so numerous. Prolonging the war meant massive devastation for both parties, along with the increasing likelihood of outside involvement by other nations not as disinterested as the British.

Instead of consoling, however, Russell found his friend Everett blunt and unforgiving in regard to the foreign secretary's inability to comprehend the meaning of the conflict in America. In early September, during the embittered Bunch affair, the arrival of Everett's letter in the Foreign Office only added to Russell's discomfiture. Everett felt betrayed by Russell. Had not their long sessions of whist and other social niceties helped to convince the British that the Atlantic relationship was positive? Despite the admitted legality of neutrality, Russell should have understood the practical necessity of bending the rules to demonstrate British affinity with the United States during its darkest hour. Recognition of southern belligerency and the reception of the Confederate commissioners had come too precipitously to a Union that had found every minute of its agony equivalent to a lifetime. Everett could not discern even a murmur of sympathy from the British; on the contrary, their "cold neutrality" suggested connivance with the southern traitors.[44]

Rather than accusing Russell of sinister motives, Everett criticized him for not making a thorough examination of the American situation before taking such decisive action. Russell exemplified the narrow-minded disposition of most British observers in failing to see that the war had grown out of slavery. The Union's most fundamental assumption at the war's outset was that Britain's antislavery views would prevent any action offering encouragement to the Confederacy. How shocking to the Lincoln administration that the British had set aside their antislavery sentiment and welcomed the breakup of the United States. Lincoln realized that great moral purpose guided his wartime effort and that he could not allow the South to leave the Union in peace. But before Adams could set foot in London to plead his case, the British ministry had declared neutrality, extended belligerent recognition to the Confederacy, and infuriated the Union by, in effect, condoning secession.[45]

Everett's assault on Russell was too severe. Even though the issues under-lying the Civil War seemed obvious to the former U.S. minister to England, he presumed too much in expecting Russell and his people to comprehend the full dimensions of a crisis three thousand miles away. Certainly Rus-sell understood the integral role of slavery in the war; yet he had no way of appreciating how political and constitutional considerations had prevented Lincoln from highlighting slavery as the root of the conflict. Reason had led the president, like Everett, to believe that the British would see this funda-mental truth. But this was war, and war seldom lends itself to rational think-ing. This hope—perhaps assumption—that the British would understand the real issues in America had proved to be a major miscalculation that con-tributed to the confusion. Had not Lincoln publicly emphasized the Union's preservation as the chief objective of the war? Had he not opposed only the expansion of slavery while recognizing the legal sanctity of the institution where it already existed? What kind of principle was this? The essence of international communications is to make messages simple and clear while leaving nothing for assumption. Just as Lincoln had little choice in his initial treatment of the war, so did Russell have little alternative to his initial reac-tion of neutrality.

As the arguments intensified over British neutrality, however, Russell had inched closer to some yet-undetermined form of intervention designed to end the American war. Seward had repeatedly warned that British inter-vention meant war with the United States—a challenge Russell did not take lightly. Yet he knew that failure to make an effort to stop the conflict meant not just forsaking his responsibility as leader of a civilized nation; doing nothing to prevent its prolongation into a more vicious war could ultimately compel a forceful intervention for both economic and humanitarian con-siderations. Not only would the war inflict widespread material destruction on both North and South, but also it would damage the British and other nations that had enjoyed a close commercial relationship with the United States. Moreover, the growing ferocity of the conflict provided another rea-son for bringing it to an end.

Russell found the remedy in a broad interpretation of international law that permitted nonbelligerent nations to do everything in their power to halt an ongoing war that threatened injury to them as well as to the prin-cipal actors. Vattel had argued that not only did a neutral nation have the obligation to help warring peoples stave off "disaster and ruin, so far as it can do without running too great a risk," but it also could intervene when its own welfare was at stake.[46] As a civilized nation, England bore a moral and legal obligation to show the way to peace. The time seemed propitious: Both northerners and southerners had ostensibly satisfied honor and principle, the former in trying to preserve the Union, the latter in reaffirming the irrevocable nature of secession.

At this point, Russell received support for intervention from across the English Channel: Emperor Napoleon III of France reiterated his interest in stopping the American conflict. Surely he was concerned about the steadily depleting supply of cotton. Doubtless he agreed with the British in concluding that the Union lacked the capacity to subjugate so much territory and so many people. Certainly he recognized the opportunity to fulfill the shattered dream of his illustrious uncle, Napoleon I, who had wanted to restore a French Empire in the New World (lost after the Treaty of Paris of 1763 ending the French and Indian War) that would swing the world balance of power away from England. Unfortunately for him, however, his search for glory in foreign policy depended too heavily on following the British lead rather than taking the initiative. As he allegedly remarked, "Other countries are my mistresses, but England is my wife."[47] The reality was that he needed the British more than they needed him, but in his world realities did not always determine his policies. Most definitely, the younger Napoleon was a notorious adventurer who repeatedly ignored danger and schemed his way into matters that furthered his own imperial interests. Those French who revered the first Napoleon may have sneeringly referred to his nephew as "Napoleon the Little" because of his short, squat stature, and they may have snickered at the remark of President Lincoln's private secretary, John Hay, who characterized the emperor's sideways walk as similar to that of a "gouty crab." But they also knew that Napoleon III had a marked propensity to act without thinking through all the consequences—and this raised questions about his motives in wanting to intervene in the American war.[48]

Russell was familiar with the longtime machinations of Napoleon III and thought his chief objective was self-aggrandizement; but he also knew that if the French emperor oftentimes acted foolishly, he was no fool. France posed a growing threat to Britain's maritime supremacy, and the two nations had noticeably cooled their relationship since its high point of triumph in the Crimean War with Russia of the previous decade. Russell realized that, as in nearly all alliances, the Anglo-French entente regarding the American contest rested solely on mutual self-interest. He also knew that a joint intervention was less dangerous than a unilateral action. Not only would the cooperating nations pose a more formidable force, but also withdrawal in the event of failure was far less dishonorable when done in the company

Napoleon III, emperor of France
(Courtesy of the Library of Congress)

of others. Also important, Russell recognized the value of keeping France preoccupied with American affairs and therefore less likely to exploit other trouble spots in the world.[49]

Mercier took the lead in talking with Lyons in October 1861 about the wisdom of a joint intervention. The French minister had recently returned to Washington after a highly publicized tour of both the Union and the Confederacy with Prince Napoleon Jerome Bonaparte. Northerners had reacted angrily to the visit, for the prince was Napoleon III's cousin and second in the line of succession to the throne. The emperor, they feared, had revived France's longtime designs on the New World, making the visit an integral part of a European movement toward recognition. Just two weeks after the Union's disaster at Bull Run, the prince had sought a pass to the battlefield. Seward had consented, but only with great reluctance. William H. Russell highlighted the problem Seward and others had with the younger Napoleon: His presence in the South appeared to underline French "recognition of the Confederates as a belligerent power." Mercier provided substance for this inflamed reaction. In a private meeting with Lyons, he focused on the contents of a letter to the prince from Thouvenel. According to the foreign minister's missive, the French need for cotton had become so critical that they sought to end the American war by some form of joint intervention with the British. The two countries, Mercier declared, should extend diplomatic recognition to the Confederacy and then warn the Union not to interfere with the Atlantic trade.[50]

Mercier emphasized, however, that the time had not yet come for intervention. The Union, he believed, had recovered from its defeat at Bull Run and was again overly confident. When the last burst of optimism disappeared, the time for Anglo-French intervention would have arrived. Mercier thought British cooperation a surety in light of their dependence on southern cotton. But he was unaware of the huge surplus afforded by the three years of bountiful harvests in the South just before the war. France likewise had an abundance of cotton on hand, but when that supply ran out it would be in trouble. Whereas England bought 80 percent of its cotton from the American South and found other sources in India, Egypt, China, and Brazil, France drew a whopping 93 percent from southern cotton growers but had been unable to find adequate alternative supplies despite a worldwide search. When Lyons indicated that his government was not prepared either to recognize the Confederacy or to challenge the blockade, Mercier assured him that if England refused to intervene, "France would not act alone."[51]

Lyons dutifully forwarded Mercier's proposal to London, but with the caveat that the only way recognition could end the war was for the intervening powers to use military force. The United States, Lyons insisted, would not stop fighting until its leaders became convinced that its restoration was impossible. That time would probably never come. Hence the British and French must have a formidable naval force that they could use "promptly and energetically and above all with no symptom of hesitation." Recognition would not halt the conflict unless accompanied by "a defensive (if not also an offensive) Alliance with the South."[52]

Palmerston agreed with Lyons's call to stand clear of the American war at the present time but cautioned that the situation could change. The hostilities had thus far inflicted no major economic damage on other nations and therefore provided no justification for intervention. Prolonged fighting, however, would change matters by causing economic problems in England and elsewhere. "This cotton question," Palmerston told Russell, "will most certainly assume a serious character by the beginning of next year; and if the American civil war has not by that time come to an end, I suspect that we shall be obliged either singly or conjointly with France to tell the northerners that we cannot allow some millions of our people to perish to please the Northern States and that the blockade of the South must be so far relaxed as to [allow] cotton loaded ships to come out."[53]

Palmerston remained cautious about becoming involved in a war that had not yet convinced northerners of the Union's dissolution. "A Rupture with the United States," he warned Russell, "would at all times be an Evil." Not only would the harsh Canadian winter obstruct a British assault from the north, but such an encounter would greatly benefit the French. They had no direct contact with the United States and would suffer fewer casualties in a war. Furthermore, the French navy was larger than the Union's and they had a smaller volume of commerce to risk. We should "lie on our oars," Palmerston insisted. The war's operations, he told Russell's undersecretary, "have as yet been too indecisive to warrant an acknowledgment of the Southern Union."[54]

At this juncture, the threat of foreign intervention in Mexico tied itself to the American Civil War by heightening the United States's apprehension of a European involvement that came through its southern neighbor. Presently deeply embroiled in postwar problems, Mexico remained a bare skeleton of a once-powerful and sprawling Spanish colony formerly known as New Spain. Mexico had borrowed heavily from England, France, and Spain, and now found itself called upon to meet its debts during a chaotic post–civil war period that made the splintered nation highly vulnerable to forced collection. The new republic under Liberal president Benito Juárez suspended debt payments and caused a firestorm abroad. As so often happens, an economic inroad can grow into a political-military involvement that, in this case, could directly challenge the Monroe Doctrine as guardian of the hemisphere. Foreign intervention would implant three European powers in the southern part of the Western Hemisphere and provide precedent for a similar joint venture above the Rio Grande.[55]

The Lincoln administration feared a European intervention in Mexico as the first step toward foreign involvement in the American war. Adams in London pointed out that European control of Mexico's coast would undermine the Union blockade by permitting the entry of foreign goods into the Confederacy through the back door. Dayton in Paris warned of "an imposing fleet" of European steamers soon stationed in the West Indies, carrying troops for the expedition but watching American affairs as much as those of Mexico. Like Adams, Dayton thought the powers could put a large fleet in the Gulf of Mexico and encourage their nationals to challenge the Union blockade. The mere presence of European warships could lead to a collision with Union vessels. French interests rather than sympathies would decide policy. The first French emperor, Dayton reminded Seward, had once asserted that "a statesman's heart should be in his head." The present emperor would act on that same principle. Despite all the "professions of good feeling," France "would, in the end, look to her own interests and, do it too, in connection with Great Britain."[56]

The Washington government had tried to circumvent this new danger by assuming Mexico's debts, but it succeeded only in drawing both domestic and foreign opposition. The U.S. minister to Mexico, Thomas Corwin, recommended a loan of perhaps $12 million in exchange for the U.S. acquisition of Baja California (believed in danger of Confederate takeover) or a major reduction in tariffs on goods imported into Mexico. The proposed arrangement (ultimately voted down by the U.S. Senate) drew Palmerston's scorn because the securities sought for the loan would come in the form of public lands and mineral rights. As he cynically observed, "A mortgage of Mexico to the United States . . . would certainly lead to foreclosing."[57]

Napoleon III's objective extended beyond collecting debts; he intended to establish a monarchy in Mexico aimed at restoring order and halting U.S. expansion into Latin America, building a French commercial empire in the Western Hemisphere, restructuring Europe by negotiating an alliance with Austria, and, most important, reshaping the world balance of power in France's favor. Granting recognition to the Confederacy would create a friendly buffer nation between the United States and a French-controlled Mexico.[58]

But Napoleon's imperial interests were not the sole guide for French behavior; like the British, many French observers regarded the war's outcome as a fait accompli whose destruction threatened to spread beyond American borders. In a private note to Mercier that he allowed Seward to read, Thouvenel expressed great concern about the impact of the American war on France and other nations. The vicious fighting indicated that no end was in sight. Compromise was out of the question, leaving "only force" to shorten the war. The "European Countries severally, unavoidably suffer more from interruption of their ordinary intercourse with the United States than they could be obliged to suffer by a similar interruption of intercourse with any other nation." The loss of cotton would hurt industry worldwide and lead to starvation in France. "The crisis in France is about to begin." To replenish the cotton supply, the Union must relax its blockade. Seward rejected any thought of doing this and, in fact, did not believe the situation that serious. Had the European countries used their "moral influence" in favor of the Union and "against the suicidal miserable attempts of our disloyal citizens to overthrow it, this civil war would well nigh have come to an end already."

Instead, they had searched for a compromise "at the cost of the Union itself." If the Union fell, the entire economic network that France was so dependent on "will disappear forever."[59]

Thouvenel was not privy to all the emperor's plans, but he knew that France's rapidly falling cotton supply had necessitated putting aside his personal support for the Union in favor of reopening the cotton flow with the Confederacy. More than 200,000 workers in France and another million in England depended on cotton. Its continued depletion, he told Dayton, would probably "destroy some of the strongest French firms" in the cities of Lyons and Bordeaux. "The pressure might become so great from these quarters that governments *could not but heed it* and look to its remedy." Dayton warned that "in the event of a war, which must necessarily follow any interference, that other interests in England and France would of necessity suffer to an extent far beyond any advantage which could be gained from an increased supply of cotton or the present opening of trade with some Port of the South." Thouvenel instructed Mercier to urge Lyons to support a joint intervention that, admittedly, raised the likelihood of Confederate recognition.[60]

The tripartite foreign intrusion in Mexico loomed as particularly dangerous to the Union because the French emperor's machinations threatened hemispheric security and provided the Confederacy with hopes of an alliance. Seward tried to secure a pledge from the European powers that they sought only to collect on their debts. Dayton met with Thouvenel, authorized to offer a U.S. guarantee on the interest on the loan. But Thouvenel rejected this proposal, declaring that his government must have the principal. The three powers sought nothing more than Mexico's payment of its debts. Dayton remained suspicious. "I cannot but feel," he wrote Seward, "that all these Governments are disposed to take advantage of the present distracted condition of the United States."[61]

Dayton could not have imagined the magnitude of Napoleon's intentions. As early as November 1861 Prince Richard Metternich, Austria's ambassador to Paris, was certain that the French emperor had decided to install Austrian Archduke Ferdinand Maximilian Joseph as monarch in Mexico. Indeed, Napoleon brazenly revealed to Metternich the procedure by which the new monarch would assume power and then build a modern state. Within a month rumors of Maximilian's ascension had become so widespread in Europe that Russell asked the Austrian ambassador in London whether the archduke had agreed to take the throne. The response was disturbing: Maximilian was waiting for suitable conditions before deciding whether to accept the offer. He and his wife Charlotte, unaware of the opposition in London,

Austrian Archduke Ferdinand Maximilian, emperor of Mexico. After an engraving by Metzmacher Pierre Guillaume. (Courtesy of the Library of Congress)

soon agreed to take the throne. The new monarch proudly proclaimed to Empress Eugénie in Austria that he was about to engage in a "holy work"— a crusade to save the Mexican people from their backward existence. As the guardian of monarchical order against the chaos engendered by republicanism, he intended to incorporate Central America into the new Mexican Empire and, with the collaboration of Maximilian's cousin, the emperor of Brazil, divide Spanish South America between them.[62]

Over the bitter objections of his cabinet colleagues, Russell emphasized the importance of cultivating French support in ending the American war and won the prime minister's approval in collecting the debts in Mexico. Lewis denounced the use of force in collecting debts from "a notoriously bankrupt, dishonest, and unsettled government." War was certain with a country in "anarchy," which would be "like fighting with the Arabs of the desert." Russell, however, told the queen that the British must send a naval force to help seize Vera Cruz and force payment of debts. He called for U.S. participation in the effort and, surely suspicious of Napoleon's broader objectives, stressed that the British government must publicly renounce any intention of interfering with the Mexican government. Failure to take these measures, he noted, would violate British adherence to nonintervention, enmesh England in Mexico's domestic turmoil, and alienate the United

States. Lewis vehemently warned against "a Foreign Office war, in which the Cabinet is to have no voice." His brother-in-law, the Earl of Clarendon, disgustedly remarked that a probable declaration of war on Mexico without cabinet consultation would be "Palmerstonian." When he urged the prime minister to seek the cabinet's advice on a blockade of Vera Cruz, Palmerston responded almost in jest, "Oh, ah! the Cabinet . . . very well; call one then, if you think it necessary."[63]

Given Russell's growing interest in ending the American war, his decision to join Napoleon III in Mexico was not surprising even if certain to alienate the Union. What better pretext for intervening in the conflict than to establish a precedent in Mexico that rested on the principles of international law? One would be hard pressed to find a more emphatic demonstration of the dangers of foreign intervention, no matter how professedly benign. England, France, and Spain dutifully agreed to pull out after collecting their debts, hoping to provide credence for their claimed disinterest. And in another weak effort to alleviate suspicions of imperial motives, they invited the United States to participate in the venture. The invitation came "somewhat late," acidly remarked Dayton to Thouvenel. On October 31 the three powers signed the Treaty of London, authorizing a military expedition to Mexico to seek "the redress of grievances."[64]

Seward rejected both their assurance and their invitation. Although he had foolishly called for war the previous April, he had matured enough to realize how imprudent it would be for the Union to challenge the three European powers while fighting the Confederacy. Indeed, with the European concert firmly entrenched in Mexico, the three powers might welcome American resistance as an opportunity to turn their attention northward and make Seward's fear of foreign intervention a self-fulfilling prophecy. Once the Union quashed the secessionists, he groused, it would deal with its new European neighbors.[65]

On the Confederate side, however, the Great Power intervention in Mexico presented the tantalizing possibility of gaining up to three allies that might, in the process of satisfying their own interests, advance those of the Confederacy. Not protesting the intervention in Mexico would be a small price to pay for a quid pro quo of recognition and perhaps an alliance to guarantee the American South's new independence. But the advantages were mutual. The Confederacy, as it knew, offered something tangible to the European nations: an ally that discouraged a Union attack. Once achieving independence, it could deal with any foreign forces still occupying Mexico after the Civil War had ended. But for the moment, the possibilities afforded by a Union clash with the intervening powers offered the Confederacy an unparalleled opportunity to establish independence.

The battle at Bull Run had opened the door to the most significant foreign threat to the United States since the War of 1812. The challenge to the Union was evident. Seward had warned of England's self-interested motives and now felt justified in his prognosis. But the danger encompassed the Confederacy as well. Even though the threat was obscured by the Confederacy's immediate needs and the goodwill assurances of all three powers, the chief mover in the Mexican enterprise was the ever-devious and greatly ambitious Napoleon III. British and French neutrality had encouraged the Richmond government to expect recognition, and it had now silently acquiesced to a joint Old World venture whose necessary by-product was southern separation. The *Times*, Charles Francis Adams noted, had asserted that the destruction of the United States removed a major threat to Europe. Henry Adams characterized the Union's supporters in England as "lukewarm" and declared that no one in Europe would help. "They all hate us and fear us.... We must depend wholly on ourselves."[66] The Confederacy, on the other hand, saw immediate advantages in the tripartite intervention—particularly with the French—and was ready to pursue a risky policy of working with the interventionist powers in an effort to secure independence. It would deal with its new postwar neighbor(s) after winning the war with the Union.

The Union's blanket criticism of England and its people was not justified, for *Russell* was the chief spokesman for those who supported intervention and believed southern independence a foregone conclusion. In pondering these weighty issues, he held to his broad definition of neutrality, which encompassed the right of neutrals to intervene in a war that damaged their welfare. Furthermore, he considered southern independence certain and the war senseless. Russell had decided that the best solution to the American problem was southern separation. The joint effort in Mexico, he seemed to believe, would signal the Union that the same corrective action could occur in the Civil War if the belligerents refused to come to the peace table. From Russell's vantage point, southern independence would help the Union by ending the bloodshed and ultimately forcing the collapse of slavery. In a stand never supported by his colleagues but one that found favor with Lord Robert Cecil and a number of other Conservatives, Russell argued that as the sole slave nation in North America, the Confederacy would come under tremendous domestic and foreign pressure to approve emancipation as a more attractive alternative to a steady drain of slaves escaping into neighboring free territories. A breakup of the United States, Russell told Lyons, guaranteed the death of slavery. "For this reason I wish for separation."[67]

But before Russell could find a way to convince the Lincoln administration that southern independence was a fait accompli, a crisis developed in Anglo-American relations in late 1861 that threatened to thrust the two Atlantic nations into a war that would virtually guarantee Confederate nationhood.

CHAPTER 3

The Trent *and Confederate Independence*

> [The Union's action was] an affront to the
> British flag and a violation of international law.
> —LORD JOHN RUSSELL TO LORD LYONS, November 30, 1861

> We will wrap the whole world in flames!
> —WILLIAM H. SEWARD, December 16, 1861

In early November 1861 the commander of the USS *San Jacinto*, Captain Charles Wilkes, forcefully removed two southern emissaries, James M. Mason and John Slidell, from the British mail packet HMS *Trent* and threatened an Anglo-American war that would all but assure the Confederacy's independence. Mason and Slidell had sought to deal a lethal blow to the Union by convincing the British and French to disavow the blockade and extend diplomatic recognition to the Confederacy. But they could not have known how close they came to achieving this objective *before* reaching Europe.

At about midnight on October 12, 1861, the CSS *Theodora* steamed out of Charleston Harbor in a rainstorm, hovering close to the coast and a bare two miles from the pale lights of the Union's blockade squadron. Among the vessel's passengers were Confederate emissaries Mason and Slidell, then on a surreptitious voyage to the Bahamas, where they planned to book passage for their final destinations of England and France, respectively. Finding that no British mail steamers went to Nassau, the *Theodora* headed for Havana, where the two diplomats received a warm welcome and an invitation to stay at a plantation on the island. Mason and Slidell intended to make connections on the Danish island of St. Thomas, which was the British point of departure for the home port of Southampton. From there Mason would travel to London and Slidell to Paris. Their mission: to secure British and French recognition of the Confederacy.[1]

Mason and Slidell bore instructions that, if consummated in London and Paris, would have granted the Confederacy nationhood status and increased its chances for winning the war. They were to present evidence to the British and French governments that the Union blockade was ineffective and to seek recognition of southern independence as the prelude to negotiating treaties of amity and commerce. To accomplish these goals, the emissaries were to use King Cotton Diplomacy in emphasizing the importance of that product to Europe's textile mills, while convincing the European powers of their opportunity to strike a blow at U.S. commercial competition and to establish a balance of power in North America that protected British and French interests in the hemisphere. As one contemporary southerner proudly put it, "We point to that little attenuated cotton thread, which a child can break, but which nevertheless *can hang the world.*" So confident was the Confederacy in the righteousness and capabilities of its cause that Mason and Slidell were not to ask for "material aid or alliances offensive and defensive, but [only] for . . . a recognized place as a free and independent people."[2]

President Davis, like European observers from overseas, thought the Confederate rout at Bull Run had assured a rapid end to the war. He therefore moved more directly for European recognition by sending his good friend Mason of Virginia as minister to England and Slidell of Louisiana as minister to France. The Confederacy wanted nothing in return for recognition, Davis told the Congress in Richmond—no assistance and no offensive or defensive treaties—just equal treatment as a nation expecting to engage in commerce with others.[3] As with his earlier selection of the three commissioners, however, Davis again underestimated the importance of choosing such key persons with care.

Mason was anything but a diplomat, both by training and temperament. Southern diarist Mary Chesnut angrily blasted his appointment as "the maddest thing yet." The move was worse than sending Yancey—"and that was a catastrophe." "My wildest imagination will not picture Mr. Mason as a diplomat. He will say 'chaw' for 'chew,' and he will call himself 'Jeems,' and he will wear a dress coat to breakfast."[4] Although Mason chaired the Senate Foreign Relations Committee for ten years, he had made a greater mark by defending slavery as the critical foundation of a romanticized Old South.

James M. Mason, Confederate minister to England (Courtesy of the National Archives)

As senator during the turbulent prewar years, Mason had made his name anathema in the North by authoring the hated Fugitive Slave Act of 1850; he followed that action four years later with his support of the Kansas-Nebraska Act, which effectively erased the boundaries around slavery by introducing the principle of popular sovereignty. Mason had apparently dedicated his life to keeping black people in bonds as the basis of a presumably superior southern civilization.

Mason's very appearance and demeanor likewise belied any suggestion of a diplomat. From under his thick eyebrows shot a cold glare at anyone who questioned Confederate independence or, for that matter, anything southern. Corpulent and eternally scowling, he had long, scraggly hair that brushed the collar of his coat and cultivated his image of disheveled dress, crude frontier manner, and hot temper. A New York paper called Mason a "cold, calculating, stolid, sour traitor" whose heart was "gangrened with envy and pride, his mien imperious and repulsive." In the House of Commons, he habitually chewed tobacco and, in the excitement of a debate, more often than not missed the cuspidor in spewing forth a vein of brown spittle that splattered

John Slidell, Confederate minister to France (Courtesy of the National Archives)

and stained the red royal carpet. "In England," Chesnut had warned almost prophetically, "a man must expectorate like a gentleman—if he expectorates at all." *Times* correspondent William H. Russell thought Mason "a fine old English gentleman—but for tobacco." Charles Francis Adams Jr. expressed the prevalent view in the Union when he dismissed Mason as a typical Virginian, slow thinking, "very provincial and intensely arrogant."[5]

Slidell was almost equally infamous in the Union. Some years earlier, he had left New York for Louisiana after wounding another man in a duel over a woman. Having found refuge in the Deep South, he established himself as a gambler and lawyer before entering politics. President James K. Polk sent him to Mexico as a special envoy during the tumultuous last days of peace between the nations in late 1845. Rebuffed by the Mexican government, Slidell indignantly called for war as the only policy capable of satisfying American honor against barbarians and, in the meantime, acquiring the lands in the Great Southwest so coveted by the expansionist-minded administration in Washington. As a U.S. senator from 1853 to 1861, he managed James Buchanan's victorious presidential campaign in 1856. Then, on the eve of secession, Slidell established himself as one of the South's most

Captain Charles Wilkes of the U.S. Navy
(Courtesy of the Library of Congress)

extreme anti-Union spokesmen in Congress. Known as manipulative and clever, he was, according to William Russell, "subtle, full of device, and fond of intrigue." If thrown into a dungeon, Slidell "would conspire with the mice against the cat sooner than not conspire at all." Northerners, wrote Charles Francis Adams Jr., considered him "the most dangerous person to the Union the Confederacy could select for diplomatic work in Europe."[6]

If anyone could scuttle Mason and Slidell's mission in Europe, it was Captain Charles Wilkes of the U.S. Navy, a crusty sixty-two-year-old explorer and scientist who had recently assumed command of the *San Jacinto*, a first-class Union steamer armed with twelve guns and presently patrolling Cuban waters. Stubborn, cocky, irascible, and self-righteous, he was an avid practitioner of gunboat diplomacy who once burned down a village in the Fiji Islands as retribution for their inhabitants having stolen items from his exploring expedition. He also was highly unpopular among his men because of his strict disciplinary practices. Court-martialed in 1842 for illegally punishing sailors, he was acquitted but publicly reprimanded. Wilkes deeply resented the fame and favor long denied him and anxiously sought to make his mark before his not-so-distinguished career came to an end. Perhaps the hot blood of his radical predecessor in England, John Wilkes, still ran in the veins of the ever-cocked descendant. Had not his famed ancestor likewise spurned authority with impunity—the crown itself during the reign of King George III?[7]

In a characteristic act of independent judgment, Wilkes ignored Washington's orders to head for Philadelphia in late August 1861 and proceeded instead to African waters in search of Confederate privateers. Once there, he heard that Confederate commerce raiders were roaming the West Indies and immediately changed course for the Caribbean. From Cuban newspapers he learned that Mason and Slidell intended to depart Havana on board the British mail packet *Trent*. This would not happen under his watch, Wilkes so determined.[8]

On his arrival in Cuba, Wilkes searched for a legal justification for seizing the two southerners from a neutral ship. The U.S. consul general in Havana, Robert Shufeldt, found no precedent for such action in a host of books on international law and finally deemed it "a violation of the rights of neutrals upon the ocean." But this argument did not stop Wilkes. In his cabin he scoured the works of international law experts James Kent, Sir William Scott (Lord Stowell), Emmerich de Vattel, and Henry Wheaton, and correctly concluded that he possessed the authority to capture vessels carrying enemy dispatches. During the Napoleonic Wars, Lord Stowell from the High Court of Admiralty in England had specifically ruled that ships bearing such papers were subject to capture. But Wilkes wanted to go further and, not so correctly, take the emissaries themselves. He was disappointed with his findings. Mason and Slidell, Wilkes admitted, "were not dispatches in the literal sense, and did not seem to come under that designation, and nowhere could I find a case in point." But suddenly he found the way. Wilkes reasoned that the two agents were "bent on mischievous and traitorous errands against our country" and, in a strikingly novel interpretation, termed them "the embodiment of dispatches"—hence contraband and subject to seizure.[9]

The *Trent* left Havana on November 7, plying its way along the Cuban coast toward St. Thomas when, a little after noon of the next day, it sighted the *San Jacinto* 10 miles offshore and 240 miles east of Havana in the Old Bahama Channel. The Union warship fired a single shot across the *Trent's* bow, signaling an intention to board. But the *Trent* continued its passage, leading Wilkes to lob a second shot a bit closer to the vessel and bring it to a standstill. As Mason noted the approaching boarding crew armed with guns and cutlasses, he quickly turned over his dispatch bag to the British mail agent, Commander Richard Williams, who locked it in the mail room and promised to complete its delivery to the three Confederate commissioners in London. Mason hid the bag with good reason. It contained official papers of the Confederacy along with the credentials and instructions assigned to the two emissaries. Heading the boarding party was Lieutenant Donald Fairfax, under orders to seize Mason and Slidell, along with their two secretaries and diplomatic papers, and to confiscate the *Trent* as a prize of war.[10]

Fairfax, however, encountered unexpected opposition on board the *Trent* and in the confusion did not follow orders. On declaring his intention to search the vessel, he met fierce resistance from its captain, James Moir. According to one eyewitness, Moir insultingly challenged Fairfax: "For a damned impertinent, outrageous puppy, give me, or don't give me, a Yankee. You go back to your ship, young man, and tell her skipper that you couldn't accomplish your mission, because we wouldn't let ye. I deny your right of search. D'ye understand that?" At this outburst, the sixty passengers (including many southerners) milling around the two parties on deck drew menacingly closer and broke out in raucous applause. "Throw the damn fellow overboard!" shouted one of them. Shaken by the confrontation, Fairfax prudently decided against taking either the *Trent* or its papers, but he ordered the seizure of the four Confederates. After some pushing and shoving, highlighted by Slidell's fiery wife's threats followed by his futile attempt to escape through a porthole, Mason and Slidell and their two assistants yielded to a mild show of force and became prisoners on the *San Jacinto*.[11]

Fairfax's failure to follow orders—combined with Wilkes's surprising approval of his behavior—provided the basis of a major Anglo-American imbroglio over the *Trent*. In a less-than-convincing defense of his actions, Fairfax explained that since the *San Jacinto* was about to participate in an attack on Port Royal in South Carolina, it could not spare the sailors necessary to take control of the *Trent*. Furthermore, its seizure would have inflicted hardship on the passengers and hurt merchants by delaying delivery of the mail and other items aboard. Fairfax's stand was inexplicable. It was absurd to argue—and for a hardened seadog like Wilkes to agree—that wartime decisions rested on whether they inconvenienced civilians. Moreover, Fairfax had no legal justification for assuming that the detachment of sailors to the *Trent* would have weakened the Union's assault on Port Royal. The U.S. Supreme Court had ruled in *The Alexander* (1814) and *The Grotius* (1815) that the assignment of a single sailor to a captured vessel was sufficient to retain a prize if it posed no danger of escape. Finally, Fairfax had the legal right to demand the ship's papers; as Wheaton contended in his treatise on international law, the evidence used in prize court proceedings "must, in the first instance, come from the papers and crew of the captured ship." Moir's refusal

HMS *Trent* and USS *San Jacinto* (Courtesy of the National Archives)

to turn over the papers had revoked the *Trent*'s status as neutral and justified its seizure as a prize.[12]

In view of these violations of neutrality on board the *Trent*, Wilkes exercised poor judgment in not seizing the vessel and its papers. In fact, he allowed it to proceed while treating his four prisoners as guests in his cabin en route to their military incarceration at Fort Warren in Boston Harbor. Even the most cursory investigation might have uncovered several breaches of neutrality. Captain Moir had resisted a legal search and was carrying enemies of the United States. Not only had Mason conspired with the mail agent to hide his diplomatic pouch, but so had Slidell asked his wife to do the same. According to a newspaper account, just before Slidell disembarked from the *Trent*, he handed his dispatches to his wife and told her to "sit at the port-hole, and that if an attempt was made to take the box from her, to drop it into the sea. Mrs. Slidell obeyed his orders, was not approached, and took the dispatches safely to England."[13]

Wilkes's failure to seize the *Trent* had opened a labyrinth of legal troubles for the Lincoln administration. His removal of agents claiming protection under a neutral flag had violated the principle of freedom of the seas and insulted British honor. Not realizing the gravity of his error, he boasted to the press that he had acted on his own initiative and proudly declared this "one of the most important days in my naval life."[14]

Most Americans learned the fate of the *Trent* in the afternoon press of November 16; by Monday, just two days later, the northern newspapers almost unanimously praised the capture of Mason and Slidell. A poem greeted Wilkes upon his arrival in Boston on November 25:

Welcome to Wilkes! who didn't wait
To study up Vattel and Wheaton,
But bagged his game, and left the act
For dull diplomacy to treat on.[15]

The only newspapers with a national circulation were in New York City, and they joined others throughout the Union in approving Wilkes's actions as a justifiable response to the arrogant maritime practices followed by the detested British. The *New York Times*, typically the voice of moderate Republicans, endorsed his move as falling within the dictates of international law and insisted that the British would not retaliate. As for Wilkes, "Let the handsome thing be done, consecrate another *Fourth* of July to him." Horace

Greeley's *New York Tribune* blasted Mason as a "degenerate son" who possessed a "brain composed of the muddiest materials" and Slidell as a "sly, cautious, dark unscrupulous traitor" known best for his "furtive glances and sinister visage." Moreover, according to Greeley, Wilkes's actions were "in strict accordance with the principles of international law . . . and," he sardonically added, "in strict conformity with English practice." He welcomed a British demand for the release of Mason and Slidell, for this act would signal the crown's acceptance of neutral rights. The Anglophobic *New York Herald*, which reached readers all over the country along with many in Europe, expected the White House to disavow Wilkes's actions and apologize, but did not advocate returning the captives.[16]

Several notable Americans commended Wilkes. The U.S. district attorney for Massachusetts, Richard Henry Dana Jr., who wrote the classic *Two Years before the Mast* and a book on maritime law, vigorously applauded what he regarded as a legal seizure of the southern emissaries. Former minister to England and secretary of state Edward Everett triumphantly cited Lord Stowell's 1813 admiralty court decision (the *Anna Maria*) defending a belligerent's right to "stop the ambassador of your enemy on his passage." Indeed, the magistrate had asserted that "in the transmission of dispatches may be conveyed the entire plan of a campaign, that may defeat all the projects of another belligerent in that quarter of the world." Adam Gurowski, a U.S. State Department adviser who taught international law at Harvard, considered Mason and Slidell a threat to the United States and thus subject to removal from a neutral vessel. As rebel emissaries, they were "political contrabands of war going on a publicly avowed errand hostile to their true government." These "traveling commissioners of war, of bloodshed and rebellion," were on a mission to destroy the United States and could not claim diplomatic immunity on board a neutral vessel.[17]

The Lincoln administration, already under siege after the Union's disastrous defeat at Bull Run, had a mixed but generally favorable reaction to the seizure. Secretary of the Navy Gideon Welles enthusiastically approved but warned that Wilkes's decision not to take the *Trent* could set a dangerous precedent. Also supporting Wilkes's action, Seward could not conceive of releasing the captives. The president, however, was deeply concerned about British retaliation. Whether or not Wilkes was legally correct, trouble with England was unavoidable—and at a time when the Union could least afford another enemy. It was satisfying to kick the British lion—but *not* at the cost of war. While Washington's residents celebrated, Lincoln allegedly told two visitors: "I fear the traitors will prove to be white elephants."[18]

From Boston, Senator Charles Sumner, who was chair of the Foreign Relations Committee and well versed in international law, privately disagreed with the exuberant American reaction to the *Trent* affair. The United States would have to surrender the captives, he believed, but he kept his views quiet out of concern for his position and a wish to avoid further entangling the situation for the White House.[19]

The strained context in which the seizure took place helps to explain the wildfire of exultation that spread throughout the Union. After the humiliation at Bull Run, the Union was starving for a victory. That the *Trent* incident came at the expense of the British provided great satisfaction to northerners still infuriated with the queen for proclaiming neutrality and bestowing belligerent status onto the Confederacy. At a public banquet in Boston held in Wilkes's honor, Governor John Andrew crowed that the captain had "fired a shot across the bows of the ship that bore the English lion's head." The House of Representatives thanked Wilkes "for his brave, adroit and patriotic conduct in the arrest and detention of the traitors."[20]

The southern reaction was equally ecstatic but, of course, for different reasons: Wilkes's seizure of Mason and Slidell had encouraged a war between the Union and England that would all but ensure Confederate independence. Whether or not the British formally aligned with the Confederacy, the result would be the same—two nations fighting the Union. The *Southern Confederacy* in Atlanta cheered Wilkes's action as "one of the most fortunate things for our cause." The *New Orleans Bee* happily summed up the Union's dilemma: To release the captives would divide the Union; to refuse would alienate the British. The *Bee* confidently predicted British recognition of the Confederacy.[21]

Southern officials in Richmond could barely contain their excitement. President Davis told the Confederate Congress that the Lincoln administration had violated maritime rights that were "for the most part held sacred, even among barbarians." Secretary of War Judah P. Benjamin echoed the *New Orleans Bee*, smiling while calling the incident "perhaps the best thing that could have happened." The secretary of the navy, Stephen R. Mallory, expected immediate recognition by the European governments. The Lincoln administration, beamed Secretary of State Robert M. T. Hunter, could not possibly justify "this flagrant violation" of international law and "gross insult" to the British flag. The London government would surely "avenge the insult," he asserted while directing his three commissioners in London to lodge a formal protest with the Palmerston ministry.[22]

Because the Atlantic cable was not functioning at this time, it took about two weeks for news to cross the ocean. But when the steamer bearing the story reached England in late November, the result was a firestorm of anger. Elated by the events, Yancey, Rost, and Mann registered the Confederacy's protest with Lord Russell, denouncing Wilkes's action as a transgression of international law. Mason and Slidell had traveled under the protection of the British flag, and the admiralty court should facilitate their release. Not by coincidence did the commissioners simultaneously send Russell a list of those vessels that ran the blockade, arguing that it was a paper blockade and therefore a violation of the Declaration of Paris. Unless the Union made restitution, later reported Rost back in Paris, "war is certain." The French supported the Confederacy, he noted, "making recognition more likely." For the moment, they chose to wait for the Union's response to British demands before formally requesting recognition. Mann, however, thought the move imminent. Ever ebullient, he noted that "British officers met me like brothers, conversed with me like brothers. I already esteemed them as allies."[23]

Just after noon on November 27, news of the *Trent* affair reached the American legation in London. Shouts of joy came from the three secretaries, restrained only by Adams's acerbic assistant secretary, Benjamin Moran, who feared the worst. Seizure of Mason and Slidell, Moran wrote in his diary, "will do more for the Southerners than ten victories, for it touches John Bull's honor, and the honor of his flag." Adams's son Henry moaned that "all the fat's in the fire." England "means to make war." The senior Adams agreed with this dire prognosis. Visiting a friend in the countryside when hearing of the *Trent*, he raced back to London in a state of despondency, only to undergo further discomfiture on having to admit to Russell—then rushing into an emergency cabinet meeting—that Seward had sent no information on the matter. Adams hurriedly completed various tasks of the legation before his expected recall. "The dogs are all let loose," he glumly confided to his diary.[24]

War seemed unavoidable. "There never was within memory such a burst of feeling," wrote an American in London to Seward. "The people are frantic with rage, and were the country polled, I fear 999 men out of a thousand would declare for immediate war." From Edinburgh came another American's confirmation of the martial spirit sweeping the kingdom: "I have never seen so intense a feeling of indignation exhibited in my life."[25]

The Palmerston government interpreted the recently arrived dispatches from the usually soft-spoken Lyons to mean that the United States *wanted* war. The Americans were "very much pleased at having . . . insulted the British Flag," the minister observed as he uncharacteristically urged a show of force to dampen this fiery mood—perhaps a military buildup in Canada and the dispatch of more warships to the British West Indies? Palmerston was furious. At the emergency cabinet meeting on November 28, he reportedly opened proceedings with a veritable declaration of war: "I don't know whether you are going to stand this, but I'll be damned if I do!" Wilkes, Palmerston told the queen, must make reparations for his affront to the British flag. To Russell, the prime minister hotly insisted that his government would not shrink before this "deliberate and premeditated insult" intended to "provoke" a conflict. Russell dryly warned that the Americans were "very dangerous people to run away from."[26]

Most British seemed to welcome war. The *London Morning Post*, so often speaking for Palmerston, firmly believed in rapid victory. "In one month," it confidently predicted, "we could sweep all the *San Jacintos* from the seas, blockade the Northern ports, and turn to a direct and speedy issue the tide of the war now raging." Even the usually staid secretary for war, George Cornewall Lewis, promised that "we shall soon *iron the smile* out of their faces." A refusal to surrender Mason and Slidell meant "inevitable war."[27]

Other members of the cabinet believed war inescapable. Although pro-Union, the Duke of Argyll told his colleagues that Wilkes's action constituted a violation of international law that Seward had surely instigated. Wilkes's "inconceivable arrogance" was the natural outgrowth "of a purely Democratic govt" that would not "*dare* to acknowledge itself in the wrong." Lord Stanley attributed the certainty of war to "the mob of America" that opposed Mason and Slidell's release.[28]

The British government did not relish a war with the United States but had to prepare for one. It needed a massive number of British troops to defend Canada against an expected U.S. invasion that could come from myriad points along the long frontier stretching from the Atlantic to the Great Lakes. British commerce would fall prey to American privateers, the Union could build more ironclads capable of decimating Britain's wooden vessels, and the chances of conquering the United States were virtually impossible. Seward's longtime heated threats of war had caused a major debate in England over the necessity of building up its defense forces in North America. The British naval squadron commander on the North American and West Indian station, Vice Admiral Sir Alexander Milne, had served the Royal Navy for four decades and knew that his fourteen vessels could not cope with the Union navy. British efforts to defend their North American possession became so extensive in early December 1861 that on one Sunday evening workers loaded enough boxes of firearms to fill eight barges on the Thames River.[29]

British anger over the *Trent* affair was intense, and the expected lack of French support did nothing to reduce the hostility. The two countries' relations had sharply deteriorated soon after their victory over Russia in the Crimean War of the mid-1850s, leaving Palmerston deeply apprehensive about a French assault on a number of British stations. Had not Napoleon III reportedly announced in January 1861 that he would make war on England if French public opinion demanded it? Just two years earlier a special study committee in England predicted that by the summer of 1862 the Royal Navy would become second to that of the French. Before the *Trent* affair, Palmerston had told the queen that Napoleon regarded the Anglo-French concert as "precarious." The Earl of Clarendon groused that the French emperor would "take this occasion to make us feel that he is necessary to us and to avenge his griefs against us by causing us to eat dirt or go to war with the North with France against us or in a state of doubtful and ill-humoured neutrality." He warned, however, that peace "never can be worth the price of national honour."[30]

Reaction outside the Palmerston ministry was similarly warlike. Britain's lord chief justice declared: "I must unlearn Lord Stowell and burn Wheaton if there is one word of defence for the American Lieutenant. . . . How a great and gallant nation can *en masse* confound safe swaggering over unarmed and weak foes with true valor, I cannot understand." A highly respected British barrister, Edward Twisleton, assured Lewis that Washington's leaders would "submit to almost anything rather than surrender their prisoners. Their false point of honor would not be so much towards England as towards the South; as they would feel humiliated and mortified beyond expression, if having had two of the Arch-rebels in their keeping three weeks and more, they should be afterwards constrained to release them." Mason and Slidell's capture exasperated British historian George Grote. "What a precious 'hash' these Yankees are preparing for themselves! Their stupid, childish rage against us, seems to extinguish all sense, in their braggart minds, even where the instinct of self-interest ought to supply it."[31]

Not everyone called for war. Two of the ministry's staunchest opponents in the House of Commons, Liberals Richard Cobden and John Bright, refused to believe that the United States wanted conflict. Cobden urged Bright to "expose the *self-evident* groundlessness of the accusation made by some of our journals that the North wish to pick a quarrel whilst fighting a life or death struggle at home. The accusation is so utterly irrational that it would be regarded as a proof that we want to take advantage of their weakness and to force a quarrel on *them*."[32]

Less than a week after writing Lewis, however, Twisleton curiously reversed his stand on Wilkes and now thought the American captain had acted in accordance with previous British admiralty court decisions during the Napoleonic Wars. In a second letter to Lewis, Twisleton pointed out: "It would seem to have been our principle in 1806 that a belligerent might seize any of his enemies on a neutral vessel, without taking them before a prize court." Wilkes had "not gone beyond" this standard. Even though Twisleton doubted the wisdom of these rulings, they raised serious questions about whether it would be "a strong measure" for England to declare war "*at once*" if Lincoln defended the legality of Wilkes's action.[33]

In the tumult on both sides of the Atlantic, only a few learned observers had the presence of mind to question whether Wilkes had acted in line with the law of nations. Natural law, of course, is the basis of international law, which means that the most basic principle in relations among nations is the right of self-defense or national preservation.[34] As Wilkes argued, and as Gurowski in the United States and Twisleton in England concurred, Mason and Slidell were avowed enemies of the Union whose mission was to secure European assistance in a war against that very Union. Wilkes's argument would have been difficult to refute had he identified the two men as emissaries of a belligerent (on board a neutral vessel) whose objective was to secure foreign help (from that same neutral country and others) in a war seeking to destroy the United States. Instead, he fogged the matter by calling them the "embodiment of dispatches" and hence contraband, when he would have stood on fairly sound legal footing by emphasizing self-defense.

The problem, of course, was that the White House could not make a decision outside the Civil War's context. The president could either support Wilkes and risk war with England while also at war with the Confederacy, or renounce the capture and experience a national humiliation that had the saving grace of permitting the Union to concentrate on defeating the Confederacy. In this instance of civil war, arguable legalities became secondary to practical realities. Clarification of the options just as readily clarified the ultimate choice of having to free the two men—*if* the Union could devise a face-saving retreat.

The British government's primary complaint focused on Wilkes's failure to take the *Trent* as a prize. In response to Russell's inquiry, the law officers stated that the Americans had violated international law and owed reparations. That information in hand, Russell spent the entire morning of November 30 drafting two dispatches calling for a seven-day ultimatum that he put before the cabinet that afternoon. A heated discussion ensued, during which Earl Granville urged the ministry to leave room for the United States to make an honorable retreat. Gladstone thought Russell too combative in calling for Lyons's departure after seven days if the Union refused to meet British demands. Lewis doubted that the Lincoln administration had ordered the seizure of Mason and Slidell but believed it would refuse to make reparations. The cabinet retained the one-week ultimatum.[35]

Russell delivered the dispatches to the queen, who turned them over to her consort, Prince Albert, for consideration. Although on his deathbed, he worked much of that night in Windsor Castle to tone down the wording of Russell's first dispatch without altering the demands for the captives' surrender and an apology within seven days. Wilkes's action, the revised version declared, was "an affront to the British flag and a violation of international law." But Prince Albert, in line with Granville's appeal, left the Union a graceful way out of the crisis. The British government hoped that Wilkes "had not acted under instructions, or, if he did, that he misapprehended them." On that basis, it expressed confidence that the Lincoln administration would "of its own accord offer to the British Government such redress as alone would satisfy the British nation, namely the liberation of the four Gentlemen . . . and a suitable apology for the aggression which has been committed."[36]

War still seemed likely. Lyons had one week to await Seward's reply. In the meantime, he was to keep Admiral Milne informed about any sign of an American assault on British holdings in North America. If his government did not comply with the demands, Lyons was to pack up his legation personnel and papers and head home. "What we want," Russell told his minister, "is a plain Yes or a plain No to our very simple demands, and we want that plain Yes or No within seven days of the communication of the despatch." But Russell left some flexibility in the ultimatum. If Lyons thought the White House was attempting to meet the demands, he could remain at his post beyond the seven-day limit. The times seemed ominous as the U.S. stock market plunged and the British government, noting that Americans were purchasing great quantities of saltpeter (the main ingredient in gunpowder), imposed an immediate embargo on all shipments to the United States.[37]

The British cabinet considered the *Trent* affair serious enough to create, for only the fourth time in the nation's history, a special War Committee. Composed of Palmerston, Russell, Lewis, the Duke of Newcastle in the Colonial Office, and other notables, the new committee focused on protecting Britain's North American possessions—particularly Canada—by dispatching more soldiers and bolstering Milne's fleet. Newcastle had received requests for assistance from Canada, New Brunswick, and Nova Scotia in constructing an intercolonial railway to help safeguard them from American invasion. In accordance with Lyons's recommendation, the British government prepared to take all necessary steps toward ensuring Union compliance with its demands.[38]

The Palmerston ministry clung to neutrality in the face of a growing popular clamor for war. Russell responded to the three southern commissioners' call for recognition with another affirmation of British neutrality, but his stand did not diminish their expectations. The *Bee-Hive* of London, whose editor supported the Confederacy because of the Union's restrictive commercial policies, urged the government to break the blockade to secure cotton and ally with France in a war against the Union. Slavery should pose no obstacle. An independent South, the journal argued, would have to accept emancipation once encased by free territory. William S. Lindsay, a shipping magnate and perhaps the Confederacy's strongest supporter in Parliament, called for an offensive and defensive treaty with the Confederacy *before* England and the Union went to war.[39]

Meanwhile, the French stridently condemned the Union's seizure of Mason and Slidell. Nothing, Dayton declared with concern, had matched the "outburst" of anger in his host country. If the United States did not renounce that action, "the almost universal impression here is that war will follow." Dayton had thought the French would stay back and let the British and Union "fight it out!" But France needed cotton, and the nation's industrial interests might push its government to intervene. Some of the French press wanted the emperor to act with England on the issue. The French joined other Europeans in believing the Union had no respect for international law and had tried "to pick a quarrel" with England.[40]

Dayton had learned from what he considered a reliable source, the pro-Union Baron Jacob Rothschild of the French banking House of Rothschild, that Thouvenel had told the British minister in Paris that the seizure of Mason and Slidell was "an unwarrantable act" and "a gross violation of international law." The baron thought that if England recognized the Confederacy, France would follow. But he was certain that "France will not go with us" if war broke out with England. The French "will sympathise (if not act) with Great Britain." That same day Dayton met with Thouvenel, who termed the Union's action a threat to all maritime powers. If war broke out between England and the United States, the French would be "spectators only," Dayton declared before adding, "not indifferent spectators."[41]

France had surprised the British by taking their side in the *Trent* crisis and repeating its earlier call for joint intervention. The Union's violation of international law, Mercier told Washington, had obligated his government to take a stand for neutral rights. France expected the White House to refuse to return the captives and planned to recognize the Confederacy in the event of an Anglo-Union war. Outside intervention might resolve the matter before it reached this dangerous point.[42]

Mercier assured Lyons that joint intervention would work if it included Russia, a friend of the Union. Admittedly, the Russians still harbored ill feelings from their defeat in the Crimean War and remained deeply suspicious of their Anglo-French rivals' imperial ambitions. But the tsar would surely see that everyone would benefit from an end to the American war. Both the British and the French became Russia's suitors, leading its foreign minister, Prince Alexander Gorchakov, to complain about how difficult it was to maintain an impartial stand. "I am sought after everywhere I go, even at the theater, and I have to dodge these attacks by all sorts of little tricks."[43]

Lyons, however, doubted that the Union would approve any type of foreign intervention. Perhaps, Mercier reasoned, the time was right for a joint "intimidation" of the Union. Only if not a bluff, Lyons responded. "Otherwise," he wrote Russell in London, "we shall only weaken the effect of any future offer, by crying out Wolf now, when there is no Wolf." The Union must realize that rejecting intervention entailed "serious consequences." The blockade was the non-negotiable issue, Lyons argued. The Union could not win the war without the blockade, whereas the Confederacy would never consider an armistice until the Union abandoned the blockade. Furthermore, Lyons noted darkly, Lincoln had become so desperate that he intended to stir up a slave rebellion and race war by announcing emancipation. War with the Union would place the intervening powers on the side of the slaveholding Confederacy.[44]

Despite the appearance of French support, the British suspected that Napoleon wanted an Anglo-Union war to boost his country's interests. Lewis felt "quite certain" that the French thought such a war would force the Union to lift the blockade and give them access to southern cotton. Britain's ambassador in Paris confirmed these beliefs. French defense of neutral rights, Lord Cowley stated, was purely expedient. They hated the British "cordially and systematically" and were "behaving well and backing us up nobly" in the event of a war with the Union that opened southern ports and made cotton available. Russell scrawled on the back of Cowley's missive that he was "quite sick" of French "intrigues" against Britain.[45]

Russell's exasperation with the American war, however, outweighed his concern over Napoleon, who uncharacteristically acted with restraint. Several factors guided the emperor's self-control, including his present involvement with British and Spanish military forces in Mexico, his wish to avoid a confrontation with the Royal Navy, and the widespread popular support in France for the British position in the *Trent* crisis. In the meantime Russell became fairly confident that the United States did not want war with England, which, paradoxically, kindled his anger because he suspected Americans of wishing to embarrass his government. Nearly "all the world is disgusted by the insolence of the American Republic," whose people would "like to draw in their horns and be disagreeable to us at the same time." All we want, he wrote Cowley, was that Lincoln "send our passengers back." The president had suggested a preference for peace when he did not mention the *Trent* in his annual message to Congress, but politics often prevailed over principle and even good sense in America, Russell knew, and congressmen owed their positions to being good politicians. The American press was easing its fire, perhaps finally realizing that "the best, if not the only chance of subduing the South is to keep Europe—i.e. England and France neutral." In a bitter twist of irony, the Union's military leaders seemed more interested in peace than did its civilian counterparts. General George B. McClellan, Russell learned, told Lincoln that Wilkes had had no justification for seizing Mason and Slidell. "I wish McClellan could be made Dictator."[46]

The French were among the Europeans in general who joined England in condemning Wilkes's action as an infringement on the rights of all nations at sea. Despite Russia's hatred for England and France, it could not defend the Lincoln administration in this matter. The Union's minister to Belgium, Henry Sanford, informed Washington that most Europeans wanted France to mediate the dispute.[47]

Even the most patriotic northerners must have realized that war with both the Confederacy and England was unthinkable—but they also understood the importance of salvaging national honor. How could the Union placate the British without backing down? In mid-December Senator Orville Browning was in the president's office when Seward burst in with England's demands. The Union's worst fears had materialized. To surrender the captives and grant an apology constituted an embarrassing retreat magnified by an admission of guilt—and to the *British* of all peoples. War or humiliation—that was the choice. Browning denounced the British for considering "so foolish a thing" as war. But if England wanted to start one, he even more foolishly exclaimed to Lincoln and Seward, "We will fight her to the death."[48]

Signs of war loomed everywhere in the Union. The day after the White House learned the British position, Congress angrily debated whether to redeem the country's honor by keeping Mason and Slidell in captivity, or to undergo national humiliation by capitulating to England's demands. At a dinner party that evening at the Portuguese legation, Seward appeared to prefer the preservation of honor—and the certainty of war. Physically and emotionally exhausted, the secretary of state cut loose a tirade of highly charged remarks as he interchanged downs of brandy with deep draws from his cigar. To an apprehensive group of listeners barely discernible in the smoke-filled room, he self-righteously proclaimed: "We will wrap the whole world in flames!" *Times* correspondent William Russell stood among the ring of stunned observers, visibly shaken by Seward's loose-winded threats. Seeing his distress, another guest tugged Russell aside to assure him that Seward had only played to his audience: "That's all bugaboo talk. When Seward talks that way, he means to break down. He is most dangerous and obstinate when he pretends to agree a good deal with you."[49]

The atmosphere in both Atlantic countries had nonetheless become so raw that mistaken perceptions of motives by either side could set off a war that only the Confederacy wanted. Charles Francis Adams Jr. anxiously wrote his brother in London that the Lincoln administration had "capstoned" its "blunders by blundering into a war with England" that would ensure southern independence. Henry Adams blasted the American reaction at home as incomprehensible. "What a bloody set of fools they are! How in the name of all that's conceivable could you suppose that England would sit quiet under such an insult. *We* should have jumped out of our boots at such a one." The United States, he declared to his brother with heightening disgust, had adopted England's contemptible search policies. "Good God, what's got into you all? What in Hell do you mean by deserting now the great principles of our fathers; by returning to the vomit of that dog Great Britain? What do you mean by asserting now principles against which every Adams yet has protested and resisted? You're mad, all of you."[50]

And through this dark period, the senior Adams dourly sat in the funereal atmosphere of his legation office, dreading the near certainty of war while lamely awaiting instructions from Washington that did not arrive until mid-December. Until that time, Henry Adams snorted with indignation, his father felt so defenseless that if he saw Lord John Russell walking down the street, he would "run as fast as he could down the nearest alley." Finally, on December 16, word arrived from Seward that Wilkes had acted without authorization. The minister's immediate sense of relief lasted no longer than it had taken to envelop him. Was it too late to make amends? A few days before Christmas, he noted war preparations in London and warned Seward that failure to comply with their demands meant the British would recognize the Confederacy and refuse to respect the Union's blockade. Little hope for peace rested in Seward's ominous directive authorizing Adams to put the Palmerston ministry on notice that recognition of the Confederacy meant war with the Union.[51]

Adams feared that the time had passed to avert war without enduring a loss of face. But neither party in the crisis seemed capable of initiating a settlement. His own government had not kept its representative in London well informed. What response could he make to Russell's repeated inquiries about American policy? What peace assurances could he offer? British leadership also seemed lacking. "Where is the master to direct this storm?" asked Adams in disbelief. "Is it Lord Palmerston or Earl Russell?" Seward's angry rhetoric had been nothing more than bluff, Adams knew, but his innate gift for drama had finally convinced the British that he preferred war as the first instrument of diplomacy. Adams wrote his namesake that most British thought Seward "resolved to insult England until she makes a war. He is the bête noire, that frightens them out of all their proprieties. It is of no use to deny it." Lyons had become a believer, and his dispatches easily validated the tenets of an already-converted ministry at home. War was not a viable option, Adams insisted. The White House must disavow Wilkes's action and surrender the captives. "I would part with them at a cent apiece!"[52]

British recognition of the Confederacy seemed irrefutable as the *Trent* furor combined with another hot issue—the growing popular clamor for running the Union blockade. A mid-December issue of the *Boston Courier* carried Henry Adams's account of his recent visit to Manchester, England, where merchants joined a newspaper editor in urging the government to challenge the blockade and recognize the Confederacy if the American war continued into the spring of 1862 and threatened the cotton flow. At the moment, according to Union supporters Cobden and Bright in Parliament, Lancashire's textile mills had sufficient cotton to temper the growing demand for breaking the blockade. But they had to admit that in the previous November 1861 almost two-thirds of 172,000 workers in 836 textile mills were on short time and another 8,000 had been released. Running the blockade, Bright warned, "would be an act of war."[53]

Additional pressure to defy the blockade came from British merchants, who had become incensed over the Union's decision to sink old ships laden with heavy stones (the "stone fleet") in order to close the channels into southern ports. Although Russell in England knew that international law allowed such action as long as the damage was not permanent, he—and even Cobden—considered the policy barbaric. Seward defended the action as only temporarily injurious and integral to the success of the blockade. The Union left two channels open to Charleston for shipping goods necessary to survival, but the ensuing controversy further heated Anglo-American emotions.[54]

To the Confederacy, the time seemed propitious for recognition. Its three commissioners in Europe assured their home government that England and France would demand that any settlement require the Union to lift the blockade. They became so excited about impending recognition that they rushed to London and Paris to be present when Palmerston and Napoleon made the announcement.[55]

Yancey was a bit more guarded in his enthusiasm than were his two companions. The British government, he reported, thought the possibility of war and peace "about evenly balanced." It had sent ten thousand troops and considerable war materials to Canada, and it had prepared a "great steam fleet." If war developed, "the English blows will be crushing on the seaboard." France, he thought, might press Britain into action. Public opinion favored the Confederacy, and when Parliament assembled, Yancey felt certain that the ministry would have "to act favorably or to resign."[56]

In the midst of this warlike atmosphere on both sides of the Atlantic, Lyons discerned a subtle but critical change within the Lincoln administration: It seemed less defiant after he formally presented his government's demands on December 23. The British minister had actually delayed this delivery a few days to allow a small passage of time that might ease tempers, and the strategy seemed to have worked. Indeed, he suddenly felt optimistic about White House compliance. That evening he wrote Russell that Seward was

> on the side of peace. He does not like the look of the spirit he has called up. Ten months of office have dispelled many of his illusions. I presume that he no longer believes in . . . the return of the South to the arms of the North in case of a foreign war; in his power to frighten the nations of Europe by great words; in the ease with which the U.S. could crush rebellion with one hand and chastise Europe with the other; in the notion that the relations with England in particular are safe playthings to be used for the amusement of the American people.

Seward faced the "very painful dilemma" of either bearing "the humiliation of yielding to England" or becoming "the author of a disastrous Foreign War."[57]

Russell nonetheless had misgivings about the manner and timing of the Lincoln administration's compliance to the demands. "I am still inclined to think Lincoln will submit," the foreign secretary lamented to Palmerston, "but not till the clock is 59 minutes past 11."[58]

The Lincoln administration found itself alone on the *Trent* issue and compelled to consider a retreat that somehow saved its honor. On Christmas Eve, Dayton confirmed the Union's fears of war with both England and France. The British, he wrote, were continuing military and naval preparations for war and would take the offensive. They had sent supplies to Gibraltar for warships coming from Malta that would then go to the United States. Their Mediterranean fleet would soon be in position to capture U.S. merchant ships in the area—perhaps more than eighty in the French port of Havre alone. Everyone assumed war unless the Union made reparations. The French government did not want war, but it sympathized with the British position and was concerned about breadstuffs if war interrupted crop growth in the United States. Supplies from the Baltic, the Danube, and the Black Sea would not be sufficient. But France would place priority on securing cotton and take its chances on wheat. Above all, the emperor would act in accordance with French interests. Dayton's note did not arrive until sometime afterward, but Mercier informed Seward the same day he received England's demands that Washington had no support from other nations. The French, Mercier emphasized, would not help the Americans.[59]

In a move that starkly demonstrated how seriously President Lincoln regarded the matter, he invited Sumner to meet with him and the cabinet at 10:00 A.M. on Christmas Day to explore the possibilities of preserving both peace and honor in resolving the crisis before the December 30 deadline. Although Seward now saw the wisdom in freeing Mason and Slidell, Lincoln remained opposed. Sumner presented letters from Bright and Cobden indicating that most of their people would fight if the president held onto the men and thereby condoned Wilkes's desecration of British honor. Even though Bright and Cobden had joined numerous church groups in England in urging arbitration, Palmerston and Russell vehemently rejected the prospect of another nation deciding their government's fate.[60]

The next day, Lincoln met for four hours with his cabinet, which, convinced of the danger of war and hearing no objection from the president, recommended the release of Mason and Slidell. Lincoln's unexpected silence mystified Seward. Just hours earlier the president had adamantly resisted their surrender. After the others had left the conference room, the secretary inquired about Lincoln's change of heart. The president smiled as he looked at Seward: "I found I could not make an argument that would satisfy my own mind, and that proved to me your ground was the right one."[61] The resolution of the problem was not that simple. Lincoln had doubtless intended to exploit the crisis for all it was worth—knowing that at the point of imminent conflict he could relent, safe in the knowledge that he had publicly opposed the surrender of Mason and Slidell but now having to comply with British demands because of the ongoing war with the Confederacy and the widespread belief that Wilkes had acted illegally.

Seward now bore the daunting responsibility of drafting a note to Lyons that camouflaged the submission to England. The captives were of "comparative unimportance" and would be "cheerfully liberated," he wrote; Wilkes had violated international law in capturing them without also taking their papers and the *Trent* itself. Wilkes had acted correctly, though without authorization, in stopping a neutral ship carrying contraband. "All writers and judges pronounce naval or military persons in the service of the enemy contraband. Vattel says war allows us to cut off from an enemy all his resources, and to hinder him from sending ministers to solicit assistance. And Sir William Scott [Lord Stowell] says you may stop the ambassador of your enemy on his passage. Despatches are not less clearly contraband, and the bearers or couriers who undertake to carry them fall under the same condemnation." Wilkes, however, had made a mistake in not seizing the *Trent* as a prize. The United States refused to grant an apology, but it would free Mason and Slidell and award reparations.[62]

Seward then made a bold argument for preserving the United States's honor. In the interests of neutral rights, the Americans were prepared "to do to the British nation just what we have always insisted all nations ought to do to us." Seward insisted that he "was really defending and maintaining not an exclusively British interest but an old, honored and cherished American cause." As Secretary of State James Madison declared in his 1804 instructions to his minister in England, James Monroe, "whenever property found in a neutral vessel is supposed to be liable on any ground to capture and condemnation, the rule in all cases is, that the question shall not be decided by the captor, but be carried before a legal tribunal." Had Wilkes taken the vessel as a prize, he would have acted in accordance with freedom of the seas and international law.[63]

Adams in London had provided Seward with the rationale for releasing

Mason and Slidell without a loss of face. The minister had stressed the importance of neutral rights and referred to Madison's instructions to Monroe in 1804. If the United States refused to comply with the British demand to free the captives, Adams asserted, it would "assume their old arrogant claim of the domination of the seas." Furthermore, the surrender of the southern emissaries would soften the negative feelings of Europeans who had universally condemned their seizure as a violation of international law.[64]

Writer James Russell Lowell expressed popular sentiment in the United States in these lines from "Jonathan to John":

> It don't seem hardly right, John,
>   When both my hands was full,
> To stump me to a fight, John,—
>   Your cousin tu, John Bull!
> We give the critters back, John,
>   Cos Abram thought 'twas right;
> It warn't your bullying clack, John,
>   Provokin' us to fight.[65]

The British had a mixed reaction to the Lincoln administration's decision to free the captives. News of their release reached London on January 8, 1862, setting off wild celebrations throughout the country; the justification did not. Even the Duke of Argyll set aside his ardent Union support to argue that the *Trent*'s passage between neutral ports had not permitted Wilkes to seize Mason and Slidell as contraband. In accordance with the French position, a vessel moving between neutral ports by its very nature could not carry contraband and was immune from search and seizure. And, as the duke asserted to Sumner in the United States, mere communications from a belligerent to a neutral did not constitute contraband. The distinguished British barrister, William Henry Harcourt (Lewis's stepson-in-law), agreed with Argyll. Writing under the pseudonym "Historicus," Harcourt declared in the *Times* that in matters affecting contraband, "the destination of the ship is everything." By definition, he asserted, a neutral vessel bound for a neutral port could not carry contraband. The crown's legal officers agreed, as did the British cabinet. Russell cited Vattel, Wheaton, and other experts on international law in claiming that neither the southern emissaries nor their papers fitted the category of contraband. It was immaterial that Wilkes had failed to take the vessel to a prize court.[66]

Seward had skillfully saved the Union's honor by disguising the capitulation in a haze of legalities, but beneath the verbiage lay an arguable defense

's conduct that in the heat of the moment escaped attention. In a
that reflected the reality of war, Seward asserted a fundamental
f natural law: "If the safety of this Union required the detention
captured persons, it would be the right and duty of this Government
to detain them." Vattel, as shown earlier, argued for the right of national
preservation as a basic principle of international law.[67] Wilkes had made
this argument, and so had Gurowski in the State Department and Twisleton
in England. Is it not the inherent right of a nation to safeguard its security?
Should people at war permit a neutral to engage in conduct that helps their
avowed enemy? Does a neutral flag protect belligerents aboard, regardless
of their purpose? Surely it guarantees the safety of ambassadors of goodwill,
but Mason and Slidell were not on a mission of goodwill. They sought British
and French recognition, which, if achieved, could have dealt a death blow to
the Union.

Mason and Slidell's objective raises questions about the widespread condemnation of Wilkes's actions. Their status constituted an arguable exception to the views of those specialists in international law who defended the
sanctity of ambassadors as well as neutral vessels passing from one neutral
port to another. No one could hold that a ship carrying such passengers was
subject to capture only if headed toward an enemy port. If military or naval
personnel in service of the enemy were subject to seizure—as they were,
according to international law—certainly Mason and Slidell were no less
dangerous because they wore civilian garb. Their purpose was to convince
the world's two leading neutral nations to recognize the Confederacy and
thereby facilitate its efforts to destroy the Union. The British commander
of the *Trent* sacrificed all claim to neutrality by knowingly transporting two
emissaries of a people at war, resisting a U.S. naval boarding party's right of
search, then permitting the concealment of their dispatches and later delivery to the three southern commissioners already in Europe. American legal
theorist Henry Wheaton maintained that the ship's destination was *not* the
key determinant. Rather, both he and Lord Stowell contended that a belligerent had the right to confiscate enemy dispatches for adjudication. Common
sense, if not natural law, presents a strong case that Wilkes's behavior was an
act of self-defense.[68]

Just as the American Civil War ushered in many features of total conflict
that previewed twentieth-century warfare, so did this nineteenth-century
war include a diplomatic front that was part of the wartime arsenal and thus
subject to broadened definitions and guidelines. President Davis looked
backward in condemning Wilkes's seizure of Mason and Slidell as an act

of barbarism. President Lincoln could have looked forward in defending his captain's action as appropriate to what the Civil War would become—an all-out war that thrust the divided nation into modern warfare and hence justified any action considered necessary to survival.

But Lincoln faced another, overriding consideration: War with England over debatable legal principles was too high a price to pay for refusing to release the captives. He did not attempt to find a legal justification for Wilkes's actions, and the massive sense of relief afforded by the settlement outweighed further thought on the subject. Lyons was correct in asserting that the British threat of war had dictated a resolution of the crisis. Indeed, he felt confident from the outset that if the Americans came to believe that Mason and Slidell's surrender did not constitute a national humiliation, they would comply with British demands.[69] Prince Albert's wise counsel had left the way open for Seward's note to accomplish these objectives. From the beginning of the American conflict, Seward thought his only leverage in blocking diplomatic recognition of the Confederacy was to threaten war with England; yet in the *Trent* affair at least, his aggressive strategy became exposed as empty rhetoric. Ironically, his repeated warnings of war with England over intervention had so embittered Anglo-American relations that they fueled the *Trent* crisis. The Lincoln administration had engaged in a dangerous game of provocation in attempting to ward off foreign intervention and had thereby intensified every issue between the Atlantic nations. Henry Adams perceptively remarked that Seward "shaves closer to the teeth of the lion than he ought." Yet Seward chose peace and thereby helped to alleviate British concern about his motives. Russell did not regret the *Trent* crisis. "The unanimity shewn here, the vigorous dispatch of troops and ships—the loyal determination of Canada, may save us in a contest for a long while to come and in fact the cost incurred may be true economy." But the chief redeeming feature was its showing that Seward's threats of war with England were "all buncom[be]."[70]

The *Trent* affair nonetheless demonstrated that British recognition of the Confederacy was a distinct possibility. Increasing numbers of observers believed southern independence a fait accompli and renounced the Union for refusing to accept reality. Others warned that the economic damage caused by the war and the Union blockade would hit England hard by the spring of 1862. A January 1862 survey revealed that the number of unemployed workers had jumped three times what they were in November and that those on short time had risen more than 50 percent.[71] A large number of British citizens wondered about their government's responsibility to intervene in the name of civilization. Popular sentiment in England favored some sort of intervention designed to end a war that many observers once thought the Confederate army had resolved at Bull Run in July 1861.

French support for the British position also pointed to intervention in the American war. Before the Diplomatic Corps in Paris, the emperor told the large gathering that an Anglo-American war would hurt the United States but be "a calamity to Europe." Dayton noted that pressure had grown on France's industrial interests and that its population was suffering, leading to the belief that removing the blockade would resolve all problems by providing cotton and a market. Despite Thouvenel's assurances, Dayton saw a real threat of France and England interfering with the blockade. The Paris government knew that the United States did not want a foreign war along with the domestic conflict, and reasonably assumed that it would "submit to much, rather than incur that hazard." The meetings of the legislative chambers in London and Paris, particularly in considering questions about the blockade's effectiveness, would undoubtedly "renew the agitation" over recognizing the Confederacy and raising the blockade. Union seizure of the Confederacy's major seaports would discourage French or British challenges to the blockade that could lead to their recognizing the Confederacy in an effort to end the war in the interests of themselves "and the world."[72]

Another point needs emphasis: British exultation over the captives' release did not signify favor for the Confederacy; rather, it was an expression of relief from having escaped war with the United States. Furthermore, the British came to realize that Seward's warnings of war were mere bluffs and felt justified in maintaining their neutrality. It appears certain that the breakdown of the Atlantic cable just before the crisis (fortuitous for the Union, not so for the Confederacy) had delayed each side's awareness of the other side's angry reaction and thereby provided a release time for emotions. The *Times* praised the preservation of honor but then assailed Mason and Slidell for doing "more than any other men to get up the insane prejudice against England which disgraces the morality and disorders the policy of the Union." They deserved no accolades. "They are personally nothing to us. They must not suppose, because we have gone to the very verge of a great war to rescue them, that therefore they are precious in our eyes. We should have done just as much to rescue two of their own Negroes."[73]

The *Trent* settlement strongly suggested that the Palmerston ministry intended to remain neutral. Indeed, the crisis forced the Atlantic nations to clarify the rights of neutrals and thereby reduced the likelihood of such problems arising again. Had the British wanted a pretext for challenging the Union blockade, they could have found it in these explosive events. But they did not, strongly signaling that their neutrality was genuine. In a tumultuous time when numerous voices called for recognizing the Confederacy, the Palmerston ministry won widespread acclaim at home for resolving the *Trent* matter short of war and thus gained greater leverage in determining foreign policy.

Palmerston's ability to maintain control augured well for the Union, even if not noticed in the Union at the time. The Confederacy, however, detected dangerous signs. One of its agents in England, Henry Hotze, warned that the crisis had hurt the southern cause by furnishing the British government with a diplomatic victory that it could use as evidence of wise leadership in resisting the popular pressure for intervention. Richmond editor E. A. Pollard later wrote that the peaceful settlement of the *Trent* affair had provided "a sharp check to the long cherished imagination of the interference of England in the war." The elder Adams offered a similar assessment while remaining leery of England's imperial nature. The Palmerston ministry had gained a much stronger political position at home, making it critical for the Union to avoid any issue that provided the British with a reason to intervene. England, he told a friend, would continue to "sit as a cold spectator, ready to make the best of our calamity the moment there is a sufficient excuse to interfere."[74]

But perhaps a clerk in the War Department in Richmond put his finger on the real importance of the *Trent* affair. The Confederacy, he believed, had lost all hope for an alliance with England. "Now we must depend upon our own strong arms."[75]

CHAPTER 4

Road to Recognition

I am heart and soul a neutral.
—LORD JOHN RUSSELL TO LORD LYONS, February 6, 1862

I think we are finally reaching the decisive moment of the crisis.
The Federals will shortly be in Richmond; there is no longer
a shadow of a doubt about that. Then we shall see whether the
Southerners are capable of persevering. . . . For myself,
I would not yet dare to say anything positive.
—HENRI MERCIER TO EDOUARD THOUVENEL, May 12, 1862

The *Trent* crisis had caused war talk on both sides of the Atlantic, further driving British interest in ending the American conflict before another problem developed that could lead to a third Anglo-American war. The two Atlantic nations had narrowly escaped conflict over a question of honor in the *Trent* affair. What if they confronted each other over the blockade? How long must the war go on before it destroyed the economic livelihood of neutral nations? How many wartime atrocities were enough to convince the antagonists to lay down their arms? The United States, the British insisted, must accept Confederate independence as a fait accompli—so amply illustrated at Bull Run. Continuing the war assured a mindless waste of human and material treasure that violated humanity while inflicting economic hardships on both Europe and America. The dictates of civilization, they concluded, necessitated a mediated settlement of the American Civil War before other nations joined the fighting.

The British government reaffirmed neutrality in the wake of the *Trent* settlement while acknowledging the dangers of a prolonged American war. Not looking beyond the present, the secretary for war noted with relief in February 1862 that the cabinet felt no great pressure to intervene in American affairs because the workers in Lancashire had "behaved with wonderful forbearance and moderation." But Lewis knew this uneasy calm could not last. By autumn the cotton supply would drop to a dangerous level, forcing extended layoffs and raising the likelihood of massive disturbances. Meanwhile, Foreign Secretary Russell tried to temper relations with the Union by announcing that, effective February 6, British waters were no longer open to privateers or warships from either Union or Confederacy. "I am heart and soul a neutral," he assured Lyons. But when Seward thought he detected a softening British attitude and asked that England show good faith by withdrawing recognition of southern belligerency, Lyons quickly opposed the move, agreeing with the French that the Union's implied quid pro quo to open southern ports and relax the blockade offered no impetus to ending the war. The British minister realized that the maintenance of neutrality kept all principals involved within the well-defined constraints of international law and avoided the vagaries of municipal law that came with port closings. Lyons urged his superiors in London to maintain pressure on the Union by keeping it uncertain about their direction. "It is when the Americans feel sure of us," he told Russell, "that they take liberties."[1]

Russell, however, raised questions in both American camps about the sincerity of his neutrality by meeting "unofficially" at his home with Mason in early February 1862. Though intending to reiterate his government's wish to stay out of the conflict, he again demonstrated his failure to understand that *any* contact with the Confederacy automatically signaled *dis*favor toward the Union. "What a fuss we have had about these men," he remarked to Lyons in dismissing the matter as inconsequential. Had not the Bunch imbroglio taught Russell the perils of public impressions? In the midst of the *Trent* troubles, he had seemingly learned this maxim by informing the three Confederate commissioners that he would not meet with them a third time and asserting that he could have no "official communication with them." But the *Trent* threat had passed, and Russell thought the time propitious to make his neutrality stance clear to the Confederacy. His well-intentioned effort satisfied neither side, as is so often the case in trying to walk the fine line of neutrality between belligerents. William Gregory took the initiative on behalf of his southern friends, first securing Russell's agreement to meet informally with Mason and then arranging for the minister to request the interview.[2] Southern hopes rose only to fall again, whereas the Union angrily denounced Russell for making another admission to the Confederacy's status as an entity.

Mason's discussion with Russell on February 10 proved "civil and kind," according to the Confederate minister's account, but it disappointed him by revealing no prosouthern sentiment. Russell refused to accept Mason's credentials but patiently listened to his request that the British extend recognition and ignore the Union blockade. The Confederacy, Mason strongly emphasized, would win independence with or without recognition. Indeed, he must have baffled Russell by stating that the Confederacy did not seek either material aid or a military alliance. Mason had thought a mere profession of self-reliance would prove the Confederacy's capacity to stand on its own, but his refusal to seek specific assistance demonstrated a wealth of self-delusion that helped to undermine its only real chance for nationhood. Mason now realized that the road to recognition ran through the battlefield. If the Confederacy administered a telling blow on the advancing Union armies in the West, "it will be a great lever by which to operate here."[3]

But that highly anticipated southern victory in the Western Theater did not come, for in mid-February Ulysses S. Grant's Union forces seized two critical points at the gateway into the Confederacy: Fort Henry on the Tennessee River and Fort Donelson on the Cumberland River twelve miles eastward. Just days later Nashville fell, putting the Union in control of Kentucky and much of Tennessee and forecasting an assault on the Mississippi River that would split the Confederacy, throw open the port at New Orleans, and thereby ease European pressure for lifting the blockade. The *New York Tribune* mirrored the widespread optimism in the Union by predicting a quick end to the war. News of Fort Henry hit the British like a "flash of lightning," Benjamin Moran gleefully declared in London. England must "desert her slave-driving allies now." Adams considered the capture of Fort Donelson the greatest military event of the war because it reduced the danger of European intervention. Davis admitted to the Richmond Congress that the fall of Forts Henry and Donelson had hurt the Confederacy, but insisted that he and fellow southerners would never give up the cause of independence. Yet the ever-confident Mason conceded that news of the Union's two conquests had "an unfortunate effect" on the southern cause in England.[4]

A combination of circumstances, including the Confederacy's twin defeats in Tennessee, brought greater attention to the need for foreign assistance and led Davis to replace Robert M. T. Hunter with a new secretary of

Judah P. Benjamin, Confederate attorney general, secretary of state (Courtesy of the Library of Congress)

state, the former attorney general and secretary of war, Judah P. Benjamin. The scion of an established Jewish mercantile family in the British West Indies, Benjamin grew up in Charleston, studied at Yale until withdrawing in a cloud of mystery, became a successful commercial attorney in New Orleans and Louisiana sugar planter with 140 slaves, was instrumental in promoting a railroad, and won election as U.S. senator in 1852. Bearded, eternally optimistic, and a raconteur of fine food and witty conversation, he loved to gamble as much as he worked hard. But if Benjamin possessed the intellectual capacity for heading the Confederate State Department, he too often showed an inability to discern reality from exaggeration. According to one close contemporary colleague, Benjamin was "the most unreliable of news reporters, believes anything, and is as sanguine as he is credulous."[5]

Benjamin and Davis made a comfortable personal and professional fit. They had developed a close friendship, but only *after* a rocky relationship during their initial days in the U.S. Senate, when Benjamin challenged the future president of the Confederacy to a duel over a remark he quickly withdrew with an apology on the Senate floor. Now, about a decade later, Davis recognized that Benjamin had had more international experience than anyone else for the position of secretary of state. Indeed, Benjamin was as cosmopolitan as Davis was provincial, having visited France on a yearly basis to see his wife and daughter who preferred Paris to America. On appointing him attorney general in 1861, Davis had called him a highly respected lawyer who had impressed him with "the lucidity of his intellect, his systematic habits and capacity for labor."[6]

Benjamin was ready for a change. In the Justice Department, he had argued for shipping cotton to England, using the money earned to purchase arms and supplies, and keeping the remaining bales for future credits. No need for such policy, his colleagues scoffed. Secretary of War Leroy P. Walker had told fellow Alabamians many times that he could easily "wipe up with my pocket handkerchief all the blood that would be shed."[7]

Benjamin's selection to head the State Department did not mean that Davis assigned top priority to securing European recognition. Doubtless because of the president's military background, his primary interest and chief concern was victory in combat. After the Confederacy's recent setbacks on the battlefield, he recognized the need for a secretary of state capable of securing outside aid, but he also admired Benjamin's courage and, perhaps even more, his loyalty. In the same month Forts Henry and Donelson collapsed, while Benjamin was still secretary of war, the Confederates met defeat at Roanoke Island in North Carolina. Benjamin shielded Davis from criticism by taking responsibility and not defending himself against a congressional censure, even though the fault lay in the lack of cannons and other military supplies. In mid-March 1862, shortly after this string of defeats, Davis appointed Benjamin secretary of state. Yet if Davis considered foreign relations critical to Confederate success, it is baffling that in his three huge volumes of postwar writings on the Confederacy (about two thousand pages), he focused almost exclusively on military affairs. Indeed, he devoted a bare dozen or so pages to foreign relations and mentioned Benjamin only three times—and not a single reference to his role as secretary of state.[8]

News of the Union's victories arrived while Parliament was in session and compounded the Confederacy's ongoing problems in convincing the British to challenge the blockade. In their meeting, Mason had given Russell 126 pages of documents allegedly proving the porous nature of the blockade, and the foreign secretary had forwarded the papers to Parliament. Gregory immediately presented a motion in the House of Commons calling on the government to renounce the blockade. But the documents were as porous as Mason had claimed the blockade to be. The statistics cited as evidence were outdated in that they did not refer to the period after October 31, 1861, when the blockade had become more effective. Moreover, William Forster delivered a devastating rebuttal showing that Gregory's glowing references to successful blockade-runners pointed only to small coastal steamers that hugged the shores en route to the West Indies. Rising cotton prices in England, Forster insisted, also proved the growing effectiveness of the blockade. England's choice was simple, he declared: Continue neutrality and maintain peace or defy the blockade and, in so doing, ally with the Confederacy in a war for slavery. Henry Adams sat in the gallery, smugly asserting that Forster's sharp response had suddenly cast the aura of a "funeral eulogy" onto the Confederacy's supporters. Gregory withdrew his motion, leaving the blockade unchallenged.[9]

Likewise in the House of Lords did the blockade prove impervious to attack. On March 10, Russell (recently made an earl) pronounced its effectiveness. His legal advisers had informed him that an "actual and effective blockade by a competent force" meant the "actual presence of an adequate naval force, either stationary or sufficiently near to each blockaded port to cause an evident danger of capture." Whether or not the blockade was effective, the Palmerston ministry had proclaimed it so, confirming its wish to avert a maritime confrontation with the Union navy.[10]

The Confederacy's leading propagandist in England, Henry Hotze, did not share Mason's gloom about the news from the battlefront and, like so many of his compatriots, deluded himself into believing his own convoluted arguments. The fall of Fort Donelson, Hotze declared to befuddled British editors, had actually *helped* the Confederacy by underlining the necessity of a British intervention aimed at ending a war that moved relentlessly toward southern separation. Even if the Union's forces overran Virginia, North Carolina, Missouri, Kentucky, and Tennessee, "the citadel would still remain untouched." The *Trent* affair had admittedly left the British government less susceptible to public pressure in determining foreign policy, but, Hotze insisted, more than a few members of Parliament staunchly supported the Confederacy. "I am for the first time, almost sanguine in my hopes of speedy recognition."[11]

Adams felt relieved by the demise of Gregory's motion, but he knew the recognition battle was not over. Many parliamentary members had expressed a visceral hatred for the United States, some touting the benefits to England of a permanent breakup of the Union. In the Lords, Adams complained, Russell's statements suggested a belief in the ultimate collapse of the Union and the necessary extension of nationhood to the Confederacy. Adams correctly suspected that jealousy driven by fear had shattered the common sense of more than a few British leaders. The United States, they charged, had recently appeared ready to challenge British maritime supremacy, making its division into two American nations particularly advantageous to the crown's interests. One parliamentary member professed continued support for the government's policy of neutrality, but he suggested the possibility of intervention by noting widespread agreement in the Commons over Gregory's claim that the blockade had caused serious economic damage at home. In an unexpected twist of fate, the Union's victories on the battlefield had *strengthened* rather than weakened the pressure for recognition.[12]

The real story behind the threat of intervention lay in England's textile industry, where the Union's military successes in the West had drawn a mixed reaction that complicated any attempt to assess the war's impact. Because of the huge prewar cotton surplus, the slowdown in imports resulting from the conflict had actually helped mill owners by providing them a welcome opportunity to cut back on labor costs, sell their back stocks, and upgrade their factories. A mill owner in Clitheroe, James Garnett, had earlier joined other manufacturers in the district in reducing their workers to short time. But with the fall of Fort Donelson to Union forces, Garnett became concerned that his stock's value would plummet because of the imminent end of the war followed by a certain glut in the cotton trade. John O'Neil, a weaver in Lancashire who worked for Garnett, probably expressed the countersentiment of fellow textile workers when he hailed Fort Donelson's collapse as signaling the end of the war and the beginning of a revived cotton trade.[13]

Russell's chief concern was to keep order at home among textile workers, and that required a stable economy. Labor unrest, he knew, meant trouble for the government. It was difficult to tell whether the mill owners actually had surplus cotton and were therefore justified in laying off workers. Perhaps, he wondered, they had created a mythical surplus, intending to make a huge profit by lowering wages while raising prices. In either case, a prolonged American war would permit this domestic economic problem to fester into violence capable of undermining the government's clamp on nonintervention. Peace at home, he believed, depended on restoring peace to North America.

The Confederacy sensed Russell's vulnerability on this domestic issue and increased its economic pressure on England, hoping to force recognition but instead making him angry. Southern leaders had placed themselves in an impossible position by arguing that the Union had installed an illegal paper blockade while finding it difficult to explain why, if the blockade was so weak, so little cotton made it to Europe. How could they risk angering the British and French by admitting to an unofficial embargo calculated to force their intervention to secure cotton? Hence the Confederacy's central dilemma—which it never resolved: How to produce a cotton famine with an embargo aimed at securing British and French support without alienating both of them and leaving the impression that the Union had imposed an effective blockade? Russell did not fool easily. In a highly charged conversation, he complained to Adams that the Confederacy's decision to withhold cotton, although unofficial, was not attributable to the blockade, but to a self-serving effort to put pressure on the London ministry to grant recognition. This question, Russell indignantly declared, should rest on "great principles, and not merely immediate interests." But he also knew that his people would soon feel the pinch, for by late summer or early fall of 1862 the British textile mills would need more cotton.[14]

Although both antagonists had denied the relevance of slavery to their conflict, the issue soon became central to the Union's war effort. Slavery remained a moral question to the small band of abolitionists on both sides of the Atlantic but not a vital concern to either the British or the French governments and therefore of little consequence to the interventionist controversy in these early stages of the war. Lincoln, however, was not aware of the Palmerston ministry's virtual dismissal of slavery as a factor in foreign policy and, as intervention became a serious threat, decided to elevate the issue to prominence in an effort to ward off outside involvement in the war. What developed was not an expected debate over the morality of slavery but a deep fear among British leaders that the president's move would stir up slave rebellions. The result, they predicted, would be a race war that crossed sectional lines and, contrary to Lincoln's intentions, *forced* other nations to intervene.

And there was another almost bizarre twist to the slavery issue: Russell told the Lords that British recognition might drive the Union into *instigating* slave insurrections to destroy the Confederacy from within and thereby salvage victory from its ruins. Within three months, he declared, the war must come to a halt on the basis of a southern separation. Otherwise, a full-scale race war would result, spiraling the American conflict upward to another level of atrocity and necessitating a British intervention intended to bring peace. This was no small concern, for Russell's warnings of a race war conjured up images among his peers of the ugly experiences in the Haitian rebellion of the 1790s, the emancipation program in the West Indies, the

Sepoy rebellion in India of the late 1850s, and the ongoing strife in Ireland. Russell's primary interests were strategic and economic, of course, but there is no reason to doubt his humanitarian concerns. In his thinking, all aspects of the American war were interrelated, meaning that prolonged fighting would have an adverse impact on British security by destabilizing the Atlantic world. He repeatedly emphasized the futility of restoring the Union. Indeed, its dissolution might promote the end of slavery. Surrounded by free territory, the Confederacy could not maintain the institution.[15]

Despite denials by both the Union and the Confederacy, slavery was emerging as the focal point of the war. Seward strongly denounced Russell's simple-sounding remedy for chipping away at slavery, but he realized that the institution had become an important concern to growing numbers of people on both sides of the Atlantic. Freedom and slavery could not coexist in peace. Abolition offered no solution, Seward insisted, for it would intensify the southern war effort. Yet he knew that the Union had to forgo its earlier claim that slavery had no bearing on the war. Adams had recently reported Mason's intimation that the Confederacy was willing to accept gradual emancipation in exchange for British and French recognition. Clearly a deception, Adams heatedly observed, but dangerous enough "to demand the most active and immediate efforts at counteraction." The White House must publicly oppose slavery. Seward needed no convincing. Emancipation, he knew, would underline the inseparability of a stronger Union and the end of slavery. "The time has probably come for the practical determination of the great issue which has thus been joined."[16]

By the spring of 1862, the Washington government had edged closer to declaring slavery a vital issue in the war. Congress had passed the Confiscation Act in August 1861, authorizing the seizure of southern property integral to the war effort—including slaves. The following February 1862, the lawmakers debated a more ambitious confiscation bill that directed the freedom after sixty days of those slaves in areas still in rebellion who escaped to Union army camps, leaving the Confederacy with the unattractive prospect of holding onto its slaves only by stopping the war. Lincoln, however, expressed concern that the new bill would antagonize the Border States by encouraging all slaves to desert the plantations. Consequently, he would support the measure only in regions where its implementation had no negative impact on restoring Union control.[17]

Lincoln's public turn against slavery greatly appealed to Europeans but surprisingly won little support in England. In early March 1862, he confronted the Border State issue by calling on Congress to authorize gradual and voluntary emancipation with federal compensation to states that voluntarily freed their slaves. Adams praised this recommendation as Lincoln's most important step in the war and thought Europeans would agree. Dayton reported that Napoleon approved the action, as did "the minds of the Christian World." Russell, on the other hand, remained skeptical about the president's motives. The pronouncement would incite slave rebellions and therefore constituted a last-ditch effort to win the war. Nothing about the measure suggested that Lincoln had taken a moral stand against the most immoral of institutions. From London, Hotze happily wrote of the widely unpopular reception given Lincoln's plan; it had "vastly brightened the prospects of speedy recognition."[18]

The Union's move against slavery continued to gain momentum when, on April 7, Seward and Lyons signed a treaty pledging their nations' opposition to the international slave trade. Like most pacts, this one rested on mixed motives. The Lincoln administration sought to curtail British interest in intervention by clarifying the differences between the Union and the Confederacy over slavery. But the White House also had such a strong interest in ending the slave traffic that it approved a provision in the treaty that had long been a source of tension between the Atlantic nations: a mutual right of search in both African and Cuban waters. Lyons agreed to the treaty even though thinking the president's motives purely political—that Lincoln sought to solidify his leadership in the Republican Party, particularly if he soon had to make concessions to the Confederacy in an attempt to repair the Union. Seward, however, correctly asserted that Lincoln supported the treaty to attract British support.[19]

The Lincoln administration considered the Seward-Lyons treaty a significant milestone in the Civil War. It illustrated the inseparability of domestic and foreign events, for the president had several reasons for endorsing the pact. However transparent his attempt to win British support, he knew they could not reject an agreement promoting the end of the slave trade. Yet he also realized that a British signature on this treaty did not guarantee their backing in the war. The British still did not fathom the severe political and legal restraints that prevented Lincoln from taking a stronger stand against slavery.[20] Any public action approaching abolition violated the principles of both his Republican Party and the U.S. Constitution, and it would automatically alienate the Border States and moderate southerners as well as those white Americans in the North who refused to shed blood for black people. Yet the treaty reiterated the Union's longtime opposition to the slave trade and made it more difficult for the British to consider recognition of the slaveholding Confederacy. But they remained unconvinced that the president's antislavery efforts were sincere, leaving them bitterly suspicious that his only motive was to stir up slave insurrections in a desperate effort to win the war.

Just three days after Seward and Lyons signed their treaty, the White House stepped up its growing campaign against slavery by pressing for gradual emancipation with compensation. On April 10, the president signed a bill authorizing the measure. His concern about the Border States' reaction again became clear when Congress ignored federal law in attempting to expand the web of confiscation by prohibiting army officers from returning fugitive slaves to their owners. Lincoln opposed such a blatant violation of the Fugitive Slave Law of 1850, believing that the most prudent approach lay in persuading the Border States to accept the new legislation. Not surprisingly, they resisted the measure, although it won approval by substantial margins in both houses. Six days later, on April 16, the president signed another bill promoting emancipation. It authorized compensation and colonization for slaves declared free in the District of Columbia.[21]

Lincoln's growing push for emancipation rested in large part on his concern over British and French intervention. The previous September, the Union's minister in Spain, Carl Schurz, had told Seward that a White House statement opposing slavery would unite the European states against the Confederacy. In January 1862 he talked with Lincoln about taking a public stand against slavery as a key step toward preventing intervention. The president pondered the matter before replying: "You may be right. Probably you are. I have been thinking so myself. I cannot imagine that any European power would dare to recognize and aid the Southern Confederacy if it became clear that the Confederacy stands for slavery and the Union for freedom."[22]

The president's position on slavery had undergone evolutionary changes. As a young lawmaker in 1837, he had maintained that Congress had "no power, under the Constitution, to interfere with the institution of slavery in the different States." *At that time in his life*, Lincoln advocated gradual emancipation with compensation to owners, followed by the colonization of free blacks. Emancipation by choice, he insisted, was preferable to emancipation by the sword. By 1860, in accordance with the Republican Party's platform, he still merely wished to contain the spread of slavery and thereby promote its "ultimate extinction."[23]

At the outset of the war, Lincoln sought to preserve the Union as he knew it in 1861. His First Inaugural Address in March highlighted a mystical and permanent Union that exalted the natural rights principles of the Declaration of Independence. Secession would destroy the Union; so the Union must destroy secession. Integrally related to the sanctity of the Union was another critical issue—the need to block foreign intervention in the contest between North and South. Preservation of the Union—the republic itself—soon became transformed into the creation of a "more perfect Union" that he hoped would lay to rest the possibility of disunion.[24]

Lincoln's carefully articulated stance on slavery at the war's beginning came at a heavy cost to his foreign policy. He believed slavery the root of the conflict but could not say so because of domestic and foreign considerations. Yet his public pronouncements about preserving the Union quickly combined with the Confederacy's dismissal of slavery's importance to the sectional struggle to have profound consequences abroad. Lincoln had wrongly assumed that the British and French would recognize slavery as the chief cause of the war and distance themselves from the Confederacy. Instead, he had been partly responsible for convincing them that slavery was *not* the core issue, inadvertently leaving the way open for an intervention in American affairs on economic, humanitarian, or, to some, strategic grounds. This unexpected position on the war by both the Union and the Confederacy led to shallow solutions such as that proposed by Foreign Secretary Russell, who attached no seminal importance to slavery in bringing on the war and called upon the Union to avoid senseless bloodshed by simply accepting southern separation.

Not surprisingly, Lincoln's efforts to end slavery derived from numerous motives and depended on a multifaceted compromise. He remained a staunch opponent of abolition but a strong supporter of gradual emancipation with compensation. Abolition, he knew, was politically volatile because it reminded contemporaries of prewar radicals who had left violence and death in their wake. The antislavery perspective, instead, offered a moderate approach that, of course, did not satisfy those opponents of slavery who regarded the institution as immoral and in need of immediate and wholesale destruction. But even the vast number of Americans who did not advocate racial equality might support an antislavery policy in which the government paid owners to liberate their slaves and incurred no further social, political, or economic obligations to the freed blacks. Lincoln also realized that the confiscation measures provided a sound military strategy that ensured the steady erosion of the Confederacy from within. Finally, the administration's move against slavery, no matter how hesitant and expedient it appeared to observers thousands of miles away in Europe, indelibly inked the Confederacy as the chief practitioner of human bondage in a world that had turned away from such medieval concepts.

Antislavery groups in England welcomed the president's new stand. On a mid-April morning, Adams greeted a large delegation of the Anti-Slavery Society, including a member of Parliament, who had come to the legation to praise the White House.[25] Lincoln the politician, the social reformer, the military strategist, the diplomatist—all aspects of effective, pragmatic leadership had merged in the slavery issue to solidify his control over the Union's war effort.

In the meantime, maritime developments provided more impetus to Russell's interest in ending the war. During the summer of 1861, Confederate naval agent James D. Bulloch had privately contracted with British manufacturers for the construction of warships (masquerading as commercial vessels) to become the basis of a Confederate navy. One of them, later named the css *Florida*, had left a Liverpool shipyard over Adams's hot protests. The vessel, Russell explained in trying to calm the indignant minister, had not been fitted for war in England and was therefore not subject to seizure under the Foreign Enlistment Act. Privately, however, Russell welcomed southern successes at sea, telling Lyons that they further demonstrated the futility of the Union cause by showing that the southern "spirit may be invincible."[26]

But in late March, the Union ironclad uss *Monitor*, surprisingly fought the Confederate ironclad css *Virginia* (formerly the *Merrimack*) to a standstill at Hampton Roads, Virginia. Not only did the *Monitor*'s performance shock Russell and other British observers and stiffen the Union's resolve, but it also raised their concern about a new maritime rival from across the Atlantic. "John Bull," Moran exuberantly proclaimed from the American legation, "is sorely frightened at the manifest weakness of his own navy and is very civil at once." Adams confirmed the anxiety of British leaders when the news arrived from Hampton Roads at an evening reception hosted by Lady Palmerston. Secretary for War Lewis acted out of character in blasting the Union for trying to crush the Confederacy. The Union was dissolved, he exclaimed with the air of an angry angel of death. Adams curtly remarked that British interest in seeing a divided United States provided the most telling reason for continuing the war. Not by coincidence did the British show greater interest in the construction of a railway linking their three major North American provinces of Canada, New Brunswick, and Nova Scotia.[27]

The perils of neutrality became increasingly clear to the British as the war ground on. The Union believed the British too anxious to extend recognition; the Confederacy considered them too cautious. Both antagonists blamed the Palmerston ministry for needlessly prolonging the war—the Union because refusal to deny any chance of recognition gave false hopes to the Confederacy, the Confederacy because such refusal encouraged the Union to believe subjugation possible. Seward's criticisms of British policy were already legend. Those of his counterpart in the Richmond State Department, Judah P. Benjamin, had not yet reached similar intensity, but they soon came close. In Washington, Seward was so pleased with recent military progress that he sent Adams a map and a long dispatch (meant for Russell as much as for Adams) setting out the Union's plan to occupy more of the Confederacy and throw open its ports. A clear pronouncement against recognition from London and Paris would hasten the inevitable Union triumph, he asserted. From Richmond, the exasperated secretary of state lambasted the British for failing to see that recognizing the Confederacy would facilitate the Peace Democrats' rise to political power in the Union and a resulting push for a negotiated end to the war. After the fighting was over, Benjamin angrily promised, the Confederacy would get even by imposing severe commercial restrictions on Britain.[28]

In the interim, the Union's international problems had opened the door for a three-power European intervention in Mexico that only lightly veiled Napoleon's real designs. Britain, France, and Spain had signed the Treaty of London in October 1861 with the ostensible purpose of collecting debts, but it quickly became evident that the French emperor was more interested in establishing control over all of Mexico. As early as January 1862, the British became suspicious of Napoleon's motives when he made known his intention to enlarge his military force after Spain sent six thousand troops into Vera Cruz the previous month. Then came rumors that Archduke Maximilian of Austria's Habsburg family had accepted the Mexican throne. The London ministry, although deeply concerned, could do nothing in light of its preoccupation with the Union over the *Trent* affair. President Ramón Castilla of Peru further embarrassed the British government when he denounced the Treaty of London as a ruse for a "war of the crowns against the Liberty Caps." Spain joined England in wanting to distance itself from Napoleon. French aims in Mexico, Dayton thought, had collided with those of Spain, with the former wanting an Austrian on the throne to promote Napoleon's dynasty and the latter preferring either the younger son of King Leopold of Belgium (the brother of Maximilian's wife Charlotte) as monarch or, in accordance with Queen Isabel II's wishes, the retention of the republic. "A Monarchy under a European prince, if not guaranteed by Europe," the Spanish minister wrote Russell in London, "would not last a year."[29]

The three powers' occupation of Vera Cruz had convinced Seward that territorial control rather than debt collection was their primary objective. All three ministries in London, Paris, and Madrid, along with other Union representatives on the Continent, confirmed his observation. Adams had alarmed the White House by observing that the French advance on Mexico City "may not stop until it shows itself in the heart of the Louisiana purchase." Dayton warned that Napoleon had "his own ends and objects," separate from those outlined by Thouvenel for the French government and the Mexicans, and that he "will prosecute them in his own way." The Lincoln administration was well aware of Napoleon's larger goals but could do nothing while at war with the Confederacy. For the moment, Seward informed Dayton, the president "has relied upon the assurance given to his government by the allies that they were seeking no political object, and only a redress of grievances." Yet the European actions in Mexico, the secretary emphasized, "are likely to be attended by a revolution in that country which will bring in a monarchical form of government there in which the crown will be assumed by some foreign prince." If any European power tried to install a monarchy, it must send military forces to secure its position, which would mark "the beginning of a permanent policy of armed European intervention, injurious and practically hostile to the most general system of government on the continent of America." In such event, Seward pointedly warned, "the permanent interests and sympathies of this country would be with the American republics." Lest there be doubt about White House resolve, Dayton was to assure his hosts in Paris of war with the Union once it had defeated the Confederacy.[30]

In response to Dayton's advisory, Thouvenel was less than candid in repeating his country's pledge against territorial designs. The French foreign minister well knew that Napoleon's reach always exceeded his grasp. Yet Thouvenel supported the idea of helping the Latin people and believed this could happen only under a monarchy. Even as Seward's note was en route to Paris, Thouvenel wrote Mercier in Washington that the war in America had afforded an opportunity for their emperor to expand his interests beyond a mere collection of debts. Less than three weeks later (and a day or so before renewing his assurances to Dayton), Thouvenel again wrote Mercier: "I have not received any information or any communication from Mr. Dayton concerning the Mexican affairs. Whatever it should be . . . you know already that it could not influence our conduct." Meanwhile, French forces alone had moved on to the capital at Mexico City, preparing to overthrow the republican government and install a monarchy under a European prince.[31] Palmerston was not surprised by Napoleon's deceit. Was not such transparent cunning consistent with the emperor's past behavior? But the prime minister derived special satisfaction from two unexpected results of the French intervention in Mexico, both beneficial to the British: Napoleon's entanglement in the weblike catacomb of Mexican affairs would keep him out of European ventures, and it would restrict further American expansion into Latin America.[32]

Russell likewise had grasped the danger in associating with Napoleon. The foreign secretary now weighed the advantages of halting American expansion southward with the near certainty of a war in Mexico resulting from Napoleon's reckless policies. The intervention appeared to be a "pretext for a continued occupation of Mexico and the assumption of the Government of the Country by a foreign Power." Had not the emperor made "excessive and exorbitant" demands of Mexico? The French had sought $15 million in bonds in return for a "fraudulent loan" of $750,000 to "a falling and bankrupt government." Mexico's rejection of the claims would provide "a *casus belli* for the Allies." Intervention to collect debts had served as a pretext for occupation and the establishment of a puppet regime. England joined Spain in negotiating separate agreements with Mexico that satisfied their reparation demands and then withdrew from that beleaguered country in early April 1862. Only the French remained.[33]

The Lincoln administration had cause for alarm about the French presence in Mexico. Could a successful intervention below the international border provide precedent for the same action above? Would southern acceptance of a new French neighbor constitute a quid pro quo for French recognition of the Confederacy? In view of the ongoing Civil War, the president could do nothing more than express reliance on the European powers' assurance that their attempt to collect debts would not lead to interference in Mexican internal matters. But he warned the British that a monarchy established in the presence of foreign armies and fleets would not lead to stability—particularly if the monarch was "a Prince of a European reigning family." This would result in "frequent European interference" and a situation "extremely offensive" to American interests.[34]

As if privy to Thouvenel's confidential communications to Mercier, Seward was adamant in his belief that a monarchy installed by France in neighboring Mexico meant trouble. In a message to the French foreign minister through Dayton, he wrote: "We have more than once informed all parties to the alliance that we cannot look with indifference upon an armed European intervention for political ends in a country situated so near and connected with us so closely as Mexico." Thouvenel immediately denied any wish to interfere with "the form of Government in Mexico." But he added a curious statement that strongly suggested an ominous change in attitude if not policy. All France wanted, the foreign minister declared, was "a *government*, not an anarchy with which other nations could have no relations." The French would not object if the Mexican people decided to create a republic. "If they chose to establish a monarchy, as that was the form of Government there, it would be charming, but they did not mean to do anything to induce such action." The rumors that France wanted to place Maximilian on the Mexican throne "were utterly without foundation."[35]

Yet Thouvenel's assertions do not fit the evidence. He had already admitted to his government's preference for a monarchy over a republic, even while guaranteeing against interference with the form of government chosen by Mexico. Months earlier, in a private letter to the French ambassador in London, Count Flahault, he had written that an improved government "for the latin races" was not "possible except under a monarchy" and that "everyone assures me that all honest and sensible people in Mexico think the same." A short time later, Thouvenel told the British ambassador to Paris, Lord Cowley, that the way to resolve the ongoing Venetian issue in Europe was to place an Austrian prince on the Mexican throne. And in early 1862 Thouvenel attributed Napoleon's hidden reason for the Mexican venture to his interest in promoting an alliance with Austria. He wished to compensate Maximilian with the throne for the loss of his position as viceroy of Lombardy-Venetia just before the war in Italy and thereby lay the basis for a French request for concessions on the Adriatic.[36]

Dayton could not have been aware of all the European maneuvers affecting French thinking, but he did discern that Napoleon had pledged not to interfere with Mexico's internal affairs because he intended to fashion its government into a monarchy acting in French interests. An election would take place, of course, but one carefully managed by Napoleon in a monarchical path. Clearly and without emotion, Dayton observed to Thouvenel "that a French army in Mexico might give to the people of Mexico a tendency toward a particular form of government and if such a government should be established it might protect its existence afterwards." Again, the foreign minister insisted that the United States could "rest assured" that the French army would not influence the Mexican government.[37]

Lincoln and Seward saw through Napoleon's transparent assault on the Americas but could do nothing to remove his forces from Mexico while the Union was at war with the Confederacy. They ignored Thouvenel's well-crafted assurances and instead praised his government's pledge against either interfering with the Mexican government or seeking Mexican territory. So did the president and secretary of state make the Union's position clear, just as England and Spain formally withdrew from the Tripartite Pact in the midst of growing insistence by European observers that Napoleon intended to establish an empire under Maximilian. The northern press, as if prodded by Seward, warned Napoleon that once the Civil War ended, the United States would eject his armies from the Western Hemisphere.[38]

Across the English Channel in Paris, Slidell had become encouraged about the prospects for recognition after learning from French officials that slavery posed no obstacle to their sentiment for the Confederacy. Like the British, Napoleon thought southern independence incontrovertible and feared that the coming cotton shortage would inflict "immense injury" on his country; similarly, Thouvenel lamented the growing unemployment that spurred petitions and memorials arriving daily for the emperor from parts of France already experiencing economic destitution and public demonstrations. To be sure, the French people regretted the presence of slavery in the Confederacy and hoped for its gradual demise. But their lukewarm feelings had placed no pressure on the emperor and government leaders to take sides, leaving them "quite indifferent" on the matter and allowing them to focus on other aspects of the war.[39]

Slidell considered this a good moment to press Thouvenel on recognition. The government's continuing refusal to grant it, Slidell complained, had made his status as "unrecognized minister" in Paris "very embarrassing." To enhance his importance, Slidell offered to keep the French government informed on the impact of the blockade and the Union's efforts to close southern harbors by sinking old ships packed with huge stones. The foreign minister was receptive to these proposals though puzzled. If so many ships had run the blockade, why did so little cotton reach neutral ports? Here, as had been Mason's experience in England, the Confederacy confronted a major dilemma of its own making: How to push France into granting recognition by an unofficial embargo that it had to conceal for fear of alienating France? The ships making it through the Union's blockading squadrons, Slidell not so convincingly replied, were primarily small vessels, and most of them carried spirits and turpentine because they yielded bigger profits than cotton. Furthermore, the possibility of capture was just strong enough to drive away captains not given to risk. The London government, Slidell declared in testing Thouvenel's reaction, had sought French and Russian opinions regarding whether the blockade and the closing of southern harbors met the conditions of international law and civilized warfare. Russell had denounced the port closings by such methods, even though knowing that international law permitted the practice as long as it inflicted no permanent damage. Slidell alleged that both England and France had declared the blockade paper in nature and the harbor closings a violation of international law and civilized warfare because they caused irreparable damage. But Thouvenel denied receiving any such inquiries from London. Slidell asserted that someone in London had sent a private note to the Confederate government, insisting that the British Foreign Office had solicited the opinion of France and Russia regarding the two issues.[40]

Slidell was more encouraged about potential recognition after talking with cabinet and other governmental figures. He met twice with Count Fialin Persigny, minister of the interior, and came away convinced that he supported the Confederacy "heart and soul." The emperor, Persigny asserted, wanted to extend recognition and renounce the blockade but preferred that England take the lead. The minister of justice, Jules Baroche, likewise spoke favorably of the southern cause, promising that he would try to persuade the emperor to grant recognition. Achille Fould, the minister of finance, also affirmed his sympathy for the Confederacy, and the Duke of Morny, president of the lower house, was "decidedly favorable."[41]

Slidell's major concern was the British. France, he believed, would extend recognition but only in conjunction with England. The French must realize that their present peace with the British could not last. When the two nations were at war over some future issue, Britain—based on the precedent of France's acquiescence to the Union blockade—could close its entire coast. British leaders had insisted that they would replenish their cotton supply from India's markets. France would be in trouble if it went to war with the British and had no southern cotton.[42]

Napoleon's crafty shifts from one stance to another on the intervention issue added further uncertainty to the crisis. Dayton reported an early April 1862 meeting in which the emperor masterfully demonstrated his propensity for creating confusion about his position toward the American war. After expressing concern about his country's growing need for cotton, he inexplicably raised the possibility of withdrawing belligerent rights from the Confederacy. These two statements, Dayton knew, did not mesh. Revoking belligerent recognition would alienate the Confederacy and cut off any chance of resuming the cotton flow. But before the Union minister could sort out these ideas in his mind, Napoleon stressed that England must take the lead in reversing Anglo-French policy toward the Confederacy. Perhaps, the emperor pondered aloud, the two nations had acted prematurely in granting belligerent standing to the Confederacy *before* it had won independence. Had not Napoleon's concession vindicated the Union's argument?

When Adams received word of this conversation, he immediately pressed England to withdraw belligerent status from the Confederacy. He met with Russell for an hour, trying to persuade him to reverse his policy. The effort was a dismal failure. Russell's arguments for continued neutrality between the belligerents, Adams confided to his diary, were sincere and honest, though by their very nature harmful to the Union.[43]

The Union minister could not have known, of course, but Napoleon's unorthodox and two-faced tactics had put additional strain on an already-tender Anglo-French relationship. Seward had recently approached Lyons with the proposal that, in exchange for withdrawing belligerent rights, the Union might "relax" the blockade. The secretary had also spoken with Mercier, posing a decidedly different proposition. If the Union permitted trade through southern ports, it must be in *American* ships. Neutrality took on a greater appeal to Mercier, who later told Lyons that it was preferable to becoming "friends to a Power engaged in suppressing a rebellion." Palmerston was livid over Napoleon's duplicity. The French, he wrote Gladstone, "hate us as a nation from the Bottom of their Hearts, and would make any sacrifice to inflict a dark Humiliation upon England." How outlandish to propose such a change in policy and then expect England to take the initiative in a program it could never support. Napoleon sought to win the Union's allegiance while advancing his long-range plans to build an army and a navy much larger than England's. He would do anything to undermine its position. Only the American war held the two European nations together.[44]

Palmerston was undoubtedly correct in his assessment of Napoleon's motives. What better way to cause trouble for England than to manufacture a French friendship with the Union by offering to withdraw belligerent rights from the Confederacy? The emperor knew that England would reject the proposal, thus building his ties with the Union by proposing the move while preserving his relationship with the Confederacy by leaving its belligerent status intact. Even if the British consented to withdrawing belligerent recognition, he could maintain that the idea came first from London and that, in keeping with his earlier statements, he had merely followed England's lead. In either case, he would maintain relations with the Confederacy at the same time he won credibility with the Union by imparting the false impression that he was on the verge of terminating the Anglo-French concert.

Napoleon's unconventional behavior continued in a series of meetings in Paris with William S. Lindsay, an outspoken southern supporter in Parliament who advocated free trade as a boon to his shipping interests and now privately sought to achieve that goal by securing French intervention in the American war. After earlier failing to convince his home government to intervene, Lindsay obtained Cowley's assistance in arranging a meeting with Napoleon. The purpose, said Lindsay, was to discuss possible revisions in the Navigation Laws. Cowley thought this request reasonable and not so wisely agreed to a meeting. But Lindsay had not told the truth. His real objective was to persuade the emperor to take the lead in recognizing the Confederacy as a means for stopping the war and reopening commercial traffic. The time was opportune, as Napoleon had been pressing the French navy to speed up the construction of ironclads.[45]

Three times in April the self-appointed British emissary made unauthorized visits to the emperor, repeatedly urging him to take the initiative. Lindsay had already talked with the minister of commerce, Eugene Rouher, who expressed great concern over the approaching dearth of cotton as a certain impetus to growing unemployment. Lindsay opened his first meeting with Napoleon on April 11 by underscoring his interest in establishing a steamer line from Bordeaux to New Orleans and then denouncing the Union blockade as ineffective and hence a violation of the Declaration of Paris of 1856. The emperor reaffirmed his willingness to challenge the blockade if England joined him in doing so. But, he groused, the Palmerston ministry had not responded to two private overtures. In about three months, Napoleon lamented, the shrinking cotton supply in France would inflict enormous personal hardships on textile workers. Recognition of the Confederacy, Lindsay quickly interjected, would remedy French economic troubles by reviving the cotton flow. If France and England did not act quickly, he warned the emperor, Spain and Belgium might take the lead. "The time for action had arrived."[46] Napoleon was dubious about others leading the way. "England was the proper power to make the suggestion," he maintained.[47]

More than Europe's interests were at stake, Lindsay argued, adding another dimension to his appeal for French involvement. "Every principle of humanity demanded prompt intervention to stop so dreadful an effusion of blood and the mutual exhaustion of both parties." Hatred had become so intense "that the Union could not be restored and . . . even if the South were overrun she could never be subjugated." The Confederacy was waging "a most unequal contest, rendered still more unequal by the submission of neutral powers to an inefficient blockade." The self-professed neutrals, he charged, were not really neutral. The Union had the capacity to purchase huge arms supplies, whereas the Confederacy was cut off from those goods and unable to produce them on its own. Seeing Napoleon's concurrence on this point, Lindsay leveled another accusation against the Union. Although claiming to oppose slavery, he had developed a friendship with Mason and Slidell in the course of which they had convinced him that slavery was benign—a position that, not surprisingly, facilitated his commercial objectives with the Confederacy. But now he had to turn the argument to fit France's antislavery feeling along with its interest in reviving trade. Washington's leaders had not gone to war to abolish slavery, Lindsay told Napoleon, "but to subjugate the South in order to reestablish their protective tariff and to restore their monopoly of Southern markets."[48]

"What then was to be done?" Napoleon asked. He was ready "to act promptly and decidedly" but had to know beforehand that the British would be receptive. He would join England in sending fleets to New Orleans to open that port to the free passage of cotton and other goods considered vital to the world's markets. He did not *want* to interfere in American affairs, but the Union had severely damaged French interests and its restoration was not possible. He asked Lindsay to relay this message to Cowley and then return to discuss his reaction in another meeting two days later.[49]

Thoroughly excited about the prospects, Lindsay rushed to Slidell's residence that same day to inform him of the meeting. The southern minister was equally elated, immediately writing Mason that he could assure the Confederacy's friends in Parliament of "positive and *authoritative* evidence that France now waits the assent of England for recognition and other more cogent measures." Lindsay then saw Cowley in the embassy. The emperor, Lindsay declared, had twice sought British collaboration to end the blockade and had received no response. Its impact now threatened France's domestic economy, raising Napoleon's support for intervening in a war he thought the Union could not win in an effort to reopen the cotton traffic. Cowley insisted that France had never asked England about challenging the blockade, but he admitted that its effectiveness had steadily grown.[50]

On April 13 Napoleon again met with Lindsay, who reported his conversation with Cowley. England was not yet ready to take action, Lindsay said. But he remained hopeful. Even though Cowley believed that the "proper moment for action had passed," a change in British policy seemed possible, for the ambassador had added that "further developments should be waited for." At this moment, Lindsay later recalled, Napoleon became "even more emphatic" in asking him to notify Palmerston and Russell of the French position. In a striking move, he urged Lindsay to share this view with the leaders of the Conservative opposition, Lord Derby and Benjamin Disraeli. Napoleon recognized the threat posed to the Anglo-French entente by his making contact with Palmerston's opponents and, in a highly improbable move, hoped to hide his hand in the transaction. The emperor cautioned Lindsay not to leave the impression that the message had come directly from the throne. "I do not want to be embarrassed by the forms and delays of diplomacy, as I feel the necessity of immediate action." Lindsay, according to Slidell, "inferred more from [Napoleon's] manner than from what he said, that he was dissatisfied with his present position, which made his action subordinate to the policy of England, and that he might be disposed to act alone."[51]

Meanwhile, Cowley had become suspicious of Lindsay's motives and wondered if he was acting on his own initiative rather than the emperor's. The same day of Lindsay's second meeting with Napoleon, Cowley asked Thouvenel about the two private notes allegedly sent to London. The French foreign minister knew nothing about them and denied that anyone had sent them. When Thouvenel noted that Lindsay had assured him that Cowley "coincided in his views," the British ambassador became livid. He denounced Lindsay's "unofficial diplomacy," declaring that his "interference" had put him in a "false position." Both Thouvenel and Cowley were career diplomats who deeply resented Lindsay's intrusion into their world. Thouvenel promised to discuss the matter with the emperor the following day. He assured Cowley that he had tried to convince Napoleon and Rouher that recognition of southern independence did not guarantee a resumed cotton flow and that resistance to the blockade would cause "a collision" with the Union.[52]

This was a "nasty intrigue," Cowley bitterly wrote Russell in London. Thouvenel had denied any knowledge of Napoleon's alleged proposals, and Cowley was inclined to believe him. "My own conviction is, from Lindsay's conversations with me, which are full of hesitations, and I fear much falsehood hidden under apparent candour, that he has told the Emperor his own views, and that those views are supported by the majority of the people of England, and by the present Opposition in Parliament, who would denounce the blockade if in power." The emperor proved "a willing listener" because of his desperate need for cotton. Lindsay would certainly raise the matter before Parliament.[53]

Thouvenel's meeting with Napoleon on April 14 proved a testy experience. The foreign minister was irate over Lindsay's claim to having French assurances of imminent recognition. Where did he get this idea? The emperor, it quickly became clear, had not consulted his advisers, and Lindsay had misinterpreted their conversations to mean much more than intended. Napoleon tried to calm Thouvenel by explaining that Rouher's report of an economic crisis over the cotton shortage had necessitated strong action. He had therefore approved Lindsay's offer to informally relay to the Palmerston ministry France's interest in working with England to reopen commercial lanes. "I can not, and will not, act without England," he assured his agitated foreign minister. Only through a private exchange of views could he learn what arrangements the British government might consider. The record does not indicate that Napoleon told Thouvenel that he had also encouraged Lindsay to speak with the London ministry's opposition. His explanation did little to assuage Thouvenel's concern.[54]

Thouvenel tried to placate Cowley by insisting that Napoleon had not understood "the intricacies of this question" and "had confounded remarks conveyed in dispatches with deliberate proposals." The French government, Thouvenel asserted, was more concerned about the growing cotton shortage than were the British. On receiving this information through Cowley, Russell acknowledged the French need for cotton but opposed any immediate action. "The evil is evident—not equally so the remedy." The British government, Russell told Cowley, "wish[es] to take no step in respect to the Civil War in America except in concert with France and upon full deliberation."[55]

Back in England, Lindsay encountered a mixed reaction to his proposals. The Palmerston ministry showed no interest in his meetings in Paris. Lindsay waited four days for an appointment, but Russell refused to see him, coldly asserting that contact with foreign governments must come only through established diplomatic channels. Palmerston was out of town and stayed out of town. Lindsay had a warmer reception from the Conservative opposition. Derby was too ill with the gout to discuss the matter, but Disraeli agreed with the French view and insisted that the Palmerston ministry would have overwhelming support if it repudiated the blockade. If France were to take the initiative in ending the war, a great majority of Parliament would approve and Russell would have to go along to save the ministry. Russell and Seward, Disraeli suspected (never proved), had entered into a "secret understanding" stipulating that England would honor the Union blockade and refuse to recognize the Confederacy.[56]

Lindsay then visited Mason and, after considerable persuasion, convinced him to cross the channel and meet with Napoleon in Paris. On April 18 Lindsay, with Mason at his side, indignantly informed the emperor that Russell had dismissed the matter in a tone that was "flippant, although intended to be sarcastic." Napoleon appeared irritated that Russell had treated Lindsay so brusquely. The emperor complained that he had twice received evasive replies from Russell on the American situation, and he did not intend to talk with England on an official basis without Russell's prior agreement to the proposition. The British, he grumbled, had acted "in a strange manner" toward France ever since its "friendly interposition" in the *Trent* affair. Russell had earlier acted "unfairly" in sharing French proposals regarding the blockade with Lyons, who had then passed this information to Seward. Had Russell lost interest in maintaining cordial relations?[57]

Napoleon's reaction to Disraeli's remarks greatly pleased Lindsay and Mason. The emperor, Slidell reported, seemed "particularly struck" by the possibility of a private agreement between Russell and Seward and asserted that it would clear up what he had never "been able to comprehend" about the hardened British attitude. He also appeared taken by Disraeli's claim that if the French took the lead, Russell had to follow. The British foreign secretary surely could not remain neutral while his people suffered from the Union's blockade. The wisest approach, Napoleon observed in a statement that he wanted kept confidential, was for him as emperor to urge the Union to open American ports and, in a striking suggestion, "to accompany the appeal with a proper demonstration of force on the Southern coasts."[58]

Lindsay and Mason were exuberant after the meetings with Napoleon. The emperor appeared so angry about the Palmerston ministry's refusal to reciprocate his support in the *Trent* crisis that he had expressed a willingness to act alone in forcing open southern ports. Napoleon was ready to take military measures, Lindsay revealed to Slidell in a breach of confidence, and the London ministry might have to take action when Parliament convened in late April. Lindsay did not know this, of course, but support for this view soon came from Hotze, who reported that the cotton famine had hit England, forcing the government to confront the growing economic distress at home. Indeed, the crisis had spread across the Continent. Germany, Hotze noted, was suffering as much as England from the sinking American market. On hearing the details of the third meeting with the emperor, Slidell believed that Napoleon had finally tired of his subordinate role to England and was poised to act—immediately and alone.[59]

On learning of the emperor's first two meetings with Lindsay, the French ambassador in London, Count Flahault, angrily wrote Thouvenel: "I cannot conceal from you that this kind of relations are helpful to no one's position, not to the emperor's or to mine." If this practice continued, "I would see no other reason for it except the emperor's lack of confidence in me, either because I lack zeal or ability. . . . I should prefer a thousand times to cease to be His Majesty's representative in London than to continue to occupy this post after I no longer possess his entire confidence." Thouvenel saw an opportunity to curtail Napoleon's indiscretions and passed this note directly to him. Less than a week later, the emperor lamely assured Flahault that he had never intended "to do anything behind your back." Napoleon guessed that his own "*easy-going*" manner had encouraged Lindsay to exaggerate the importance of their conversation.[60]

Napoleon also tried to calm Cowley, who had sent him a similar complaint. In a response dated April 20, which Cowley enclosed in a note to Russell two days later, the emperor reiterated his concern over the diminishing cotton supplies, then made a series of statements that directly contradicted Lindsay's account summarized in a message from Slidell to Richmond. "I have not been at all shocked that Lord Russell did not receive Mr. Lindsay," Napoleon declared. All Lindsay asked was "my permission to report our conversation to the principal secretary of state, and I had given my consent and that's all there is to it."[61]

Lindsay and Mason's elation proved fleeting, for they had joined British enthusiasts of the Confederacy (like southerners themselves) in a marked propensity for self-delusion. Lindsay had acted without government authorization in urging a European challenge to the blockade that aimed to restore commerce at the risk of going to war with the Union. Looking for every conceivable sign of French favor, he relayed the truth as he wanted it to be in asserting that the emperor stood poised to act on his own. Dayton informed Seward of Mason's presence in Paris with Slidell, reporting that the two southern ministers were in high spirits over the prospect of recognition, intervention, "or some other great good the character and extent of which, I think, neither they, nor I, distinctly understand." Napoleon's unguarded statements had certainly left that impression. He had been sorely tempted to take matters into his own hands, but even he, reckless as he often was, quickly reconsidered his position in light of the not-so-gentle remonstrance from his advisers about the hazards of unilateral intervention. Had he not already undergone a similar upbraiding for his ongoing venture in Mexico? Thouvenel, Cowley, and Flahault had brought the imperious emperor to his senses by warning that any flirtation with Lindsay's unconventional methods invited trouble. Napoleon had blundered in not consulting his advisers. To Cowley, he conceded: "I quite agree that nothing is to be done for the moment but to watch events." Lindsay and Mason returned to England empty-handed.[62]

The threatened French involvement in American affairs had deepened on another front when Mercier, like Lindsay's acting without authorization, engaged in a peace-seeking mission to Richmond in mid-April. After the Union's victories at Forts Henry and Donelson, Thouvenel had instructed his minister in Washington to inquire whether Seward would consider mediation now that the Union armies had restored their prestige on the battlefield. But the U.S. secretary of state was so ebullient over the recent turn of military events—since capped by another victory, however narrow and brutal, at Shiloh (or Pittsburg Landing) in southern Tennessee—that Mercier decided against making the recommendation. The Union was near restoration, Seward proudly proclaimed in his State Department office in early April. Mercier remained skeptical, remarking that "I wish I could be as sure of it as you are." He then added in a near-casual manner, "It's just too bad I can't go down to Richmond and find out for myself what is the condition of things there." Seward shocked his visitor by welcoming the idea. The insurrection, he later wrote Dayton, was "sinking and shriveling into very narrow dimensions," and Mercier might convince the Confederacy to accept peace. Even if he failed, Seward doubtless hoped to subvert the Anglo-French relationship by encouraging Mercier to make the trek alone. "Have one of your ships take you to Norfolk," Seward told him, "and I'll give you a pass. Your visit at this time could have a very good effect and do us a real service."[63]

Mercier had the presence of mind to ask for time to reflect on the matter but sensed an opportunity to end the war and immediately informed Stoeckl of the meeting with Seward. According to the Russian minister, Mercier proposed that the two ministers "make the trip together in the hope, if not of beginning negotiations, at least of looking over the situation and seeing if we could open some avenue of reconciliation." Mercier had ensured trouble for himself in extending this invitation without Thouvenel's knowledge. How would the British react to a Franco-Russian peace delegation? The French foreign minister would certainly disapprove of Mercier's acting alone and thereby jeopardizing the Anglo-French entente; to go with Stoeckl could tear it apart.[64]

If Stoeckl saw this opportunity, he could not take advantage of it. Certainly the proposition was tempting. He had long favored a private French overture to the belligerents in light of Russia's opposition to intervention and the certainty of Union rejection of a British proposal. But he turned down Mercier's invitation because, as he explained to his superiors at home, "I did not see any chance that this project would succeed."[65]

Mercier knew that Thouvenel supported the Anglo-French understanding and, with a reluctant sense of duty, presented the matter to Lyons on April 10. The British minister, Mercier had long complained, was overly cautious and would doubtless oppose the idea. He was correct. Lyons was under strict instructions to remain neutral toward the American conflict and could not have gone to Richmond had Mercier extended an invitation. Mercier nonetheless argued that if southerners were demoralized by recent defeats, he could speak frankly about their plight and thereby administer "a knock-down blow" that might convince them to give up the war. The British minister strongly disapproved of the mission, warning that unilateral action might suggest that the Anglo-French concert had collapsed. In a statement that contradicted Stoeckl's account of having received an invitation, Mercier, not wanting Lyons to know about his previous discussions with the Russian minister, wondered out loud whether he should ask Stoeckl to accompany him to Richmond. Lyons rejected that idea as well, saying it would give the appearance that Russia had undermined the Anglo-French entente. Mercier already knew of Stoeckl's decision against going and, as he reported to Thouvenel, "did not hesitate to make that concession to [the British minister]." Lyons recognized Mercier's determination to make the trip and approved his proposal to reaffirm the entente by telling Seward that the two ministers had agreed on the mission. Mercier would inform the Confederacy that recognition was unlikely in view of its recent battlefield reversals and that it should accept an armistice followed by a negotiated settlement. The Confederacy, he agreed to emphasize at Lyons's urging, should expect no European alliance.[66]

Two days after meeting with Lyons, Mercier returned to Seward's office to announce his intention to go to Richmond. The secretary of state expressed great pleasure in the decision. Inform the southerners, he said, that they need fear "no spirit of vengeance" and that their representatives "would be cordially welcomed back to their seats in the Senate, and to their due share of political influence. I have not said so to any other person, but I'll tell you that I am willing to risk my own political station and reputation in pursuing a conciliatory course towards the South, and I am ready to make this policy and to stand or fall by it." Without Thouvenel's sanction, Mercier and his first secretary and chargé, Louis de Geoffroy, boarded a French frigate on the morning of April 15 and proceeded to the Confederate capital.[67]

Despite his outward confidence, Mercier entertained no illusions about achieving peace. Two days before his departure, he had written Thouvenel about the mission, knowing it would take two or more weeks for the note to reach Paris; by then he would have already returned to Washington. "I am

... thoroughly convinced beforehand," Mercier declared, "that my words will not bring the men of the Richmond government to accept the reestablishment of the Union, any more than they would bring Mr. Seward to accept separation. Each side is too much committed to be able to draw back." But he hoped to uncover the "secret" that might draw the two warring parties into peace talks.[68]

Mercier arrived in Richmond on April 16 and immediately headed to the office of the secretary of state. If any chance existed for peace, Mercier knew, it lay with his longtime friend Judah P. Benjamin, whom he had met before the war when Benjamin was a Louisiana senator alongside Slidell. The battlefront news had also seemed encouraging. McClellan's Union forces had just launched the highly heralded Peninsula campaign, reaching Yorktown in the first week of April en route to Richmond. Gazing around at the city as he rode to Benjamin's office, Mercier thought that surely the Confederacy had come to realize its plight. Granted, the Union blockade had not been a resounding success, but it had denied the Confederacy a number of goods to which it had long been accustomed. Mercier, a connoisseur of fine drink and gourmet food, would find nothing of the sort in Richmond. "Mercier did not taste tea, coffee, wine or Brandy while in Dixie," according to one contemporary. "All Richmond could not furnish him a cup of coffee or a bottle of claret." In addition to the shortages resulting from the blockade, the government had outlawed the production of spirits in an effort to halt the rising instances of intoxication in the army and among civilians. How disappointed Mercier must have been that, in the midst of widespread economic misery stemming from the war and the blockade, the Confederate secretary of state seemed impervious to his dismal surroundings and staunchly supported continued fighting. Even if the Federals "take our cities, they will find only women, old men, and children. All the people who can bear arms will withdraw into the hinterland. . . . In the face of such resistance, the North must decide to yield."[69]

But, Mercier asked, if the Union offered "substantial guarantees, more than you have ever asked for, would you refuse to engage in a compromise?"

"It's too late for that kind of patching up," Benjamin replied bitterly. "In fact we are two distinct peoples and should each have a separate life. Our population today hates the Yankees as much as the French have ever hated the English. Look at the women. They are the first to push their husbands, sons, and fathers to take up arms. They single out those who don't and pursue them with sarcasm. Things have come to the point that the North must make up its mind either to exterminate us or to accept our separation."

Mercier remained skeptical of the Confederacy's chances for independence. "With numbers, money, and the sea against you, it is a very unequal fight."

"Not so much as you think," responded Benjamin.[70]

"But aren't you a little worried about your slaves?"

"Not a bit," Benjamin declared. "As we retreat into the back country, we will take them with us, losing a few it's true, but we have to resign ourselves to that as with any property. As to getting them to revolt, if they try, they won't succeed. We're quite sure on that score."[71]

When Benjamin complained about Europe's refusal to grant recognition, Mercier insisted that the Confederacy had not grasped the complexities of this issue. The French regretted the breakup of the Union, the minister asserted, but as long as restoration seemed possible, they could do nothing to shape the outcome. Premature recognition would alienate the Union while doing nothing to end the blockade. France must retain the use of recognition as leverage for achieving peace at the appropriate time.[72]

"I understand all that," Benjamin answered. "Also, we do not complain precisely about not yet being recognized. But what surprises us is the readiness you have shown in accepting the blockade as effective. . . . I can show you more than twenty ports before which a warship has never been stationed."[73]

Mercier found it difficult to counter this argument and, thoroughly exasperated by Benjamin's stubbornness, finally grasped the irreconcilable nature of the conflict. "How can anybody talk to either side?" he exclaimed to Benjamin as the meeting drew to a close. "I dare not utter to you a single sentence that does not begin by the word 'independence,' nor can I say a syllable to the other side on any other basis than union."

Benjamin vainly tried to close the conversation on a friendly and unofficial note. "Why should you say anything to either side? I know your good feeling for us, and we require no proof of it. But you know we are hot-blooded people, and we would not like to talk with anybody who entertained the idea of the possibility of our dishonoring ourselves by reuniting with a people for whom we feel unmitigated contempt as well as abhorrence."[74]

Mercier stayed in Virginia for three more days, glumly learning that most southerners shared Benjamin's unyielding opposition to stopping the war. He met a number of notables, including former secretary of state Robert M. T. Hunter and General Robert E. Lee, who remained undeterred about achieving ultimate victory. Mercier returned to Washington on April 24 and reported the failed mission to the secretary of state and then to the president. Seward appeared stunned, expressing consternation about the Confederacy's continued refusal to face reality; Lincoln sat in silence. How could southerners remain defiant in the face of so much adversity?[75]

Mercier's visit was not a total failure, for he provided considerable first-hand information that supported his government's wisdom in maintaining neutrality. The Confederacy would not quit its war for independence, he became convinced, no matter how hopeless the situation, and the Lincoln administration demonstrated the same tenacity, demanding a restored Union as the sole prerequisite to peace. Mediation offered no hope for a compromise. Moreover, Mercier came away from his inspection of the massive destruction at Fredericksburg and Yorktown with a profound respect for the Union's military and economic power. France must avoid any policy that risked war with the Union, he warned his superiors in Paris. "I think we are finally reaching the decisive moment of the crisis," he wrote Thouvenel. "The Federals will shortly be in Richmond; there is no longer a shadow of a doubt about that. Then we shall see whether the Southerners are capable of persevering. . . . For myself, I would not yet dare to say anything positive."[76]

Mercier's final report arrived in Paris on the evening of May 14, eliciting Thouvenel's immediate insistence on a continued policy of "strict neutrality." The foreign minister remained embarrassed by his emissary's unilateral decision to visit the Confederacy and, like Lyons, feared that it could endanger the Anglo-French concert. But he considered Mercier correct in warning against a challenge to Washington and suggesting that the war was approaching its end. New Orleans had just fallen to Union forces, perhaps signifying that the Confederate withdrawal from Shiloh was the first in a pattern of southern reversals. A certain military confrontation in Richmond would determine whether the French should change its policy. "More than ever it is best to wait before modifying, if at all, our line of conduct."[77]

The collapse of New Orleans in early May 1862 seemingly ended the chances of foreign intervention. "New Orleans is gone," lamented Mary Chesnut in her diary, "and with it the Confederacy! Are we not cut in two?" In London, Adams rejoiced at the news and felt even more relieved on hearing that General McClellan was finally moving toward Richmond. The British were in shock, he happily reported to Seward. Assistant Secretary Moran termed the collapse of the port city a devastating blow to the Confederacy; the British "refuse to believe it, simply no doubt, because they don't want it should be so." Mill owners expressed alarm at the recent developments in the American war. Were not the reports of southerners burning cotton to force British intervention further proof of an impending Union victory?[78]

The irony was that, despite Lincoln's proclamation that New Orleans and other ports were open after June 1, the Union successes had actually *heightened* European interest in intervention. British mediation suddenly seemed prudent—particularly since the Union had satisfied honor and presumably would see no point in continuing the war. French intervention also seemed wise. Although, Slidell conceded to Thouvenel, the outcome at New Orleans had seriously damaged the Confederate war effort, it had done nothing to undermine southern morale. Foreign intervention, the Confederate minister declared, would quicken the inevitable southern victory. In preparation for negotiations, he suggested terms. If France extended recognition, the Confederacy would accept a six-month armistice as long as the Union lifted the blockade during that period. Both Russell in England and Thouvenel in France would continue the policy of neutrality until the proper moment for mediation. That time had come.[79]

Despite claims by Adams and others, Union victories on the battlefield had not closed the door on foreign intervention in the war. The Mississippi River was not completely open to commerce, and the resumption of trade in New Orleans did not automatically lead to a massive injection of cotton into the foreign market. More important, the Union victory did not satisfy honor; instead, it increased the likelihood of a longer conflict by greatly enhancing the Union's drive to subjugate the Confederacy. And as the government in Washington intensified its efforts to win the war, so did England and France increase their determination to end it.

CHAPTER 5

Union and Confederacy at Bay

The war has become one of Separation—or Subjugation.
—LORD LYONS TO LORD JOHN RUSSELL, June 9, 1862

While I do not wish to create or indulge false expectations,
I will venture to say that I am more hopeful than I have
been at any moment since my arrival in Europe.
—JOHN SLIDELL TO JUDAH P. BENJAMIN, July 25, 1862

The threat of European intervention intensified in the summer of 1862, highlighted by the first pitched debate on the issue in Parliament. The Union's victory at New Orleans had not quieted the advocates of British and French involvement in the war. Indeed, Russell rejected Adams's appeals to revoke the belligerent status of the South, as did Napoleon in overriding Dayton's protests, repeatedly expressing interest in intervention but holding back until England took the lead. Russell infuriated Adams by declaring again that neutrality was "exceedingly advantageous" to the Union. Relations became so raw that William H. Russell warned his fellow British citizens that the Union might turn on England next.[1]

How bitter for the Union that its victory at New Orleans had failed to undercut the pressure for British and French intervention! Surging economic problems in both countries forced legislators to consider interceding. Some British observers regarded the fall of the southern port city as an aberration, one that misled the Union into believing it possible to defeat the Confederacy. The result would be prolonged fighting that hurt their own economy and that of France as well. French cotton supplies had already dropped to a

145

dangerous level, and by the autumn of 1862, the British surplus would have disappeared. Challenging the Union blockade meant certain hostilities, leaving mediation as the only viable solution to the war. The process was less provocative than an arbitration in that mediation entailed no binding terms—simply a friendly offer to sit with the two adversaries and explore avenues for peace that they *both* must accept before becoming final. But when Richard Cobden, no southern sympathizer, broached this idea at a breakfast meeting with Adams, the minister sternly replied that the European powers participating in such a venture must have a detailed peace plan. Slavery was the central issue, Adams maintained; the Union, he believed, would reject any arrangement that permitted the institution to survive, whereas southerners regarded its continuation as vital to their future. There was no room for compromise: Lincoln insisted on union, Davis on disunion. "It was the failure to comprehend this truth," Adams wrote in his diary that evening, "that clouded every European judgment of our affairs."[2]

Anglo-French interest in intervention after the collapse of New Orleans greatly alarmed the Union. The threat of a joint action seemed so real to the Lincoln administration, according to Lyons, that it had temporarily toned down criticisms of the Palmerston ministry in an effort to avoid a confrontation and defuse interest in stepping into the fight. Lyons believed that Seward thought the French involvement in Mexico might undermine the entente and reduce the danger of intervention, but the truth was that Napoleon had become more determined to see the American conflict end with southern independence, even if that entailed intervention. Though not yet clear to his foreign contemporaries, the emperor's purpose was to fashion a Confederacy both beholden to him for achieving independence and powerful enough to ward off Washington's opposition to his expansionist aims in northern Mexico as well as in the southwestern part of the present United States. But what form should intervention take? What territorial spoils would he demand without antagonizing the Confederacy? And, most important, how would intervention ensure an influx of cotton? Mercier had expressed concern that the Confederacy would fight at the risk of its own destruction and, thinking like the British, that the Union's expected demand for immediate emancipation would spark a race war that disrupted the southern economy and stopped the cotton flow. Such a conflict could spread beyond sectional boundaries and drag in other nations. Lyons thought Mercier correct in his summary of the dilemma confronting the powers: A decision *not* to intervene guaranteed massive economic destruction in America that could hurt world commerce, whereas intervention meant involvement in the war without assured benefits. If the Union's military advances continued, the southerners would destroy more cotton to force Anglo-French intervention. The only remedy, Lyons asserted, lay in the war itself—a major Confederate victory in the field was needed to convince the Union of its inability to win. Russell agreed, lamenting that northerners mistakenly believed that their success in New Orleans "portend[ed] the conquest of the South." The only "fair solution" was southern separation.[3]

Ironically, Lyons's dire forecast of a long war raised the possibility of a British intervention that he vehemently opposed. Outside involvement in the conflict, he believed, could come only when the Union had lost its will to fight—and no signs of a diminished spirit had appeared. A defensive pact with the Confederacy, even if tied solely to protecting the cotton flow, could cause war with the Union. The only chance of a bloodless involvement lay in the willingness of either antagonist to accept peace "*at any price.*" Even then, he noted, the war would be over at that point because one side would have compelled the other to lay down its arms. Mercier concurred, arguing that intervention was inseparable from recognition and that success could come only after the Union had exhausted itself on the battlefield and realized it was pursuing a hopeless cause. Poor health would soon force Lyons to return home for a time, when he intended to discuss the situation with his superiors. "The war," he wrote Russell, "has become one of Separation—or Subjugation."[4]

The Lincoln administration prepared to fend off what it regarded as a certain Anglo-French intervention. The *National Intelligencer* in Washington ran an unsigned piece in mid-May that contained ideas expressed by Seward to Lyons less than a week earlier. In "Rumoured Foreign Intervention," the writer argued that the only acceptable path was a "moral intervention" aimed at restoring the Union. Any involvement condoning southern separation to satisfy European economic interests would be tantamount to a military alliance with the Confederacy. The Union would consider this step an "act of hostility" and resist "to the last extremity." The Confederacy had become desperate, as shown by its burning of hundreds of thousands of cotton bales to reduce the 1862 crop and force outside intervention. "Can a rebellion claim recognition by virtue of its weakness, or sympathy because of the recklessness of its leaders?" Southerners had not "vindicated their independence among the commonwealth of States."[5]

In a note to Adams, Seward asserted that British intervention would spark widespread slave insurrections and a climactic race war having no sectional boundaries. How ironic that Russell had recently expressed a similar concern but, of course, from the British perspective—that *failure* to intervene would prolong the war and likewise lead to slave uprisings and racial conflict throughout America. Slaves looked to the Union armies as their ticket to freedom, Seward wrote. Outside interference would undermine this new hope by bolstering the Confederacy's chances for separation. Who could then prevent the conflict from "degenerating into a servile war?" The outcome would be massive economic destruction at home that would, in turn, hurt European interests. If the Palmerston ministry showed any signs of intervening, Adams was to share this note with Russell—not realizing that its contents would actually *encourage* British intervention.[6]

Thus another irony of this Civil War and the outside powers' course of neutrality: Just as the British and French advocates of intervention warned that failure to stop the war would lead to a slave insurrection followed by racial violence that dragged in other nations, so did the opponents of intervention contend that any foreign involvement would produce the same results. And even though Seward dreaded such an outcome, the British came to believe that he encouraged it.

The Lincoln administration's fear of intervention made it extremely sensitive to any British actions. When Union occupation forces in New Orleans encountered bitter female resistance, General Benjamin Butler just as stubbornly decreed that any woman who insulted his men would "be treated as a woman of the town plying her avocation." A note from Palmerston indignantly denouncing the "woman order" persuaded Adams that the prime minister had purposely overblown the matter to justify intervention. Russell tried to calm Adams, assuring him that the statement had resulted from anger and was unofficial, therefore signifying no change in ministerial policy. Palmerston, however, did not abandon the issue. He refused to speak with Adams, and Lady Palmerston no longer invited the minister and his wife to receptions. This was no small matter, for at these social affairs the minister had on numerous occasions picked up useful information from conversations with British figures.[7]

Further events in June 1862 elevated White House apprehension and raised southern expectations of British involvement. Lindsay announced his plan to introduce a motion in Parliament calling on the government to recognize the Confederacy. "All this I hope," Mason excitedly informed his superiors in Richmond, "indicates that some movement is to be made at last." Adams was so alarmed that he showed Russell the note from Seward warning that intervention could incite slave insurrections. The motion would "come to nothing," Russell insisted. The ministry, he emphasized in a response that was by no means assuring, had no mediation plan under consideration. The implication was clear: The timing was wrong though the concept was right. British leaders still failed to realize that the Union regarded any outside expression of interest in the war as an unwarranted intrusion that benefited the Confederacy. Both Russell and Palmerston refused to renounce a mediation that was their preferred way to peace but nonetheless, by definition, rested on southern separation. Eternally vigilant in detecting anti-Union feeling, Moran thought that most of the British press had been calling for "the mediation to be all on one side, and that of the South." The prime minister only postponed a confrontation with the Union by informing Russell that "no intention at present exists to offer mediation." A move at this time would be like asking two boxers to stop their fight after only "the third round." Mediation would become likely only after the war had convinced the Lincoln administration of the impossibility of reunion.[8]

The time appeared propitious for intervention when General McClellan shocked Washington by failing to take Richmond in the Peninsula campaign of early June. Moran conceded that the news from the Eastern Theater had hurt the Union's cause in Europe and heightened the chances for intervention. Henry Adams discerned surging support for the Confederacy. Lyons meanwhile had arrived in London, where he expressed great concern about the Union's reversal. "I'm afraid no one but me is sorry for it." The call for intervention, he feared, would swell as the war seemed certain to continue for an indefinite period. A parliamentary debate over recognition would make matters worse. "I do not think we know here sufficiently the extent of the disaster to be able to come to any conclusion as to what the European Powers should do."[9]

The irony was evident: Neither the Union's conquest of New Orleans nor its rebuff at Richmond had stemmed the talk of intervention. Nothing turned the British from what the Union angrily denounced as their southern course. Whether or not they favored the Confederacy, the British refused to budge from their belief in southern separation as the inevitable outcome of the war.

Lindsay, like his contemporaries, had not comprehended the depth of the Union's resolve and felt confident that his peers in Parliament would approve his July call for recognition. Russell had requested a copy of the motion beforehand; it arrived along with a note from Lindsay effusively claiming that 90 percent of the Commons supported immediate recognition and that the majority would vote for the motion even without the ministry's endorsement. The government, Lindsay stoutly asserted, had a *"right"* to extend recognition. The Union, he assured Russell, would not make war on England. Furthermore, in an utterly baseless argument, he said that most northerners would welcome foreign recognition of the Confederacy. Indeed, so would Seward, who desperately wanted the fighting to end.[10]

The Palmerston ministry nevertheless opposed extending recognition at this juncture in the war. The Union controlled the entire Atlantic coast and every important inland waterway, the prime minister noted, and one of the Confederacy's largest armies lay "split into Fragments." Admittedly, southerners would not quit, "but we ought to know that their separate independence is a Truth and a Fact before we can declare it to be so." The war's verdict had not become clear, meaning that recognition at this point would make England a virtual ally of the Confederacy.[11]

As the British failed to grasp the importance of Union, so did Adams find the Palmerston ministry's support for mediation incomprehensible. Only in semantics was there a difference between southern separation and recognition as a nation. Yet Palmerston and Russell insisted that mediation posed no threat to the Union because, even though confirming the Confederacy's status as a belligerent, the action did not imply recognition of national sovereignty. Hence the conundrum: The British argued in good faith that their motives were pure in calling for a mediation aimed only at ending a war between belligerents and not nations; the Union countered, in equally good faith, that mediation constituted interference in domestic affairs and further acknowledgment of the South as a belligerent that placed it one step closer to nationhood. Such a mutual feeling of distrust guaranteed trouble over any form of intervention.[12]

The steadily diminishing supply of cotton had become a driving force in England's foreign policy by the summer of 1862. British workers, Cobden explained to Adams, had gathered in huge meetings to decide how to convince the ministry to work with France in making a "joint representation" to the Lincoln administration. Impressions obscured realities as contemporaries erroneously believed that popular sympathy for the Confederacy had grown to such intensity that only a massive injection of cotton could ease the clamor for intervention. But they failed to consider that the British (and French) need for cotton did not automatically translate into support for the American South. A Union admission of its inability to subjugate the Confederacy would stop the war and ensure a reopened cotton flow and the ultimate end of slavery. Yet these arguments did not penetrate the emotions carrying the war and the popular pressures demanding government action. On reading Adams's note detailing his conversation with Cobden, Seward conceded that Europe's leaders were perhaps acting in good conscience, but, he charged, they had no understanding of America's reverence for the Union. Foreign involvement would stiffen northern resolve, prolong the war, promote a violent end to slavery, and, by wreaking havoc throughout the Confederacy, cut off the flow of cotton.[13]

In the interim, McClellan's troops had not only failed to take Richmond, but also had sustained a major defeat at the hands of Lee's forces in the Seven Days' battle of late June and early July, which had serious internal and diplomatic consequences. The war had taken a vicious turn in the Eastern Theater. Seven Days left more than thirty thousand Union and Confederate casualties—a number that matched those slain in *all* battles in the Western Theater up to this point, including Shiloh—and deflating the Union's hopes for victory despite its capture of Forts Henry and Donelson in Tennessee the previous February. Had McClellan's campaign succeeded, it might have ended the war in the summer of 1862—with slavery largely untouched. Instead, Lee won his first victory, causing widespread jubilation among his people that, in retrospect, prolonged the fighting and threatened total war. Lincoln countered with a harder line toward the Confederacy. This shift brought him a step closer to emancipation by supporting the Militia Act, which instituted the draft and the use of "persons of African descent" as soldiers, and the Second Confiscation Act of July, which authorized the seizure of traitors' property, including slaves who "shall be deemed captives of war and shall be forever free." The death toll and the inability of McClellan's forces to take Richmond reinforced Europe's interest in intervening in a war that it did not believe the Union could win.[14]

Seward had become exasperated with the European flirtations with intervention and warned again that such a move meant war with the United States. Adams met with Lyons in London to emphasize Russell's failure to understand the gravity of the issue. Adams was relieved by Lyons's admission that foreign involvement in the war would make matters worse, yet highly concerned that his opinion did not always shape that of his superiors. From Paris, Dayton reported Napoleon's growing doubts that the Union could subjugate the Confederacy. But it was the British attitude that infuriated Seward. Military successes, they had once professed, must determine the question of intervention. Yet when the Union won a string of battles in Louisiana and in the West, the ministry virtually discounted them while underscoring the earlier reverses at Richmond and Corinth along with the lukewarm Union sentiment in Norfolk and New Orleans. Expressing his total frustration to Adams in London, Seward wrote: "Ah, well! Skepticism must be expected in this world in regard to new political systems, insomuch as even Divine revelation needs the aid of miracles to make converts to a new religious faith." It was ironic, he noted, that the Union finally took Corinth on the same day the British people proclaimed that Confederate control of that city confirmed the permanent dissolution of the Union. When the Union seize Memphis, Moran sarcastically predicted, the British would surely dismiss the conquest as meaningless. British aristocrats, Adams sourly complained, maintained their "ill-disguised antipathy" for the Union.[15]

In the midst of the news of McClellan's failure, Mercier paid a visit to the U.S. secretary of state and reiterated his call for mediation. Seward could no longer contain his rage. The emperor, he declared, "can commit no graver error than to mix himself in our affairs. At the rumor alone of intervention all the factions will reunite themselves against you and even in the border states you will meet resistance unanimous and desperate." Obviously shaken after the encounter, Mercier repeated his May warning to leaders in Paris that intervention meant war with the Union.[16]

The Confederacy meanwhile widened its attempt to gain foreign recognition. In April 1862 it appointed Edwin De Leon, a friend of President Davis and a wealthy South Carolina attorney, to the State Department post of confidential agent to Europe. In that capacity De Leon was authorized to spend $25,000 in secret service funds to commission press articles aimed at winning support for the Confederacy. Previously, he had served as a consul general and diplomatic agent in Egypt before also agreeing in the spring of 1861 to become an unofficial adviser to the three southern commissioners sent abroad. De Leon arrived in Paris in May and in London shortly afterward, where as part of his job he wrote letters to the press on behalf of the Confederacy. Only after the *Trent* crisis had ended did he return home to seek a military commission from Davis. Although impressed by De Leon's arguments appearing in newspapers, the Confederate president preferred that he continue to serve as a propaganda agent.[17]

From the beginning of De Leon's mission, the outlook was not auspicious. On his second Atlantic voyage in the spring of 1862, he broke a diplomatic trust by opening and reading Richmond's dispatches he carried to Mason and Slidell. From them he learned that Confederate secretary Benjamin had instructed Slidell to bribe Napoleon to challenge the Union blockade by offering cotton and the promise of free trade. Slidell never forgave De Leon for violating the sanctity of the diplomatic seal, refusing to work with him or even to introduce him to French leaders. Furthermore, the Confederate government made no effort to foster cooperation between De Leon and its agent already in London, Henry Hotze. They met shortly after De Leon's arrival and just as Hotze had begun publishing the *Index*; but *if* De Leon was aware of Hotze's actions as propaganda agent, he disapproved of the publication as too openly pro-Confederate to win converts. Benjamin would finally recall De Leon in February 1864 after New York newspapers intercepted and published a letter he had written to Davis criticizing Slidell and the French press. Until then, however, De Leon met unofficially with Palmerston on one occasion and, though Napoleon claimed to be too preoccupied with an ongoing crisis in Italy to see him, wrote monthly dispatches to Benjamin, emphasizing in the critical summer of 1862 that British involvement in the war was unlikely but that French intervention on behalf of the Confederacy was almost certain. Partly due to De Leon's assessment, Richmond's diplomatic focus gradually shifted from London to Paris.[18]

On his arrival in London in late June 1862, De Leon quickly used his connections with Palmerston's closest friends to arrange a meeting—as a private citizen—with the prime minister. Stating that his purpose was to share information on the Confederacy, De Leon aroused Palmerston's interest and received an invitation to his home in Piccadilly at noon the following day. The timing was not the best for the Confederacy in that the British public's enthusiasm for its cause had diminished following the Union's victories at Forts Henry and Donelson in February, and at Shiloh, Fort Pulaski, and New Orleans in April. But Mason had been unable to meet with Russell on an official basis, making De Leon's conference with Palmerston all the more important.[19]

At the appointed hour De Leon appeared and was led into the library, where Palmerston rose from his chair to extend a warm welcome. As the prime minister slowly made his way toward his visitor, De Leon noticed a limp resulting from a heavily cushioned foot necessitated by an attack of the gout—"the old foe of 'all fine old English gentlemen' who live at ease," he thought, "'not wisely but too well.'" How gracefully and self-assuredly did the once-fiery leader move, De Leon later recalled, and how convincingly did he belie his age with his full head of gray hair sprouting from atop his tall and well-preserved stature. Palmerston could not have been aware of his visitor's clandestine but official ties with the Confederate government when he remarked that his friends had spoken so highly of De Leon that a meeting with him as a private individual seemed acceptable. Palmerston smiled before establishing the parameters of their conversation. "You must remember in talking to me you are not talking to the Secretary of Foreign Affairs; that is Lord John Russell's field; and also, that I am only speaking to a private Southern gentleman, and that the expression of our opinions is personal entirely." After De Leon agreed with these guidelines, Palmerston went directly to the point: "Now, tell me, what do your people think England ought to do, and what they expect?"

Southerners, De Leon replied, thought the British should extend recognition to the Confederate government on at least a de facto basis. "All the precedents were in their favor."

"Briefly cite some of these precedents to which you refer."

Belgium, Greece, and the South American republics, responded De Leon.

"Your argument is plausible," Palmerston admitted, "but you seem to forget that as yet you have not established your right to recognition, and are in the first stage only—that of revolutionists. We recognize you as belligerents, and you must sustain yourselves in that position before we recognize that revolution as successful." Showing his detailed knowledge of the war, he observed: "At the present moment your great city of New Orleans is in the hands of the Federals; your other cities are all blockaded, and your capital itself is in a state of siege." Both Seward and Adams had insisted that the Union's forces would soon put down the rebellion.

If De Leon believed the stories that Palmerston's sympathies lay with the Confederacy, the prime minister crushed those hopes by a blunt remark that demonstrated his realistic outlook toward foreign affairs. "I do not think your people have yet done enough to prove the falsity of this or establish their right to recognition."

Palmerston could not ignore the irony in the present situation. With what De Leon termed "a sly twinkle in his eyes," the prime minister added: "Besides, you Southerners, as well as Northerners, have always insisted that European Governments must not interfere in affairs on the American Continent. We are adopting your Monroe doctrine in our non-intervention."

"But," De Leon objected, "Mr. [George] Canning recognized the revolted provinces of Spain on our continent, when their situation without it would have been hopeless, and both Greece and Belgium were recognized, without doing or being able to do a tithe as much as we have done." It could not have escaped Palmerston's notice that De Leon did not understand the profound difference between those situations and the present case (or did he try to hide this reality?)—that in the American war, recognition of the Confederacy could pull the outside nation into the fighting.

De Leon also embellished the Confederacy's position, whether in error or in a further attempt to mislead his host. "We have a regularly organized government, whose authority is recognized by twelve States and twelve millions of people." The southern agent must have known that only eleven states had seceded, bringing with them 5.5 million southerners. If intentionally misleading, his inflated calculations could not have fooled the crafty statesman, for the only way to reach such lofty figures was to include 4 million slaves plus the residents of Missouri and Kentucky, Border States that never seceded but had unofficial representatives in the Confederate Congress. Only then did the number come close to 12 million, though still falling short by 600,000.

Palmerston said nothing as De Leon continued to praise the Confederate position, just days after the prime minister had opposed Lindsay's announced intention to propose a parliamentary motion for recognition—one based on the successes of the *Union*. "We have been accorded all the rights of belligerents by the Federal Government," De Leon asserted, "your own and that of France. Is not this enough to establish our claim?"

"I think not," the prime minister responded. "You must do much more to establish it. We always have recognized, and still do recognize the Government in Washington, and its representative to-day represents the people of the United States to us."

"Well," remarked De Leon, "the Confederate forces to-day menace the city of Washington, and it is not impossible they may compel Mr. Lincoln and his Cabinet to evacuate that city and transfer the seat of government to Philadelphia or some other Northern city. If it is the 'Government of Washington' which you alone recognize, would you recognize its representative in the person of one who brought his commission from that place, only bearing the sign[ed] manual of Jefferson Davis instead of Abraham Lincoln?"

"No," asserted Palmerston. "I do not say that; that is not what I mean." The Confederacy must do more than force the evacuation of Washington and change the government representative. It had to demonstrate its capacity to stand as a nation. "You must break through the blockade that makes you prisoners within your limits, and makes all communication with you contracted. You must strike some decisive blows to free yourselves, and to compel the recognition of foreign nations, and of the old Government."

"But," said De Leon, revealing the southern naïveté about diplomatic realities, "we only ask fair play to do this." He then lodged a complaint that unknowingly mirrored the Union's repeated plea: "We insist that European neutrality is not the real thing; that it is one-sided, and interpreted in such a way as always to injure us and aid our adversary. For example, the acknowledgment of the validity of this paper blockade, which is defied with impunity by the blockade runners, who earn millions of money by breaking through its paper meshes."

"We have considered that question of blockade," the prime minister noted, "and accepted the existing one as sufficient." "Tell me," he asked with what De Leon called "a laughing twinkle in his eye," "did you find the blockade such an imaginary thing when you went into and came out of the Confederacy? My friends tell me not."

De Leon considered this a "hard hit" that brought "the matter home with a vengeance." His crossing had been a harrowing experience that he now tried to dismiss as merely an annoyance. But Palmerston's observation, given as if he had witnessed De Leon's tribulations firsthand, rubbed deeply and made the point. Gathering his composure, he lamely replied: "What might occasion inconvenience or difficulty to individuals was not sufficient to shut up the ports of a whole country, and that the Law of Nations—"

Palmerston interrupted his guest, saying "It's useless to dwell on that point, for we have recognized the validity of the blockade, and there is an end of it; but the same complaint your people make about our neutrality your Yankee neighbors make too; so, as both sides abuse us, we think we must be pretty impartial. It is the fate of neutrals to be complained of by both parties."

This was a disabling rebuttal that De Leon vainly tried to parry. "Lord Palmerston must admit," replied De Leon with some degree of sharpness, "that his name hitherto has not been regarded in Europe as a synonym of neutrality, but rather the reverse."

Palmerston laughed aloud, appearing to relish his new image as a moderate who had mellowed after a career-long reputation as a wild-eyed, overly aggressive sword bearer. "Live and learn, I suppose; it is high time that I should prove myself a man of peace and quietness, and not a stirrer up of strife, as they have long considered me on the Continent; but, as I said before, Lord Russell is Foreign Secretary, not I, and the consideration of this matter is more in his province than mine."

De Leon knew, however, that Palmerston remained the acknowledged head of the ministry and repeated his earlier hollow assertion that the South sought only "fair play in this fight."

"Oh, certainly, certainly," the prime minister quickly replied. "You have a right to demand and to expect even-handed justice at the hands of the

English Government; but," he keenly observed, "both your people and the Northerners ask more. Each of you wants us to take your side, and as we had no hand in getting up this quarrel, we really do not see why we should meddle in it."

But in pursuing such a policy, De Leon persisted, "England will make two enemies, instead of securing one friend, as she would by taking either side."

"No, no," Palmerston objected. "This is an exceptional case; it is a family quarrel—like interfering between man and wife—both would combine to assail the intermeddler. Besides, we are no more bound to your side than to the other. Suppose we were to take the Northern, what then?"

"We should consider it as very disinterested as it is against your interest," De Leon replied. "But that we do not fear. We think that both the precedents and the interests of England are in our favor, and we only complain that the same neutrality which openly furnishes the North with all the supplies she needs, under Lord John Russell's construction of it, makes us, and everything intended for us, contraband of war."

Palmerston strongly disagreed. "Dr. John [Russell] has [a] great reputation as a constitutional lawyer, and can have no particular reason to construe the law more harshly in your case than in the other. It is the misfortune of your position at the start." Thus did Palmerston put his finger on the innate legal advantages that the parent country had over its recalcitrant citizenry seeking to break familial ties (advantages the Union still failed to comprehend): the long-standing status of the established state—the United States—and all the commercial and military benefits accrued; and the people striking out on their own—the Confederacy—having to prove, beyond any doubt, their claim to independence and nationhood status to observer nations that must out of their own interests remain skeptical.

Perhaps enjoying the discomfort the Confederacy had inflicted on itself by imposing a cotton embargo (whether or not official), Palmerston threw down a challenge: "Break through this blockade, get some decisive advantage, and no country will recognize you more cheerfully when you have earned your right to it, than England will."

Then laughing, he expressed pride in his neutrality. "You know that I am accused of having strong Confederate sympathies, and you are a gallant people. Yes, a very gallant people; nobody can gainsay that. But our talk to-day satisfies me, that whatever my personal feelings or wishes may be, I have not given any grounds in my public course for the accusation of partiality."

Trying to ease the sudden tension, Palmerston briefly inquired about Confederate military matériel, leadership, and commitment before speaking candidly again. "The common idea of England is that the Southern people are more like us in character than the Yankees, who have too much of the old Puritan leaven in them to suit us. You Southerners we consider only as transplanted Englishmen of the old stock. Probably the truest reflection of real English feeling is to be found in *Punch*, and you will observe the Yankee is generally caricatured very freely there."

De Leon sensed that the interview had come to an end and fired what he called a "parting shot" as a warning. "Has it not occurred to your lordship, that in the desperation of obtaining aid and countenance here in our mother country, we may turn towards France, the traditional rival of England, and more so now than ever before, practically, and offer her such tempting inducements as may secure her intervention, to the great detriment of English interests?"

Palmerston paused a moment at this bald threat before fixing his eyes on his visitor. "Yes," he replied, "we have considered that point, and I will not pretend to mistake your meaning, but I tell you candidly, your hopes are vain. You will not succeed in detaching France from England on this question, nor in breaking the *entente cordiale* which is stronger than you suppose. French and English interests are identical in these matters, and not conflicting as your people think; and you will fail to divide them. There was a time when such a thing was feasible, but not now, not now." Lest there be doubt, he reemphasized: "Do not deceive yourselves with that idea. Whatever action may be taken, will be joint action, not separate. Our understanding with France is perfect."

De Leon remained unconvinced about the closeness of Anglo-French ties but thought Palmerston sincere. "The sharpest arrow I had kept in reserve in my quiver," he told himself, "was pointless for him." As he rose from his seat, Palmerston did also and asked one last question. "Now tell me frankly, what do your people think and say of us, and how do they regard the attitude of England? Speak freely, for I am curious to know."

"If your lordship really wishes to know the whole unvarnished truth, I must answer, that the Southern people generally think and say precisely what your lordship's conversation with me to-day confirms, . . . that the Government and people of England, entertaining the most sympathetic feelings possible towards them, will intervene in this quarrel, and give them the aid of their countenance and assistance, precisely at the moment they are convinced the Southern States stand in no need of either."

"That is—hum! Ha!—putting it rather strongly, is it not?" The prime minister, according to De Leon, was "slightly staggered by this unexpected answer, but not at all offended."

"I think not," De Leon returned, "but believe such to be the sentiment, which, I fear, the frank admissions your lordship makes of the future as well as the past policy of the Government, will confirm."

"I am sorry for that," Palmerston asserted. "They do not do us justice. Our embarrassments and the difficulties of taking another course are greater than they dream of. But I hope time will set it all right. Your people are fine fellows—very fine fellows."[20]

After securing Palmerston's hesitant approval to share their nonofficial conversation with "friends at home," De Leon forwarded his assessment of what he termed a mixed and discouraging British reaction to the Confederacy's appeal for intervention. He thought the prime minister privately sympathized with the Confederacy but had become more conservative in his elder years and therefore more cautious. Russell was "the most ungracious of private as of public men" and had alienated northerners *and* southerners by his "impertinence" but leaned toward the Union and therefore balanced Palmerston's southern inclination. Gladstone showed his "usual brilliant inconsistency," appearing to be "on both sides or neither alternately." Lewis opposed the Confederacy, and the radical members of the coalition cabinet, led by the president of the Board of Trade, Thomas Milner Gibson, and the head of the Admiralty, James Stansfeld, were "violently Northern." The cabinet thus remained "in equipoise, and preserved its equilibrium like a boy standing midway on a see-saw, putting down his foot first on one side and then on the other, an attitude not very dignified for a great power to maintain, and which subjected it to severe buffeting from both sides alternately."[21]

Despite this rare firsthand glimpse into Palmerston's thinking, De Leon had gained at best a superficial understanding of British sentiment toward the war. Yet his prognosis about the slim chances of securing recognition must have been disheartening although not surprising to his superiors in Richmond. The *Trent* affair had presented the best chance for southern independence but did not pull the London ministry into the war. Mason had repeatedly been denied an official meeting with Russell, while making no headway in convincing the British to challenge the blockade, and Palmerston opposed Lindsay's imminent motion for recognition. Whatever the prime minister's private feelings toward the Confederacy, he remained pragmatic in policy, refusing to act unless in the national interest. And so far, as he made plain to De Leon, intervention did not benefit the crown—and certainly not on the Confederate side. Nor did he mention slavery. Furthermore, it was not the foreign secretary's alleged pro-Union feeling that dissuaded Palmerston from extending recognition. Rather, as the prime minister emphasized: Only success on the battlefield could lead to recognition. Yet De Leon refused to accept this hard reality.

De Leon failed to grasp the realistic positions of other British leaders as well. To De Leon, Russell did not cut a figure nearly as impressive as Palmerston's towering silhouette and domineering manner, old in years but young in carriage. In Parliament the foreign secretary sat "like a small boy perched on a high stool, . . . with the large head, crabbed countenance and dwarfish," his "worn and haggard face" carrying the "expression of a roguish little bull terrier."[22] But De Leon's spite for Russell clouded recognition of his hard core. The admittedly diminutive and deceptively weak-looking foreign secretary firmly maintained a neutral course that, from the southern point of view, appeared to support the Union, just as from the Union perspective that same policy seemed to favor the Confederacy. Gladstone, too, De Leon mistakenly dismissed as driven solely by politics and not by his oft-expressed abhorrence of the American war. Probably Gladstone's allegiance to neutrality had likewise left the impression of wavering from one side to the other, never knowing where he stood. And Lewis was less anti-Confederacy than he was a stone-cold legalist and realist who believed that intervention in the American war meant British participation in that war—as an opponent of the Union and thus, by default, as a friend of the Confederacy. Neutrality was the only possible British policy, yet it spawned all manner of difficulties that by its very nature alienated *both* American antagonists. De Leon joined his southern compatriots along with his northern enemies in never comprehending this fundamental reality.

De Leon and most other contemporaries similarly failed to understand another critical element of Russell's conception of neutrality: It contained the potential for an intervention aimed at bringing an increasingly destructive war to a close—and on the basis of a southern separation that could lead only to recognition.

The Union, of course, was unaware of De Leon's private conversation in London and continued to fear an Anglo-French intervention during the summer of 1862. Neither battlefield victories nor battlefield defeats had dissuaded the proponents of involvement, and, most ominous, the prewar cotton glut was virtually gone. Nearly half of England's labor force was out of work, cotton stocks had plummeted in tandem with rising prices, and the overall crop yield was dismal. In France, the economic situation was comparable if not worse. The Union must crush the Confederacy, Henry Adams declared— and quickly.[23]

The chief saving factor for the Union was Britain's continued refusal to renounce the blockade. Mason had accused the Palmerston ministry of unilaterally altering the Declaration of Paris by introducing a new definition of an effective blockade. The original text had stipulated that the blockading nation must maintain "a force sufficient really to prevent access to the coast of the enemy." Thus Russell shocked the Confederacy by declaring a blockade effective if the force managed "*to create an evident danger of entering or leaving*" a port [emphasis Mason's]. President Davis, Mason complained in a note to Russell, was not aware of these words until they appeared in recently published correspondence before Parliament. Russell, however, had already clarified the ministry's position by unofficially telling Mason that documentation of ships passing through the blockade did not automatically make the blockade ineffective. Mason nonetheless forwarded the names of numerous vessels entering and leaving southern ports, calling this evidence of a paper blockade. "Not one in 10, in the large number of voyages so made, it is believed, has been captured." The Lincoln government, he wrongly charged, had hardened British policy by circulating lies that the Confederacy had ordered the burning of cotton. Perhaps Mason was unaware of the recent March 1862 decision by the Confederate Congress to approve crop destruction as a means for drawing an Anglo-French intervention. If so, his inability to maintain communications with home provided further proof of the Confederacy's difficulties in running the blockade. Any drop in the cotton supply, Mason bitterly insisted, was "because Europe has not thought it proper to send her ships to America for cotton."[24]

Washington's fear of foreign intervention had become so intense that it helped push the Lincoln administration into an antislavery position. Months earlier, the president had hinted at an impending change in policy when, in an unprecedented move, he convinced Congress of the wisdom in extending recognition to the black governments in Haiti and Liberia. A little more than a month later, in mid-July 1862, he invited Border State congressmen to the White House and argued for compensated emancipation. Lincoln had long supported the principles of the American Colonization Society and now insisted that the freed blacks could relocate in South America. The legislators rejected the proposal, leaving him no alternative but to take the final step.

The next day, July 13, Lincoln won the approval of Seward and Secretary of the Navy Gideon Welles in calling for emancipation in order to "strike at the heart of the rebellion." Taking a stand against slavery, the president argued, was "a military necessity, absolutely essential to the preservation of the Union."[25]

Not by coincidence did Lincoln make this pivotal move at precisely the time recognition of the Confederacy appeared certain. Cobden had warned that only a reopened cotton flow could undercut the move toward intervention. To ease the threat of domestic disturbances, Palmerston approved a massive relief program for unemployed mill workers. Mason jubilantly reported to Confederate leaders in Richmond that the cotton shortage had generated widespread public pressure in England for recognition. Slidell detected the same feelings in France. And Mann noted that Belgium, the Germanic States, Switzerland, and Holland would follow suit because their manufacturing districts were hurting badly. The cotton famine, he thought, would cause those European countries to extend recognition and put pressure on England and France to do the same. With Lyons temporarily at home, British chargé William Stuart had become the chief barometer of Union behavior in Washington, and he sensed a turning point in the war. Numerous observers in Louisiana suspected that Lincoln was ready to proclaim emancipation. A U.S. State Department representative in New Orleans, Reverdy Johnson, warned the president that his growing stand against slavery had alienated southern Unionists.[26]

Adams praised the timing of emancipation in warding off intervention and urged Seward to strengthen the Union's moral position by proclaiming freedom the central issue of the war. He also informed the secretary that a mediation offer seemed imminent. If its proponents pushed the measure as "the most benevolent aspect possible, the effect would be to concentrate in a degree the moral sense of the civilized nations of Europe in its behalf." Palmerston might submit to the call for mediation from Russell, Gladstone, and many textile workers, as well as from numerous British observers who believed that McClellan's retreat from Richmond had signaled the Union's collapse and the necessity of intervention. The atmosphere in London, Adams reported, was similar to that air of exhilaration following the Union debacle at Bull Run. Buoyed by the latest battlefield news, Lindsay triumphantly announced that his motion before Parliament would link intervention with recognition and that he intended to invite other European powers to join England in a mediation offer. Lindsay had built a strong and vocal following in Parliament that included the outspoken southern sympathizer, John

Roebuck, and the Conservative opposition leader in the Commons, Benjamin Disraeli. Adams doubted that the ministry and most opposition party members supported recognition, but "it is a good deal nursed by the rank and file of the latter [the Conservatives], and by a portion of the ministerialists." This growing push for intervention could succeed, especially because the line between southern separation and southern nationhood appeared so thin. Adams could not have known that Mason had already assured Russell of the Confederacy's willingness to accept a British mediation aimed at ending the war and ensuring southern independence.[27]

The economic problems fostered by the American war had combined with the dangerous Mexican situation to intensify the clamor for intervention. England's cotton supply had plummeted from a high of 1.2 million bales in 1861 to a mere 200,000 bales by the summer of 1862. The *Economist* warned that "the time when mills must stop and Lancashire must starve from an actual exhaustion of the whole supply of raw materials may be very near at hand." Of 1,678 textile mills in Manchester, only 497 were operating full time; 903 were open two to five days a week, and the remaining 278 had shut down. As Americans celebrated their Fourth of July holiday, almost 80,000 British textile workers were out of work and 370,000 were on half time, drastically cutting the average total weekly wage by more than half—from £250,000 to £100,000. "These are the figures of the cotton famine," dourly reported the paper.[28]

The French need for cotton overrode the nation's sentiment against slavery, attracting interest in an intervention aimed at bringing peace to America. In March 1862 Paris legislators praised the Union as "defender of the right and of humanity"; a Union victory would guarantee an end to slavery, they declared. And yet they wondered how long they could wait for that to happen. As the American war wore heavily on the French economy, so did public support for intervention grow. Lincoln's initial moves against slavery in early 1862—the Confiscation Acts, the Seward-Lyons Treaty, the gradual emancipation bill, and the colonization of blacks freed in Washington, D.C.—had failed to arouse popular support. The cotton surplus in France, as in England, had dropped dramatically, forcing many mill owners to close their factories. The once high backlog of 578,000 bales in 1861 had plunged to 311,000 in 1862, lowering the weekly average consumption by nearly half— from 11,114 bales in 1861 to 5,981 in 1862. Slavery remained a French concern, but, as Thouvenel emphasized, the French need for cotton played a more critical role in recognition discussions. The likelihood of a prolonged war raised talk of challenging the Union's blockade.[29]

By mid-July 1862, Napoleon III had become Europe's most ardent supporter of intervention—but for reasons having little to do with the American war. He had expressed concern over the threat that republicanism posed to monarchies, and he wanted to fulfill a long-cherished dream of constructing a canal between the Atlantic and Pacific oceans that would make Central America the crossroads of international commerce. To promote this ambitious scheme, Napoleon privately directed Major General Elie Frédéric Forey, his friend and commander of French forces in Mexico, to assure its people of good treatment if they cooperated with France. "As for the prince who may mount the Mexican throne," Napoleon continued, "he will always be forced to act in the interests of France, not only by gratitude but especially because those of his new country will be in accordance with ours and he will not be able to sustain himself without our influence." To stem the dangerous spread of republicanism, he sought to implant a monarchy in Mexico that would promote the conversion of the other Spanish American republics to monarchies patterned after the Second Empire of France. Such a bold but risky move would block U.S. expansion into Latin America and give Mexico the opportunity to take advantage of a massive injection of talented European immigrants to become the most powerful nation in the region. Recognition of the Confederacy would encourage Mexico to become a commercial partner with France and thereby promote what Napoleon called his "Grand Design for the Americas."[30]

It was thus no coincidence that as the British Parliament prepared to debate Lindsay's motion for recognizing the Confederacy, Napoleon met again at his Vichy retreat with Slidell at noon on July 16 and left the distinct impression that he had moved closer to a unilateral intervention. In this way he would gain the upper hand with the Confederacy by acting on his own, rather than in the wake of the British. The emperor appeared satisfied with the news of the Union army's retreat from Richmond and observed that Lincoln's call for 300,000 more troops had demonstrated a sense of desperation resulting from significant manpower losses. It was in the French interest that the United States remain sufficiently strong to balance English maritime power, he asserted, and yet he admitted to admiring the Confederacy's drive for independence. In a blatant attempt to advance his Grand Design, he praised the Confederacy's break with the United States. "My sympathies," declared the lifelong champion of monarchy, "have always been with the South, whose people are struggling for the principle of self-government, of which I am a firm and consistent advocate." The Union's restoration was impossible. The Palmerston ministry, however, had shown no interest in his proposals.

"I have several times intimated my wish for action in your behalf," he assured Slidell, "but have met with no favorable response." Still, he wanted to preserve good relations with England and could not act without its lead. He insisted that his neighbor across the channel had more to gain from granting recognition to the Confederacy than did France and wanted him "to draw the chestnuts from the fire for her benefit."[31]

In respecting the blockade, Napoleon admitted, "I have committed a great error, which I now deeply regret." France and the other European powers should have recognized the Confederacy in the summer of 1861, when it controlled its ports and threatened Washington. "But what," he asked in feigned exasperation, "can now be done?" A forceful opening of southern ports would constitute an act of war, and the Union would reject mediation—"probably in insulting terms." Recognition would do little to help the Confederacy and would undoubtedly pull France into the war. To exploit this remarkable concession, Slidell agreed that the Union would refuse mediation and that the Confederacy would accept the offer. Such an outcome, he argued, would benefit the Confederacy by enlisting other countries' sympathies and, in a thinly veiled invitation to use force, provide reasons for a "more potent intervention." The Union would capitulate to pressure as it did during the *Trent* crisis, and France would be justified under international law to take action. "I think you're right," Napoleon responded. "I regret to say that England has not properly appreciated my friendly action in the affair of the *Trent*."

Anglo-French differences over Mexico gave Slidell a chance to widen the gap by praising the French military intervention as helpful to the southern cause. Yet he must have suspected that Napoleon's long-standing interest in North America did not stop in Mexico. Once established in Central America, the emperor's New World Empire would put Texas, New Mexico, and Louisiana within his grasp. But the present needs of the war drove Slidell to ignore this certain postwar danger. Better to cross the bridge, he realized, before worrying about what was on the other side. The Confederacy, Slidell assured Napoleon, trusted him to bring about a "respectable, responsible, and stable government" in Mexico. Admittedly without clearance from Richmond, Slidell mentioned the possibility of a Franco-Confederate alliance. Since the Union supported France's opposition leader in the Mexican conflict, President Benito Juárez, the Confederacy had "no objection to make common cause with you against the common enemy."

Napoleon seemed tempted by a military alliance, repeating that "simple recognition" would not help the Confederacy and that the Union would refuse mediation. Southern independence, he knew, depended on commercial and military alliances. Slidell insisted that the Union's expected rejection of mediation would help the Confederacy by drawing other nations into a multilateral intervention aimed at ending the war on the basis of a southern separation. "But we do not ask for mediation," Slidell asserted; "all we ask for is recognition." Napoleon must have appeared puzzled as Slidell tried to explain the southern position. The Lincoln administration had resorted to a "reign of terror" in clamping down on those northerners who sought peace at the price of disunion. Recognition would boost the Democrats' chances for victory in the coming congressional elections and thereby encourage France and other nations to stop a war that threatened the economies of both North America and Europe.

"What you say is true," Napoleon allowed, "but the policy of nations is controlled by their interest and not by their sentiments, and ought to be so."

Slidell agreed but said that the European nations needed to consider the long-term impact of a devastating war. England had ignored its obligation to the world by pursuing "a tortuous, selfish, and time-serving policy" that had alienated other nations—including the Confederacy. "We should never hereafter consider her our friend."

Napoleon appeared to be pondering the question of intervention, as he concurred with Slidell on the weakness of the Union's blockade and admitted to the importance of southern cotton. "If you do not give it to us," the emperor conceded, "we cannot find it elsewhere."

"Your Majesty has now an opportunity of securing a faithful ally, bound to you not only by the ties of gratitude, but by those more reliable of a common interest and congenial habits."

"Yes," Napoleon acknowledged, "you have many families of French descent in Louisiana who yet preserve their habits and languages."

Slidell could not deny it, pointing out that his own family regularly spoke French.

Would the Confederacy have any problem with its slaves? asked Napoleon.

Slidell's response, so grounded in southern culture and history, could not have surprised the emperor. "They have never been more quiet and more respectful and no better evidence could be given of their being contented and happy." With no small measure of relief, Slidell later reported to his home office that this was the only time the subject of slavery arose in the discussion.

The emperor then raised the most penetrating issue. "Do you expect that England will agree to cooperate with me in your recognition?"

Slidell assured him that his English friends were more confident than ever before, and that, for the first time, Mason felt good about the prospect. Lindsay intended to introduce a motion for recognition in Parliament, a move that would force Palmerston to take a stand.

What would Cobden do? asked Napoleon.

Slidell considered him "unfriendly" to the Confederacy, though not as unfriendly as Bright. Most observers thought that a great majority in the House of Commons favored the Confederacy, but that Lord Derby was not ready to take office and no one would do anything that might push Palmerston into resigning.

At this point Napoleon flashed "a very significant smile," noting: "It is very singular that while you ask absolute recognition, Mr. Dayton is calling upon me to retract my qualified recognition of you as belligerents." Such a demand, Slidell retorted, was further proof of the Lincoln administration's "insolence." If France and England intervened, Napoleon asked, what would be the peace terms? The boundary question was a major problem—especially for the four Border States. Slidell thought the solution clear. Those states that had voted in conventions for separation would remain with the Confederacy; Kentucky, Missouri, Delaware, and Maryland should have a popular referendum on whether to join. Slidell had no doubts that they would do so. Did not the emperor pursue this policy in Italy with other nations' approval? Then, in a mistake not discerned by Napoleon because he had no map on hand, Slidell inadvertently left Maryland and Delaware to the Union by delineating the Chesapeake, Potomac, and Ohio rivers as the Confederacy's natural boundaries.

To push Napoleon closer to intervention, Slidell held out the prospect of a cotton subsidy as a thinly disguised bribe that his home office had authorized sometime earlier.[32] He also emphasized that the emperor must understand that the Union's restoration was not possible, and that peace was out of the question without some form of European intervention at the earliest possible date. An armistice must first take place, accompanied by the opening of southern ports.

Slidell also informed Napoleon that Lincoln had sent the U.S. Senate a treaty with Mexico, which approved a congressional allotment of $11 million to help finance Juárez's war against France. The emperor expressed confidence that "the Senate will not ratify it." Perhaps, Slidell replied, but he reminded Napoleon that Lincoln controlled foreign affairs. A reliable source had claimed that the first installment of $2 million had already reached Juárez, meaning that his army was already using Union funds to fight French troops.

In closing the discussion, Slidell explained that he intended to present Thouvenel with a "formal demand" for recognition on his return from England. Napoleon did not object, although he did not intimate what his response would be.

Slidell emerged from the seventy-minute meeting very optimistic about French intervention. He found the emperor "frank, unreserved, I might perhaps say cordial, placing me entirely at my ease by the freedom with which he spoke himself." The emperor made no commitments, but Slidell felt certain that "if England long persevered in obstinate inaction, he would take the responsibility of moving by himself."[33]

Slidell correctly noted the importance of cotton to Napoleon's thinking, but he still had not fathomed the reasoning behind the emperor's refusal to take the initiative in any interventionist proposal. When the moment for action came, Slidell appeared to believe, Napoleon would move with or without British participation. Was he trying to thrust ahead of the British, thereby cultivating southern favor before Parliament passed Lindsay's motion? Slidell could not see how it was *not* in the French interest to act without England, particularly if the Union carried out its threats of war against an intruder. Nor could he have known how clearly Palmerston emphasized to De Leon that it was not in the ministry's interests to intervene. Whether or not Slidell suspected Napoleon's motives, he showed no concern about how the emperor's push into Mexico might someday pose a threat to the Confederacy—particularly if his expansionist interests turned toward Texas and Louisiana. Slidell had dismissed the danger of slave disturbances, permitting the emperor to consider an intervention based on his people's need for cotton—and on his own imperial designs on Mexico.

Napoleon, however, still hesitated to take the lead because of the resistance of both the British and his own advisers. The highly anticipated debate over recognition in the House of Commons led him to believe the time had come to push the Palmerston ministry into a joint intervention. He telegraphed Thouvenel, then in England on an unrelated matter: "Ask the English government if they don't think the time has come to recognize the South." Thouvenel pondered his country's financial problems along with the troubles over its military expedition in Mexico and concluded that an Anglo-French involvement in the American war would be a certain impetus to further difficulties. He warned Napoleon that "our haste in starting a conflict with the United States is unwise and dangerous."[34]

The emperor did not heed this advice; instead, he explored the possibility of inviting Russia to join an Anglo-French mediation effort. Collaboration with the Union's trusted friend might not only ensure success, but also help to mend relations with France and England after their recent war against Russia in the Crimea. Soon after his conversation with Slidell, Napoleon raised the issue with the Russian foreign minister, Prince Alexander Gorchakov. Russia supported the Union, Gorchakov affirmed, and deplored the war's destruction. But, he added, his government could never work with England because of the Union's animosity toward that country. Furthermore, a cooperative effort with England and France would grant stature to the Confederacy and appear to be a hostile act against the Lincoln administration. Russia had no pressing need for cotton, and it stood outside the European community of nations that the United States so roundly distrusted. In fact, Russia had a natural affinity with the Union. "Both of them being young nations in the life of the civilized world," Gorchakov observed, "Russia and America have a special regard for each other which is never adversely affected because they have no points of conflict."[35] As in the *Trent* crisis, Russia refused to pursue any policy that offended the Union. The United States, the Russians well remembered, had been the only nation to make its good offices available to them during the Crimean War.

Russia remained outside the circle of British and French peoples considering intervention, but the Palmerston ministry held the pivotal position and, to Napoleon, appeared certain to approve Lindsay's motion in Parliament for recognition. That done, so would the French follow the British lead, with or without the Russians.

By mid-July 1862 both the Union and the Confederacy thought that popular pressure would force British and French intervention in a war that had become a violation of humanity and destructive to the Atlantic economy. The *Economist* called for the "friendly interposition" of the European powers to stop this horrendous war. A mediation could halt the economic calamity resulting from a vastly reduced cotton trade and its devastating impact on Atlantic commerce. The Union could not defeat the Confederacy, making the war a senseless waste of humanity and economic resources. Slavery was *not* the issue. Southern independence would isolate and confine slaveholders, meaning the end of profits and the end of slavery. The British government had the right to intervene on the basis of the war's destruction of the economy. "We participate in the ruin that is going on," proclaimed the paper's editor, Walter Bagehot. "We have, therefore, a right to speak and to be heard."[36]

French arguments were similar. By mid-June 1862, French governmental leaders were discussing mediation and what actions to take if it was refused. The semiofficial *Constitutionnel* insisted that the Union could not conquer the Confederacy, that neither side could stop the war, and that mediation was the only way to find peace, end slavery, and satisfy France's economic needs. Other Conservative papers agreed that North-South differences were irreconcilable and, according to one writer, had caused both camps to become "drunk with raging insanity." Two Conservative journals supported mediation, one in the name of humanity and civilization, the other calling it "the best guarantor of abolition of slavery."[37]

Recognition of the Confederacy seemed a certainty. Although the Palmerston ministry opposed Lindsay's motion for recognition, it remained open to making a mediation offer that the *Times* appeared to believe would lead to recognition, regardless of the outcome of mediation. But Lindsay wanted to act quickly and decisively. He had drummed up popular support for his recognition proposal by putting it before the public and by working with Roebuck and Disraeli in lining up endorsements in the House of Commons. In the excitement of the moment, southern sympathizers had heralded McClellan's setback in Virginia as a sign of defeat not just there but for the entire Union cause. In a letter to Slidell, Mason could scarcely contain his exuberance: "I am happy to say that the rout before Richmond has had the happiest effect here in all quarters, and things look well for Lindsay's motion tonight." The British permanent undersecretary of state for foreign affairs, Edmund Hammond, thought the Confederacy deserved recognition; the Union had sustained a sound defeat, though still not "sufficiently humbled to seek for peace." Adams suspected that southern supporters had exaggerated the McClellan reversal to round up more votes in the Commons for recognition. Henry Adams wrote that anti-Union feeling was "rising every hour and running harder against us than at any time since the *Trent* affair." Believing the moment had come, Benjamin instructed Mason to formally request recognition.[38]

Thus on the outside, it appeared that Palmerston would go along with Parliament and popular sentiment in recognizing the Confederacy. But the proponents of recognition were not aware of the prime minister's strong feelings against such a move that he had revealed so clearly to De Leon.

On the evening of July 18, Parliament resonated with anticipation, driven to a fever pitch when Palmerston entered the great hall in response to Lindsay's intention to make a motion for recognition. Joining the proceedings were Mason and, as Moran contemptuously described them, "two or three vulgar looking Confederates." A short and testy exchange broke out over their seating in the chamber; as a result, an usher escorted Mason and one of his companions to seats just below the gallery (Moran's perch), and the others had to trudge upstairs. The electricity in the air suddenly intensified as a legislator dashed in, excitedly waving a newspaper with the headline: "Capitulation of McClellan's Army; Flight of McClellan on a Steamer." While a large number of colleagues squeezed in to learn the details, Henry Adams stood back, watching them and remarking that "Southern liars" had concocted the story. McClellan had *not* surrendered, according to reliable reports that had earlier reached the Union's London legation and were, most crucially, dated two days *after* the article ravenously devoured by members of the Commons.[39]

When order returned to the hall, Lindsay stood to bring his motion to the floor. The Union was dissolved, he proclaimed with the finality of an undertaker; the Confederacy was engaged in a just war for independence. Steering around the volatile issue of recognition, he emphasized the need for mediation as a wedge for getting to his real objective. Cotton was running out in Lancashire, he told the lawmakers, leading workers to support southern independence in an effort to replenish nearly depleted cotton stores. Palmerston had yanked his cap over his eyes, feigning sleep, while numerous members abruptly stalked out of the chamber, disgusted with the obviously gross distortions highlighted by Lindsay's fumbling delivery. His assault on the Union drummed on for nearly an hour before he admitted to his real purpose: to support "the disruption of the American Union, as every honest Englishman did, because it was too great a Power and England sh'd not let such a power exist on the American continent." Mason had become increasingly animated as Lindsay continued. "Old Mason," Moran observed, "spat tobacco more furiously at this than ever, and covered the carpet." In the excitement of the moment, Moran added, Mason failed to realize that Lindsay had cavalierly considered the Confederacy's independence as important only in destroying England's chief commercial rival. Surely the legislators had more lofty reasons for intervening in the war.[40]

The ensuing debate over Lindsay's motion convinced Moran that most Commons members questioned the advisability of intervention. To cultivate this growing doubt, Moran circulated a private telegram throughout the hall, attesting that McClellan had not surrendered. "It seemed to me," he later recorded in his diary, "that fear of us, and fear alone, was the check to action." The Conservative opposition railed against Leicester's P. A. Taylor, a member of the London Emancipation Society who had recently won election to the Commons and now came to the ministry's defense. In the midst of the tumult, those who had departed the hall now returned, and the prime minister began to stir as if a bear awakened from his winter slumber. Pushing back his cap, he listened intently as Taylor attempted to speak above the heckling. The American conflict marked a significant chapter in the epic battle between slavery and freedom, he insisted. Lincoln played a vital role in this struggle, according to Taylor while trying to shout above, as Moran put it, a "burst of horse-laughter and ridicule" that marked a "disgrace to the age." Any policy helping the Confederacy, Taylor thundered, made England an ally of slavery. Not so, countered—just as loudly—Lord Adolphus Vane-Tempest, son-in-law of the Duke of Newcastle. In a fierce rejoinder, he defended Lindsay's stand but embarrassed his comrades when, clearly inebriated, he repeatedly fell over the bench in front of him. Union advocate William E. Forster then delivered a brief but spirited argument in support of the ministry, concluding with an ominous warning that intervention could incite a slave insurrection followed by a race war.[41]

Into the early morning hours the debate hammered on, until the climactic point when Palmerston pulled himself from his seat and, now standing, pronounced his opposition to intervention. His ministry's only concern about the American war, he declared, was "that it should end." Implicitly reminding the House members that his government had kept the peace during the popular outcry for war over the *Trent*, he emphasized the danger in basing foreign policy on sentiment in the streets. The hot criticisms coming from all sides to the controversy could only inflame both American belligerents and prolong the war. The ministry alone must make foreign policy decisions. The Commons lacked sufficient information to deal with such sensitive issues "according to the varying circumstances of the moment." Intervention, he insisted, must not rest on emotion but solely on that moment when Confederate independence was "firmly and permanently established." A premature grant of recognition would not guarantee nationhood unless "followed by some direct active interference." Gazing around the room at his rapt listeners, Palmerston sternly warned that such provocative action ensured "greater evils, greater sufferings, and greater privations." History had never recorded "a contest of such magnitude between two different sections of the same people." Mediation had no chance for success at this point in the war, for neither side had expressed any interest in ending the fight. Indeed, he darkly added, "Mediation meant war." Lindsay's motion must not pass. The ministry must retain the power to decide "what can be done, when it can be done, and how it can be done."[42]

Palmerston's three-minute speech had been cryptic and decisive. The ministry would not act at this moment, but the situation in America could change and force a reconsideration. The silence that had enveloped the room so quickly after the ceaseless bantering of the past few hours just as suddenly gave way to booming applause. Lindsay withdrew his motion, angrily shouting that he would "wait for king cotton to turn the screws still further." As Moran walked out with colleagues after adjournment, he cheerfully observed Mason still sitting, "looking sullen and dejected." Southern enthusiast William H. Gregory also saw Mason and tried to console him as they left the building. The next day's papers confirmed Moran's telegram declaring that McClellan had not capitulated at Richmond. They then praised Lindsay's decision to withdraw his motion.[43]

Palmerston's words had nonetheless unsettled American observers in the Union, further encouraging Adams's growing interest in turning the war's focus to a fight against slavery. The Union's narrow escape from British recognition had been only a reprieve, for the prime minister had made clear that Confederate successes on the battlefield pointed to an intervention aimed only at ending the war. Adams, however, considered the recognition question still very much alive in light of what he regarded as the upper class's unbending objective of seeing the United States permanently disabled. Mixed results from the military campaigns had promoted the confused reaction in England. The Union victory at New Orleans had rung hollow after McClellan's failure to seize Richmond, affirming the widespread belief in the impossibility of defeating the Confederacy. Henry Adams's earlier prognosis seemed correct: A Union failure to take Virginia by July meant certain outside interference. Only the European powers' inability to agree on mediation had restrained their involvement. Adams joined his father in urging the White House to shift the war into an antislavery direction.[44]

Palmerston's strategy of waiting for the war to determine the fate of intervention was not entirely final. He could not ignore the certain cotton shortage in autumn that would cause an economic crisis and heighten pressure for British involvement in the conflict. At that point, the hard feelings toward the Confederacy for withholding cotton would give way to the exigencies of a nationwide emergency caused by its diminished supply. A balancing factor, of course, was the fear of war with the Union, which boasted an army larger than England's and a navy uniquely strong in ironclads. Furthermore, the logistical problems in waging a war three thousand miles away would be horrendous while exposing British North America to Union conquest. Mediation stood as the only possible means for ending the war—but even that measure rested on the Union's realization that it could not subjugate the Confederacy.

Thus with no feelings of bias, the British insisted they were not taking the Confederate side in the war by hoping for a major southern military victory. Indeed, a close analysis of the parliamentary debate over recognition, followed by the overwhelming vote against the motion and the praise its defeat drew from the press afterward, strongly suggests that most British lawmakers and their constituents did *not* support the Confederacy and that they simply wanted to bring the war to a close.[45] According to their convoluted argument, a decisive battle might convince northerners that they had only two options: Either fight until both antagonists had sustained irreparable destruction, or agree to an armistice engineered by outside powers and followed by a negotiated peace. Not surprisingly, the Union considered this a phony rationale that underlined British hostility toward the United States.

Slidell moved quickly after the Lindsay motion failed, meeting with Thouvenel on July 23 to present a formal demand for recognition. The Confederate minister remained enthusiastic after talking with the emperor, so sure of singlehanded French intervention that he sought immediate action. "Had you not better withhold it for the present?" asked Thouvenel. "In a few weeks, when we shall have further news from the seat of war, we can better judge of the expediency of so grave a step, and the English Government may perhaps then be prepared to cooperate with us, which they certainly are not now; that the refusal to acknowledge us, however worded, could not fail to be prejudicial to our cause; that the answer could only be couched 'en banalités' and unmeaning generalities."

Slidell refused to withdraw his demand. He had wanted to act some weeks earlier but did not do so because Mason claimed to have had encouraging discussions with southern friends in Parliament. Slidell now felt he could no longer wait. Napoleon was ready to act alone, or so Slidell believed. Thinking that Thouvenel had not yet seen the emperor, Slidell purposely implied that he was privy to information not yet revealed to French officials. "Your Excellency does not probably know that I have had the honor of an audience with the Emperor."

Thouvenel apparently had not been aware of this meeting, for the revelation suddenly made him more receptive to Slidell's demand for recognition.

Had Napoleon once again made a foreign policy decision without consulting his chief foreign policy adviser? Uncertain about what Slidell knew, Thouvenel asked: Would Mason make a similar demand of Russell?

Mason would do so either that day or the next, Slidell responded.

Thouvenel was glad to know this, for, based on his most recent conversation with the emperor, Slidell must make a demand for recognition simultaneously with that made by Mason in England. Both Lyons and Mercier thought a mediation offer would infuriate the Union. Slidell noted that the Confederacy did not prefer mediation but would accept the offer. It wanted only recognition—a principle that both the emperor and England had always respected.

Mercier and "everyone in France" felt the same way, Thouvenel added, reiterating his belief that the Union's restoration was impossible.

Slidell was confident of success. He expected an answer to his demand by mid-August—the contents of which depended on the war's progress. "While I do not wish to create or indulge false expectations," he wrote Benjamin, "I will venture to say that I am more hopeful than I have been at any moment since my arrival in Europe."[46]

Slidell's optimism was unwarranted, resting as it did on numerous questionable assumptions and his belief in the justice of the Confederate cause. If Napoleon had a history of acting independently of his advisers and the public, and if he were willing to move without the British, Slidell would have been correct in anticipating an imminent intervention. But the emperor usually did not act on his own and, despite his blustery talk, remained reluctant to intervene without a British initiative. His senior advisers were nonetheless concerned that he would do something rash. Both Thouvenel and Mercier warned him that premature recognition of the Confederacy meant war with the Union. To his ambassador in London, Count Flahault, Thouvenel expressed concern that Napoleon would act as hastily in America as he had done in Mexico. "I see with great satisfaction," Thouvenel wrote, "that, on this point as on others, we are in agreement, and I shall perhaps need your help in order to guard us from an adventure even more serious than the Mexican one."[47]

Slidell did not become concerned even after learning that the British had not changed their position. Russell had coldly declined Mason's request for a meeting, explaining that only the war could determine British policy. Yet Mason remained optimistic because of Slidell's favorable reports on Napoleon's attitude. If France called for recognition, Mason insisted, the British "may be dragged into an ungraceful reversal of their decision."[48]

Thouvenel had long recognized the difficulty in discouraging Napoleon's interest in intervention; in the early summer of 1862 he had directed his staff to draft a detailed set of terms that the intervening powers could propose after a mediation. The proposal came before him on July 4 under the title, "Note for the Minister, the American Question." Based on the premise of a southern separation, the staff recommended a boundary between the two American republics that depended on a compromise between free and slave states and the military front at the time of the armistice. Northern Virginia and the four Border States of Delaware, Kentucky, Maryland, and Missouri would remain in the Union, and the Confederacy would retain slavery along with the Union's agreement to return fugitive slaves. In late August Thouvenel called for "the formation of two *federated confederations*," a formula strikingly similar to the solution posed by Russell and others in England. He invited Mercier to forward his own ideas, adding that in the event of a mediation, "it would be helpful to have a sketch of an arrangement in my pocket."[49]

De Leon had crossed the channel to Paris in August, convinced that France alone offered hope for Confederate recognition. Like Slidell, however, he ignored the realities of European politics in believing that France would act without a British lead. In failing to win an audience with the emperor (Napoleon was too bogged down in the Italian question to discuss American affairs, he was told), De Leon should have realized that his mission was futile. Undeterred by this rebuff, he focused on the press, using his ample funds to secure propaganda support from the Paris journal *Patrie* as a cross-channel partner with Hotze's sparsely financed *Index* in London. De Leon felt certain that Napoleon's primary objective was to advance French interests over those of England's but soon realized that popular opposition to slavery posed a major obstacle in his consideration of intervention. As Slidell had done earlier, De Leon defended bondage—slaves were loyal servants and constituted an efficient workforce in producing the cotton France needed. Confederate vice president Alexander H. Stephens had been even more emphatic about the virtues of slavery, calling it the "corner stone" of the South that rested on "the great truth that the negro is not equal to the white man—that slavery, subordination to the superior race, is his natural and moral condition." But De Leon believed that even though the British and French people favored the Confederacy, they could not support a society whose "corner stone" was loudly "proclaimed to be slavery; and whose chief public men boastfully announced their ability to compel such recognition, basing their ability on the meanest of all motives of human action, self-interest." On the other hand, whereas England "had everything to gain and nothing to risk by the policy of inaction," France had too many economic interests at stake to stand quietly aside.[50]

De Leon emphasized that Napoleon's advisers, like Palmerston's, were divided on the American conflict. Napoleon wished to be "Emperor of the French" and not merely emperor of France. A powerful egotist, he never made decisions based on private sentiment but always listened carefully to his people in trying to govern in harmony with their wishes. Yet his policies rested on secrecy. "His left hand never knows what his right hand is doing." And he had a "great talent for silence," leaving his ministers to guess his intentions. He was closest to Jean François Mocquard, his confidential secretary, and to the Duke of Morny, president of the French legislature. De Leon thought Morny sympathetic to the Confederacy but never willing to act without first protecting French interests. He and the Duke of Persigny, another confidante of Napoleon, proved helpful to the Confederacy. Empress Eugénie admired the Confederacy's free spirit and regarded the struggle as pitting the Puritan descendant of the Anglo-Saxon northerner against its Catholic or "semi-Catholic Episcopalian of French or Spanish descent." Thus the people closest to the emperor were pro-Confederate. But strong opposition came from Thouvenel and Prince Napoleon. The foreign minister supported the French understanding with England, keeping his distance from the Confederacy. The prince, although related to the emperor, opposed Confederate recognition and insisted that the Union would win. But he was enormously unpopular in France. Indeed, De Leon observed, one might describe this attitude in the words of King Charles II to his brother James: "No one will ever kill me to make you king!"[51]

In a rare southern nod to realistic diplomacy, De Leon urged Davis and Benjamin to negotiate offensive and defensive alliances with the European powers rather than rely on cotton. London and Paris acted out of "selfish" motives, not sentiment or principle. "Let us, therefore, appeal to that selfishness and make it a fulcrum for our lever." Confederate diplomacy should focus on France. Napoleon, who sought to surpass England in commerce and industry, would welcome a southern alliance. The Confederacy should therefore make some concessions—perhaps a gradual emancipation program that would appeal to the French people and put pressure on their government to ally with the American South. But he never convinced the Confederate decision makers to change policy.[52]

De Leon's findings in England and France confirmed what leaders in both nations had already made clear—that neither government would extend recognition until the Confederacy proved its independence on the battlefield. This meant, as he had cynically remarked to Palmerston, that recognition could come only after the British were persuaded that the Confederacy no longer needed them in the war. De Leon also denounced as a fallacy the southern profession that "cotton is king," making it a product of former secretary of state Robert Toombs's imagination. Such public declarations had fostered "the Southern hallucination" that England was a "sure ally" because its "principles were supposed to be deposited in [its] pockets." Palmerston maintained his pragmatic stance, refusing to recognize the Confederacy until it had established independent status and the Union realized it could not win a war of subjugation. Regardless of Napoleon's southern sympathies, he was too preoccupied with European affairs to intervene in the American war without a British initiative. Thus England remained the key to outside intervention, and it refused to act.[53]

Mediation nonetheless maintained its appeal to numerous British contemporaries, both inside and outside the government. Strategists warned that a prolonged war would eventually lead to a servile insurrection and a transsectional race war capable of dragging in other nations and leading to international confrontations. Humanitarians insisted that civilized nations had a moral obligation to end such vicious and pointless carnage. Business interests stressed the importance of reestablishing American stability as the chief means for resuming the importation of northern grain as well as southern cotton. And legal theorists argued that the doctrine of neutrality encompassed the right of neutrals to intervene in a war that damaged their wellbeing. But the central enigma remained: how to convince the Union of the war's futility.[54]

The Lincoln government continued to miss the central thrust of Europe's growing interest in intervention. Instead of analyzing the foreign position, Seward simply noted the great resentment among Americans caused by all this needless meddling. The direction of the war should be the sole barometer of foreign reaction to it, and that direction pointed in the Union's favor. Yet this was not the case. Europeans regarded the Union's failure in one battle as indicative of the failure of its entire war effort; yet its growing number of victories had not forced the Confederacy to submit, thus rendering those successes "ineffectual and valueless." Seward had unknowingly put his finger on the problem. England and France, and perhaps the other European players, were less concerned about which side won the conflict than how quickly the fighting came to an end. Both powers had their own interests.

England wanted peace for various economic, humanitarian, and strategic reasons, with the last focusing on blocking French expansion in Europe and in the Americas. France sought cotton along with Napoleon's wish to restore the family's New World Empire. The latter could be achieved only with the cooperation of a new Confederate nation—by acting as a buffer against a postwar Union. Neither victory nor defeat for the Union swayed the Anglo-French view, except insofar as the battle outcomes directly led to the termination of hostilities.[55]

Seeing great danger ahead, the Lincoln administration prepared to play its trump card in undercutting the Anglo-French move toward intervention: Take the moral high ground by converting the war into a crusade for freedom dependent on the death of slavery.

CHAPTER 6

The Paradox of Intervention

> At first the [Union] government was considered as unfaithful to
> humanity in not proclaiming emancipation, and when it appeared
> that slavery, by being thus forced into the contest, must suffer,
> and perhaps perish in the conflict, then the war had become an
> intolerable propagandism of emancipation by the sword.
> —WILLIAM H. SEWARD, July 28, 1862

> Any proposal to recognize the Southern Confederacy would
> irritate the United States, and any proposal to the Confederate
> States to return to the Union would irritate the Confederates.
> —LORD JOHN RUSSELL, July 31, 1862

> We shall prosecute this war to its end.
> —WILLIAM H. SEWARD, September 8, 1862

Immediately after Lindsay's motion failed, rumors swirled around London
that Baltimore had fallen to Confederate forces, edging England and France
closer to a joint mediation that implied southern independence. Russell felt
relieved about recent events on the battlefield, hoping the collapse of Washington's neighboring city would break the Union's resolve and lead it to the
peace table. Southern separation, repeated many British observers, would
benefit both antagonists. But the rumors from the battlefield proved unfounded, and, despite the swelling popular interest in mediation, the Palmerston government felt no inordinate pressure from mill workers and other
constituents. Time had not yet become a factor, for most economic indicators
suggested that the growing cotton shortage would not have a major impact

on families until the spring of 1863. Russell noted, however, that the Union's stubborn refusal to accept its dissolution could still force British involvement in the war. Seward had done nothing "to prevent the cry that may arise here, from the obstinacy and passion of the North." France likewise seemed poised to intervene. Slidell informed Mason that Napoleon appeared ready to step into the conflict, with or without England's involvement. In a highly questionable assertion, Mercier assured William Stuart in a conversation in Washington that most Americans would approve a joint mediation.[1]

By late July two of the most powerful figures in England, John Russell and William E. Gladstone, had agreed on joint mediation as the chief means for halting the war before it spread beyond American borders. The Lincoln administration, complained Stuart, was about to wage a war on slavery intended to incite disturbances throughout the southern plantations and pull Confederate soldiers home from battle to protect their families. Emancipation, confiscation of property in slaves, incorporation of freed blacks into the Union army—all these measures ensured widespread racial upheaval having both national and international repercussions. The British must somehow stop the conflagration. From Washington came the counterargument that, ironically, forecast the same devastating outcome if Britain interfered in the war. Seward had told Russell that intervention would cause a disaster. But the British foreign secretary misconstrued Seward's cautionary note to mean that to block intervention, the White House planned to *instigate* a slave uprising. Out of this would come a race war, Russell wrote Stuart in a note shared with Seward, that would "only make other nations more desirous to see an end of this desolating and destructive conflict." Intervention or nonintervention— either avenue promised a calamity of international proportions if the war continued its widening path of mutual destruction.[2]

If proclaiming the war a crusade against slavery at the outset would have turned England against the Confederacy, that moment had passed. The expected shift in Lincoln's objective to antislavery infuriated most British contemporaries because, they charged, it rested on expediency rather than morality. In the initial fighting, the president had surprised the British by focusing on preserving the Union. Slavery was not the issue, he had argued; indeed, he had maintained his prepresidential policy (and that of the Republican Party) of renouncing any legal right to disturb the institution short of halting its expansion and thereby promoting its extinction over a period of time. Political considerations had weighed heavily on his mind. When the war erupted, Lincoln could not risk driving the Border States into the Confederate camp by calling for emancipation. He also knew that Americans were deeply divided over slavery. Many had quietly condoned bondage by refusing to oppose it. Some preferred compensated emancipation. Others rejected the abolitionists' call for racial equality. Finally, he and Seward had feared that emancipation would undermine reported Union sentiment in the South. None of these arguments had convinced British observers of the Union's need for caution in the early stages of the war. Now, in late July 1862, the Lincoln administration had incurred a severe setback at Richmond's gates and discovered there was no substantial Unionist sentiment in the South. The president, many British bitterly charged, had adopted emancipation in a desperate attempt to avert defeat by encouraging slave insurrections aimed at destroying the cotton kingdom from within. Only an intervention leading to southern separation could counter his hypocrisy.[3]

The mutual misperceptions continued as Seward furiously accused the British of supporting the "slaveholding insurgents." How could the Palmerston ministry be so blind as to fall under the spell of traitors who wanted to overthrow the duly constituted U.S. government? How could it sympathize with a people who sought to protect slavery by posing as a friend to the British (and the French) while withholding cotton to force recognition? The Confederacy was waging a war against humanity that the British had prolonged by holding out the hope of intervention. A Union victory "does not satisfy our enemies abroad. Defeats in their eyes prove our national incapacity." Even the White House call for emancipation had drawn little support. "At first the [Union] government was considered as unfaithful to humanity in not proclaiming emancipation, and when it appeared that slavery, by being thus forced into the contest, must suffer, and perhaps perish in the conflict, then the war had become an intolerable propagandism of emancipation by the sword." British intervention, Seward darkly predicted, would escalate the American conflict into "a war of the world."[4]

Their diametrically opposite stands on intervention permeated every issue between the Washington and London governments and threatened to cause a third Anglo-American war surely conducive to Confederate statehood. Each side dreaded an already horrific contest made worse by the certain outbreak of slave insurrections and the onset of a race conflict that crossed sectional and perhaps national boundaries. Intervention, the Lincoln administration warned, would intensify the fighting, extend the war, and pull in other nations. Failure to intervene, the Palmerston ministry feared, ensured the same results. Such was the paradox of intervention.

First reading of the Emancipation Proclamation, July 22, 1862. Francis B. Carpenter's painting presented to Congress in 1878. Cabinet members, *left to right:* Secretary of War Edwin M. Stanton, Secretary of the Treasury Salmon P. Chase, President Abraham Lincoln, Secretary of the Navy Gideon Welles, Secretary of the Interior Caleb B. Smith, Secretary of State William H. Seward, Postmaster General Montgomery Blair, and Attorney General Edward Bates (out of picture). (Courtesy of the National Archives)

Lincoln had diplomatic, political, and military objectives in mind when in mid-July 1862 he decided on emancipation. Secretary of War Edwin M. Stanton had urged him to meet with New York Democrat Francis B. Cutting, a prominent attorney who had proposed a spotlight on antislavery as a means for winning the war. Two hours later, Lincoln emerged from their discussion convinced that emancipation would block recognition of the Confederacy while satisfying the Republican Party's antislavery proponents. The president also realized he had to take stronger measures in light of McClellan's inability to seize Richmond. At a meeting with his cabinet that same day, he declared his intention to support emancipation as a "necessary military measure." According to his draft of the Emancipation Proclamation read to advisers, all slaves in states still in rebellion by January 1, 1863, would be free.[5]

All cabinet members but one supported the measure. Postmaster General Montgomery Blair felt that emancipation would undermine the Republican Party's control of Congress after the fall elections. The next day, however, he changed his position, conceding that emancipation might discourage outside intervention in the war. Secretary of the Treasury Salmon P. Chase strongly endorsed Lincoln's proposal. A longtime advocate of abolition, Chase recommended that the president facilitate the new policy by directing his generals to arm the slaves. Stanton had made the same argument and now called for immediate emancipation. But Seward thought the timing was not right. He had never wanted "to proselyte with the sword" and now, in a perceptive prophecy of England's worst fears, warned that the British government would regard emancipation as an insidious effort to incite a slave uprising and thus feel compelled to intervene. Wait until the Union won another battle, he urged the president. Premature emancipation would appear to be "the last measure of an exhausted government, a cry for help . . . our last *shriek*, on the retreat." Lincoln agreed to hold the Proclamation until the Union secured a decisive victory on the battlefield.[6]

Lincoln had become convinced that the exigencies of war demanded a forceful end to slavery. He considered himself patient and forgiving. "Still I must save this government if possible. What I *cannot* do, of course I *will* not do; but it may as well be understood, once for all, that I shall not surrender this game leaving any available card unplayed." He reiterated his stand to Democrat August Belmont, a financial magnate from New York: "This government cannot much longer play a game in which it stakes all, and its enemies stake nothing. Those enemies must understand that they cannot experiment for ten years trying to destroy the government, and if they fail still come back into the Union unhurt." Belmont concurred but cautioned that a dramatic pronouncement would provoke southerners. They had already accused the Union of seeking "conquest and subjugation" and thereby hurt its chances for ginning up support from within the Confederacy. A public stand against slavery must not take on a vengeful appearance that substantiated the Confederacy's arguments in Europe. Lincoln, however, had run out of patience—particularly with the Border States, whose slaveholders had hampered the war effort. He told a Union supporter in the South that by insisting that "the government shall not strike its open enemies, lest they be struck by accident," the Border States had caused a "paralysis—the dead palsy—of the government in this whole struggle." The time had come for action. "The truth is, that what is done, and omitted, about slaves, is done and omitted on . . . military necessity."[7]

Lincoln decided on emancipation for several reasons, the most important being to facilitate victory in the war. He had first suggested colonization, then gradual emancipation with compensation, and, finally, confiscation, but the war's demands had pushed him further into the antislavery camp and now necessitated the revolutionary measure of emancipation. Success meant the death of the Old South. Had not Confederate vice president Alexander H. Stephens called slavery the cornerstone of southern civilization? Inherent in emancipation was the possibility of violence between slave and owner or of slave abandonment of the plantation, either of which would destroy the institution from within and bring down the Confederacy. Lincoln sought no slave rebellion, but he knew that emancipation in wartime had the potential for stirring up hatreds between blacks and whites that would not end even after all slaves were free. He had no choice. The Union's failure to administer a lethal blow on the battlefield forced him to change strategy.[8]

Lincoln's intention to preserve the Union had thus tied the Confederacy's defeat to slavery's death and the growing sense of higher purpose in the war. Continued setbacks on the battlefield had encouraged him to adopt a progressively harder stance against slavery that became vital to victory. To wrap his military objective in universal humanitarian principles would give added meaning to the war and perhaps raise Union morale. This was a risky proposition, he knew, for few northerners cared about emancipation except as it hurt the Confederacy. But the desire to win the war, he also knew, would override any reservations about considering antislavery a moral as well as a military good. Lincoln's intensely personal religion rested on the eternal laws of necessity, leading him to believe in a divine plan in which he as president acted as God's instrument in effecting great social change whose present priority was to end slavery in order to win the war. In his Inaugural Address of March 1861, he had called for a mystical and permanent Union that grew out of the natural rights undergirding the Declaration of Independence. Fulfillment of those principles dictated the abolition of slavery.[9]

The Civil War, Lincoln had come to believe, must beget a spiritual rebirth of the republic. As a master of rhetoric, he often used biblical imagery in focusing on the "born again" concept found in the New Testament Gospel of John. During the 1850s, Lincoln had set out a belief he adhered to throughout the ensuing conflict: "Our republican robe is soiled, and trailed in the dust," he declared. "Let us repurify it. Let us turn and wash it white, in the spirit, if not the blood, of the Revolution."[10] Thus the same synergy that drove the great document of 1776 was now moving the American nation closer to the ultimate goal of freedom for all. The Declaration of Independence had provided the spirit of the Constitution, which itself served as the first real attempt to manifest that ideal, to be shaped by evolutionary development in accordance with the steady progression toward universal liberty. The end of slavery became morally inseparable from the sanctity of representative government through a vastly improved Union. By viewing the war for the Union as a moral crusade, the president attempted to vindicate the massive suffering as crucial to convincing Americans to accept profound social change; as the reward, he suggested, divine intervention would ensure victory. Lincoln's appeal to the universal principles of right and wrong led him to conclude that the destruction of the southern government and the southern way of life was necessary to creating a better republic.

In line with Lincoln's thinking, the Union and the Confederacy were engaged in an ideological conflict that, ironically, revolved around the ways each antagonist selectively interpreted the same two sacred documents: the Declaration of Independence and the Constitution. According to northern nationalists, the longevity of the Union proved its constitutional legitimacy to anyone seeking its dissolution. Southern states' rightists countered that their growing minority status had left them vulnerable to northern oppression and that the right to withdraw from the governing pact derived from a fundamental precept of the Declaration. Had not the contract theory of seventeenth-century English philosopher John Locke provided justification for the American colonies' break with Mother England in 1776? Yet southerners refused to address the natural rights principles of the Declaration and argued instead for the constitutionality of secession by charging the Washington government with interfering in their domestic concerns— especially their right to property in slaves as guaranteed by the due process clause in the Fifth Amendment of the Bill of Rights. Lincoln responded that the promises of freedom contained in the Declaration of Independence had gone unfulfilled in the Constitution and that his responsibility as president was to redeem those ideals by forming a more perfect Union.

Lincoln recognized that a central problem lay unresolved during the first eighty-five years of the Union's existence: the eternal struggle between human and property rights. The ideals of the Declaration of Independence, he believed, provided the moral and intellectual framework of the Civil War. Liberty in this self-professed republic was not yet available to all Americans; black people in the United States did not enjoy the natural rights guaranteed by the Declaration's underlying philosophy. Lincoln firmly believed that the present conflict rested primarily on Union-Confederate differences over slavery and thereby constituted an integral part of the larger problem of ensuring freedom to every American. The most profound complication in freeing enslaved blacks lay in the property rights protected by the Constitution. Lincoln thought that the human rights exalted in the Declaration of Independence took priority over all else and soon considered it his responsibility as president to kill slavery by using its protector—the Constitution—as its executioner. Only by constitutional amendment could the peculiar institution finally be destroyed.

Lincoln's calculated change in direction promised to escalate the war to another level of ferocity, for the Confederacy also claimed to be fighting against slavery—the enslavement by Union oppressors in violating its people's right to own slaves. "Sooner than submit to Northern Slavery, I prefer death," wrote a South Carolina officer to his wife. Or as a Kentucky doctor and soldier put it, "We are fighting for our liberty, against tyrants of the North . . . who are determined to destroy slavery." Freedom to own slaves was crucial, according to a Mississippi officer, for "without slavery little of our territory is worth a cent." A Georgian insisted that southerners had the choice of being "either *slaves in the Union or freemen out of it.*" Just as fervently did southerners declare their support for freedom, a term they broadly conceived to include their right to own slaves.[11]

By mid-1862 Lincoln had decided to incorporate antislavery into his military effort to save the Union and, at the same time, drive home the point that a republic based on the Declaration of Independence could not coexist with a Constitution that safeguarded human bondage. Casting universal meaning onto such vicious fighting, he also knew, would justify the sacrifices and maintain unity, cause, and morale. Freedom and slavery could not live in harmony together—requiring the latter to become the chief casualty of the war. Union and freedom—the longtime objective of Daniel Webster, one of Lincoln's most revered figures in history—could at last become one.[12]

Lincoln was not alone in believing that emancipation offered both moral and military benefits to the Union. Those on both sides of the issue recognized that emancipation, even though a wartime measure, would culminate in the end of slavery and, by definition, topple the Old South as well. In a Sunday cabinet meeting in early August, Chase asserted that quashing the rebellion and killing slavery were inseparable. Seward likewise emphasized the importance of black freedom in eroding the Confederacy from within. Lincoln's conversion to emancipation as a wartime expedient became evident in his concession that he was "pretty well cured of objections to any measure except want of adaptedness to put down the rebellion." From the Western Theater of the war came support for black liberation as a military instrument. General Ulysses S. Grant, who had made his mark in brutal, hammer-like victories at Forts Henry and Donelson, Shiloh, and Corinth, now hailed emancipation as essential to victory. An officer under his command affirmed that the best policy was "to be terrible on the enemy. I am using Negroes all the time for my work as teamsters, and have 1,000 employed." Grant assured his family that his sole purpose was "to put down the rebellion. . . . I don't know what is to become of these poor people in the end, but it weakens the enemy to take them from them."[13]

To Lincoln, the wisdom of the policy was indisputable as the danger of outside intervention became more pronounced. In mid-July, French writer Count Agénor-Etienne de Gasparin had sent him a note expressing astonishment at the Union's failures on the battlefield and claiming he had done everything to discourage European intervention. The Confederacy could not win without foreign assistance, Gasparin wrote. Only when the Lincoln administration shifted its wartime objective to abolition would the interventionists lose their fire. The president agreed that a cry for black freedom would reduce the threat of outside interference.[14]

Ideal and reality had meshed in shaping Lincoln's decision, combining his longtime animosity toward slavery with the Union's misfortunes on the battlefield to formulate a new policy that initially drew little support. Numerous white northerners actively opposed a war on behalf of black people, while others remained silent, feeling no moral responsibility to slaves. Abolitionists denounced any action short of freeing all slaves with no compensation, perceiving remuneration to slaveowners as a compromise with sin. Antislavery groups called for a moderate approach, warning that a radical solution would spawn more violence. Northern Democrats blasted the Republicans as fanatics who stirred up racial hatreds that guaranteed more antiblack riots similar to those in northern cities during that summer of 1862. Lincoln realized that many Union soldiers would refuse to fight a war against slavery, but he also knew that they wanted to win the war and that necessity had forced him into a limited form of emancipation. And yet, though he stipulated that only those slaves in states still in rebellion would go free, he knew that once the shackles of a few were broken, the cracks would run through the entire edifice.[15]

Lincoln could not have known at the time that Mason had failed to budge Russell from his stance of neutrality. Nor would the British foreign secretary meet with Mason. Russell (like Palmerston) did not believe the Confederacy had won independence. Foreign intervention must *not* determine the fate of recognition, he repeated in response to Mason's written appeals; the Confederacy must first establish its status as a nation. Russell clarified his government's dilemma: "Any proposal to recognize the Southern Confederacy would irritate the United States, and any proposal to the Confederate States to return to the Union would irritate the Confederates." Mason refused to give up. The Confederacy had demonstrated "the capacity and the determination to maintain its independence," obligating other governments to extend recognition. Then, adding to the confusion, he repeated his perplexing assertion first expressed in his February meeting with Russell (one similar to that made by Slidell to Napoleon): The Confederacy sought simple recognition—"no aid from, nor intervention by, foreign Powers." Such a statement conveyed a dreamlike quality—that merely being "right" guaranteed victory. Other nations must understand, Mason held, that "for whatever purpose the war was begun, it was continued now only in a vindictive and unreasoning spirit." Refusal to grant recognition ensured a longer war that hurt Europeans as well as Americans. Russell coldly repeated that only the war could shape British policy.[16]

More likely, differing interpretations of the struggle rather than ulterior motives dictated the British response to the war. Russell opposed recognition but strongly considered mediation if staying out of the war hurt his government's interests. To him, there were vast differences between the two interventionist measures being debated. Mediation aimed only to end the war, whereas recognition granted nationhood and made Britain the Confederacy's partner in the war. Secession was a constitutional issue that did not concern the British; whether the South had succeeded in withdrawing from the Union was of no consequence. The London ministry's chief objective was to stop the fighting before it spread beyond the United States. To the Lincoln administration, however, there was no distinction between mediation and recognition: Indeed, the first would lead to the second. Moreover, both measures constituted outside interference in American domestic affairs and hence violated national sovereignty. Russell regarded continued British neutrality to be the most feasible policy at this time. Southerners claimed to have won independence; northerners thought they were on the way to restoring the Union. This core issue still unresolved, Russell could take no action. "In the face of the fluctuating events of the war, the alternations of victory and defeat . . . ; placed, too, between allegations so contradictory on the part of the contending Powers, Her Majesty's Government are still determined to wait." Recognition, he wrote Mason, would come of "an independence achieved by victory, and maintained by a successful resistance to all attempts to overthrow it. That time, however, has not, in the judgment of Her Majesty's Government, yet arrived."[17]

Mason remained embittered over the British refusal to grant recognition outright but optimistic that mediation could lead to the same end. Russell, Mason groused, had ignored every piece of evidence confirming the Confederacy's credibility as a nation and would extend recognition only after its military forces had won decisively on the battlefield—at precisely the point it no longer needed recognition. He might have added that in winning the war, the Confederacy would have achieved nationhood and thereby would be entitled to recognition without having to ask. What a needless expenditure of blood, he thought. An Anglo-French mediation, probably joined by Austria, Prussia, and Russia, seemed likely that summer. If so, the Union would come under great pressure to reconsider the feasibility of continuing the war. Intervention was nigh, Mason wrote his wife. He appeared correct, for Gladstone had moved deeper into that camp. "This bloody and purposeless conflict should cease," the chancellor exclaimed to a friend. To his wife, he triumphantly wrote that Palmerston "has come exactly to my mind about some early representation of a friendly kind to America, if we can get France *and* Russia to join."[18]

Although Russell had discouraged Mason by insisting on continued neutrality, the truth was that such a stand helped the Confederacy by offering the possibility of mediation. Short of force, the only avenue to ending the war lay in convincing the warring parties to negotiate a settlement. And that moment would come only after both sides had exhausted themselves in combat and welcomed mediation as an honorable way out. But even that scenario carried a result that the British had highlighted and the Union had vehemently rejected: southern separation. Perhaps with that thought in mind, the Union had no choice but to express confidence that it would win the war despite repeated reversals on the battlefield. Edmund Hammond cautioned the ministry to offer mediation only after the Union realized that subjugation was impossible. Lyons thought his government, as the representative of a civilized people, bore the responsibility to end the war and warned that coming cotton shortages would dictate an intervention.[19] Whatever Russell's true motives, his pledge of neutrality created the appearance of unbending resistance to intervention when in reality it opened the way to mediation— an outcome Mason must have known encompassed southern separation because he had already welcomed mediation as a step toward recognition.

Further pressure for intervention had come from the ongoing controversy between the Union and the British ministry over the Confederacy's shipbuilding program in England. Adams had protested that this year-old business— allegedly engaged in the construction of warships for Italy or Spain—was a poorly disguised attempt to build a Confederate navy. Moreover, British refusal to stop such activities constituted a blatant breach of neutrality that favored the Confederacy. Russell said his government lacked the authority to act on Adams's complaints. The Foreign Enlistment Act of 1819, he explained, stipulated that for a violation to occur, the equipping and manning of war vessels must take place *in* British territory. The British admiralty would take action against the shipbuilding firms only if the United States proved that the construction teams had armed the ships *in England* and for the Confederacy. Adams, Russell insisted, had never amassed such evidence. The Union minister vehemently disagreed, suspecting that Russell had cited municipal law to defend a violation of British neutrality.[20]

The shipbuilding issue threatened to mesh with the recognition crisis in the summer of 1862, when the first ships rolled off the line that Confederate naval agent James D. Bulloch had contracted a year earlier with Laird Brothers of Liverpool—vessels that satisfied the letter but not the spirit of British law. Bulloch, a native of Georgia, had been assigned to Liverpool to fit out privateers and purchase war munitions. An uncle of the future president Theodore Roosevelt, he had served as a U.S. naval officer before becoming a merchant marine captain in New York City. When he arrived in England in June 1861, Bulloch's instructions were to arrange for the building of cruisers fast enough to raid Union commerce and to purchase blockade-runners to keep the Confederacy supplied. Within a year he had assumed responsibility for another project: the construction of two ironclad rams, equipped with iron piercers extending six or seven feet beyond the prow and beneath the water, to destroy the Union's wooden-hulled blockade vessels. In promoting these objectives, he secured financial backing from the Liverpool firm of Fraser, Trenholm and Company, and he did not hide in the shadows. Bulloch boarded his ships almost every day, inspecting their progress and visibly establishing himself as the person in control. The State Department in Washington had already alerted the acting consul in Liverpool, Henry Wilding, that Bulloch headed the Confederate Secret Service in England.[21]

Bulloch confronted all manner of obstacles—including Union spies along with a prying British press that printed every detail it uncovered about his operations. His chief antagonist as of late 1861 was the Union's new consul at Liverpool, Thomas Haines Dudley, a Quaker with strong antislavery sentiments who proved resourceful and persistent. On arriving, in November, at his post, which was a pro-Confederate hotspot, Dudley managed to hire a host of local detectives and Union supporters to gather information about two gunboats suspected of being under construction for the Confederacy and built for speed—the *Oreto*, by W. C. Miller and Sons and Messrs. Fawcett, Preston and Company, and the twin-engined No. 290, by Laird Brothers. But he was unable to counter Bulloch's skill in subterfuge. From the Birkenhead Ironworks on the Mersey River emerged in March 1862 the *Oreto*, ostensibly built for an Italian owner from Palermo but under a British captain and flag and destined for the Confederacy. The unarmed warship headed for Nassau in the British Bahamas, where Confederates fitted it with guns as a privateer and renamed it the css *Florida*.[22]

More menacing was the construction of a larger ship fitted for cannon but innocuously referred to as No. 290 (called the *Enrica* at first launch in May 1862) because it was the 290th vessel built in the Lairds' Birkenhead shipyard. From two officers of the Confederate commerce raider css *Sumter*, Dudley had testimony that No. 290 was for the Confederacy. Soon afterward, a number of reliable observers, including the foreman in the Lairds' shipyard, confirmed the allegation.[23]

Dudley asserted that No. 290 was a gunboat built to destroy Union commerce. It had magazines, powder canisters, and platforms attached to the decks for carrying swivel guns. It had a two-ton steam device that could lift the propeller from the water, a feature that enhanced speed by diminishing drag. And it could spend long periods at sea because its combined steam and sail power freed the vessel from the need for coal, and its condensing device cooled the water tanks and provided fresh water for the crew. Shipbuilders marveled at the sight, claiming that "no better vessel of her class was ever built." Dudley agreed. "When completed and armed, she will be a most formidable and dangerous craft, and if not prevented from going to sea, will do much mischief to our commerce."[24]

The Laird brothers, John and Henry, did not deny that No. 290 was a war vessel, but they said that it had been commissioned for the Spanish government. Dudley asked Adams to make inquiries at the Spanish embassy in London to confirm the claim. When the Spanish minister denied it, Dudley concluded that the ship was indeed for the Confederacy.[25]

The case against No. 290 seemed irrefutable—or so Dudley thought. The critical hole in his information was its lack of documented wrongdoing and his consequent dependence on hearsay. No matter how firm his belief, he had to *prove* that the builders had violated the Foreign Enlistment Act by "fitting out or equipping" the vessel for the Confederacy while in England. Dudley wanted to send a formal note to Liverpool's customs officials, asking them to seize the vessel. But Adams preferred to send the request to Russell through diplomatic channels. The minister then prematurely heated up the matter by including in his June 23 "formal remonstrance" Dudley's in-house note containing the charges. Concerned that the Confederacy was using England as a base of military operations against the Union, Adams insisted that the Palmerston ministry abide by its professed neutrality to stop this conduct. In an implicit reference to the Birkenhead firm's elder John Laird, who had founded the company and later became a member of Parliament, Adams accused the Confederacy of pursuing this project in "the dockyard of a person now sitting as a member of the House of Commons."[26]

In this rife atmosphere, Adams's suspicions rose unjustifiably when he did not receive a prompt response to his complaint. The foreign secretary had sought counsel from his legal advisers, who caused further delay by turning for information to the customs surveyor at Liverpool, Edward Morgan. Under orders of the customs collector and reputed Confederate sympathizer Samuel Price Edwards, Morgan personally inspected the vessel on June 28 and concluded that Dudley had been correct in reporting that the vessel had powder canisters on board but no guns or gun carriages. The builders permitted access to the ship and did nothing "to disguise what is most apparent to all—that she is intended for a ship of war." They did not deny that the vessel was under contract to a foreign power but refused to reveal its destination once completed.[27]

The case, according to customs officials, was not strong enough to justify government action. According to Felix Hamel, the solicitor for the Board of Customs Commissioners in London, the American claim did not contain sufficient grounds for intervening in the matter. Government officials should not take action "without the clearest evidence of a distinct violation of the Foreign Enlistment Act." A wrongful seizure could have serious legal consequences.[28]

Despite these findings, the crown's law officers—Attorney General William Atherton and his associate, Solicitor General Roundell Palmer—recommended on June 30 that Russell examine the accusations contained in Adams's note. If Adams was correct, they declared to Russell, the action had violated the law and the ship must not leave the yard. Dudley's charges raised "grounds of reasonable suspicion" about the vessel that a shipyard foreman reinforced by declaring it bound for the Confederacy. If so, the law officers asserted, the ship "must be intended for some warlike purpose." Liverpool officials should investigate whether the evidence was sufficient to invoke the Foreign Enlistment Act.[29]

Yet two days later, on July 1, Treasury officials agreed with Hamel's argument against government intervention and recommended that Dudley submit the evidence he had gathered if he wished to begin prosecution proceedings. The Treasury officials sent their thoughts to Edmund Hammond, permanent undersecretary at the Foreign Office, who forwarded them to Russell.[30]

For some unexplained reason, Russell ignored his law officers' advice to conduct an inquiry into Dudley's accusations and followed the more cautious approach advocated by his Treasury Department. On July 4 he asked Adams for Dudley's evidence, which three days later the minister agreed to send. Nothing in the record suggests that the foreign secretary acted out of an oft-alleged pro-Confederate sentiment; rather, he seems to have relied on his customs officials' belief that the evidence of wrongdoing appeared inconclusive and not worth the risk of a wrongful seizure. The onus for proving the case was Dudley's. Thus did the matter settle into a drawn-out process that inadvertently bought time for the builders of No. 290 to complete its construction.[31]

The London ministry quickly realized that Dudley's charges rested almost entirely on hearsay—largely because Bulloch had shrewdly refrained from arming or equipping No. 290 while it was in England and had therefore broken no law in contracting for and building the vessel. Dudley had collected accurate information on the ship's purpose but was unable to substantiate his suspicion of a Confederate connection. His so-called evidence included no names of informants and thus lacked "legally certified affidavits from firsthand witnesses." He could not divulge his sources because they were Union supporters in a hotbed of Confederate sympathizers, and he suspected Edwards of being a Confederate agent. On July 9 Dudley told the Liverpool customs officials what he knew without identifying his informants.[32]

Two days later Hamel expanded on his views, leading Edwards to inform Dudley that the British government must *not* seize the vessel. Most of the evidence, "if not all," Hamel insisted, was "hearsay and inadmissible." In calling no witnesses to appear and providing no names, Dudley had failed to present any information "amounting to prima facie proof sufficient to justify a seizure, much less to support it in a court of law." Hamel sent these observations to Treasury officials the next day, July 12.[33]

Dudley nonetheless persisted. Edwards reported that the consul and his recently hired British solicitor, A. T. Squarey, had appeared with witnesses and affidavits, asking him to seize the gunboat based on the allegation that Laird Brothers had fitted it out for the Confederacy. But Dudley's only piece of important evidence was that of William Passmore, who had signed on as a sailor on the vessel, and the only item placed on board was coal. Passmore had learned that Laird Brothers was constructing a war vessel and applied for duty to Captain Matthew Butcher on June 21. The captain explained that the ship was going to the Confederacy. Passmore had had fighting experience on a British warship during the Crimean War and, after asking to serve as signalman, was given a password to use when boarding in two days—the number 290. He could see that the ship was fitted for fighting: It had a magazine and shot and canister racks on deck, and it was pierced for guns with the sockets for the bolts already in place. It carried ample provisions, nearly three hundred tons of coal, and about thirty hands, most of whom had served on war vessels. Indeed, one of them had been on the Confederate steamship *Sumter*. All of the men understood that No. 290 was commissioned for Confederate service. Butcher was the sailing master and Bulloch the fighting captain. The vessel, to be known as the css *Alabama*, was to be used in the Confederacy's war against the Union.[34]

Two other testimonials affirmed that No. 290 was built for the Confederacy. Henry Wilding, now U.S. vice consul at Liverpool, and private detective Matthew Maguire of that city who also worked for Dudley, learned from an apprentice employed at the Laird yard, one Richard Brogan, that the firm had built the vessel to carry guns. Bulloch had selected the timber for the ship and had asked Brogan to serve as carpenter's mate for three years. The vessel would carry 120 men, about 30 of them already signed on—as Passmore had attested. The petty officers had agreed to a three-year service, the seamen to five months. Wilding and Maguire also confirmed Passmore's testimony given that same day—that all hands knew No. 290 to be a Confederate warship.[35]

To advise in preparing their case, Adams and Dudley had hired the queen's counsel, Robert P. Collier, who was a member of Parliament and one of England's acknowledged experts on admiralty and maritime law, and the Foreign Enlistment Act. After reviewing the documentation they had compiled, Collier completed his study and his findings reached Russell perhaps on July 23. The Americans' evidence, Collier wrote, was "almost conclusive" that the vessel "is being fitted out" for the Confederacy in violation of the Foreign Enlistment Act. The chief customs officer at Liverpool must "seize the vessel, with a view to her condemnation." It would be difficult, Collier concluded, "to make out a stronger case of infringement of the Foreign Enlistment Act, which, if not enforced on this occasion, is little better than a dead letter." Russell directed his undersecretary to send the case materials to the law officers. The British government, it appeared, was going to take action.[36]

But the Palmerston ministry did not issue a detention order, primarily because of an unforeseen event. The papers containing Collier's views had arrived in two batches at the home of the crown's chief law officer, Queen's Advocate Sir John Harding, the first on July 23 and the other three days later. But at this crucial moment Harding had a mental breakdown. Only his wife, Lady Harding, knew the state of her husband, but she was so distraught that she said nothing about his condition. Staying with friends, he had carried the papers with him.[37]

On the evening of July 28, Atherton retrieved the case materials from Harding and with Palmer studied them through the night and into the next morning before endorsing Collier's conclusions. Russell should detain No. 290 until a full-scale investigation could take place, the two law officers declared. The depositions presented by Dudley, "coupled with the character and structure" of the ship, made it "reasonably clear" that its destination was the Confederacy. Passmore's testimony made it impossible to deny that the vessel was a warship. A jury might decide against the seizure, largely because "neither guns nor ammunition have as yet been shipped" and the crew had not signed on as "a military crew." But given the clear impression of wrongdoing, the owners had to prove innocence. Atherton and Palmer agreed with Collier that the government should *not* adhere to a strict interpretation of the terms "equip," "furnish," "fit out," or "arm"—all found in the Foreign Enlistment Act. This narrow approach "would fritter away the act, and give impunity to open and flagrant violation of its provisions." The lack of guns on board did not prove innocence. "The vessel, cargo, and stores may be properly condemned."[38]

In the meantime, however, Bulloch managed No. 290's escape from Birkenhead—also on July 28—while it was taking on coal and provisions. Now known as the *Enrica*, it pulled away from the dock that evening, dropped anchor off Seacombe on the Mersey River, and left the next morning for a purported trial cruise. A large number of party-minded men and women were on deck, some of the men admitting they were part of the crew for the gunboat. But the vessel had aroused no suspicion, leaving port in the company of the steam tug HMS *Hercules*. No beams were on board the gunboat, despite Dudley's claims. The master of the *Hercules*, Thomas Miller, attested to seeing no guns; in fact, he saw nothing except coal. Miller transported up to thirty men to the vessel to serve as either sailors or firemen, but he carried no guns, powder, or ammunition.[39]

When the tug's master returned, however, it became clear that Bulloch had perpetrated a massive hoax. Miller reported that the *Enrica*, which was cruising off Point Lynus, had six guns hidden below and was taking on powder from another ship. Too late Dudley demanded a stop to "this flagrant violation of neutrality," for Bulloch had masterfully arranged its escape.[40]

Meanwhile, the foreign secretary was out of town and the law officers' urgent message did not reach him until early in the afternoon of July 29. Again for some unexplained reason, Russell did not send the detention order to Liverpool until late in the evening of July 31. Although Edwards had not found evidence to substantiate Dudley's allegation of guns on the *Enrica*, the Board of Customs Commissioners instructed Liverpool officials to detain the ship. By that time, the *Enrica* had been at sea for fifty-five hours. The delay caused by Harding's illness proved costly. If Atherton and Palmer had possessed the July 23 information on the twenty-fourth or even the twenty-fifth, they undoubtedly would have approved the detention at that time and blocked the ship's departure.[41]

The British had evidence that the *Enrica* had taken on cargo from the *Bahama*, a steamer that had arrived in Liverpool the previous evening out of Angra, the capital of Terceira Island in the Azores, after its clearance from Liverpool for Nassau. To inquiries about the cargo, the master said he had taken on sixteen cases of unidentified goods, presumably arms, and transferred them to a Spanish vessel before returning to Liverpool with a supply of coal. Off the Western Islands, he saw the *Enrica*, well armed and with a 100-pounder pivot gun mounted on the stern that he thought capable of destroying seaport towns along the north Atlantic coast. The master of the *Bahama* had transferred nineteen cases of goods to the *Enrica*, and Captain Raphael Semmes, former commander of the Confederate steamer *Sumter*, had arrived on the *Bahama*, along with about fifty others, to become captain and crew of the gunboat, now called the *Alabama*.[42]

Bulloch had taken the *Alabama* from British waters to a spot near the northwest coast of Ireland. He had then returned to Liverpool to arrange the transportation of Captain Semmes and his officers, along with the battery and ordnance stores, men's clothing and other supplies, and 250 tons of coal. The two vessels met at Praya, on Terceira Island. Captain Semmes and his officers arrived from Nassau around August 8 and five days later joined Bulloch on the *Bahama*, bound for the *Alabama*. They reached Praya on August 20 and boarded the cruiser; good weather allowed them to finish the exchange on the late morning of August 22. After mounting the last gun and stowing other ammunition, they completed the coaling process by ten the following night. On Sunday morning, August 25, the *Alabama* and the *Bahama* steamed out into Portuguese waters and, with the crews of both vessels giving three cheers, raised Confederate colors on the new cruiser. By midnight, the officers had made all the arrangements for the men on the *Alabama*, and Captain Semmes prepared to cross the Atlantic. Bulloch climbed off the vessel, noting that he felt like he was leaving his home.[43]

Dudley and Adams had mishandled the process by failing to understand all the legal steps involved in detaining a vessel. This was all the more inexcusable in light of their experiences in trying to stop the *Florida*'s departure. Dudley had been watching No. 290 since his arrival in Liverpool months earlier. His detectives had kept him fully apprised of the ship's character. Thus, along with Bulloch's expert maneuvering, poor preparation was primarily responsible for the *Alabama*'s escape, *not* British collusion or purposeful delay. Dudley and Adams did not *start* gathering evidence for a detention until July 16 and forwarded their findings to British customs officials on July 21–23. Adams had thought—erroneously—that his mere request for detention would suffice and had not taken into account the intricacies of the British legal system.[44]

Union officials had mistakenly accused the Palmerston ministry of hiding behind legal technicalities to implement a pro-Confederate policy. Seward sharply dismissed Stuart's claim that his government had been unable to act without evidence of wrongdoing. Dudley asserted that because of the *Alabama*'s escape, "we are in more danger of intervention than we have been at any previous period. . . . They are all against us and would rejoice at our downfall." Seward had in hand a letter written to a British colleague by the undersecretary of state for foreign affairs, Sir Austen Henry Layard, who criticized London's policies. The ministry's slowness to act had exposed it to accusations of violating neutrality.[45] Only when the Confederacy met defeat at Gettysburg and Vicksburg the following July 1863 did it appear that the Union might win the war and that Russell could seize the war vessels and stifle the shipbuilding program.

Another outcome of the Union's battlefield victories was increased pressure on the British Foreign Office by Adams and Dudley to detain the two Laird rams. "If these ships go," Moran confided to his diary, "nothing will prevent a war between the two countries." Russell assured Adams that his protest had gone to the proper authorities in an effort to determine how to legally carry out the seizure. But Hamel found Dudley's evidence again insufficient to justify the action and warned that failure to win the case in court would result in "serious consequences in the shape of damages and costs." After a lengthy delay caused by the annual vacation in August, Russell penned a note on September 1 declaring that his government would not seize the rams. On reading Russell's note two days later, Adams predicted that "a collision must now come of it." In an uncharacteristic loss of control, he wrote Russell on September 5: "It would be superfluous in me to point out to your Lordship that this is war." Adams's nerves had frayed so badly that he lashed out in a manner setting aside all diplomatic tact and apparently conceding the probability of war. He was not threatening war; rather, he was warning that the issue was moving in that direction and wanted to emphasize the danger. Nevertheless, he had made a poor choice of words.[46]

And all so unnecessary, for on the day before Adams's note arrived, September 4, Russell decided on his own volition to detain the rams for further investigation. The foreign secretary directed Layard to hold the rams "as soon as there is reason to believe that they are actually about to put out to sea, and to detain them until further orders." Russell intended to test the Foreign Enlistment Act, knowing that British policy strongly suggested that ships with iron plates, rotating turrets (capable of housing guns and crew), and rams were warships and that the government had to assure Americans that it would not follow a policy of "neutral hostility." Palmerston agreed with the decision, admitting that the government might ultimately have to free the rams because of the necessity of proving that they were for Confederate use against the Union. Although Adams complained that this action was not strong enough, Russell responded that with the *Alabama*, his government could not "admit assertions for proof, nor conjecture for certainty." At long last, however, the Royal Navy provided a solution: It purchased the two rams in May 1864 and commissioned them as war vessels.[47]

Would the rams have made a difference in the war? Pure speculation, of course, but an accident in which one of the two former Confederate rams ran into another British vessel and did not draw its attention casts serious doubt on whether they had the capacity to raise the blockade and open southern ports. Yet the widespread perception of these ironclads disabling the wooden Union vessels and wreaking havoc along the Atlantic coast threatened to diminish the reality. The Union's consul general in Paris, John Bigelow, later asserted that the rams "would not only have opened every Confederate port to the commerce of the world, but they might have laid every important city on our seaboard under contribution."[48]

By the time the rams' crisis subsided, the *Alabama* had sunk a Union warship and either burned or bonded more than sixty Union merchant vessels (including a large number of whaling ships that carried the oil necessary to keep Union machinery running), but it went to the bottom after an hour-long battle with the Union gunboat uss *Kearsarge* off Cherbourg, France,

CSS *Alabama* sunk by USS *Kearsarge* off Cherbourg, France, in the English Channel on June 19, 1864 (Courtesy of the Library of Congress)

while spectators watched on shore and in yachts. More so than the Laird rams, the *Alabama*'s destructive activities created deep animosities toward the British that lingered for years after the war. Not until 1871 did the Treaty of Washington resolve the *Alabama* claims controversy with England by an arbitration settlement reached the following year that awarded the United States $15.5 million in damages. Russell later admitted that he should have ordered the ship's seizure while waiting for the law officers' report. "In a single instance, that of the escape of the 'Alabama,'" he lamented, "we fell into error."[49]

Seward had considered the danger of intervention so serious by the summer of 1862 that he threatened to break off diplomatic relations with the British if they got involved in the war. In a section of a dispatch to Adams in London so explosive that it did not appear in the executive documents sent to Congress, the secretary declared that if Russell offered to "dictate, or to mediate or to advise or even to solicit or persuade," the U.S. minister was to respond that he was "forbidden to debate, to hear or in any way receive, entertain, or transmit any communication of the kind." Whether the British acted alone or with other nations in extending recognition to the Confederacy, Adams was to "immediately suspend" his functions as minister. If they followed recognition with "any act or declaration of War against the United States," he was to sever diplomatic relations and return home. "You will perceive," Seward gravely concluded, "that we have approached the contemplation of that crisis with the caution which great reluctance has inspired."[50]

Seward's concerns were justified, for Gladstone had urged the ministry to support mediation. The chancellor of the exchequer not only cited economic and humanitarian reasons, but he also wished to halt a chain of events that would drag in other nations hurt by the war and culminate in their own clash over its spoils. In his diary, he recorded numerous attempts to devise a formula for peace. An unnamed "Southern Gentleman" highlighted the problems in drawing a border between the "Northern and Southern Republics." Gladstone praised a best-selling pamphlet entitled *The American Union*, now in its fourth edition, in which Liverpool businessman James Spence rejected slavery as a cause of the war. Having served as a financial agent for the Confederacy, Spence seemed to have intimate knowledge of the situation as he argued for southern recognition. According to one biographer, Gladstone's primary motivations in life were religion and morality, which helped to guide his humanitarian concerns regarding the American war. Spence's interest rested on more practical considerations. He wanted to establish a steamship line between England and a southern port and a railroad from the Confederacy to Matamoros, Mexico, both permitting an evasion of the Union blockade that would translate into huge profits. Regardless of motives, the two men were strong voices for intervention.[51]

Gladstone sought only to end the war, though he had little grasp of its causes. After an early August cabinet meeting, he walked out with "a bad conscience" because his colleagues would not support recognition until *both* American antagonists agreed to it. This was an immoral stance, Gladstone wrote the Duke of Argyll. To permit the war to render its own verdict would extend the fighting and place the burden of guilt for the ensuing destruction on the European powers. England should join France and Russia in offering mediation—"Something, I trust, will be done before the hot weather is over to stop these frightful horrors." Recalling his feelings some three decades after these events, Gladstone still maintained that he had regarded intervention as "an act of friendliness to all America."[52]

Like numerous British contemporaries, the London press failed to comprehend the tenacity behind the issues between Union and Confederacy when advocating intervention as a humane gesture to end a war that the

Union had brought on but that neither American antagonist understood. The *Times* termed the Union an "insensate and degenerate people" then pursuing a "hateful and atrocious war." No one in Europe supported "this horrible war." The Union, according to the *Morning Post*, had made many mistakes in waging this conflict. "Blinded by self-conceit, influenced by passion, reckless of the lessons of history, and deaf of warnings which everyone else could hear and tremble at, the people of the North plunged into hostilities with their fellow-citizens without so much as a definite idea what they were fighting for, or on what condition they would cease fighting." Not realizing that the two sides fought so viciously because they so well understood what was at stake, the *Morning Post* accused the Union of going to war "without a cause," "without a plan," and "without a principle." The fighting had swelled into a "suicidal frenzy" characterized by a "ferocity unknown since the times when Indian scalped Indian on the same continent."[53]

The Lincoln administration had reason to worry about British and French intervention during the autumn of 1862. Palmerston informed the queen that October presented the most opportune time of the year for an armistice. The approach of winter would force a pause in the fighting, allowing each side to reflect on the wisdom of accepting outside mediation in a pointless war. Russell concurred with Palmerston's assessment. "Mercier's notion that we should make some move in October agrees very well with yours." The queen did not object to an October intervention, although she preferred prior consultation with Austria, Prussia, and Russia. According to Adams some years afterward, King Leopold of Belgium (Victoria's uncle) had the greatest influence on her, and he urged Napoleon to convince England that it was in the interests of the European powers to end the American war, whether to recognize the Confederacy or, in the former Union minister's words, "take any other course likely to put an end to the American struggle." In the hands of Napoleon, this was an invitation to use force.[54]

The growing fear of a slave uprising instigated by the Union had pushed England closer to an intervention. The Border States might abandon the Union in light of their dissatisfaction with Lincoln's call for emancipation. McClellan's rebuff at Richmond had shaken the Union's confidence. In arranging a mediation, Russell reminded Palmerston, its sponsors must have a peace program in hand. "I quite agree with you that a proposal for an armistice should be the first step; but we must be prepared to answer the question on what basis are we to negotiate?" If they had no satisfactory terms and the Union's leaders decided to resume the war, "it will be of little use to ask them to leave off." At that point, he remarked with studied vagueness, the intervening powers might have to engage in some stronger action. An October cabinet meeting seemed advisable.[55]

The British stood on the verge of intervention primarily because the three most powerful figures in the government—Palmerston, Russell, and Gladstone—spoke favorably of mediation. Earl Granville was no proponent of intervention, but he admitted to great difficulty in halting a movement that had the support of his three esteemed colleagues. On an earlier occasion and on a different issue, he had remarked that Palmerston, Russell, and Gladstone constituted "a formidable phalanx when they are united in opposition to the whole Cabinet in foreign matters." Most cabinet members supported mediation, Granville thought, but he considered it "decidedly premature" and "a great mistake."[56]

The ministry encountered mixed interest in Parliament on suggesting a joint mediation. In early August, Russell notified the legislators that the ministry had the idea under consideration and that, if pursued, it intended to invite Russia's participation because of its well-known pro-Union sentiment. Argyll also supported the Union but opposed any British involvement until its leaders showed "some symptoms of doubt and irresolution." Otherwise, he agreed with Russell that premature involvement could grow into "*armed interference*." Mediation had a chance to work only if *both* antagonists accepted the offer. Argyll doubted that the Union could win the war, though he knew it did not share this belief. John Bright was confused. "I don't quite understand Lord Russell's American Declarations [in Parliament] last night," he wrote Cobden. Either Charles P. Villiers or Thomas Milner-Gibson from the cabinet had assured him that Russell was "quite Northern in feeling and wishes." If so, Bright cynically observed, the foreign secretary appeared "very unwilling to let anybody discover this from his official sayings." But this lack of clarity did not matter. Russia, Bright declared, would not participate in a mediation without the Union's prior approval. Furthermore, slavery as an issue of morality lay behind the American contest, and humanity might profit from a longer war if it led to the death of that southern institution. Cobden concluded that his earlier argument made to Adams still held true: A mediation sponsored by all European powers was the "safest form of intervention."[57]

At this point, it did not appear that Seward's belligerent strategy could block intervention. On the surface an outside involvement seemed unlikely. Parliament was prorogued on August 7, just two days after Russell expressed the ministry's interest in mediation, and the queen in her speech appeared to lean toward noninvolvement. Yet in the quiet recesses of the political stage, the Palmerston ministry had begun exploring other nations' sentiments for mediation. Russell and fellow proponents of intervention had naively dismissed the Union's opposition to all forms of intervention and continued to distinguish between mediation and recognition. To the Union, mediation was interchangeable with recognition in that both forms of intervention implied the existence of two entities. And that the Union could not accept.

Russia had become the key to a mediation, even though its opposition to intervention was well known in British and French governing circles. Russian ties with the Union ran deep and not only because Washington had made its good offices available in the Crimean War. The St. Petersburg government welcomed Lincoln's emancipation pronouncement as similar in spirit to Tsar Alexander's decision to free the serfs in March 1861. Moreover, the tsar had other considerations. He opposed rebellions against the established order, recognized that his country's primarily agricultural economy had incurred no hardships from the American war, and considered the Union a friend that had helped to balance off his Anglo-French rivals in the post–Crimean War era. In addition, the Russian minister to the United States, Baron Edouard de Stoeckl, had lived in Washington for two decades and was married to an American woman. He blamed irresponsible demagogues for bringing on the war and argued that the Union would staunchly oppose recognition of the Confederacy. And, according to Stuart, Stoeckl was confident that the Lincoln administration would turn down any interventionist offer. Yet the Russian minister feared that the Union was nearing exhaustion and would not risk a war with intervening powers over a mediation proposal. But, he added ominously, to push anything other than mediation carried a high risk; no people were more unpredictable than the Americans. The British chargé remained oblivious to the danger, insisting that recognition of the Confederacy would gain British "respectability" in the Union. "Peace might thus be accelerated."[58]

In a twist of logic the British never understood, the Union's repeated failures on the battlefield paradoxically fueled its determination to defeat the Confederacy. The *Times* had pronounced McClellan's retreat from Richmond as proof of military weakness. In the Foreign Office, Hammond praised the South for waging a well-orchestrated war and noted its forward thinking in building a navy based on rams and ironclads. Stuart hailed the Union's losses in combat as necessary to persuade its leaders that mediation presented the only option to certain defeat. Secretary for War Lewis had a word of caution, however. The Lincoln administration might denounce mediation as an outside threat and exploit that fear to win more recruits. Seward

had vehemently attacked intervention in any form as potentially "fatal to the United States." Indeed, he had authorized Adams to warn England that if it intervened, he would suspend diplomatic relations. In the U.S. embassy in London, Moran recorded in his diary that the situation had become so tense that he had "placed the dispatch [containing these instructions] under lock and key for security's sake."[59]

The perception of certain intervention confirmed the White House's determination to stand behind emancipation as a military and diplomatic instrument that, the president knew, had profound postwar implications. Lincoln explained his broadly based stand on slavery in a published letter written in response to Horace Greeley's late August editorial in the *New York Tribune* supporting black liberation, addressed to the president as "The Prayer of Twenty Millions." "My paramount object in this struggle," Lincoln declared, "*is* to save the Union, and is *not* either to save or to destroy slavery. . . . If I could save the Union without freeing *any* slave I would do it, and if I could save it by freeing *all* the slaves I would do it; and if I could save it by freeing some and leaving others alone I would also do that." Realistic considerations had shaped his position. Emancipation had become a major means to win the war but *not* its chief objective.[60]

The Lincoln administration's opposition to slavery infuriated British observers because it did not rest on moral considerations. Stuart noted the assessment of Senator Charles Sumner, staunch abolitionist and chair of the Foreign Relations Committee. Most members of the president's cabinet, according to Sumner, supported emancipation as a way to salvage political control at home while preventing foreign intervention in the war. In a letter to Argyll, Sumner emphasized that the administration had united behind a battle for emancipation whose outcome depended on victory in the war. Argyll realized that the Union would never approve mediation and that compromise was impossible in a "Life or Death" struggle.[61]

But it was one thing to convince a pro-Unionist such as Argyll; it was another to ease the widespread indignation aroused by Lincoln's new policy of emancipation. Most Europeans complained that the Union had acted out of desperation and that the war itself, not the president's hollow claim to opposing slavery, would determine the question of intervention. Thus the mixed signals coming from the battlefield continued to stymie the proponents of intervention. Neither the British nor the French would act until the war's outcome had become clear. Stuart told Russell that only "another Bull Run" would increase the chances for peace. Although Hammond opposed the Union and thought its plight hopeless, he recommended against mediation until both sides had suffered extensive damage. Perhaps, he thought, a prolonged struggle would benefit his country's interests. The more destruction suffered by North *and* South, "the less likely will they be to court a quarrel with us or to prove formidable antagonists if they do so." In France, Slidell's confidence in imminent recognition had wavered. Thouvenel had cooled Napoleon's ardor for acting independently of England and pointedly advised Slidell *not* to ask for recognition. When the southern minister sought to take advantage of recent Union setbacks in Richmond by seeking an interview with the emperor at Vichy, he was denied an audience. The Palmerston ministry would not act until both American antagonists were so spent that they welcomed mediation, and Napoleon refused to move without a British initiative.[62]

Not everyone in England wanted to shelve intervention until the war had run its course. Both Cobden and Argyll wrote Senator Sumner, expressing concern about the debilitating impact of imminent cotton shortages on mill families in Lancashire. Bright, on the other hand, supported the present policy of neutrality, arguing that the workers would not feel the brunt of the American war for at least another year. The Palmerston ministry and the news media, he charged, "had done all they can, short of direct interference by force of arms, to sustain the hopes of the Southern conspirators" who had tried to force England "to spill her blood and treasure in [their] Godless cause!" Gladstone admitted that the time was not yet right for mediation, but the European powers must not "stand silent without limit of time and witness these horrors and absurdities, which will soon have consumed more men, and done ten times more mischief than the Crimean War." The extended conflict in the Crimea had been justified because of an unclear verdict on the battlefield. But no one could defend the fighting in America, for the outcome was "certain in the opinion of the whole world except one of the parties." Mediation, Gladstone insisted, was the proper course in light of the "frightful misery which this civil conflict has brought upon other countries, and because of the unanimity with which it is condemned by the civilized world."[63]

British textile workers had remained silent primarily because they had not yet experienced extreme economic hardships from the American war. Although the booming economy had declined initially, England's shipping and industrial production had continued to grow throughout the conflict. True, about three of every four mill workers were unemployed or on short time, and, reported Henry Adams, the misery in Lancashire (as well as in France) had spread at a disturbing rate. Both Gladstone and Lyons feared that mounting unrest would force the ministry to intervene. But these dire assessments were not accurate. Cotton continued to flow into England—from the American South, delivered by vessels that had run the Union blockade, from southern cotton confiscated by Union forces, and from expanded purchases in Brazil, China, Egypt, and India. Hotze further disheartened Benjamin by concluding that British workers had not banded with the Confederacy because public and private charities had alleviated much of the suffering and numerous mills had resumed production if only on a part-time basis.[64]

A further ameliorating factor was the evidence suggesting that British workers based their sentiments toward the war on the importance of freedom as well as on their economic welfare. Lincoln's reference to "a People's Contest" had confirmed the growing conviction that the Union supported liberty while the Confederacy fought for slavery. Had not the president told

Congress that the Union advocated equal opportunity for all people, regard-less of color or class? Karl Marx, the outspoken proponent of the working class, called on workers everywhere to rejoice over the path-breaking events in America. Lincoln led a "world-transforming . . . revolutionary movement" against the "slave oligarchy," declared Marx from his place of exile in En-gland. "As the American War of Independence initiated a new era of as-cendancy for the middle class, so the American anti-slavery war will do for the working classes." Thus did domestic reform agendas help to determine the workers' reaction to the war and doubtless contribute to the shaping of government policies. Hotze also recognized the importance of slavery. The Lancashire workers, he reported to Richmond, were the only "class [that] continues actively inimical to us. . . . With them the unreasoning . . . aversion to our institutions is as firmly rooted as in any part of New England. . . . They look upon us, and . . . upon slavery as the author and source of their present miseries."[65]

France's economic situation, however, had become more serious than England's and resulted in great pressure on the Napoleonic regime to in-tervene in America. Shipping and industrial production, though remaining fairly solvent, showed signs of imminent problems. By the spring of 1862, at a social function in Paris, Thouvenel uncharacteristically exclaimed to the Union minister in Brussels, Henry Sanford: "We are nearly out of cotton, and cotton we *must have.*" More telling, the French foreign minister elaborated on these feelings that same evening by assuring Sanford that "we are going to have cotton even if we are compelled to do something ourselves to obtain it." Mercier likewise revealed a propensity to act. A mediation decision should await the outcome of the November congressional elections in America, he observed to Stuart. If the peace party made a strong showing, the European powers should offer joint mediation with "the greatest courtesy" as a prelude to recognition. So confident was he of this result that he recommended that the intervening powers' representatives in the United States carry a "Mani-festo" authorizing them to grant recognition of the Confederacy on the spot when they thought the time appropriate. Stuart questioned the procedure but not the objective. Only the home governments involved in mediation should decide when to extend recognition, he asserted, not their spokesmen thousands of miles away. Furthermore, the intervening nations should skip mediation and immediately grant recognition. Mercier opposed this move, maintaining that it would provoke the Union while "playing away one of our best cards without doing us any good."[66]

Both the French and the British had openly adopted the position that the

Lincoln administration most feared: Mediation, they had finally announced, constituted the first step toward recognition. Mercier urged his superiors in Paris to work out a mediation program with the London ministry. A joint offer, the French minister said, might stiffen the resolve of the Peace Democrats. If the White House turned down the hand of friendship, the intervening powers must recognize the Confederacy. Russia's involvement in the plan would probably ensure Union compliance, but this arrangement was not vital in view of the Republican Party's expected defeat in the upcoming elections combined with the army's continued failures on the battlefield. Stuart had softened his stand, now supporting Mercier in a mediation and thinking that Russia would privately urge the Union to accept the offer while publicly opposing southern separation. If England did not join the French program, Stuart warned Russell, it would appear to have "some ulterior object in continuing to look quietly on."[67]

Argyll continued to resist intervention, arguing that slavery was the primary issue and that only the war should decide the outcome. His stand was not surprising, given that his mother-in-law, the Duchess of Sutherland, had long fought slavery. Those who defined the issue as southern independence versus northern empire were wrong, Argyll wrote Gladstone. At stake was "one great cause, in respect to which both parties have been deeply guilty, but in respect to which, on the whole, the revolt of the South represents all that is bad, and wrong." Slavery was "rotting the very heart and conscience of the Whites—all over the Union—in direct proportion to their complicity with it." Only intense fighting could sear this great evil from America. England, Argyll insisted, must not permit its textile mills to become dependent again on southern cotton. Once the war had resolved these moral issues, "*then* I sh[oul]d not object to *help* in the terms of peace."[68]

Arguments on both sides of the intervention issue drummed on, but the Palmerston ministry had clearly maintained its interest in mediation. More than a few British observers urged the prime minister to reconsider the impact of ending the flow of southern cotton. Would it not be better to turn to alternative sources of supply rather than continue to depend on the Confederacy? China, Egypt, India, Morocco, and Turkey—all of these countries were potential sources of cotton that, British investors assured the Foreign Office, could be developed. Stuart informed the ministry that southern armies were about to invade the Union and thereby convince its people that the time had come to make peace. Bright, however, noted that his own contacts in New York predicted a Union victory. Gladstone leaned toward Stuart's assessment and suggested to Argyll that the ministry propose recognition rather than mediation. "It is our absolute duty to recognise, when it has become sufficiently plain to mankind in general that Southern independence is established, i.e. that the South cannot be conquered." Intervention would constitute "an act of charity." Ignore White House threats about switching to a war against slavery. In a statement that again demonstrated Gladstone's failure to understand the enormity of the issues confronting the Union, he said that the intervening powers would only make matters worse if they warned the administration against "resorting in [its] extremity to a proclamation of Emancipation[,] for that I cannot think Lincoln would do."[69]

If Henry Adams had been privy to Gladstone's thoughts, he would have countered that the Lincoln administration was serious in assuming its anti-slavery stand and would adopt any approach that destroyed the Confederacy. The Union would not accept peace "so long as the southern people exist." To his brother, he wrote: "I don't much care whether they are destroyed by emancipation, or in other words a vigorous system of guerrilla war carried on by negroes on our side, or by the slower and more doubtful measures of choaking [sic] them with their own cotton." The Union "must exterminate them in the end, be it long or be it short, for it is a battle between us and slavery."[70]

The argument for allowing the war to return its own verdict gained great momentum in early September 1862, when the British learned that Union forces had recently sustained another huge defeat—a second time at Bull Run. The war was virtually over, Russell told Palmerston with relief. Adams in London sank into despair on receiving the shocking news. The government in Washington initially reacted in a similar manner, but its mood quickly shifted to anger when reports arrived that McClellan had been close to Bull Run but stood idly by, refusing to assist fellow soldiers because of the need, he said, to save his men for the defense of Washington. A demand for the general's removal came in a letter to the president signed by Secretary of War Stanton, Secretary of the Treasury Chase, Secretary of the Interior Caleb Smith, and Attorney General Edward Bates. The capital was about to fall, Bates warned, and the president "seemed wrung by the bitterest anguish," even mumbling that he was "almost ready to hang himself." Yet Lincoln rejected his advisers' recommendation. McClellan might not be able to fight himself, the president conceded, but "he excels in making others ready to fight." At the same time, Lincoln realized that McClellan's repeated failures on the battlefield not only encouraged the Confederacy to continue the war, but also provided more impetus for outside intervention. Russell had now taken a step closer to fleshing out Seward's worst nightmare: like France, tying mediation to recognition. Turning to Thouvenel, the British foreign secretary inquired about French interest in a joint appeal for an armistice that, if rejected, would lead to British, French, Austrian, Prussian, and Italian recognition of the South as "Independent Confederate States." Such a step might "dispose the North to Peace." Above all, Russell stressed, neither England nor France must "act alone."[71]

The British and French had often cited the July 1861 Confederate victory at Bull Run as evidence of the Union's incapacity to win the war. How ironic that climactic proof came again at Bull Run. Stuart had taken on the air of a prophet in earlier asserting that only "another Bull Run" would ensure an end to the war. Surely the Union would now realize that its blue-shirted forces should agree to a mediated peace before they (along with the Confederacy) suffered utter devastation.[72]

But the Union surprised the external judges again by refusing to quit. More so than at First Bull Run, its remarkable resiliency refueled its determination to stave off intervention while resuming its efforts to win the war.

If slavery was emerging as a major issue in Anglo-French thinking about the war, it had still not replaced the widespread belief within England and France in the futility of the Union's drive to subjugate the Confederacy. Thouvenel, Dayton was convinced, considered slavery the root of the rebellion. "I only wish he was as well satisfied of our power to suppress the insurrection as I believe him to be satisfied of our right to do so."[73]

In the aftermath of the Confederacy's second major victory at Bull Run, Mercier passed on Thouvenel's renewed plea for mediation to Seward. "I think now that the Union is no longer possible," the French foreign minister observed. "So . . . if there must be two confederacies, . . . they should be confederated confederacies."

Seward replied that "it would be a great misfortune if the powers should wish to intervene in our affairs. There is no possible compromise, tell Mr. Thouvenel, and at any price, we will not admit the division of the Union."

France sought only to end the fighting, Mercier calmly asserted.

"We do not doubt your sentiments," Seward not so calmly shot back, "but the best testimony that you are able to give us of it is that you will stay out of our affairs."

Why not create two "confederated Confederacies"? asked Mercier.

Separation was impossible, Seward sternly interjected before Mercier could explain his idea. France must realize that "this Government neither has the thought, nor can entertain it by whomsoever it may be suggested, that there are or cannot be two confederacies here or any other government than this Union just as it constitutionally exists and has always been."

But the situation seemed "very unfavorable," Mercier said.

Seward stubbornly insisted that "this Government saw nothing in the change of circumstances but a new phase in the ever changing panorama, which would probably be followed by a new and different phase tomorrow." Regardless of future battles and their outcomes, "do not for a moment believe that either the President, Congress, myself or any person connected with this Government, will in any case entertain any proposition or suggestion or arrangement or accommodation or adjustment from within or without upon the basis of a surrender of the Federal Union." Let there be no doubt, Seward coldly emphasized; "We shall prosecute this war to its end."[74]

The war continued to produce paradoxes seemingly incapable of resolution. The Lincoln administration had resorted to emancipation in an effort to facilitate victory by blocking intervention, but the move instead deepened the distrust between the Union and England and *encouraged* intervention. In the Union's worst-case scenario, the British government and people interpreted White House opposition to slavery as a cheap stunt designed to destroy the Confederacy by fomenting black unrest and, contrary to Lincoln's objective, became more supportive of an intervention that would automatically place an antislavery nation on the side of a slaveholding people. By the autumn of 1862, the British virtually dismissed Seward's warnings of war in the belief that they could finesse a mediation without risk of conflict. Like those in England who opposed intervention, the leaders in Washington came to believe that Union forces must win big on the battlefield before the Palmerston ministry decided on an intervention—ostensibly intended to end this horrible war but that would succeed only in prolonging it.

CHAPTER 7

Antietam and Emancipation

Let us do something, as we are Christian men.
. . . Let us do something to stop this carnage.
—*London Morning Herald*, September 16, 1862

We are now passing through the very crisis of our fate.
—CHARLES FRANCIS ADAMS, October 9, 1862

British intervention appeared certain after the Union's second defeat at Bull Run in the autumn of 1862. Its attempt to defeat the Confederacy had again proved impossible, a truth that seemed obvious to contemporaries three thousand miles across the Atlantic. Surely the Lincoln administration would recognize the futility of continuing a war that could destroy both antagonists. Southern separation posed the only viable alternative to mounting atrocities. From the *Times* and the *Morning Post* came appeals to the Palmerston ministry to recognize the Confederacy. The *Morning Herald* expressed the growing popular sentiment: "Let us do something, as we are Christian men." Whether "arbitration, intervention, diplomatic action, recognition of the South, remonstrance with the North, friendly interference or forcible pressure of some sort . . . , let us do something to stop this carnage."[1]

The London ministry, indeed, thought the time had come for intervention. "The Federals," Palmerston observed to Russell, "got a very complete smashing, and it seems not altogether unlikely that still greater disasters await them, and that even Washington or Baltimore may fall into the hands of the Confederates. If this should happen, would it not be time for us to consider whether . . . England and France might not address the contend-

215

ing parties and recommend an arrangement upon the basis of separation?" If either or both antagonists rejected mediation, the prime minister added, the two European governments should "acknowledge the independence of the South as an established fact." Russell concurred. If mediation failed, "we ought ourselves to recognize the Southern States as an independent State." The cabinet should meet in late October to discuss the proposal.[2]

Second Bull Run encouraged the Palmerston ministry to consider southern separation as the key to stopping a war that the Union must accept as over. In light of their growing desperation, the prime minister and his foreign secretary refused to believe that Washington had any resiliency left. Palmerston and Russell thus linked either approval or rejection of mediation by the Union with an admission to independence that, by definition, pointed to ultimate recognition of a Confederate nation. Yet the Lincoln administration continued to renounce mediation as an unwarranted interference in American affairs that would prolong the war by holding out the prospect of southern recognition. The British again ignored the Union's warnings against *any* kind of intervention and insisted that they sought only to bring the two warring parties to the peace table. But the White House correctly suspected that mediation marked the first step in a process that as a matter of course would lead to a foreign acclamation of separation and then, finally, to recognition. What other outcome could there be once the Union refused a public offer of mediation from one or more European powers that claimed only to want the war to end? Recognition, the Union realized, would open the Confederacy to commercial and even military agreements, making the European nations virtual if not actual allies of the new nation. With the welfare of one or more continental powers then tied to the Confederacy, the peacemakers would be under enormous pressure to use force to end the conflict.

These events might have played out in the autumn of 1862, had not Confederate general Robert E. Lee followed his victory at Second Bull Run with a raid into Maryland.

Palmerston had accepted the probability of mediation after Second Bull Run, but remained uneasy about the Union's stubborn insistence on continuing the fight. Consequently, he welcomed Lee's trek into the north, for it provided the likelihood of more southern victories that would finally convince the Lincoln administration of the hopelessness of its cause. Palmerston wrote Russell: "Though the time for making a communication to the United States is evidently coming, yet perhaps it is partly actually come." With the two huge armies approaching each other above Washington, "another great conflict is about to take place" that should put us "in a better State than we now are in, to determine as to our course." The "northern Fury has not as yet sufficiently spent itself," but additional losses in the field should force the Union into "a more reasonable state of mind." Russell agreed and recommended inviting the French to join the British in a mediation attempt before pursuing the queen's proposal to broaden the list of participants to include Austria, Prussia, and Russia. Now was the time to act! Mercier had just underlined the escalating fear that if England did not take the lead in intervention, the war would pound on until the Union's "complete exhaustion."[3]

Given this moment for reflection, Palmerston revealed his own concern about mediation leading to recognition (as the Lincoln administration had insisted would occur) and, for that reason, preferred French and Russian involvement. A mediation proposal, he told Russell, could raise the question of whether "the fact of our meddling would not of itself be tantamount to an acknowledgement of the Confederate as an independent State." The Union's expected rejection of mediation would compound the difficulties. French collaboration was not enough. Russia must be part of the team, for its friendship with the Union would add credibility to the offer. Even if the Russians declined (and Palmerston admitted to this probability), the invitation itself would strengthen the mediation effort while perhaps assuaging their hatred for the British stemming from the Crimean War. Although those bitter memories lay in the not-too-distant past, he hoped that the leaders in St. Petersburg would set animosity aside and grasp the overarching importance of achieving peace in America. Palmerston agreed with the queen's recommendation to contact other European powers about mediation, but he hesitated to involve them in the process. Perhaps he remembered the old adage that the more parties to an agreement, the weaker it becomes.[4]

Thus the mediation effort came to a temporary standstill as Palmerston opted to await word of additional southern conquests on the battlefield. The Union would finally realize what most contemporaries already knew—that the Confederacy had demonstrated its separate status at First Bull Run and had now reaffirmed that truth by holding Richmond after the setbacks at Forts Henry and Donelson. Second Bull Run had driven home this point, and the two armies under Lee and McClellan would shortly engage each other again. What harm could come from postponing mediation a few days? The prime minister appeared to be correct. "It is evident," he soon wrote Russell, "that a great conflict is taking place to the north-west of Washington, and its issue must have a great effect on the state of affairs. If the Federals sustain a great defeat they may be at once ready for mediation, and the Iron should be struck while it is hot. If, on the other hand, they should have the best of it, we may wait awhile and see what may follow."[5]

Initial reports from America indicated that northern and southern forces were on the verge of a major battle in Maryland, one that could put the final touches on a mediation offer that, for the first time, contained peace terms stipulating the Union's dissolution. Palmerston had informed Gladstone of Russell's support for a plan that included French and Russian involvement and would go before the cabinet for approval. The three powers should propose an armistice requiring the Union to lift its blockade and negotiate a peace premised on southern separation. Russell then stated the stronger position recently introduced by the prime minister. To Gladstone, the foreign secretary advocated an "offer of mediation to both parties in the first place, and in the case of refusal by the North, to recognition of the South." In an inexplicable attempt to maintain goodwill while licensing interference in American domestic affairs, Russell recommended that "a [renewed] declaration of neutrality" accompany a proposed mediation "on the basis of separation and recognition."[6]

British neutrality had already deeply offended the Union, but Russell had put a new twist on the policy that he somehow thought Washington might accept. Rather than appeal to neutrality as the chief means for keeping the British out of the war, he now used it as the major justification for their intervention. In an all-encompassing interpretation of neutrality, he argued that international law permitted intervention when a war endangered the neutral nations' interests. As shown earlier, Russell had drawn on Vattel's writings in formulating British policy toward the American war by proposing an involvement that only at first glance seemed to contradict neutrality.[7] Yet no matter how "legal" this stance might be, it would inflame the Union. How could Russell hope to temper the Lincoln administration's certain furious reaction to the ministry's assurance of continued neutrality while advocating an intervention that meshed mediation with recognition?

These issues, if they concerned Russell, did not slow his interventionist course. He did not think the Union could defeat the Confederacy and suggested that England and France propose that Russia join them in offering mediation. If the Union refused, the British should remain neutral while offering mediation to the Confederacy on the same basis of separation; once it accepted the arrangement, the British would extend recognition and insist on its compliance with all treaties made by the United States before the war. Russell wanted a mid-October cabinet meeting and notified his ambassador in Paris of the ministry's interest in an Anglo-French mediation initiative that included the Russians should they choose to participate. If the Union refused mediation, England would recognize the Confederacy while softening the blow with a renewed pledge of neutrality. "Palmerston agrees entirely in this course," Russell assured Cowley in Paris.[8]

London's strategy once again demonstrated its failure to understand the implications of intervention. Indeed, Palmerston and Russell had taken their allegedly innocent program a monumental step forward by specifically promising recognition should the Union reject the mediation. Furthermore, they based their hopes on the dubious argument that the Union would lose another battle and then call off the war. No basis existed for this assumption. Had not First and Second Bull Run underlined both the Union's resilience and its capacity to make the best out of disaster? How could another Union defeat (if it occurred) ensure capitulation? Could Palmerston and Russell guarantee against their nation's direct intervention in the war if the Union refused mediation? What assurances could they give that an intervention intended to end an atrocious war would not actually expand the conflict by increasing the number of players?

The ministry nonetheless prepared to act on the basis of several questionable and dangerous assumptions. Palmerston and Russell had not considered how the Union's string of victories in the Western Theater helped to balance losses in the East and maintain the belief in ultimate victory. They had too readily accepted Stuart's conclusions that the Confederacy would never surrender and that the Peace Democrats would seize the initiative in stopping the war after certain Republican defeats in the November congressional elections. Palmerston and Russell naively assumed that a renewed pledge of neutrality would protect their government from the charge of self-interest; they still did not realize that the Lincoln administration regarded *any* form of intervention—even an allegedly altruistic neutrality—as a deadly threat to the Union. The imminent onset of winter, they surmised, would temporarily halt the fighting and provide time for the Union to reconsider the appeals for peace by outside nations. The prime minister and his foreign secretary were reasonable men who assumed that leaders in the Lincoln administration were also reasonable. Somehow dismissing the reality—that war is seldom conducive to rational thought—they insisted that the Union would agree to southern separation and that neither side would wish to restart the fighting once having had the opportunity to assess the costs.

Gladstone sensed an impending close to the American war and urged the ministry to act immediately. But contrary to his colleagues, he did not welcome further Union defeats. If the Confederacy won more battles, he warned, it would demand more concessions in the negotiations and further reduce the chances for a settlement. Before initiating mediation proceedings, England should make "a friendly effort" to persuade the Union to call off the war before it incurred more battlefield losses and faced a harder peace. Mediation seemed timely for another reason. Gladstone's constituency in Lancashire had been suffering "with a fortitude and patience exceeding all example, and almost all belief." If violence broke out before the government intervened in the war, the Americans would accuse the British and French of self-interest rather than acting as an "influence for good." And Russia's participation would add "moral authority" to the offer.[9]

As the Palmerston ministry made final preparations for a mediation proposal, the huge armies of Lee and McClellan met on September 17 at Antietam, a creek near the village of Sharpsburg, Maryland, in a battle that would go down in history as the bloodiest single day of fighting in the Civil War. The Confederacy's first incursion into the North came to a resounding halt as tens of thousands of America's youths fought viciously into the afternoon. Photography, a fledgling art at the time of the Civil War, allowed Americans for the first time to gaze with horror at pictures of the lifelike, unmoving dead scattered across the battlefield and gathered in ghostly images that were displayed at Mathew Brady's showing on Broadway in New York City. In a story that Stuart must have read and sent home from his post in Washington, the *New York Times* remarked that if Brady "has not brought bodies and laid them in our dooryards and along the streets, he has done something very like it." Decapitated, mutilated, twisted, mangled, rotting, and bloated corpses strewn haphazardly among carcases of horses and mules and in greater numbers than ever before—Antietam brought home in photographs the stark reality of war in a sudden and grotesque manner.[10]

In the foggy aftermath, more than 23,000 soldiers were casualties, including nearly 6,000 dead—every one of them Americans distinguished only by their contrasting blue and gray uniforms. On the evening of the next day Lee's forces staggered back into Virginia, leaving McClellan's army on the scene, equally battered and stunned but claiming victory by its presence. Lincoln, however, was not satisfied. Rushing to the battle scene, he urged McClellan to pursue Lee and finish the job. But the general claimed that his forces were not prepared to give chase, indignantly writing his wife that he would not "submit to all this from men whom I know to be my inferior!" In fact, he bitterly added, "There never was a truer epithet applied to a certain individual than that of the 'Gorilla.'" Lincoln simply remarked that McClellan had "the slows."[11]

Judah P. Benjamin's assessment of the battle of Antietam differed radically from that of McClellan's. After Lee's victory at Bull Run (or Second Manassas), Benjamin reported to Mason in London, Union forces had fled back to nearby Washington and McClellan took charge of the army to defend the capital. Lee meanwhile established headquarters at Frederick, Maryland, before capturing more than eleven thousand Union soldiers at Harpers Ferry, Virginia, and posing a distinct threat to Washington. McClellan's arrival, followed by reinforcements, led Lee to withdraw to Sharpsburg for the purpose of joining up with Generals Stonewall Jackson and A. P. Hill, en route from Harpers Ferry. The combined Confederate defense blunted the Union assault just before nightfall.[12]

The next morning, Benjamin continued, Lee was ready to resume the battle when he discovered that McClellan's army had left the field. Lee therefore gathered the wounded and buried the dead before moving across the river to Shepherdstown to rest and to round up stragglers before heading back into Virginia. At this point, according to Benjamin, McClellan erroneously claimed a victory.[13]

Benjamin believed that the Confederacy's military fortunes had soared dramatically in the last three months, raising again the possibility of recognition by the European powers. Confederate forces had been successful in western Virginia and in the Mississippi valley. Major General Kirby Smith had entered Richmond to rout a Union army of ten thousand on August 30, the same day Lee won at Second Manassas. In the battle of Antietam alone, Benjamin rejoiced, Confederate forces killed or wounded eleven Union generals, including four major generals. The Union's losses, he claimed, matched those of Napoleon I's disastrous retreat from Moscow in the early part of the century.[14]

Within a couple of weeks, the news of Antietam reached England, where the ministry initially believed the premature accounts of Confederate victory and resumed its interest in a mediation to stop the blood fest. The Earl of Shaftesbury, Lady Palmerston's son-in-law and of considerable influence in ministerial circles, had visited Paris a few days before the battlefield news had reached the Continent and, according to Slidell, assured French officials of imminent British intervention. From the outbreak of the war, Shaftesbury told Slidell, he had supported the South's struggle for independence against the Union's quest for empire. He had been nearly alone in that stand, for his

President Abraham Lincoln and General George B. McClellan face each other at Antietam, Maryland, in September 1862. (Courtesy of the Library of Congress)

associates had defined the issue as slavery versus freedom. But British public opinion had undergone a revolution in feeling. Lincoln's recent speech to the black delegation from New York and his published letter on slavery to Horace Greeley had alienated those English people calling for abolition. They now believed it more beneficial to black liberation if the Confederacy became independent.[15]

Slidell agreed with Shaftesbury, declaring that southerners could resolve the issue after a calm assessment of the economic and social values of the slave system. "If the day should ever arrive when slave labor ceased to be profitable and the slave could safely be liberated," he insisted, "slavery would soon cease to exist." What about the chances for gradual emancipation?

asked Shaftesbury. If President Davis implemented such a policy, the European governments would grant recognition and take all steps necessary to end the war. Slidell responded that the slavery issue was for the states to decide and not the president. British recognition, Shaftesbury nonetheless felt certain, would take place in a few weeks. If so, Slidell declared, it seemed strange that London's ministers held back despite the French emperor's well-known interest in recognition. The Confederacy could only believe that Britain wanted to prolong the war in an effort to exhaust the Union. Shaftesbury denied that allegation and promised to do everything possible to convince his leaders to recognize the Confederacy.[16]

Shaftesbury assured Slidell that the battle of Antietam had not changed

British interventionist sentiment. "There is every reason to believe that the event so strongly desired of which we talked when I had the pleasure of seeing you in Paris is very close at hand." Shaftesbury did not speak on an official basis, of course, but he, once observed Charles Francis Adams, was a "good key" to understanding British policy.[17]

Regardless of which side won, the battle had *not* ended the talk of intervention. Lee's retreat into Virginia had shocked the British into realizing that his invasion of the North had not only failed to deliver a widely anticipated victory, but it had also restored the Union's morale so badly shaken at Second Bull Run. The Confederacy tried to minimize the impact of Antietam by boasting that McClellan had not destroyed Lee's forces, leaving them in a position to establish control over the vast region extending from the Atlantic to the Mississippi. Northerners had lost their senses, many British contemporaries seemed to believe. Lewis cynically remarked that the Union had come to realize what it meant to be governed by a "village attorney appointed Prime Minister for 4 years certain, during a period of civil war." Hammond downgraded the importance of Lee's rebuff, asserting that his crossing the Potomac had been "more in the nature of a feeler" than a military offensive. Moran, however, saw through the self-serving charade, terming the outcome "a bitter draught and a stunning blow" to the British. "They express as much chagrin as if they themselves had been defeated." Gladstone, too, welcomed the news, although for different reasons. "I am not sorry for the apparent ill success of the Confederates as invaders," he wrote Argyll. "They might have become intoxicated, and entangled, by good Fortune."[18] In tactical terms, the outcome at Antietam proved indecisive; but for diplomatic purposes, the battle made clear that the Union would never accept mediation. Yet the Palmerston ministry more fervently felt the need to do something. It had delayed action for too long and now confronted a growing call at home for intervention on humanitarian grounds.

The debatable results at Antietam left the impression overseas that Union and Confederacy had reached a lethal stalemate that only outside intervention could break. The unparalleled toll of casualties in a single day's fighting confirmed the necessity for civilized nations to intercede. According to Stuart's erroneous assessment, Lee had not wanted the swollen waters of the Potomac River behind his forces and decided against taking an offensive against McClellan that would have yielded victory. Failing to understand the importance of holding the field after an engagement, Stuart called Antietam "as near a drawn Battle as could be, only that the Federals have since held the ground." Palmerston agreed that the two sides had become locked in a death grip that was, he informed Russell with notable relief, "just the case for the stepping in of friends." Now that the two antagonists had satisfied honor, they would surely listen to reason. "One thing must be admitted and that is that both sides have fought like bull dogs." They were "pretty equally balanced," with neither party able to subjugate the other.[19]

The French, too, considered the time right for mediation and urged the British to take the lead. Mercier had proposed that he and Lyons announce their joint interest in an armistice that permitted an opportunity for Union and Confederate officials to negotiate peace. The two mediators' good offices would be available if needed, but they should retain the option to act in accordance with their own interests. Above all, Mercier stressed, the proposal must make no reference to the word *separation*. Naively hoping to alleviate the Union's fears over separation by not mentioning the word, Mercier moved to two more questionable premises—that Antietam's horrors had assured the acceptance of an armistice by both sides, and that no one would want to resume hostilities. Yet, as noted earlier, death for honor on the battlefield impelled northerners *and* southerners, ensuring a heavenly aftermath that, in turn, created momentum for continuing the fight and thereby increasing the number of deaths. Still not grasping the furor of the struggle, Stuart thought his government could feel "perfect safety" in pursuing Mercier's proposal. Most northerners, the chargé emphasized, wanted peace.[20]

The British governing triumvirate most interested in mediation was powerful, but it did not command a unanimous following. In the cabinet, Argyll and Earl Granville recognized the humanitarian importance of ending the war, and yet they did not wish to provoke the Union. Argyll admitted to Gladstone that mediation had intrinsic appeal as long as it had a "reasonable chance" of acceptance by *both* sides. But the Union still believed it could defeat the Confederacy, making mediation an impossible proposition. Argyll also insisted that the Confederacy had not demonstrated its capacity to stand as a nation, although he conceded that the present direction of the war made that only a matter of time. Granville believed that the ministry lacked the requisite familiarity with American politics to formulate a viable peace plan. A member of the Liberal Party, Granville was a former foreign minister now sitting in the Lords who had long opposed his nation's involvement in other countries' affairs. He warned Russell that the British people did not support either the Union or the Confederacy on the explosive slavery issue, that the boundary questions involved not only the two principals in the war but also the American West, and that the French need for cotton dictated their participation in any negotiations. The mere announcement of recognition would not throw open the Union blockade and ensure a renewed cotton flow. Indeed, the American North would probably rally against the new foreign threat and oppose any peace initiative. England might get pulled into the war, freeing Napoleon to pursue his imperial objectives on the Continent. The ministry must maintain neutrality while calming desperate mill workers at home with relief assistance.[21]

British reactions to the American war were enormously complex, especially in the manufacturing districts. Workers, of course, favored a rapid end to the fighting and a restored cotton economy in the South. The Earl of Clarendon, who had earlier served Palmerston as foreign secretary, saw strategic value in the war's continuance until both sides were too spent to threaten British interests in the Americas. But he also sympathized with the workers, a position encouraged by his brother Charles P. Villiers, a cabinet member who headed the Poor Law Board. Clarendon denounced the mill owners for profiting from the war. To another of his relatives in the cabinet, Secretary for War Lewis, Clarendon asserted that the American war had saved the mill owners from having to close their factories by providing markets for their huge backlog of cotton stocks caused by massive overproduction in the halcyon pre–Civil War days. Moreover, the high prices resulting from wartime demands did not provide their only profit. "They have sold their raw cotton at 50% profit. They have shut up every mill that could not be worked at a profit and they have contributed little or nothing to their starving work people. In the worship of the almighty dollar they have acted exactly in accordance with their hard and grinding instincts."[22]

Clarendon's assessment pointed to the difficulties in understanding the British textile industries' response to the war, but it does not diminish the reality of the workers' hardships. The abundant cotton yield in the South during the three years before the war had banked up so much raw cotton in British warehouses that British (and French) producers had flooded the markets with finished goods, while making drastic cutbacks in production that forced numerous laborers into short time or layoffs. James Garnett, a leading mill owner in Clitheroe, did not welcome a quick end to the war. He had taken advantage of the drop in cotton imports to sell his overload of manufactured items at higher prices. Lee's advance into Maryland had concerned him because it might force the Union into peace. In Manchester, the anticipation over the expected battles had virtually halted business. Garnett knew a Confederate victory would shorten the war and drive down prices, whereas a Union conquest would prolong the war and push them up. During the sharply reduced work hours in the winter of 1862–63, mill workers suffered while mill owners used the downtime to update the machines in their factories. John O'Neil, a leader in the trade union movement, was "too sad and weary" to record anything in his diary for two years following the slow-down. Finally, in the spring of 1864, he penned an entry: "It has been a very poor time for me all the time owing to the American war, which seems as far of being settled as ever." O'Neil's emphasis on distress continued through his last entry in early October, when he noted the large number of mill closures in Lancashire.[23]

Was this a cotton famine that, according to some observers, heightened support for the Confederacy? More than a few writers suggest that no cotton famine occurred because cotton remained plentiful. Indeed, the manufac-turers had so much cotton on hand that they slowed production to drive up the prices of finished goods. The overproduction from the prewar period led to a cotton surplus that allowed owners to cut work time for their employees and modernize facilities; but the surplus ran out by the end of 1862 and led to a dearth in cotton that shortened work hours. Thus the initial surplus led to reduced work time, and its eventual depletion extended the layoffs. It there-fore seems more accurate to say that a rapid drop in cotton stock—hence a "famine"—contributed to a desperate economic situation that had its great-est impact on textile workers. Yet this reality does not change the findings of recent studies—that the great majority of these workers did *not* therefore support the Confederacy in an effort to secure cotton.[24]

Many British, perhaps most of them, appeared to be pro-Union because of its stand against slavery and for reform. Close to forty thousand British emigrants had returned home from the United States in the tumultuous two years before Lincoln's election and educated their people about the issues tearing apart the American nation. Of the many points of division, slavery stood at the top of the list. If the president's approach to antislavery did not seem strong enough, his support for emancipation nonetheless turned in-creasing numbers of British citizens against the Confederacy. "It is slavery from the top to the bottom, and slavery in the middle, and slavery all the way through," insisted a British reformer and attorney. Leicester parliamen-tary member Peter Taylor publicly praised the Union for using antislavery to "surround the scorpion slavery with a ring of fire, so that it must either die or sting itself to death."[25]

Thus the most thorough research to date suggests that the great bulk of textile workers, along with British reformers, leaned toward the Union. A British worker tied antislavery and reform together: "We have a general im-pression amongst us that the once despised and enthralled African will not only be set free, but enfranchised, and in spite of his master; and when the slave ceases to be, and becomes enfranchised free men, that then the British workman's claim may be listened to." In a division remindful of the Hamiltonians and Jeffersonians in early America, British support for the Union came mainly from business and manufacturing leaders, trade union proponents, Dissenting ministers, and others in urban sectors, whereas the Confederacy drew sympathy from aristocrats, women, professionals, Anglican ministers, and those from small towns and rural areas. Interest in the American war was high among British observers, and the division was deep, but they were united in believing that the responsibilities of civilization provided them with a mandate for intervening in the war and helping to determine its outcome.[26]

The ironies continued to unfold as Antietam's impact became clear. The Lincoln administration felt confident that the outcome had provided a vital impetus to its campaign against intervention. Adams and Seward concluded that the danger had eased, and the president prepared to inflict the final blow on the foreign threat by issuing his proclamation of emancipation. A war against slavery, he firmly believed, would dissuade any further thought in Europe about interfering in American domestic affairs and thereby helping a slaveholding people. But just as Lee's failure at Antietam had paradoxically raised the British interest in mediation, so did Lincoln's emancipation pronouncement intensify this sentiment by spreading their fear of a larger war. Some British observers became incensed over what seemed to them a hypocritical policy designed to achieve victory by inciting slave rebellions that would ensure widespread racial conflict. To the British, intervention seemed a foregone conclusion by the autumn of 1862.[27]

The warm reception to the preliminary Proclamation at home had encouraged Lincoln to turn his restrained support of emancipation into a full-fledged crusade against slavery. In mid-September he met with an organization called Chicago Christians of All Denominations, whose members argued that black liberation would underline the moral purpose of the war and attract European support. Lincoln concurred for several reasons: "No other step would be so potent to prevent foreign intervention." Union soldiers would fight harder for such a "glorious principle." Slaves would abandon the plantations, depleting the southern workforce and furnishing labor and soldiers to the Union. "What the rebels most fear," the president said in emphasizing his military objective, "is what we should be most prompt to do; and what they most fear is evident from the hot haste with which, on the first day of the present session of the Rebel Congress, bills were introduced threatening terrible vengeance if we used blacks in the war." The delegation exhorted him to promise the slaves freedom.[28]

If Lincoln had not yet focused on the moral aspects of an antislavery crusade, he had come closer to that position by now pronouncing slavery the major cause of the Civil War. His response to the Chicago Christians, which appeared in the *Chicago Tribune* and other newspapers, demonstrated this revolutionary change in perspective. He admitted to mulling over the issue for some time but had hesitated to broaden emancipation into a moral stand because of its impracticality:

> I do not want to issue a document that the whole world will see
> must necessarily be inoperative, like the Pope's bull against the comet!
> Would *my word* free the slaves, when I cannot even enforce the Con-
> stitution in the rebel States? . . . And what reason is there to think
> it would have any greater effect upon the slaves than the late law of
> Congress, which I approved, and which offers protection and free-
> dom to the slaves of rebel masters who come within our lines?

If the slaves flocked to the Union, "*what should we do with them* [emphasis Lincoln's]?" How were they to feed and clothe so many destitute people? "Nor do I urge objections of a moral nature, in view of possible consequences of insurrection and massacre of the South. I view the matter as a practical war measure, to be decided upon according to the advantages or disadvantages it may offer to the suppression of the rebellion." Emancipation would convince Europe that "we are incited by something more than ambition." Slavery, he insisted, was "the root of the rebellion."[29]

Lincoln remained the pragmatist, however, deciding on September 22 to release his preliminary Emancipation Proclamation while ignoring the mounting pressure to publicly declare a war on slavery that crossed all political and territorial barriers. At noon he met with his cabinet to make his intentions known. "Gentlemen," he explained, "I have, as you are aware, thought a great deal about the relation of this war to Slavery." He could no longer wait. The victory at Antietam had not been as pronounced as he would have liked, but Lee's forces *had* retreated into Virginia, leaving Maryland secure. When the rebels quartered at Frederick posed a threat to Washington, Baltimore, and Harrisburg, he had sworn to announce emancipation if their efforts failed. "I said nothing to anyone; but I made the promise to myself, and (hesitating a little)—to my Maker. The rebel army is now driven out, and

I am going to fulfill that promise." He gazed down at the paper on the desk for a moment before telling his advisers that he wanted them only to hear the words of his Proclamation before he released it to the public. "I do not wish your advice about the main matter—for that I have determined for myself." He read the document, making relevant remarks as he proceeded. On January 1, 1863, the president affirmed that all slaves in states still in rebellion were "forever free."[30]

Lincoln had carefully skirted a moral war against slavery, but at the same time he realized that the sheer momentum of an antislavery campaign would extend beyond the bounds of "military necessity." Abolitionists complained about the Proclamation's limitations but prepared to use it as a stepping-stone toward liberating all slaves. Lincoln had acted legally and constitutionally in granting freedom to only those slaves residing in rebellious states. He demonstrated political astuteness in refusing to provoke the Border States, southern Unionists, and northerners who opposed abolition. He also knew the Proclamation would transform the war into a humanitarian effort and thereby undermine European sympathy for southerners as an oppressed people who deserved outside intervention. Finally, he recognized that emancipation would erode the Confederacy from within by encouraging blacks to walk off plantations and perhaps join the Union army. The president doubtless wished to avoid racial violence, but in this period of mass upheaval, he knew his action would raise a black cry for freedom that intensified southern resistance. To an official in the Department of Interior, Lincoln admitted that "the character of the war will be changed. It will be one of subjugation. . . . The [Old] South is to be destroyed and replaced by new propositions and ideas."[31]

McClellan bitterly complained that his president sought to stir up slave rebellions in an attempt to win the war. The general found it easy to believe the worst of Lincoln, who had criticized him for both the failed Peninsula campaign and his refusal to pursue Lee's army into Virginia after the battle of Antietam. Lincoln, McClellan charged, was a civilian who knew nothing about the military profession and therefore did not understand that no army could take the offensive without sufficient numbers and tight organization. Never should a soldier use racial unrest as a military weapon. McClellan wrote his wife that he could not "fight for such an accursed doctrine as that of a servile insurrection."[32]

To ease the widespread concern about racial violence, Lincoln revised parts of the Proclamation. He followed Seward's advice to add two passages. First, he urged freedmen "to abstain from all violence, unless in necessary self-defense," and second, he asserted that, "in all cases, when allowed, they labor faithfully for reasonable wages." Furthermore, during the hundred days between the preliminary and final Proclamations, Lincoln struck passages criticized as inducements to rebellion—assurances against executive interference with the blacks' efforts to win freedom and references to colonization and compensated emancipation. These cosmetic changes, however, could not alter the expanding course of emancipation. On the evening of the presidential announcement, Treasury secretary Chase invited friends into his home to celebrate. The Confederacy deserved a round of thanks, he announced to his incredulous guests. Then in a satirical vein, he explained. "This was a most wonderful history of an insanity of a class that the world has ever seen. If the slaveholders had staid [sic] in the Union they might have kept the life in their institution for many years to come. That what no party and no public feeling in the North could ever have hoped to touch they had madly placed in the very path of destruction." Trouble would come, warned a Union official in New Orleans. The Proclamation, he wrote Chase with some exaggeration, had led to "the organizing and arming of the colored population throughout the South."[33]

News of the Emancipation Proclamation infuriated the British and the French. From Washington, Stuart indignantly informed Russell that Lincoln had enacted an antislavery decree in areas where the Union had no "*de facto* jurisdiction*." The purpose of the measure was to "render intervention impossible." It bore no "pretext of humanity" and was "cold, vindictive, and entirely political." The president sought only to offer "direct encouragement to servile Insurrections." His action had angered Confederate lawmakers who mouthed "threats of raising the Black Flag and other measures of retaliation." Bring in the French guillotine, declared a northern governor. If Lincoln and his Republican Party remained in control, Stuart warned, "we may see reenacted some of the worst excesses of the French Revolution." Hammond joined Cobden in fearing the worst. To block the Confederacy's quest for nationhood, Cobden moaned, the Union would "half ruin itself in the process of wholly ruining the South." The use of blacks in the war effort would cause "one of the most bloody and horrible episodes in history." The French concurred, complaining to London that the danger of a slave rebellion provided another reason for a joint intervention to end the war. A few days later, Stuart wrote Russell with no hint of dissatisfaction that Lincoln's Proclamation seemed to be causing many in the Union armies and the Border States to desert to the Confederacy.[34]

The British press launched a blistering attack on the decree. The *Times* bitterly ridiculed Lincoln for considering himself "a sort of moral American Pope." Taking advantage of the war, he sought to stir up a slave uprising during which the blacks would "murder the families of their masters" while they were away at war. "Where he has no power Mr. LINCOLN will set the negroes free; where he retains power he will consider them as slaves." His seemingly moral pronouncement was "more like a Chinaman beating his two swords together to frighten his enemy than like an earnest man pressing on his cause." Though it supported the Union, the *Spectator* of London found the Proclamation exasperating. "The principle is not that a human being cannot justly own another, but that he cannot own him unless he is loyal to the United States." London's *Bee-Hive*, sympathetic to the Confederacy until the paper changed editors in January 1863, accused Lincoln of refusing to take action against slavery in the Border States in which he had authority and attempting to end the institution in the Confederacy where he did not. The *Times* bitterly asked whether "the reign of the last PRESIDENT [was] to go out amid horrible massacres of white women and children, to be followed by the extermination of the black race in the South? Is LINCOLN yet a name not known to us as it will be known to posterity, and is it ultimately to be classed among that catalogue of monsters, the wholesale assassins and butchers of their kind?" *Blackwood's Edinburgh Magazine* renounced the Proclamation as "monstrous, reckless, devilish." To defeat the Confederacy, the Union "would league itself with Beelzebub, and seek to make a hell of half a continent."[35]

Both Conservative (government-supported) and Liberal newspapers in France were almost as venomous. The Conservative press thought the Proclamation would cause slave rebellions and a "fratricidal war" that would envelop America in "blood and ruins." The president's decree freed only those slaves in rebellious areas and thus intended to punish and avenge the South. Lincoln, snidely charged one paper, "wishes to abolish slavery where he is not able to achieve it and to save it where he would be able to abolish it." He sought "the ruin of the Southern states" by instigating servile war. In October a Liberal newspaper joined in the attacks, accusing Lincoln of using emancipation as a wartime measure and not as an act of justice. Another paper contended that it would have been better if the Union had simply abolished slavery at the outset of the war. "All spirits, or philosophers or Christians would have immediately rallied to the cause of the North, which would have been that of humanity." The same month a Conservative paper maintained that neither side was able to win and that "an intervention by a third party was necessary to break the equilibrium."[36]

Palmerston remained the pivotal figure in any interventionist effort, and he had suddenly returned to his wait-and-see position. The Confederacy, he knew, would welcome mediation "upon the Basis of Separation," but, he emphasized to Russell, the Union would continue to refuse the offer because Antietam had further deluded the White House into believing that victory was possible. In fact, the Confederacy's failure to win a decisive battle left the Union not only free to reject mediation, but also to take the field against any nation interfering in American affairs. Mediation "has been lately checked" by the recent battle, suggesting that the ministry should wait another ten days for "future prospects." If the Union threatened war on the mediating party (or parties), it would be wise to wait until spring weather reopened British communications to Canada and allowed naval operations along the Atlantic coast. The only approach that might work was a multilateral recognition of the Confederacy. "If the acknowledgement were made at one and the same time by England, France and some other Powers, the Yankee would probably not seek a quarrel with us alone, and would not like one against a European Confederation."[37]

Palmerston again insisted that the fortunes of the American war must determine the timing of mediation, which he considered unavoidable. The ministry, he thought, should first deliver a "friendly suggestion" that the Union accept separation as "the inevitable result of the contest, however long it may last." An armistice would be difficult to secure, for it required a resolution of the blockade issue. If lifted, the Confederacy would gain the advantage; if not lifted, the Union would retain the upper hand. The best outcome at present, the prime minister believed, was to bring the two parties to the peace table and let them settle the details. Any disputes during those talks "would do us no harm if they did not lead to a renewal of war." But at this point, neither side appeared receptive to a cease-fire, leaving continued British inaction as the most prudent policy. "The whole matter is full of difficulty, and can only be cleared up by some more decided events between the contending armies."[38]

Palmerston's hesitation did not deter Russell. "This American question," the foreign secretary admitted, "must be well sifted." He noted that Lewis was also "against moving." But Russell opposed further delay. "I think unless some miracle takes place this will be the very time for offering mediation, or as you suggest, proposing to North and South to come to terms." A mediation proposal must contain the ministry's recommendation for southern separation along with a statement that England "shall take no part in the war unless attacked." Russell dismissed Palmerston's concern that British acknowledgment of separation meant war with the Union. "My only doubt," he asserted, "[is] whether we and France should stir if Russia holds back. Her separation from our move would ensure the rejection of our proposals." Yet if the Russians declined to participate, the British and French should still act. "If no fresh battles occur, I think the suggestion might be adopted, tho' I am far from thinking with Mercier that the North would accept it. But it would be a fair and defensible course, leaving it open to us to hasten or defer recognition if the proposal is declined."[39]

The British did not know it yet, but if they acted it would be without the Russians. The slavery issue was of no consequence in Russian thinking. The war's collateral damage had not threatened the Russian economy. And, despite the Anglo-French insistence on southern separation as certain, the St. Petersburg government preferred that the war—not military prophets—determine its outcome. From the Russian embassy in Washington, Stoeckl wrote his home office that Lincoln (as both the British and the French had charged and the president himself acknowledged) had used the Emancipation Proclamation primarily as a military tool against the Confederacy and not as a humane call for freedom. The Russian ambassador in London, Baron Philip Brunow, was struck by the Palmerston ministry's insistence on "doing something" before Parliament reconvened after the first of the year. Gorchakov, however, had already informed Stoeckl that their government would do nothing to jeopardize its friendship with the United States.[40]

Despite Lincoln's high hopes, the Union victory at Antietam had combined with his preliminary Emancipation Proclamation to encourage, rather than undermine, intervention. Russell justified mediation on the growing atrocities of the war, the endless nature of the fighting, the rapidly developing economic crisis caused by diminishing cotton supplies, and a certain race war that would drag in other nations. In the ultimate irony, Lincoln had adopted an antislavery posture in part to prevent outside interference in the war but had instead raised the likelihood of a foreign involvement by, according to the British and the French, attempting to stir up a servile insurrection in a desperate attempt to defeat the Confederacy. From Paris, Dayton praised the Emancipation Proclamation for appealing to "the enlightened conscience of the Christian world," but he warned that the foreign press had twisted the president's motives and that the interventionists would demand action on humanitarian grounds, when their real concern was that black liberation would hurt the Confederacy and interfere with cotton production. Seward had been correct in recognizing the need for a major battlefield victory as a prelude to the Proclamation. But the Union conquest at Antietam had not been decisive, and the war now threatened to get out of hand.

ABE LINCOLN'S LAST CARD; OR, ROUGE-ET-NOIR.

President Abraham Lincoln plays the emancipation card. (*Punch*, October 18, 1862)

Lincoln had played "his last card," charged the *Times*. "He will appeal to the black blood of the African; he will whisper of the pleasures of spoil and of the gratification of yet fiercer instincts; and when blood begins to flow and shrieks come piercing through the darkness, Mr. LINCOLN will wait till the rising flames tell that all is consummated, and then he will rub his hands and think that revenge is sweet."[41]

Contrary to the traditional story, the battle of Antietam and the Emancipation Proclamation did not stop the British movement toward intervention; rather, they only slowed down a process that once again had gotten under way. Palmerston preferred waiting a few days; Russell wanted to act now. Gladstone and others joined the foreign secretary in warning against a war of subjugation made worse by a certain slave insurrection destined to grow into a racial conflict. Russell sought an immediate mediation leading to an armistice that culminated in recognition. The time had come to stop the war in the name of peace.[42]

Thus, even as the mutual slaughter at Antietam had heightened British interest in intervention, the lack of a clear-cut victory had deeply divided the government over when to take action. Russell had emerged as the chief proponent of stepping in immediately to spare the antagonists and other nations continued destruction. Gladstone wholeheartedly agreed, citing humanitarian and economic reasons. Yet Palmerston had again revealed his reluctance to act without ironclad assurances of success. All three leaders wanted to stop the fighting, but they disagreed on the timing. The prime minister did not believe the Confederacy had earned nationhood status on the battlefield and feared that premature intervention would make his government a virtual ally of the Confederacy and cause war with the Union.

Most of the cabinet appeared to agree with Palmerston. The lord chancellor, Baron Westbury, was the only other member who joined Russell and Gladstone in advocating immediate intervention. Formidable opposition came from Lewis and Argyll, but also from Granville, Villiers, the Duke of Newcastle in the Colonial Office, Sir George Grey from the Home Office, and Thomas Milner-Gibson from the Board of Trade. Lewis argued that intervention did not guarantee an end to the war and that, because the ministry could offer no peace terms acceptable to both antagonists, it must remain neutral and outside the conflict. Both he and Argyll warned that the Union would use force to block any form of outside intervention.[43]

The divisions within the ministry had not been made public, however, and recognition seemed definite when, on October 7, 1862, Gladstone praised the Confederacy in an emotional speech at Newcastle. Amid thunderous applause, he proclaimed: "We may have our own opinions about slavery, we may be for or against the South; but there is no doubt that Jefferson Davis and other leaders of the South have made an army; they are making, it appears, a navy; and they have made what is more than either—they have made a nation." Then came his ringing conclusion: "We may anticipate with certainty the success of the Southern States as far as regards their separation from the North."[44]

Both Union and Confederacy considered this address the Palmerston government's signal of intervention. The ebullient and ever-optimistic Confederate minister in Belgium, Ambrose D. Mann, celebrated recognition as all but achieved and effusively described the warm welcome that Gladstone's public proclamation had received throughout the Continent. His assertion "clearly foreshadows our early recognition, as no member of the British cabinet is in closer cordial relations with the premier than the chancellor of the exchequer." More than two months later, the high hopes remained as Francis Lawley, a pro-Confederate correspondent for the *Times* who had close ties with Richmond's leaders, wrote Gladstone of the widespread excitement

William E. Gladstone, British chancellor of the exchequer (H. C. G. Matthew, ed., *The Gladstone Diaries*, 9 vols. [Oxford, England: Clarendon Press, 1978], 6:frontispiece)

over "establishing hereafter mutually beneficial relations between the two countries." William Forster's tight relationship with Adams became evident when he urged the minister to warn Russell of Seward's instructions to break relations if the ministry recognized the Confederacy. Adams was distraught but wisely waited for the official reaction to Gladstone's fiery words. The British government, Adams informed Seward, would reveal its decision when Parliament assembled. "We are now passing through the very crisis of our fate," the minister penned in his diary.[45]

Gladstone's speech infuriated fellow Liberals Cobden and Bright, who had long fought against intervention and considered it bad policy to take a public stand on American affairs. Cobden was livid: "I could not help wishing that Cabinet Ministers would apply to their tongues the principle of non-intervention which they profess to adopt in their diplomacy." Bright bitterly noted that Gladstone had never sympathized with blacks in America and had now capitalized that cold stance by becoming "the first public man who has complimented Jeff Davis." The chancellor's family had owned slaves in the West Indies and, even though he had renounced human bondage, he had refused to join the abolition movement and later spoke out only for gradual emancipation. The "taint" of slavery appeared "ineradicable." Gladstone insisted that he "pities the North—bears with it in its trials—and unduly believes in and hopes for the success of its deadly enemies!"[46]

Argyll also criticized Gladstone's public declaration, arguing that the ministry must maintain neutrality. Cobden was correct in warning against intervention. Gladstone ignored what British labor had already realized—that the Union could retaliate by stopping its exportation of corn and flour. Had not British workers voted down every resolution for intervention? Argyll assured Russell that Gladstone's claim to the South's having "made a nation" had embarrassed the government. "Whatever you may do—He, at least, has 'recognised' the South!" Wait a while longer, Argyll pleaded. The Union would doubtless acknowledge southern independence during the quiet winter months. Recognition now would be "wholly premature." The move would be "followed up by other measures; and in this case, w[oul]d probably involve us in a war."[47]

Gladstone's speech had crystallized the interventionist issue, causing a political firestorm in which the ministry's opponents accused the chancellor of meddling in other countries' domestic affairs and risking England's involvement in the American war. If so, they cynically remarked, Palmerston had returned to his old imperial form. Both Conservatives and Liberals protested a recognition decision apparently already made in the ministry's inner chambers. Lord Derby spoke for his Conservative colleagues in calling for private relief to workers rather than trying to acquire cotton by interfering in the conflict. Did not Gladstone's pronouncements signal imminent recognition of the Confederacy? He "must be considered as speaking in the name of his colleagues and it will be awkward if they don't agree with him, and even if they do I think it is a strong measure to say what he did." From the Liberals came concurrence from Clarendon, who denounced Gladstone's provocative stance. The American combatants, Clarendon reminded Palmerston, "had not yet marked out the stipulations of a Treaty of Peace." And even if the intervening powers had devised peace terms, the proposal would alienate the Union and give it further reason to continue the war.[48]

Gladstone denied supporting the Confederacy and insisted that he remained neutral. Both publicly and privately, he argued that his sole intention at Newcastle had been to clarify the Confederacy's establishment of independence and thus encourage other nations to help end the war. He conceded that he had committed a political blunder in making statements that were open to wildly distorted interpretations by the press and the public. To Russell, Gladstone emphasized that he had not meant to send a message that recognition was nigh. Yet the damage had been done. The *Times, Saturday Review,* and *Illustrated London News* perhaps reflected the views of many British contemporaries in opposing an intervention that Gladstone wanted and insisting that the battlefield determine the victor. But in Liverpool, as Gladstone noted, southern sympathizers had already established an organization to promote the Confederate cause.[49]

Ever the pragmatic politician, Palmerston bounced from one side to the other, searching for a safe middle position. He initially told Russell that Gladstone was "not far wrong in pronouncing by anticipation the National independence of the South." But the rising tumult soon caused him to modify his stance. Gladstone should have "steer[ed] clear of the Future unless authorized by his colleagues to become . . . the organ of the Govt. for announcing Decisions come to upon suitable Deliberation." Palmerston later distanced himself even further from the episode by asserting that "Gladstone ought not to have launched into Confederate acknowledgement."[50]

Gladstone could not have been oblivious to the political risks he had taken in publicly anointing the Confederacy as a nation. He was a leading and highly visible cabinet member. A discerning observer would have noted that his views toward American events had remained constant. At the outset of the Civil War, he had pronounced southern separation a fait accompli. He had expressed the same sentiment before a huge gathering at Manchester the previous April and repeated it in a private letter less than a month before his Newcastle appearance. To his correspondent, Gladstone wrote: "It has long been (I think) clear that Secession is virtually an established fact and that Jeff. Davis and his comrades have made a nation." He had repeatedly stated that hesitation was a mistake. As the war intensified by the autumn of 1862, Gladstone became convinced that intervention was imperative to bring the war to a close. Not only had the fighting at Antietam reached a new level of atrocity, but, in an argument consonant with Russell's, its continuation would threaten the British economy by cutting off any chance of replenishing a nearly depleted cotton supply. Gladstone had hoped his Newcastle speech would increase public pressure on the government to intervene. But he had misread the expected reaction, both by the public and by his government colleagues.[51]

In the Foreign Office, Hammond opposed Gladstone's argument but thought it had the saving grace of forcing a careful consideration of the dangers in recognition. To Layard, Hammond wrote: "You will be amused by Gladstone's attempts to write himself out of the scrape which his tongue brought him into." The permanent undersecretary supported the Confederacy but felt nothing good could come from recognition. Confederate forces, he argued, had fought well at Antietam, but Lee's departure from the field had provided the Union with a pretext for claiming victory. Lincoln's decision for emancipation was "a great mistake," for it would alienate the Border States, divide northerners while motivating southerners, and culminate in a race war. The British must give the Confederacy time to convince the Union that it could not win.[52]

Russell found himself in an awkward position. He agreed with Gladstone that intervention was necessary for humanitarian and economic reasons, yet he thought foreign policy should result from decisions made in the quiet confines of the Foreign Office—not from the tumult in the streets. Recognition should *follow* mediation, not preempt it. Gladstone's tactics had encouraged irrational thinking that pushed the ministry into a direction it was not yet ready to take. Russell chastised the chancellor for going "beyond the latitude which all speakers must be allowed." His statements had led the public to believe that the ministry was ready to recognize the Confederacy. "Negotiations would seem to follow, and for that step I think the Cabinet is not prepared."[53]

Gladstone's public indiscretion had left Russell with the difficult task of convincing Adams that his government had not made a decision to intervene. The Union minister had already mentioned his concern in his diary: "If Gladstone be any exponent at all of the views of the cabinet, then is my term likely to be very short." Moran expressed the sentiments of those in the American legation who asserted that Gladstone's words had confirmed their long-held beliefs that Palmerston's ministry favored the Confederacy. The Newcastle speech, Moran believed, marked the prelude to recognition. Russell tried to ease Adams's fears by assuring him that Palmerston and others in his government "regretted the speech" and that Gladstone "was not disinclined to correct, so far as he could, the misinterpretation which had been made of it." Britain's policy had not changed, Russell assured Adams; indeed, the ministry had no changes in mind. Would the British government maintain neutrality? Yes, Russell replied.[54]

Russell had not been honest with Adams, for the battle at Antietam had led the Palmerston ministry to consider several policy changes, all pointing to intervention. The prime minister preferred an armistice followed by negotiations; Russell dropped his call for a mediation tied to recognition but held fast to his belief in intervention as a defensible part of neutrality when the war threatened British interests. Palmerston wanted an Anglo-French appeal to the American antagonists to find some basis for agreement. But this approach could work only after Union and Confederate forces had reached a stalemate on the battlefield. If either side held a military advantage at the time of a proposed armistice, the intervening nation (or nations) had no chance for success. He admitted that both belligerents might exploit a cease-fire to reload their arsenals for resumed fighting in the spring. An "armistice without some agreement as to a Basis of negotiations, and that Basis can be none other than separation, would only be like breathing Time allowed to Boxers between Rounds of a Fight, to enable them to get fresh wind." The Union would reject a separation unless its armies underwent "a good deal more pummeling by the South." Palmerston wanted the cabinet to discuss the feasibility of an armistice proposal. The next ten days were crucial to a program for peace.[55]

The uproar over Gladstone's speech had caused Russell to shift his support from mediation to an armistice offer, although he first wanted to ease northern suspicions of British motives by securing French and Russian cooperation. He shared Palmerston's concern that both Union and Confederacy might take advantage of a cease-fire to prepare for renewed fighting. But Russell also realized the importance of making the first move toward peace. He told Cowley in Paris that the initial overture to the Union should come from the French; it must be of "the most confidential kind, and yet certain and official enough to enable me to lay something tangible before the Cab[ine]t." Through it all, he emphasized again in a telling demonstration of his naïveté, the British must "remain neutral, even were we to recognize the South and acknowledge that Jeff. Davis has made a 'Nation.'"[56]

Russell prepared for the cabinet meeting, scheduled for October 23, by sending a memorandum to his colleagues urging support for an armistice. If the war did not end soon, Lincoln's emancipation decree would incite his armies to commit "acts of plunder, of incendiarism, and of revenge" that would destroy the South. The continental powers must stop the conflict before Lincoln excited "the passions of the slave to aid the destructive progress of armies." Europe must "ask both parties, in the most friendly and conciliatory terms, to agree to a suspension of arms for the purpose of weighing calmly the advantages of peace against the contingent gain of further bloodshed and the protraction of so calamitous a war."[57]

Argyll supported Russell's efforts for peace but cautioned against any action beyond recommending an armistice. England should work with the European powers in a "friendly and conciliatory spirit" to secure a cease-fire and peace talks. But it must not pursue any further act leading to "direct interference." Such a step would involve the ministry in the dangerous issue of slavery. The Lincoln administration, he reminded Russell, called for

George Cornewall Lewis, British secretary for war (Gilbert F. Lewis, ed., *Letters of the Right Hon. Sir George Cornewall Lewis* [London: Longmans, Green, 1870], frontispiece)

emancipation on a limited basis—*not* abolition throughout the South. "I have always looked to the irresistible tendency of events, rather than to the *intentions* of the North, for the AntiSlavery effects of the War." Trouble would come from any proposal other than one for an armistice.[58]

Lewis strongly opposed Russell's position. *Any* form of intervention, warned the secretary for war, would be a monumental mistake. Lewis commanded respect because of his quiet, unassuming manner and impressive intellect. A respected philosopher and scholar who had authored numerous works, he was a man of principle, measured in temperament, and extremely cautious about getting involved in other countries' affairs. Military force, he had believed from the outset, could not preserve the Union. "You may conquer an insurgent province," Lewis had written a friend, "but you cannot conquer a seceding State." To another correspondent, he had predicted that secession would lead to "arbitration of the sword." The Union would resort to force "to gratify passion or pride," whereas the Confederacy would fight for independence as the essence of survival. England must not intervene.[59]

In a speech and in a memo to the cabinet, Lewis expanded on his argument against intervention. Within a week of Russell's proposal, the secretary for war told a large gathering at Hereford that the Confederacy had *not* justified its claim to independence. Clarendon (Lewis's brother-in-law) and Derby agreed. British recognition, Derby warned, would constitute a challenge to the blockade and hence a hostile act against the Union. Neither antagonist considered a reconciliation possible and had therefore rejected mediation. An armistice proposal, too, would not work; despite its altruistic purpose, the measure still amounted to an intervention that the Union opposed at the risk of fighting the intervening nations. Lewis realized that Clarendon had shared Derby's thoughts with Palmerston and added support to their argument by warning that a suggested cease-fire would come under consideration not by a "conclave of philosophers" but by "heated and violent partisans" in both Union and Confederacy who had no interest in compromise. Whether a mediation or an armistice proposal, Lewis argued, the step implied the existence of a southern entity that the Union would reject. Even a temporary cease-fire would not have equal impact on the two sides. An armistice would be acceptable only when both antagonists wanted to stop fighting. But the Union sought restoration, and the Confederacy demanded independence. No common ground existed between them, making compromise impossible.[60]

If ever intervention were to be acceptable, Lewis insisted, that time had not yet come. Russell, Lewis continued, was correct in asserting that Lincoln *wanted* emancipation to incite slave rebellions in the South. But that was no reason to intervene; rather, that danger supported the argument for staying out of American affairs. The fighting had reached such a "moment of peculiar bitterness and exasperation" that the Union would oppose an offer of armistice as a virtual recognition of southern independence. Union resentment might lead to war against England, leaving Canada particularly vulnerable to attack as winter weather made reinforcements difficult. The November congressional elections, Lewis said, should indicate whether there was enough support in the Union for a peace based on southern independence.[61]

In the meantime, Lewis contended, the war—not England—must define the terms for peace. Either mediation or an armistice offer necessitated a peace plan that resolved the major issues between Union and Confederacy. What slavery settlement would satisfy both sides? What boundaries were mutually acceptable? Would the Border States and territories be slave or free? "The sword has not yet traced the conditions of a treaty recognizing the independence of the South." In "looking to the probable consequences of this philanthropic proposition, we may doubt whether the chances of evil do not preponderate over the chances of good, and whether it is not—

> 'Better to endure the ills we have,
> Than fly to others which we know not of.'"[62]

Russell reluctantly but only temporarily shelved his call for intervention. He had insufficient cabinet support for an armistice proposal; he also was aware that a ministerial crisis had brought the French government to a standstill. Napoleon's sudden silence on intervention had concerned Russell, but more important were the recent dismissals of Foreign Minister Thouvenel and his ambassador to London, Count Flahault. Dayton thought Napoleon's differences with Thouvenel on the Italian question had been the decisive factor, noting that observation expressed in the semiofficial journal, *La France*. "The moral of the late events at Paris," Russell wrote Cowley, "is that it is dangerous to trust a man [Napoleon] whose counsels are so very secret, whose professions are so little to be trusted, and whose actions are so little to be foreseen." Russell lamented the departure of Thouvenel—"a true European statesman"—even though his successor in the Foreign Office, Edouard Drouyn de Lhuys, was an "old friend" who would surely support continued Anglo-French cooperation. But now was not the time to intervene, Russell conceded. He wrote Stuart that the cabinet would meet in the next few days and that Lyons would return to his Washington post on October 25. "But I do not expect to have any decisive instructions to give him." Russell then notified Palmerston of the need to delay action. The St. Petersburg government had not yet expressed its feelings on the matter, and "we ought not to move *at present* without Russia."[63]

Palmerston needed little persuasion to agree that immediate action was premature and that the war itself must convince the two belligerents to accept a cease-fire. Lewis's memo and the growing public opposition to Gladstone's Newcastle speech had confirmed the wisdom of returning to a wait-and-see posture. Each belligerent thought it was winning the war, and Palmerston could not come up with satisfactory terms for resolving the slavery issue. Could his ministry, he asked Russell, "without offence to many People here[,] recommend to the North to sanction Slavery and to undertake to give back Runaways, and yet would not the South insist upon some such Conditions[,] especially after Lincoln's Emancipation Decree[?]" And practically speaking, Palmerston added, a delay was advisable in light of winter's approach and the uncertain American political and military situation. Any form of intervention must come with terms suitable for negotiation. An armistice was unworkable as long as one side had the advantage in the war. England's only recourse was to urge the antagonists to make "an arrangement between themselves." Yet a reconciliation was highly unlikely, he admitted, for the Union insisted on reunion and the Confederacy on independence. "I am therefore inclined to change the opinion on which I wrote to you when the Confederates seemed to be carrying all before them, and I am very much come back to our original view of the matter." We must remain "lookers on till the war shall have taken a more decided turn."[64]

Russell had no choice but to postpone the October 23 cabinet meeting. Some members did not receive the message in time to cancel their trip into London, but so strongly did they oppose the armistice proposal that they met informally with the foreign secretary to tell him so. With Palmerston lodged at his Broadlands retreat in the south of England, Lewis took the lead in assuring Grey, Newcastle, and others that intervention was wrong. They had thoroughly discredited the idea, or so Lewis thought afterward. He felt "greatly relieved" by Russell's "voluntary abandonment of the scheme of interfering in the American quarrel, which could only have led to mischief." On the same afternoon, Russell assured Adams that neutrality remained the British government's policy.[65]

Clarendon praised Lewis's memo, rejoicing that it had put Russell's interventionist plan to rest. "Johnny [Russell] always loves to do something when to do nothing is prudent, and I have no doubt that he hoped to get support in his meddling proclivities when he called a Cabinet for yesterday." But Lewis had exposed the "idiotic position" Russell had taken, "either in having presented our face gratuitously to the Yankee slap we should receive, or in being asked what practical solution we had to propose after an armistice had been agreed to at our suggestion." The ministry had no peace terms to recommend, forcing Russell "to draw in his horns."[66]

But Russell realized that the prime minister's absence from this rump meeting of cabinet members made their sentiments unofficial and did not give up on his plan for intervention. On the same day Clarendon celebrated the so-called defeat of intervention, Russell underlined his unbroken support for taking the lead in ending the war. "As no good could come of a Cabinet," he later explained to Palmerston, "I put it off." He agreed with Palmerston's restraint "for the present," but he blasted Lewis for having "made a proposition for me which I never thought of making." He had *not* proposed that the ministry work with France and Russia in urging the Americans to accept a cease-fire. Although technically true that Russell had made no formal proposal, to Cowley he had expressed his preference for an Anglo-French-Russian intervention based on an armistice and follow-up negotiations. But he had changed his approach. "Less than the whole five [England, France, Russia, Austria, and Prussia] would not do." A five-power call for an armistice offered the only feasible solution.[67]

Russell had still not grasped the Union's visceral opposition to *any* form of outside involvement as a violation of its sovereignty. An armistice, he now argued with Palmerston, had the best chance for acceptance because it offered the least intrusive form of involvement. Surely the Lincoln administration would soon recognize the futility of its efforts. A mediation, Russell now admitted, was more provocative because it implied ultimate recognition. Had he not regarded the two measures as inseparable? An armistice procedure carried no such connotation. Yet he had earlier proposed an armistice followed by a negotiated peace premised on southern separation. The truth was that no matter how Russell packaged the interventionist proposal, it constituted a major step toward southern recognition. Regardless of his argument, the Lincoln administration *would* question the innocence of a proposed cease-fire followed by peace talks.

Russell continued to ignore reality. A cease-fire proposal implied the existence of a belligerent entity, as did the suggestion of negotiations. Unlike Palmerston, the foreign secretary did not understand that the success of an armistice rested on *both* sides' realization that the war had stalemated and that only the certainty of mutual destruction could lead them to the peace table. Seward, of course, remained confident that the Union would prevail and that it must crush the Confederacy—not out of a brutal hatred but because this was the only way to convince it to lay down its arms. The insurrectionists, he argued, "prefer a common ruin, a complete chaos, to any composition whatever that could be made under any auspices." It was a "conflict between universal freedom and universal slavery" that had led to civil war. Mediation or compromise had never resolved a conflict that had developed into a "trial of arms." Never had such a struggle "ended except by exhaustion of one or both of the parties." Surely it was obvious that exhaustion would hit the Confederacy first. "The Union is distracted, but it is not broken nor even shaken."[68] As long as one of the warring parties believed victory a possibility, both a cease-fire and negotiations were out of the question. In this case, however, *both* sides expected to win.

Russell nonetheless pushed forward, convinced that the war's intensification made British involvement a selfless, humanitarian act. A British agent in America had recently highlighted the lack of support for the president's policy of emancipation. Those Americans interested in destroying the Confederacy welcomed the measure; others denounced abolition and expressed no concern about freed blacks. No one favored their migration into the free states. The Union sought to subjugate the Confederacy; the Confederacy promised resistance to the end. Only outside intervention, Russell insisted, could bring this conflict to a close.[69]

Russell still had Gladstone's support. The chancellor had been upset with the decision to postpone the cabinet meeting and circulated among his colleagues his own memo entitled "The War in America." England's choice, he argued, was either to sit by while Union and Confederacy destroyed each other or to engage in an "interference limited to moral means" that aimed to stop the war by employing its good offices in suggesting mediation, an armistice, or recognition. England as a civilized state had the responsibility to intervene. Antietam had unveiled new terrors in the war, making it incumbent on "the civilized world" to put pressure on Union and Confederate leaders to reach a peace. Russia provided "the one vital element" to success—its friendship with the Union. "Again, if we desire the war to continue, either with a view to the possible success of the North, or to the extinction of slavery through a servile war or otherwise, or on any other ground, then of course all room for argument is gone. But I assume that we wish the war to end, and that we see no early probability of its ending if left to itself." The Union could not reject a proposal based on "the common interests of humanity." The nations of "civilized Europe" must stop "this horrible war."[70]

Lewis's memo, Russell wrote in a rebuttal for the Foreign Office file, had distorted his argument. The foreign secretary denied having made an interventionist proposal and insisted that he would not do so without cabinet concurrence. Nor had he ever advocated unilateral action. At one point he had asserted, "It has now become a question for the *Great Powers of Europe*." Later, he had said, "It has become a question, in the sight of these afflictions, and the prospect of more and worse, whether it is not a duty *for Europe*." He had earlier called for a tripartite intervention comprised of England, France, and Russia, but now he expanded the list to include Austria and Prussia. "In this shape, I think, the recommendation would be accepted." Russia's participation in an armistice proposal, he knew, was critical. And perhaps he calculated that the longer list of four would convince the Russians to join. Now was the time to initiate the process. Negotiations following a cease-fire would extend into the winter months, providing time for reflection by both belligerents. "It can hardly be said that either side will be a loser by an armistice." He would present his case before the cabinet at a later time.[71]

A delayed cabinet meeting seemed wise, Palmerston wrote Russell, for it would give more time for the Union to reconsider its position. He rejected "Lewis's Doctrine" of opposing recognition until the Union accepted southern independence. This idea was neither "sound in Theory, [nor] consistent with historical events." At some point, Palmerston appeared to believe, the two sides would recognize the reality of a lethal stalemate that could lead only to mutual devastation. That time had not yet come. Lincoln's emancipation pronouncement and the highly anticipated November elections had escalated the bitterness to such a level in both warring camps that any proposed peace talks "would be as useless as asking the winds during the last week to let the waters remain calm." Palmerston concluded that "the Pugilists must fight a few more Rounds before the Bystanders can decide that the State Should be divided between them."[72]

Russell discarded Lewis's argument and moved forward with intervention. Lewis admitted to having made a mistake in claiming that Russell had presented a formal proposal for intervention but repeated his warning against an involvement even if the five European powers participated. The secretary for war doubted that Russia, Austria, and Prussia would join England and France, and even if they did, the combined interference in American affairs would necessitate "some element of dictation, either in form or substance." If they cooperated "cordially in the event of hostilities becoming necessary, the intervention would doubtless be effectual." The cost, however, could be horrendous. "*Some* separation is inevitable," but the chances were that "the disintegration will go still further." France favored recognition, Russell responded. Russia had not yet taken a position. He did not prefer the use of force, but if the Union rejected an intercession, the powers were within the boundaries of international law in extending recognition to the Confederacy. The "most suitable" time to act was in the spring—with Parliament in session and the warring parties contemplating another horrifying military season.[73]

Russell likewise refused to consider Grey's call for steering clear of the war. An armistice proposal, the home secretary asserted, was dangerous because it was "not a separate form of proceeding, as it could only be proposed with a view to mediation." Russell had contradicted his earlier stance, now reasoning that an armistice proposal implied nothing more than a cease-fire and was therefore less challenging than a mediation pointing to recognition; Grey had taken the hard, realistic position, showing the inseparability of all three measures by warning that an armistice necessarily led to a mediation that, by implication, preceded recognition. War could develop with the

Union. Both Russell and Grey were doubtless unaware that they had confirmed the correctness of Seward's long-standing complaint that *any* form of intervention was injurious to the Union and therefore conducive to an Anglo-American conflict.[74]

Russell relentlessly pushed for action on the basis of an argument riddled with holes. Lewis, the foreign secretary hotly declared, "sprang a mine upon me, but I cannot agree with any part of what he said. No country has ever waited to make peace till it was unable to carry on war." If the British and French invited Russia to participate in an armistice offer, Russell remarked, its emperor "would not like to say that he preferred war and desolation." Russian involvement would guarantee the proposal's success. The chances for peace were admittedly slim, but the European powers owed it to civilization to make the effort. "If a friend were to cut his throat, you would hardly like to confess, he told me he was going to do it, but I said nothing as I thought he would not take my advice.'"[75]

The battle of Antietam had encouraged Gladstone to deliver his Newcastle speech, which had inadvertently mobilized the forces on both sides of the interventionist issue and thereby drawn attention to its perils. Russell had to convince his colleagues that the Great Powers could achieve the virtually impossible: Sponsor an armistice without getting involved in the war, devise peace terms acceptable to both sides, and secure Russian participation. But Gladstone's proclamations had encouraged the ministry to examine every aspect of intervention, particularly whether it could find a solution that did not force the British themselves into the conflict.

Gladstone's address had combined with Lewis's memo to undermine what Granville had earlier perceived as widespread cabinet support for mediation. The Union's narrow victory at Antietam and the succeeding Emancipation Proclamation had heightened the pressure for European intervention. The war had intensified, threatening the dictates of humanity along with the British and French economies. Yet once the risks of an interventionist enterprise became clear, Palmerston and others had become more cautious. The prime minister had agreed with Russell and Gladstone after Second Bull Run that the time had come for mediation. But events afterward had slowed this fervor, ultimately revealing the pitfalls in this seemingly innocuous effort and shifting his interest to an armistice proposal.

Palmerston raised a host of legitimate concerns. France, as always, was mercurial and seldom trustworthy. Russian cooperation remained uncertain though highly doubtful. Peace terms were elusive. An armistice did not guarantee an end to the fighting; indeed, the downtime afforded by a cease-fire might permit both sides to gear up for renewed hostilities on a grander scale. Palmerston joined Lewis in fearing that intervention could cause a third Anglo-American war. The prime minister conceded one point to Russell: "I believe you are right in fixing next Spring for the period for the acknowledgement of the Confederate States." But then he quickly backtracked into a familiar position: Confederate "independence can be converted into an Established Fact by the Course of Events alone."[76]

From information before the U.S. State Department, Seward noted that England and France were "seriously considering" recognition of the insurgents as "a sovereign State." The president and others were surprised, given the failure of the Confederacy's broadly advertised military campaign throughout Europe to invade the loyal Border States of Maryland, Kentucky, and Missouri and threaten Philadelphia and New York, while capturing Baltimore and New Orleans and forcing Washington to surrender. Yet the southern armies were in retreat. Furthermore, the president had proclaimed slaves in states still in rebellion to be free after January 1, 1863. "Are the enlightened and humane nations Great Britain and France to throw their protection over the insurgents now?" Are they willing to enter this conflict that had become "a war between freedom and bondage?" Recognition would fail without intervention, and intervention could succeed only with the help of "permanent and persisting armies," all the while committed to maintaining slavery in an area where it no longer existed. Russell was correct in saying they were fighting for empire. "But the empire is not only our own already, but it was lawfully acquired, and is lawfully held."[77]

Europeans had still not grasped the possibility that the Union would subdue the Confederacy—that prolongation of the war was senseless and atrocious and that the outcome had been clear from the first threat of fighting. Thouvenel had thought British recognition of the Confederacy imminent, because the government was under the pressure of the press and widespread economic troubles. "As we speak unofficially (you know my sympathies)," Thouvenel told Dayton, "I must say, I no longer believe you can conquer the South; and, further, I am confident that at this time there is not a reasonable statesman in Europe who believes you can succeed in carrying out your first conception" of preserving the Union. Dayton reminded Seward that both Thouvenel and the emperor had shared this belief, but that it had now grown into "a matured conviction." Thouvenel admitted that he had no official knowledge of an imminent British move for recognition. Dayton warned

Seward, however, that if England took the initiative, "France would probably follow."[78]

If Lincoln's Proclamation had not worked exactly the way he intended, it had forced the issue of intervention in England and led to a more cautious approach. Furthermore, his move toward emancipation had come as a result of Antietam and had great potential for ultimately reshaping the direction of the war into a crusade against slavery—an objective that Argyll, Bright, and Cobden had earlier insisted would happen.

CHAPTER 8

Union-Confederate Crisis over Intervention

[Union refusal of an armistice would provide] good reason
for recognition and perhaps for more active intervention.
—NAPOLEON III, October 28, 1862

Can nothing be done to stop this dreadful war?
—ALEXANDER GORCHAKOV, October 29, 1862

Was there ever any war so horrible?
—LORD JOHN RUSSELL, November 1, 1862

This destructive and hopeless war [has to end].
—WILLIAM E. GLADSTONE, November 27, 1862

If there is a worse place than Hell, I am in it.
—ABRAHAM LINCOLN, December 16, 1862

European interest in intervention remained very much alive by the autumn of
1862. From their vantage point thousands of miles away, the British, French,
Russians, Belgians, and others on the Continent had become increasingly
concerned about the American struggle, hoping to see an end to the fighting
before it endangered onlooking nations and required direct intervention. The
American battlefield, it seemed clear after Antietam, would not determine a
winner; rather, it promised endless carnage as both antagonists stubbornly
fought on, each side resolved to grind out an ultimate victory that rested on
virtual annihilation of the other's forces. The dictates of civilization and the
principles of international law condoned an intervention when an ongoing
war threatened the belligerents' neighbors. But the Union viscerally rejected

any form of outside involvement as a challenge to its integrity and pledged war on the intruders. Furthermore, to step in at this point in the stalemated fighting would be tantamount to extending recognition to the Confederacy, allying with a slaveholding people, and deciding the war's outcome. The entire matter was ridden with complexities that baffled the strategists and political leaders, along with the learned philosophers and scholars, the hard-line veteran warriors, the commercial magnates, the concerned civilians, and the workforce now beginning to suffer on a broad scale in the Old World's manufacturing districts.

Russell's waning hopes for intervention jumped dramatically in late October 1862, when Napoleon III took the lead in proposing a joint mediation based on an armistice. This was not his first attempt to sell this idea; he had suggested it to Slidell a few months earlier and had received a favorable reception. The emperor's ongoing problems with Italy had eased, allowing him to focus on domestic economic issues and to assuage a swelling national sentiment for southerners as victims of northern aggression. Russell welcomed the offer, although fully aware of the risks attached to working with the imperious leader.[1]

Further encouragement came from Washington, where Stuart reported both Russian and French interest. Stoeckl had conceded that intervention might become "useful" if the Peace Democrats won the congressional elections in November. Mercier felt optimistic about securing a peace after talking with leaders of both political parties in New York. Democrats in the state favored a mediation that did not stipulate a gradual end to slavery. Stuart thought Mercier "rather too anxious to precipitate matters" but held high hopes for Democrat Horatio Seymour in New York's gubernatorial contest, confident that such a high-profile victory would intensify the movement toward mediation. A special emissary from Europe should come to America to extend recognition as the way to end the war. "If independence has ever been nobly fought for and deserved," Stuart sighed, "it has been so in the case of the Confederacy." Mercier concurred but expressed concern about anti-British sentiment in the United States. Stoeckl, the French minister warned, might suggest a Franco-Russian mediation that ostensibly aimed to relieve this ill feeling but also drove a wedge between England and France. For that reason, Mercier insisted that all three powers make the proposal.[2]

Stuart had inaccurately gauged the Russian position. In late October 1862, Bayard Taylor, famous traveler and lecturer and secretary to Union minister

Simon Cameron in St. Petersburg, met with Gorchakov and found him anxious to see the war end. The Russian foreign minister assured his country's friendship but thought "the chances of preserving the Union were growing more and more desperate." He then asked in exasperation, "Can nothing be done to stop this dreadful war?" The Union had "few friends among the Powers. England rejoices over what is happening to you: she longs and prays for your overthrow." France "is not your friend. Russia, alone, has stood by you from the first, and will continue to stand by you." The other powers will propose intervention, but "we believe that intervention could do no good at present. *Proposals will be made to Russia, to join in some plan of interference. She will refuse any invitation of the kind.* Russia will occupy the same ground, as at the beginning of the struggle. *You may rely upon it, she will not change.* But we entreat you to settle the difficulty. I cannot express to you how profound an anxiety we feel—how serious are our fears." Gorchakov emphasized that Russia would participate in the peace process only after *both* Union and Confederacy agreed to negotiate.[3]

Thus the republic remained in peril—from the outside as well as from within because now, with the slavery issue on the way to resolution, the French interventionists could act for economic and imperial reasons without alienating anyone over moral questions. Nonetheless, the new French foreign minister, Edouard Drouyn de Lhuys, assured Dayton that "France had no intention of intruding into American affairs," either alone or with another nation. The emperor sought only to convey "the expression of a wish to be useful if it could be done with the assent of both parties." His chief concern was the growing slaughter of the war. If Drouyn told the truth, and Dayton believed in the sincerity of his assurances, there remained Napoleon's mercurial behavior. Nothing was certain without his specific approval, and that appears "to have no fixed purpose but grows out of circumstances."[4] No matter how fervently denied, the strongest proponent of intervention in the fall of 1862 was France—or, more specifically, Napoleon. For the first time in the American war, he could support the Confederacy without fearing domestic repercussions over slavery.

Ironically, the prospect of French intervention endangered *both* the Union and the Confederacy, rising and falling in intensity throughout this tumultuous period in proportion to Napoleon's imperial designs and the capacity of his advisers to restrain him. The emperor considered recognition of the Confederacy as not only a means for securing cotton but also for satisfying his expansionist aims in Mexico. The Union minister to Belgium, Henry Sanford, repeatedly warned Seward of Napoleon's expansionist intentions in the Americas. Nor did Confederates lose sight of the reality that Napoleon would support them only if the act promoted his objectives. Mann in Belgium cautioned Secretary Benjamin about Napoleon's treachery: "I shall be agreeably disappointed if we do not in after years find France a more disagreeable neighbor on our southern border than the United States." Benjamin was aware of its interest in Texas; French consular officials in Texas and Virginia had bluntly asked about reacquiring territories that Mexico had lost in its recent war with the United States. Indeed, the inquiries were not spontaneous because both consuls had used the same words in questioning the wisdom of Texas's staying in the Confederacy.[5]

Mercier's recommendation for immediate action led Napoleon to notify the Palmerston ministry of his interest in a tripartite intervention aimed at bringing the war to a close. Despite his rebuff by Russia just months earlier, the emperor led the British to think that the collaboration of a third party remained a distinct possibility. He met with Lord Cowley on October 27 to suggest an Anglo-French-Russian mediation offer that included an armistice and a suspension of the Union blockade, both for six months. This two-pronged approach, he told the British ambassador in Paris, would "give time for the present excitement to calm down" and for peace talks to begin. Russian participation was imperative. Drouyn later assured Cowley that the emperor's only objective was to end the war. Drouyn preferred waiting a while, thinking the Confederacy would amass more victories in the field. If the Union rejected the proposal, he warned, Russia would probably refuse to join England and France in extending recognition to the Confederacy. Napoleon, however, preferred to act now—but for reasons not confided to his advisers.[6]

The following day, October 28, Napoleon met with Slidell and revealed more ambitious intentions than those shared with Cowley. Less than three months earlier, he had declined a meeting with Slidell, largely because of his preoccupation with European affairs and his desire for the British to take the lead in any interventionist move. What had changed? On the surface, the emperor had become impatient with British hesitation and therefore pushed for Russian involvement. Furthermore, Italy was less on his mind, giving him more time to work with other nations in resolving the American question. But he had also seen an opportunity to acquire territory in North America—even if at southern expense. Although expressing support for the Confederacy, he noted his perplexity in demonstrating how to make his feelings known. Slidell believed that Napoleon did not wish to act alone. England, the emperor doubtless feared, would not join him in a mediation, wanting instead to "embroil with the United States" and thereby hurt French commerce. Russia was the key. "What do you think," asked Napoleon, "of the joint mediation of France, England, and Russia? Would it, if proposed, be accepted by the two parties?"[7]

At first the emperor's proposal did not strike Slidell as any more hopeful than his previous ideas. Had they not discussed an Anglo-French undertaking the previous summer, raising Confederate hopes only again to see them dashed? The Union, he thought, would approve if Russia were involved, although he was uncertain of his own government's reaction. Russia would probably support the Union, but England's participation remained doubtful. Just that day Slidell had learned from a reliable source close to Palmerston that most members of his ministry opposed recognition at this time and that, despite Gladstone's public declarations about Confederate nationhood, nothing had changed. The Confederacy, Slidell stressed to Napoleon, could not favor a three-power mediation. In such an arrangement, "France could be outvoted." Slidell had an alternative suggestion. A joint Anglo-French mediation might be acceptable if accompanied by "certain assurances" to the Confederacy—namely, recognition. Indeed, southerners welcomed his "umpirage."[8]

Understanding the importance of winning Confederate support, Napoleon sweetened the offer. "My own preference," he asserted, "is for a proposition of an armistice of six months, with the Southern ports open to the commerce of the world. This would put a stop to the effusion of blood, and hostilities would probably never be resumed. We can urge it on the high grounds of humanity and the interests of the whole civilized world." But Slidell knew that the assurance of reopened trade to France did not go far enough; he had gotten nowhere on bringing this identical proposal to Thouvenel nearly nine months earlier. At this point, however, Thouvenel was no longer in office, and the emperor added a provision having profound ramifications. Union refusal of an armistice, he said, would provide "good reason for recognition and perhaps for *more active intervention* [emphasis added]."[9]

Napoleon's allusion to force was unmistakable. Slidell could barely contain himself as he pushed the emperor to guarantee action. "Such a course," the Confederate minister responded, "would be judicious and acceptable." But, he warned, Palmerston would probably reject any plan pointing to recognition. Neither Slidell nor the emperor, of course, could have known how close this proposal approached present thinking within London's leadership. They were unaware of the pressure growing for a mediation that everyone knew would lead to recognition. Nor could they have known that Russell, too, had intimated a resort to strong measures if either American belligerent refused mediation. Perhaps also unknown to Slidell, Napoleon was not concerned about whether England would oppose an intervention pointing to recognition, for he had not told Cowley of any further recourse if the Union rejected an armistice offer.[10]

Napoleon nevertheless hoped for British participation, even if the intervention entailed the possibility of military action. As a further assurance, he told Slidell of a letter in his possession from King Leopold of Belgium dated October 15 and written while Queen Victoria (his niece) was in Brussels, which contained a recommendation that one could interpret as an approval of force. The king first appealed to humanity in urging France, England, and Russia to end the war as a means for securing cotton for depressed mill workers across the Continent. The Union should concede southern independence, making it incumbent on the European powers to extend recognition. If the Union refused to do so, Leopold said that the intervening powers should adopt "any other course" necessary to end the war. Slidell was elated. "It is universally believed," he wrote Benjamin, that "King Leopold's counsels have more influence with Queen Victoria than those of any other living man."[11]

To determine the emperor's sincerity, Slidell asserted that Cowley and others in British governing circles claimed that the French had not expressed interest in intervention. Indeed, Slidell had recently informed Benjamin of Cowley's claim that his government had received no official notification of the French emperor's views on recognition, despite his oft-expressed sympathy for the Confederacy. Thouvenel had been surprised by Cowley's assertion, insisting that the French had consistently made clear that leadership must come from England and that his government's sole intention was to secure an armistice as the initial step toward peace. Slidell suspected that either the London government did not keep Cowley informed or he had purposely twisted the situation.[12]

The emperor smiled at Cowley's contention, remarking how the canons of diplomacy dictated that nothing existed unless it appeared in a formal note. Thouvenel, Napoleon stated, had doubtless spoken with Cowley about the matter and perhaps had not pressed it far enough. This response satisfied Slidell, who had long suspected that the former foreign minister had not acted strongly on the Italian issue as well, perhaps helping to explain why the emperor had removed him from office.[13]

Napoleon offered further support for the Confederacy by proposing that its emissaries contract for the construction of a navy in France. With a minimal number of ships, the Confederacy could inflict serious damage to Union commerce, and with only three or four steamers it could open some of its ports. Slidell jumped at the opportunity. "If the Emperor would give only some kind of verbal assurance that his police would not observe too closely when we wished to put on board guns and men we would gladly avail ourselves of it."[14]

Napoleon cagily replied with a question: "Why could you not have them built as for the Italian Government? I do not think it would be difficult, but will consult the minister of marine about it." The possibility of force now combined with the emperor's invitation to deception in surreptitiously building a Confederate navy. Certainly Napoleon's suggestion of force combined with his invitation to deception could not do much more to demonstrate his support for the Confederacy. Confederate officers in Mexico had expressed concern over the presence of so many French troops and ships— that more were there than required and that Napoleon had "ulterior views." But, as earlier, Slidell dismissed the long-range costs of entering into such a pact and focused on the immediate need.[15]

Whatever thoughts Slidell tossed around in his mind, he regarded this moment as an opportunity to repeat his request for recognition. At Vichy the previous July, he reminded the emperor, he had sought a closer relationship between the Confederacy and France; now, to further entice him, Slidell asserted that his government in Richmond would not object to French reoccupation of Santo Domingo. Napoleon appeared receptive, mentioning a letter from a New Yorker attesting that many leading Democrats believed that recognition would help end the war. Slidell affirmed the writer's reliability; he had already seen the letter, which the British Parliament had sent to Lindsay and shown to Lord John Russell before sharing it with Michel Chevalier, a writer and economist who had great influence with the emperor.[16]

As if to justify his proposal for intervention, Napoleon turned his attention to the growing bloodshed in the American war. He praised Jeb Stuart's cavalry for its recent thrust into Pennsylvania and asked Slidell to trace its route on the map. As the Confederate minister enthusiastically did so, the emperor expressed amazement at Stuart's audacity along with the magnitude of Union casualties. Were the numbers exaggerated? Slidell said that the figures were much larger than released and that the Lincoln administration had intentionally kept them lower to maintain morale. "Why, this is a frightful carnage," Napoleon declared with astonishment—worse than at Magenta in the recent war with Austria. "But," Slidell commented, with a less-than-subtle nudge toward intervention, "Solferino and Magenta produced decisive results, while with us successive victories do not appear to bring us any nearer to a termination of the war." When the rivers in the West were again navigable, he added, the war's atrocities would increase. French involvement would save numerous lives and earn the world's appreciation.[17]

An hour had passed, and the emperor brought the meeting to a close. Slidell, ever watchful for favorable signs, reported that Napoleon shook his hand, a European custom that further demonstrated his warm feeling for the Confederacy.[18] But the reality ran counter to the perception. Napoleon had masterfully played to Slidell's emotions, winning his confidence and laying the basis for a Franco-Confederate friendship that, not by coincidence, promoted the emperor's Grand Design for the Americas.

Napoleon's interventionist proposal drew an exuberant reaction in the Confederate capital, tempered only by James Mason's recent reminder that any French move still depended on British participation. Slidell nonetheless remained optimistic. Sources from within the emperor's inner circle had privately assured him that the Paris government would not interfere with Confederate shipbuilding in France; they had already encouraged Bulloch in England to cross the channel and begin the process. This news did not surprise Benjamin. Before Slidell's note on the meeting arrived in Richmond, Mason had reported Napoleon's interest in an "ulterior action which would probably follow the offer of mediation." The emperor had made the identical proposal—that the British and Russians join him in offering the American antagonists a six-month armistice accompanied by a lifted blockade for the same period. Reports were that Russia had agreed to it and, if so, Mason felt certain that England would likewise concur. Benjamin was so jubilant that he entered into a long discourse with Mason on the postwar problems facing the victorious Confederacy. Suspending the blockade, the secretary asserted, would ease the most pressing economic issues. Mason, however, cautioned that Napoleon's views had "lost their value to us, as his purpose not to act independently seems unaltered." Benjamin nonetheless remained optimistic.[19]

Napoleon's proposal had raised the Confederacy's hopes while deepening its anger with England for refusing to take the initiative. Russell's support for intervention had remained within the ministry, unknown to southern leaders who continued to berate England over its rigid opposition to recognition. Before Napoleon had revealed his intentions, Benjamin complained to Mason about London's "unfriendly" treatment of the Confederacy. Russell had first ignored the Declaration of Paris in acquiescing to a paper blockade, then had committed a "rude incivility" in rejecting the minister's request for a meeting. Most exasperating, the British foreign secretary used Seward's words to warn that British intervention would cause a slave uprising. This charge was "derogatory to the government and without foundation in fact." Russell had no "well-founded reason" for refusing to grant recognition. But southerners felt confident that change was coming. They believed, however erroneously, that there was considerable popular support in England for recognition and that Russell and his colleagues would soon be out of office because they had ignored this sentiment. Benjamin instructed Mason to lodge a protest against the British refusal to challenge the blockade and thereby give Russell time to reconsider the wisdom of denying recognition. Napoleon's proposal, doubtless by design, thus widened the impasse between Richmond and London while drawing France and the Confederacy closer together.[20]

Confederate leaders were unaware of Russell's support for the French proposal. Admittedly, he was not sanguine about its success, but he considered any measure worthwhile if it offered the slightest chance of stopping the war. To Lyons, the foreign secretary bitingly remarked that Napoleon expected both American antagonists to accept his plan, "the one on the ground of Union, and the other on the ground of separation!" Nothing suggested that either side was willing to lay down its arms. But the endless nature of this atrocious war justified the effort. Even the pro-Union Cobden had bitterly declared that "to preach peace" to northerners was "like speaking to mad dogs." Most appalling, Lyons reported, was Seward's cold assertion that only the Confederacy's "extermination" would bring peace. Despite these obstacles, Russell insisted that the war's growing bloodshed necessitated any peace attempt, no matter how futile it seemed. Russell complained to Cowley that the Lincoln administration sought to "wear out the South by mutual slaughter. Was there ever any war so horrible?"[21]

Russell's desperate search for peace had led him deeper into a world of illusion. Not only did Napoleon's proposal offer scant hope for Union acceptance, but its implied resort to force escalated the potential for widening the American war to include all three prospective intervening powers along with other nations. Furthermore, a joint mediation built on an armistice confirmed the existence of two belligerents and had already proved unacceptable to the Lincoln administration. Moreover, the Union could never agree to a six-month suspension of the blockade, which guaranteed a Confederate buildup.[22] How would Napoleon react to the Union's certain rejection of his plan? Was not the use of force more than a possibility? Russell was aware of

Washington's continued adamant resistance to any form of intervention, and he had witnessed the emperor's perfidy in the recent Anglo-French-Spanish debt-collecting venture in Mexico. Had not Napoleon devised an imperialist scheme that England and Spain had felt compelled to abandon? The cabinet, Russell knew, would strenuously object to the emperor's new enterprise, regardless of its alleged humanitarian base. A peace-seeking project in the American war would facilitate the Napoleonic family's long-sought return to North America and thereby tip the world balance of power in France's favor. Yet more significant to Russell was that if a prolonged war endangered the economic stability of other countries, international law justified an intervention to stop the fighting. Russia might join that pristine effort, particularly if France were involved to ease St. Petersburg's concern over both England's acquisitive nature and the Union's distrust of the Palmerston ministry. If the powers could persuade Union and Confederacy to enter into peace talks, the pressure from Peace Democrats and other antiwar groups might mesh with the certainty of continued mutual destruction to dictate an end to the hostilities.

Thus Russell thought the French proposal worth pursuing. He admitted to Palmerston that there was "little chance of our good offices being accepted in America," but, he added, "we should make them such as would be creditable to us in Europe." Those nations joining Napoleon's plan "ought to require both parties to consent to examine, first, whether there are any terms upon which North and South would consent to restore the Union; and secondly, failing any such terms, whether there are any terms upon which both would consent to separate." Russell did not explain how the intervening powers would "require" the two sides to consider peace terms, nor did he posit any response to a rejection of terms by one or both warring parties. But a resort to force seemed likely in either case. And, of course, he could not assume Russian involvement, which both England and France considered indispensable. This was only a "rough sketch" of the project, Russell acknowledged in a clear instance of faith without works. But he intended to flesh out the details at the cabinet meeting. It would be an "honourable proposal," although he raised more doubt about its efficacy by concluding that "the North and probably the South will refuse it."[23]

Palmerston remained wary, still believing mediation a sound if premature approach. He had asked the Belgian king whether "the time had come to offer a mediation and to recognize the Southern States." To turn down

Napoleon's overture, Leopold replied, would help those in France who supported the Union as a postwar obstacle to England's imperialist ambitions. Palmerston weighed the alternatives, then directed Russell to delay any action until the cabinet discussed the "French Scheme." The prime minister did not trust Napoleon, and he doubted that the Union would accept the proposal. The Lincoln administration knew that if the Confederacy opened its cotton stores to European buyers, it would "contrive somehow or other to get the value back in muskets and warlike Stores." Furthermore, Palmerston repeated, the intervening powers had no solution to the slavery problem. The French, he cynically remarked, could pose as disinterested peacemakers because they were not bound by the "Shackles of Principle and of Right and Wrong on these Matters, as on all others than we are." The ministry must wait for the Union's congressional elections.[24]

Continued hesitation seemed wise in light of Stuart's prediction that the Peace Democrats would win in a landslide and support mediation. He and Mercier agreed that Seymour's expected victory in the New York governor's race would ensure an intervention aimed at ending the war. Stoeckl concurred, thinking "the time may be very near." One good sign, the Russian minister observed, lay in a recent conversation with Seward in which the secretary of state no longer threatened military retaliation against nations extending recognition. The time had arrived, insisted Stuart. "We might now recognize the South without much risk to ourselves."[25]

But Stuart was wrong in his assurance of an overwhelming Democratic success in the November elections. So excited was he over the early returns that he prematurely notified his home office of a major victory and proclaimed that the time had come for intervention. Elated by the news, Russell told his colleague in the cabinet, Sir George Grey, that the new Democratic leaders would doubtless block the resurgence of war in the spring. "I heartily wish them success." But later reports all but crushed Russell's hopes. The Republicans had *not* fared badly in the elections. Granted, the Democrats had gained thirty-four congressional seats and had won the gubernatorial contests in New York and New Jersey. They had also secured control of the legislatures in Illinois, Indiana, and New Jersey. But the Republicans had held on to all but two of the nineteen free state governors' houses and all but three of the same nineteen legislatures. In the Senate, the Republicans gained five seats, and in the House they maintained a twenty-five–vote lead. Furthermore, in six of the states controlled by Democrats, their lead was precariously narrow. As these truths slowly sank in, Stuart's enthusiasm for intervention slipped away—along with Russell's excitement.[26]

In truth, political chaos reigned in the Union. It was driven to a fever pitch first by Lincoln's long-anticipated decision to relieve George McClellan (a Democratic stalwart) of command of the Army of the Potomac following his refusal to pursue Lee into Virginia after the battle of Antietam, and second by the Democrats' public statements of interest in foreign mediation. Many observers regarded the president's personnel action as a victory for the war effort. Did he not seek a warrior rather than a priest? McClellan's supporters demanded revenge for what they charged was a purely political move. Lyons arrived back in Washington just as Democrats boisterously proclaimed their intention to handcuff the president and throw him in jail. Some party members advocated an armistice, followed by a special convention to change the Constitution in ways that would convince southerners "to return to the Union." Lyons, however, noted the private opinions of numerous other Democrats who sought an armistice as a "preliminary to peace—and for the sake of peace would be willing to let the Cotton States at least depart."[27]

If most Democratic Party spokesmen leaned toward southern separation, Lyons observed, they could not say so publicly. Instead, they called for a more aggressive war effort to embarrass the White House, gain a stronger position on the battlefield before accepting an armistice, and secure more territory in the event of a separation. Mediation would be acceptable to the Democrats if they could establish control over the present administration and if the offer came from "*all* the Powers of Europe"—which Lyons interpreted as "principally *Russia* in addition to England and France, and perhaps 'Prussia.'" But he was not optimistic. The Democrats were uneasy about inviting other nations to help determine American affairs, and southerners did not have a "shadow of a desire to return to the Union." For the moment, "foreign intervention, short of the use of force, could only make matters worse here."[28]

Meanwhile, Slidell had become more hopeful about France's intervention in the war. He reported that three agents from the French banking house of Émile Erlanger and Company were en route to Richmond with a loan proposal. Two days after his October 28 meeting with Napoleon, Slidell noted, Mercier received instructions to make clear to the Lincoln administration that the emperor considered southern independence a fait accompli and that continuation of the war would hurt all civilized countries. On November 2, *before* the election returns in the United States, the French government sent a circular note to all European heads of state except those in England and Russia, inviting them to appeal to both Union and Confederacy to accept an armistice accompanied by a raised Union blockade. To England and Russia went special invitations to join the proposal; Slidell believed that the emperor had earlier received Russia's concurrence. The British, Slidell thought, would join either with France and Russia or with France and other governments, but not with France alone. Spain, Belgium, Denmark, Sweden, and others would undoubtedly support the proposal. Although uncertain about Austria, he thought it would probably be more supportive than Russia. Slidell was not concerned. Even if England and Russia declined the overture, "I now believe that France will act without them."[29]

Mercier, in fact, urged his government to act alone and, ignoring Drouyn's October 30 assurance against force, to threaten military measures in attempting to persuade the Union to accept intervention. Like Stuart, Mercier had declared a Democratic victory in the congressional elections and thought the party "timid" for not seeking mediation. France must secure the Palmerston ministry's public approval of a unilateral approach that would imply Europe's acceptance of the move. The drawback of Russia's involvement, he warned, was that its friendship with the Union would remove "the element of *intimidation*, which though kept in the background, must be felt by the United States to exist." Admittedly, participation in a joint mediation effort by all the continental powers "might have the effect of reconciling the pride of the United States to negotiation with the South." But, Mercier said, the program might have a greater chance if Russia were *not* a party and the use of force remained a viable option to ending the war. The Lincoln administration would find it difficult to reject a mediation led by France alone (or with England). It knew that both nations would resort to naval power to protect their "obvious and pressing interest" in stopping the war.[30]

Lyons acknowledged that the implied use of force must lay behind any successful intervention but, contrary to Mercier, found that factor a major reason for *opposing* the move. While he was in London, several cabinet members told Lyons that they resisted interfering in the war but feared that growing popular pressure might force them to approve that step. The Democrats did not control the U.S. government, he wrote Russell, and Lincoln's recent removal of McClellan from command had forged unusual ties between moderates and radicals within the Republican Party who believed that reconciliation with the South was not possible until the Union "ruined and subjugated if not exterminated" the Confederacy. Democrats warned that Lincoln would drum up more support for the war by denouncing mediation as a violation of his nation's sovereignty—particularly if the British were involved. Recognition by itself, Lyons insisted, was of no value to the

Confederacy. "I do not clearly understand what advantage is expected to result from a simple recognition of the Southern Government." Nor could he envision the Great Powers "breaking up the blockade by force of arms, or engaging in hostilities with the United States in support of the independence of the South." They also had no terms conducive to a compromise settlement. "All hope of the re-construction of the Union appears to be fading away, even from the minds of those who most ardently desire it."[31]

Lyons argued that British involvement would undermine any mediation effort. The Americans were so suspicious of the London ministry that they would reject a proposal even if the Russians participated in its formulation. Then, "if nothing followed, we should have played out a good card without making a trick." A unilateral French intervention would have a greater chance for acceptance by the Union than one that included the British, and a multilateral intervention might work as long as the British were *not* involved. "The bitter portion of the draft which the Americans would have to swallow in a case of joint mediation would be the English portion, and the more it is diluted by the mixture of foreign elements the better." Mercier knew, as did all Europeans, that a resumption of the fighting in the spring of 1863 would further diminish the cotton crop and heavily damage the textile industries across the Continent. Intervention was necessary, he insisted, even if France acted alone and the effort benefited the Confederacy by challenging the blockade. The Union must realize that its rejection of mediation would lead to "something more in favour of the South than naked recognition." Russian participation, Lyons argued, was "essential" to winning Union compliance, but Stoeckl had already made clear that his government would not follow "in the wake of the French and English governments." Lyons conceded that Mercier was correct in believing that some intimidation was vital and that the blockade was the "critical point." The Union understood that reopening southern ports would "give up the war forever," whereas the Confederacy recognized that an armistice without a lifted blockade was meaningless. For these reasons, Lyons reasoned, if England and France threatened force and failed to follow through, they would be "crying out Wolf now, when there is no Wolf."[32]

Napoleon's proposal had introduced the reality of a wider war to the intervention controversy. Russell was not taken aback. He had earlier supported an armistice that most likely would have led to recognition and possible conflict; he now leaned toward the emperor's plan, which sharply increased the likelihood of forceful actions after the extension of recognition. The foreign secretary had learned from the Mexican experience that Napoleon was capable of any action needed to satisfy his imperial interests. Why would the emperor act with restraint when both his reputation and a French toehold on the North American continent were at stake? Russell, however, considered the French proposal the final opportunity to end the American war and refused to let that moment pass.

Secretary Lewis strongly opposed the French program as a catalyst for war. In early November he circulated a lengthy memorandum among his cabinet colleagues citing the dangers of intervention and denying that the Confederacy deserved recognition. His 15,000-word paper, entitled "Recognition of the Independence of the Southern States of the North American Union," was a collaborative work with his stepson-in-law, William Vernon Harcourt, who later became the first scholar to hold the Whewell Chair of International Law at Cambridge University. In London, the *Spectator* identified Harcourt as coauthor of the essay and lauded his use of history and international law to undermine the rationale for intervention.[33]

Under the pseudonym "Historicus," Harcourt also wrote a string of letters opposing intervention that appeared in the *Times*. His central theme, "The International Doctrine of Recognition," contained the same arguments found in Lewis's memorandum. According to Historicus, "Rebellion, until it has succeeded, is Treason"; "when it is successful, it becomes independence. And thus the only real test of independence is final success." A joint mediation "would practically place our honour in the hands of our copartners in the intervention." This business was not "child's play." A European intervention did not guarantee peace. "To interpose without the means or the intention to carry into effect a permanent pacification is not to intervene, but to intermeddle." Although the step might be "wise," "right," and "necessary," it could not be "short, simple, or peaceable." Past experience showed that intervention "almost inevitably . . . results in war." The intervening powers could not succeed "except by recourse to arms; it may be by making war upon the North, it may be by making war upon the South, or, what is still more probable, it may be by making war upon both in turns." To argue that an armistice could end an "irrepressible conflict" was "childish in the extreme." The Great Powers lived in a "Paradise of Fools" if they intervened in the American war with neither peace terms nor a readiness to use force. "We are asked to go we know not whither, in order to do we know not what." England must maintain neutrality.[34]

Lewis meanwhile assured his colleagues that Russell was correct in saying that the American war had threatened neutral nations. The fighting had stalemated, with the blockade inflicting "greater loss, privation, and suffering to England and France, than was ever produced to neutral nations by a war." Many British observers believed that southern separation would eliminate the blockade and reopen the cotton flow to their textile mills. The war's atrocities had led numerous British citizens to the "rational and laudable desire" for their government to intervene and stop the conflict. But, Lewis noted, intervention between "two angry belligerents, at the moment of their greatest exasperation, [was] playing with edge tools." With the outcome of the war not yet decided, intervention would promote the southern cause and result in war with the Union.[35]

The decisive point in the recognition controversy was whether the Confederacy had established its independence. "A state whose independence is recognized by a third state is as independent without that recognition as with it." It was "the acknowledgment of a fact." No nation had the right to grant recognition to a group of people in revolt against their government until they were "virtually an independent community according to the principles of international law." Two conditions were vital: First, the "community claiming to be independent should have a Government of its own, receiving the habitual obedience of its people." Second, the insurgents' "habit of obedience" to the old government must have stopped as a result of a severed relationship. Lewis urged caution: "It is easy to distinguish between day and night; but it is impossible to fix the precise moment when day ends and night begins." The great English legal scholar John Austin noted that "it was impossible for neutral nations to hit that juncture with precision." The British government must not bestow recognition if it saw any "reasonable chance of an accommodation." According to international law, it must withhold any action while a *"bona fide* struggle with the legitimate sovereign was pending."[36]

The war's verdict, Lewis argued, remained undecided. Part of the proof for this claim lay in the Union's resort to black liberation. The Lincoln administration had termed the Emancipation Proclamation a military action that, Lewis charged, was "intended to impoverish and distress the Southern planters, possibly even to provoke a slave insurrection." Additional evidence of the ongoing war was the Confederacy's continued pleas for recognition. "If the independence of the seceding States was equally clear, they and their English advocates would not be so eager to secure their recognition by European Governments." Premature intervention would make England an ally of the Confederacy and lead to war with the Union. Intervention came laden with problems. "If the Great European Powers are not contented to wait until the American conflagration has burned itself out, they must not expect to extinguish the flames with rose-water."[37]

The neutral nations, Lewis admitted in a concession to Russell's claim, could justify a forceful intervention only if the fighting had so badly damaged them economically that it threatened their survival. To stop the loss of life or to secure cotton, international law condoned "an avowed armed interference in a war already existing." The "Southern champion" (Napoleon) wanted an "armed mediation" or "dictation." Such a step, Lewis later acknowledged, might have been advisable, but this was not what the proponents of "*moral force*" intended. No one spoke of "*coercing* the North a few weeks ago." Foreign governments had advocated using their "good offices" in seeking peace. If mediation failed, however, they could follow the law of nature in judging the merits of the struggle and helping the party believed to be in the right *if* that party asked for assistance or accepted it.[38]

But, Lewis warned, the use of force guaranteed monumental problems that raised the question of whether intervention was "expedient." England, France, Russia, Austria, and Prussia (assuming they cooperated in the effort) would confront great logistical difficulties in moving armed forces across the Atlantic. How would their wooden ships fare against the Union's ironclads? If the intervening nations brought an end to the war, did they have peace terms capable of maintaining that peace? A "Conference of Plenipotentiaries of the Five Great Powers" would have to meet in Washington, D.C., to negotiate a settlement. "What would an eminent diplomatist from Vienna, or Berlin, or St. Petersburg, know of the Chicago platform or the Crittenden compromise?" The "Washington Conference," as Lewis called it, would confront numerous other questions after it presumably settled the independence issue. Boundaries? Partition of the western territories? Slavery both in the South and in the territories? Navigation of the Mississippi River? "These and other thorny questions would have to be settled by a Conference of five foreigners, acting under the daily fire of the American press."[39]

Would the powers retain their cooperative arrangement once the war ended and its spoils became available? "In the same proportion that, by increasing the number of the intervening powers, you increase the military or moral force of the intervention, you also multiply the chances of disagreement." A five-power mediation would be "an imposing force," Lewis conceded, "but it [was] a dangerous body to set in motion." The sovereigns would not only have to satisfy the Union and the Confederacy but themselves as well. The arbiters might dispute with each other, "and this well-intentioned intervention might end in inflaming and perpetuating the discord." England would have a "peculiar interest" in North America that the other four powers did not share. England and France could find themselves on one side against the others. "England might stand alone."[40]

Lewis had presented a powerful argument against intervention. Involvement in another country's affairs always guaranteed complex problems, the most important being the chances of causing a war with either or both antagonists. That northerners and southerners had gone to war constituted strong evidence that no outside power could devise peace terms that satisfied both sides. Either that power must stay out of the conflict and let the battlefield yield the verdict, or it must engage in a forceful intervention whose ramifications could spread beyond the present war.

Gladstone's spirited speech calling the Confederacy a nation had launched a national debate over intervention that forced the Palmerston ministry to confront an issue having enormous implications for both sides in the American war. The main focus was the widespread destruction and loss of life in a contest without meaning, one that would not have happened had the Union recognized its inability to subjugate the Confederacy. The British now faced the awesome prospect of risking conflict with one or both American antagonists by attempting to stop an atrocious war that damaged other nations, or simply ignoring its obligation as a civilized nation and allowing the war to wind down on its own. Particularly noteworthy was the absence of slavery from the discussions both outside and within the halls of government, but that did not mean the issue was inconsequential. Nor was the possibility of a French-led intervention totally advantageous to the Confederacy. Napoleon III had long sought to fulfill his illustrious predecessor's dream of reestablishing a French Empire in the New World following its humiliating withdrawal from the Continent after the French and Indian War. Only at the Confederacy's expense could he acquire the territory needed to flesh out his Grand Design.

On November 11, Russell convened a cabinet meeting that stretched over two days and focused on the issues raised in Lewis's memorandum. The foreign secretary recognized the problems inherent in intervention but made no attempt to deal with them. He had wrestled with these same matters while trying to justify his own proposal in October, and he knew that Napoleon's involvement in this new interventionist venture had erected additional obstacles. Rumors had already hit the London streets about a tripartite intervention proposed by the emperor and comprised of England, France, and

Russia. In this uncertain atmosphere, Russell opened the meeting by announcing that the previous day the French ambassador had forwarded an invitation from Napoleon to join France and Russia in asking the two warring parties in America to accept a six-month armistice and a suspended blockade to provide an opportunity to reach a peace settlement. Russia refused to participate on an official basis but, according to a note just received from the British ambassador in St. Petersburg, had agreed to support any Anglo-French effort that the Union found satisfactory. Russell understood that Russia's conditional acceptance—requiring the Union's highly unlikely compliance with the proposal—was tantamount to a refusal. But he warned that British rejection of the armistice plan might encourage Russia to reverse its position and join France in an attempt to break up the Anglo-French relationship. He therefore recommended British cooperation with the French as a way to maintain their entente cordiale and as an incentive to peace proponents in the Union.[41]

The ensuing discussion quickly became hot and divisive. Palmerston briefly highlighted the positive features of the French proposal, but his support was, according to Lewis, not "very sincere" and "certainly was not hearty." British participation, the prime minister declared, would demonstrate to suffering mill workers the ministry's concern over their plight. Lewis countered that the outcome might be just the opposite. British focus on the American problem could suggest the government's "indifference" to their problems. The proposal then went to the cabinet, which, Lewis wrote, "proceeded to pick it to pieces." Every member except Gladstone and Baron Westbury "threw a stone at it." The blockade proposal was "so grossly unequal, so decidedly in favour of the South," that even Russell admitted that the Union would turn it down. Lewis had failed to grasp the prime minister's position—that he opposed the timing of an armistice offer but not the offer itself—and later recorded that Palmerston had broken with Russell once the cabinet's overwhelming opposition became clear. Gladstone, too, had not comprehended the cautious support for intervention in his two colleagues' stance and felt betrayed. Russell had "turned tail . . . without resolutely fighting out his battle," whereas Palmerston had given him only "feeble and half-hearted support." Sensing impending victory, Lewis concluded that Russell's "principal motive was a fear of displeasing France, and that Palmer[ston's] principal motive was a wish to seem to support *him*."[42]

The outcome was predictable. At the end of the day, the cabinet overwhelmingly voted against the French proposal and asked Russell to write a note to Napoleon informing him of the decision. The foreign secretary ("under protest," Lewis asserted) agreed to undertake the task. The cabinet would reconvene the following morning to review the draft.[43]

Russell managed to word the note in such a manner as to leave open the chance for an intervention. The destruction of the war, he wrote, had affected not only the two American antagonists but also the European observers. The French proposal was laudable for attempting to "smooth obstacles, and only within limits which the two interested parties would prescribe." Indeed, it might cause the two sides to consider laying down their arms. His government's rejection of the proposal, Russell continued, did not signify an end to British cooperation with the French on "great questions now agitating the world." Had not the Paris government "assisted the cause of peace" in the *Trent* crisis? The Palmerston ministry, however, had decided there was "no ground *at the present moment* [emphasis added] to hope that the Federal Government would accept the proposal suggested, and a refusal from Washington at present would prevent any speedy renewal of the offer." It urged a close following of American public opinion to determine whether a tripartite "friendly counsel" might become appropriate in the future.[44]

Russell's carefully crafted reply to Napoleon's proposal, *with the cabinet's approval*, implied four times that intervention might become acceptable at some time in the war. Gladstone triumphantly wrote his wife that the response was "put upon grounds and in terms which leave the matter very open for the future." Palmerston likewise voiced no opposition to the draft, demonstrating again his resistance to the timing but *not* to an intervention itself. Lewis admitted that the cabinet decision "was only provisional." Lyons, too, approved the cabinet's action and assured Russell that the Union would have rejected Napoleon's proposal.[45] Russell had not given up on intervention but had adopted Palmerston's wait-and-see posture—that the outside powers would refrain from stepping in until the fortunes of the battlefield had convinced the Union that it could not subjugate the Confederacy. Perhaps most if not all cabinet members and Lyons agreed with this stand, objecting to the proposed intervention primarily because it had come from Napoleon.

If so, the ministry's suspicions of Napoleon's motives were justified, for his ambitions extended beyond a humanitarian desire to end the American conflict. The emperor knew the Union could not accept the plan without abandoning all hope of defeating the Confederacy. To throw open southern ports during an armistice would permit the enemy to stockpile matériel and resume the war fully armed. But a forcefully reopened cotton trade would alleviate the widespread suffering of his own people. And, as Dayton later observed, even if the emperor failed to acquire cotton, his effort would let his distressed people know he had tried. Two contemporaries on opposite sides of the American conflict believed that Napoleon had more in mind. Dayton from the Union and De Leon from the Confederacy both thought that Napoleon had intended his armistice offer to curry southern favor and thereby promote his expansionist goals in Mexico. Southerners and the French, Dayton warned Washington, would find mutual benefits in working together. The emperor thought southern separation probable and would believe that his policy had helped bring it about. De Leon also argued that Napoleon had used the proposal to win moral standing among Europeans—hence, his attempt to put England and Russia in an awkward position by having the offer published in the *Moniteur* on November 13 before they could reply. After the British and Russians rejected the proposal, the *Moniteur*, again speaking for the emperor, attempted to salvage the situation by insisting that their actions "did not constitute a refusal, but only an adjournment," and that "the hesitations of the Cabinets of London and St. Petersburg are apt soon to terminate. A feeling prevails in America, North as well as South, favorable to peace, and that feeling gains ground daily."[46]

Napoleon had several reasons for advocating this armistice proposal, but he mainly sought to tie the Confederacy to his Mexican project. Economic problems in France had placed him under great political pressure to help end the American war and reopen the cotton flow so crucial to his industrial program. His Conservative supporters wanted to stop the "needless effusion of blood" and help Europeans in economic distress. Liberal proponents of the Union countered that intervention would favor the Confederacy and meet rejection by the Lincoln administration. Restoration of the Union, they argued, was the best way to secure cotton. But Napoleon's proposal rested on the belief—shared throughout France—that neither antagonist would prevail, along with his calculation that an armistice would win Confederate favor and facilitate his aims in Mexico.[47]

In the meantime, the American legation in London heard rumors of a French interventionist proposal that Adams, unaware of the secret meetings at the Palmerston ministry to discuss the matter, at first dismissed as nonthreatening even if true. Russell, after all, had assured him that neutrality remained the government's policy and that he would inform the minister if anything changed. The day after the cabinet's deliberations, however, the *Times* published the French offer (the same day it appeared in the *Moniteur*) with the assertion that the Palmerston ministry had only placed intervention on hold and that "the present is not the moment for these strong measures." Not only had the French presented a proposal, but also the Palmerston government had discussed it. Furthermore, the ministry had left the issue open for future consideration. Clearly, Adams reacted to these explosive revelations with mixed emotions: indignation over Russell's apparent false assurances of neutrality, anger that the European powers had considered a forceful intervention in *American* affairs, and surely a bitter sense of relief tempered by alarm that the proposal had failed but only for "the present."[48]

Two days later, on November 15, Russell (while keeping his own position private) calmed the minister with another carefully crafted statement of truth—that the cabinet "never intended agreeing to the mediation." That same day the Russian government publicly turned down the French proposal (though he privately instructed Stoeckl that if France and England went ahead with a mediation offer, he was "to lend to both his colleagues, if not official aid, at least moral support"). Despite the *Times*'s suggestion that the French offer remained a possibility, Adams felt confident after their public disavowals of the French venture that the British and the Russians would reject similar proposals in the future. Russell, Adams believed, had been forthright and honest, and the Russian ambassador in London, Baron Philip Brunow, had made every effort to maintain friendly relations with the Union. Moreover, a recent article in Russia's semiofficial organ, the *Journal of St. Petersburg*, had expressed the same sentiments.[49]

The ever-suspicious assistant secretary, Benjamin Moran, did not feel assured. He called the French offer "a piece of weak insolence" that had originated from that "prince of intriguers Slidell." Also on November 15, word arrived from the American legation in Paris that Drouyn had earlier stated that if England and Russia rejected it, the proposal would die. "I hope so," Moran tersely remarked.[50]

The Lincoln administration, however, was infuriated on learning that the French and the British had discussed a proposal for intervening in American affairs. Seward seethed with anger as he specifically asked Lyons to make the Union's resentment known to Mercier. Only the Russians had understood the Civil War as America's business—not the Europeans'. Anglo-French interest in mediation, Seward told Adams, substantiated Napoleon's "aggressive designs" in North America. Lincoln remained cautious about taking on additional problems in the midst of the Civil War and discreetly attributed the French proposal to a "mistaken desire to counsel in a case where all foreign counsel excites distrust." But whatever its roots, the offer had raised southern hopes and assured a longer war. "This Government will in all cases,"

Seward wrote Dayton in Paris, "seasonably warn foreign Powers of the injurious effect of any apprehended interference on their part." After the fighting was over, "the whole American people will forever afterward be asking who among the foreign nations were the most just—and the most forbearing to their country in its hour of trial."[51]

The Confederacy also reacted bitterly to the episode, although for different reasons. Francis Lawley, the pro-Confederate correspondent for the *Times*, witnessed firsthand the disappointment felt in Richmond. Like many southerners, he tied England's refusal to the existence of slavery and found it difficult to believe that that single institution could prove so decisive. Once independent, the Confederacy would be in a better position to resolve that problem than if it rejoined the Union and continued to be "on the defensive" with abolitionists. The *Index* was livid over the British reluctance to act: "Has it come to this? Is England, or the English Cabinet, afraid of the Northern States?"[52]

Both American antagonists mistakenly thought Russell the chief obstacle to British intervention. Years later, Adams remained unaware of the foreign secretary's support for British involvement in the war and fondly recalled his strong resistance to the measure. Russell was a leader of "unquestioned integrity," making it "fortunate I had just such a person to deal with during my difficult times." In 1868 Adams recorded in his diary that Russell had brought the French proposal before the cabinet "with his own opinion adverse to it. It had then been declined without dissent." The view was no different from the Confederate side. Slidell and the *Index* were likewise ignorant of Russell's real sentiments and blasted him for opposing Napoleon's proposal.[53]

Some contemporaries, however, compounded Adams's mistake in judgment by attributing England's rejection of intervention to Palmerston as well as Russell. According to the *Richmond Whig*, the prime minister and his foreign secretary were "two old painted mummies" who had sought to prolong the war until it destroyed both Union and Confederacy. Harcourt also demonstrated an amazing lack of astuteness in finding Palmerston equally responsible for blocking intervention. He thought it a "little amusing that the whole wrath of the South and the imputation of being the real obstacle to Intervention should fall on Lord John. It only shows how little is known of the real history of affairs. Probably when the history of 1862 is written," he observed in a letter to Lewis, "it will be apparent that Ld. Palmerston and Russell were the two men who decided the question against interference. It reminds me of what Sir R[obert] Walpole said[:] 'Don't tell me of History[;] I know that *can't* be true [Harcourt's emphasis]."[54]

Russell and Gladstone had always been the strongest proponents of immediate British intervention, whereas Palmerston (and some if not most cabinet members) had wanted to hold off until both American antagonists had realized the futility of continuing the war. But the interventionist sentiments of the prime minister and his foreign secretary remained hidden behind the policy of neutrality, while the chancellor had trumpeted his feelings both publicly and privately. Palmerston and Russell had wanted to remain neutral until the Union realized that it could not subjugate the Confederacy and that mediation had become necessary. The foreign secretary, however, did not want to wait any longer. When the moment for mediation never came, Russell supported Napoleon's armistice plàn even though it included the potential for force. The growing bloodshed sickened the secretary; that carnage combined with the burgeoning cotton famine caused him to support any approach that offered the slightest hope for success. Palmerston only lukewarmly discussed the merits of Napoleon's project but did not rule out intervention. In mid-December 1862, the prime minister assured Russell that the government could extend recognition "with less Risk in the Spring" to the safety of Canada. He told King Leopold that England would have accepted the French proposal if it had had a chance for success. Intervention in two to three months might work. Gladstone, however, opposed a further delay because of the rising atrocities of the war and the rapidly spreading economic misery at home. To New York financial magnate Cyrus Field in New York, Gladstone insisted that "this destructive and hopeless war" had to end. "Is this not enough?"[55]

Slidell, meanwhile, had uncovered part of the truth about the Confederacy's real supporters in the British government and now felt more certain about French action. The "entente cordiale," he thought, had collapsed because of growing French distrust of the British. Napoleon had expected London to comply with his October 30 proposal and, failing that, would act on his own in the next few weeks or months. "Who would have believed," Slidell asked Mason in November 1862, "that Earl Russell would have been the only member of the Cabinet besides Gladstone in favor of accepting the Emperor's proposition?" *Palmerston*, Slidell mistakenly believed, had been the main barrier to intervention.[56]

Slidell was correct in expecting a greater French push for intervention: The question soon became entangled in the slavery issue and in Napoleon's imperial interests in Mexico. In turning the war in an antislavery direction, the Lincoln administration had confronted the Confederacy with its greatest threat. Not only did the president hope that emancipation would eventually knock out the chief cornerstone of the South's existence, but he also counted on increasing its difficulties in securing outside assistance in the war. The Confederacy, of course, was well aware of the challenge that emancipation posed to foreign intervention, but what both antagonists failed to realize was that the changed orientation in the war had thoroughly angered the British and *increased* the impetus for Anglo-French involvement. Yet even as this anger worked in the Confederacy's favor, another danger threatened its future: Its willingness to negotiate a devil's bargain with Napoleon would open the door for his imperial interests in the Western Hemisphere. The British, he had learned from the failed armistice proposal, would not intervene in American affairs and most certainly would do nothing to obstruct his intentions in Mexico.

President Davis, too, ignored Napoleon's past record of treachery and remained optimistic about winning French recognition. To a crowd in Jackson, Mississippi, on the day after Christmas, he declared: "We have expected sometimes recognition and sometimes intervention at the hands of foreign nations, and we have had a right to expect it." Never in history "had a people for so long a time maintained their ground, and showed themselves capable of maintaining their national existence, without securing the recognition of commercial nations." Although it was unwise to depend on foreign governments, there were encouraging signs from abroad. "England still holds back," but France seemed ready to extend "the hand of fellowship." If so, "right willingly will we grasp it."[57]

In Washington, Lincoln considered the Emancipation Proclamation integral to his initial goal of preserving the Union and then, as the war progressed, to improving that Union along with stemming the interventionist urge. In terms of the war, he asserted his authority as commander in chief to employ any method necessary to achieve victory. On legal grounds, he pronounced slaves free only in states still in rebellion. Lincoln knew that only a constitutional amendment could end slavery, but he also recognized the importance of creating an atmosphere conducive to such a momentous change. Finally, for diplomatic reasons, he used emancipation to curtail the chances for foreign intervention. Critics at home and abroad denounced the document for lacking moral fiber, but they failed to consider its broad impact as the first major step taken by the federal government against slavery. Even Stoeckl joined the chorus of skeptics, grousing that the administration had issued an "impolitic and impractical" decree intended to incite slave insurrections in the South. Once the Proclamation went into effect on January 1, 1863, Lincoln hoped, the call for black freedom would become integral to the establishment of a more perfect Union. Emancipation would finally mesh with liberty and, with Union, become one and inseparable.[58]

Jefferson Davis also grasped the significance of the Proclamation in terms of its potential impact both at home and abroad. The measure, he insisted, meant that "several millions of human beings of an inferior race, peaceful and contented laborers in their sphere, are doomed to extermination, while at the same time they are encouraged to a general assassination of their masters by the insidious recommendation 'to abstain from violence unless in necessary self-defense.'" British and French neutrality had already prolonged the war and resulted in "scenes of carnage and devastation on this continent, and of misery and suffering on the other, such as have scarcely a parallel in history." In refusing to treat the Confederacy as independent, these nations had emboldened the Union to believe it could conquer the Confederacy. Lincoln had now directed the war onto a path that would lead to one of three consequences: the slaves' extermination, the exile of all whites in the Confederacy, or complete separation from the United States.[59]

The mixed reaction to Lincoln's call for emancipation revealed a widespread failure to grasp the long-range thrust of the document. Some observers ridiculed the lack of eloquence in his words and the absence of a moral condemnation of slavery. Count Adam Gurowski, Harvard professor of international law and translator for the U.S. State Department, remarked that the Proclamation was "written in the meanest and the most dry routine style; not a word to evoke a generous thrill, not a word reflecting the warm and lofty . . . feelings of . . . the people." Karl Marx, coauthor with Friedrich Engels of the *Communist Manifesto* in 1848 and now correspondent for a London newspaper, likewise decried the document's terse tone.[60]

But Marx's attack actually highlighted the Proclamation's greatest strengths. He conceded that the "most formidable decrees which [the president] hurls at the enemy and which will never lose their historic significance, resemble—as their author intends them to—ordinary summons, sent by one lawyer to another." Skeptics unfairly denounced Lincoln for freeing the slaves only in areas where he had no jurisdiction; the truth was that he acted correctly in freeing them in regions that fell within his domain as a commander in chief exercising his war powers. In exempting the Border States, his sole purpose was to restore "the constitutional relation between the United States, and each of the states, and the people thereof."[61]

The British attitude toward the Proclamation gradually changed, suggesting that the Lincoln administration had finally achieved its central objective in foreign affairs of keeping England out of the war. British indignation over

Union and Emancipation meeting in Exeter Hall, London (*Harper's Weekly*, March 14, 1863)

the missing moral principles steadily gave way to the realization that the Confederacy's defeat necessarily meant slavery's demise. Foresighted spokesmen such as Argyll, Bright, and Cobden had made this argument on the eve of emancipation, but they had failed to convert their colleagues. In early October 1862, however, the *Morning Star* of London broke with Lincoln's critics. The Emancipation Proclamation marked "a gigantic stride in the paths of Christian and civilized progress . . . the great fact of the war—the turning point in the history of the American Commonwealth—an act only second in courage and probable results to the Declaration of Independence."[62]

Workers north of London, too, had praised the U.S. president's action, spurred by the presence of nearly forty African Americans from the Union who advocated its cause by lecturing and holding meetings that exalted the movement against slavery. In huge, highly charged rallies beginning in December 1862, British labor groups cheered Lincoln for promoting the rights of people everywhere. His preliminary Proclamation encouraged the establishment of pro-Union clubs such as the Committee on Correspondence with America on Slavery to resist recognition of the Confederacy, and the Union and Emancipation Society in Leicester, which included a large number of workers who condemned slavery as a violation of liberty. "The great body of the aristocracy and the commercial classes," Adams observed from the embassy, "are anxious to see the United States go to pieces," whereas "the middle and lower class sympathise with us." They "see in the convulsion in America an era in the history of the world, out of which must come in the end a general recognition of the right of mankind to the produce of the labor and the pursuit of happiness." Adams received countless letters, petitions, and resolutions from labor organizations and emancipation societies, all lauding the president. The public outpouring for emancipation virtually muted the southern sympathizers in England.[63]

Lincoln also helped shape British workers' opinions on the war. Charles Sumner, who had many contacts in England, worked closely with the president in writing notes to textile workers expressing concern over unemployment and blaming the cotton shortage on the Confederates—"our disloyal citizens." Self-interest, Lincoln wrote workers in Manchester, could easily have drawn them into the Confederate camp; instead, they acted on high principles in supporting the Union. This was an example "of sublime Christian heroism which has not been surpassed in any age or in any country." To workers in London, Lincoln declared the war a test of "whether a government, established on the principles of human freedom, can be maintained against an effort to build one upon the exclusive foundation of human bondage."[64]

By early 1863, however, the British government realized that the White House's move against slavery, regardless of the motive, had made intervention even more difficult to endorse. Southern enthusiasts outside British governing circles remained active, establishing organizations such as the Manchester Southern Independence Association, the London Southern Independence Association, and the London Society to Promote the Cessation of Hostilities in America. But, as shown earlier, the appearance of widespread popular support for the Confederacy was deceptive. Even Russell had grown weary of the struggle, writing Lyons in mid-February that "till both parties are heartily tired and sick of the business, I see no use in talking of good offices." William Gregory felt the same way. Although he had been the first vocal supporter of intervention in 1861, he now gloomily told Mason that the House of Commons opposed any such action as "useless to the South" and a possible cause of war with the Union. "If I saw the slightest chance of a motion being received with any favour I would not let it go into other hands, but I find the most influential men of all Parties opposed to it."[65]

The war, meanwhile, offered no solution to the overarching objective of stopping the bloodshed. Two major battles in December 1862 and early 1863 had failed to break the will of either antagonist—Fredericksburg in Virginia, which resulted in a devastating Union defeat, and Murfreesboro or Stones River in Tennessee, which ended in a narrow victory for the Union. The engagement at Murfreesboro left the northern Army of the Cumberland unable to take the offensive for months after sustaining the highest casualty rates of the war in relation to the numbers fighting. The slaughter at Fredericksburg particularly bedeviled the Union, heightened by a mid-December cabinet crisis driven by Chase's efforts to remove Seward, one that Lincoln masterfully defused. "If there is a worse place than Hell," the president moaned in the midst of these troubles, "I am in it."[66]

For the moment, however, he had to maintain the fight by enlarging the Union army and raising his people's morale. The Union's shattering defeat at Fredericksburg had combined with the shared butchery at Murfreesboro to force the administration to institute a military draft. As it went into effect on March 3, 1863, Lincoln fervently defended the war effort as a necessary baptism by blood that would renew hope. At the end of the month, he issued a presidential proclamation that established a national day of fasting on April 30 and appealed to higher principles in justifying such a terrible war. "Insomuch as we know that, by His divine law, nations like individuals are subjected to punishments and chastisements in this world, may we not justly fear that the awful calamity of civil war, which now desolates the land, may be but a punishment, inflicted upon us, for our presumptuous sins, to the needful end of our national reformation as a whole People?"[67]

The president's new emancipation policy inspired black enlistment in the Union army, which conjured up the Confederacy's worst nightmare: ex-slaves killing their white masters. In March 1863 Lincoln wrote Andrew Johnson, military governor of Union–occupied Tennessee: "The bare sight of fifty thousand armed, and drilled black soldiers on the banks of the Mississippi, would end the rebellion at once. And who doubts that we can present that sight, if we but take hold in earnest?" By autumn fifty thousand blacks would be in uniform, prompting the president to declare publicly that "the emancipation policy, and the use of colored troops, constitute the heaviest blow yet dealt to the rebellion."[68]

Lincoln continued to insist that the chief justification for the Proclamation rested on its military usefulness. In that way, he told Chase, emancipation had a constitutional or legal base. "If I take the step must I not do so, without the argument of military necessity, and so, without any argument, except the one that I think the measure politically expedient, and morally right? Would I not thus give up all footing upon constitution or law?" Yet Lincoln's emphasis on military necessity had become inseparable from emancipation, tying antislavery to the war effort and eventually convincing the British and the French that the Proclamation waged an all-out war on the Confederacy that could only end with its unconditional surrender and the death of slavery.[69]

Only in this manner can one understand the strong reaction to emancipation by both northerners and southerners, along with their equally intense feelings toward foreign intervention. Each side considered itself the principal defender of republicanism. Both called for self-government and liberty in combating tyranny—whether emanating from the government in Washington (the Confederate view) or from white slaveholders below the Mason-Dixon Line (the Union view). Above and below that line, the staunchest supporters of the war considered the republic in peril and sought to preserve its heritage as the true progenitors of the American Revolution. From the Union's perspective, emancipation defined northerners as patriots and southerners as traitors. To the Confederacy, emancipation constituted the first step in a long-range program to squelch states' rights, thereby defining northerners as traitors and southerners as patriots. Such was the central paradox of the Civil War.

The American Civil War is replete with myth and irony, not the least of which is that the Union victory at Antietam, followed by the Emancipation Proclamation, decisively blocked British intervention. Events afterward do not bear out this traditional claim—at least not in the immediate sense. The truth is that Lewis's arguments had confirmed Palmerston's wisdom in *postponing* an involvement until the Confederacy had amassed enough victories on the battlefield to substantiate its claim to independence.[70] The final decision, of course, was Palmerston's, but it was Lewis who provided historical and legal evidence supporting the prime minister's desire to wait for a more opportune time to intervene. Antietam and the Emancipation Proclamation did not quash the threat of intervention; on the contrary, they temporarily *heightened* the demand for intervention. The British were appalled and angered by the Union's failure to deliver a convincing victory, then by following up that horrific battle with what many contemporaries regarded as a lackluster, amoral stand against slavery along with continued struggles in the field.

Slavery was *not* the defining factor in Britain's November 1862 decision against intervention; rather, it only belatedly contributed to the November 1862 decision by proving Bright, Cobden, Argyll, and others correct in claiming that the war itself would destroy the institution. At the outset of the fighting, both American antagonists had denied the importance of slavery to the nation's division, leading the British to interpret the conflict as northern oppression versus southern independence and to examine every form of intervention possible to achieve peace by persuading the Union that it could not conquer the Confederacy. The Lincoln administration's tardy stand against slavery, or so the British regarded the president's autumn 1862 Proclamation, appeared to be a hypocritical and desperate step to salvage victory in the face of certain defeat. The measure, they argued, would justify intervention by inciting slave uprisings followed by a race war that spread beyond America's borders and inflicted irreparable damage on all nations dependent on the ravaged economies of North and South. But nothing of the sort happened, affording time for British observers to grasp the profound implications of a document they so heartily condemned for its restraint in opposing slavery as immoral.

If British leaders (and those on the Continent) had finally joined working people in grasping the impact of the Emancipation Proclamation, they still struggled to understand how the war had reached such a level of ferocity. As nationalism in Europe had not yet become a powerful force appreciated by continental statesmen, so did they continue their skepticism about the rationale for the conflict raging in North America. It seemed inconceivable that the attempt to preserve the Union against so many states and so many people merely wanting independence could arouse such mutual, visceral hatred.

Perhaps the explanation lay in the words of the participants. As an Illinois officer told his wife: "We are fighting for the Union . . . a high and noble sentiment, but after all a sentiment. They are fighting for independence and are animated by passion and hatred against invaders." Confederate soldiers wrote of protecting their homes from "hordes of Northern Hessians," fighting "in defence of innocent girls and women from the fangs of lecherous Northern hirelings," and avenging "the Vandal hordes, who would desecrate and pollute our Southern Soil." One southerner said he would never allow his homeland to be "polluted by a horde of Abolition incendiaries" or by the "lowest and most contemptible race upon the face of God's earth"—"the thieving hordes of Lincoln." As a Missouri Confederate asserted, *"vengeance will be our motto."*[71] Duty, honor, family, country, protectors of the true republic, a heavenly reward—all made death worth the price—to *both* sides.

Yet as long as the war continued on its murderous path, the possibility of British intervention posed a crisis to both the Union and the Confederacy. If the British intervened, the French (and perhaps other European nations) would follow suit and, coming while the outcome of the war remained unclear, doubtless ensure the Union's dissolution. The Confederacy would emerge an independent nation, free to float loans abroad and to negotiate military and commercial agreements capable of solidifying its new status. Britain (and other countries) would expect to trade with the South, which necessitated a challenge to the blockade; but such a challenge could spark the outbreak of a war with the United States that would shape Anglo-American relations into the twentieth century. For the same reasons did French intervention offer only a short-run benefit to the Confederacy's drive for independence; in the long run, Richmond's leaders would confront Napoleon's imperial objectives—a situation that could cost the Confederacy dearly.[72]

Both the Confederacy and the Union realized that the British were the key to their futures and were furious with them for maintaining neutrality. Southern hopes had risen dramatically when the Palmerston ministry granted the Confederacy belligerent status, only to plummet into bitterness when diplomatic recognition failed to follow. The Union's fortunes had dipped just as dramatically when the Confederacy won belligerent standing and seemed certain to receive recognition as a nation soon afterward. Seward denounced the British recognition of belligerency; the extension of "British sympathy, aid, and assistance" had made England's leaders "active allies" of the Confederacy and thereby gave it false hope. By meddling in America's domestic affairs, the secretary bitterly charged, the British prolonged the war and threatened "the life of the nation itself."[73] The Confederacy, however, believed it had repeatedly proved itself on the battlefield and, on failing to achieve formal recognition of independence, felt mistreated by the British in particular and by France and the other powers in general. As is so often the ill-starred fate of a neutral nation in wartime, the British were damned if they intervened and damned if they did not.

The threat of British intervention in the war had eased, but the chances for a French involvement had just as quickly intensified into a potential action that endangered *both* Union and Confederacy—and hence the republic itself.

CHAPTER 9

Requiem for Napoleon—and Intervention

If [General Robert E.] Lee should take Pennsylvania and
drive the government out of Washington, the effect would be
immediate recognition from all of the European States.
—WILLIAM L. DAYTON, July 10, 1863

Truthfulness is not, as you know, an element in French diplomacy or manners.
No man but a Frenchman would ever have thought of [Charles] Talleyrand's
famous *bon mot*, that the object of language was to conceal thought.
—WILLIAM L. DAYTON, September 7, 1863

French interest in intervention continued after the British rebuff and, like
their counterpart, for reasons unrelated to slavery. Napoleon had long favored the Confederacy though restrained by his people's distaste for slavery, which partly explained his reluctance to act without a British initiative.
But by late 1862 domestic economic problems had threatened violence and
provided a strong motivation for leading an intervention ostensibly aimed
at ending the American war and securing access to southern cotton. Napoleon, however, had more in mind. A close relationship with the Confederacy would combine with control over Mexico to facilitate his predecessor's
dream: Reestablish French influence in the New World and tip the world
balance of power toward Paris.

As the American war drummed on, the French government proposed another intervention plan. Russell's note rejecting Napoleon's November pro-

posal had led Foreign Minister Drouyn to believe that the Palmerston ministry would support an intervention if the Union agreed. The Confederate victory at Fredericksburg in mid-December 1862 had underlined the war's atrocities and renewed interest in an armistice. Perhaps the Union's recent defeat would make the Lincoln administration realize it could not win the war. Popular dissatisfaction with its army had spread, further enhancing the prospects for peace.[1]

Consequently, in January 1863 Drouyn and his cabinet colleagues devised a new form of intervention shorn of any references to armistice, blockade, mediation, or recognition: Invite northern and southern representatives to meet at a neutral location and, with no European power present, engage in "an argumentative discussion" of reconciliation. France simply wanted to make its good offices available to help end a war that was becoming "comparable to the most terrible distractions of the ancient republics, and whose disasters multiply in proportion to the resources and the valor which each of the belligerent parties develop." The suggestion, approved by the emperor a month earlier, went to Slidell and then to Washington. Slidell immediately opposed the idea, fearing it might result in some solution other than recognition of the Confederacy; but his superiors in Richmond agreed to a meeting *if* the Lincoln administration first publicly announced its willingness to attend. To ease the Union's concern over intervention, Drouyn assured the White House that the proposal did not signify either a cease-fire or increased status for the Confederacy. If the Union "believes that it ought to repel any foreign intervention, could it not honorably accept the idea of direct informal conferences with the authority which may represent the States of the South?"[2]

William Dayton distrusted France and arranged a meeting with the foreign minister. "This is not an effort to mediate," Drouyn told his anxious visitor. "It proposes no interference of any kind by a foreign power in the American affairs, and it does not even suggest a cessation of hostilities pending the negotiation." But Drouyn had clearly joined Russell in England in failing to grasp the Union's sensitivity to intervention or even to the *impression* of intervention. Dayton remained unconvinced. "Such a suggestion from abroad, however well-intentioned, is unnecessary." When it was time for peace talks, he told Drouyn, the two belligerents would send delegates on their own and *not* at the behest of a foreign power. Americans already mistrusted Napoleon's motives because of his armistice proposal and continued involvement in Mexico. They "would not like to see His Majesty's hand always in this business." Drouyn defended the emperor, denying any long-term objectives in Mexico and, in fact, calling that inference "a great annoyance." The French sought only to recover their debts and "leave Mexico as soon as we have obtained satisfaction."[3]

Despite these assurances, Dayton's suspicions were justified even though not based on specific evidence. Drouyn in the early 1850s had pledged to Mexico that France would oppose further territorial acquisitions by the United States. And he was a strong proponent of a Franco-Austrian alliance that, regardless of his disapproval, had become entangled with the emperor's Mexican project. If Drouyn considered his response to Dayton an honest promise of restraint, it did not ease the Union minister's fears of Napoleon's well-known imperial instincts along with his propensity to act without his advisers' blessing. Drouyn sensed this skepticism and, as the meeting drew to a close, again tried to allay Dayton's concerns. "As to any purpose or design upon the United States in connection with their proceedings in Mexico, *it would be madness* to think of it."[4]

Drouyn's very cloak of innocence demonstrated Napoleon's skillful duplicity. As a professional diplomat, the foreign minister was often at odds with the emperor's personal brand of diplomacy. Yet Drouyn felt certain that Napoleon sought neither colonies nor exclusive political and economic gains from the venture in Mexico. The emperor's ulterior purpose remained secret though transparent: Facilitate French dominance in the New World by proposing peace talks that won Confederate support while assuring his economically distressed people that he had taken the lead in stopping the war and acquiring southern cotton. Dayton, who had read a series of newspaper articles that often reflected the government's views, conceded that French leaders wanted to show "they are making every possible effort to relieve" their people's economic hardships. Napoleon's proposal, even if it failed to attract Union interest, would convince unemployed workers that he was still trying to stop the war. That the French press published Drouyn's dispatch to Mercier advising the appointment of commissioners to negotiate with the Confederacy—*before* that dispatch reached Mercier—was an attempt to prove its domestic purpose: to mollify the workers and manufacturers.[5] But Dayton also was aware of Napoleon's well-deserved reputation for satisfying his acquisitive interests. His intervention in Mexico provided ample warning of a similar action in North America.

Napoleon won his legislature's support for mediation when, in his annual address in mid-January 1863, he declared that "the Empire would be flourishing if the war in America had not exhausted one of the most fruitful of our industries." The previous November he had acted out of "sincere sympathy" in inviting Britain and other nations to work with him in ending the war, but they had not "thought themselves yet able." So he had postponed "to a more propitious season the mediation which had for its object the checking of bloodshed and the prevention of the devastation of a country whose future should not be indifferent to us." The legislature approved the effort, expressing regret that mediation had failed to bring the war to a close and thereby resolve the problems it had caused for the French economy.[6]

Meanwhile, Napoleon's credibility had risen in some Union circles when the Peace Democrats (bitterly termed "Copperheads") invited France to mediate a settlement. After their successes in the fall 1862 congressional elections, they viciously attacked Lincoln for pursuing a war the public opposed, and his Emancipation Proclamation for threatening the West with a mass influx of black freedmen from the South. Ohio representative Clement Vallandigham called the war an "utter, disastrous, and most bloody failure," blasting the White House as "one of the worst despotisms on earth" and welcoming the intervention of an impartial outside nation to secure "an informal, practical recognition" of the Confederacy. The question of reunion was irrelevant, he insisted. "Stop fighting. Make an armistice—no formal treaty." French mediation was the solution. "I would accept it at once."[7]

The idea also appealed to Horace Greeley, the powerful editor of the *New York Tribune*. Although an arch-supporter of the Union and emancipation, he so desperately wanted the war to end that he was willing to forego the administration's progress against slavery and restore "the Union as it was." He told his northern colleagues that he welcomed mediation "in a conciliatory spirit" by either England, France, or Switzerland. Especially attractive was Napoleon's shift from the armistice program to a straightforward mediation, a proposal brought to Greeley from France by businessman William Cornell Jewett. Excited about the prospects for peace, Greeley rushed to Washington to seek Mercier's assistance in securing Napoleon's intervention, and to discuss the idea with the president, Sumner, and other leading Republicans. The French minister thought the Union cause hopeless and told Lyons he was considering asking Drouyn for authority to offer mediation. In the meantime, Mercier pushed the proposal with Sumner along with western Republican congressmen, while Jewett took it to the new Democratic governor of New York, Horatio Seymour, and the influential editor of the *New York Herald*, James G. Bennett.[8]

Greeley, however, undermined his own efforts by trying to publicly recast Napoleon into a peace-loving humanitarian. In a series of articles in the *New York Tribune*, the editor directly contradicted his own previous writings. Whereas formerly the Union's "one substantial enemy in Europe" and the "destroyer of the French republic," the emperor now, by some strange metamorphosis, was the most ardent republican in Europe and "more popular with his people than any other European monarch." Unable to win over Bennett, Greeley attacked the *Herald* for its criticism of Napoleon, praising his abortive armistice proposal as "an excellent act" and denouncing anyone opposed to foreign mediation for providing "aid and comfort to the Rebels."[9]

Not surprisingly, Greeley's call for mediation did not spark any interest in Washington. No one could believe in the sudden transformation of the imperious French emperor into a selfless advocate of peace. Lincoln refused to consider a foreign intervention, regardless of its surface innocence. Any such arrangement, he knew, awarded governmental status to the Confederacy. Under no conditions would he accept a breakup of the Union; his soldiers had shed too much blood for him to change direction and concede that their supreme sacrifice had been in vain. How could he support an action that would undermine more than two years' resistance to any outside involvement? How could he revert to a prewar Union that condoned slavery and thus cast aside the Emancipation Proclamation? Sumner urged Greeley to be patient; Union forces would prevail on the battlefield. But Greeley refused to drop the idea. He shared it with Henry Raymond, editor of the *New York Times* and his longtime friend. Asked the president's reaction, Greeley confidently told Raymond: "You'll see . . . I'll drive Lincoln into it."[10]

The Lincoln administration at first ignored the French proposal but soon recognized the danger it presented and decided to quash it. The president approved Seward's recommendation to reject the proposal. The secretary persuaded Raymond to publish a piece charging Greeley with illegally pursuing "personal negotiations" with Mercier. If the accusation was true, the *New York Times* declared, Napoleon must recall his minister. Not only had Mercier meddled in domestic matters, but also Greeley had violated the Logan Act of 1799, which forbade private negotiations with foreign governments. Lincoln tried to shuck off the mediation proposal with his characteristic humor. Greeley's attempt to bring peace, the president quipped, had probably done more "to aid in the successful prosecution of the war than he could have done in any other way." His plea had, "on the principles of antagonism, made the opposition urge on the war." But Lincoln thought the plan a product of Napoleon's machinations and hence a threat to the Union.[11]

Lincoln's action won widespread support. Nearly all American newspapers praised his decision, including the usually critical *New York Herald*, which, in a remarkable change of form, lauded Seward's "masterly diplomacy" and Lincoln's "sagacity, consistency and steadiness of purpose" in keeping him in the administration when so many Americans demanded his removal.[12]

Economic, political, and imperial objectives guided Napoleon's American policy, making him outwardly amenable to southern interests and hence extremely dangerous to the Union. But for these same reasons, he posed a silent though lethal threat to a postwar Confederacy. The Emancipation Proclamation had eliminated slavery as a factor in French thinking, freeing Napoleon from moral and political restraints to pursue his territorial objectives in the Western Hemisphere. Lincoln had been only partly correct in believing that emancipation would kill the idea of foreign intervention. In the immediate sense, his Proclamation encouraged interventionists in both England and France to fear a racial war and to continue their efforts to stop the fighting; but over the long term, the document convinced the British to drop the cause of intervention when it became clear that slavery would be the chief casualty of the president's action. What remained largely unnoticed initially was that when the Proclamation resolved the slavery question in French minds, it virtually invited Napoleon to use intervention as a lever for quenching his imperial thirst in Mexico as a stepping-stone into the American South and West. Thus the price for recognition was Confederate acquiescence to French expansion from the Gulf of Mexico to the Pacific. The result was a two-headed crisis—one for the Union that it recognized and would deal with after the war, and the other for the Confederacy, which understood the threat but intended to resolve it *after* exploiting French assistance in achieving independence.

The chances for British intervention also seemed to revive in light of the recent public criticism of the ministry for appearing to capitulate to the Union on two important maritime cases. In February 1863 a Union cruiser had captured the British steamship *Peterhoff* near the Danish West Indies, charging its captain with transporting contraband to the Confederacy via Matamoros, Mexico. That same year, amid the ongoing heated controversy over the *Alabama*, British authorities impounded the warship *Alexandra*, then also under construction for the Confederacy. Instead of demanding hard evidence, Russell ordered its seizure because it was "apparently intended for the Confederate service." But the government lost its case when a jury agreed with the judge that it was legal to provide such ships "to be used against a power with which we are at peace." If there was no law against the sale of weapons, how could there be one prohibiting the sale of ships? To violate the Foreign Enlistment Act, he told the jury, the arming of such a vessel must take place in England.[13] Battlefield events then combined with British frustration over the war to renew interest in intervention. Lee's army had just routed Union forces at Chancellorsville, perhaps finally persuading the Lincoln administration that it could not win the war.

Thus the ironies continued to appear in Civil War diplomacy. The imminent demise of slavery in the United States had presumably convinced the Palmerston ministry *not* to intervene—that such a step would put England in the camp of the slaveholding Confederacy. But even while the Emancipation Proclamation was finally working to keep the British out of the war, it had freed Napoleon to mastermind a major threat not just to the United States but to the entire Western Hemisphere: the establishment of a monarchy in Mexico as the first step toward ending republicanism throughout the Americas and greatly enhancing French power in both the New World and the Old World.

By early 1863 Napoleon appeared certain to intervene in the American war. He had a new ruler in mind to assume the throne in Mexico, the French National Assembly had quieted domestic unrest by providing relief for distraught workers, and the Confederacy had negotiated a substantial loan through the Paris banking firm of Erlanger and Company and seemed receptive to mediation. Furthermore, he had devised what he considered to be a respectable resolution of the slavery issue.

The Confederacy remained under the illusion that it could accept French intervention without experiencing any negative repercussions from Napoleon's involvement in Mexico. Speaking to the Confederate Congress in mid-January 1863, President Davis praised the French for proposing the armistice offer that the British had rejected. But the emperor was not a friend. His past imperialist actions made him a threat to southern interests in the region, if not during the war then soon afterward. The isthmus linked the Atlantic with the Pacific and provided a land bridge integral to the cotton trade. It afforded refuge for blockade-runners as well as the chance to seize Union gold that passed from California to Asia via either the Panama Railroad or the waterways cutting through Nicaragua. Most important, the French presence in Mexico could block Confederate expansion both west and south while also endangering Texas and Louisiana. Was a French alliance worth such risks?[14]

The Confederacy revealed no concern about French motives in Mexico in early February 1963, when it tried another means for winning recognition—

the use of treasury bonds and cotton certificates as collateral for negotiating funds and credit in Europe. More than a year earlier, Secretary Benjamin had failed to secure a $1 million loan from the Baring Brothers of London's agent in New Orleans resting on cotton as collateral. A few months later he attempted to use cotton as the basis for a free trade agreement with France, one that might encourage Napoleon to dispatch ships off the southern coast to protect the new French commerce. Neither the French government nor the pro-Union banking firm would agree to such an arrangement, though Benjamin's proposals suggested more realistic financial thinking than some southerners had urged early in the war.[15]

The new approach had also become evident in early November 1862, when Confederate treasury secretary Christopher Memminger approved the sale of cotton certificates as the basis for credit in Europe. By the following February the Confederacy had $6 million in treasury bonds and another $3 million in cotton certificates either in hand or changing hands on the Continent. Managing the new enterprise was one of the Confederacy's most fervent supporters abroad—James Spence, its propaganda and financial agent in England and author of a widely read pamphlet defending the South, entitled *The American Union*. Buyers rejected the bonds—$5 million at a mere fifty cents on the dollar—but the cotton certificates had attracted enough interest to cause Confederate officials to seek one huge loan using cotton as collateral rather than rely on a disparate issuance of cotton certificates that competed with each other on the market. Besides offering more promise of success, a national loan would legitimize the Confederacy and perhaps lead to its recognition. Mason worked with his friend in Parliament and shipping magnate, William S. Lindsay, in crafting this loan proposal.[16]

But Slidell had been negotiating a larger loan through the Erlanger banking firm in Paris. The result was an arrangement in late January 1863 that floated a twenty-year loan in Europe of £3 million ($14.5 million) and, for the first time in the war, was convertible in cotton certificates. The terms were not particularly favorable to the Confederacy, but its desperate need for money left no choice but to accept a deal that awarded funds in advance. The strongest argument for the loan, however, was the respect it might afford the Confederacy as an impetus to England and France to extend recognition. In late March the bonds became available for purchase at 90 percent of face value in Amsterdam, Frankfurt, Liverpool, London, and Paris. London's *Economist*, no supporter of making loans to the American South, found it "startling" that the Confederacy could "borrow money in Europe while the Federal Government has been unable to obtain a shilling." Perhaps the loan had uplifted President Davis, who, according to Mercier, had recently given up on receiving help from the European powers. Slidell triumphantly declared that the loan marked the "financial recognition of our independence, and Mason proclaimed that "cotton is king at last."[17]

While the Confederacy celebrated its financial breakthrough, Napoleon took advantage of Europe's preoccupation with the ongoing Polish uprising against Russian rule to deepen his involvement in Mexico and, among other objectives, attempt to shape the outcome of the American conflict. France and England had adopted different policies toward the European crisis since its eruption in February 1863. Russell repeatedly urged Drouyn to act on behalf of the Polish people; yet England itself refused to furnish support. The French populace likewise pressed Napoleon to help the rebels, but he wished to avoid such a move, which would alienate Russia and Prussia, the former still seeking revenge after the Crimean War and the latter wanting him toppled so badly that it would go to war with France less than a decade later. When Napoleon adhered to his familiar American policy of following England's lead, he drew heavy domestic and foreign criticism. Drouyn meanwhile sought a diplomatic settlement that would maintain a European balance of power. As trouble threatened to envelop the Continent, Union minister Henry Sanford in Belgium acidly remarked to Seward: At the bottom of nearly all international turmoil was that "perpetual nightmare, the Emperor."[18]

Napoleon's policy of noninvolvement in Poland's domestic emergency also provided an opportunity for the Union to cultivate its friendship with Russia in a further effort to block Confederate recognition. In the fall of 1863, the Lincoln administration welcomed two highly publicized visits by the Russian Imperial Fleet—in New York and San Francisco—as an expression of support for Russia's role in the Polish uprising. Most studies suggest that the Russian presence was motivated primarily by the tsar's desire to avoid entrapment in his frozen home waters of the Baltic in the event of war with England or France over his forces' treatment of the Poles. The tsar did not want to repeat the experience of the Crimean War of the 1850s, when British and French warships had prevented Russian vessels from leaving the Baltic. Although this argument is compelling, it says nothing about the public impressions of the fleet's visit to the United States. Russian leaders wanted to demonstrate friendship with the Union and to have the imperial navy engage in training exercises that advertised its new capabilities in the Atlantic. The ships, according to recent research, were capable of withstanding British and French pressure and in no danger of confinement to the Baltic in the event of war over Poland. At the time, numerous American, British, French, and even Russian contemporaries were convinced that the fleet was there to show support for the Union. The Lincoln administration knew that the visit did not signify either favor for the Union or opposition to slavery, but the president and his secretary of state exploited Russia's presence to suggest its support in the war and thereby discourage Confederate chances for recognition.[19]

If the Polish crisis benefited the Union through Russia, it nonetheless facilitated Napoleon's objectives in Mexico. In exchange for Austrian concessions in Europe that promoted French defenses on the Continent and led to their acquiring parts of Denmark, Italy, and Poland, he secretly agreed to sponsor Habsburg Archduke Ferdinand Maximilian of Austria as emperor of Mexico.[20]

Napoleon's clandestine program of conquest—the so-called Grand Design for the Americas—depended on his intervening in the American war while establishing a foothold in Mexico. He intended to block both Union and Confederate expansion southward by constructing a North American balance of power based on a "hyphenated confederation" similar to that in Germany. The confederation would consist of the North, the South, the West, and Mexico, each having equal power. The plan would thus break up the United States, leaving Mexico under French control to eventually incorporate Texas and perhaps the former colony of Louisiana.[21]

It was an ambitious and provocative plan, but neither the Confederacy nor the Union could have been surprised. In Richmond, Benjamin had long suspected the emperor of wanting Texas in order to contain southern expansion. From Belgium the year before, Ambrose D. Mann had warned of Napoleon's threat, and again in early 1863 he expressed concern that the emperor's territorial aims would cause "general uneasiness in the minds of our citizens"; his chief goal was "the restoration of Mexico as it was prior to the independence of Texas." Napoleon, Mann added in May, "will remain anxious for us to believe that he is silently our friend. Mexico first, and then Mexico as she was previous to her dismemberment in the resolutely and faithfully cherished end at which he aims." The Union also was on alert. Veteran diplomat Edward Everett, now an adviser in the State Department, had apprised the Lincoln administration that Napoleon intended to resurrect a scheme first tried nearly two decades earlier: creating a state comprised of Texas and all Mexican territories west to the Pacific, including California and Louisiana. Sanford, too, had long warned Seward of the emperor's imperial interests in the Western Hemisphere, and reported loud talk almost "*ad nauseum*" in Parisian salons about his advancing the "Latin race." To Napoleon, control over Mexico was inseparable from his intervention in the American war.[22]

In the spring of 1863, several reports from America reached Napoleon that, although at times contradictory, led him to think it was time to mediate an end to the war. A French consul in Boston, one Shouchard, asserted in March that New Englanders were thoroughly disenchanted with Washington's leaders and sought peace so desperately that they threatened secession. The next month, however, he reported the opposite, insisting that support for the war had revived as a result of the Peace Democrats' failure to arrange peace talks. From the Confederacy came conflicting assessments of the blockade. On one occasion, Benjamin triumphantly announced that the Union had given up on closing Charleston, Galveston, and Sabine Pass; but less than a month later, the French consul in Richmond, Alfred Paul, informed his home government that the blockade had caused an "economic and commercial crisis" of "alarming proportions" for the Confederacy. Whatever the truth, the conflict continued, leaving its verdict in doubt and thus increasing the chances of a foreign involvement.[23]

In early April, Napoleon again tried to convince England to take the initiative toward an intervention based on outright recognition rather than mediation. "If Great Britain would recognize the Confederacy," he reminded Cowley, "cotton would become available." French economic troubles, he implied, would compel the Paris government to follow suit. Napoleon felt encouraged. The Union had suffered setbacks at Vicksburg and Chancellorsville. Confederate agents in Europe had negotiated the Erlanger loan. Lindsay had approached the emperor a year earlier about extending recognition and, failing in that effort, was working with Mason to persuade the British to take the first step. In May, Lindsay invited Mason to his country residence outside London to meet with him and John A. Roebuck, a staunch southern supporter in the House of Commons, to discuss a parliamentary resolution aimed at forcing the Palmerston ministry to recognize the Confederacy. Soon afterward Roebuck informed the Commons of his intention to introduce a motion for recognition.[24]

Slidell meanwhile requested another meeting with Napoleon, hoping to prevail on him to grant recognition without waiting for a British lead. England, the Confederate commissioner thought, opposed recognition to prolong the war and disable a major commercial competitor; France, however, preferred two American republics capable of challenging the British maritime position. Slidell therefore considered French intervention more important than the threat Napoleon posed to Confederate expansion south and to Texas and Louisiana. Without foreign intervention, the hostilities would grind on endlessly, eating away at the Confederacy (as well as the Union) and helping only the British. Confederate concerns about French territorial ambitions were secondary to the need for intervention. Once established as a nation, the Confederacy could deal with Napoleon's expansionist schemes.[25]

Roebuck's objective soon meshed with Slidell's persistence to revive hope for recognition. The Palmerston ministry opposed Roebuck's planned motion and sought to undermine the interventionists by claiming that Napoleon, too, had decided against recognition. Suspecting trickery, Roebuck invited Lindsay to accompany him on a special visit to the emperor. Mason meanwhile informed Slidell of the Roebuck-Lindsay mission.[26]

Slidell met with Napoleon on June 18, when he again appealed for joint Anglo-French intervention and noted Roebuck's imminent motion for recognition. Intervention, Napoleon explained, probably meant war with the Union, and he could not take that chance without British naval support. Slidell assured him that the European powers would join France in recognizing the Confederacy and that they could count on the Spanish fleet for support. Had the emperor a moment to reflect, he might have wondered why Spain would ally with him now after pulling out of the Mexican expedition of 1861. But Slidell had quickly moved on with a question: Was Palmerston correct in asserting that France no longer supported recognition? No, Napoleon emphatically replied; Slidell could assure Roebuck of French support. Told of the Roebuck-Lindsay mission, Napoleon said that he "would be pleased to converse with them on the subject of Mr. Roebuck's motion." In fact, he cagily observed, "I think that I can do something better—make a direct proposition to England for joint recognition. This will effectually prevent Lord Palmerston from misrepresenting my position and wishes on the American Question." Slidell was elated, later telling Mason that the emperor's decision to approach England with a joint proposal was "by far the most significant thing that [he] has said, either to me or to the others."[27]

Slidell's euphoria did not last long, however; Napoleon inserted a qualification that left him a way out. "I shall bring the question before the cabinet meeting today," he asserted; "and if it should be decided not to make the proposition now, I shall let you know in a day or two . . . what to say to Mr. Roebuck."[28]

The emperor had failed to win British support for his armistice proposal, and his cabinet opposed his again taking the lead in a joint Anglo-French move for recognition; yet his ministers left the door open for an intervention by declaring the timing "inopportune." Furthermore, they "did agree to deny, as far as the British cabinet is concerned, the reports which falsely attribute to us sentiments and a policy less favorable for the South." Several times, they wanted London to know, their government had proposed an intervention that the Palmerston ministry rejected. France's position had not changed— "quite the contrary." Napoleon could inform the British that the French "shall be charmed to follow them up, and if they have any overtures to make to us in a like spirit to that which has inspired ours, we shall receive them with quite as much eagerness as pleasure."[29]

In the meantime, Slidell had asked Drouyn about the likelihood of recognition and came away convinced that the French had refused to act because they did not trust the British. If the French took the initiative, Drouyn explained, the British would probably decline and inform the Lincoln administration of the proposal. The Union would be infuriated and demand that French forces leave Mexico. The confrontation might "compel the Emperor to declare war, a contingency which he desires to avoid and which England would aid in creating."[30]

French advisers certainly distrusted the British, but they now found themselves in the unlikely position of having to oppose Confederate recognition because the move might push the Union into some military action that undermined their status in Mexico. Napoleon knew that Confederate independence would weaken the United States and do more to guarantee the French presence in the New World than would a Union victory followed by a reunited North and South. Only out of self-interest did he consider Confederate recognition. But now that the French faced the probability of conflict with the Union—and without British naval support—they had to avoid any action that favored the Confederacy. Ironically, the French had encouraged southern hopes by intervening in Mexico, only now to refuse to help the Confederacy because of their intervention in Mexico.[31] Slidell failed to grasp the nuances involved in a French decision to recognize the Confederacy and erroneously believed that only their rivalry with England stood in the way.

Like the Confederacy, Napoleon lived in a world of delusion, this time demonstrated by his regarding the unauthorized visit of Lindsay and Roebuck as a way of putting pressure on the Palmerston ministry to intervene in the war. The questionable reputations of these two maverick politicians should have provided clear warning against the chances of their prevailing in England. Not only were they operating outside diplomatic channels, but Roebuck had few friends after long ignoring domestic political propriety with impunity. Hotze thought Roebuck held "a singularly isolated position" in the Commons by always opposing the government, regardless of its leadership. One of Roebuck's colleagues derisively called him "a mock Robespierre who had no guillotine to command." Writer and social critic Thomas Carlyle described him as "an acrid, barren, sandy character, dissonant speaking dogmatist, with a singular exasperation: restlessness as of diseased vanity written over his face when you came near it." Henry Adams simply pronounced him "rather more than three-quarters mad." But Napoleon's obsession with restoring French hegemony in the Americas blinded him to reality. At last, or so it appeared to the wishful emperor, the moment had come for a joint Anglo-French action aimed at ending the American war and entrenching his forces in North America.[32]

On June 22, just four days after Slidell's meeting with Napoleon, Roebuck and Lindsay joined the emperor at his Fontainebleau retreat to discuss a joint intervention. Accounts of this conference vary, the truth depending on each participant's interpretation of the talks. Lindsay asserted that Napoleon refused to take the lead again (as in the previous fall) because, the emperor charged, the British had "immediately transmitted" his proposal to the Lincoln administration in an effort "to create bad blood between me and the United States." Instead, he had instructed his ambassador in London, Baron Gros, to ask whether the Palmerston ministry intended to recommend "any mode for proceeding for the recognition of the Southern States which I so desire." At the end of the meeting, according to Lindsay, the emperor authorized his British visitors to assure Parliament of his continued support for recognition.[33]

Napoleon's memory of the discussion sharply differed from Lindsay's. The emperor denied making any assurance of recognition or authorizing Lindsay and Roebuck to tell the House of Commons that he had agreed to cooperate with the British. Their rejection of his November call for an armistice had led him to oppose submitting another proposal without prior acceptance. He said that he directed his ambassador in London to inform the Palmerston ministry that he would support recognition to stop the war only if the proposal came from the British government. To Drouyn, Napoleon conceded that he should not have been so blunt in his talks with Lindsay and Roebuck. They had spoken in English, the emperor noted, and this could have caused misunderstandings. "It was enough to make [Roebuck] understand that I could not address to the English Government an official proposition to recognize the South without first knowing its intentions, because the official act of the month of last October was not accepted, and it came back to me (which however I doubted) that the English Government boasted in Washington for having refused our offer of mediation."[34]

In Paris, Dayton suspected that Napoleon's involvement with Lindsay and Roebuck had led to some secret arrangement for recognition—a hunch bolstered by an article in the progovernment *La France* that suggested a conspiracy. According to the writer, the emperor had met privately with Slidell, then Lindsay and Roebuck; the Confederacy praised the recent French military victories in Mexico; and Spain, the writer erroneously stated, had talked with the Confederacy about granting recognition in exchange for assurances regarding Cuba. "The cause of the Confederates," the writer continued, "gains new sympathies every day and their heroic resistance on the one side, on the other the impotence of the armies of the North prove that there is in them a people strongly organized, worthy in fact to be admitted among the independent states." Dayton rushed to Drouyn's office to ask "if any change in the policy of this government towards us is contemplated?"[35]

Drouyn tried to calm Dayton by assuring him there had been no official change in policy, but he admitted to not knowing what Napoleon might have decided on his own. "I have not seen the emperor for some days, and I could not therefore answer for what he had said and done." Napoleon, Drouyn admitted, had seen Slidell in Paris and perhaps Lindsay and Roebuck in Fontainebleau. Slidell, Dayton reported to Seward, had approved French actions in Mexico to curry the emperor's favor. The French sought "to make the South a basis of operations against that country," and Slidell gave "most satisfactory assurances." Despite Drouyn's repeated defense of Napoleon, "I am always somewhat distrustful." Dayton trusted the foreign minister, "but he did not have command of the situation." Behind him was "a self-judging, governing and reticent power." Although Dayton did not anticipate "actual forcible interference," he was apprehensive about recognition because "these foreign Governments do not believe it would be a just cause for war, nor that it would lead to it."[36]

Dayton had drawn attention to a major threat to the Union, particularly because Napoleon had seemingly acted without his advisers' knowledge. His interest in recognizing the Confederacy was inseparable from his intervention in Mexico: French recognition in exchange for Confederate support of the latter. Dayton had brought clarity to a severe challenge not only to the Union, but also to the Confederacy and, indeed, to all the Americas.

On June 30 Roebuck rose in Parliament to present his motion for recognizing the Confederacy in a joint effort with the French. But instead of focusing on ending the war, he soured his cause by showing that his real motive was to destroy the Union. Raised in Canada shortly after the War of 1812, Roebuck had developed a visceral hatred for America that had not abated over the years as he and others accused the United States of causing the conflict and trying to annex his homeland. Perhaps the Civil War afforded an opportunity to end that threat once and for all. Southerners were transplanted English gentlemen, he asserted; northerners were the cast-out "scum of Europe." His colleagues and the Palmerston ministry had denied the Confederacy a recognition it richly deserved. He then revealed his underlying anti-American purpose. Doubtless heartened by the Confederacy's rout of Union forces at Chancellorsville in early May, Roebuck argued that dismemberment of the United States would guarantee cotton for Lancashire's mills and permanently weaken England's maritime competition and most-despised rival. Mockingly, Roebuck noted that, until the ongoing war in America, that proud nation

> . . . bestrode the narrow world
> Like a colossus; and we petty men
> Walked under her huge legs and peeped about
> To find ourselves dishonoured graves.[37]

Roebuck then shocked his peers by sharing the substance of his and Lindsay's private discussion with Napoleon. The emperor, Roebuck proudly reported, still supported a joint intervention. "France is the only power we have to consider," he maintained, "and France and England acknowledging the South, there would be an end of the war." After detailing the conversation, he related Napoleon's claim that the Palmerston ministry had betrayed him by informing the Union of his interventionist proposal.[38]

Roebuck's arrogance alienated his listeners, even embarrassing fellow Confederate supporters, who quickly distanced themselves from him. Bright went on the attack, Henry Adams later wrote from firsthand observation, and "with astonishing force, caught and shook and tossed Roebuck, as a big mastiff shakes a wiry, ill-conditioned, toothless, bad-tempered Yorkshire terrier." Russell had already denied receiving a French proposal, making it difficult for Roebuck to convince his colleagues that Napoleon had agreed to act once the British took the initiative. Members of Parliament were angry that Roebuck had risked antagonizing both the Union and France over this explosive issue. Why would Napoleon act outside diplomatic channels and with someone not officially sanctioned by the British government?[39]

In the midst of this angry debate, William Forster's reaction perhaps confirmed a changing British attitude toward intervention in the American war and the issue of slavery. Forster warned that a war with the Union not only would wreck British commerce and endanger Canada, but also would be "unpopular on far higher grounds, because it would be a war against our own kinsmen, for slavery." How had the line of division emerged between North and South? "Exactly by slavery," Forster proclaimed. Northerners realized "they could not uphold that Union and preserve slavery." The outcome of the ongoing siege of Vicksburg, he maintained, would determine "peace and freedom." If the fortress fell, "the other side of the Mississippi [would be] cut off from the slave territory, [and] we would see an end of the war." Northerners would have blocked the extension of slavery and prevented the establishment of "a powerful slavery confederation." Interference at this critical time would stop northerners from resolving this question and spread "the horrors of war" and "at the risk of involving ourselves in its miseries." Not only would England suffer, but also the "great Anglo-Saxon race would be torn, not merely by a double but triple civil war, and every despot, civil and religious, throughout the world would rejoice to see them destroying each other." This was more than a war; it was a "tremendous social revolution" that might lead to a "purification from the evils of slavery."[40]

Predictably, Russell and his supporters in the Commons defeated Roebuck's motion. Hotze reported nationwide ridicule of Napoleon's antics as "a sort of farce in which Mr. Roebuck acted a broadly comic part." Surely this episode marked the end of the Confederacy's hopes for recognition. Mason, however, believed Roebuck's story and called the whole episode a "mess" that resulted from Napoleon's duplicity. In early July Roebuck tried again to muster support for his motion, but less than two weeks later, on July 13, he gave up and formally announced its withdrawal.[41]

Roebuck had dropped the matter primarily because of Palmerston's pressure. Stricken with an attack of the gout, the prime minister had missed the opening exchanges but appeared in the Commons on July 13 to praise Roebuck and Lindsay for withdrawing the motion and to express his hope that this would be "the last time" a House member thought it "his duty to communicate to the British House of Commons that which may have passed between himself and the sovereign of a foreign country." Although they had acted with "the best intentions," it was "most irregular" for Parliament to receive foreign communications." Palmerston's low-key scolding was not a surprise, for he had privately assured Roebuck (and Lindsay) four days earlier that Napoleon "was completely wrong" in accusing the ministry of trying to cause trouble with the Union by sending the armistice proposal to Washington. The proposal had first appeared in the *Paris Moniteur* before going to Dayton and then to Mercier, who passed it on to Seward. Palmerston chastised Roebuck for his "very irregular" behavior in revealing to the Commons his private discussion with the emperor. Nothing good could come from either pursuing this issue or blaming Napoleon. In fact, to do so might damage Anglo-French relations. "I am very anxious that neither you nor Mr. Lindsay should mention these matters any more."[42]

The overwhelming opposition to Roebuck's motion by Palmerston, members of the Commons, and the British press again suggests the absence of strong Confederate sympathy throughout the country. Expressing the Conservative view, the *Economist* warned that recognition would violate international law while doing nothing to end the war, secure cotton, and ease the plight of distressed textile workers. With no benefits gained, the British by extending recognition would "intervene by war," "break the blockade," and "create the 'South.'" The *Saturday Review* likewise vehemently opposed recognition, contending that Roebuck had accepted the certainty of war and tried to "strengthen his case by pointing out the expediency of diminishing the formidable strength of the former Union." He had undermined all claim to morality. "The legitimate greatness of a foreign country is no excuse for projects against its prosperity." The *Illustrated London News* belittled the motion by giving it barely any attention, except to note Roebuck's "sarcasm and bitterness."[43]

Dayton was so upset by what had transpired in Parliament that he again went to Drouyn for an explanation. Roebuck, the foreign minister conceded, should not have divulged the contents of "an unofficial and private conversation." Surely the emperor had not authorized him to do so. Moreover, "*no official communication of any kind*" [Dayton's emphasis] had recently passed between France and England. Napoleon probably affirmed his continuing support for a joint recognition with England. But if so, Drouyn assured Dayton, these statements were unofficial, *not* a formal proposal.[44]

What *was* the truth behind this strange episode? On June 22, just after his meeting with Roebuck and Lindsay, Napoleon wrote Drouyn: "I wonder whether Baron Gros may not be instructed to state unofficially to Lord Palmerston that I am resolved on recognizing the independence of the Southern Provinces. We could not be compromised by such a declaration, and it might determine the British Government to take a step." The next day, Drouyn wired Gros: "See Lord Palmerston and in the course of conversation give him to understand that the Emperor has no objection to recogniz[ing] the independence of the South." Napoleon's directive markedly differed from Drouyn's telegram. Whereas Napoleon stated that he was "resolved on recognizing" the Confederacy's independence, Drouyn wrote that the emperor had "no objection to recogniz[ing]" its independence. The distinction could *not* have been accidental. Gros later admitted to Drouyn that in talking with Russell in London, "it is very likely that I incidentally said to him that having no official communication to make to him on the recognition of the Southern States, I was personally persuaded that the emperor was disposed to recognize them." Drouyn assured Dayton that Napoleon had made no formal proposal of joint recognition.[45]

Drouyn had told the truth as he knew it, but he did not ease Dayton's anxieties. The emperor's tendency to act independently of his advisers sometimes created potentially dangerous situations. Dayton also noted that both Drouyn and Russell had carefully denied any *official* overtures, strongly suggesting that Roebuck had told the truth about an informal proposal. Dayton therefore argued that even if Napoleon had not sent an official note to London, his authorization of Roebuck to reveal the contents of a private discussion took on a "quasi-official character" and was subject to an inquiry and required an explanation. Drouyn, however, denied that the emperor had granted Roebuck this authority. As the tense meeting came to a close, the French foreign minister pledged to consider any British recommendation aimed at ending the American war. "It certainly will not be brought to a close by a recognition of the South," Dayton tersely replied. Such action could widen the war by drawing in other nations. Dayton knew that Lee's forces had recently engaged the Union armies at Gettysburg, but he had not yet heard the outcome. "If Lee should take Pennsylvania and drive the government out of Washington," Dayton warned Seward after the meeting with Drouyn, "the effect would be immediate recognition from all of the European States."[46]

The Lincoln administration soon learned of two major Union victories on the battlefield in early July and felt confident that the news would discourage foreign intervention once it reached Europe. Union armies had defeated Lee's forces at Gettysburg and pushed them back into Virginia, while in the Western Theater Union general Ulysses S. Grant had captured the Confederate fortress at Vicksburg after a long siege. Seward's elation was tempered by concern that slow communication of these outcomes to France and England might provide time for them to jointly intervene in the apparently endless, brutal war.

In this dangerous interlude Seward hurriedly sent Dayton two special delivery letters instructing him to warn the French not to recognize the Confederacy. "Any new demonstration of activity by [Napoleon] prejudicial to the unity of the American people," Seward emphasized, would be "necessarily regarded as unfriendly." If the emperor approved any "official act" endangering the Union, *your functions will be suspended* [Seward's emphasis]." At no other time during the Civil War did the Union come so close to severing diplomatic relations with France.[47]

Yet unknown in the Union, the Confederate reverses at Gettysburg and Vicksburg had had another positive impact on its diplomatic fortunes: They severely shook the credibility of the Erlanger loan and further damaged the Confederacy's hopes for independence.

In truth, the financial bubble had already begun to leak in almost direct harmony with the continuation of the war. From the beginning of the arrangement, investors backed off when reading the conditions at the bottom of the advertisements: Bondholders must redeem their papers in cotton coming only from inside the Confederacy. Indeed, the exchange could not take place at an Atlantic port because of the dangers posed by the Union blockade; it could occur only at a spot within ten miles of either a Confederate railroad station or a navigable river. Thus the transaction involved running the blockade to get into the Confederacy, arranging for the carriage of the cotton to a port, and then running the blockade again to escape into the Atlantic. Even the Erlangers' innovative creation of the European Trading Company as a fleet of blockade-runners did little to encourage continued investments because of high shipping and insurance costs. Furthermore, the Union army's advances combined with the increasing effectiveness of the blockade had caused retreating Confederate forces to burn cotton reserves rather than have them fall into enemy hands. Finally, Lincoln's implementation of the Emancipation Proclamation, which moved the war in an antislavery direction, made the British reluctant to do anything that helped the Confederacy. By April 1863 the bonds had fallen slightly below the opening price, making it nearly certain that buyers would default on their next payment. The Union's victories at Gettysburg and Vicksburg in July led to further depreciation of the bonds, which made it virtually impossible for Richmond to borrow again from European investors.[48]

If judged on whether the Erlanger loan provided arms and other war matériel, it was a success in underwriting close to £1.8 million ($8.5 million) of the South's purchases in Europe in 1863 through the early part of 1864. But the negative political and diplomatic impact of the loan on Confederate credibility as an entity deserving recognition far outweighed its numeric value.[49]

In Washington, Seward sought to buy time by asking the French to clarify their policy toward the war. He had learned of Napoleon's growing interest in recognizing the Confederacy, either with or without the British. Yet at the same time, Seward wrote, Mercier had informed his superiors in Paris that after the Confederate defeats at Gettysburg and Vicksburg, recognition no longer seemed viable. The secretary of state therefore directed Dayton to seek "an explanation" from Foreign Minister Drouyn of the emperor's intentions. Napoleon must understand that recognition would be "an unfriendly proceeding."[50]

Before Seward's hard-nosed instructions arrived, however, the French crisis had passed. News of the Union's recent battlefield conquests undercut recognition's appeal. Drouyn assured Dayton that "the Emperor had, at no time, made any proposition to England to acknowledge the South." Lindsay and Roebuck had "pressed him hard to do so," insisting that *England was ready to acknowledge the South and would do so if it were not believed that France would refuse to follow* [Dayton's emphasis]." If the emperor "would but say *the word*," the two emissaries claimed, the Commons would immediately pass the motion for recognition. Napoleon had replied that he had given England no reason to think he would oppose a joint action and that the Palmerston ministry had rejected the only proposal he had made on the matter. He now refused to propose recognition. When asked if they could relay his position to their peers, Napoleon consented, knowing his views were "no secret," but "he never dreamed of their attempting to use them as they afterwards did in the House of Commons." He had told them "he would not act alone upon any important matters either on the Continent or in America, and more especially would he not act alone in our affairs."[51]

Dayton pursued the matter. Did Gros say that the emperor intended to make another proposal that England join France in recognizing the Confederacy and that if turned down he would act alone? Dayton could barely complete the question before Drouyn, shaking his head, emphatically denied that he had done so. "Baron Gros never made such remarks; he had never said anything of the kind official or unofficial, public or private." As for the emperor's policy toward the American war, Drouyn insisted that "he had none; he waited on events." Dayton felt certain that the Union's battlefield triumphs had impressed the French and turned them against intervention.

Seward did not know it, but the victories had also dampened Confederate enthusiasm about Napoleon's actions in North America. The French consul in Richmond wrote home that the Confederacy's support for the French as its new neighbor in Mexico mirrored "the dreams of an unhappy people" whose hopes had been shattered.[52]

Drouyn had toned down Napoleon's instruction to Gros because it guaranteed trouble with the Union. The foreign minister had been alarmed by Napoleon's unorthodox diplomacy regarding Roebuck and Lindsay, as well as by his reckless involvement in another country's affairs.[53] The emperor had earlier called for an armistice that he outwardly professed to be innocent because it carried no promise of recognition. But as Slidell knew at the time and others correctly suspected, recognition would have followed a cease-fire and Napoleon stood prepared to use force if the British joined the project. His personal style of diplomacy was unique in showing no concern for the consequences, a feature that often resulted from his failure to consult advisers before acting.

Drouyn knew that any interventionist proposal guaranteed a bitter reaction by the Lincoln administration. Consequently, in accord with the cabinet's wishes, he chose to wait until the British took the lead and to temper the emperor's directive without closing the door on recognition. Furthermore, the thrust of Gros's message to Russell leaned heavily toward Drouyn's instruction. Thus Napoleon upheld his promises to Slidell, Roebuck, and Lindsay, while Drouyn acted with his colleagues in avoiding a policy conducive to war.[54]

Napoleon had mistakenly accused the British of revealing his November 1862 proposal to the Lincoln administration in an effort to hurt French relations with the Union. The charge was unfounded, for the French press had published the proposal two days *before* it appeared in British newspapers. Now, in mid-July 1863, whether or not he had just discovered his error, Napoleon wrote Drouyn that he no longer thought the British had tried to damage the Union-French relationship. His change of heart also came from the realization that any form of intervention would enrage the Union, and he did not wish to face a potential encounter alone. "I did not want to put myself in the wrong," he remarked to Drouyn, "without being sure of the help of England." Napoleon acknowledged his indiscretion. "I spoke to the misters Lindsay and Roebuck openly; I should have been more diplomatic."[55]

The Roebuck-Lindsay affair had needlessly threatened international relations. Napoleon's poorly considered use of personal diplomacy had taken place in English, where his vague and noncommittal language had left the matter vulnerable to misunderstanding. He had then ill-advisedly permitted Roebuck and Lindsay to repeat the exact words of their conversation to the members of Parliament. "They are no secret," he declared. Not everyone thought the episode accidental. The British undersecretary of state for foreign affairs, Sir Austen Layard, noted that many believed Napoleon had "told a deliberate lie."[56] Whatever the truth, the Anglo-French concert suffered a severe blow from Napoleon's armistice proposal that clouded all issues afterward. Not only did hard feelings continually plague any possible joint peace effort in American affairs, but they also disrupted the two nations' cooperation in the Polish crisis. Moreover, Napoleon's lingering interest in intervention, combined with his ongoing involvement in Mexico, encouraged the Confederacy and infuriated the Union, ensuring raw Franco-American relations in the postwar period.

Soon after the Roebuck affair, in August 1863, the Confederate government directed Mason to leave England. His mission had failed to persuade the Palmerston ministry either to grant recognition or to challenge the Union blockade. President Davis's reading of the parliamentary debates showed little chance of achieving recognition from the British, and he wanted Mason to relocate in France. Within a short time, the Davis cabinet voted to expel the British consuls from Richmond, probably as a face-saving measure but officially because they had told British nationals that they were under no obligation to serve the Confederacy's armed forces. When Mason informed Russell of his departure, the foreign secretary coldly emphasized that nothing had changed. His reasons for refusing to accept the emissary on an official basis were "still in force," and it was "not necessary to repeat them." Mason joined Slidell in Paris before accepting a new appointment as commissioner in Europe.[57]

The Confederacy nevertheless maintained its warm relationship with French representatives, largely because King Cotton Diplomacy had collapsed and France was its last hope. The British had made clear their opposition to intervention; the Russians had never deviated from their pro-Union stance; and the Spanish, who at an earlier time would doubtless have followed a European alignment with the Confederacy, now feared a victorious Union seeking to grab Cuba or any of their other remaining American possessions as retribution for Madrid's neutrality.[58] Napoleon, southerners calculated, would soon have to work with them in holding on to Mexico. Perhaps the Confederacy could help him in exchange for French recognition. Thus did southern leaders continue the illusion of expecting to achieve independence by surviving the war rather than winning it.

Napoleon's involvement in Mexico had become so tangled that the entire project threatened to unravel. He had to maintain a delicate balance between Union and Confederacy. The future of his Mexican venture greatly rested on an independent Confederacy, but so also must he weigh the potential benefits against the certainty of alienating the United States. Seward kept the heat on by repeatedly warning the emperor against staying in Mexico. This dilemma wore heavily on Napoleon as he pondered recognizing the Confederacy in exchange for its support in the Western Hemisphere.[59]

The Confederacy decided to push the issue in the fall of 1863, when it learned that the rumors were true—that Napoleon intended to install Maximilian as emperor of Mexico. Richmond's leaders prepared to guarantee against interfering with the new monarch in exchange for either an alliance with France or its intervention on the Confederacy's behalf.[60]

Not by coincidence did that same fall of 1863 mark the beginning of sharply deteriorating relations between the Union and Mexico. The Lincoln administration became uneasy about the prospect of Maximilian's ascension to the throne, and Dayton again trooped over to Drouyn's office. France did not seek either Mexican territory or governmental control, assured the foreign minister. As asserted many times, the emperor intended to withdraw from Mexico once he had resolved the debt problem and restored stability to that deeply divided nation. But when Dayton expressed concern that the French might "leave a puppet behind," Drouyn coyly replied: "No, the strings would be too long to work." Dayton found no humor in the remark and warned the White House not to trust the French. The commander of the French army, General Forey, was "the real governor of Mexico" and "the mouth piece of the Emperor." Its people would follow the direction of a conquering military force. "Truthfulness is not, as you know, an element in French diplomacy or manners. No man but a Frenchman," he told Seward, "would ever have thought of [Charles] Talleyrand's famous *bon mot*, that the object of language was to conceal thought."[61]

In exonerating Napoleon of intrigue, Drouyn either twisted the truth or was incredibly naive in believing the emperor's motives altruistic. In November 1862 the *Moniteur* had published an article highlighting Napoleon's defense of his Mexican policy. The following January the *Documents diplomatiques* elaborated on his goals. Soon afterward, an anonymous pamphlet, appearing in Paris under the title *La France, le Mexique et les États-Confédérés*, strongly advocated Confederate independence as a step toward regenerating Spanish America. In late September 1863 the *New York Times* published a translation, which infuriated Americans over the emperor's audacity. Within two weeks, another translation appeared in New York City. William Henry Hurlbert, celebrated journalist and editorial writer for the *New York Times* and now editor of the *New York World*, wrote a preface to this version, claiming that the pamphlet deserved "world-wide notoriety as embodying the first coherent view which has been made public of the designs of Napoleon III in the New World." Doubtless inspired by Napoleon, the *La France, le Mexique et les États-Confédérés* was seemingly the work of longtime adviser Michel Chevalier.[62]

A noted entrepreneur, Chevalier had for some time promoted these ideas and had a great influence on Napoleon. In the 1830s Chevalier had visited the United States to inspect its canals and railroads; he also traveled across the country and into Mexico and Cuba, studying their economic potential. His subsequent books and pamphlets exalted the New World's future. In late 1851, he supported Napoleon's successful coup and, as a reward, became a high-ranking official of the Second Empire who was well positioned to advance his socialist ideas. Chevalier and Napoleon developed a bond over their mutual interest in building an isthmian canal connecting the Atlantic and Pacific oceans. In addition, Chevalier detailed Mexico's poor economic conditions in two articles appearing in the *Revue des deux mondes* in 1862. The following year he published *Le Mexique, ancien et moderne*, a two-volume work on the French expedition in Mexico, which emphasized the need to halt U.S. expansion, stabilize Spanish America with monarchical rule, and encourage a mass influx of talented Europeans to ensure economic and social reforms. In this way, the Old World would acquire a vast wealth of raw materials and a host of new markets, making Napoleon the chief benefactor of the Latin peoples in both Europe and the Americas. Thus armed with material goods and world stature, he would block "the absorption of Southern America by Northern America" and prevent "the degradation of the Latin race on the other side of the ocean." French recognition of the Confederacy would ensure its independence along with a bright future for Mexico and its neighbors.[63]

Thus did Chevalier publicly set out Napoleon's Grand Design for the Americas, a program that hinged on recognition of the Confederacy. France would protect the Latins in the New World by working closely with the southern states. In an appeal to French aristocrats and military leaders, Napoleon proclaimed his intention to "regenerate" French commerce in the Atlantic as a major impetus to the nation's industry. Mexican grain and gold would furnish the basis for growth, but only after a new monarchical government had restored stability and control. The French Empire had eliminated anarchy at home by a progressive program of socialism. "This it is that the empire is to do in Mexico, and this it cannot do securely and properly until the Confederate States have been recognized."[64]

The most novel feature of Napoleon's reform program was its elimination of slavery as an obstacle to recognizing the Confederacy. *Le Mexique, ancien et moderne* derisively noted that America's brutal treatment of the Native Americans showed a lack of respect for human rights and a certain resistance to abolishing slavery. And even if the Union won the war, "the poor negroes would find their way to liberty a path of thorns." France would remedy that situation. As the first European nation to recognize the Confederacy, it would gain "a right to obtain much more for the negro than the Federals could secure for him through their 'Union by victory.'" Only in peacetime could abolition take place; "an alliance with the South will effect that great social renovation." Thus, according to the pamphlet, "Slavery cannot possibly be made a serious argument against the recognition of the South." France could bring about "the gradual emancipation of the slaves without making slavery a ground for refusing recognition." Once it had removed slavery from the intervention issue, other powers—including the British, Spanish (with interests in Havana), and Austrians (with Maximilian on the Mexican throne)—would likewise recognize the Confederacy. The Union, facing the French navy in alliance with the Confederacy, would have to give up the war.[65]

Napoleon considered Confederate independence crucial to the military and commercial bastion he envisioned in the Western Hemisphere. The Confederacy would ally with France in protecting Mexico from Union encroachments while the new monarchy reigned over an industrial and agricultural mecca underwritten by the rich silver mines of Sonora in northern Mexico—located at the top of a vast area extending west two thousand miles from the Rio Grande's opening into the Gulf of Mexico to the southern rim of Baja California at the Pacific Ocean. Napoleon had recently instructed one of his military commanders in Mexico to acquire "confidential information about the mines of Sonora and advise me if it would be possible to occupy that state." To populate this huge domain, France planned to entice American and European immigrants with generous tax reductions on mining. French military forces would ensure Mexico's security and thereby avoid the charge of imperialism.[66]

Drouyn was intimately familiar with the emperor's intentions regarding Mexico, even if he chose to emphasize the redeeming qualities of protecting it against American invasion and providing economic assistance to both the Latin and French people. And there is little doubt that he disapproved of the Mexican project as a possible source of conflict. But he was a loyal servant who believed his responsibility was to "carry out the wishes of the emperor." In writing instructions to General Achille François Bazaine in Mexico City, Drouyn referred to the Grand Design as "the Emperor's highest expression of policy," as found in his letter of July 3, 1862, to General Forey; "it is always to this memorable document that we must return."[67]

In pursuing his dream of reestablishing a French Empire in the New World, Napoleon had convinced Maximilian to join him in this world of illusion. The young, impressionable Austrian had come from a long heritage of emperors and readily accepted Napoleon's invitation to become a king and thus replace the chaos of republicanism with the order of monarchy. From the quiet of the American legation in Austria, Union minister and historian John Lothrop Motley watched these proceedings unfold. In wonder, he asserted that the archduke "firmly believes . . . he is going forth . . . to establish an American empire, and that it is his divine mission to destroy the dragon of democracy."[68]

With justification, President Lincoln remained concerned about French objectives and sent troops to Texas under the command of General Nathaniel Banks. Perhaps their presence would discourage Napoleon from expanding northward.[69]

Seward traced this threat back to the emperor's original assumption that the Union could not prevail over the insurrection. At the American war's outbreak, Napoleon "adopted the current opinion of European Statesmen that the efforts of this Government to maintain and preserve the Union would be unsuccessful." Seward complained that this prejudgment had prolonged the war. Acting in concert, France and England had conceded belligerent rights to the Confederacy, called on the Union to accept a separation, and conferred on recognition. The emperor had encouraged the insurrection by raising questions about "our position as a sovereign" and suggesting an "equality with the seditious disturbers of our peace."[70]

The United States, Seward asserted, did not wish to intervene in Mexico's war with France, just as it did not expect any European government to intervene in the American contest. If France adopted a policy in Mexico contrary to American sentiments, the result might be a "collision between France and the United States and other American Republics." Rumor was that France intended to take the Rio Grande and Texas, seize control of the Mississippi River, and form a coalition under French control between "the regency established in Mexico and the insurgent cabal at Richmond." The president, Seward alleged, did not believe these stories but worried that they might cause trouble.[71] Whether or not Seward had expressed the real feelings of the president, he treaded carefully on this matter, not wishing to provoke France but wanting to make the Union's message clear—that the United States would not abide by any action threatening its sovereignty or that of Mexico.

In an early October 1863 conversation with Drouyn, Dayton again expressed apprehension about the French involvement in Mexico. How rich the irony when assured that Maximilian would take the throne only after the democratic exercise of a popular vote. Drouyn assured a countrywide election that encompassed all Mexican departments, whether or not in French possession. If it appeared that a large majority of the entire population (Spanish and Native American) supported a monarchical form of government, Drouyn would consider that "sufficient." He foresaw no difficulty in showing that a large majority favored the archduke as a monarch. Dayton was cynical about the honesty of a vote, explaining to Seward how the system guaranteed a monarchy. The French would probably seize control of the larger cities and more populous departments and then institute voting by registry, allowing them to control the people within reach of their armies. "None else will vote save those who are favorable to the French programme, and the result announced will probably be a vast majority. There will seem to be nothing of republicanism left in all Mexico!" Dayton, however, said nothing publicly because Seward had instructed him not to pursue the matter.[72]

Drouyn contended that once the United States established relations with Maximilian's government, France would leave Mexico. In an assertion that belied a central premise of the Grand Design, he again renounced any interest in Texas or permanent control of Mexico. Yet Napoleon's plan highlighted French interest in Texas, and the implantation of an Austrian on the Mexican throne did not mean that he intended to give up control of Mexico after the departure of French troops. Dayton surely knew that Maximilian would maintain close ties with the emperor. Drouyn nonetheless continued to stress his country's goodwill, even assuring Dayton that America's proximity to Mexico "entitled us [Americans] to an influence there paramount to that of distant European countries, and that France at her great distance from the scene would not be guilty of the folly of desiring or attempting to interfere with us."[73]

Seward realized that a rigged election would put an Austrian monarch on the Mexican throne but could do nothing until the Civil War had ended. The French knew, he noted, that the United States would not extend recognition to any government in Mexico until the war had resolved the issue. To worried members of Congress, the secretary declared it "quite as likely" for the administration to recognize Jefferson Davis as "King of Richmond" than to recognize Maximilian as emperor of Mexico. Drouyn nonetheless stated that an early U.S. acknowledgment of the proposed empire "would be convenient to France" by relieving it of complications in Mexico. Dayton responded that the United States did not intend to recognize a Mexican monarchy in view of its good relations with the existing Juárez government. But just before Christmas he told Seward of the stories circulating in Paris that if Maximilian accepted the Mexican throne, the Confederacy would promptly recognize his government and France would recognize the Confederacy.[74]

The Lincoln administration realized that Napoleon's plan threatened the hemisphere. Although the ongoing Civil War prevented an immediate and direct reaction, the Union's recent victories at Gettysburg and Vicksburg had permitted Seward to sharpen his tone toward France. Its denial of imperial ambitions in Mexico, he asserted, had encouraged the Union to remain neutral during the conflict. But Maximilian's imminent arrival had changed the situation. Once the French resolved their financial issues, they must pull out of Mexico without disturbing its "unity and independence." The Union wished to avoid alienating France but would deal with the matter after defeating the Confederacy. "The sensibility I have described," warned Seward, "increases with every day's increasing of the decline of the insurrection in the United States."[75]

Without the cooperation of an independent Confederacy, Napoleon could not succeed in Mexico. Maximilian won the throne in the fall of 1863 after a so-called plebiscite, but he must have felt some trepidation after most observers concluded that the election did not reflect the popular will. So uneasy was Maximilian that he reached out to the Confederate government before it had reacted to the outcome of the vote. In November he told a friend of President Davis then in Europe that he supported the Confederacy's independence and compared its precarious position to that of Mexico. England and France, Maximilian said, should recognize the Confederacy before he assumed the Mexican throne. Soon afterward he told another southerner that Confederate victory in the war was "identical with that of the new Mexican empire." Slidell considered this a renewed opportunity for recognition and requested a meeting with Maximilian while he was in Paris discussing the Mexican venture with Napoleon. But, surprisingly, the archduke did not respond. From Belgium, Mann suspected that something had gone awry and indignantly declared that Napoleon had "enjoined upon Maximilian to hold no official relations with" Confederate officials, either in France or in Mexico.[76]

Aware of the Confederacy's integral role in Napoleon's plan, Davis and other officials in Richmond could not understand why neither the emperor nor Maximilian would grant recognition. Indeed, southern hopes had risen, only to fall again. In early December, Davis had informed the Confederate Congress that British neutrality had become "positively unfriendly." Yet in what could be interpreted as an indirect offer of alliance, officials in France had made it clear that the Confederacy must not interfere with French occupation of Mexico and its move toward self-government. Napoleon, Davis stressed, had given his solemn pledge that he would not force any form of government upon Mexico. Monarchy or republic—that was for the Mexican people to decide. In January 1864, Davis appointed a minister to Mexico. General William Preston, who had served in the same position in Spain, was then in Havana and expecting to proceed to Mexico City at any moment. The following month Slidell assured Benjamin that Maximilian considered recognition of the Confederacy "essential to the successful establishment of his Government." And now this studied insult by the newly elected monarch was too much to bear.[77]

Slidell expressed his anger to Maximilian's aide-de-camp. "Without the active friendship of the South," he declared in a transparent warning, the new monarch "will be entirely powerless to resist Northern aggression." Benjamin could not fathom why neither Napoleon nor Maximilian realized that "the safety of the new empire is dependent solely upon our success in interposing a barrier between northern aggression and the Mexican territory." Slidell warned Drouyn along with the Mexican ministers in Paris and London that the American war would soon end with Confederate independence and that the two new governments in North America would enter an "offensive and defensive alliance, for the establishment of an American policy on our continent, which will result in the suppression of monarchical institutions in Mexico."[78]

What had caused Maximilian's abrupt change in policy? In early March 1864, just before departing for Mexico, he spent a week in Paris during which he refused to meet with either Union or Confederate representatives, or with French minister Mercier, who was home at the time. Maximilian had isolated himself from the Confederacy following a discussion with Napoleon and after the rumored promise by Lincoln to extend recognition to Mexico in exchange for his refusal to recognize the Confederacy. Lincoln's thinly veiled threat of war had altered the emperor's plan. On April 10 Maximilian formally accepted the throne and four days later left for Mexico, but never recognizing the Confederacy. Preston remained in Havana through mid-summer, waiting for notification to assume his new post that never came.[79]

Napoleon's fear of war with the Union had led him to withhold recognition, ignoring the Confederacy's virtual invitation of alliance as well as its threat to join the Union in defending the Americas against French violations of the Monroe Doctrine. He also withdrew his approval of the Confederacy's building a navy in France, rescinding the government's authorization to arm the vessels and blocking all but one of six ironclads from reaching the Confederacy by selling them to other countries. Paradoxical as it may seem, the emperor could take no action on behalf of the Confederacy, even though he believed its independence would practically guarantee success in Mexico. The reason was that in a war with the Union, his only ally would be a Confederacy that might develop second thoughts about a foreign intrusion in the hemisphere. A few months earlier, he had told a British diplomat that such a war "would spell disaster to the interests of France and would have no possible object."[80]

Davis was livid, complaining to the lawmakers in Richmond that England and France had ignored morality and law in accepting the Union invasion of the South as an alleged effort to put down a rebellion. The Confederacy would not quit, he declared. Let not the world think that the Confederacy's interest in peace suggested exhaustion; it preferred "any fate to submission to their savage assailants."[81]

The chief irony in this affair is that Maximilian's mid-June 1864 arrival in Mexico City assured trouble with the Union because his assumption of the throne violated Napoleon's pledge to seek only a claims settlement. Although the emperor insisted that a popular election was responsible for Maximilian's rise to power, the Lincoln administration doubted the honesty of the proceedings and refused to recognize the new monarch as the legitimate ruler. At the risk of antagonizing the Confederacy by withholding recognition, Napoleon could only hope that it would win the war on its own and thus secure his control in Mexico. How he could expect such an outcome provided further evidence of the world of illusion in which he lived.[82]

Napoleon's last-minute ploy showed, once again, his dismissal of reality: He accused Lincoln of agreeing to recognize Maximilian's government in exchange for a French promise not to negotiate with the Confederacy. This charge was simply not true, yet Mercier had left Washington for Paris in early March 1864 to inform Slidell of the so-called arrangement while London's *Globe* reported the same story. Napoleon probably based the claim on Dayton's assurance to Drouyn that the United States did not oppose the upcoming monarchy in Mexico and would "enter into relations with it." Yet at this very time, the House of Representatives in Washington passed resolutions against recognizing the new government in Mexico and the Senate seemed ready to do the same. Both the French press and Mercier maintained that Napoleon would proceed as planned despite the congressional resolutions. The *Moniteur* and the *Constitutionnel* did not expect Union interference in Mexican affairs. Slidell protested that Mercier had masqueraded as the Confederacy's friend while trying to be "everything to everybody."[83]

The Confederacy's chief enemy in this shady episode was Napoleon, for he was prepared to sell it out to secure the Union's acceptance of Maximilian. Judah P. Benjamin failed to see the betrayal, attributing the emperor's refusal to grant recognition to Seward's warnings of war. The U.S. secretary of state's strategy was "so transparent," Benjamin hotly asserted, that Napoleon should not have been fooled. Yet Confederate leaders had underestimated the impact of Seward's angry threats abroad, deluding themselves that recognition would come once they convinced the Europeans of the righteousness of their cause. Nor did their other strategies work—either King Cotton Diplomacy or their use of Mexico as leverage. Their naive approach to foreign affairs prevented them from realizing that self-interest guided British and French policies throughout the American war. Recognition of the Confederacy did not offer anything so vital to their interests that it outweighed the risk of war with the Union.[84] Nonetheless, Napoleon's provocative diplomacy had combined with Britain's neutrality to give the South false hope, doubtless prolonging the war, while leaving a legacy of Union hostility for both European governments that lasted for decades.

In the summer of 1864, Lincoln confronted a major problem with the Peace Democrats, who had attracted expressions of Confederate interest in their proposal for an armistice with the intention of negotiating a reunion. Such a cease-fire at this time, the Confederates knew, effectively meant their victory in the war. Lincoln also knew this and decided that both sides must publicly pronounce their conditions for peace before they met to negotiate. The Union, of course, would insist on restoration of the Union and the cessation of slavery; the Confederacy would call for independence and the protection of slavery, thereby proving to peace groups in the Union that only victory on the battlefield could end the war. Events, however, did not play out that way.

To prepare for peace talks, Confederate and Union representatives met at Niagara Falls in Canada on July 18 to discuss how to arrange safe passage for Confederate emissaries to Washington. It was an impressive gathering. Representing the Confederacy were Clement C. Clay, former senator from Alabama; James P. Holcombe, former congressman from Virginia; and Jacob Thompson, former cabinet member under President James Buchanan. The Union sent Horace Greeley, editor of the *New York Tribune*, and John Hay, the president's private secretary. Hay gave the Confederate delegation a letter from Lincoln agreeing to peace talks premised only on "the integrity of the whole Union, and the abandonment of slavery." Davis, however, had not authorized his delegation to mention peace terms. The conference never took place. Davis publicly blamed Lincoln for the debacle, claiming he had purposely sabotaged the meeting by demanding unconditional surrender.[85]

But a propaganda victory did not translate into victory on the battlefield, and ultimately Union forces under General William T. Sherman took Atlanta in the fall of 1864, helping to usher in the reelection of Lincoln in a November landslide over George B. McClellan and the Democratic Party. It thus became evident that military events alone would decide the outcome of the war.

With Confederate fortunes sinking on both the domestic and foreign fronts in early 1865 and more than a few congressmen calling for a change in leadership, Davis hoped to rally his people's support by agreeing to peace discussions intended to publicly expose the Union's insistence on total victory. In January he considered a peace plan in Richmond with longtime friend and veteran Jacksonian Francis P. Blair, whose son Montgomery served as postmaster general in Lincoln's cabinet. Lincoln had been highly skeptical when first approached by Blair with his chief proposal—to ally northerners and southerners in forcing the French out of Mexico. But the president did not want to reject even the slightest chance for peace and approved Blair's crossing the battle lines into the Confederacy.

The Blair-Davis conversation led to a four-hour meeting on February 3 at Hampton Roads, Virginia, on board the Union steamship *River Queen*. The meeting had almost aborted when Davis approved a discussion aimed at bringing peace "to the two countries" and Lincoln responded by expressing hope that they might achieve peace for "our one common country." Davis expected another Union demand for total surrender that would kill any formal talks. Indeed, to undermine the peace advocates at home, he hoped to tie them to that expected failure by sending a delegation comprised of three known proponents of negotiations: Vice President Alexander H. Stephens, former secretary of state and president pro tem of the Confederate Senate Robert M. T. Hunter, and Assistant Secretary of War and former U.S. Supreme Court justice John A. Campbell. Seward, soon joined in the talks by President Lincoln, read the administration's terms of settlement: restoration of the Union, no retreat from its stand against slavery, and unconditional surrender. The president expressed no interest in Stephens's proposed joint effort to throw Napoleon's armies out of Mexico. Nor did he welcome Hunter's call for an armistice and a meeting of the states. Hunter was perplexed. Even King Charles I of England had reached agreements with armed rebels during its civil war. "I do not profess to be posted in history," Lincoln wryly remarked. "All I distinctly recollect about the case of Charles I, is, that he lost his head."[86]

Lincoln's stipulations for peace had not changed throughout the war, and yet Davis feigned surprise and indignation over the meeting's collapse. To the Confederate Congress in Richmond three days later, he denounced Lincoln for acting as a "conqueror" in demanding "unconditional submission." That same night, he publicly swore "unconquerable defiance" to the "disgrace of surrender" and dubbed his chief enemy "His Majesty Abraham the First." Within a year, Davis promised, the "Yankees" would "petition us for peace on our own terms."[87]

But the war continued to go badly for the Confederacy until, in the spring of 1865, it made a last-ditch effort to salvage victory by offering Benjamin's proposal of emancipation in exchange for British and French recognition. Duncan F. Kenner, a Louisiana congressman and wealthy slaveowner, had made the suggestion to his friend and former law partner Benjamin (along with Slidell) shortly after the Emancipation Proclamation went into effect in 1863, arguing that slavery posed the major barrier to foreign recognition. Davis had objected, noting that each state had laws protecting slave ownership and the Confederate constitution prohibited any measure "denying or impairing the right of property in negro slaves." By late 1864, however, the Confederate military was in such desperate straits that the southern press urged the use of slaves to defend the South. Kenner now revived the idea and this time won Davis's support. The president sent Kenner to Europe with instructions to Slidell and Mason to pursue the arrangement. The proposal was so sensitive that Davis kept it secret from both the Confederate Congress and people.[88]

Yet Kenner's secret mission was anything but secret. Reports about it appeared in the *Richmond Enquirer* and *Sentinel* in late December 1864. Seward notified the Union embassy in London of the mission on January 10, and the news appeared in the Paris press on March 2. Kenner had left Richmond in disguise on January 18, 1865, lamenting that he would have had a better chance in early 1863, when both England and France were well aware of the Confederacy's diminishing resources and the battles at Gettysburg and Vicksburg had not yet occurred. "I would have succeeded" in securing a £15 million loan when "slavery was the bone of contention."[89]

Now, neither Napoleon nor Palmerston showed interest in the proposal. To Kenner and Mason, the emperor explained that he refused to move without England and that he "had never taken [slavery] into consideration" regarding recognition. On March 14, 1865, Mason met with Palmerston for more than an hour at Cambridge House, where the prime minister also rejected the plan, insisting that slavery was not the obstacle to intervention; the Confederacy had not proven its independence on the battlefield. The *Richmond Dispatch* glumly noted, "No one would receive us as a gift."[90]

The responses should not have surprised the Confederacy. Napoleon's reply contained nothing different from his initial determination to follow the British lead. Palmerston's argument against recognition correlated with his long conversation with De Leon in the summer of 1862. On neither side of the English Channel did slavery emerge as the critical consideration.

In perhaps the darkest irony, the death knell for recognition came in late March 1865, when Mason's friend and Confederate sympathizer, the Earl of Donoughmore, told him that, contrary to prevailing thought, slavery "had always been in the way" of recognition. In fact, he added, had it not been for slavery, the Confederacy would have won recognition after Lee's victory at Second Bull Run in August 1862 or when he posed a threat to Washington before his defeat at Gettysburg in July 1863. When Mason asked what chance Richmond had for recognition if he went back to Palmerston and offered immediate abolition, Donoughmore (who opposed slavery) replied that "the time had gone by now."[91]

In the meantime, the Union's string of military victories in late 1864 and early 1865 had forced Napoleon to abandon his Mexican project and soon to begin a phased withdrawal of troops that would conclude in February 1867. With the war finally coming to a close, the emperor considered it expedient to pull out before confronting an angry and reunited American nation. Sherman's forces had cut a broad swath of destruction through Georgia while making their way from Atlanta to the sea and taking Savannah in December, and Grant's army hammered Lee into surrender at Virginia's Appomattox Courthouse in April 1865. Just days later Lincoln died from an assassin's bullet, bringing to the White House Vice President Andrew Johnson, of Tennessee, who had publicly promised military retribution against the French for invading Mexico. In a final act of duplicity, Napoleon announced in January

1866 that France had accomplished its objective for civilization and was re-calling its troops. Mexico was ready to stand on its own.[92]

Maximilian made the ill-fated decision to remain on the throne. In a fit-ting climax to this fiasco, President Juárez's troops captured him in mid-May 1867. After a court-martial found the new emperor of Mexico guilty of sub-verting the republic, he was executed by a firing squad a month later.[93]

Thus the French, like the British, finally realized it was in their best interest to stay out of the American war and avert a conflict with the United States. Ironically, Lincoln's move for emancipation had ultimately restrained Britain while releasing France to pursue Napoleon's Grand Design for the Americas, a plan that presented an even greater threat to the United States and the hemisphere than did England's flirtations with intervention. But Lincoln's actions had helped to spur a social revolution, one highlighted by the Eman-cipation Proclamation, the Gettysburg Address of November 1863 heralding "a new birth of freedom," and the Thirteenth Amendment of December 1865, which abolished slavery and in so doing helped heal the Union. "Amidst all the horrors of war," British minister Lyons solemnly observed, "the one con-solation for all the evils of this wretched war" was the death of slavery.[94]

Epilogue

The Civil War was America's greatest crisis, for it imperiled the republic both from within—the struggle between North and South—and from without—the threat of intervention by England and France. Whichever side won the war would largely determine the direction of the republic, and, as pure as the British and French claimed their neutrality to be, their actions would likewise shape its future to their advantage.

Thus the story of the Civil War cannot be complete without an exploration of its international dimensions. Yet historians of Blue and Gray diplomacy remain small in number, particularly compared with the military and political historians of the conflict. Battles, generals, and politicians all helped to determine the outcome of the war; but so did diplomats. Had the Confederacy secured recognition from England (and then France and perhaps others), it would have gained the right as a nation to negotiate alliances, both military and commercial; call on its allies to help challenge the Union blockade; and float loans necessary to finance the war. With the outcome hanging in the balance during the critical first eighteen months of the fighting, recognition might have tipped the scales in the Confederacy's favor and ended the war by the close of 1862 or in mid-1863 with southern independence. But despite the countless discussions about intervention in London and Paris, Washington and Richmond, that moment never came.

The Confederacy's failure to win recognition did not by itself determine the victor in the war. But its inability to gain acknowledgment as a nation certainly contributed to its defeat. If so, why did the Confederacy fail to win recognition?

Jefferson Davis was a poor diplomat, according to many writers. He did little to help the Confederacy's case, both in his demeanor and in his actions.

He appeared cold and stubborn, often inflexible about changing decisions, rigidly formal, and out of touch with his people. He was among the first to see no chance for recognition, yet among the last to concede defeat. So occupied with military matters, he did not give needed attention to foreign affairs. Davis remained shackled to legality, never understanding the European powers' emphasis on national interests over international law and criticizing British neutrality as pro-Union in thrust because it was not pro-Confederate.[1]

Abraham Lincoln, on the other hand, personified a diplomat, as shown in his appointments, his realization that international (and domestic) law became flexible in wartime, and his ability to make meaningful public pronouncements. What he lacked in knowledge, he made up with a determination to learn. Admittedly, Lincoln miscalculated the British response to his wartime objective of preserving the Union, expecting the government and public to understand his political obstacles to tying slavery to the war effort. He also mistakenly assumed that the British government and people would react favorably to the Emancipation Proclamation and drop all thoughts of intervention. Yet, in his defense, they ultimately realized that he had taken a major step toward abolition regardless of the document's lack of moral emphasis. In this and other public declarations such as the Gettysburg Address and his First and Second Inaugural Addresses, Lincoln's words inspired listeners to seek those higher goals envisioned by the Founding Fathers.[2]

Nevertheless, the realistic considerations helping to shape a policy of foreign intervention far outweighed the role of personalities. Slavery was always an obstacle in British thinking, as the Earl of Donoughmore asserted to Mason in the spring of 1865. Confederate diplomacy was inept, according to many writers, beginning with Davis's choice of emissaries abroad and continuing with King Cotton Diplomacy and a long record of fiscal and commercial mismanagement. Richmond's leaders helped to undermine foreign relations by refusing to use cotton as collateral for loans until too late in the war, failing to develop a centralized purchasing program in Europe, and deciding against regulating business in the national interest. Another factor was Russia, which never seriously considered intervention and thereby undercut any Anglo-French action by eliminating itself as the only foreign power trusted by the Union. New research suggests that the great majority of British and French workers, and doubtless the bulk of British and French citizens, did not support the Confederacy despite their need for cotton. The Confederacy never proved its claim to independent status by winning decisively on the battlefield. And, finally, Seward's repeated threats of war helped to ward off intervention.[3]

Was there ever a moment in the war when recognition was a distinct possibility? There were, in fact, two such times: in late August 1862, when Palmerston supported a mediation immediately after Lee's victory at Second Bull Run, and in early 1863, when Napoleon appeared ready to recognize the Confederacy as well as install the Maximilian government in Mexico. In both instances, the European leaders had become convinced that a combination of interests justified intervention—the British to stop a war that threatened the Atlantic economy and shocked the conscience of Victorian England; the French to protect Mexico from Union invasion, improve the lot of Latin peoples, and build another Napoleonic empire. Yet in both instances, the interventionists backed away when the Union rebounded with battlefield victories and the Lincoln administration repeated its threat to wage war against the intruder.

The central question remains: Was there anything the Confederacy had that either the British or the French considered so vital to their interests that it was worth fighting a war with the United States?

Both European powers opposed slavery, wanted to end what they considered a senseless war in which southern separation was a fait accompli, and shared a humanitarian and economic interest in stopping a conflict that committed monstrous atrocities at home while inflicting collateral damage on other nations. Yet none of these considerations shook the foundations of British and French security. The risk of war with the United States was always greater than the benefits gained from supporting Confederate independence.

Thus the answer to the question is no; yet it took more than two years for both British and French policymakers to reach this conclusion. In the meantime, their talk of intervention posed a serious threat to the republic, both North and South, by adding another dimension to the crisis Americans already confronted from within.

Once the British and the French realized they had no vital interests worth fighting for in the American war—the British in the fall of 1862, the French during the following spring—the Confederacy had lost its last chance for recognition and the war's outcome would turn only on the battlefield— where the Union held insurmountable advantages in manpower and material resources.

In one of those all-too-rare instances in history, a country—in this case

England, followed by France—resisted the temptation to intervene in another country's domestic affairs. The Civil War demonstrates the dangers of foreign interference. So often the intervening power does not understand the issues and cannot determine who is "right"; finds it impossible to establish trust by eliminating suspicions of self-interest; is unable to render a fair, informed verdict that satisfies all sides; does not understand what caused the hostilities in the first place and thus cannot offer mutually satisfactory terms of peace; and must resort to force. Secretary for War Lewis in England had reminded his colleagues of these considerations, convincing them of the dangers in making a rash decision for recognition that might drag the British (and others) into the American war.

And so the Confederacy's greatest fear came to pass: To win recognition, it had to win in battle; but to win in battle, it had to have the foreign aid that could come only from recognition. In more ways than one, the South had fought a lost cause.

Notes

ABBREVIATIONS

Add. Mss., Brit. Lib.
　Additional Manuscripts,
　British Library, London
AR
　Duke of Argyll
BFSP
　Great Britain, Foreign Office,
　British and Foreign State Papers
Bodleian Lib.
　Bodleian Library, Oxford
　University, Oxford
BPP
　Great Britain, *British
　Parliamentary Papers*
CFA
　Charles Francis Adams
CFA Diary, Letterbook
　Adams Family Papers,
　Historical Society, Boston
CFA Jr.
　Charles Francis Adams Jr.
CG
　Congressional Globe
CL
　Fourth Earl of Clarendon
CWL
　Roy P. Basler, ed., *Collected
　Works of Abraham Lincoln*

Dip. Instructions, France (NA)
　U.S. Department of State,
　Diplomatic Instructions to U.S.
　Ministers to France (National
　Archives), Washington, D.C.
Dip. Instructions, Russia (NA)
　U.S. Department of State, Diplomatic
　Instructions to U.S. Ministers to
　Russia, 1801–1906 (National
　Archives), Washington, D.C.
Disp.
　Diplomatic Dispatches
Disp., France (NA)
　U.S. Department of State,
　Diplomatic Dispatches from U.S.
　Ministers to France (National
　Archives), Washington, D.C.
Disp., GB (NA)
　U.S. Department of State,
　Diplomatic Dispatches from U.S.
　Ministers to Great Britain (National
　Archives), Washington, D.C.
DS
　Department of State, United States
FO
　Foreign Office, Great Britain
FRUS
　U.S. Department of State, *Papers
　Relating to Foreign Affairs*

GB
  Great Britain
GC
  General Correspondence
JD
  Jefferson Davis
LC
  Library of Congress,
  Washington, D.C.
MHS
  Massachusetts Historical
  Society, Boston
NA
  National Archives, Washington, D.C.
NFBL, GB (NA)
  U.S. Department of State, Notes
  from the British Legation in the
  United States to the Department
  of State, 1791–1906 (National
  Archives), Washington, D.C.
NFFL, France (NA)
  U.S. Department of State, Notes
  from the French Legation in the
  United States to the Department
  of State, 1789–1906 (National
  Archives), Washington, D.C.

NTFL, France (NA)
  U.S. Department of State, Notes to
  Foreign Legations in the United
  States, from the Department of
  State, 1834–1906, France (National
  Archives), Washington, D.C.
NTFL, GB (NA)
  U.S. Department of State, Notes to
  Foreign Legations in the United
  States, from the Department of State,
  1834–1906, Great Britain (National
  Archives), Washington, D.C.
ORN
  U.S. Department of the Navy,
  Official Records of the Union
  and Confederate Navies in the
  War of the Rebellion
Parl. Debates
  Thomas C. Hansard, ed.,
  Hansard's Parliamentary Debates
PM/J
  Prime Minister/Journal
PRO
  Public Record Office, Kew, England
RU
  Lord John Russell

PROLOGUE

1. For the horrors and high casualties of trench warfare, see Hess, *Trench Warfare*, 91–98, 193–202, 208–12. Glatthaar examines the impact of atrocities and the rising number of deaths on the soldiers' growing turn to religion in his study, *General Lee's Army*, 57, 144, 163, 174, 330–32, 371, 380–81.

2. Sexton, *Debtor Diplomacy*, 1, 3–6, 12, 15, 17, 19; Potter, "Atlantic Economy." A recent study by Myers (*Caution and Cooperation*) highlights the Anglo-American ties that had developed before the Civil War, but then contains the questionable argument that this rapprochement overrode the importance of the recognition issue and virtually eliminated the chance of British intervention.

3. Schantz, *Awaiting the Heavenly Country*, 2, 10; Wills, *Lincoln at Gettysburg*, 76, chap. 2. For the war's atrocities, see Faust, *This Republic of Suffering*.

4. Vattel, *Law of Nations*, bk. 2, chap. 1, secs. 114–15, chap. 12, secs. 196–97; bk. 3, chap. 3, sec. 249, chap. 7, secs. 269–70, chap. 18, sec. 340.

5. Coletta, "Recognition Policy," 889–90.

6. Adams cited ibid., 888–89.

7. For a useful examination of the legal issues relating to diplomatic recognition, see Lauterpacht, *Recognition in International Law*.

8. For some of the important works used in writing this book, see the "Historiographical Note" following this section. Full citations for all works consulted are in the Bibliography.

CHAPTER 1

1. JD Inaugural Address, Feb. 18, 1861, in Richardson, *Messages and Papers of the Confederacy*, 1:183, 188. For the Confederate argument, see McPherson, *What They Fought For*, 10–11, 13, 27, 30.

2. Lincoln's original manuscript, [July?] 1861, *CWL*, 4:434 n. 83; Lincoln's First Inaugural Address, Mar. 4, 1861, *CWL*, 4:264–65, 268.

3. For Davis's legal approach to the war, see Eaton, *Davis*, chap. 17. For the Confederacy's belief that foreign recognition would come because of its righteous cause, see E. M. Thomas, *Confederate Nation*, 169.

4. Jenkins, *Britain*, 1:1–2; Blackett, *Divided Hearts*, 26, 54, 56, 87–88; D. A. Campbell, *English Public Opinion*, 47–49; Lorimer, "Role of Anti-Slavery Sentiment."

5. E. D. Adams, *Great Britain*, 2:2 (Hammond); *CG*, 36th Cong., 2nd sess., pt. 1, 73 (Wigfall). See also Hoslett, "Southern Expectations"; Owsley, *King Cotton Diplomacy*, 15–16; S. R. Cockerill (the leading southerner), Arkansas planter, politician, and soldier, to Gen. J. H. Walker, June 2, 1861, cited in Owsley, 19. Owsley's work is the classic study of this economic argument.

6. D. P. Crook, *The North, the South*, 120; Jenkins, *Britain*, 1:2–3; Owsley, *King Cotton Diplomacy*, 3. Nearly 17 percent of the British people were dependent on cotton and the textile industry. Ball, *Financial Failure*, 66.

7. Jenkins, *Britain*, 1:3; *Richmond Whig*, Dec. 12, 1861, quoted in D. P. Crook, *The North, the South*, 21.

8. Owsley, *King Cotton Diplomacy*, 1–5; *Economist*, Apr. 13, 1861, quoted ibid., 5.

9. *Times*, Apr. 29, June 1, 1861, quoted in Owsley, *King Cotton Diplomacy*, 11; Maj. W. H. Chase (of Florida), "The Secession of the Cotton States: Its Status, Its Advantages, and Its Power," *De Bow's Review* 30 (January 1861): 93–101 (quote, 95); V. H. Davis, *Jefferson Davis*, 2:160, 165.

10. *Saturday Review*, Jan. 12, 1861, quoted in D. A. Campbell, *English Public Opinion*, 50; *Economist*, Jan. 26, 1861, quoted in Campbell, 51; Campbell, 49–54; D. P. Crook, *The North, the South*, 7; Sexton, *Debtor Diplomacy*, 137–38; Eaton, *History*, 68–69; E. M. Thomas, *Confederate Nation*, 172; Case and Spencer, *United States and France*, 158, 161–64, 178–79, 181, 184; Khasigian, "Economic Factors"; Schmidt, "Influence of Wheat and Cotton"; *Economist*, Feb. 2, 1861, quoted in D. A. Campbell, *English Public Opinion*, 51; Pecquet, *Diplomacy of the Confederate Cabinet*, 35. In sharp disagreement on the northern grain issue are two less convincing articles and E. D. Adams's two-volume study: Ginzberg's "Economics of British Neutrality," which argues that wheat did *not* have a major impact on British neutrality; Robert H. Jones's "Long Live the King?" which insists that Britain experienced no shortage in either cotton or wheat and that the products had no impact on government policy toward the American war; and E. D. Adams's *GB and*

the American Civil War (2:13–14 n. 2), which found no expressions of concern among cabinet members about wheat shortages but numerous worries about cotton.

11. Case and Spencer, *United States and France*, chaps. 4–5; Blumenthal, "Confederate Diplomacy"; Sexton, *Debtor Diplomacy*, 136–37; Eaton, *Davis*, 167; W. H. Russell, *My Diary*, 79 (Apr. 16, 1861).

12. Robert Mure (private citizen in Charleston) to W. H. Russell, Dec. 13, 1860, FO 5, vol. 744 (PRO), cited in Jenkins, *Britain*, 1:6; Jenkins, 1:78; Confederate States of America, *Journal of the Congress*, 1:27.

13. Blackett, *Divided Hearts*, 75–77, 80–81, 91, 102, 119–20; D. P. Crook, "Portents of War"; Park, "English Workingmen"; Greenleaf, "British Labor"; R. Harrison, "British Labour"; *Economist*, Mar. 2, 1861, quoted in D. A. Campbell, *English Public Opinion*, 47; Campbell, 100–101; *Punch*, Feb. 9, 1861. Campbell shows that British Conservative reaction to the American conflict was much more complex than the traditional claim that political conservatives and aristocrats supported the Confederacy and radicals and working classes were pro-Union. See his study cited above, pp. 2–3, and numerous other references throughout the book. For examples of the traditional argument, see Bellows, "British Conservative Reaction," and Hernon, "British Sympathies." The pendulum threatened to swing the other way, when Ellison, in *Support for Secession*, argued that Lancashire's textile workers supported the Confederacy because of the need for cotton. But Blackett's highly important and well-researched study, *Divided Hearts*, brought a much needed balance to the literature by showing the deep divisions in Britain while establishing that most workers supported the Union. Wilbur D. Jones ("British Conservatives") likewise challenges the traditional argument, asserting that most members of the Conservative Party followed the problems in Denmark and Poland more than they did those in America.

14. W. R. West, *Contemporary French Opinion*, 10, 17, 113, 136; Blackburn, *French Newspaper Opinion*, 26–31; Gavronsky, "American Slavery" and *French Liberal Opposition*; Pecquet, *Diplomacy of the Confederate Cabinet*, 25, 28–29, 105.

15. Jenkins, *Britain*, 1:9–10; W. C. Davis, *Jefferson Davis*, 690, 693; Eaton, *Davis*, 272.

16. Jenkins, *Britain*, 1:14–15; JD speech in Stevenson, Ala., Feb. 14, 1861, in JD, *Papers*, 7:42; Hendrick, *Statesmen*, 140; D. P. Crook, *The North, the South*, 16.

17. Hendrick, *Statesmen*, 141; *New York Tribune*, Jan. 1, 1861; Bunch to RU, Mar. 21, 1861, FO 5/780 (PRO). For a first-rate biography, see Walther, *Yancey*.

18. Williams, *Diary from Dixie*, 126 (1st quote); Woodward, *Chesnut's Civil War*, 25 (2nd quote); Jenkins, *Britain*, 1:15–17; Myers, *Caution and Cooperation*, 196.

19. Bunch to RU, Mar. 21, 1861, FO 5/780 (PRO); French noble (Marquis de Lapressange) to Pecquet du Bellet, quoted in Hendrick, *Statesmen*, 140. Du Bellet acted as an agent of the South; he likewise considered Rost a poor choice. Pecquet, *Diplomacy of the Confederate Cabinet*, 30. See also D. P. Crook, *The North, the South*, 28; W. C. Davis, *Jefferson Davis*, 384–86.

20. Jenkins, *Britain*, 1:15–16; Owsley, "Mann"; V. H. Davis, *Jefferson Davis*, 1:557 (JD); Eaton, *Davis*, 166.

21. Cobb to wife, Feb. 21, 1861, quoted in Jenkins, *Britain*, 1:19.

22. Sickles quoted in *CG*, 36th Cong., 2nd sess., p. 1153 (Feb. 23, 1861).

23. *Times*, Mar. 20, 1861.

24. Confederate States of America, *Journal of the Congress*, 1:113; Cobb to wife, Mar. 7, 1861, quoted in Jenkins, *Britain*, 1:19–20.

25. Commissioners' directives of Mar. 16, 1861, in Richardson, *Messages and Papers of the Confederacy*, 2:3–8; D. P. Crook, *The North, the South*, 22; Du Bose, *Yancey*, 600 (Rhett); Hendrick, *Statesmen*, 142; Blumenthal, "Confederate Diplomacy," 151–52, 155, 162–64, 169.

26. Lutz, "Rudolph Schleiden," 210. Schleiden was the minister from Bremen.

27. Bancroft, *Seward*, 2:151 (Seward); Jenkins, *Britain*, 1:29–30, 90. During the Canadian rebellions against the crown in 1837–38, British sheriff Alexander McLeod allegedly killed an American in the destruction of a rebel gun-running steamer, the *Caroline*, in December 1837. Four years later American authorities brought him to trial in New York, where, after British prime minister Lord Palmerston threatened war, the jury returned an acquittal. Seward, then governor of the state, stirred up Anglophobia in the crisis by publicly attacking the crown. See H. Jones, *Webster-Ashburton Treaty*, chaps. 2, 4; Stevens, *Border Diplomacy*; and H. Jones and Rakestraw, *Prologue to Manifest Destiny*, chaps. 2–3.

28. Lyons to RU, Dec. 18, 1860, in Barnes and Barnes, *American Civil War*, 1:12; Jenkins, *Britain*, 1:44.

29. Lyons to RU, Feb. 4, 1861, RU Papers, PRO 30/22/35; CFA to CFA Jr., Dec. 20, 1861, in Ford, *Adams Letters*, 1:88 (contemporary quote).

30. For this argument, see Ferris, *Desperate Diplomacy*. On the decision by the British foreign secretary, Lord John Russell, to meet with the Confederate representatives on an unofficial basis, see RU to Lyons, Apr. 6, 1861, RU Papers, PRO 30/22/96.

31. Jenkins, *Britain*, 1:87. Britain and France had defeated Russia in the Crimean War of 1854–56.

32. Lyons to RU, May 8, Nov. 25, 1860, RU Papers, PRO 30/22/34; Lyons to RU, Dec. 4, 18, 1860, FO 5/740 (PRO).

33. RU to Lyons, Feb. 16, 1861, cited in Jenkins, *Britain*, 1:91; H. Jones, *Union in Peril*, 14–15; Lyons to RU, Mar. 18, 26, 1861, RU Papers, PRO 30/22/35.

34. Lyons to RU, Mar. 26, 29, May 6, June 18, 1861, RU Papers, PRO 30/22/35; Ferris, *Desperate Diplomacy*, 214 n. 26 (Lyons's warning to Seward).

35. Lincoln to Seward, Apr. 1, 1861, *CWL*, 4:316–17; Seward memo, "Some Thoughts for the President's Consideration," Apr. 1, 1861, *CWL*, 4:317–18. See Brauer, "Seward's 'Foreign War Panacea,'" 136–37, 153–55; H. Jones, *Union in Peril*, 15. For a defense of Seward, see Ferris, *Desperate Diplomacy*, 10–12. According to Landry ("Slavery and the Slave Trade," 184–207), in the memorandum Seward tried to promote nationalism over the slavery issue.

36. Lincoln to Seward, Apr. 1, 1861, *CWL*, 4:317; Brauer, "Seward's 'Foreign War Panacea,'" 156–57; Sowle, "Reappraisal of Seward's Memorandum"; H. Jones, *Union in Peril*, 15. Lincoln and Seward soon developed a close relationship, although the president maintained control over foreign affairs, particularly during crises. Van Deusen, *Seward*.

37. Brauer, "Slavery Problem," 441, 443–45; McPherson, *Tried by War*, 11, 34–35; H. Jones, *Union in Peril*, 15–16.

38. According to D. A. Campbell, the British never fathomed the depth of northern commitment to the Union and yet understood the southerners' drive for nationhood.

See his *English Public Opinion*, 244. For Confederate emphasis on the liberty inherent in American Revolutionary ideology, see Eaton, *History*, 67.

39. St. Clair, "Slavery as a Diplomatic Factor," 262; Charles Greville (the Englishman) to CL (former foreign secretary), Jan. 26, 1861, in Maxwell, *Clarendon*, 2:237; E. D. Adams, *Great Britain*, 1:35; H. Jones, *Union in Peril*, 16; Crawford, *Anglo-American Crisis*.

40. Monaghan, *Lincoln Deals*.

41. Brauer, "Slavery Problem," 450; Beale, *Diary of Edward Bates*, 179 (Mar. 31, 1861); Dennett, *Lincoln and the Civil War*, 22 (May 10, 1861); H. Jones, *Union in Peril*, 17.

42. RU to Lyons, Dec. 29, 1860, RU Papers, PRO 30/22/96; W. H. Russell, *My Diary*, 51 (Mar. 28, 1861).

43. *Boston Evening Transcript*, Mar. 19, 1861; CFA to CFA Jr., Nov. 8, 1861, in Ford, *Adams Letters*, 1:68; CFA Jr., *Autobiography*, 112; Jenkins, *Britain*, 1:32–33. Seward had recommended Adams's appointment.

44. Jenkins, "William Gregory" and *Britain*, 1:21 (Ravenel).

45. *Economist*, Apr. 27, 1861 (Forster), cited in Jenkins, *Britain*, 1:92; T. W. Reid, *Forster*; D. A. Campbell, *English Public Opinion*, 55; Palmerston to RU, Apr. 27, 1861, RU Papers, PRO 30/22/21. After succeeding William Wilberforce in Parliament, Buxton campaigned for the Slavery Abolition Act of 1833 ending slavery in the British Empire and fought against the African slave trade for the remainder of his life.

46. Hardman, *Letters and Memoirs*, 8 (British observer); CFA to Everett, Jan. 24, 1862, Adams Papers (MHS); *Economist*, Jan. 19, 1861; *Times*, Jan. 7, 1861.

47. *London Morning Post*, May 4, 1861, quoted in Jenkins, *Britain*, 1:81.

48. *Cornhill Magazine* 4 (Aug. 1861), 153, cited ibid., 1:81; *Times*, Apr. 30, May 9, 1861; Blackett, *Divided Hearts*, 17–18, 26, 34–35; D. A. Campbell, *English Public Opinion*, 55, 102, 104; Jenkins, *Britain*, 1:81–82; D. P. Crook, "Portents of War"; W. R. West, *Contemporary French Opinion*, 18–19; Blackburn, *French Newspaper Opinion*, 57, 95, 137; Lorimer, "Role of Anti-Slavery Sentiment"; Ausubel, *Bright*; Trevelyan, *Bright*; Zorn, "Bright and the British Attitude"; AR, *Argyll*.

49. Lewis to Lord Clarendon, Jan. 24, 1861, Clarendon Papers, ca. 533 (Bodleian Lib.); *Times*, May 10, 1861; *Punch*, n.d., and *London Morning Post*, Apr. 30, 1861, cited in Jenkins, *Britain*, 1:82.

50. Palmerston to RU, Dec. 30, 1860, Apr. 14, 1861, RU Papers, PRO 30/22/21; Bell, *Palmerston*, 2:276–77, 291; H. Jones, *Union in Peril*, 20; Palmerston to [?] Normanby, Feb. 28, 1848 (1st quote), in Ashley, *Palmerston*, 1:73; Palmerston to RU, Apr. 25, 1862, RU Papers, PRO 30/22/21.

51. Jenkins, *Britain*, 1:84–85; Maxwell, *Clarendon*, 2:206 (quote by contemporary). For Russell and Palmerston's collaboration in diplomacy, see Scherer, "Partner or Puppet?"

52. Jenkins, *Britain*, 1:85–86. The name "Peelites" came from the followers of Sir Robert Peel, who had been prime minister during the early 1830s and again in the 1840s; he died in 1850. Gladstone and others had allied with the Whigs to become the Liberal Party in 1859 led by Palmerston. Peel's eldest son was now chief secretary for Ireland. Ibid., 2:240.

53. RU to Lyons, Mar. 22, 1861, *BFSP 1860–1861*, 51:177; George Dallas (Union minister to London) to Seward, Apr. 9, 1861, *FRUS 1861*, 81; RU to Lyons, Apr. 12, 1861, Gladstone

Papers, Add. Mss., 44,593, vol. 508 (Brit. Lib.); Tilby, *Russell*, 19–20, 72, 156; H. Jones, *Union in Peril*, 20–22.

54. Palmerston to Somerset, Dec. 29, 1860, Palmerston Letterbooks, Add. Mss., 48582 (Brit. Lib.); Morley, *Gladstone*, 2:82.

55. AR to Gladstone, Dec. 25, 1860, Add. Mss., 44098 (Brit. Lib.); D. A. Campbell, *English Public Opinion*, 55; AR, *Argyll*.

56. Lyons to RU, Mar. 26, 1861, RU Papers, PRO 30/22/35; Lyons to RU, Apr. 9, 1861, FO 5/762 (PRO), quoted in Jenkins, *Britain*, 1:89–90.

57. Donald, *Sumner and the Rights of Man*, 21 (Seward); H. Jones, *Union in Peril*, 32.

58. W. H. Russell, *My Diary*, 65–66 (Apr. 8, 1861).

59. Seward to CFA, Apr. 10, 1861, *FRUS 1861*, 72–79.

60. Bunch to RU, Apr. 18, 1861, encl. in Lyons to RU, Apr. 26, 1861, in Barnes and Barnes, *American Civil War*, 1:65.

61. Palmerston to Queen Victoria, Jan. 1, 1861, in Ridley, *Palmerston*, 548; RU to Lyons, Jan. 10, 1861, RU Papers, PRO 30/22/96; W. H. Russell, *My Diary*, 110 (Apr. 30, 1861— Georgian's quote); H. Jones, *Union in Peril*, 22–24.

62. Palmerston to RU, Apr. 14, 1861, RU Papers, PRO 30/22/21. For a masterful discussion of the South's interests in the Caribbean, see May, *Southern Dream*.

63. Bunch quoted in JD, *Jefferson Davis*, 5:62–63.

64. Lincoln quoted in Wheaton, *Elements of International Law*, 570 n. 235; Seward to CFA, May 21 (p. 89), June 8, 1861 (p. 103), *FRUS 1861*; H. Jones, *Union in Peril*, 27–28.

65. Lyons to Seward, Apr. 29, 1861, NFBL, GB (NA); Lyons to RU, May 2, 1861, *BPP: Civil War*, 16:22.

66. Vattel, *Law of Nations*, bk. 3, chap. 7, secs. 103–4, and chap. 18, secs. 293–94, 338, 340; Tilby, *Russell*, 185; H. Jones, *Union in Peril*, 22, 27–28.

67. H. Jones, *Union in Peril*, 42. See RU to CFA, Aug. 28, 1861, encl. in CFA to Seward, Sept. 7, 1861, *FRUS 1861*, 146.

68. Lyons to RU, Apr. 27, 1861, RU Papers, PRO 30/22/35; RU to Lyons, May 18, 1861, Gladstone Papers, Add. Mss., 44,593, vol. 508 (Brit. Lib.); Case and Spencer, *United States and France*, 122; Monaghan, *Lincoln Deals*, 82 (Lyons's 2nd quote).

69. RU to Lyons, June 1, 1861, encl. in RU to Lords Commissioners of Admiralty, June 1, 1861, *BPP: Civil War*, 16:80; Lyons to RU, June 14, 1861, RU Papers, PRO 30/22/35; CFA to Seward, June 14, 1861, *FRUS 1861*, 105; H. Jones, *Union in Peril*, 42–43. The Confederacy changed its maritime strategy in June 1861.

70. Jenkins, *Britain*, 1:43, 45–46. Seward's dispatch appeared on May 5. Seward had earlier told his minister in Paris, William Dayton, that the Lincoln administration regarded intervention of any type as making "allies of the insurrectionary party," which necessitated "war against them as enemies." Seward to Dayton, Apr. 22, 1861, Dip. Instructions, France (NA).

71. Jenkins, *Britain*, 1:91–92; H. Jones, *Union in Peril*, 20–21; GB, Parliament, *Brit. Sess. Papers*, 3rd ser., 167:1378–79 (Commons, May 2, 1861).

72. Law Officers Memorandum, undated, RU Papers, PRO 30/22/25; RU to Lyons, May 4, 1861, cited in Jenkins, *Britain*, 1:93; H. Jones, *Union in Peril*, 47.

73. Owsley, *King Cotton Diplomacy*, 56–57. Rost soon met informally with the Paris government, where he learned of an Anglo-French understanding to cooperate regard-

ing American affairs. The French people, their government, and the public journals appeared favorable to the southern cause. Those interested in restoring the French Empire did not oppose a permanent division of "the late United States," but others were concerned that the destruction of the U.S. Navy would open the door to British maritime domination. France intended to postpone any attempt to deal with the recognition issue. The commission recommended that President Davis send letters of credence to the queen of Spain with the objective of opening discussions with that government. Yancey, Rost, and Mann to Toombs, June 1, 1861, *ORN*, 2nd ser., 3:219–21. The last item, known as the "Pickett Papers," is a large compilation of diplomatic and consular papers and correspondence that Col. John T. Pickett took from the State Department in Richmond and hid in a Virginia barn in order to deny their confiscation by federal authorities. Negotiations ultimately led to their transfer to the U.S. government.

74. RU to Lyons, May 11, 1861, *BFSP 1860–1861*, 51:186–87; Lyons to RU, May 6, June 10, 1861, RU Papers, PRO 30/22/35; RU's (May 21, 1861) and Palmerston's (May 23, 1861) comments on the need for strengthening British North America, RU Papers, PRO 30/22/35; Bourne, *Britain*, 212–15; Jenkins, *Britain*, 1:93, 98–99.

75. See Whiting, *War Powers*, 38–57; Claussen, "Peace Factors," 512; Merli, *Great Britain*, 58–59; Spencer, *Confederate Navy*, 9–10; H. Jones, *Union in Peril*, 29.

76. Sexton, *Debtor Diplomacy*, 134 (Cushing); Coulter, *Confederate States*, 184–85, 195. Huse overcame many of these obstacles by buying numerous arms and other supplies in England along with 100,000 rifles and 60 cannons from Austria. Boaz, *Guns for Cotton*, 13–18, 46, 52–53, 68–69.

77. CFA Jr., *Charles Francis Adams*, 107–8 (quote, 111); *Richmond Whig*, May 18, 1861, quoted in Jenkins, *Britain and the War*, 1:109. Sumner quoted in Graebner, "Northern Diplomacy," 60–61 (Seward). For the *Prize Cases*, see *U.S. Supreme Court Reports, 17 Law. Ed.*, 2 Black [U.S. 67], secs. 665–74. See also Bernath, *Squall across the Atlantic*, 25; Kelly, Harbison, and Belz, *American Constitution*, 304; Randall, *Constitutional Problems*, 51 n. 2, 53–54; Merli, "American War"; and Seward to CFA, June 3, 1861 (97–98), June 8, 1861 (100–101), *FRUS 1861*; "British Proclamation for the Observance of Neutrality in the Contest between the United States and the Confederate States of America, May 13, 1861," *BFSP 1860–1861*, 51:165–69; and Wheaton, *Elements of International Law*, 167 n. 84. The French had also decided on neutrality between "two belligerents" shortly after Lincoln's announcement. Thouvenel to Mercier, May 11, 1861, NTFL, France (NA). France declared neutrality on June 10, followed by Spain a week later. Spain, however, never formally awarded belligerent status to the Confederacy. H. Jones, *Union in Peril*, 235 n. 21; Case and Spencer, *United States and France*, 59; Cortada, *Spain*, 54, 58. The Spanish court opposed emancipation and the democratic reforms advocated in the Union because of their impact on its control of Cuba and its hold on home government. Some in the Spanish cabinet supported recognition of the Confederacy to protect slavery in Cuba. Cortada, 55, 60. For Britain's practical considerations in announcing neutrality, see B. Adams, "British Proclamation of May, 1861," and R. H. Jones, "Anglo-American Relations." For British concern about Canada, see Winks, *Canada and the United States*. D. A. Campbell (*English Public Opinion*, 241–42) sharply disagrees, arguing that the British did not fear losing Canada and that the dominion was not as vulnerable to American

attack as numerous writers have claimed. Given the heated context of the times, the British did not want to risk a policy of inaction.

CHAPTER 2

1. "Act Passed by the Confederate Congress, Prohibiting the Exportation of Cotton except through Southern Seaports, May 21, 1861," quoted in *BFSP 1860–1861*, 51:200; Bourne, *Foreign Policy*, 90; D. P. Crook, *The North, the South*, 20; Bernath, *Squall across the Atlantic*, 12; *Charleston Mercury*, June 4, 1861, quoted in Owsley, *King Cotton Diplomacy*, 24; W. H. Russell, *My Diary*, 79 and 82 (Apr. 16), 92 (Apr. 18), 95 (Apr. 20), 107 (Apr. 28), 112 (May 2), 130 (May 7, 1861).

2. CFA to Seward, May 21, 1861, *FRUS 1861*, 91–93. Seward approved Adams's strong statements to Russell and emphasized the Union's "integrity" above everything while expressing the wish to avoid all controversy with England. Seward to CFA, June 8, 1861, ibid., 100–101.

3. CFA Diary, May 18, 1861 (MHS); CFA to Seward, May 21, 1861, *FRUS 1861*, 95. Seward published the entire dispatch in the annual Diplomatic Correspondence series he inaugurated in the following autumn of 1861. See Seward to CFA, May 21, 1861, *FRUS 1861*, 87–90; H. Jones, *Union in Peril*, 32; and Warren, *Fountain of Discontent*, 68–69. Warren termed Russell "One of the few British leaders who favored the Confederacy" (p. 74).

4. Wallace and Gillespie, *Journal of . . . Moran*, 2:820 (May 28, 1861); CFA Diary, May 27, 1861 (MHS); *Parl. Debates*, 168:134 (Commons, May 27, 1861); CFA to Seward, May 31, 1861, *FRUS 1861*, 96; Tilby, *Russell*, 196–97 (Russell).

5. CFA to Seward, June 7, 1861, *FRUS 1861*, 98–99.

6. RU to Lyons, May 6, 1861, Gladstone Papers, Add. Mss., 44,593, vol. 508 (Brit. Lib.); Bourne, *Foreign Policy*, 92; Vattel, *Law of Nations*, bk. 3, chap. 18, secs. 292, 292k. See also Wheaton, *Elements of International Law* (1836 ed.), pt. 1, sec. 23; Kelly, Harbison, and Belz, *American Constitution*, 306–7; and Randall, *Constitutional Problems*, 60–65.

7. "British Proclamation of Neutrality," May 13, 1861, *BFSP 1860–1861*, 51:165–69.

8. CFA Diary, May 26, 1861 (MHS); CFA to Seward, June 14, 1861, *FRUS 1861*, 104–5.

9. Yancey and Rost (from Paris) to Toombs, June 10, 1861, *ORN*, 2nd ser., 3:221 (Gregory motion); CFA to Seward, June 14 (104, 106), June 21 (109–10), June 28, 1861 (111), *FRUS 1861*.

10. T. W. Reid, *Forster*, 1:337–39; H. Jones, *Union in Peril*, 29; Wheaton, *Elements of International Law* (1836 ed.), pt. 1, secs. 21, 23. See also Dana's extensive notes in Wheaton (1866 ed.), 31 n. 15. Since at least the 1720s, blockades had existed without recognition of the existence of war. R. E. Johnson, "Investment by Sea," 46. For the argument that British neutrality benefited the Union, see Baxter's two articles, "British Government and Neutral Rights," 29, and "Some British Opinions as to Neutral Rights," 518.

11. McPherson, *Battle Cry*, 500, and *Tried by War*, 4–5, 269; Lincoln, "Reply to Emancipation Memorial Presented by Chicago Christians of All Denominations," Sept. 13, 1862, *CWL*, 5:419.

12. Dayton to Seward, May 22, 30, 1861, Disp., France (NA); Thouvenel to Mercier,

May 16, 1861, NFFL, France (NA); Seward to Mercier, May 23, 1861, NTFL, France (NA); Seward to Dayton, May 30, June 8, 1861, Dip. Instructions, France (NA).

13. W. R. West, *Contemporary French Opinion*, 14, 27–28; *Constititionnel*, May 7 (28), May 16, 1861 (29), quoted in West; Blackburn, *French Newspaper Opinion*, x–xi, 5, 8; Case and Spencer, *United States and France*, 38–43.

14. RU to Lyons, June 27, 1861, RU Papers, PRO 30/22/96; W. H. Russell, *My Diary*, 218–19 (June 25–30, 1861). For the cotton crisis in France, see Case and Spencer, *United States and France*, 161–64, 374–81.

15. Seward to CFA, June 8, 1861, *FRUS 1861*, 102–3. On the port closing issue, see Brauer, "Seward's 'Foreign War Panacea,'" 147–48, and Anderson, "1861: Blockade vs. Closing Confederate Ports." For the constitutional provision on ports, see U.S. Constitution, art. 1, sec. 9.

16. Lyons to RU, Mar. 18, 1861, in Barnes and Barnes, *American Civil War*, 1:44; Lyons to RU, Apr. 15, June 14, 24, 1861, RU Papers, PRO 30/22/35; RU to Lyons, July 6, 1861, *BPP: Civil War*, 16:89. For French opposition to the port closings and their growing closeness to the British, see Case and Spencer, *United States and France*, 150–57.

17. Lyons to RU, June 8, 1861, Barnes and Barnes, *American Civil War*, 1:113; Palmerston to RU, Dec. 11, 30, 1860, RU Papers, PRO 30/22/21; RU to Lyons, June 21, 1861, Gladstone Papers, Add. Mss., 44,593, vol. 508 (Brit. Lib.). For *Tropic Wind*, see 28 Federal Cases 218–22 (case no. 16, 541a). In the *Prize Cases* of 1863, the U.S. Supreme Court upheld the earlier decision by declaring the blockade proclamation an act of war and drawing no distinction between a public war and a civil war. U.S. Supreme Court, *Reports, 17 Law. Ed.*, 2 Black U.S. 67, secs. 635–99.

18. Wheaton, *Elements of International Law* (1866 ed.), Dana's notes, 575 n. 239; Seward to CFA, July 21, 1861, *FRUS 1861*, 120–21; Lyons to RU, July 8, 19, 20, Aug. 12, 1861 (PRO 30/22/35), and RU to Lyons, July 6, 1861 (PRO 30/22/96), RU Papers; Lyons to RU, July 12, 1861, *BPP: Civil War*, 16:97–98; Pease and Randall, *Diary of . . . Browning*, 1:489 (July 28, 1861).

19. RU to First Earl of Cowley (Henry Richard Charles Wellesley), June 12, 1861, RU Papers, PRO 30/22/104; F. W. Seward, *Reminiscences*, 179–80; Lyons to RU, June 17, 1861, *BFSP 1864–1865*, 55:558–61; Seward to Dayton, June 17, 1861, Dip. Instructions, France (NA); Case and Spencer, *United States and France*, 69–71; Blumenthal, *Reappraisal*, 127; Seward to CFA, June 19, 1861, *FRUS 1861*, 106–9; Carroll, *Mercier*, 78–79 (Seward to Lyons).

20. Seward to CFA, June 19 (107, 109), July 1 (112), and July 21, 1861 (117–21), *FRUS 1861*; W. H. Russell, *My Diary*, 227–28 (July 4, 1861).

21. Dayton to Seward, June [20?], 1861, Disp., France (NA).

22. RU to Cowley, June 12, July 13, 1861, RU Papers, PRO 30/22/104.

23. CFA to Seward, Aug. 16, 1861, *FRUS 1861*, 128; CFA to CFA Jr., July 18, 1861, in Ford, *Adams Letters*, 1:19–20; Henry Adams to CFA Jr., June 10 (1:238), July 4, 1861 (quote, 1:243), in Levenson et al., *Letters of Henry Adams*; CFA to Richard Henry Dana Jr., June 4, CFA to Seward, June 21, and CFA to Edward Everett, July 26, 1861, CFA Letterbook (MHS); CFA Diary, July 25, 1861 (MHS); *Economist*, July 6, 1861, quoted in Sexton, *Debtor Diplomacy*, 152; *Saturday Review*, July 13, 1861, quoted in D. A. Campbell, *English Public Opinion*, 50.

24. Lyons to RU, June 4, 1861, Barnes and Barnes, *American Civil War*, 1:106; *New York Herald*, July 22, 26, 1861, cited in E. D. Adams, *Great Britain*, 1:178 n. 2; Adams, 1:177–78; *Times*, Aug. 20 (p. 7), Aug. 24, 1861 (p. 10); W. H. Russell, *My Diary*, 267–77 (July 21), 278–79 (July 22), 304 (Aug. 1, 1861); Crawford, "William Howard Russell"; Ridley, *Palmerston*, 551 (Palmerston); Bell, *Palmerston*, 2:292.

25. Sexton, *Debtor Diplomacy*, 84–87, 91; Katz, *Belmont*, 100–101.

26. Sexton, *Debtor Diplomacy*, 88–89; Katz, *Belmont*, 97–98.

27. Sexton, *Debtor Diplomacy*, 91–92; D. A. Campbell, *English Public Opinion*, 41–43; Katz, *Belmont*, 101–3.

28. Sexton, *Debtor Diplomacy*, 152–53.

29. Lyons to RU, July 30, 1861, in Barnes and Barnes, *American Civil War*, 1:149; W. H. Russell, *My Diary*, 279 (July 22, 1861).

30. Yancey and Mann to Toombs, Aug. 1, 1861, *ORN*, 2nd ser., 3:339–30; Yancey, Rost, and Mann to Toombs, Aug. 7, 1861, ibid., 3:235–37; Yancey, Rost, and Mann to RU, Aug. 14, 1861, *BFSP 1860–1861*, 51:219–28.

31. RU to Yancey, Rost, and Mann, Aug. 24, 1861, *ORN*, 2nd ser., 3:248; RU to Yancey, Rost, and Mann, Aug. 7, 1861, encl. in Yancey, Rost, and Mann to Toombs, Aug. 7, 1861, ibid., 3:237; RU to Yancey, Rost, and Mann, Aug. 24, 1861, ibid., 3:248; CFA to CFA Jr., Sept. 7, 1861, Adams Papers (MHS); CFA to Seward, Aug. 8, 1861, quoted in Warren, *Fountain of Discontent*, 89.

32. Lyons to RU, July 30, 1861, RU Papers, PRO 30/22/35.

33. Seward to CFA, Aug. 17, 1861, *FRUS 1861*, 131; H. Jones, *Union in Peril*, 62.

34. Seward to CFA, Aug. 17, 1861, *FRUS 1861*, 131. See also Ferris, *Desperate Diplomacy*, 99–116; E. D. Adams, *Great Britain*, 1:184–96; Jenkins, *Britain*, 1:136–39, 157; and Case and Spencer, *United States and France*, 116–17.

35. Seward to CFA, Aug. 17, 1861 (no. 63), *FRUS 1861*, 131–33; Seward to CFA, Aug. 17, 1861 (no. 64), ibid., 133.

36. CFA Diary, Sept. 2, 1861 (MHS); CFA to RU, Sept. 3, 1861, encl. (151–53), CFA to Seward, Sept. 9 (149–50), and CFA to Seward, Sept. 14, 1861 (155–57), *FRUS 1861*; Case and Spencer, *United States and France*, 117–18.

37. RU to Palmerston, Oct. 29, 1861, RU Papers, PRO 30/22/35; Palmerston to RU, Sept. 9, 1861, ibid., PRO 30/22/31; RU to Palmerston, Sept. 11, 1861, Palmerston Papers, GC/RU/670 (U. of Southampton); RU to Palmerston, Nov. 12, 1861, GC/RU/680 (U. of Southampton); Bell, *Palmerston*, 2:293.

38. RU to Lyons, Nov. 21, 1861, RU Papers, PRO 30/22/96; Bunch to Lyons, Sept. 30, 1861, encl. in Lyons to RU, Oct. 8 (16:626–27), RU to Lyons, Oct. 26 (16:627), and Bunch to Lyons, Oct. 31, 1861, encl. in Lyons to RU, Nov. 14, 1861 (633–34), *BPP: Civil War*.

39. Case and Spencer, *United States and France*, 115; *Baltimore Sun*, Aug. 16, 1861, cited in Lyons to RU, Aug. 16, 1861 (55:579), and *Charleston Mercury* (n.d.), cited in Lyons to RU, Aug. 23, 1861 (579–80), *BFSP 1864–1865*.

40. Gladstone to Lewis, Sept. 21, 1861, Gladstone Papers, Add. Mss., 44,236, vol. 151 (Brit. Lib.); Lyons to RU, Sept. 24, 1861, RU Papers, PRO 30/33/35.

41. Seward to CFA, Oct. 22 (p. 163), and Oct. 23, 1861 (pp. 165–66), *FRUS 1861*.

42. CFA to RU, Aug. 15, 1861, *BFSP 1860–1861*, 51:229–30; CFA to RU, Oct. 1, 1861, ibid., 51:237; Ferris, *Desperate Diplomacy*, 172–73; Robert M. T. Hunter, Confederate

Secretary of State, to Hotze, Jan. 16, 1863, *ORN*, 2nd ser., 3:659; Eaton, *History*, 72–73; E. M. Thomas, *Confederate Nation*, 177–78; Cullop, *Confederate Propaganda*; Hanna and Hanna, *Napoleon III*, 33. The full title of Hotze's publication was *Index: A Weekly Journal of Politics, Literature, and News*. For a first-rate introductory analysis of Hotze's work as a propagandist, along with a collection of his writings on the recognition issue, see Burnett, *Hotze*, 1–33, 130–57.

43. Reference to RU to Everett, July 12, 1861, in Everett to RU, Aug. 19, 1861, RU Papers, PRO 30/22/39. For characterizations of Russell, see miscellaneous draft in unidentified hand and undated, ibid., PRO 30/22/118A, and Tilby, *Russell*, 50. For Russell's hatred of slavery, see Tilby, 197, and RU to Cowley, Apr. 15, 1865, RU Papers, PRO 30/22/106.

44. Everett to RU, Aug. 19, 1861, RU Papers, PRO 30/22/39.

45. Ibid.

46. Vattel, *Law of Nations*, bk. 2, chap. 1, sec. 114; bk. 3, chap. 3, sec. 249, and chap. 7, secs. 269–70.

47. Napoleon III quoted in Blackburn, *French Newspaper Opinion*, 6.

48. Quotes in Evans, *Benjamin*, 156.

49. RU to Cowley, Sept. 24, 1861, RU Papers, PRO 30/22/104; Bourne, *Foreign Policy*, 96.

50. W. H. Russell, *My Diary*, 290 (Aug. 2, 3), 292 (Aug. 6, 1861); Lyons to RU, Oct. 4, 1861, RU Papers, PRO 30/22/35. For the prince's visit, see Carroll, *Mercier*, 86–90, and H. Jones, *Union in Peril*, 73–74.

51. Mercier's views in Lyons to RU, Oct. 4, 1861, RU Papers, PRO 30/22/35. For British and French cotton interests, see Duberman, *Adams*, 277; Case and Spencer, *United States and France*, 127, 374–75; Blumenthal, *Reappraisal*, 154–55; H. Jones, *Union in Peril*, 155; and Pomeroy, "French Substitutes." France tried to secure cotton in North Africa, Central America, Mexico, Haiti, Italy, Cambodia, Cyprus, and Syria. See Pomeroy.

52. Lyons to RU, Oct. 4, 1861, RU Papers, PRO 30/22/35.

53. Palmerston to RU, Oct. 18, 1861, Palmerston Papers, GC/RU/1139/1–2 (U. of Southampton); Palmerston to RU, Oct. 6, 1861, RU Papers, PRO 30/22/21.

54. Palmerston to RU, Oct. 18, 1861, Palmerston Papers, GC/RU/1139/1–2 (U. of Southampton); Palmerston to Sir Austen Henry Layard, Undersecretary of State for Foreign Affairs, Oct. 20, 1861, Layard Papers, Add. Mss., 38,987, vol. 57 (Brit. Lib.).

55. Hanna and Hanna, *Napoleon III*, 39.

56. CFA Diary, Sept. 12, 1861 (MHS); CFA to Seward, Sept. 28, 1861, CFA Letterbook (MHS); Seward to Dayton, Sept. 24, Oct. 11, 1861, Dip. Instructions, France (NA); Dayton to Seward, Nov. 6, 1861, Disp., France (NA).

57. Hanna and Hanna, *Napoleon III*, 38–39, 53; Schoonover, *Dollars over Dominion*, 56–58; Blumenthal, *Reappraisal*, 152–53; Ferris, *Desperate Diplomacy*, 161–62 (Palmerston, 162).

58. Barker, "France, Austria," 225–27, 229, 243, "French Legation," 423, and "Monarchy in Mexico," 53–59, 62–65; D. P. Crook, *The North, the South*, 338–39. See also Hanna, "Roles of the South."

59. Thouvenel to Mercier, Sept. 29, 1861, NTFL, France (NA); Seward to Dayton, Oct. 30, 1861, Dip. Instructions, France (NA).

60. Dayton to Seward, Nov. 6, 1861, Disp., France (NA); Dayton to Seward, Dec. 6, 24, 1861, cited in Owsley, *King Cotton Diplomacy*, 71–72; Hanna and Hanna, *Napoleon III*, 38–39. The three powers signed the London Treaty on Oct. 31, 1861. For an exhaustive treatment, see Bock, *Prelude to Tragedy*.

61. Dayton to Seward, Sept. 27, 1861, quoted in Owsley, *King Cotton Diplomacy*, 509.

62. Barker, "France, Austria," 225, "French Legation," 409, 423–24, and "Monarchy in Mexico," 51, 68; Hanna and Hanna, *Napoleon III*, 98–100, 183 (Maximilian, 100).

63. RU to Queen Victoria, Sept. 27, 1861, in Gooch, *Later Correspondence*, 2:320–21; RU to Cowley, Sept. 27, 1861, *BFSP 1861–1862*, 52:329–30; Lewis to Gladstone, Oct. 5, 1861, Gladstone Papers, Add. Mss., 44,236, vol. 151 (Brit. Lib.); Clarendon to Lewis, Oct. 4, 1861, in Maxwell, *Clarendon*, 2:240 (Clarendon on Palmerston); Blumenthal, *Reappraisal*, 167.

64. Dayton to Seward, Nov. 6, 1861, Disp., France (NA); Ferris, *Desperate Diplomacy*, 167 (quote from three European governments). See also Ferris, 154–70; Hanna and Hanna, *Napoleon III*, 39–40; Schoonover, *Dollars over Dominion*, 145–46; and Blumenthal, *Reappraisal*, 169.

65. Van Deusen, *Seward*, 365–70.

66. CFA to CFA Jr., Sept. 20, 1861, in Ford, *Adams Letters*, 1:48; Henry Adams to CFA Jr., Oct. 25, 1861, ibid., 1:61–62; Henry Adams to CFA Jr., Nov. 7, 1861, in Levenson et al., *Letters of Henry Adams*, 1:262.

67. RU to Lyons, Nov. 2, 1861, RU Papers, PRO 30/22/96; Bellows, "British Conservative Reaction," 512–13, 522. Cecil counted on world pressure persuading the Confederacy to emancipate its slaves. See Lorimer, "Role of Anti-Slavery Sentiment," 409; see also 407, 420.

CHAPTER 3

1. Mason to Hunter, Oct. 12, 1861, *ORN*, 2nd ser., 3:283; Charles J. Helm (special agent to Spanish, English, and Danish islands) to Hunter, Oct. 22, 1861, ibid., 3:284; Helm to Hunter, Nov. 8, 1861, ibid., 3:284–85. For the voyage, see Mason to Hunter, Oct. 9, 1861, ibid., 3:280; William H. Trescott (lawyer and former diplomat) to Hunter, Oct. 12, 1861, ibid., 3:281; Mason to Hunter, Oct. 18, 1861, *ORN*, 1st ser., 1:151–52; and V. Mason, *James M. Mason*, 200, 202, 209–13. Spain's neutrality and concern over Cuba encouraged its consul on the island to extend cordial treatment to Mason and Slidell. Cortada, *Spain*, 55–56.

2. Hunter to Mason and Slidell, Sept. 23, 1861, *ORN*, 2nd ser., 3:257–73; Mason to Hunter, Oct. 12, 1861, ibid., 3:282–83; Coulter, *Confederate States*, 184–85 (contemporary's quote). See also Hammond, *Cotton Industry*, 252–54, and Owsley, *King Cotton Diplomacy*, 3, 8.

3. JD to Confederate Congress, Nov. 18, 1861, in Richardson, *Messages and Papers of the Confederacy*, 1:142.

4. Woodward, *Chesnut's Civil War*, 170–71.

5. Ibid., 170 (Russell); H. C. Perkins, *Northern Editorials* (New York paper), 2:1028; CFA Jr., *Adams*, 215.

6. W. H. Russell, *My Diary*, 164 (May 24, 1861) (1st Russell quote); *Times*, Dec. 10, 1861, p. 9 (2nd Russell quote); Warren, *Fountain of Discontent*, 6–7 (CFA Jr.).

7. G. S. Smith, "Charles Wilkes," 136–38; Long, "Glory-Hunting off Havana," 133; Rawley, *Turning Points*, 77.

8. Warren, *Fountain of Discontent*, 11–13.

9. Shufeldt to Seward, Nov. 9, 1861, cited in Ferris, *Trent*, 209 n. 6; D. P. Crook, *The North, the South*, 108 (Stowell's decision); Kent, *Commentaries*, 1:47; Wilkes to Welles, Nov. 16, 1861, *ORN*, 1st ser., 1:130; *Times*, Dec. 5, 1861. Wilkes later attested that he had consulted these specialists in international law in deciding to remove Mason and Slidell. U.S. Cong., *Senate Exec. Docs.*, 1, 37 Cong., 2nd sess., 3:123.

10. The Confederate secretaries were George Eustis and James Macfarland. Hunter to Yancey, Rost, and Mann, Nov. 20, 1861, *ORN*, 2nd ser., 3:297; Rawley, *Turning Points*, 77.

11. Fairfax, "Wilkes's Seizure," 141 (Fairfax's account); Warren, *Fountain of Discontent*, 18 (passenger's quote); Ferris, *Trent*, 20, 23–24, 232 n. 4; D. P. Crook, *The North, the South*, 106; Hunter, "Capture of Mason and Slidell," 797–98 (eyewitness account). Rawley (*Turning Points*, 79) believes that Fairfax apparently did not think of seeking the dispatches. Warren (*Fountain of Discontent*, 192), however, concludes that Fairfax tried to seize them but failed. See also Crook, *The North, the South*, 106 n. 13, and Ferris, *Trent*, 209 n. 10.

12. Ferris, *Trent*, 25–26; Warren, *Fountain of Discontent*, 22 (Supreme Court cases, 192); *The Dos Hermanos, U.S. Supreme Court, Reports*, 17 *Law. Ed.*, 2 Wheaton 78 (1817).

13. *New York Times*, Dec. 19, 1861, p. 1; Mason to wife, Nov. 15, 1861, *ORN*, 2nd ser., 3:296.

14. Mason to wife, Nov. 17, 1861, *ORN*, 2nd ser., 3:296; U.S. Cong., *House Exec. Doc. 102*, 38th Cong., 1st sess., 1864, p. 157 (Wilkes).

15. Ferris, *Trent*, 32; Warren, *Fountain of Discontent*, 26–27 (poem).

16. *New York Times*, Nov. 18, 19, 22, 1861, *New York Daily Tribune*, Nov. 18, 22, 23, 1861, and *New York Herald*, Nov. 17, 1861, all cited in Warren, *Fountain of Discontent*, 39–40.

17. Warren, *Fountain of Discontent*, 28 (Everett, 28; Stowell, 196); Gurowski, *Diary*, 1:109. For Gurowski's views on the Civil War, see Fischer, *Lincoln's Gadfly*.

18. Warren, *Fountain of Discontent*, 37–38 (Lincoln, 38); Ferris, *Trent*, 130; D. P. Crook, *The North, the South*, 116–17.

19. Donald, *Sumner and . . . the Civil War*, 129, and *Sumner and the Rights of Man*, 31–32; Long, "Glory-Hunting off Havana," 140; Cohen, "Sumner and the *Trent* Affair," 208–9; Warren, *Fountain of Discontent*, 29–30.

20. Rawley, *Turning Points*, 80 (Governor Andrew); *CG*, 37th Cong., 2nd sess., pt. 1, p. 5; D. P. Crook, *The North, the South*, 100.

21. *Atlanta Southern Confederacy*, Nov. 19, 1861, quoted in Warren, *Fountain of Discontent*, 43; *New Orleans Bee*, Dec. 24, 1861, cited ibid.; *New Orleans Bee*, Dec. 19, 1861, cited in Ferris, *Trent*, 128.

22. Rawley, *Turning Points*, 81 (Davis); Ferris, *Trent*, 117 (Benjamin); Mallory to Bulloch, Nov. 30, 1861, *ORN*, 2nd ser., 2:113; Hunter to Yancey, Rost, and Mann, Nov. 20, 1861, *ORN*, 2nd ser. 3:297.

23. H. Jones, *Union in Peril*, 83; Rost to JD, Dec. 24, 1861, *ORN*, 2nd ser., 3:311–12; Mann to Hunter, Dec. 2, 1861, ibid., 3:307; Yancey, Rost, and Mann to Hunter, Dec. 2, 1861, ibid., 3:305; Yancey, Rost, and Mann to RU, Nov. 27, 1861, *ORN*, 1st ser., 1:154; Yancey,

Rost, and Mann to RU, Nov. 29, 1861, *ORN*, 2nd ser., 3:298–301; Yancey, Rost, and Mann to Hunter, Dec. 2, 1861, *ORN*, 1st ser., 1:156; Mann to Benjamin, Dec. 18, 1862, *ORN*, 2nd ser., 3:631.

24. Henry Adams, *Education of Henry Adams*, 119; Wallace and Gillespie, *Journal of . . . Moran*, 2:914 (Nov. 27, 1861), 915 (Nov. 28, 1861); Henry Adams to CFA Jr., Nov. 30, 1861, in Levenson et al., *Letters of Henry Adams*, 1:263–64; CFA Diary, Nov. 29, 30, Dec. 1, 1861 (MHS).

25. E. D. Adams, *Great Britain*, 1:217 (Americans' quotes); CFA to Seward, Nov. 29, 1861, *FRUS 1861*, 6–7.

26. Lyons to RU, Nov. 19, 1861, FO 115/258 (PRO); Warren, *Fountain of Discontent*, 109 (Palmerston in cabinet meeting); Palmerston to Queen Victoria, Nov. 29, 1861, in Benson and Esher, *Letters of Queen Victoria*, 3:469; Palmerston to RU, Nov. 29, 1861 (2 letters), RU Papers, PRO 30/22/21; RU, *Recollections*, 275.

27. *London Morning Post*, Nov. 30, 1861, cited in D. P. Crook, *The North, the South*, 130; Ferris, *Trent*, 57; Lewis to Twisleton, Nov. 30, 1861, in G. F. Lewis, *Letters of . . . George Cornewall Lewis*, 406; Lewis to Palmerston, Nov. 27, 1861, Palmerston Papers, GC/LE/147 (U. of Southampton).

28. Palmerston to Gladstone, Nov. 29, 1861, cited in Warren, *Fountain of Discontent*, 110–11; AR, *Argyll*, 2:182; AR to Gladstone, Nov. 29, 1861, Gladstone Papers, Add. Mss., 44,099 (Brit. Lib.); Mitford, ed., *Stanleys*, 321.

29. D. P. Crook, *The North, the South*, 145, 147; Bourne, "British Preparations for War" and *Britain*, 35, 44, 53, 223, 236; Warren, *Fountain of Discontent*, 82–85, 136; Bernath, *Squall across the Atlantic*, 162–63; Baxter, "British Government and Neutral Rights," 10; Courtemanche, *No Need of Glory*, 40–56; Palmerston to Lewis, Nov. 27, 1861, Palmerston Papers, GC/LE/234 (U. of Southampton); Ferris, *Trent*, 67.

30. Palmerston to Gladstone, July 19, 21, 1861, Gladstone Papers, Add. Mss., 44,272 (Brit. Lib.); Warren, *Fountain of Discontent*, 84–85; Wellesley, *Secrets of Second Empire*, 223–25 (Clarendon).

31. Ferris, *Trent*, 58 (Lord chief justice [John Duke Lord Coleridge]); Twisleton to Lewis, Nov. 28, Dec. 4, 1861, ibid., 103; Twisleton to Lewis, Dec. 4, 1861, ibid., 107–8; Grote to Layard, Dec. 1, 1861, Layard Papers, Add. Mss., 38,987 (Brit. Lib.).

32. Cobden to Bright, Dec. 3, 1861, quoted in Ferris, *Trent*, 71–72.

33. Twisleton to Lewis, Dec. 10, 1861, ibid., 239–40 n. 28.

34. Vattel, *Law of Nations*, v–xv, bk. 1, chap. 2, secs. 18, 19, bk. 2, chap. 4, sec. 49.

35. Law officers to RU, Nov. 28, 1861, cited in Warren, *Fountain of Discontent*, 109–10; Confidential memo for use of cabinet, Dec. 4, 1861, ibid., 120–21; Fitzmaurice, *Granville*, 1:402; Gladstone to AR, Dec. 3, 1861, Gladstone Papers, Add. Mss., 44,099 (Brit. Lib.); Lewis to Twisleton, Nov. 30, 1861, in G. F. Lewis, *Letters of . . . George Cornewall Lewis*, 405–6; RU to Palmerston, Dec. 1, 1861, Palmerston Papers, GC/RU/681 (U. of Southampton).

36. Queen Victoria to RU, Dec. 1, 1861, RU Papers, PRO 30/22/21; Martin, *Prince Consort*, 5:421–23; RU to Lyons, Nov. 30, 1861 (1st dispatch), FO 5/758; Ferris, "Prince Consort," 154–55, and *Trent*, 51–52.

37. RU to Lyons, Nov. 30, 1861, *BPP: Civil War*, 16:646–47; RU to Lyons, Nov. 30, 1861,

ibid., 16:647; "British Proclamation, Prohibiting the Export of Gunpowder, Saltpetre, Nitrate of Soda, and Brimstone," Nov. 29, 1861, *BFSP 1860–1861*, 51:170; Ferris, *Trent*, 62; Bell, *Palmerston*, 2:294–95.

38. Palmerston to Lewis, Dec. 6, 1861, Palmerston Papers, GC/LE/237 (U. of Southampton); Memorials from Canada, New Brunswick, and Nova Scotia to Newcastle, Dec. 2, 1861, *BPP: Papers Relating to Canada, 1861–63*, 24:293–307; MacKintosh, *British Cabinet*, 147–48; Bourne, *Britain*, 220; Ferris, *Trent*, 65. The War Committee had come into existence during the Crimean War, the Indian Mutiny, and the expanded defense campaign against the French in 1859.

39. RU to Yancey, Rost, and Mann, Dec. 7, 1861, FO 5/807 (PRO); K. J. Logan, "*Bee-Hive* Newspaper"; H. Jones, *Union in Peril*, 85–86, 246 n. 8; Lindsay to Layard, Dec. 10, 1861, Ripon Papers, Add. Mss., 43,512, vol. 22 (Brit. Lib.); *Bee-Hive*, Nov. 23, Dec. 7, 1861, cited in Foner, *British Labor*, 29.

40. Dayton to Seward, Nov. 30, Dec. 3, 1861, Disp., France (NA).

41. Dayton to Seward, Dec. 5, 6, 1861, ibid.

42. Thouvenel to Mercier, Dec. 3, 1861, *ORN*, 1st ser., 1:164–65. Three days later, Thouvenel emphasized to Dayton that the Union had violated international law. Dayton to Seward, Dec. 6, 1861, Disp., France (NA). See also Dayton to Seward, Nov. 30, 1861, Disp., France (NA).

43. Case and Spencer, *United States and France*, 207 (Gorchakov). For Russian ties with the Union, see Saul, *Distant Friends*, 320–26.

44. Lyons to RU, Nov. 24, 1861 (PRO 30/22/36), and Nov. 29, 1861 (PRO 30/22/14C), RU Papers,; Newton, *Lord Lyons*, 1:59.

45. Case and Spencer, *United States and France*, 196; Rawley, *Turning Points*, 85; Lewis to Twisleton, Nov. 30, 1861, G. F. Lewis, *Letters of . . . George Cornewall Lewis*, 406–7; Ferris, *Trent*, 80 (Cowley); RU to Cowley, Dec. 5, 1861 (PRO 30/22/104), and Dec. 7, 1861 (PRO 30/22/106), RU Papers.

46. D. P. Crook, *The North, the South*, 128–29; Warren, *Fountain of Discontent*, 154–55; Case and Spencer, *United States and France*, 199–201; Carroll, *Mercier*, 105–18; Bourne, "British Preparations for War," 631; RU to Cowley, Dec. 5, 9, 11, 16, 1861, RU Papers, PRO 30/22/104; RU to Gladstone, Oct. 13 [Dec.], 1861, Gladstone Papers, Add. Mss., 44,292, vol. 207 (Brit. Lib.); RU to Clarendon, Dec. 9, 1861, in Gooch, *Later Correspondence*, 2:321. The three powers sent military forces to Mexico, ostensibly to collect debts.

47. Warren, *Fountain of Discontent*, 159, 162–63; Ferris, *Trent*, 77–78; B. P. Thomas, *Russo-American Relations*, 129.

48. Pease and Randall, *Diary of . . . Browning*, 1:515 (Dec. 15, 1861).

49. *CG*, 37th Cong., 2nd sess., 101 (House, Dec. 16, 1861), 119–22 (House, Dec. 17, 1861); W. H. Russell, *My Diary*, 331 (Dec. 16, 1861); Warren, *Fountain of Discontent*, 174–75.

50. CFA Jr. to Henry Adams, Dec. 10, 1861, in Ford, *Adams Letters*, 1:79, 81; Henry Adams to CFA Jr., Dec. 13, 1861, in Levenson et al., *Letters of Henry Adams*, 1:265–66.

51. CFA to Seward, Dec. 11, 12, 1861, CFA Letterbook (MHS); Duberman, *Adams*, 280–81; Henry Adams to CFA Jr., Dec. 13, 1861, in Levenson et al., *Letters of Henry Adams*, 1:265–66; Seward to CFA, Nov. 27, 1861 (arrived December 16), vol. 18, Dip. Instructions, GB (NA). See also Seward to CFA, Nov. 30, 1861, Disp., GB (NA), and CFA to CFA Jr., Dec. 20, 1861, in Ford, *Adams Letters*, 1:88.

52. CFA to CFA Jr., Dec. 20, 1861, in Ford, *Adams Letters*, 1:88–89.

53. Silver, "Henry Adams' 'Diary of Visit to Manchester'"; Cobden to Bright, Dec. 7, 18, 1861, Cobden Papers, Add. Mss., 43,651, vol. 5 (Brit. Lib.); Bright to Cobden, Nov. 16, 1861, Jan. 10, 1862, Bright Papers, Add. Mss., 43,384, vol. 2 (Brit. Lib.); J. M. Mackay (businessman) to Layard, Dec. 9, 1861, Layard Papers, Add. Mss., 39,102, vol. 172 (Brit. Lib.); Jenkins, *Britain*, 1:205; Carroll, *Mercier*, 134–35.

54. Lyons to RU, Nov. 29, 1861, *BPP: Civil War*, 16:155; RU to Lyons, Dec. 20, 1861, ibid., 16:156; Lyons to RU, Jan. 14, 1862, ibid., 16:179–80. For the legality of the stone fleet, see Wheaton, *Elements of International Law*, Dana's notes, 360–61 n. 166.

55. Rost to JD, Dec. 24, 1861, *ORN*, 2nd ser., 3:311–12; Mann to JD, Jan. 18, 1862, ibid., 3:318.

56. Yancey to Hunter, Dec. 31, 1861, ibid., 3:313.

57. Lyons to RU, Dec. 23, 1861, cited in Ferris, *Trent*, 135. Although Lyons had unofficially furnished Seward with a copy of the dispatch on December 19, they agreed to meet in the State Department on December 21 for its official delivery and the beginning of the seven-day countdown. When Seward asked for two additional days, Lyons consented and made the formal presentation of British demands on the morning of Monday, December 23. The Lincoln administration thus had to make a decision by December 30. Case and Spencer, *United States and France*, 216; Ferris, *Trent*, 133.

58. RU to Lyons, Dec. 19, 1861, FO 115/250 (PRO); RU to Cowley, Jan. 1, 2, 1862, RU Papers, PRO 30/22/105.

59. Lyons to RU, Dec. 23, 1861, RU Papers, PRO 30/22/14C; Dayton to Seward, Dec. 24, 1861, Disp., France (NA); Carroll, *Mercier*, 8, 69, 110.

60. Ferris, *Trent*, 181; Rawley, *Turning Points*, 89; Pease and Randall, *Diary of . . . Browning*, 1:516 (Dec. 21, 1861); Parish, *Civil War*, 412; Cohen, "Sumner and the *Trent* Affair" (Sumner recommended the king of Prussia or some other European sovereign to arbitrate the dispute); Warren, *Fountain of Discontent*, 178.

61. Warren, *Fountain of Discontent*, 148, 151–63, 167, 179, 181–82; Cohen, "Sumner and the *Trent* Affair"; Ferris, *Trent*, 76, 78–79; Parish, *Civil War*, 412; Sumner to Bright, Dec. 23, 1861 (2:85–87), Sumner to Francis Lieber (lawyer and friend), Dec. 24, 1861 (2:88–89), Sumner to Seward, ca. Dec. 24, 1861 (2:90), Sumner to Bright, Dec. 27, 1861 (2:91), and Sumner to Cobden, Dec. 31, 1861 (2:92–94, 87 n. 2, 90 n. 1), all in Palmer, *Selected Letters of . . . Sumner*; Pease and Randall, *Diary of . . . Browning*, 1:518–19 (Dec. 25, 1861); W. H. Seward, *Autobiography*, 3:26 (Lincoln).

62. W. H. Seward, *Autobiography*, 1:52, 2:586; Seward to Lyons, Dec. 26, 1861, NTFL, GB (NA). See Welles, "Capture and Release," for the navy secretary's summary of the Lincoln administration's legal views providing the basis for releasing the two Confederate emissaries.

63. W. H. Seward, *Autobiography*, 1:52, 2:586; Seward to Lyons, Dec. 26, 1861, NTFL, GB (NA); Lyons to Seward, Dec. 27, 1861, NFBL, GB (NA); Pease and Randall, *Diary of . . . Browning*, 1:519 (Dec. 27, 1861); Warren, *Fountain of Discontent*, 183–84; Ferris, *Trent*, 183–84; D. P. Crook, *The North, the South*, 161; E. D. Adams, *Great Britain*, 1:232–33.

64. CFA to Seward, Dec. 3, 1861, cited in Ferris, *Trent*, 184–85.

65. Lowell quoted in Rawley, *Turning Points*, 90–91.

66. Ferris, *Trent*, 192, 194–96; RU to Lyons, Jan. 23, 1862, cited ibid., 196; *Times*, Jan. 14,

1862, p. 6. Warren (*Fountain of Discontent*, 197–98) argues that the *Trent* was passing lawfully between neutral ports, that Mason and Slidell were civilians and therefore not subject to removal, and that neutral nations had the right to deal with belligerents.

67. Seward to Lyons, Dec. 26, 1861, NTFL, GB (NA). See Vattel, *Law of Nations*, v–xv, bk. 1, chap. 2, secs. 18–19, bk. 2, chap. 4, sec. 49.

68. Wheaton cited Lord Stowell's decision in the *Anna Maria* case of 1813 in arguing that a belligerent has the right of visit and search to inquire whether the ship was free of contraband and warranted seizure. Wheaton, *Elements of International Law*, pt. 4, secs. 525–26, p. 578. See also D. P. Crook, *The North, the South*, 108. An American specialist in international law, Francis Wharton, later argued that if emissaries carried dispatches designed to promote belligerent goals, those dispatches became contraband and thus subject to confiscation. Crook, 109.

69. Lyons to RU, Dec. 27, 31, 1861, RU Papers, PRO 30/22/35.

70. Henry Adams to CFA Jr., Dec. 28, 1861, in Levenson et al., *Letters of Henry Adams*, 1:267; Gooch, *Later Correspondence*, 2:324; RU to Lyons, Feb. 8, 1862, cited in Gooch; RU to Lyons, Jan. 11, 1862, RU Papers, PRO 30/22/96; RU to Gladstone, Jan. 26, 1862, cited in Ferris, *Trent Affair*, 198.

71. Survey cited in Cobden to Bright, Jan. 8, 1862, Cobden Papers, Add. Mss., 43,652, vol. 6 (Brit. Lib.).

72. Dayton to Seward, Jan. 2, 20, 27, 1862, Disp., France (NA).

73. *Times*, Jan. 9, 1862, p. 8, Jan. 10, 11, 1862, both p. 6.

74. Rawley, *Turning Points*, 92 (Pollard); Hotze to Hunter, Mar. 11, 1862, cited in Ferris, *Trent*, 191; CFA to Seward, Jan. 10, 24, 1862, CFA to Everett, Feb. 21, 1862, and CFA to Richard Henry Dana Jr. (the friend), Feb. 6, 1862, all in CFA Letterbook (MHS)

75. Clerk quoted in Ferris, *Trent*, 191.

CHAPTER 4

1. Lewis to William Vernon Harcourt (stepson-in-law), Feb. 4, 1862, Harcourt Papers, box 12 (Bodleian Lib.); RU to Lyons, Feb. 1, 1862, encl. in RU to Lords Commissioners of the Admiralty, Jan. 31, 1862, *BPP: Civil War*, 16:181–82; RU to Lyons, Feb. 8, 1862 (PRO 39/22/96), and Lyons to RU, Feb. 11, 1862 (PRO 30/22/36), RU Papers; Lyons to RU, Mar. 3, 1862, FO 146/1023, Cowley Papers (PRO).

2. RU to Lyons, Feb. 8, 1862, RU Papers, PRO 39/22/96; RU to Confederate Commissioners, Dec. 7, 1861, Mason Papers (LC); Mason to Hunter, Feb. 7, 1862, and Gregory to Mason, Feb. 7, 1862, *ORN*, 2nd ser., 3:332–33.

3. Mason to Hunter, Feb. 22, 1862, plus encls.: Mason to RU, Feb. 8, 1862, and RU to Mason, Feb. 8, 1862, Mason Papers, Disp. (LC); H. Jones, *Union in Peril*, 102; Blumenthal, "Confederate Diplomacy" and *Reappraisal*, 158–59.

4. *New York Tribune* (n.d.), quoted in McPherson, *Battle Cry*, 396–404; Moran Diary, Feb. 20, Mar. 6, 1862 (LC); CFA Diary, Mar. 5, 1862 (MHS); JD to Confederate Congress in Lyons to RU, Mar. 3, 1862, cited in Barnes and Barnes, *American Civil War*, 1:302; V. Mason, *James M. Mason*, 266.

5. Eaton, *Davis*, 165 (quotes). The contemporary colleague was Robert Kean, head of the War Bureau. At the age of fourteen at Yale, Benjamin was accused of thievery, a

charge never proved. Benjamin was the first Jew to hold a U.S. Senate seat. Evans, *Benjamin*, 47–48.

6. Evans, *Benjamin*, 17–48, 98–99, 156; Eaton, *Davis*, 164–65, and *History of the Southern Confederacy*, 69; Meade, "Relations between . . . Benjamin and . . . Davis," and *Benjamin*; JD, *Rise and Fall of the Confederate Government*, 1:242. Evans and Meade establish Benjamin's integral role in Confederate foreign relations.

7. Walker quoted in Evans, *Benjamin*, 116.

8. Ibid., 146, 154–56. See also JD, *Rise and Fall of the Confederate Government* (2 vols.) and *Short History of the Confederate States of America*.

9. Owsley, *King Cotton Diplomacy*, 211; E. D. Adams, *Great Britain*, 1:267, 268 n. 2, 271; Forster to Ellis Yarnall, May 10, 1861, in T. W. Reid, *Forster*, 1:334; *Parl. Debates*, 165:1158–1230 (Commons, Mar. 7, 1862), 1233–43 (Lords, Mar. 10, 1862); Henry Adams to CFA Jr., Mar. 15, 1862, in Ford, *Adams Letters*, 1:119–20.

10. A. S. Green of British FO, "Memorandum relative to Blockades" (for cabinet use and based on Wheaton and other international legal theorists), Mar. 3, 1862, Gladstone Papers, Add. Mss., 44,594, vol. 509 (Brit. Lib.). Russell had been promoted to the Lords on July 30, 1861. Historians disagree on the effectiveness of the blockade. Wise claims that the Confederate blockade-runners repeatedly ran the Union blockade and could have done more had the Richmond government supported the effort from the beginning of the war. See his work, the first to examine the entire blockade, *Lifeline of the Confederacy*. Neely ("Perils of Running the Blockade") argues that international law and uncertain Union policies limited the blockade's effectiveness. Lebergott ("Through the Blockade") insists that Confederate blockade-runners profited from cotton smuggling but often declined follow-up voyages because of the risks in challenging the blockade. Laas ("'Sleepless Sentinels'") shows the Union's problems in implementing the blockade in the North Atlantic during the crucial first two years of the war. According to Coddington ("Civil War Blockade Reconsidered"), the British took a pragmatic approach to the Union blockade in acknowledging its effectiveness.

11. Hotze to Hunter, Mar. 11, 1862, *ORN*, 2nd ser., 3:360–62; Addendum to above letter, Mar. 18, 1862, ibid., 3:363; Burnett, *Hotze*, 144.

12. CFA Diary, Mar. 8, 1862 (MHS); CFA to Seward, Mar. 13 (pp. 47–48), Mar. 20 (p. 51), and Mar. 27, 1862 (53–54), *FRUS 1862*.

13. E. D. Adams, *Great Britain*, 2:7–9, 12; Jenkins, *Britain*, 2:74–75; Ashmore, "Diary of James Garnett," vol. 1, 121:77–78, vol. 2, 123:112–14 [Sept. 5, 1861]; Brigg, *Journals of a Lancashire Weaver*, 122:130 (Nov. 16, 1861), 131 (Dec. 31, 1861), 132 (Jan. 1, 1862), 134 (Mar. 4, 1862).

14. Parish, *Civil War*, 398–400; E. M. Thomas, *Confederate Nation*, 174–75; Owsley, *King Cotton Diplomacy*, 43, 211, 213–14; RU to Cowley, Apr. 19, 1862, RU Papers, PRO 30/22/105.

15. E. D. Adams, *Great Britain*, 1:271–72, 272 n. 1. For the sources of England's racial fears, see D. P. Crook, *The North, the South*, 237–38, and McPherson, *Battle Cry*, 558.

16. CFA to Seward, Feb. 21, 1862, CFA Letterbook (MHS); Seward to CFA, Mar. 10 (p. 46), Apr. 1, 1862 (p. 60), *FRUS 1862*; D. P. Crook, "Portents of War," 175. Lincoln did not reveal his decision for emancipation until mid-July 1862, about four months after Seward had moved in that direction.

17. McPherson, *Battle Cry*, 353.

18. CFA Diary, Mar. 19, 1862 (MHS); Dayton to Seward, Mar. 26, 1862, Disp., France (NA); RU to Lyons, Mar. 22, 1862, RU Papers, PRO 30/22/96; E. D. Adams, *Great Britain*, 2:82–83; Hotze to Hunter, Mar. 24, 1862, *ORN*, 2nd ser., 3:371.

19. Lyons to RU, Mar. 31, Apr. 8, 1862, RU Papers, PRO 30/22/36; Seward to CFA, Apr. 8, 1862, *FRUS 1862*, 65; treaty text in *BPP: Papers Relating to Slave Trade, 1861–74*, 91:161–70; Milne, "Lyons-Seward Treaty," 511; Henderson, "Anglo-American Treaty of 1862," 314. E. D. Adams (*Great Britain*, 1:275, 2:10, 90) rejects Lyons's calculating view of Lincoln's motives and insists that both reconstruction and antislavery were important to the president.

20. St. Clair, "Slavery as Diplomatic Factor."

21. E. D. Adams, *Great Britain*, 2:83–84; Thomas and Hyman, *Stanton*, 232–33; Lincoln to U.S. Congress, Apr. 16, 1862, *CWL*, 5:192, 370–71 n. 1.

22. References to Schurz and to Lincoln quote in E. D. Adams, *Great Britain*, 2:91–92.

23. Lincoln's speech at Springfield, Ill., June 16, 1858, *CWL*, 2:461; Lincoln's speech at Peoria, Ill., Oct. 16, 1854, *CWL*, 2:248; Protest in Illinois Legislature on Slavery (signed by Congressman Lincoln), Mar. 3, 1837, *CWL*, 1:75. On Lincoln's evolving views toward slavery, see H. Jones, *Lincoln* and "Toward a More Perfect Union."

24. Lincoln's First Inaugural Address, Mar. 4, 1861, *CWL*, 4:265. The phrase, of course, comes from the U.S. Constitution. For a superb analysis of the threat of disunion from 1789 to 1859, see Varon, *Disunion*.

25. Moran Diary, Apr. 16, 1862 (LC).

26. Ibid., Mar. 20, 1862; CFA to Seward, Feb. 27, 1862, encl.: CFA to RU, Feb. 18, 1862, RU to CFA, Feb. 26, 1862, and CFA to RU, Feb. 27, 1862 (encl.: report of British Commissioners of Customs, Feb. 22, 1862), all in *FRUS 1862*, 39–40; RU to Lyons, Mar. 22, 1862, RU Papers, PRO 30/22/96. For the *Florida*, see Maynard, "Escape of the *Florida*," and Owsley Jr., *C.S.S. Florida*. For the agent's activities in Europe, see Roberts, "Bulloch and Confederate Navy."

27. Moran Diary, Apr. 5, 1862 (LC); CFA to Seward, Apr. 3, 1862, *FRUS 1862*, 62; CFA Diary, Mar. 29, 1862 (MHS); Duke of Newcastle to Governor Gen. of Canada, and to Lt. Governors of New Brunswick and Nova Scotia, Apr. 12, 1862, *BPP: Papers Relating to Canada, 1861–1863*, 24:314–15; Bourne, *Foreign Policy*, 96.

28. Seward to CFA, Apr. 14, 1862, *FRUS 1862*, 67–70; Van Deusen, *Seward*, 320–21; Benjamin to Mason, Apr. 12, 1862, Mason Papers (LC).

29. Carroll, *Mercier*, 280; Hanna and Hanna, *Napoleon III*, 183 (Castilla), (Spanish minister, 101), 102; Dayton to Seward, Feb. 13, 1862, Disp., France (NA). Europe was a tangled web of familial relationships. In addition to Princess Marie Charlotte Amélie and her brother, the Count of Flanders—their father and king of Belgium—was the uncle of Queen Victoria of England.

30. CFA to Seward, Jan. 24, 1862, CFA Letterbook (MHS); Dayton to Seward, Feb. 21, 1862, Disp., France (NA); Seward to Dayton, Mar. 3, 1862, quoted in Owsley, *King Cotton Diplomacy*, 510. For Lincoln's efforts to block European intervention in North America, particularly the French in Mexico, see Tyrner-Tyrnauer, *Lincoln and the Emperors*.

31. Dayton to Seward, Mar. 31, 1862, Disp., France (NA), and Thouvenel to Mercier,

Mar. 7, 27, 1862, both cited in Owsley, *King Cotton Diplomacy*, 511; Barker, "Monarchy in Mexico," 63, and *French Experience*, 185.

32. Palmerston to RU, Jan. 19, 1862, RU Papers, PRO 30/22/22; Jenkins, *Britain*, 1:177; Bourne, *Foreign Policy*, 89.

33. Lyons to RU, Mar. 3, 1862 (FO 146/1024), and RU to Cowley, Mar. 8, 1862 (FO 146/1022), Mar. 11, 1862 (FO 146/1023), Apr. 29, 1862 (FO 146/1029), all in Cowley Papers (PRO); Hanna and Hanna, *Napoleon III*, 42–44; Bock, *Prelude to Tragedy*, 447; Jenkins, *Britain*, 1:176–77; Crook, *The North, the South*, 183–84; E. D. Adams, *Great Britain*, 1:259–60.

34. Lyons to RU, Mar. 3, 1862, FO 146/1024, Cowley Papers (PRO).

35. Seward to Dayton, Mar. 31, 1862, Dip. Instructions, France (NA); Dayton to Seward, Apr. 22, 1862, Disp., France (NA).

36. Thouvenel to Flahault, Sept. 19, 1861, quoted in Barker, "Monarchy in Mexico," 63. British foreign secretary Russell also considered the proposed connection between Mexico and Europe a useful idea. But he had reservations. In addition to his fear of the project's alienating the Union, he thought Maximilian should occupy the throne of Greece; the Mexican people, Russell warned, would never accept a prince sponsored by the French army. Maximilian, however, was not interested in Greece. Barker, "France, Austria," 224–27; Cunningham, *Mexico*, 48–49; Cowley to RU, Oct. 2, 1861, cited in Cunningham, 51; Ridley, *Maximilian and Juárez*, 67–71, 79, 90–91, 106.

37. Dayton to Seward, Apr. 22, 1862, Disp., France (NA).

38. Owsley, *King Cotton Diplomacy*, 513–14.

39. Dayton to Seward, Mar. 4, 16, 25, 1862, Disp., France (NA); Slidell to Hunter, Feb. 11, 1862, *ORN*, 2nd ser., 3:336.

40. RU to Lyons, Dec. 20, 1861, *BPP: Civil War*, 16:156. For the legality of the stone fleet, see Wheaton, *Elements of International Law*, Dana's notes, 360–61 n. 166. See also Confidential memo from London to the State Department in Richmond, Jan. 31, 1862, Mason Papers (LC); and Mann to JD, Feb. 1, 1862 (3:324–25), and Slidell to Hunter, Feb. 11, 1862, encl. in Notes of interviews with Thouvenel, Persigny, Baroche, and Fould (3:340–41), *ORN*, 2nd ser.

41. Notes of interviews with Thouvenel, Persigny, Fould, and Baroche, encl. in Slidell to Hunter, Feb. 11, 1862, *ORN*, 2nd ser., 3:339–41; Case and Spencer, *United States and France*, 260 (Morny).

42. Slidell to Hunter, Feb. 26, 1862, *ORN*, 2nd ser., 3:347–49.

43. CFA to Seward, Apr. 16 (70–73—Dayton's meeting and Adams's reaction), Apr. 25 (77), and May 8, 1862 (83–84), *FRUS 1862*; CFA Diary, Apr. 7, 15, May 3, 1862 (MHS); Moran Diary, Apr. 17, 1862 (LC).

44. Lyons to RU, Mar. 3, 1862, FO 146/1023 (PRO); Palmerston to Gladstone, Apr. 29, 1862, Gladstone Papers, Add. Mss., 44,272, vol. 187 (Brit. Lib.).

45. Case and Spencer, *United States and France*, 269; E. D. Adams, *Great Britain*, 1:289; D. A. Campbell, *English Public Opinion*, 56–58.

46. Case and Spencer, *United States and France*, 269; Slidell to Benjamin, Apr. 14, 1862, encl. in Memo of dispatch no. 5, *ORN*, 2nd ser., 3:393–94.

47. Slidell to Benjamin, Apr. 14, 1862, encl. in Memo of dispatch no. 5, *ORN*, 2nd ser., 3:394.

48. Ibid.; D. A. Campbell, *English Public Opinion*, 161.

49. Slidell to Benjamin, Apr. 14, 1862, encl. in Memo of dispatch no. 5, *ORN*, 2nd ser., 3:394.

50. E. D. Adams, *Great Britain*, 1:292; Case and Spencer, *United States and France*, 270–71.

51. Case and Spencer, *United States and France*, 271; Slidell to Benjamin, Apr. 14, 1862, encl. in Memo of dispatch no. 5, *ORN*, 2nd ser., 3:394–95.

52. E. D. Adams, *Great Britain*, 1:293; Case and Spencer, *United States and France*, 271.

53. E. D. Adams, *Great Britain*, 1:291–92.

54. Case and Spencer, *United States and France*, 271–72.

55. E. D. Adams, *Great Britain*, 1:293–94.

56. Ibid., 1:295 (Disraeli); Owsley, *King Cotton Diplomacy*, 280.

57. Slidell to Benjamin, Apr. 18, 1862, *ORN*, 2nd ser., 3:395–96; Mason to Benjamin, Apr. 21, 1862, ibid., 3:398.

58. Slidell to Benjamin, Apr. 18, 1862, ibid., 3:395–96; Mason to Benjamin, Apr. 21, 1862, ibid., 3:397–98; Case and Spencer, *United States and France*, 273; Owsley, *King Cotton Diplomacy*, 280–81.

59. Slidell to Benjamin, Apr. 14 (3:393–95—Memo encl.), Apr. 18, 1862 (3:395–96), Mason to Benjamin, Apr. 21, 1862, (3:397–99), and Hotze to Hunter, Apr. 25, 1862 (3:399–400), all in *ORN*, 2nd ser.; Case and Spencer, *United States and France*, 269–73.

60. Case and Spencer, *United States and France*, 273. Napoleon's response came in a note dated Apr. 23, 1862.

61. Ibid., 273–74.

62. Dayton to Seward, May 5, 1862, Disp., France (NA); Case and Spencer, *United States and France*, 273–75 (Napoleon, 275).

63. Case and Spencer, *United States and France*, 277; Carroll, *Mercier*, 148–50.

64. Carroll, *Mercier*, 151. Napoleon, like Thouvenel, knew nothing about Mercier's mission until afterward. If the emperor had wanted to side with the South, he could have done so by challenging the Union blockade. That he refused to act except in conjunction with England provides evidence that he would not have risked breaking up the entente by sending Mercier to Richmond. Ibid., 180. Blumenthal (*Reappraisal*, 141–42) agrees that Napoleon had nothing to do with the trip. But Owsley (*King Cotton Diplomacy*, 268, 273, 282–91) argues—with no documentary evidence—that Mercier's mission was part of Napoleon's well-orchestrated plan to learn the Confederacy's potential for independence. Both Slidell and Mason believed that Napoleon had masterminded Mercier's visit without telling Thouvenel. Owsley, 291–92; E. D. Adams, *Great Britain*, 1:288. Although the evidence does not support their conclusion, such a belief certainly encouraged the Confederacy's hopes for French intervention.

65. Stoeckl to Gorchakov, Apr. 25, May 5, 1962, quoted in Saul, *Distant Friends*, 334. See also Carroll, *Mercier*, 151, and Woldman, *Lincoln and the Russians*, 94–95.

66. E. D. Adams, *Great Britain*, 1:281–82, 283 n. 1; Case and Spencer, *United States and France*, 275–78; Carroll, *Mercier*, 146–47, 151–52; Owsley, *King Cotton Diplomacy*, 284; Blumenthal, *Reappraisal*, 141. England originally believed that the Confederacy had won at Shiloh, but Grant had rallied his forces on the second day and, at horrendous

cost, held the field. For the battle, see McPherson, *Battle Cry*, 405–15. Slidell and Mason thought it possible that the emperor had directed Mercier to Richmond without consulting Thouvenel. Slidell to Benjamin, May 9 (3:415), May 15, 1862 (3:419–20), and Mason to Benjamin, May 15, 1862 (3:421), all in *ORN*, 2nd ser. But no evidence has appeared to support their claim. See Carroll, *Mercier*, 176. Mason found everyone "mystified" by Mercier's visit. Mason to JD, May 16, 1862, *ORN*, 2nd ser., 3:425.

67. Case and Spencer, *United States and France*, 278–79; Carroll, *Mercier*, 155.

68. Carroll, *Mercier*, 154–55; Owsley, *King Cotton Diplomacy*, 283.

69. Case and Spencer, *United States and France*, 279; Carroll, *Mercier*, 155–56, 160–61 (Benjamin, 161). The contemporary was Sam Ward, a Washington lobbyist and himself a gourmet. Carroll, 156.

70. This and the preceding paragraphs are from Carroll, *Mercier*, 161.

71. Mercier and Benjamin quotes on slavery in Case and Spencer, *United States and France*, 280.

72. Carroll, *Mercier*, 162–63.

73. Ibid., 163.

74. Quotes in this and the following paragraph are from Case and Spencer, *United States and France*, 281.

75. Ibid., 279–82; Carroll, *Mercier*, 157, 158; Blumenthal, *Reappraisal*, 142; Evans, *Benjamin*, 174–75; Benjamin to Slidell, July 19, 1862, *ORN*, 2nd ser., 3:463–64.

76. Mercier to Thouvenel, May 12, 1862, quoted in Carroll, *Mercier*, 173.

77. Case and Spencer, *United States and France*, 283, 285; Carroll, *Mercier*, 182, 184.

78. Seward to CFA, Apr. 28, 1862, *FRUS 1862*, 78; CFA to Seward, May 15, 1862, ibid., 91; Williams, *Diary from Dixie*, 215 (Apr. 27), 216 (Apr. 29, 1862); Woodward, *Chesnut's Civil War*, 326–27, 330, 333, 339; Moran Diary, May 12, 1862 (LC); Ashmore, "Diary of James Garnett," vol. 2, 123:115 (May 12, 1862); McPherson, *Battle Cry*, 418–20; Duberman, *Adams*, 287.

79. Presidential proclamation, May 12, 1862, encl. in Seward to CFA, May 12, 1862, *FRUS 1862*, 88–89; Slidell to Benjamin, May 15, 1862, *ORN*, 2nd ser., 3:419–20; Case and Spencer, *United States and France*, 282–85; Blumenthal, *Reappraisal*, 142.

CHAPTER 5

1. Henry Adams to CFA Jr., May 16, 1862, in Levenson et al., *Letters of Henry Adams*, 1:297–98; CFA to Seward, Dec. 20, 1861, CFA Letterbook (MHS); CFA to Seward, May 22, 1862 (98–99), RU to CFA, May 17, 1862, encl. (99), and CFA to Seward, May 23, 1862 (100), *FRUS 1862*; Atkins, *Russell*, 1:vii, 2:3; Dayton to Seward, Mar. 25, 1862, Disp., France (NA).

2. CFA Diary, May 3, 1862 (MHS).

3. Lyons to RU, May 16, 26, 1862, RU Papers, PRO 30/22/36; RU to Lyons, May 17, 1862, ibid., PRO 30/22/96. Russell also mentioned the Union's military successes in Yorktown, Va., and Corinth, Miss.

4. Lyons to RU, May 23, June 9, 1862, ibid., PRO 30/22/36.

5. Lyons to RU, May 16, 1862, *BFSP 1864–1865*, 55:514–18 (*National Intelligencer*, 516–18). For southerners' destruction of cotton, see Owsley, *King Cotton Diplomacy*, 43–50.

6. Seward to CFA, May 28, 1862, Disp., GB (NA). Moran thought Seward's note a "wholesome threat." Moran Diary, June 16, 1862 (LC).

7. For the extensive correspondence on this issue, see Palmerston to CFA, June 11, 1862, PM/J/1, Palmerston Letterbook, Palmerston Papers (U. of Southampton); CFA to Palmerston, June 12, 16, 20, 1862, CFA to Seward, June 13, 1862 (2 notes), and Palmerston to CFA, June 15, 1862, all in CFA Letterbook (MHS); CFA Diary, June 12, 13, 19, 20, 29, 1862 (MHS); Palmerston to RU, June 14, 1862, in Gooch, *Later Correspondence*, 2:325–26; Seward to CFA, June 28, 1862, Disp., GB (NA). Seward later expressed regret for failing to see the danger in the "woman order." Seward to CFA, July 5 (124), July 9 (127), and Sept. 8, 1862 (188), *FRUS 1862*. See also H. Adams, *Education*, 137, and Duberman, *Adams*, 288–91.

8. CFA Diary, June 13, 19, 20, 1862 (MHS); Moran Diary, June 12, 13, 24, 1862 (LC); Graebner, "Northern Diplomacy," 66–67; Mason to State Department in Richmond, June 13, 1862, Mason Papers (LC); Palmerston to RU, June 13, 1862, RU Papers, PRO 30/22/22. For a convincing refutation of the charge that the *Times* was biased toward the Confederacy, see Crawford, *Anglo-American Crisis*.

9. Graebner, "Northern Diplomacy," 66 (Henry Adams and Lyons, 67–68); Moran Diary, June 14, 1862 (LC).

10. Lindsay to Mason, June 18, 1862, Mason Papers (LC).

11. Palmerston to Layard, June 19, 1862, Layard Papers, Add. Mss., 38,988, vol. 57 (Brit. Lib.); CFA to Seward, June 20, 1862, *FRUS 1862*, 115.

12. CFA to Seward, June 20, 1862, *FRUS 1862*, 115; H. Jones, *Union in Peril*, 128–29.

13. CFA Diary, June 29, 1862 (MHS); CFA to Seward, July 3, 1862 (122–23), and Seward to CFA, July 18, 1862 (142–44), *FRUS 1862*. For convincing refutations of the arguments for strong Confederate sympathy in England, see Blackett, *Divided Hearts*, and D. A. Campbell, *English Public Opinion*. Ellison (*Support for Secession*) focuses on Lancashire in offering the most detailed claim for southern support among the British. Her argument is not persuasive in that she relies on the local press rather than worker sentiment, and on petitions urging recognition that she does not show to be signed by workers and that, she admits, the British government ignored. For a critical analysis of Ellison's work, see Frank J. Merli's review in *Civil War Times Illustrated* 13 (February 1975): 49–50.

14. McPherson, *Battle Cry*, 471, 490–91, 500; Gallagher, *Confederate War*, 137–38, 145–46, *Richmond Campaign*, ix–x, and "Civil War Watershed," 3, 8, 17; Blair, "Seven Days," 153–54, 173–76; Blackburn, *French Newspaper Opinion*, 57; H. Jones, *Union in Peril*, 133–36. For the best narrative of the Seven Days' battle, see S. W. Sears, *To the Gates of Richmond*.

15. CFA Diary, July 1, 1862 (MHS); Seward to CFA, June 24, 1862 (116–17), and CFA to Seward, June 26, 1862 (118–19), *FRUS 1862*; Moran Diary, June 21, 1862 (LC).

16. Seward exchange with Mercier, ca. July 1, 1862, in Graebner, "Northern Diplomacy," 73, and Owsley, *King Cotton Diplomacy*, 309. See also Carroll, *Mercier*, 200.

17. De Leon, *Secret History*, xiii–xiv; Owsley, *King Cotton Diplomacy*, 162; Monaghan, *Lincoln Deals*, 223. This section draws primarily from Davis's version of De Leon's account.

18. Owsley, *King Cotton Diplomacy*, 155, 163–68. See also Monaghan, *Lincoln Deals*, 223. Monaghan mistakenly claims that the instruction to bribe Napoleon went to De

Leon; Owsley shows that the instruction went to Slidell. Benjamin to Slidell, Apr. 12, 1862, *ORN*, 2nd ser., 3:390; Eaton, *History*, 81, and *Davis*, 171; E. M. Thomas, *Confederate Nation*, 178, 256; Cullop, *Confederate Propaganda*, 77–84; De Leon, *Secret History*, xiv, xvi–xvii, xix, xxiv.

19. De Leon to JD and Benjamin, Spring 1962, in De Leon, *Secret History*, 103, 112–13, xvi. De Leon published his account of this meeting of June 30, 1862 in the *New York Citizen*, Feb. 22, 1868, chap. XIII. One can perhaps question the reliability of De Leon's rendition of his conversation with Palmerston, particularly since it first appeared in published form just six years afterward. But the spirit of the conversation fits well with other evidence showing the Confederacy's growing disenchantment with the prime minister's reluctance to intervene in the American contest and its increasing turn toward the French.

20. This and the preceding paragraphs are from De Leon, *Secret History*, 113–15, 115 n. 8, 116–19.

21. Ibid., 110–12, 119.

22. Ibid., 70.

23. Henry Adams to CFA Jr., July 4, 1862, in Levenson et al., *Letters of Henry Adams*, 1:305–6; Owsley, *King Cotton Diplomacy*, 136–37, 140–42.

24. Mason to RU, July 7, 1862, encl. in Mason to Benjamin, July 30, 1862, *ORN*, 2nd ser., 3:495–96; Benjamin to Mason, Apr. 8, 1862, ibid., 379–83; Owsley, *King Cotton Diplomacy*, 45–46.

25. Monaghan, *Lincoln Deals*, 183, 226; "Appeal to Border State Representatives to Favor Compensated Emancipation," July 12, 1862, in *CWL*, 5:317–19; McPherson, *Battle Cry*, 503–4; Current, *Lincoln Nobody Knows*, 221–22; Thomas and Hyman, *Stanton*, 238; Beale, *Diary of Gideon Welles*, 1:70–71 (July 13, 1862). For an extended treatment of Lincoln's views, see Cox, *Lincoln and Black Freedom*. Cox does not think Lincoln merely followed Congress in making emancipation policy. The president, she argues, led the way (pp. 14–15). For an analysis of Lincoln's evolving views toward slavery, see H. Jones, *Lincoln*, chaps. 1–2, and "Toward a More Perfect Union," 15–28.

26. Mason to Benjamin, June 23, 1862 (3:445–46), Slidell to Benjamin, June 1, 1862 (3:428–29), and Mann (in Brussels) to Benjamin, June 3 (3:429), July 5, 1862 (3:453), *ORN*, 2nd ser; Cobden to Bright, July 12, 1862, Cobden Papers, Add. Mss., 43,652, vol. 6 (Brit. Lib.); Palmerston to Queen Victoria, July 14, 1862, quoted in Bell, *Palmerston*, 2:327; Mason to State Department in Richmond, July 15, 1862, and Slidell to Mason, July 16, 1862, Mason Papers (LC); Stuart to RU, July 15, 1862, RU Papers, PRO 30/22/36; Johnson to Lincoln, July 16, 1862, in *CWL*, 5:343 n. 1. Johnson was in New Orleans investigating charges of undisciplined behavior by the Union occupation force. See also L. M. Sears, "Confederate Diplomat," 262–63. Stuart headed the British legation in Washington until Lyons returned from England in early November.

27. CFA Diary, July 14, 17, 1862 (MHS); CFA to Seward, July 17, 1862, *FRUS 1862*, 139–40; Mason to RU, July 17, 1862, encl. in Mason to Benjamin, July 30, 1862, *ORN*, 2nd ser., 3:499; CFA to Seward, July 17, 1862, *FRUS 1862*, 136–37; CFA Diary, July 15, 1862 (MHS); Jenkins, *Britain*, 2:94; *Parl. Debates*, 168:569–73 (Commons, July 18, 1862); Matthew, *Gladstone Diaries*, 6:136 (July 18, 1862); Mason to Slidell, July 11, 13, 1862, Mason Papers (LC).

28. *Economist*, July 5, Aug. 2, 1862, quoted in Owsley, *King Cotton Diplomacy*, 137; Owsley, 137–38, 142. By September the cotton stock in England had plunged to 100,000 bales, with a weekly drain of 30,000 to either industrial use or exportation. Unemployment and hardship would peak the following December 1862. The cotton stores on hand would meanwhile climb back up, primarily because of supplies confiscated by the Union blockade vessels and by new sources in Brazil, China, Egypt, and India. Even though the latter goods were of inferior grade, their availability permitted an increase in working hours that eased unemployment numbers. But all this did not come until the end of the year. Owsley.

29. Owsley, *King Cotton Diplomacy*, 152; Case and Spencer, *United States and France*, 159, 162, 164–66, 319–23. The autumn of 1862 found thousands of French workers unemployed and marked the country's worst period of unemployment and deprivation. Case and Spencer.

30. Hanna and Hanna, *Napoleon III*, xiii–xiv, 4, 19, 79, 199, 303 (Napoleon, 78); Barker, "Monarchy in Mexico," 59, 63, and "French Legation," 411, 423.

31. Slidell's July 16 meeting with Napoleon (here and in the following paragraphs) in Slidell memo of conversation, encl. in Slidell to Benjamin, July 25, 1862, *ORN*, 2nd ser., 3:479, 482–83, 485–87, and Case and Spencer, *United States and France*, 300–305.

32. Davis, Benjamin, and the Confederate Congress approved an effort in the spring of 1862 to bribe the French to challenge the Union blockade by offering free trade and 100,000 bales of cotton. Eaton, *Davis*, 171. This was the arrangement De Leon read about in the dispatches.

33. Slidell's confidence in French intervention even without the British becomes plain in L. M. Sears, "Confederate Diplomat."

34. Case and Spencer, *United States and France* (Napoleon, 307; Thouvenel, 308). Napoleon's prognosis on the Union loan to Mexico was correct. Less than a week before this conversation (hence unknown to the emperor), the U.S. Senate had tabled the proposal after Lincoln had sent it up without a recommendation. Hanna and Hanna, *Napoleon III*, 72. Dayton had recently emphasized to the emperor that French withdrawal of belligerent rights from the Confederacy would break the rebellion and end the war. The "moral support" gained from the concession had given the Confederacy hope that recognition of independence would soon follow and thereby prolonged the war. Dayton to Seward, Mar. 25, 1862, Disp., France (NA).

35. Case and Spencer, *United States and France* (Gorchakov, 309).

36. *Economist*, Feb. 15, June 14, 1862 (Bagehot). Both issues are cited in Sexton, *Debtor Diplomacy*, 153–54.

37. Blackburn, *French Newspaper Opinion*, 95.

38. *Parl. Debates*, 168:569–73 (Commons, July 18, 1862); Matthew, *Gladstone Diaries*, 6: 136 (July 18, 1862); Mason to Slidell, July 11, 13, 18, 1862, and Benjamin to Mason, July 19, 1862, Mason Papers (LC); Henry Adams to CFA Jr., July 19, 1862, in Levenson et al., *Letters of Henry Adams*, 1:307–8; Hammond to Layard, July 18, 1862, Layard Papers, Add. Mss., 38,951, vol. 21 (Brit. Lib.); CFA to CFA Jr., July 18, 1862, in Ford, *Adams Letters*, 1:166; CFA Diary, July 18, 1862 (MHS). See also Blumenthal, "Confederate Diplomacy." For the claim that the *Times* had already seemingly admitted that a failed mediation would lead to recognition, see W. R. West, *Contemporary French Opinion*, 79.

39. Moran Diary, July 19, 1862 (LC); Henry Adams to CFA Jr., July 19, 1862, in Levenson et al., *Letters of Henry Adams*, 1:308.

40. Moran Diary, July 19, 1862 (LC); Henry Adams to CFA Jr., July 19, 1862, in Levenson et al., *Letters of Henry Adams*, 1:308; CFA Diary, July 18, 1862 (MHS); Graebner, "Northern Diplomacy," 67.

41. Moran Diary, July 19, 1862 (LC); Wallace and Gillespie, *Journal of . . . Moran*, 2:1041 n. 13; *Parl. Debates*, 168:511–12 (Lindsay in Commons, July 18, 1862), 522–27 (Taylor in Commons, July 18), 527–34 (Vane-Tempest in Commons, July 18), 534–38 (Forster in Commons, July 18); E. D. Adams, *Great Britain*, 2:22.

42. *Parl. Debates*, 168:569–73 (Commons, July 18, 1862); Moran Diary, July 19, 1862 (LC); Wallace and Gillespie, *Journal of . . . Moran*, 2:1044.

43. Moran Diary, July 19, 1862 (LC); Graebner, "Northern Diplomacy," 67.

44. CFA Diary, July 19, 1862 (MHS); CFA to Seward, July 10, 1862, CFA Letterbook (MHS); CFA to Seward, July 31, 1862, no. 197, *FRUS 1862*, 159–60; Henry Adams to CFA Jr., July 19, 1862, in Levenson et al., *Letters of Henry Adams*, 1:308.

45. For the argument that the great numbers of British were *not* southern sympathizers, see D. A. Campbell, *English Public Opinion*, chap. 5. According to Blackett (*Divided Hearts*, 102, 119–20, 143), most British workers and a large number of cotton manufacturers favored the Union because of its interest in political reform. He also argues that exchanges between editors and readers demonstrate that most of the British press did *not* support the Confederacy.

46. Slidell's July 23 meeting with Thouvenel (here and in the preceding paragraphs) is from Slidell to Benjamin, July 25, 1862, *ORN*, 2nd ser., 3:480–81.

47. Case and Spencer, *United States and France*, 311–12 (Thouvenel, 312).

48. Mason to Benjamin, July 30–Aug. 4, 1862, with encls., *ORN*, 2nd ser., 3:490–504; E. D. Adams, *Great Britain*, 2:25–29.

49. Case and Spencer, *United States and France* (Thouvenel, 313–14). Two years after the Civil War, the Austro-Hungarian dual monarchy came into existence, exemplifying many of the principles advocated by Thouvenel regarding the American war.

50. De Leon, *Secret History*, xvii, 22, 42–44, 122, 126–27, 142, 216. De Leon even shared some of his own funds with Hotze. Ibid., xvii. De Leon argued for recognition in a pamphlet entitled *La Vérité sur des États Confédérés (The Truth about the Confederate States of America)*, published in August 1862; it included a picture of Davis intended to impress Europeans with his magisterial bearing. Ibid., xiii. For a reprint of the entire pamphlet, see ibid., app. 3, pp. 209–19. De Leon published his French views in the *New York Citizen*, Dec. 21, 1867, Jan. 4, Feb. 22, 29, 1868. See also Benjamin to Slidell, Apr. 12, 1862, *ORN*, 2nd ser., 3:390; Eaton, *History*, 81; E. M. Thomas, *Confederate Nation*, 178, 256; Cullop, *Confederate Propaganda*, 77–84; and Owsley, *King Cotton Diplomacy*, 163–68.

51. De Leon, *Secret History*, 23–26, 131.

52. Ibid., 103.

53. Ibid., 32, 43. De Leon published his conclusions on England in the *New York Citizen*, Feb. 15, 1868.

54. Adams warned the Union government that England needed grain from abroad— and mainly from the United States. See CFA to Seward, July 24, 1862, Disp., GB (NA). For British interest in grain as a counterbalance to their need for cotton, see Schmidt,

"Influence of Wheat and Cotton," 431, 437, 439, and Khasigian, "Economic Factors." British wheat needs, however, were never great enough to have an important impact on the intervention issue. See Ginzberg, "Economics of British Neutrality," 151, 155; R. H. Jones, "Long Live the King?," 167–69; and E. D. Adams, *Great Britain*, 2:13–14 n. 2.

55. Seward to Dayton, July 10, 1862, Dip. Instructions, France (NA).

CHAPTER 6

1. RU to Stuart, July 19, 1862, RU Papers, PRO 30/22/96; Stuart to RU, July 21, 1862, ibid., PRO 30/22/36; Slidell to Mason, July 20, 1862, Mason Papers (LC); Slidell memo, July 25, 1862, encl. in Slidell to Benjamin, July 25, 1862, *ORN*, 2nd ser., 3:481–87; Bourne, *Foreign Policy*, 91.

2. Seward to CFA, July 28, 1862, *FRUS 1862*, 157; Stuart to RU, July 21, 29, Aug. 4, 1862 (PRO 30/22/36), and RU to Stuart, July 25, 1862 (PRO 30/22/96), RU Papers; Stuart to RU, July 21, 1862, *BFSP 1864–1865*, 55:519; RU to Stuart, Aug. 7, 1862, *BPP: Civil War*, 17:29; Brauer, "Slavery Problem," 450. Stuart thought Russell's dispatch of July 28 important enough to read it to Seward on August 16; two weeks later, Stuart gave Seward a copy. See Stuart to Seward, Aug. 30, 1862, with encl.: RU to Stuart, July 28, 1862, NFBL, GB (NA).

3. H. Jones, *Union in Peril*, 139–40; Blair, "Seven Days," 153–54, 175.

4. Seward to CFA, July 28, 1862, *FRUS 1862*, 156–58.

5. Gallagher, "Civil War Watershed," 17; Beale, *Diary of Gideon Welles*, 1:70–71 (July 13, 1862); Lincoln, "Emancipation Proclamation—First Draft," July 22, 1862, in *CWL*, 5:336–37; Thomas and Hyman, *Stanton*, 238–40; H. Jones, *Lincoln*, 86.

6. Blair to Lincoln, July 23, 1862, in *CWL*, 5:337 n. 1; Donald, *Inside Lincoln's Cabinet*, 99–100. On Lincoln's fear of alienating the Border States, see his "Remarks to Deputation of Western Gentlemen," Aug. 4, 1862, in *CWL*, 5:357; W. H. Seward, *Autobiography*, 3:74 (1st Seward quote); Brauer, "Slavery Problem," 452; McPherson, *Battle Cry*, 505 (2nd Seward quote); H. Jones, *Lincoln*, 86–87; and Van Deusen, *Seward*, 328–29.

7. Lincoln to Reverdy Johnson, July 26, 1862, in *CWL*, 5:343 (Lincoln's 1st quote); Lincoln to Belmont, July 31, 1862, ibid., 5:350 (Lincoln's 2nd quote); Belmont to Lincoln, Aug. 10, 1862, ibid., 5:351 n. 1 (Belmont); Lincoln to Cuthbert Bullitt, July 28, 1862, ibid., 5:344–45 (remainder of Lincoln's quotes); Randall, *Constitutional Problems*, 377–78; H. Jones, *Lincoln*, 88.

8. Pease and Randall, *Diary of . . . Browning*, 1:562 (July 24, 1862); E. D. Adams, *Great Britain*, 2:87.

9. For Lincoln's religious views, see Donald, *Lincoln*, 15, 114, 337, 514–15, and Thomas, *Lincoln*, 108–9. For an expanded treatment of Lincoln's views toward slavery and their relation to the concept of Union, see H. Jones, *Lincoln*.

10. Lincoln's speech at Peoria, Ill., Oct. 16, 1854, *CWL*, 2:276.

11. McPherson, *What They Fought For* (South Carolina officer, 49; Kentuckian, 51), *For Cause and Comrades* (Mississippi officer, 171), and *Drawn with the Sword* (Georgian, 60).

12. On Lincoln's view that a better Union depended on the death of slavery, see H. Jones, *Lincoln*; Diggins, *On Hallowed Ground*; Jaffa, *New Birth of Freedom*; and Striner, *Father Abraham*.

13. Donald, *Inside Lincoln's Cabinet*, 105–6 (Aug. 3, 1862); McPherson, *Battle Cry* (Grant and Grenville Dodge [officer], 502).

14. Gasparin to Lincoln, July 18, 1862, in *CWL*, 5:355 n. 1; Lincoln to Gasparin, Aug. 4, 1862, ibid., 5:355–56.

15. McPherson, *Battle Cry*, 505–8; Cox, *Lincoln and Black Freedom*, 5, 14; Fehrenbacher, "Only His Stepchildren," 293–310; Fredrickson, "A Man but Not a Brother," 53; Oates, *With Malice toward None*, 41, and "'Man of Our Redemption,'" 15–16, 19–20; Randall, *Constitutional Problems*, 370; Guelzo, *Lincoln*, 338–44; Carnahan, *Act of Justice*, chap. 7. For Lincoln's longtime aversion to slavery, see, among numerous examples, his protest in the Illinois legislature on slavery, Mar. 3, 1837, in *CWL*, 1:75; Lincoln to Williamson Durley, Oct. 3, 1845, in *CWL* 1:348; and Lincoln's speech at Bloomington, Ill., Sept. 26, 1854, in *CWL*, 2:239. In the 1854 speech he called slavery "a moral, social and political evil."

16. RU to Mason, July 31, 1862, Mason Papers, Disp. (LC); RU to Mason, July 24, 1862 (3:499), and Mason to RU, July 24, 1862 (3:501), encls. in Mason to Benjamin, July 30, 1862, *ORN*, 2nd ser.; Mason to RU, Aug. 1, 1862, *BFSP 1864–1865*, 55:731–33.

17. RU to Mason, Aug. 2, 1862, Mason Papers, Disp. (LC).

18. Mason to Benjamin, Aug. 4, 1862, ibid.; Mason to Mrs. Mason, July 20, 1862, quoted in McPherson, *Battle Cry*, 555; Gladstone to Col. [?] Neville, July 26, 1862, quoted in E. D. Adams, *Great Britain*, 2:26; Gladstone to wife, July 29, 1862, quoted in Morley, *Gladstone*, 2:75; Randall and Donald, *Civil War and Reconstruction*, 507.

19. Hammond to Layard, July 20, 28, 1862, Layard Papers, Add. Mss., 38,951, vol. 21 (Brit. Lib.); Lyons to Stuart, July 29, 1862, quoted in E. D. Adams, *Great Britain*, 2:26.

20. CFA to Seward, July 31 (p. 162), Aug. 1, 1862 (p. 163), *FRUS 1862*; CFA Diary, July 31, 1862 (MHS); Ridley, *Palmerston*, 557; Duberman, *Adams*, 293–94; E. D. Adams, *Great Britain*, 2:35, 118–22. See reference to British Foreign Enlistment Act of 1819 in "British Proclamation for the Observance of Neutrality in the Contest between the United States and the Confederate States of America, May 13, 1861," *BFSP 1860–1861*, 51:165, 167. For Confederate shipbuilding activities in England, see Merli, *Great Britain*, and Spencer, *Confederate Navy*.

21. Merli, *Alabama*, 24, 199 n. 4, and *Great Britain*, 136–37, 178; Milton, *Lincoln's Spymaster*, 19, 29, 34; Dudley to Edwards, July 9, 1862, encl. in Alabama docs. requested by House of Commons, Mar. 20, 1863 (2:379), and Testimony by Dudley to Edwards at customhouse in Liverpool, July 21, 1862 (2:385–86), *ORN*, 2nd ser. Spencer (*Confederate Navy*) maintains that both Britain and France hurt the Confederacy's shipbuilding efforts by adhering to a neutrality based on self-interest.

22. Jenkins, *Britain*, 2:120–21; Milton, *Lincoln's Spymaster*, xix; Cross, *Lincoln's Man in Liverpool*; Merli, *Great Britain*, 63–65, 68–69, and *Alabama*, 54–57, 92; Owsley, *King Cotton Diplomacy*, 395–96; Tucker, *Blue and Gray Navies*, 274; Hearn, *Gray Raiders of the Sea*, 53–55.

23. Merli, *Great Britain*, 62–65; Dudley to Samuel Price Edwards (customs collector, Liverpool), July 9, 1862, encl. in Alabama docs. requested by House of Commons, Mar. 20, 1863, *ORN*, 2nd ser., 2:378–79.

24. Merli, *Alabama*, 48–49. Captain Matthew Butcher wrote in his diary that "290" was used to conceal the intended name of *Alabama* (p. 129).

25. Dudley to Customs Collector, Liverpool, July 9, 1862, encl. in Alabama docs. requested by House of Commons, Mar. 20, 1863, *ORN*, 2nd ser., 2:380.

26. Merli, *Alabama*, 49–50.

27. Milton, *Lincoln's Spymaster*, 37; Merli, *Alabama*, 56; Report by Edward Morgan (customs surveyor), June 28, 1862, encl. in Samuel Price Edwards (customs collector, Liverpool) to Commissioners of Customs, June 28, 1862, encl. in Alabama docs. requested by House of Commons, Mar. 20, 1863, *ORN*, 2nd ser., 2:377.

28. Merli, *Alabama*, 57.

29. Ibid., 55–56.

30. Ibid., 58.

31. Ibid., 58–62.

32. Ibid., 61–62, 73; Jenkins, *Britain*, 2:122; Milton, *Lincoln's Spymaster*, 43; Maynard, "Union Efforts"; Edwards to Commissioners of Customs, July 10, 1862, and Report by Morgan, July 10, 1862, both encl. in Alabama docs. requested by House of Commons, Mar. 20, 1863, *ORN*, 2nd ser., 2:378; Frederick Goulburn and R. W. Grey to Customs Collector, Liverpool, July 15, 1862, 381.

33. Merli, *Alabama*, 65.

34. Cross, *Lincoln's Man in Liverpool*, 48; Milton, *Lincoln's Spymaster*, 44; Edwards to commissioners of customs, July 21, 1862, and Testimony by William Passmore to Edwards at customhouse, Liverpool, July 21, 1862, 381–82, both encl. in Alabama docs. requested by House of Commons, Mar. 20, 1863, *ORN*, 2nd ser., 2:381; Merli, *Alabama*, 67–68. For a useful collection of essays and annotated bibliography of primary and secondary materials, see Merli, *Journal of Confederate History*.

35. Testimonies by Henry Wilding and Matthew Maguire to Edwards at customhouse, Liverpool, July 21, 1862, *ORN*, 2nd ser., 2:384.

36. Opinion of Collier, July 16, 23, 1862, in *FRUS 1862*, 151–52; Merli, *Alabama*, 66–72, 82–83.

37. T. F. Fremantle and G. C. L. Berkeley (the commissioners of customs) to Edwards, July 22, 1862, encl. in Alabama docs. requested by House of Commons, Mar. 20, 1863, *ORN*, 2nd ser., 2:386; Merli, *Alabama*, 82–83; Jenkins, *Britain*, 2:124–25; Milton, *Lincoln's Spymaster*, 46; MacChesney, "*Alabama*."

38. Merli, *Alabama*, 86–88; Jenkins, *Britain*, 2:125.

39. Morgan to Edwards, July 30, 1862, encl. in Alabama docs. requested by House of Commons, Mar. 20, 1863, *ORN*, 2nd ser., 2:387–88; Edwards to Commissioners of Customs, July 30, 1862, ibid., 2:388; Edwards to F. G. Gardner, July 31, 1862, ibid., 2:388–89; Examination of Thomas Miller by collector at customhouse, Liverpool, Aug. 1, 1862, ibid., 2:390; Hearn, *Gray Raiders of the Sea*, 156–57.

40. Dudley to Edwards, July 30, 1862, encl. in Alabama docs. requested by House of Commons, Mar. 20, 1863, *ORN*, 2nd ser., 2:387; Maynard, "Plotting the Escape" and "Union Efforts." Two recent works attribute the *Alabama*'s escape to a bungled British policy and not to complicity. See Merli, *Alabama*, chap. 4, and D. A. Campbell, *English Public Opinion*, 245.

41. Edwards to Commissioners of Customs, Aug. 1, 1862, encl. in Alabama docs. requested by House of Commons, Mar. 20, 1863, *ORN*, 2nd ser., 2:389; Merli, *Alabama*, 84.

42. W. G. Stewart (assistant collector, Liverpool) to Commissioners of Customs, Sept. 3, 1862, encl. in Alabama docs. requested by House of Commons, Mar. 20, 1863, *ORN*, 2nd ser., 2:391; Report from J. Hussey (assistant surveyor, Liverpool), Sept. 2, 1862, ibid., 2:391–92; Report from E. Morgan (surveyor), Liverpool, Sept. 3, 1862, ibid., 2:392.

43. Bulloch to Mallory, Sept. 10, 1862, ibid., 2:263–64.

44. Merli, *Alabama*, 61.

45. Ibid., 88; Stuart to RU, Aug. 16, 1862, *BFSP 1864–1865*, 55:520–21; McPherson, *Battle Cry*, 555 (Dudley); Layard to [?] Horsfall, July 5, 1862, encl. in RU to CFA, Aug. 4, 1862, encl. in CFA to Seward, Aug. 7, 1862, *FRUS 1862*, 171.

46. Wallace and Gillespie, *Journal of . . . Moran*, 2:1182 (July 11, 1863); Merli, *Great Britain*, 197–201.

47. Merli, *Alabama*, 23, and *Great Britain*, 202, 203 (Palmerston), 204, 211; E. D. Adams, *Great Britain*, 2:122; Krein, "Russell's Decision." For a detailed examination of British policy leading to seizure of the rams, see W. D. Jones, *Confederate Rams at Birkenhead*. The two rams became the HMS *Scorpion* and the HMS *Wivern*.

48. Merli, *Great Britain*, 216–17; Owsley, *King Cotton Diplomacy*, 418 (Bigelow).

49. Merli, *Great Britain*, 95–99; Robinson, *Shark of the Confederacy*; Fox, *Wolf of the Deep*; Taylor, *Confederate Raider*; Marvel, *Alabama*; RU, *Recollections*, 235; Eaton, *Davis*, 171; Tucker, *Blue and Gray Navies*, 286. Bonding meant that the Confederate captain allowed a commercial vessel carrying passengers or neutral goods if that vessel's captain signed a paper promising to pay a condemnation fee after the war. Tucker, 272. For the *Alabama* claims settlement, see Cook, *Alabama Claims*.

50. Seward to CFA, Aug. 2, 1862, Disp., GB (NA).

51. E. D. Adams, *Great Britain*, 2:154; Matthew, *Gladstone Diaries*, 6:139 (July 31, 1862), 6:142 (Aug. 12, 1862), 6:142 n. 2, 6:154 n. 10; Gladstone memo on "Southern Gentleman," July 31, 1862, and Gladstone to RU, Oct. 17, 1862, in Guedalla, *Gladstone and Palmerston*, 230–31. See also R. L. Reid, "Gladstone's 'Insincere Neutrality'"; Butler, *Gladstone*, 122; Spence to Mason, Apr. 28, 1862, encl. in Mason to Benjamin, May 2, 1862, *ORN*, 2nd ser., 3:401–4.

52. Gladstone to AR, Aug. 3, 1862, in AR, *Argyll*, 2:191; Morley, *Gladstone*, 2:81; Magnus, *Gladstone*, 153.

53. *Times*, July 9, 12, 1862, and *London Morning Post*, Aug. [?], 1862, quoted in CFA Jr., *Before and after the Treaty of Washington*, 43–44.

54. Palmerston to Queen Victoria, Aug. 6, 1862, quoted in Bell, *Palmerston*, 2:327; CFA Jr., "Crisis of Foreign Intervention," 13–14. One of Victoria's biographers, Elizabeth Longford (*Queen Victoria*, 26, 66), points out that Leopold was not only the queen's uncle but also a father figure.

55. RU to Palmerston, Aug. 6, 1862, GC/RU/721, Palmerston Papers (U. of Southampton); RU to Stuart, Aug. 7, 1862, *BFSP 1864–1865*, 55:519; RU to Stuart, Aug. 8, 1862, RU Papers, PRO 30/22/96.

56. Granville to Lord Stanley, Oct. 1, 1862, in Fitzmaurice, *Granville*, 1:442. Granville made his remark to Stratford Canning, British minister to Washington, during the early 1820s.

57. CFA Jr., "Crisis of Foreign Intervention," 12; AR to Gladstone, Aug. 6, 1862, Gladstone Papers, Add. Mss., 44,099, vol. 14 (Brit. Lib.); Bright to Cobden, Aug. 6, 1862,

Bright Papers, Add. Mss., 43,384, vol. 2 (Brit. Lib.); Cobden to Bright, Aug. 7, 1862, Cobden Papers, Add. Mss., 43,652, vol. 6 (Brit. Lib.). Cobden's argument for joint intervention is summarized in CFA Diary, June 29, 1862 (MHS). See also Bright, *Speeches*, and Gwin, "Slavery and English Polarity."

58. CFA Diary, Aug. 7, 1862 (MHS); Stuart to RU, Aug. 8, 1862, RU Papers, PRO 30/22/36; Parish, *Civil War*, 393; Eaton, *History*, 84; D. P. Crook, *The North, the South*, 226–27; Golder, "American Civil War," 454, 456–57; Adamov, "Russia and the United States," 596–97; Saul, *Distant Friends*, 321–23, 331; Woldman, *Lincoln and the Russians*, viii, 125, 127–30.

59. *Times*, Aug. 15, 1862, p. 6; Hammond to Layard, Aug. 17, 1862, Layard Papers, Add. Mss., 38,951, vol. 21 (Brit. Lib.); Stuart to RU, Aug. 18, 1862, RU Papers, PRO 30/22/36; Lewis to Sir George Grey, Aug. 27, 1862, Ripon Papers, Add. Mss., 43,533, vol. 43 (Brit. Lib.); Seward to CFA, Aug. 18, 1862, circular no. 20, *FRUS 1862*, 179; Moran Diary, Aug. 18, 1862 (LC). Moran was referring to Seward's dispatch to CFA of Aug. 2, 1862, Disp., GB (NA).

60. Greeley to Lincoln, Aug. 19, 1862, in *CWL*, 5:389 n. 1; Lincoln to Greeley, Aug. 22, 1862, ibid., 5:388.

61. Stuart to RU, Aug. 22, 1862, RU Papers, PRO 30/22/36; AR to Gladstone, Aug. 26, 1862, Gladstone Papers, Add. Mss., 44,099, vol. 14 (Brit. Lib.); AR to Palmerston, Sept. 2, 1862, GC/AR/25/1, Palmerston Papers (U. of Southampton).

62. Stuart to RU, Aug. 26, 1862, RU Papers, PRO 30/22/36; Hammond to Layard, Aug. 28, 1862, Layard Papers, Add. Mss., 38,951, vol. 21 (Brit. Lib.); Dayton to Seward, Aug. 8, 1862, Disp., France (NA) (Slidell's rebuff); Slidell to State Department in Richmond, Aug. 24, 1862, in Graebner, "Northern Diplomacy," 69–70.

63. Cobden to Bright, Aug. 28, 1862, Cobden Papers, Add. Mss., 43,652, vol. 6 (Brit. Lib.); Bright to Cobden, Aug. 30, 1862, Bright Papers, Add. Mss., 43,884, vol. 2 (Brit. Lib.); Gladstone to AR, Aug. 29, 1862, and Gladstone to RU, Aug. 30, 1862, Gladstone Papers, Letter-Book, 1862–63, Add. Mss., 44,533, vol. 448 (Brit. Lib.); Zorn, "Bright and the British Attitude," 145.

64. Mitchell, *European Historical Statistics*, 355 (British industrial figures), 618 (British shipping); Henry Adams to CFA Jr., May 8, 1862, in Ford, *Adams Letters*, 1:139; Lyons to Stuart, July 29, 1862, quoted in E. D. Adams, *Great Britain*, 2:26; Owsley, *King Cotton Diplomacy*, 137, 140; McPherson, *Battle Cry*, 548–51; Hotze to Benjamin, Dec. 20, 1862, *ORN*, 2nd ser., 3:632–33. From 1861 on, the amount of cotton imported from India increased; in 1864, 67 percent of Britain's supply came from India and during the American war, 55 percent. See Logan, "India—Britain's Substitute for American Cotton," 475–76. England eventually found India's cotton inferior to that from the Confederate South and turned to Egypt, whose cotton equaled the quality of that from the South, except for the Sea Island variety. See Earle, "Egyptian Cotton," 527. New York business leaders and philanthropists worked to feed unemployed textile workers in Lancashire, helping to ease the pressure for Britain's intervention in the war. Carpenter, "New York International Relief Committee."

65. Jenkins, *Britain*, 1:214; Lincoln, "Message to Congress in Special Session," July 4, 1861, in *CWL*, 4:438; McPherson, *Battle Cry*, 550 (8); Eaton, *History*, 75–76 (Hotze). See also Marx and Engels, *Civil War in the United States*. Workers supported the Union as

guardian of freedom, according to Park, "English Workingmen," and Greenleaf, "British Labor." Textile workers favored the Confederacy, argues Ellison in *Support for Secession*. For the most convincing refutation of the argument for southern sympathy, see Blackett, *Divided Hearts*, and D. A. Campbell, *English Public Opinion*.

66. Mitchell, *European Historical Statistics*, 355, 618; Case and Spencer, *United States and France*, 289–90 (Thouvenel); Stuart to RU, Sept. 1, 1862, RU Papers, PRO 30/22/36.

67. Stuart to RU, Sept. 9, 1862, RU Papers, PRO 30/33/36.

68. Henry Adams to CFA Jr., Feb. 13, 1863, in Ford, *Adams Letters*, 1:253; AR to Gladstone, Sept. 2, 1862, Gladstone Papers, Add. Mss., 44,099, vol. 14 (Brit. Lib.).

69. F. O. Mitchell to Layard, Sept. 3, 1862, Layard Papers, Dipl. Ser., Add. Mss., 39,104, vol. 174 (Brit. Lib.); Stuart to RU, Sept. 5, 1862, RU Papers, PRO 30/22/36; Bright to Cobden, Sept. 6, 1862, Bright Papers, Add. Mss., 43,384, vol. 2 (Brit. Lib.); Gladstone to AR, Sept. 8, 1862, Gladstone Papers, Letter-Book, 1862–63, Add. Mss., 44,533, vol. 448 (Brit. Lib.).

70. Henry Adams to CFA Jr., Sept. 5, 1862, in Levenson et al., *Letters of Henry Adams*, 1:309–10.

71. CFA Diary, Sept. 14, 1862 (MHS); *CWL*, 5:404 n. 1 (top) (Bates), 486 n. 1 (top); RU to Cowley, Sept. 13, 1862 (PRO 30/22/105), Palmerston to RU, Sept. 14, 1862, and RU to Palmerston, Sept. 17, 1862 (PRO 30/22/14), all in RU Papers; Walpole, *Lord John Russell*, 2:349; Duberman, *Adams*, 294; McPherson, *Battle Cry*, 528, 555–56 (Lincoln, 533); Brauer, "British Mediation," 57; E. D. Adams, *Great Britain*, 2:38, 41.

72. Stuart to RU, Aug. 26, 1862, RU Papers, PRO 30/22/36.

73. Dayton to Seward, Sept. 13, 1862, Disp., France (NA).

74. Seward conversation with Mercier is from Seward to Dayton, Sept. 8, 1862, Dip. Instructions, France (NA). See also CFA Diary, Sept. 21, 1862 (MHS). In a recommendation made by his staff in early summer of 1862 (see chap. 5), Thouvenel proposed a boundary between Union and Confederacy that created two republics, one slave and one free. Case and Spencer, *United States and France*, 313–14; Owsley, *King Cotton Diplomacy*, 330–31; Graebner, "Northern Diplomacy," 73–74. Russell had advocated this kind of solution at the beginning of the conflict.

CHAPTER 7

1. *Times*, Sept. 16, 1862, p. 6; *London Morning Post* and *Morning Herald*, both Sept. 16, 1862, quoted in Jenkins, *Britain*, 2:151; Jenkins, 167.

2. Palmerston to RU, Sept. 14, 1862, RU Papers, PRO 30/22/14D; RU to Palmerston, Sept. 17, 1862, GC/RU/728, Palmerston Papers (U. of Southampton). Lewis agreed that the Union's great defeat had eased British fear of an invasion of Canada that winter of 1862. Lewis to Sir George Grey from the Home Office, Sept. 18, 1862, Ripon Papers, Add. Mss., 43,533, vol. 43 (Brit. Lib.).

3. Palmerston to RU, Sept. 22, 1862, RU Papers, PRO 30/22/14D; RU to Palmerston, Sept. 22, 1862, GC/RU/729, Palmerston Papers (U. of Southampton). Mercier's comment in Stuart to RU, Sept. 9, 1862, RU Papers, PRO 30/33/36.

4. Palmerston to RU, Sept. 23, 1862, RU Papers, PRO 30/22/14D. One writer argues, erroneously, that by mid-September Palmerston was still unaware of Russia's opposition

to intervention or of Seward's dependence on Russia for assistance. B. P. Thomas, *Russo-American Relations*, chap. 8.

5. Palmerston to RU, Sept. 23, 1862, RU Papers, PRO 30/22/14D.

6. Palmerston to Gladstone, Sept. 24, 1862, in Morley, *Gladstone*, 2:76; RU to Gladstone, Sept. 26, 1862, Gladstone Papers, Add. Mss., 44,292, vol. 207 (Brit. Lib.).

7. See Chapter 2 of this book. For the legal argument, see Vattel, *Law of Nations*, bk. 2, chap. 1, sec. 114, and bk. 3, chap. 3, sec. 249, chap. 7, secs. 269–70.

8. RU to Cowley, Sept. 26, 1862, RU Papers, PRO 30/22/105.

9. Gladstone to Palmerston, Sept. 25, 1862, Gladstone Papers, Add. Mss., 44, 272, vol. 187 (Brit. Lib.).

10. Faust, *This Republic of Suffering*, xvi–xvii, 37, 66.

11. McPherson, *Crossroads*, 177 n. 56, and *Battle Cry*, 545 (McClellan, 569). For the most balanced coverage of the battle, see McPherson, *Crossroads*. See also Murfin, *Gleam of Bayonets*, L. M. Sears, *Landscape Turned Red*, and two edited works by Gallagher, *Antietam* and *Antietam Campaign*.

12. Benjamin to Mason, Sept. 26, 1862, *ORN*, 2nd ser., 3:538–39; Gallagher, *Antietam Campaign*, ix–x.

13. Benjamin to Mason, Sept. 26, 1862, *ORN*, 2nd ser., 3:539–40.

14. Ibid., 3:540–43. In the context of recognition expectations, Benjamin noted that the United States and Denmark had recently signed an agreement pertaining to Africans captured from slave ships at sea. Union officials intended to transfer Africans from captured slavers to Danish colonies in the West Indies in an attempt, he argued, to pull Denmark into the war against the Confederacy. The Lincoln administration had already made the war one of "indiscriminate robbery and murder" by authorizing the confiscation of property—including slaves—from anyone participating in the so-called rebellion. That law effectually emancipated the slaves, for an executive order directed Union military commanders to employ them as workers in the army. Union generals had already made it a practice to arm the slaves against their masters in an effort to instigate an insurrection. The Union's racial prejudice blocked a black migration into its states, so this treaty with Denmark was an attempt to rid the Union of freed slaves. President Davis had linked this potential problem with the Danish treaty. Ibid., 3:543; Benjamin to Mann, Aug. 14, 1862, ibid., 3:512–13.

15. CFA Jr. claimed that the news of Antietam reached England on September 26. CFA Jr., "Crisis of Foreign Intervention," 32. Case and Spencer (*United States and France*, 339–40) show that the first stories of the battle appeared in the *Paris Moniteur* on September 27 and 30, 1862. In England, Moran first referred to the Union victory on September 30. Moran Diary, Sept. 30, 1862 (LC). For the Shaftesbury episode, see Slidell to Benjamin, Sept. 29 (3:546), and Oct. 9, 1862 (3:551), *ORN*, 2nd ser.

16. Slidell to Benjamin, Sept. 29, 1862, *ORN*, 2nd ser., 3:546–47.

17. Ibid., 3:546, and Slidell to Benjamin, Oct. 9, 1862, ibid., 3:551. For Adams's assessment of Shaftesbury, see CFA to Everett, May 2, 1862, CFA Letterbook (MHS). Brauer ("British Mediation," 50–51) argues that Antietam exemplified the war's futility and thereby explains the British move toward mediation.

18. Benjamin to Mason, Sept. 26, 1862, Mason Papers (LC); Lewis to Grey, Sept. 27, 1862, Ripon Papers, Add. Mss., 43,533, vol. 43 (Brit. Lib.); Hammond to Layard, Oct. 6,

1862, Layard Papers, Add. Mss., 38,951, vol. 21 (Brit. Lib.); Moran Diary, Sept. 27, 1862 (LC); Gladstone to James Hudson, Sept. 27, 1862, and Gladstone to AR, Sept. 29, 1862, Gladstone Papers, Add. Mss., 44,533, vol. 448 (Brit. Lib.).

19. Stuart to RU, Sept. 29, 1862, RU Papers, PRO 30/22/36; Palmerston to RU, Sept. 30, 1862, ibid., PRO 30/22/14D.

20. Stuart to RU, Sept. 23, 1862, ibid., PRO 30/22/36; Case and Spencer, *United States and France*, 326–28, 338.

21. AR to Gladstone, Sept. 23, 1862, Gladstone Papers, Add. Mss., 44,099, vol. 14 (Brit. Lib.); Granville to RU, Sept. 27, 1862, in Fitzmaurice, *Granville*, 1:443–44; Granville to RU, Sept. 29, 1862, RU Papers, PRO 30/22/25. Granville sent Russell two letters from correspondents who argued that the Union would not approve mediation and that England had missed opportunities to ask the Russian tsar to propose the good offices of England, France, and Russia. J. Winslow to Lord Henry Brougham, Aug. 30, 1862, and Joseph Parkes to Brougham, Sept. 11, 1862, both encl. in Granville to RU, Sept. 30, 1862, RU Papers, PRO 30/22/25. See also D. P. Crook, *The North, the South*, 225.

22. Jenkins, *Britain*, 2:63, 68; Clarendon to Lewis, Sept. 29, 1862, Clarendon Papers (Bodleian Lib.); CFA to Seward, Sept. 12, 1862, *FRUS 1862*, 189–90.

23. Ashmore, "Diary of James Garnett," 2:115 (May 14, 19, July–Aug., Sept. 23, 1862), 126. Garnett served as mayor of Clitheroe from November 1863 to November 1865. Ibid., 2:131. For the introduction of improved equipment and methods, see Blaug, "Productivity of Capital," 360. See also Brigg, *Journals of a Lancashire Weaver*, 138 (Apr. 10, 1864), 144 (Oct. 9, 1864). Cobden wrote Bright that all England was "thriving" except Lancashire. Cobden to Bright, Sept. 19, 1862, Cobden Papers, Add., Mss., 43,652, vol. 6 (Brit. Lib.).

24. For the argument against a cotton famine, see Brady, "Reconsideration of the Lancashire 'Cotton Famine'"; Broadbridge, "Lancashire Cotton 'Famine'"; R. H. Jones, "Long Live the King?" In *The Lancashire Cotton Famine*, W. O. Henderson argues that a shortage of cotton affected nearly a half million Lancashire textile workers. Owsley (*King Cotton Diplomacy*, 136) also claims there was a cotton famine, dating its beginning in late 1862. Mill owners, mill workers, and residents of London attested to the hard times in Lancashire during the winter of 1862–63. James Garnett recorded in his diary that the cotton famine reached its worst level in Low Moor. He made many references throughout October 1862 to relief for the distressed. Clitheroe and other cotton towns had local relief committees who secured assistance from poor law officials. The previous month the Garnetts furnished their own relief at first. Ashmore, "Diary of James Garnett," 2:115–19, 131. See also Foner, *British Labor*, 5. For the argument that textile workers supported the Confederacy, see Ellison, *Support for Secession*. For the more convincing counterargument, see Blackett, *Divided Hearts*, and D. A. Campbell, *English Public Opinion*.

25. Blackett, *Divided Hearts*, 24, 119–20, 143. Ernest Jones was the reformer and lawyer.

26. Ibid., 24 (quote), 243.

27. CFA to Seward, Oct. 3, 1862, *FRUS 1862*, 205; Seward to CFA, Oct. 18, 1862, ibid., 212–13. According to one writer, the Emancipation Proclamation led to a "battle for democracy" in England as well as the United States. St. Clair, "Slavery as a Diplomatic Factor," 275.

28. Lincoln, "Reply to Emancipation Memorial Presented by Chicago Christians of All Denominations," Sept. 13, 1862, in *CWL*, 5:422–23.

29. Ibid., 5:419–21, 423; *Chicago Tribune*, Sept. 23, 1862, and *National Intelligencer*, Sept. 26, 1862, both cited ibid., 5:419 n. 1.

30. Seward to CFA, Sept. 8, 1862, *FRUS 1862*, 188; Seward to CFA, circular, Sept. 22, 1862, ibid., 195; Donald, *Inside Lincoln's Cabinet*, 149–51 (Sept. 22, 1862); Lincoln, "Preliminary Emancipation Proclamation," Sept. 22, 1862, in *CWL*, 5:434.

31. Jenkins, *Britain*, 2:153; Franklin, *Emancipation Proclamation*, 129–40; McPherson, *Battle Cry*, 510, 557–58; Oates, "'Man of Our Redemption,'" 17, 19–20; McPherson, *Abraham Lincoln*, 34–35; T. J. Barnett to Samuel L. M. Barlow, Sept. 25, 1862 (Lincoln), quoted in McPherson, *Battle Cry*, 558.

32. McClellan to Mary Ellen (wife), Sept. 25, 1862, in S. W. Sears, *Civil War Papers of George B. McClellan*, 481.

33. Brauer, "Slavery Problem," 467; Van Deusen, *Seward*, 333; McConnell, "From Preliminary to Final Emancipation Proclamation," 275; Dennett, *Diaries and Letters of John Hay*, 50 (Sept. 26, 1862); George S. Denison (collector of internal revenue for Louisiana after Lincoln lifted the blockade) to Chase, Oct. 8, 1862, American Historical Association, *Diary and Correspondence of Salmon P. Chase*, 319.

34. Stuart also told Lyons about the Confederate retreat from Maryland and the announcement of the preliminary Emancipation Proclamation. Stuart to Lyons, Sept. 23, 1862, RU Papers, PRO 30/22/36; Stuart to RU, Sept. 23, 26, Oct. 7, 10, 1862, ibid.; Hammond to Layard, Oct. 6, 1862, Layard Papers, Add. Mss., 38,951, vol. 21 (Brit. Lib.); Cobden to Bright, Oct. 6, 1862, Cobden Papers, Add. Mss., 43,652, vol. 6 (Brit. Lib.); E. D. Adams, *Great Britain*, 2:103 n. 5.

35. Heckman, "British Press Reaction"; *Times*, Oct. 7, 1862 (p. 8), Oct. 21, 1862 (p. 9); *Spectator*, n.d., quoted in Whitridge, "British Liberals," 694; *Bee-Hive*, Oct. 11, 1862, quoted in K. J. Logan, "*Bee-Hive* Newspaper," 341; "The Crisis of the American War," *Blackwood's Edinburgh Magazine* 92 (November 1862): 636–46 (quote, 636).

36. Blackburn, *French Newspaper Opinion*, 65–66, 95. The Conservative papers cited included the *Pays*; among the Liberal papers was the *Temps*. For a breakdown of the French newspapers by political affiliation, see Blackburn, 9.

37. Palmerston to RU, Oct. 2, 3, 1862, RU Papers, PRO 30/22/14D.

38. Ibid.; Jenkins, *Britain*, 2:170. Merli (*Great Britain*, 118, 257, 259) shows Palmerston's reluctance to consider mediation after the battle of Antietam.

39. RU to Palmerston, Oct. 2, 4, 6, 1862, GC/RU/731–33, Palmerston Papers (U. of Southampton).

40. Stoeckl to Gorchakov, Sept. 25, 1862, in Brauer, "Slavery Problem," 463. Brunow quoted and Gorchakov cited from E. D. Adams, *Great Britain*, 2:45 n. 2.

41. Dayton to Seward, Oct. 14, 1862, Disp., France (NA); *Times*, Oct. 7, 1862, p. 8.

42. Seward to CFA, Sept. 26, 1862, *FRUS 1862*, 202. McPherson (*Battle Cry*) argues that the battle of Antietam "frustrated Confederate hopes for British recognition and precipitated the Emancipation Proclamation. The slaughter at Sharpsburg therefore proved to have been one of the war's great turning points. . . . Thus ended the South's best chance for European intervention. . . . By enabling Lincoln to issue the Emancipation Proclamation the battle . . . ensured that Britain would think twice about intervening against a government fighting for freedom as well as Union" (pp. 545, 556–57). S. W. Sears (*Land-*

scape Turned Red) largely agrees: "If Antietam abruptly halted the movement toward foreign intervention, the proclamation on emancipation put the seal on the matter." He admits that the latter impact "was not immediately apparent" because of the venomous reaction in England to the belief that Lincoln was trying to stir up slave revolts. Sears then claims that Lincoln's Proclamation "made it virtually impossible for any civilized power to enter the conflict on the side of the South" (p. 334). Owsley (*King Cotton Diplomacy*) declares that Antietam marked "the death-blow of Confederate recognition," for Palmerston "turned against present mediation when the news of Confederate military failure arrived" (p. 347). For the counterargument that the Emancipation Proclamation had no substantial impact on British public opinion, see Hernon, "British Sympathies."

43. See CFA Jr., "Crisis of Foreign Intervention," 24; Jenkins, *Britain*, 2:33, 63–64, 71; Brauer, "British Mediation"; Graebner, "European Interventionism."

44. Matthew, *Gladstone Diaries*, 6:152 n. 6; *Times*, Oct. 8, 1862 (p. 7), Oct. 9, 1862 (pp. 7–8); Ridley, *Palmerston*, 558.

45. Mann to Benjamin, Oct. 7, 1862, *ORN*, 2nd ser., 3:551 (1st quote); Mann to Benjamin, Oct. 26, 1862, ibid., 3:567; Lawley to Gladstone, Dec. 23, 1862, Gladstone Papers, Add. Mss., 44,399, vol. 314 (Brit. Lib.); CFA to Seward, Oct. 10, 1862, *FRUS 1862*, 209. Lawley had been a member of Parliament and a private secretary to Gladstone but left England because of financial problems caused by gambling. See also CFA Jr., "Crisis of Foreign Intervention," 32–33; CFA Diary, Oct. 8, 9, 12, 1862 (MHS); Crawford, *Anglo-American Crisis*, 132, 172 n. 8; and Jenkins, "Frank Lawley" and *Britain and the War*, 2:47–50. Two writers have found no evidence for the charge that Gladstone's speech was the cabinet's "trial balloon" to gauge popular feeling. Rather, they believe it likely that Gladstone was out of touch with the cabinet. See Merli, *Great Britain*, 100, 107–8, and Matthew, *Gladstone*, 133.

46. Cobden to Bright, Oct. 7, 1862, Cobden Papers, Add. Mss., 43,652, vol. 6 (Brit. Lib.); Bright to Cobden, Oct. 8, 1862, Bright Papers, Add. Mss., 43,384, vol. 2 (Brit. Lib.). See also D. P. Crook, *The North, the South*, 241.

47. AR to RU, Oct. 11, 1862, RU Papers, PRO 30/22/25.

48. Clarendon to Lewis, Oct. 13, 1862, Clarendon Papers (Bodleian Lib.) (Derby); Clarendon to Palmerston, Oct. 16, 1862, GC/CL/1207, Palmerston Papers (U. of Southampton); D. P. Crook, *The North, the South*, 241.

49. Gladstone to RU, Oct. 17, 1862, Gladstone Papers, Add. Mss., 44,292, vol. 207 (Brit. Lib.); D. A. Campbell, *English Public Opinion*, 178–79. See also R. L. Reid, "Gladstone's 'Insincere Neutrality.'"

50. Palmerston to RU, Oct. 12, 1862, RU Papers, PRO 30/22/22; Palmerston to RU, Oct. 17, Dec. 17, 1862, ibid., PRO 30/22/14D.

51. CFA Jr., "Crisis of Foreign Intervention," 32; Matthew, *Gladstone*, 133–34, 186; Gladstone to Arthur Gordon (the correspondent), Sept. 22, 1862, in Matthew, 134; Jenkins, *Britain*, 2:22–23. Palmerston expressed to Clarendon the same reservations about Gladstone's speech. See Palmerston to Clarendon, Oct. 20, 1862, in Maxwell, *Clarendon*, 2:267.

52. Hammond to Layard, Oct. 12, 18, 26, 27, 1862, Layard Papers, Add. Mss., 38,951, vol. 21 (Brit. Lib.).

53. RU to Gladstone, Oct. 20, 26, 1862, Gladstone Papers, Add. Mss., 44,292, vol. 207 (Brit. Lib.).

54. CFA Diary, Oct. 8, 9, 23, 1862 (MHS); Morley, *Gladstone*, 2:80; Moran Diary, Oct. 9, 24, 1862 (LC); CFA to Seward, Oct. 24, 1862, *FRUS 1862*, 224.

55. Palmerston to RU, Oct. 8, 1862, RU Papers, PRO 30/22/14D.

56. RU to Cowley, Oct. 11, 1862, ibid., PRO 30/22/105.

57. All quotes in RU, "Memorandum" for FO, Oct. 13, 1862, Gladstone Papers, Add. Mss., 44,595, vol. 510 (Brit. Lib.). See also E. D. Adams, *Great Britain*, 2:49–50.

58. AR to RU, Oct. 15, 1862, RU Papers, PRO 30/22/25.

59. G. F. Lewis, *Letters of . . . George Cornewall Lewis*, vi, viii–ix, xi; Earl of Aberdeen to Lewis, Nov. 6, 1858, ibid., 352; Lewis to W. Twisleton (first friend), Jan. 21, 1861, ibid., 391–92; Lewis to Sir Edmund Head, governor of Canada (second friend), Mar. 10, 1861, ibid., 393; Lewis to Head, May 13, Sept. 8, 1861, ibid., 395, 402; Head to Twisleton, Nov. 30, 1861, ibid., 405–6. Characterization of Lewis by Argyll in AR, *Argyll*, 1:540.

60. CFA Jr., "Crisis of Foreign Intervention," 37 (Lewis at Hereford); Clarendon to Lewis, Oct. 13, 1862 [Derby's view], Clarendon Papers (Bodleian Lib.); Palmerston to Clarendon, Oct. 20, 1862, in Maxwell, *Clarendon*, 2:267; Clarendon to Palmerston, Oct. 16, 1862, GC/CL/1207/1–3, Palmerston Papers (U. of Southampton); Lewis, "Memorandum on the American Question," Oct. 17, 1862, Gladstone Papers, Add. Mss., 44,595, vol. 510 (Brit. Lib.); Morley, *Gladstone*, 2:80; Merli, *Great Britain*, 107–9. There were rumors that Palmerston had arranged for Lewis to deliver the speech at Hereford, but they now seem unfounded. See E. D. Adams, *Great Britain*, 2:50, 50 n. 1; D. P. Crook, *The North, the South*, 233.

61. Regarding Lewis's mention of the Emancipation Proclamation, Gladstone inserted a marginal comment on the memo: "May have about played their last very *great* card." Lewis, "Memorandum on American Question," Oct. 17, 1862, Gladstone Papers, Add. Mss., 44,595, vol. 510 (Brit. Lib.).

62. Ibid. Lewis's quote was a loose rendition of Hamlet's words in William Shakespeare's play *The Tragedy of Hamlet, Prince of Denmark*, act 3, scene 1.

63. Dayton to Seward, Oct. 17, 1862, Disp., France (NA); RU to Cowley, Oct. 18, 1862 (PRO 30/22/105), and RU to Stuart, Oct. 18 [?], 1862 (PRO 30/22/96), RU Papers; RU to Palmerston, Oct. 18, 20, 1862, GC/RU/734–35, Palmerston Papers (U. of Southampton). As Dayton thought at the time, Thouvenel's dismissal probably stemmed primarily from his disagreements with Napoleon over Italian policies. Case and Spencer, *United States and France*, 346, 352.

64. Palmerston to RU, Oct. 20, 21, 22, 1862, RU Papers, PRO 30/22/14D.

65. Russell claimed that Palmerston had decided against a cabinet meeting and only told him the day before. RU to Grey, Oct. 28, 1862, in Gooch, *Later Correspondence*, 2:331–32. See also Lewis to Grey, Oct. 23, 1862 [Lewis quote], Ripon Papers, Add. Mss., 43,533, vol. 43 (Brit. Lib.); CFA Diary, Oct. 23, 1862 (MHS); CFA to Seward, Oct. 14, 1862, *FRUS 1862*, 224; E. D. Adams, *Great Britain*, 2:55; and Clarendon to Lewis, Oct. 24, 1862, in Maxwell, *Clarendon*, 2:265.

66. Clarendon to Lewis, Oct. 24, 1862, in Maxwell, *Clarendon*, 2:265–66.

67. RU to Palmerston, Oct. 24, 1862, GC/RU/736, Palmerston Papers (U. of Southampton). See also RU to Cowley, Oct. 11, 1862, RU Papers, PRO 30/22/105.

68. Seward to Dayton, Oct. 8, 1862, Dip. Instructions, France (NA).

69. H. Percy Anderson (British agent) to Stuart, Oct. 1, 1862, encl. in Stuart to RU, Oct. 7, 1862, Gladstone Papers, Add. Mss., 44,595, vol. 510 (Brit. Lib.).

70. Gladstone, "The War in America," Oct. 24, 1862, Gladstone Papers, Add. Mss., 44,595, vol. 510 (Brit. Lib.).

71. RU Memo for FO, Oct. 23, 1862, Gladstone Papers, ibid.

72. Palmerston to RU, Oct. 23, 24, 1862, RU Papers, PRO 30/22/14D.

73. Lewis to RU, Oct. 25, 1862, ibid., PRO 30/22/25; RU to Lewis, Oct. 26, 1862, ibid., PRO 30/22/14D; Jenkins, *Britain*, 2:177.

74. Grey to RU, Oct. 27, 1862, RU Papers, PRO 30/22/25.

75. RU to Grey, Oct. 28, 1862, in Gooch, *Later Correspondence*, 2:332.

76. Palmerston to RU, Oct. 26, 1862, RU Papers, PRO 30/22/14D.

77. Seward to Dayton, Oct. 20, 1862, Dip. Instructions, France (NA).

78. Dayton to Seward, Oct. 2, 1862, Disp., France (NA).

CHAPTER 8

1. D. P. Crook, *The North, the South*, 248; E. D. Adams, *Great Britain*, 2:60; Owsley, *King Cotton Diplomacy*, 335; Carroll, *Mercier*, 239–40; Case and Spencer, *United States and France*, 356–61. Case and Spencer argue that Napoleon "apparently" based his plan on Russell's September objectives (p. 356).

2. Stuart to RU, Oct. 17, 24, 26, 1862, RU Papers, PRO 30/22/36. Stuart expressed his support for intervention to George Elliott (Stuart to Elliott, Oct. 24, 1862, ibid.). For Mercier's proseparatist feelings, see Case and Spencer, *United States and France*, 353. Stuart's pro-Confederate sympathies become plain in his dispatches to Russell while Lyons was in London from June through early November 1862.

3. Taylor to Seward, Oct. 29, 1862, cited in Saul, *Distant Friends*, 333 (emphases are Taylor's); Gorchakov to Stoeckl, Oct. 27, 1862, cited ibid., 335.

4. Dayton to Seward, Nov. 6, 21, 1862, Disp., France (NA).

5. E. D. Adams, *Great Britain*, 2:153, 155; Sanford to Seward, Aug. 13, Sept. 2, 1862, both cited in Hanna and Hanna, *Napoleon III*, 81; Hanna and Hanna, 118; Mann to Benjamin, Sept. 1, 1862, *ORN*, 2nd ser., 3:523; C. E. Crook, "Benjamin Théron."

6. Cowley to RU, Oct. 27, 1862, RU Papers, PRO 30/22/14D; Cowley's memo of his conversation with Drouyn, Oct. 28, 1862, FO 27/1446 (PRO).

7. Slidell memo on interview with Napoleon, encl. in Slidell to Benjamin, Oct. 28, 1862, *ORN*, 2nd ser., 3:575.

8. Slidell to Benjamin, Oct. 28, 1862, ibid., 3:573–74; Slidell memo on interview with Napoleon, encl. ibid., 3:575.

9. Slidell to Benjamin, Oct. 28, 1862, ibid., 3:575. See also Case and Spencer, *United States and France*, 356–57, and Owsley, *King Cotton Diplomacy*, 333–36. Whether Drouyn did not know of Napoleon's implied assurance of military action or had convinced him to change course, the new foreign secretary two days later assured Mercier that the Paris government would not attempt to force the Union into accepting the proposal. Probably Drouyn was unaware of Napoleon's assurance. Drouyn to Mercier, Oct. 30, 1862, cited in

Owsley, 336. Owsley does not explore this important matter, simply stating that Drouyn assured Mercier that there should be no use of force against the Union.

10. Slidell to Benjamin, Oct. 28, 1862, *ORN*, 2nd ser., 3:576.

11. Memo of Slidell interview with Napoleon, encl. ibid.; Slidell to Mason, Oct. 29, 1862, Mason Papers (LC). Although Slidell's note of October 29 did not reach Richmond until December 31, he wrote Mason the same day—October 29—about the interview. Mason presumably informed Benjamin soon afterward (and long before December 31), for on December 11 Benjamin wrote Mason of the Confederacy's support for a six-month armistice (in Mason Papers). See also Case and Spencer, *United States and France*, 356–57, 364.

12. Slidell to Benjamin, Oct. 20, 1862, *ORN*, 2nd ser., 3:561.

13. Slidell to Benjamin, Oct. 28, 1862, ibid., 3:576.

14. Ibid., 3:576–77.

15. Ibid., 3:577.

16. Ibid. For Chevalier's influence on Napoleon III, see Hanna and Hanna, *Napoleon III*, 60 n. 3, 60–68, 199.

17. Slidell to Benjamin, Oct. 28, 1862, *ORN*, 2nd ser., 3:578. The heavy casualties at the battles of Solferino and Magenta in June 1859 convinced Napoleon III to seek a truce with Austria that soon ended the Second War of Italian independence and contributed to the country's unification.

18. Slidell memo on interview with Napoleon, encl. ibid., 3:577–78.

19. Mason to Benjamin, Nov. 8, 1862, ibid., 3:603; Benjamin to Mason, Jan. 15, 1863, ibid., 3:656; Bulloch, *Secret Service*, 2:23–24; Benjamin to Mason, Dec. 11, 1862, Mason Papers (LC); Mason to Benjamin, Nov. 6, 1862, in Richardson, *Messages and Papers of the Confederacy*, 2:359.

20. Benjamin to Mason, Oct. 28, 31, 1862, Mason Papers (LC).

21. Cowley to RU, Oct. 31, 1862, FO 27/1446/1236 (PRO); RU to Lyons, Nov. 1, 1862 [Seward's assertion], RU Papers, PRO 30/22/96 (Cobden); RU to Cowley, Nov. 1, 1862, RU Papers, PRO 30/22/105.

22. Case and Spencer, *United States and France*, 361. E. D. Adams (*Great Britain*, 2:60 n. 2) argues that Napoleon never offered a mediation, although it was implied.

23. RU to Palmerston, GC/RU/739, Nov. 3, 1862, Palmerston Papers (U. of Southampton).

24. Leopold to Palmerston, Oct. 30–Nov. 3, 1862, RU Papers, PRO 30/22/14D; Leopold to RU, Oct. 31, 1862, in Gooch, *Later Correspondence*, 2:332; Palmerston to RU, Nov. 2, 1862, RU Papers, PRO 30/22/14D. Palmerston focused on Greek problems in his November 2 letter and in others through December. Palmerston to RU, Nov. 2, 1862, and after. See RU Papers, PRO 30/22/14D.

25. Stuart to RU, Nov. 4, 1862, RU Papers, PRO 30/22/36.

26. Stuart to RU, Nov. 7, 1862, ibid., RU to Grey, Oct. 28, 1862, in Gooch, *Later Correspondence*, 2:332; McPherson, *Battle Cry*, 561–62; Graebner, "Northern Diplomacy"; Brauer, "British Mediation."

27. Lyons to RU, Nov. 11, 1862, RU Papers, PRO 30/22/36.

28. Ibid.

29. Slidell to Benjamin, Nov. 11, 1862, *ORN*, 2nd ser., 3:603–4.

30. Mercier's views reported in Lyons to RU, Nov. 14, 1862, RU Papers, PRO 30/22/36.

31. Lyons to RU, Nov. 14, 1862, ibid., PRO 30/22/36; Lyons to RU, Nov. 17, 1862, *BFSP 1864–1865*, 55:534–39. Russell demonstrated his lack of understanding of the American political system when he asked Lyons if the election of the next president would be in autumn 1864. RU to Lyons, Nov. 8, 1862, RU Papers, PRO 30/22/96. Lyons's biographer remarks in vague terms that while the minister was home in London, he was in "constant communication with the cabinet" and that the ministers opposed interference in the American war but thought it "might be forced upon them." See Newton, *Lord Lyons*, 1:89–90. Lincoln had relieved McClellan on November 7, saying the general had moved too slowly toward Richmond. When McClellan kept "delaying on little pretexts of wanting this and that," the president complained to his private secretary: "I began to fear that he was playing false—that he did not want to hurt the enemy." McPherson, *Battle Cry*, 562, 569–70.

32. Lyons to RU, Nov. 14, 18, 24, 1862, RU Papers, PRO 30/22/36; Lyons to RU, Nov. 18, 1862 (confidential), FO 5/838, PRO.

33. Gardiner, *Life of . . . Harcourt*, 1:125, 127, 132–37; Jenkins, *Britain*, 2:179–80; D. P. Crook, *The North, the South*, 241; Merli, *Great Britain*, 114–15.

34. Historicus letter dated Nov. 4, 1862, in *Times*, Nov. 7, 1862, pp. 6–7; Letter reprinted in Harcourt, *Letters by Historicus*, 3–15 (quotes, 8, 9–10); Historicus, "Neutrality or Intervention," in Harcourt, *Letters*, 41–51 (quotes 42–43, 46–51) (letter in *Times*, Nov. 17, 1862, p. 9). Historicus claimed that in October Palmerston had been wrong in defining "Lewis's Doctrine" as an argument for England to postpone recognition until the Union first recognized the Confederacy; Lewis had called instead for "*de facto* independence" (Letter of Nov. 8, 1862, in Harcourt, *Letters*, 8). See also E. D. Adams, *Great Britain*, 2:63; D. P. Crook, *The North, the South*, 251; and CFA Jr., "Crisis of Foreign Intervention," 40–41. Hotze wrote Benjamin that the *Times*'s refusal to print his rebuttal to Historicus demonstrated that it was partial to the Palmerston ministry. Hotze to Benjamin, Nov. 22, 1862, *ORN*, 2nd ser., 3:611–12.

35. Lewis, "Recognition of the Independence of the Southern States of the North American Union," Nov. 7, 1862, Gladstone Papers, Add. Mss., 44,595, vol. 510 (Brit. Lib.) (hereafter cited as Lewis, "Recognition of Independence). The original draft (though incomplete) is in the National Library of Wales in Aberystwyth. See Lewis Papers, War Office and India, 3509, 3510, and 3514. The assistant keeper of the Department of Manuscripts and Records, Gwyn Jenkins, assured me that Lewis's papers contain no other references to this aspect of the Civil War.

36. When Lewis wrote that recognition of independence by a foreign government was "recognition of a fact," Gladstone responded in the margin: "in what sense?" Lewis, "Recognition of Independence." The United States itself sent a secret agent to Hungary in 1850 to determine how far the revolt had progressed before deciding whether to extend recognition. Austria lodged a formal complaint, causing the U.S. government to refrain from making a decision. In supporting his argument regarding recognition, Lewis cited and quoted John Austin, *The Province of Jurisprudence Determined* (1832), 215 (quote). See also Austin, 206–7. Austin was the first professor of jurisprudence (philosophy of law) at the University of London on its founding in 1826. Two years later, Lewis was

among a number of Benthamites who attended Austin's lectures on jurisprudence. In 1836 Austin joined Lewis as a commissioner to offer advice on constitutional and legal reforms in Malta. See Introduction to Austin by H. L. A. Hart, viii. Lewis's other historical examples were the Netherlands, Portugal, Greece, Belgium, the South American colonies and Spain, and the South American colonies and Portugal. Lewis, "Recognition of Independence." Lewis also cited Wheaton, *Elements of International Law* (1836 ed.), pt. I, sec. 26. The Benthamites were followers of the mid-eighteenth-century British reformer, Jeremy Bentham.

37. Lewis, "Recognition of Independence." Lewis cited Vattel, *Law of Nations*, bk. 3, sec. 295. Lewis's reference to recognition was to Mason's letter, which appeared in the *Times* on October 22, 1862, p. 8. On the question of what recognition could have done for the South, Gladstone wrote in the margin of Lewis's memo that the action would "accelerate the issue" of independence.

38. Lewis, "Recognition of Independence"; Lewis to Harcourt, Nov. 21, 1862, Harcourt Papers, box 12 (Bodleian Lib.). Lewis cited Vattel, *Law of Nations*, bk. 3, sec. 295; see also sec. 296. The law of nature is, of course, the basis of international law.

39. Lewis, "Recognition of Independence."

40. Ibid.

41. Lord Napier (Brit. ambassador in St. Petersburg) to RU, Nov. 8, 1862, cited in E. D. Adams, *Great Britain*, 2:63, 66; Lewis to Clarendon, Nov. 11, 1862, in Maxwell, *Clarendon*, 2:268; Jenkins, *Britain*, 2:180. Russell had first learned of the French proposal unofficially on November 1.

42. Lewis to Clarendon, Nov. 11, 1862, Clarendon Papers (Bodleian Lib.); Gladstone to wife, Nov. 12, 13, 1862, in Morley, *Gladstone*, 2:85. On November 13 an article appeared in the *Times*, Lewis noted, "throwing cold water on the invitation." He assumed that someone had informed the editor, John Delane, of the cabinet's decision. See *Times*, Nov. 13, 1862, p. 8. Palmerston, one might note, maintained close ties with Delane. See Crawford, *Anglo-American Crisis*, 18.

43. Lewis to Clarendon, Nov. 11, 1862, Clarendon Papers (Bodleian Lib.).

44. RU to Cowley, Nov. 13, 1862, Cowley Papers, FO 146/1046 (PRO); Cowley to RU, Nov. 18, 1862, cited in Case and Spencer, *United States and France*, 363.

45. Lewis to Harcourt, Nov. 11, 1862, Harcourt Papers, box 12 (Bodleian Lib.); Gladstone to wife, Nov. 12, 1862, in Morley, *Gladstone*, 2:85; Lyons to RU, Nov. 28, 1862, RU Papers, PRO 30/22/36.

46. Case and Spencer, *United States and France*, 358–59; D. P. Crook, *The North, the South*, 247, 254; Owsley, *King Cotton Diplomacy*, 336, 355, 357; Dayton to Seward, Nov. 14, 21, 24, 1862, Disp., France (NA); De Leon, *Secret History*, 157 (*Moniteur* quote, 158).

47. W. R. West, *Contemporary French Opinion*, 88; Blackburn, *French Newspaper Opinion*, 92 (quote), 98.

48. Moran Diary, Nov. 11, 12, 1862 (LC); *Times*, Nov. 13, 1862, p. 8.

49. Moran Diary, Nov. 15, 1862 (LC); CFA Diary, Nov. 15, 1862 (MHS); Russian letter in *Journal of St. Petersburg*, Nov. 15, 1862, published in *Times*, Nov. 17, 1862, p. 12, and enclosed in CFA to Seward, Nov. 15, 1862, *FRUS 1863*, 3; CFA to Seward, Nov. 13, 1862, *FRUS 1863*, 1. (Adams was referring to the *Journal of St. Petersburg*.) See also Saul, *Distant Friends*, 334–35, and Woldman, *Lincoln and the Russians*, 133–35.

50. Moran Diary, Nov. 12, 13, 15, 1862 (LC).

51. Lyons to RU, Dec. 2, 1862, *BFSP 1864–1865*, 55:539–40; Seward to Dayton, Nov. 30, 1862, Dip. Instructions, France (NA); Seward to CFA, Dec. 8, 1862, *FRUS 1863*, 12–13; Seward to Bayard Taylor, Dec. 7, 1862, Dip. Instructions, Russia (NA). Taylor had sent dispatches dated Nov. 11, 12, and 15, all assuring Lincoln of the tsar's friendly policy.

52. Lawley to Gladstone, Dec. 23, 1862, Gladstone Papers, Add. Mss., 44,399, vol. 314 (Brit. Lib.); *Index*, Nov. 20, 1862, p. 56, quoted in E. D. Adams, *Great Britain*, 2:68.

53. E. D. Adams, *Great Britain*, 2:69; CFA Diary, Nov. 15, 1862, May 3, 1868 (MHS); Seward to CFA, Aug. 2, 1862, *FRUS 1862*, 165–66; Duberman, *Adams*, 297–98; CFA, "Reminiscences of His Mission to Great Britain, 1861–1862" (begun in September 1867), in CFA, Miscellany, Adams Family Papers, reel 296 (MHS).

54. *Index*, Jan. 15, 1863, p. 191 (*Richmond Whig*), quoted in E. D. Adams, *Great Britain*, 2:68; Harcourt to Lewis [1863?], Harcourt Papers, box 12 (Bodleian Lib.).

55. Palmerston to RU, Dec. 17, 1862, RU Papers, PRO 30/22/14D; Palmerston to Leopold, Nov. 18, 1862, PM/J/I, Palmerston Letterbook, Palmerston Papers (U. of Southampton); Gladstone to Field, Nov. 27, 1862, Gladstone Papers, Add. Mss., 44,399, vol. 314 (Brit. Lib.). Field helped develop the transatlantic cable.

56. Slidell to Benjamin, Nov. 29, 1862, *ORN*, 2nd ser., 3:612–13; Slidell to Mason, late November 1862, quoted in CFA Jr., "Crisis of Foreign Intervention," 51.

57. JD speech in Jackson, Miss., Dec. 26, 1862, in JD, *Papers*, 8:576.

58. McPherson, "'Whole Family of Man,'" 131–32; Stoeckl to Gorchakov, Dec. 24, 1862/Jan. 5, 1863, cited in Saul, *Distant Friends*, 335.

59. JD to Confederate Congress, Jan. 12, 1863, in Richardson, *Messages and Papers of the Confederacy*, 1:280–81, 290, 292; Lyons to RU, Jan. 19, 1863, in Barnes and Barnes, *American Civil War*, 2:303.

60. Gurowski, *Diary*, 278; Lincoln, Emancipation Proclamation, Jan. 1, 1863, *CWL*, 6:30; Franklin, *Emancipation Proclamation*, 86–87.

61. Paludan, *Presidency of Abraham Lincoln*, 187–88 (Marx); Lincoln, Preliminary Emancipation Proclamation, Sept. 22, 1862, *CWL*, 5:433–34.

62. *London Morning Star*, Oct. 6, 1862, quoted in Nevins, *War Becomes Revolution*, 270.

63. Bright to Cobden, Dec. 24, 1862, Bright Papers, Add. Mss., 43,384, vol. 2 (Brit. Lib.); Henry Adams to CFA Jr., Jan. 27, 1863 (1:243–45), and CFA to CFA Jr., Dec. 25, 1862 (1:220–21), both in Ford, *Adams Letters*; CFA Diary, Jan. 2, 13, 16, 17, Feb. 27, 1863 (MHS); CFA to Seward, Jan. 2, 1863, Disp., GB (NA); Blackett, "Pressures from Without," 71–74, 90–91, and *Divided Hearts*, 75–77, 80–81; Jordan and Pratt, *Europe and the American Civil War*, 145–63; E. D. Adams, *Great Britain*, 2:152. For intervention as the real threat to Anglo-American relations but coming to an end in November 1862, see Beloff, "Historical Revision," 47. For the argument that commercial concerns helped maintain Anglo-American ties, see Claussen, "Peace Factors."

64. Lincoln to Workingmen of Manchester, England, Jan. 19, 1863, *CWL*, 6:64; Lincoln to Workingmen of London, Feb. 2, 1863, *CWL*, 6:88–89; Donald, *Lincoln*, 415.

65. Blackett, "Pressures from Without," 77–81, 87–90; Owsley, *King Cotton Diplomacy*, 177; RU to Lyons, Feb. 14, 1863, quoted in E. D. Adams, *Great Britain*, 2:155; Gregory to Mason, Mar. 18, 1863, Mason Papers (LC). On the lack of significant southern support in England, see Blackett, *Divided Hearts*, and D. A. Campbell, *English Public Opinion*.

66. McPherson, *Battle Cry*, 568–75 (Lincoln, 574), 580–83, 645–46. For the definitive account of the battle, see Rable, *Fredericksburg! Fredericksburg!*

67. Lincoln, "Proclamation Appointing a National Fast Day," Mar. 30, 1863, *CWL*, 6:156.

68. McPherson, *Abraham Lincoln*, 35; Lincoln to Johnson, Mar. 26, 1863, *CWL*, 6:149–50; Lincoln to James C. Conkling, Aug. 26, 1863, *CWL*, 6:408–9; Paludan, *Presidency of Abraham Lincoln*, xv; McPherson, *Negro's Civil War*, 158. Before the war ended, some 180,000 black soldiers had worn Union blue (along with 29,000 more in its navy, or a fourth of its rolls), which made up nearly 12 percent of the Union's fighting force in 1865 while depleting much of the Confederacy's labor supply.

69. Lincoln to Chase, Sept. 2, 1863, *CWL*, 6:428–29; Cox, *Lincoln and Black Freedom*, 15; H. Jones, "To Preserve a Nation," 174–75.

70. Other writers who have noted Lewis's role in countering the interventionists are E. D. Adams, *Great Britain*, 2:44–46, 52–58, 62–63, 73–74; Ellsworth, "Anglo-American Affairs in October 1862," 94–95; Merli and Wilson, "British Cabinet and the Confederacy," 254, 256, 258, 261–62; Merli, *Great Britain*, 109–15; D. P. Crook, *The North, the South*, 233–36, 240–41, 251; and Jenkins, *Britain*, 2:169–70, 173–76, 179. Merli and Wilson attribute nonintervention primarily to Palmerston. Their argument, however, does not show that the prime minister had opposed the *timing* of an intervention rather than the step itself.

71. McPherson, *What They Fought For*, 19, and *For Cause and Comrades*, 148–49. On nationalism in Europe, see Barker, "Monarchy in Mexico," 52.

72. For thought-provoking speculation on what British intervention would have meant for Anglo-American relations, see Nevins, *War Becomes Revolution*, 2:242.

73. Seward to CFA, Aug. 27, 1866, folder 6302: DS Printed Material, Seward Papers (U. of Rochester).

CHAPTER 9

1. Case and Spencer, *United States and France*, 385.

2. Ibid., 386–88; Drouyn to Mercier, Jan. 9, 1863, NFFL, France (NA).

3. Drouyn and Dayton conversation quoted in Dayton to Seward, Jan. 15, 1863, Disp., France (NA).

4. Ibid. (Drouyn); Barker, "Monarchy in Mexico," 58, and "France, Austria," 230; Case and Spencer, *United States and France*, 371, 548.

5. Dayton to Seward, Jan. 27, 30, 1863, Disp., France (NA). See also Hanna and Hanna, *Napoleon III*, 93, 117. Owsley did not believe Drouyn trustworthy; see, e.g., *King Cotton Diplomacy*, 516.

6. Napoleon's Annual Address to the National Assembly, Jan. 15, 1863, cited in Case and Spencer, *United States and France*, 392; ibid., 393.

7. Donald, *Lincoln*, 416–18 (1st three quotes). *CG*, 37th Cong., 3rd sess., Jan. 14, 1863, p. 314, app., 52–60 (last two quotes).

8. Donald, *Lincoln*, 414–15 (quotes); Case and Spencer, *United States and France*, 393–94. See also Spencer, "Jewett-Greeley Affair."

9. *New York Tribune*, Jan. 28, 29, 1863, quoted in Case and Spencer, *United States and France*, 394.

10. Carroll, *Mercier*, 251–57; Donald, *Sumner and the Rights of Man*, 103, and *Lincoln*, 414 (quote).

11. Case and Spencer, *United States and France*, 393–95; Donald, *Lincoln*, 414–15.

12. Donald, *Lincoln*, 415.

13. Merli, "Crown versus Cruiser," 167–77, *Great Britain*, 161–77, and *Alabama*, 88 (judge), 179; E. M. Thomas, *Confederate Nation*, 183; Owsley, *King Cotton Diplomacy*, 398–99 (Russell, 399), 407–8, 410 (Russell, 399). Bernath gives the *Peterhoff* case exhaustive treatment within the context of international law and national self-interest; see his *Squall across the Atlantic* and his two articles: "British Neutrality" and "Squall Across the Atlantic." For the *Peterhoff* and other cases, see Hanna, "Incidents of the Confederate Blockade."

14. JD to Confederate Congress, Jan. 12, 1863, in Richardson, *Messages and Papers of the Confederacy*, 1:288. For reference to Davis's January 12 address to the Confederate Congress, see Lyons to RU, Jan. 19, 1863, in Barnes and Barnes, *American Civil War*, 2:303. See also Schoonover, "Napoleon Is Coming!," 107, 112–14, 121; Blumenthal, *Reappraisal of Franco-American Relations*, 172.

15. Sexton, *Debtor Diplomacy*, 159–60.

16. Ibid., 161–62; Owsley, *King Cotton Diplomacy*, 365.

17. Sexton, *Debtor Diplomacy*, 162–65 (*Economist*, 165); Lyons to RU, Mar. 6, 1863, in Barnes and Barnes, *American Civil War*, 3:17 (reference to Mercier); Gentry, "Confederate Success," 159–61. The loan offer originated in September 1862. Gentry, 182.

18. McPherson, *Battle Cry*, 683–84; Kutolowski, "Effect of the Polish Insurrection"; Orzell, "'Favorable Interval'"; Sanford to Seward, May 19, 1863, cited in Hanna and Hanna, *Napoleon III*, 90.

19. For the European context of the visits, see Golder, "Russian Fleet and the Civil War"; Adamov, "Russia and the United States"; Nagengast, "Visit of the Russian Fleet"; Higham, "Russian Fleet on the Eastern Seaboard"; and Orzell, "'Favorable Interval.'" Pomeroy ("Myth after the Russian Fleet") agrees with the argument, asserting that the American press understood at the time that the visit did not indicate support for the Union or opposition to slavery. Kushner ("Russian Fleet") argues that Lincoln and Seward exploited the fleet's presence to suggest Russian support for the Union. For the more convincing and broader argument, see Saul, *Distant Friends*, 340–45.

20. McPherson, *Battle Cry*, 683–84; Hanna and Hanna, *Napoleon III*, 110–11; Barker, "France, Austria," 224–45.

21. Case and Spencer, *United States and France*, 399–401; Owsley, *King Cotton Diplomacy*, 441, 513–14; D. P. Crook, *The North, the South*, 264–65, 335–36; Hanna, "Roles of the South," 9–10; Hanna and Hanna, *Napoleon III*, 90.

22. Mann to Benjamin, Mar. 19, 1863, in Richardson, *Messages and Papers of the Confederacy*, 2:419; D. P. Crook, *The North, the South*, 336; Berwanger, "Union and Confederate Reaction." C. E. Crook ("Benjamin Théron") analyzes two letters from the French consular agent and vice-consul for Spain in Galveston indicating French interest in detaching Texas from the Confederacy. Hanna ("Roles of the South") shows that the Con-

federacy welcomed the French intervention in Mexico as a way to block Union soldiers from entering northern Mexico en route to attack Texas.

23. Case and Spencer, *United States and France*, 401–2; Paul to Drouyn, Mar. 15, 1863, cited ibid., 401.

24. Cowley to RU, Apr. 10, 1863 (Napoleon), cited in Case and Spencer, *United States and France*, 402; ibid., 402, 404, 408; Owsley, *King Cotton Diplomacy*, 369–82; E. D. Adams, *Great Britain*, 2:158–63; Hubbard, *Burden of Confederate Diplomacy*, 128–29; Dayton to Seward, Mar. 13, 20, 27, 1863, Disp., France (NA).

25. Case and Spencer, *United States and France*, 408.

26. Ibid., 409.

27. Ibid.; Slidell memo on meeting of June 18, 1863, encl. in Slidell to Benjamin, June 21, 1863, *ORN*, 2nd ser., 3:812–14; Slidell to Mason, June 29, 1863, Mason Papers (LC). Why Slidell thought Spain would send its fleet to help France remains a mystery. The Madrid government had remained neutral throughout the war, joining other powers in arguing that reunion seemed impossible but that the Confederacy must prove itself on the battlefield. It did not want to risk alienating the Union or the Confederacy, for either one as victor could pose a postwar threat to Cuba and other Spanish possessions in the hemisphere. Furthermore, Spain faced a host of foreign problems as well as political instability at home. Finally, Spain's earlier withdrawal from Mexico suggested disenchantment with Napoleon's intentions. For Spain's adherence to neutrality, see Cortada, *Spain*, 58, 63.

28. Slidell memo, *ORN*, 2nd ser., 3:812–14 (quote, 813). See also Case and Spencer, *United States and France*, 409.

29. Slidell to Benjamin, June 21, 1863, *ORN*, 2nd ser., 3:810–12. See also Case and Spencer, *United States and France*, 409–10.

30. Case and Spencer, *United States and France*, 410–11; Slidell to Benjamin, June 21, 1863 (Drouyn), cited ibid., 411.

31. Slidell to Benjamin, June 21, 1863, *ORN*, 2nd ser., 3:811; Case and Spencer, *United States and France*, 411.

32. Hotze to Benjamin, June 6, 1863, *ORN*, 2nd ser., 3:783–86; Bigelow, *Retrospections*, 2:26 (Carlyle); Henry Adams to CFA Jr., June 25, 1863, in Ford, *Adams Letters*, 2:40; Case and Spencer, *United States and France*, 398. See also Leader, *Roebuck*. A. W. Kinglake, Liberal MP from Bridgewater, made the Robespierre comparison; quoted in D. A. Campbell, *English Public Opinion*, 175. Maximilien Robespierre was a leader of the radical Jacobins during the French Revolution. As a powerful member of the Committee of Public Safety, he pushed for the execution of King Louis XVI during the Reign of Terror that ended with his own execution in 1794.

33. Lindsay's account in Owsley, *King Cotton Diplomacy*, 449.

34. Case and Spencer, *United States and France*, 412–16; Napoleon to Drouyn, July 14, 1863, cited ibid., 415–16.

35. Ibid., 331, 403, 420 (*La France*); Dayton to Seward, May 29, 1863, cited 420; D. P. Crook, *The North, the South*, 315.

36. Dayton to Seward, June 26, 1863, Disp., France (NA).

37. U.S. DS, *Correspondence concerning Claims*, June 30, 1863, pp. 650–54, 674 (Roebuck); D. A. Campbell, *English Public Opinion*, 175. For the full debate, see U.S. DS,

Correspondence concerning Claims, pp. 650–80. The State Department account comes from *Parl. Debates*, 171:1769, 1771–1841.

38. U.S. DS, *Correspondence concerning Claims*, June 30, 1863, p. 653.

39. H. Adams, *Education*, 187; Monaghan, *Lincoln Deals*, 317–19; Myers, *Caution and Cooperation*, 203. See also Owsley, *King Cotton Diplomacy*, 452–56, and D. P. Crook, *The North, the South*, 313–14.

40. U.S. DS, *Correspondence concerning Claims*, June 30, 1863, pp. 669–70.

41. Hotze to Benjamin, July 11, 1863, *ORN*, 2nd ser., 3:839–41; Mason to Slidell, July 1, 1863, Mason Papers (LC); Case and Spencer, *United States and France*, 413; Myers, *Caution and Cooperation*, 203.

42. Palmerston to Roebuck, July 9, 1863, GC/RO/5, Palmerston Papers (U. of Southampton); Palmerston's speech of July 13 in the Commons, in U.S. DS, *Correspondence concerning Claims*, July 13, 1863, pp. 684–85.

43. *Economist*, July 4, 1863, quoted in D. A. Campbell, *English Public Opinion*, 172; *Saturday Review*, July 4, 1863, quoted ibid., 173; *Illustrated London News*, July 4, 1863, quoted ibid., 172.

44. Case and Spencer, *United States and France*, 420–21; Dayton to Seward, July 2, 1863, Disp., France (NA) (Drouyn).

45. Napoleon to Drouyn, June 22, 1863, quoted in Case and Spencer, *United States and France*, 417; Drouyn to Gros, June 23, 1863, quoted ibid.; Gros to Drouyn, July 1, 1863, quoted ibid., 418.

46. Dayton to Seward, July 2, 10, 1863, Disp., France (NA).

47. Case and Spencer, *United States and France*, 422–23; Seward to Dayton, July 8, 1863, cited ibid.

48. Sexton, *Debtor Diplomacy*, 165–69; Gentry, "Confederate Success," 160, 163, 165; Lester, "Confederate Finance."

49. Sexton, *Debtor Diplomacy*, 162–74; *Economist*, Mar. 21, 1863, quoted ibid., 165; Gentry, "Confederate Success," 157, 188; E. M. Thomas, *Confederate Nation*, 188. Sexton sharply disagrees with Gentry, who argues that the Erlanger loan was the only one by either side in the Civil War and that it was a success in securing arms, matériel, and ships for the Confederacy until early 1864. Sexton's argument is more persuasive because it places the issue within the broader context of the recognition question. Ball (*Financial Failure*) contends that poor financial management and economic problems were largely responsible for the Confederate defeat in the war.

50. Seward to Dayton, July 10, 1863, quoted in Case and Spencer, *United States and France*, 423; Seward to Dayton, July 29, 1863, quoted in Owsley, *King Cotton Diplomacy*, 464.

51. Dayton to Seward, July 30, 1863, Disp., France (NA).

52. Case and Spencer, *United States and France*, 423–24; Paul to Drouyn, Aug. 24, 1863, cited ibid., 424; Dayton to Seward, July 30, 1863, Disp., France (NA).

53. Case and Spencer, *United States and France*, 414.

54. Ibid., 417–18.

55. Owsley, *King Cotton Diplomacy*, 357; Napoleon to Drouyn, July 14, 1863, cited in Case and Spencer, *United States and France*, 416.

56. Case and Spencer, *United States and France*, 416 (Napoleon); Owsley, *King Cotton Diplomacy*, 460–61; Layard to Cowley, July 15, 1863, PRO/FO 519/195.

57. Benjamin to Mason, Aug. 4, 1863, *ORN*, 2nd ser., 3:852–53; Mason to RU, Sept. 21, 1863, and RU to Mason, Sept. 25, 1863, both encl. in Mason to Benjamin, Oct. 19, 1863, ibid., 3:934–35; Benjamin to Mason, Nov. 13, 1863, ibid., 3:950–51; Eaton, *Davis*, 170; Owsley, *King Cotton Diplomacy*, 465–66.

58. Saul, *Distant Friends*, 344; Cortada, "Florida's Relations with Cuba," 48–51, and *Spain*, 57–58.

59. Owsley, *King Cotton Diplomacy*, 508.

60. Ibid., 507–8.

61. Dayton to Seward, Apr. 9, Aug. 21 (Drouy), Sept. 7, 1863, Disp., France (NA). Charles Maurice de Talleyrand-Périgord was French foreign minister during the late eighteenth and early nineteenth centuries.

62. Hanna and Hanna, *Napoleon III*, 58 (*Moniteur* and *Documents diplomatiques*); *New York Times*, Sept. 25, 1863, and pamphlet, both cited ibid., 60.

63. Hanna and Hanna, *Napoleon III*, 66–68. In suggesting that American historians have focused too much on Napoleon's anti-American motives for intervening in Mexico, Cunningham (*Mexico*, 127) argues that Chevalier nowhere indicated that his views "reflected the Emperor's ideas." Yet Napoleon's actions followed many of those ideas expressed by Chevalier. On Chevalier's influence on Napoleon, see Barker, "Monarchy in Mexico," 56–57, and Hanna and Hanna, *Napoleon III*, 60–68.

64. Hanna and Hanna, *Napoleon III*, 60–64 (quote, 63); Schoonover, "Napoleon Is Coming!," 106.

65. Hanna and Hanna, *Napoleon III*, 64–66.

66. Napoleon to Gen. Achille François Bazaine (commander in Mexico City), Sept. 12, 1863, cited ibid., 169; ibid., 170–71; Black, *Napoleon III and Mexican Silver*, 2; Ridley, *Maximilian and Juárez*, 67. In a questionable argument, Cunningham (*Mexico*, 4, 127) downplays Black's emphasis on Napoleon's silver interests and hence his goal to build a dominant France by asserting that the emperor's correspondence during the venture did not emphasize the mineral and that he wanted all countries to use the markets and commodities in Mexico in an effort to regenerate its economy. An examination of Napoleon's Grand Design for the Americas makes it difficult to refute his interest in tying the Mexican project to his objectives in Europe. For Napoleon's strong interest in Sonora's silver, see Barker, "Monarchy in Mexico," 68. See also Schoonover, *Dollars over Dominion*, chap. 6.

67. Drouyn to Bazaine, Aug. 17, 1863, quoted in Hanna and Hanna, *Napoleon III*, 93; Case and Spencer, *United States and France*, 548.

68. Motley to Oliver Wendell Holmes, Sept. 22, 1863, quoted in Hanna and Hanna, *Napoleon III*, 130.

69. McPherson, *Battle Cry*, 683; Harrington, *Fighting Politician*, 128, 130–31.

70. Seward to Dayton, Sept. 26, Oct. 5, 1863, Dip. Instructions, France (NA).

71. Seward to Dayton, Sept. 26, 1863, ibid.

72. Dayton to Seward, Oct. 9, 1863, Disp., France (NA).

73. Ibid.

74. Seward to Dayton, Oct. 23, 1863, Dip. Instructions, France (NA); Lyons to RU, Feb.

23, 1864 (Seward's assurances to U.S. Congress), in Barnes and Barnes, *American Civil War*, 3:149; Dayton to Seward, Nov. 27, Dec. 21, 1863, Disp., France (NA).

75. Seward to Dayton, Sept. 21, 1863, Dip. Instructions, France (NA); Seward to Dayton, Feb. 14, 1864, cited in Owsley, *King Cotton Diplomacy*, 517.

76. Maximilian to Slidell, Nov. 7, 1863, encl. in Slidell to Benjamin, Dec. 3, 1863, *ORN*, 2nd ser., 3:968–70; Contacts with Davis's friend and another southerner reported ibid.; Mann to Benjamin, Mar. 11, 1864, ibid., 1057–59; D. P. Crook, *The North, the South*, 335, 339–41. Owsley (*King Cotton Diplomacy*, 521) believes that Mann's source for this information was King Leopold of Belgium.

77. JD to Confederate Congress, Dec. 7, 1863, in Richardson, *Messages and Papers of the Confederacy*, 1:348, 359–60; JD to Maximilian, Jan. 7, 1864, in JD, *Papers*, 10:158; Slidell to Benjamin, ca. early February 1864, ibid., 337 n. 8.

78. Slidell to Mason, Mar. 22, 1864, Mason Papers (LC) (Slidell's conversation with Maximilian's aide); Slidell to Benjamin, Mar. 16, 1864 (3:1063–65), and Benjamin to Slidell, June 23, 1864 (3:1156–57; quote, 1157), *ORN*, 2nd ser.; Owsley, *King Cotton Diplomacy*, 508, 521–22, 524–25 (Slidell warning, 524).

79. JD, *Papers*, 10:337–38 n. 8; Mann to Benjamin, Mar. 11, 1864, ibid.; Slidell and Mason to Benjamin, Mar. 16, 1864, ibid.

80. Dayton to Seward, Oct. 23, 1863, Mar. 11, May 16, 1864, Disp., France (NA); McPherson, *Battle Cry*, 684; Owsley, *King Cotton Diplomacy*, 525–26; Hanna and Hanna, *Napoleon III*, 122 (Napoleon). Confederate agent James Bulloch went to court to gain control over the ships he had contracted for construction. He won back one ironclad, the CSS *Stonewall*, which did not arrive in American waters until a month after Lee's surrender at Appomattox. McPherson, *Battle Cry*, 684. Questions remain about whether the rams would have had any impact on the war because of design and construction problems. See Strong, Buckley, and St. Clair, "Odyssey of the CSS *Stonewall*."

81. JD to Confederate Congress, May 2, 1864, in Richardson, *Messages and Papers of the Confederacy*, 1:444–45.

82. Owsley, *King Cotton Diplomacy*, 525–26; Hanna and Hanna, *Napoleon III*, 125, 133.

83. Slidell to Benjamin, Mar. 16, 1864, *ORN*, 2nd ser., 3:1063–65; Slidell to Benjamin, Apr. 7, 1864, ibid., 1077–79; Slidell to Mason, May 2, 1864, ibid., 1107–11; Dayton to Seward, Mar. 21, 1864, cited in Owsley, *King Cotton Diplomacy*, 527; Owsley, 526–28 (Slidell on Mercier, 527).

84. Benjamin to Slidell, June 23, 1864, *ORN*, 2nd ser., 3:1156–57.

85. McPherson, *Battle Cry*, 766–67; Hubbard, *Burden of Confederate Diplomacy*, 166; Coulter, *Confederate States*, 547–48.

86. Blair memo of conversation with JD, Jan. 12, 1865, in JD, *Papers*, 11:315–19; JD memo of meeting with Blair, Jan. 12, 1865, ibid., 320; JD to Blair, Jan. 12, 1865, ibid., 323; Stephens, Hunter, and Campbell to JD, Feb. 5, 1865, ibid., 378–79; Lincoln to Seward, Jan. 31, 1865, *CWL*, 8:279; McPherson, *Battle Cry*, 821–24 (Lincoln, 823); E. B. Smith, *Francis Preston Blair*, 363–68.

87. JD's Message to Confederate Congress, Feb. 6, 1865, in JD, *Papers*, 11:378; McPherson, *Battle Cry*, 824.

88. Art. I, sec. 9, clause 4, Confederate Constitution, in Richardson, *Messages and*

Papers of the Confederacy, 1:43; Benjamin to Slidell, Dec. 27, 1864, ibid., 2:694–97; Hubbard, *Burden of Confederate Diplomacy*, 168–69; Bauer, "Last Effort" and *Kenner*; Meade, "Relations between . . . Benjamin and . . . Davis"; Evans, *Benjamin*, 262–64, 268–69, 275, 278–79; Sexton, *Debtor Diplomacy*, 184–86; D. P. Crook, *The North, the South*, 356–59; Coulter, *Confederate States*, 194–95. Both Mason and Slidell had predictably opposed the deal but gave in when shown Kenner's instructions.

89. JD, *Papers of Jefferson Davis*, 11:271 n. 7, 271–72 n. 9; Hubbard, *Burden of Confederate Diplomacy*, 170.

90. H. Jones, *Union in Peril*, 272 n. 4; Owsley, *King Cotton Diplomacy*, 532, 536–41; Bauer, "Last Effort"; Mason to Benjamin, Mar. 31, 1865 (2:709), Minutes of Mason's conversation with Palmerston, Mar. 14, 1865, encl. in Mason to Benjamin, Mar. 31, 1865 (2:713–17), and Mason to Benjamin, Mar. 31, 1865 (2:710), all in Richardson, *Messages and Papers of the Confederacy*; Hubbard, *Burden of Confederate Diplomacy*, 170–71; Evans, *Benjamin*, 279; Levine, *Confederate Emancipation*, 111–12 (*Richmond Dispatch*, Feb. 6, 1865, quoted on 111); Myers, *Caution and Cooperation*, 197–98.

91. Minutes of Mason's conversation with Donoughmore, Mar. 26, 1865, encl. in Mason to Benjamin, Mar. 31, 1865, in Richardson, *Messages and Papers of the Confederacy*, 2:717. See also Owsley, *King Cotton Diplomacy*, 530, 540–41. Donoughmore was Richard John Hely-Hutchinson, Fourth Earl of Donoughmore of the Peerage of Ireland and a Conservative Party member; he had served in Lord Derby's second administration as paymaster general and president of the Board of Trade.

92. Hanna and Hanna, *Napoleon III*, 153, 271, 296.

93. Ibid., 300.

94. McPherson, *Battle Cry*, 859; Wills, *Lincoln at Gettysburg*, 58–62, 90; Donald, *Lincoln*, 460–66; Final text of Gettysburg Address, Nov. 19, 1863, *CWL*, 7:22–23 ("a new birth of freedom"); Lyons to RU, July 26, Nov. 1, 1864, PRO 30/22/38.

EPILOGUE

1. See, among other studies cited earlier, W. C. Davis, *Jefferson Davis*, and Eaton, *Davis*.

2. For Lincoln, see, e.g., H. Jones, *Union in Peril* and *Lincoln and a New Birth of Freedom*; Monaghan, *Diplomat in Carpet Slippers*; and Wills, *Lincoln at Gettysburg*.

3. Among numerous studies, see Sexton, *Debtor Diplomacy*; Ball, *Financial Failure*; Saul, *Distant Friends*; Blackett, *Divided Hearts*; D. A. Campbell, *English Public Opinion*; Blackburn, *French Newspaper Opinion*; W. R. West, *Contemporary French Opinion*; and Ferris, *Desperate Diplomacy*.

Historiographical Note

The foreign relations of the Civil War has not yet received its fair due from scholars, although they have made considerable progress toward filling that gap in the literature. Among the many first-rate studies of Civil War diplomacy, I have found the following works particularly helpful in preparing this book.

The starting point for any historiographical examination of the Civil War is chapter 8 in volume 1 of Robert L. Beisner's two-volume edited work, *American Foreign Relations since 1600: A Guide to the Literature*, 2nd edition (2003). But see also chapter 11 of the first edition, *Guide to American Foreign Relations since 1700*, edited by Richard D. Burns (1983). Still useful for locating both primary and secondary works is Samuel F. Bemis and Grace G. Griffin, eds., *Guide to the Diplomatic History of the United States, 1775–1921* (1935), chapter 13.

Pioneering studies of the international dimensions of the war include Ephraim D. Adams's two-volume work, *Great Britain and the American Civil War* (1925), and Donaldson Jordan and Edwin J. Pratt's *Europe and the American Civil War* (1931). David P. Crook offers a sweeping analysis of foreign relations in *The North, the South, and the Powers, 1861–1865* (1974), and in his slimmer account, *Diplomacy during the American Civil War* (1975). For Union and Confederate relations with the British, see (in addition to E. D. Adams's work mentioned above) Brian Jenkins's two-volume study, *Britain and the War for the Union* (1974, 1980), which highlights the British belief that southern independence was a fait accompli, that a prolonged war would hurt international trade, and that concern about a Union-British war shaped Canadian-American relations. Jay Sexton's important study, *Debtor Diplomacy: Finance and American Foreign Relations in the Civil War Era, 1837–1873* (2005), ties investments to diplomacy and is especially strong on the Erlanger loan. For Confederate foreign relations, see Frank L. Owsley's classic study, *King Cotton Diplomacy* (1959, 2009), which was the first to examine British and French archival materials but is overtly pro-Confederate in thrust and heavy in its economic orientation. A useful synthesis is Charles M. Hubbard, *The Burden of Confederate Diplomacy* (1998). Indispensable to any discussion of the war is James M. McPherson's Pulitzer Prize–winning *Battle Cry of Freedom: The Civil War Era* (1988).

Numerous secondary works cover various aspects of British-American diplomacy during the war. For the interventionist issue, see Howard Jones, *Union in Peril: The Crisis over British Intervention in the Civil War* (1992). And for the slavery issue in the Union's relations with both England and France, see Howard Jones, *Abraham Lincoln and a New Birth of Freedom: The Union and Slavery in the Diplomacy of the Civil War* (1999). The legalities of the *Trent* crisis receive careful attention in Gordon H. Warren's *Fountain of Discontent: The Trent Affair and Freedom of the Seas* (1981). Also important are two books by Norman B. Ferris, *The Trent Affair: A Diplomatic Crisis* (1977) and *Desperate Diplomacy: William H. Seward's Foreign Policy, 1861* (1976), both emphasizing the secretary of state's role in opposing British intervention in the Civil War. For the Confederacy's shipbuilding efforts in England, see Frank J. Merli's classic study, *Great Britain and the Confederate Navy, 1861–1865* (1970), and his posthumously published work, *The Alabama, British Neutrality, and the American Civil War* (2004). British reaction to the Civil War was diverse but primarily pro-Union in the labor sector, according to Richard J. M. Blackett in his major revisionist work, *Divided Hearts: Britain and the American Civil War* (2001). In a controversial account that deserves attention, *English Public Opinion and American Civil War* (2003), Duncan A. Campbell charges that historians have exaggerated both pro-Confederate and pro-Union sentiment in England.

For Union and Confederate relations with France, see Lynn M. Case and Warren F. Spencer, *The United States and France: Civil War Diplomacy* (1970). Alfred J. Hanna and Kathryn A. Hanna explore the French emperor's Grand Design for the Americas in *Napoleon III and Mexico: American Triumph over Monarchy* (1971). French public opinion about the American war becomes clear in two studies: George M. Blackburn, *French Newspaper Opinion on the American Civil War* (1997) and W. Reed West, *Contemporary French Opinion on the American Civil War* (1924).

Norman E. Saul examines Russia's critical though underemphasized relationship with the United States during the Civil War in *Distant Friends: The United States and Russia, 1763–1867* (1991).

Bibliography

PRIMARY MATERIALS

Manuscript Sources

Adams, Charles Francis. Diary. Adams Family Papers. Massachusetts Historical Society, Boston.

———. Letterbook. Adams Family Papers. Massachusetts Historical Society, Boston.

———. Miscellany. Adams Family Papers. Massachusetts Historical Society, Boston.

Bright, John. Papers. British Library, London.

Clarendon, Fourth Earl of (George William Frederick Villiers). Papers. Bodleian Library, Oxford University, Oxford.

Cobden, Richard. Papers. British Library, London.

Cowley, Lord (Henry Richard Charles Wellesley, First Earl Cowley). Papers. FO 146. Public Record Office, Kew, England.

Gladstone, William E. Papers. British Library, London.

Great Britain. Foreign Office. FO 115, Embassy and Consular Archives, America, United States. Public Record Office, Kew, England.

———. Foreign Office. FO 146, Embassy and Consular Archives, France, Public Record Office, Kew, England.

———. Foreign Office. FO 27, France, General Correspondence, Public Record Office, Kew, England.

———. Foreign Office. FO 5 (series 2), America, United States, Public Record Office, Kew, England.

———. Foreign Office. FO 83, Great Britain and General, Law Officer's Reports, America, 1866–68, Public Record Office, Kew, England.

Harcourt, William Vernon. Papers. Stanton-Harcourt Collection, Bodleian Library, Oxford University, Oxford.

Layard, Sir Austen Henry. Papers. British Library, London.

Lewis, George Cornewall. Papers. National Library of Wales, Aberystwyth.

Mason, James M. Papers. Manuscript Division, Library of Congress, Washington, D.C.

Moran, Benjamin. Diary. Manuscript Division, Library of Congress, Washington, D.C.

Palmerston, Lord (Henry John Temple). Letterbooks. British Library, London.
———. Papers. University of Southampton, Southampton, England.
Ripon, First Marquis of (Earl de Grey, George Frederick Samuel Robinson). Papers. British Library, London.
Russell, Lord John. Papers. Public Record Office, Kew, England.
Seward, William H. Papers. Rush Rhees Library, University of Rochester, New York.
U.S. Department of State. Diplomatic Instructions of the Department of State, 1801–1906, France. National Archives, Washington, D.C.
———. Diplomatic Instructions of the Department of State, 1801–1906, Great Britain. National Archives, Washington, D.C.
———. Diplomatic Instructions of the Department of State, 1801–1906, Russia. National Archives, Washington, D.C.
———. Dispatches from the United States Ministers to France, 1789–1906. National Archives, Washington, D.C.
———. Dispatches from United States Ministers to Great Britain, 1791–1906. National Archives, Washington, D.C.
———. Domestic Letters of the Department of State, 1784–1906. National Archives, Washington, D.C.
———. Miscellaneous Letters of the Department of State, 1789–1906. National Archives, Washington, D.C.
———. Notes from the British Legation in the United States to the Department of State, 1791–1906. National Archives, Washington, D.C.
———. Notes from the French Legation in the United States to the Department of State, 1789–1906. National Archives, Washington, D.C.
———. Notes to Foreign Legations in the United States from the Department of State, 1834–1906, France. National Archives, Washington, D.C.
———. Notes to Foreign Legations in the United States from the Department of State, 1834–1906, Great Britain. National Archives, Washington, D.C.

Published Sources

Adams, Charles Francis, Jr. *Charles Francis Adams, 1835–1915: An Autobiography.* Boston: Houghton Mifflin, 1916.
Adams, Henry. *The Education of Henry Adams: An Autobiography.* Boston: Houghton Mifflin, 1918.
American Historical Association. *Annual Report of the American Historical Association for the Year 1902.* 2 vols. Vol. 2: *Sixth Report of Historical Manuscripts Commission: With Diary and Correspondence of Salmon P. Chase.* Washington, D.C.: Government Printing Office, 1903.
Argyll, Duchess of, ed. *George Douglas, Eighth Duke of Argyll (1823–1900): Autobiography and Memoirs.* 2 vols. London: John Murray, 1906.
Ashmore, Owen, ed. "The Diary of James Garnett of Low Moor, Clitheroe, 1858–65." Vol. 1: "Years of Prosperity, 1858–60." In *Transactions of the Historical Society of Lancashire and Cheshire for the Year 1969* 121:77–98. Liverpool: Printed for Society, 1970. Vol. 2: "The American Civil War and the Cotton Famine, 1861–65."

In *Transactions of the Historical Society of Lancashire and Cheshire for the Year 1971* 123:105–43. Liverpool: Printed for Society, 1972.

Austin, John. *The Province of Jurisprudence Determined*. London: Weidenfeld and Nicolson, 1832.

Barnes, James J., and Patience P. Barnes, eds. *The American Civil War through British Eyes: Dispatches from British Diplomats*. 3 vols. Kent, Ohio: Kent State University Press, 2003.

———, eds. *Private and Confidential: Letters from British Ministers in Washington to the Foreign Secretaries in London, 1844–1867*. Selinsgrove, Pa.: Susquehanna University Press, 1993.

Baxter, James P., ed. "Papers Relating to Belligerent and Neutral Rights." *American Historical Review* 34 (October 1928): 77–91.

Beale, Howard K., ed. *The Diary of Edward Bates, 1859–1866*. Washington, D.C.: U.S. Government Printing Office, 1933.

———. ed., *Diary of Gideon Welles: Secretary of the Navy under Lincoln and Johnson*. 3 vols. New York: Norton, 1960.

Beisner, Robert L., ed. *American Foreign Relations since 1600: A Guide to the Literature*. 2nd ed. 2 vols. Santa Barbara, California: ABC-CLIO, Inc., 2003.

Bemis, Samuel F., and Grace G. Griffin, eds. *Guide to the Diplomatic History of the United States, 1775–1921*. Washington, D.C.: U.S. Government Printing Office, 1935.

Benson, Arthur C., and Viscount Esher, eds. *The Letters of Queen Victoria, 1837–1861*. 3 vols. London: John Murray, 1908.

Bernard, Mountague. *A Historical Account of the Neutrality of Great Britain during the American Civil War*. London: Longmans, Green, Reader, and Dyer, 1870.

Bigelow, John. *France and the Confederate Navy, 1862–1868*. New York: Harper and Brothers, 1888.

———. *Retrospections of an Active Life*. 5 vols. New York: Baker and Taylor Co., 1909–13.

Bourne, Kenneth, and D. Cameron Watt, eds. *British Documents on Foreign Affairs: Reports and Papers from the Foreign Office Confidential Print: Part 1, Series C: North America, 1837–1914*. Vols. 5 and 6 of *The Civil War Years, 1859–1865*. Bethesda, Md.: University Publications of America, 1986.

Brigg, Mary, ed. *The Journals of a Lancashire Weaver, 1856–64, 1872–75*. Vol. 122 of *The Record Society of Lancashire and Cheshire*. Liverpool: Printed for Society, 1982.

Bright, John. *Speeches of John Bright, M.P., on the American Question*. 1865. Kraus Reprint, 1970.

Buckle, George E., ed. *The Letters of Queen Victoria, 1862–1878*. 2nd series. 2 vols. New York: Longmans, Green, 1926–28.

Bulloch, James D. *The Secret Service of the Confederate States in Europe; or, How the Confederate Cruisers Were Equipped*. 2 vols. 1883. Reprint, New York: Thomas Yoseloff, 1959.

Burnett, Lonnie A., ed. *Henry Hotze, Confederate Propagandist: Selected Writings on Revolution, Recognition, and Race*. Tuscaloosa: University of Alabama Press, 2008.

Burns, Richard D., ed. *Guide to American Foreign Relations since 1700*. Santa Barbara, Calif.: ABC-CLIO, Inc., 1983.

Campbell, Ina E. M., ed. *Autobiography and Memoirs: George Douglas, Eighth Duke of Argyll.* 2 vols. London: J. Murray, 1906.

Confederate States of America. *Journal of the Congress of the Confederate States of America, 1861–1865.* 7 vols. Washington, D.C.: Government Printing Office, 1904–5.

Connell, Brian, ed. *Regina vs. Palmerston: The Correspondence between Queen Victoria and Her Foreign and Prime Minister, 1837–1865.* Garden City, N.Y.: Doubleday, 1961.

Crawford, Martin, ed. *William Howard Russell's Civil War: Private Diary and Letters, 1861–1862.* Athens: University of Georgia Press, 1992.

Davis, Jefferson. *Jefferson Davis, Constitutionalist: His Letters, Papers, and Speeches.* 10 vols. Edited by Rowland Dunbar. Jackson: Mississippi State University Press, 1923.

——. *The Papers of Jefferson Davis.* 11 vols. to date. Edited by Lynda L. Crist and Mary Seaton Dix. Baton Rouge: Louisiana State University Press, 1971–97.

——. *The Rise and Fall of the Confederate Government.* 2 vols. New York: D. Appleton, 1881.

——. *A Short History of the Confederate States of America.* New York: Belford Co., Publishers, 1890.

Davis, Varina H. *Jefferson Davis: A Memoir by His Wife.* New York: Belford Co., 1890.

De Leon, Edwin. *Secret History of Confederate Diplomacy Abroad.* Edited by William C. Davis. Lawrence: University Press of Kansas, 2005.

Dennett, Tyler, ed. *Lincoln and the Civil War in the Diaries and Letters of John Hay.* New York: Dodd, Mead, 1939.

Donald, David, ed. *Inside Lincoln's Cabinet: The Civil War Diaries of Salmon P. Chase.* New York: Longmans, Green, 1954.

Dudley, Thomas H. "Three Critical Periods in Our Diplomatic Relations with England during the Late War: Personal Recollections of Thomas H. Dudley, Late United States Consul at Liverpool." *Pennsylvania Magazine of History and Biography* 17 (1893): 34–54.

Fairfax, D. MacNeill. "Captain Wilkes's Seizure of Mason and Slidell." In *Battles and Leaders of the Civil War,* edited by Robert U. Johnson and Clarence C. Buel, 135–42. 1887–88. Reprint, New York: Thomas Yoseloff, 1956.

Ford, Worthington C., ed. *A Cycle of Adams Letters, 1861–1865.* 2 vols. Boston: Houghton Mifflin, 1920.

Gooch, G. P., ed. *The Later Correspondence of Lord John Russell, 1840–1878.* 2 vols. London: Longmans, Green, 1925.

Great Britain. *British Parliamentary Papers, 1801–1899.* 1,000 vols. Shannon: Irish University Press, date varies by volume.

——. Foreign Office. *British and Foreign State Papers.* 116 vols. London: William Ridgway, 1812–1925.

——. Parliament. *British Sessional Papers (House of Commons and Lords), 1801–1900.*

Guedalla, Philip, ed. *Gladstone and Palmerston: Being the Correspondence of Lord Palmerston and Mr. Gladstone, 1851–1865.* Covent Garden, England: Victor Gollancz, 1928.

Gurowski, Adam. *Diary: From March 4, 1861 to November 12, 1862.* 2 vols. 1862. Reprint, New York: Burt Franklin, 1968.

Hansard, Thomas C., ed. *Hansard's Parliamentary Debates.* 3rd series. 356 vols. London: Wyman, 1830–91.

Harcourt, William V. *Letters by Historicus on Some Questions of International Law.* London: Macmillan, 1863.

Hardman, Sir William. *The Letters and Memoirs of Sir William Hardman.* 2nd series: 1863–65. Annotated and edited by S. M. Ellis. New York: George H. Doran, 1925.

Hunter, Robert M. "The Capture of Mason and Slidell." In *Annals of the War Written by Leading Participants, North and South,* 797–98. Philadelphia: Times, 1879.

Jones, John B. *A Rebel War Clerk's Diary.* 1866. Reprint edited by Earl S. Miers, New York: Sagamore Press, 1958.

Jones, Robert H. "The American Civil War in the British Sessional Papers: Catalogue and Commentary." *Proceedings of the American Philosophical Society* 107 (October 1963): 415–26.

Kent, James. *Commentaries on American Law.* 10th ed., 4 vols. Boston: Little, Brown, 1860.

Levenson, J. C., et al., eds. *The Letters of Henry Adams.* 6 vols. Cambridge: Harvard University Press, 1982–88.

Lewis, Gilbert F., ed. *Letters of the Right Hon. Sir George Cornewall Lewis.* London: Longmans, Green, 1870.

Lincoln, Abraham. *The Collected Works of Abraham Lincoln.* 8 vols. and Index. Edited by Roy P. Basler et al. New Brunswick, N.J.: Rutgers University Press, 1953–55.

———. *Complete Works of Abraham Lincoln.* Edited by John G. Nicolay, John Hay, and F. D. Tandy. New ed. 12 vols. New York, 1905.

Lloyd's of London. Register of Shipping, 1861–66.

MacCarthy, Desmond, and Agatha Russell, eds. *Lady John Russell: A Memoir with Selections from Her Diaries and Correspondence.* New York: John Lane, 1911.

Mason, Virginia. *The Public Life and Diplomatic Correspondence of James M. Mason.* Roanoke, Va.: Stone Printing and Manufacturing Co., 1903.

Matthew, H. C. G., ed. *The Gladstone Diaries.* 9 vols. Oxford, England: Clarendon Press, 1978.

Mitchell, Brian R., comp. *European Historical Statistics, 1750–1970.* New York: Columbia University Press, 1975.

Monroe, Haskell M., Jr., et al., eds. *The Papers of Jefferson Davis.* 5 vols. Baton Rouge: Louisiana State University Press, 1971–85.

Moore, John B. *History and Digest of the International Arbitrations to Which the United States Has Been a Party.* 6 vols. Washington, D.C.: Government Printing Office, 1898.

Moran, Benjamin. "Extracts from the Diary of Benjamin Moran, 1860–1868." *Massachusetts Historical Society Proceedings* 48 (1915): 431–92.

Palmer, Beverly W., ed. *The Selected Letters of Charles Sumner.* 2 vols. Boston: Northeastern University Press, 1990.

Pearson, H. G., ed. "Letters of the Duke and Duchess of Argyll to Charles Sumner." *Massachusetts Historical Society Proceedings* 47 (1914): 66–106.

Pease, Theodore C., and James G. Randall, eds. *The Diary of Orville Hickman Browning.* 2 vols. Springfield: Illinois State Historical Library, 1925.

Pecquet du Bellet, Paul. *The Diplomacy of the Confederate Cabinet of Richmond and Its Agents Abroad: Being Memorandum Notes Taken in Paris during the Rebellion of the Southern States from 1861–1865.* Edited by William Stanley Hoole. Tuscaloosa, Ala.: Confederate Publishing Co., 1963.

Perkins, Howard C., ed. *Northern Editorials on Secession.* 2 vols. New York: D. Appleton-Century Co., 1942.

Reclus, Elisée. "Le cotton et la crise américaine." *Revue des deux mondes* 37 (January 1862): 176–208.

Reid, Robert L., ed. "William E. Gladstone's 'Insincere Neutrality' during the Civil War." *Civil War History* 15 (December 1969): 293–307.

Richardson, James D., ed. *A Compilation of the Messages and Papers of the Confederacy, Including the Diplomatic Correspondence, 1861–1865.* 2 vols. Nashville, Tenn.: U.S. Publishing Co., 1905.

———. ed. *A Compilation of Messages and Papers of the Presidents.* [1789–1917]. 20 vols. and *Supplement.* New York: Bureau of National Literature, 1917.

Russell, John Earl. *Recollections and Suggestions, 1813–1873.* Boston: Roberts Brothers, 1875.

Russell, William Howard. *My Diary North and South.* Edited by Eugene H. Berwanger. Philadelphia: Temple University Press, 1988.

———. *My Diary North and South.* Edited by Fletcher Pratt. New York: Harper, 1954.

Sears, Stephen W., ed. *The Civil War Papers of George B. McClellan: Selected Correspondence, 1860–1865.* New York: Ticknor and Fields, 1989.

Seward, Frederick W. *Reminiscences of a Wartime Statesman and Diplomat, 1830–1915.* New York: Putnam's, 1916.

Seward, William H. *Autobiography of William H. Seward from 1801 to 1834: With a Memoir of His Life, and Selections from His Letters from 1881 to 1846.* Edited by Frederick W. Seward. 3 vols. New York: D. Appleton, 1877.

Silver, A. W., ed. "Henry Adams' 'Diary of a Visit to Manchester.'" *American Historical Review* 51 (October 1945): 74–89.

U.S. Congress. *Congressional Globe.* Washington, D.C.

———. House. *House Executive Documents.* Washington, D.C.

———. Senate. *Senate Executive Documents.* Washington, D.C.

U.S. Department of the Navy. *Official Records of the Union and Confederate Navies in the War of the Rebellion.* 1st series, 30 vols; 2nd series, 3 vols. Washington, D.C.: Government Printing Office, 1894–1927.

U.S. Department of State. *Correspondence concerning Claims against Great Britain: Transmitted to the Senate of the United States in Answer to the Resolutions of December 4 and 10, 1867, and of May 27, 1868.* Papers Relating to Claims against Great Britain: Parliamentary and Judicial Appendix No. 26. Washington, D.C.: Government Printing Office, 1870.

———. *Papers Relating to Foreign Affairs, Accompanying the Annual Message of the*

President to the Second Session of the Thirty-Seventh Congress, 1861. Washington, D.C.: Government Printing Office, 1861.

————. *Papers Relating to Foreign Affairs Communicated to Congress, December 1, 1862.* Washington, D.C.: Government Printing Office, 1863.

————. *Papers Relating to Foreign Affairs, Accompanying the Annual Message of the President of the First Session of the Thirty-Eighth Congress.* Washington, D.C.: Government Printing Office, 1864.

————. *Papers Relating to Foreign Affairs: Executive Documents Printed by Order of the House of Representatives during the Second Session of the Thirty-eighth Congress, 1863–64.* 15 vols. Washington, D.C.: Government Printing Office, 1865.

U.S. Supreme Court. *U.S. Supreme Court Reports: Cases Argued and Decided in the Supreme Court of the United States,* 5, 6, 7, 8. In Henry Wheaton, *Lawyers' Edition.* Rochester, N.Y.: Lawyers' Co-operative Publishing Co., 1918.

Vattel, Emmerich de. *The Law of Nations; or, Principles of the Law of Nature Applies to the Conduct and Affairs of Nations and Sovereigns.* Philadelphia: Abraham Small, 1817.

Wallace, Sarah A., and Frances E. Gillespie, eds. *The Journal of Benjamin Moran, 1857–1865.* 2 vols. Chicago: University of Chicago Press, 1949.

Welles, Gideon. "The Capture and Release of Mason and Slidell." *Galaxy* (May 1873): 640–51.

Wellesley, F. A., ed. *Secrets of the Second Empire: Private Letters from the Paris Embassy, Selections from the Papers of Henry Richard Charles Wellesley, 1st Earl Cowley, Ambassador at Paris, 1852–1867.* New York: Harper, 1929.

Wheaton, Henry. *The Elements of International Law.* 1836. 8th ed. Edited by Richard Henry Dana Jr. Boston: Little, Brown, 1866.

Whiting, William. *War Powers under the Constitution of the United States.* 10th ed. Boston: Little, Brown, 1864.

Williams, Ben A., ed. *A Diary from Dixie by Mary Boykin Chesnut.* Boston: Houghton Mifflin, 1949.

Woodward, C. Vann, ed. *Mary Chesnut's Civil War.* New Haven: Yale University Press, 1981.

Newspapers, Magazines, and Contemporary Journals

Blackwood's Edinburgh Magazine (England)
Boston Advertiser
Boston Evening Transcript
Boston Post
Charleston Mercury
De Bow's Review
Economist (London)
London Morning Herald
National Intelligencer (Washington, D.C.)
New Orleans Picayune
New York Commercial Advertiser

New York Herald
New York Times
New York Tribune
Niles' Register (Baltimore)
North American Review (Boston)
Punch (London)
Quarterly Review (London)
Richmond Enquirer
Richmond Whig
Times (London)
Washington Globe

SECONDARY MATERIALS

Books

Adams, Charles Francis, Jr. *Before and after the Treaty of Washington: The American Civil War and the War in the Transvaal.* New York: New-York Historical Society, 1902.

Adams, Ephraim D. *Great Britain and the American Civil War.* 2 vols. New York: Longmans, Green, 1925.

Ashley, Evelyn. *The Life and Correspondence of Henry John Temple Palmerston.* 2 vols. London: Richard Bentley and Son, 1879.

Atkins, John B. *The Life of Sir William Howard Russell: The First Special Correspondent.* 2 vols. New York: E. P. Dutton, 1911.

Ausubel, Herman. *John Bright: Victorian Reformer.* New York: Wiley, 1966.

Ball, Douglas B. *Financial Failure and Confederate Defeat.* Urbana: University of Illinois Press, 1991.

Bancroft, Frederic. *The Life of William H. Seward.* 2 vols. New York: Harper and Brothers, 1900.

Barker, Nancy N. *The French Experience in Mexico, 1821–1861: A History of Constant Misunderstanding.* Chapel Hill: University of North Carolina Press, 1979.

Bauer, Craig A. *A Leader among Peers: The Life and Times of Duncan Farrar Kenner.* Lafayette: Center for Louisiana Studies, University of Southwestern Louisiana, 1993.

Bell, Herbert C. F. *Lord Palmerston.* 2 vols. London: Longmans, Green, 1936.

Beringer, Richard E., Herman Hattaway, Archer Jones, and William N. Still Jr. *Why the South Lost the Civil War.* Athens: University of Georgia Press, 1986.

Bernath, Stuart L. *Squall across the Atlantic: American Civil War Prize Cases and Diplomacy.* Berkeley: University of California Press, 1970.

Berwanger, Eugene H. *The British Foreign Service and the American Civil War.* Lexington: University of Kentucky Press, 1994.

Black, Shirley J. *Napoleon III and Mexican Silver.* Silverton, Colo.: Ferrell Publications, 2000.

Blackburn, George M. *French Newspaper Opinion on the American Civil War.* Westport, Conn.: Greenwood Press, 1997.

Blackett, Richard J. M. *Divided Hearts: Britain and the American Civil War.* Baton Rouge: Louisiana State University Press, 2001.

Blumberg, Arnold. *The Diplomacy of the Mexican Empire, 1863–1867.* Philadelphia: Transactions of the American Philosophical Society, 61, part 8, 1971.

Blumenthal, Henry. *France and the United States: Their Diplomatic Relations, 1789–1914.* New York: W. W. Norton and Co., 1970.

———. *A Reappraisal of Franco-American Relations, 1830–1871.* Chapel Hill: University of North Carolina Press, 1959.

Boaz, Thomas. *Guns for Cotton: England Arms the Confederacy.* Shippensburg, Pa.: Burd Street Press, 1996.

Bock, Carl H. *Prelude to Tragedy: The Negotiation and Breakdown of the Tripartite Convention of London, October 31, 1861.* Philadelphia: University of Pennsylvania Press, 1966.

Bonham, Milledge L., Jr. *The British Consuls in the Confederacy*. New York: Columbia University, Longmans, Green, 1911.

Bourne, Kenneth. *Britain and the Balance of Power in North America, 1815–1908*. Berkeley: University of California Press, 1967.

———. *The Foreign Policy of Victorian England, 1830–1902*. Oxford, England: Clarendon Press, 1970.

Boykin, Edward C. *Ghost Ship of the Confederacy: The Story of the Alabama and Her Captain, Raphael Semmes*. New York: Funk and Wagnalls, 1957.

———. *Sea Devil of the Confederacy: The Story of the Florida and Her Captain, John Newland Maffitt*. New York: Funk and Wagnalls, 1959.

Bradlee, Francis B. *Blockade Running during the Civil War and the Effect of Land and Water Transportation on the Confederacy*. Philadelphia: Porcupine Press, 1974.

Browning, Robert M., Jr. *From Cape Charles to Cape Fear: The North Atlantic Blockading Squadron during the Civil War*. Tuscaloosa: University of Alabama Press, 1993.

Burn, W. L. *The Age of Equipoise: A Study of the Mid-Victorian Generation*. London: Allen and Unwin, 1964.

Butler, Perry. *Gladstone: Church, State and Tractarianism—A Study of His Religious Ideas and Attitudes, 1809–1859*. New York: Oxford University Press, 1982.

Callahan, James M. *Diplomatic History of the Southern Confederacy*. New York: Frederick Ungar, 1901.

Campbell, Charles S. *From Revolution to Rapprochement: The United States and Great Britain, 1783–1900*. New York: Wiley, 1974.

Campbell, Duncan A. *English Public Opinion and the American Civil War*. Woodbridge, Suffolk, United Kingdom; Rochester, New York: Royal Historical Society/Boydell Press, 2003.

Carnahan, Burrus M. *Act of Justice: Lincoln's Emancipation Proclamation and the Law of War*. Lexington: University Press of Kentucky, 2007.

Carroll, Daniel B. *Henri Mercier and the American Civil War*. Princeton: Princeton University Press, 1971.

Case, Lynn M., and Warren F. Spencer. *The United States and France: Civil War Diplomacy*. Philadelphia: University of Pennsylvania Press, 1970.

Cook, Adrian. *The Alabama Claims: American Politics and Anglo-American Relations, 1865–1872*. Ithaca, N.Y.: Cornell University Press, 1975.

Cortada, James W. *Spain and the American Civil War: Relations at Mid-Century, 1855–1868*. Philadelphia: American Philosophical Society, 1980.

Coulter, E. Merton. *The Confederate States of America, 1861–1865*. Baton Rouge: Louisiana State University Press, 1950.

Courtemanche, Regis A. *No Need of Glory: The British Navy in American Waters, 1860–1864*. Annapolis, Md.: Naval Institute Press, 1977.

Cox, LaWanda. *Lincoln and Black Freedom: A Study in Presidential Leadership*. Columbia: University of South Carolina Press, 1981.

Crawford, Martin. *The Anglo-American Crisis of the Mid-Nineteenth Century: The Times and America, 1850–1862*. Athens: University of Georgia Press, 1987

Crook, David P. *Diplomacy during the American Civil War*. New York: Wiley, 1975.

————. *The North, the South, and the Powers, 1861–1865*. New York: Wiley, 1974.

Cross, Coy F., II. *Lincoln's Man in Liverpool: Consul Dudley and the Legal Battle to Stop Confederate Warships*. De Kalb: Northern Illinois University Press, 2007.

Cullop, Charles C. *Confederate Propaganda in Europe, 1861–1865*. Coral Gables, Fla.: University of Miami Press, 1969.

Cunningham, Michele. *Mexico and the Foreign Policy of Napoleon III*. New York: Palgrave, 2001.

Current, Richard N. *The Lincoln Nobody Knows*. New York: Hill and Wang, 1958.

Daddysman, James W. *The Matamoros Trade: Confederate Commerce, Diplomacy, and Intrigue*. Newark: University of Delaware Press, 1984.

Dalzell, George W. *The Flight from the Flag: The Continuing Effect of the Civil War upon the American Carrying Trade*. Chapel Hill: University of North Carolina Press, 1940.

Davis, William C. *Jefferson Davis: The Man and His Hour*. New York: HarperCollins, 1991.

Diggins, John P. *On Hallowed Ground: Abraham Lincoln and the Foundations of American History*. New Haven: Yale University Press, 2000.

Donald, David H. *Charles Sumner and the Coming of the Civil War*. New York: Alfred A. Knopf, 1960.

————. *Charles Sumner and the Rights of Man*. New York: Alfred A. Knopf, 1970.

————. *Lincoln*. New York: Simon and Schuster, 1995.

Duberman, Martin. *Charles F. Adams, 1807–1886*. Boston: Houghton Mifflin, 1961.

Du Bose, John W. *The Life and Times of William Lowndes Yancey: A History of Political Parties in the United States, from 1834 to 1864*. Birmingham, Ala.: Roberts and Son, 1892. Reprint, New York: Peter Smith, 1942.

Durkin, Joseph T. *Stephen R. Mallory: Confederate Navy Chief*. Chapel Hill: University of North Carolina Press, 1954.

Eaton, Clement. *A History of the Southern Confederacy*. New York: Free Press, 1954.

————. *Jefferson Davis*. New York: Free Press, 1977.

Ellison, Mary. *Support for Secession: Lancashire and the American Civil War*. Chicago: University of Chicago Press, 1972.

Evans, Eli N. *Judah P. Benjamin: The Jewish Confederate*. New York: Free Press, 1988.

Faust, Drew G. *This Republic of Suffering: Death and the American Civil War*. New York: Alfred A. Knopf, 2008.

Ferris, Norman B. *Desperate Diplomacy: William H. Seward's Foreign Policy, 1861*. Knoxville: University of Tennessee Press, 1976.

————. *The Trent Affair: A Diplomatic Crisis*. Knoxville: University of Tennessee Press, 1977.

Fischer, LeRoy H. *Lincoln's Gadfly: Adam Gurowski*. Norman: University of Oklahoma Press, 1964.

Fitzmaurice, Lord Edmond George Petty-Fitzmaurice, 1st Baron. *The Life of Granville George Leveson Gower, Second Earl Granville, K.G., 1815–1891*. 2 vols. London: Longmans, Green, 1905.

Foner, Philip S. *British Labor and the American Civil War*. New York: Holmes and Meier, 1981.

Fox, Stephen. *Wolf of the Deep: Raphael Semmes and the Notorious Confederate Raider CSS Alabama*. New York: Alfred A. Knopf, 2007.

Franklin, John Hope. *The Emancipation Proclamation*. Garden City, N.Y.: Doubleday, 1963.

Freeman, Douglas S. *R. E. Lee: A Biography*. 4 vols. New York: Scribner, 1934–35.

Gaddis, John L. *Russia, the Soviet Union, and the United States: An Interpretive History*. 2nd ed. New York: McGraw-Hill, 1990.

Gallagher, Gary W. *The Confederate War*. Cambridge: Harvard University Press, 1997.

———, ed. *The Antietam Campaign*. Chapel Hill: University of North Carolina Press, 1999.

———, ed. *Antietam: Essays on the 1862 Maryland Campaign*. Kent, Ohio: Kent State University Press, 1989.

———, ed. *The Richmond Campaign of 1862: The Peninsula and the Seven Days*. Chapel Hill: University of North Carolina Press, 2000.

Gardiner, A. G. *The Life of Sir William Harcourt*. 2 vols. New York: George H. Doran, 1923.

Gavronsky, Serge. *The French Liberal Opposition and the American Civil War*. New York: Humanities Press, 1968.

Glatthaar, Joseph T. *General Lee's Army: From Victory to Collapse*. New York: Free Press, 2008.

Grant, Alfred. *The American Civil War and the British Press*. Jefferson, N.C.: McFarland and Co., 2000.

Guelzo, Allen C. *Abraham Lincoln: Redeemer President*. Grand Rapids, Mich.: William N. Eerdmans Publishing Co., 1999.

Hammond, M. B. *The Cotton Industry*. 1897. New York: Johnson Reprint, 1966.

Hanna, Alfred J., and Kathryn A. Hanna. *Napoleon III and Mexico: American Triumph over Monarchy*. Chapel Hill: University of North Carolina Press, 1971.

Harrington, Fred H. *Fighting Politician: Major General N. P. Banks*. Philadelphia: University of Pennsylvania Press, 1948.

Hearn, Chester G. *Gray Raiders of the Sea: How Eight Confederate Warships Destroyed the Union's High Seas Commerce*. Camden, Maine: International Marine Publishing, 1992.

Henderson, William O. *The Lancashire Cotton Famine, 1861–1865*. 1934. Reprint, New York: Augustus M. Kelley, 1969.

Hendrick, Burton J. *Statesmen of the Lost Cause: Jefferson Davis and His Cabinet*. New York: Literary Guild, 1939.

Hess, Earl J. *Trench Warfare under Grant and Lee: Field Fortifications in the Overland Campaign*. Chapel Hill: University of North Carolina Press, 2007.

Hubbard, Charles M. *The Burden of Confederate Diplomacy*. Knoxville: University of Tennessee Press, 1998.

Hyman, Harold M., ed. *Heard round the World: The Impact Abroad of the Civil War*. New York: Alfred A. Knopf, 1969.

Jaffa, Harry V. *A New Birth of Freedom: Abraham Lincoln and the Coming of the Civil War*. Lanham, Md.: Rowman and Littlefield, 2000.

Jenkins, Brian. *Britain and the War for the Union*. 2 vols. Montreal: McGill-Queen's University Press, 1974, 1980.

Johannsen, Robert W. *Lincoln, the South, and Slavery: The Political Dimension*. Baton Rouge: Louisiana State University Press, 1991.

Jones, Howard. *Abraham Lincoln and a New Birth of Freedom: The Union and Slavery in the Diplomacy of the Civil War*. Lincoln: University of Nebraska Press, 1999.

——. *To the Webster-Ashburton Treaty: A Study in Anglo-American Relations, 1783–1842*. Chapel Hill: University of North Carolina Press, 1977.

——. *Union in Peril: The Crisis over British Intervention in the Civil War*. Chapel Hill: University of North Carolina Press, 1992.

Jones, Howard, and Donald A. Rakestraw. *Prologue to Manifest Destiny: Anglo-American Relations in the 1840s*. Wilmington, Del.: Scholarly Resources, 1997.

Jones, Wilbur D. *The Confederate Rams at Birkenhead: A Chapter in Anglo-American Relations*. Tuscaloosa, Ala.: Confederate Publishing Co., 1961.

Jordan, Donaldson, and Edwin J. Pratt. *Europe and the American Civil War*. Boston: Houghton Mifflin, 1931.

Katz, Irving. *August Belmont: A Political Biography*. New York: Columbia University Press, 1968.

Kelly, Alfred H., Winfred A. Harbison, and Herman Belz. *The American Constitution: Its Origins and Development*, 6th ed. New York: Norton, 1983.

Lauterpacht, Hersch. *Recognition in International Law*. Cambridge: Cambridge University Press, 1947.

Leader, Robert E. *Life and Letters of John Arthur Roebuck*. London: Edward Arnold, 1897.

Lester, Richard I. *Confederate Finance and Purchasing in Great Britain*. Charlottesville: University Press of Virginia, 1975.

Levine, Bruce. *Confederate Emancipation: Southern Plans to Free and Arm Slaves during the Civil War*. New York: Oxford University Press, 2006.

Longford, Elizabeth. *Queen Victoria: Born to Succeed*. New York: Harper and Row, 1964.

MacKintosh, John P. *The British Cabinet*. 2nd ed. London: Smith, Elder, 1880.

Magnus, Philip M. *Gladstone: A Biography*. New York: E. P. Dutton, 1954.

Mahin, Dean B. *One War at a Time: The International Dimension of the American Civil War*. Washington, D.C.: Brassey's, 1999.

Martin, Theodore. *Life of the Prince Consort*. 5 vols. London: Smith, Elder, 1880.

Marvel, William. *The Alabama and the Kearsarge: The Sailor's Civil War*. Chapel Hill: University of North Carolina Press, 1996.

Marx, Karl, and Frederick Engels. *The Civil War in the United States*. New York: International Publishers, 1937.

Matthew, H. C. G. *Gladstone, 1809–1874*. New York: Oxford University Press, 1986.

Maurois, André. *Disraeli: A Picture of the Victorian Age*. Translated by Hamish Miles. New York: D. Appleton and Co., 1928.

Maxwell, Herbert. *The Life and Letters of George William Frederick, Fourth Earl of Clarendon*. 2 vols. London: Edward Arnold, 1913.

May, Robert E. *The Southern Dream of a Caribbean Empire, 1854–1861*. Baton Rouge: Louisiana State University Press, 1973.

McPherson, James M. *Abraham Lincoln and the Second American Revolution*. New York: Oxford University Press, 1990.

———. *Battle Cry of Freedom: The Civil War Era*. New York: Oxford University Press, 1988.

———. *Crossroads of Freedom: Antietam*. New York: Oxford University Press, 2002.

———. *Drawn with the Sword: Reflections on the American Civil War*. New York: Oxford University Press, 1996.

———. *The Negro's Civil War: How American Negroes Felt and Acted During the War for the Union*. New York: Alfred A. Knopf, 1965.

———. *Ordeal by Fire: The Civil War and Reconstruction*. Boston: McGraw-Hill, 1982, 3rd ed., 2000.

———. *For Cause and Comrades: Why Men Fought in the Civil War*. New York: Oxford University Press, 1997.

———. *Tried by War: Abraham Lincoln as Commander in Chief*. New York: Penguin Press, 2008.

———. *What They Fought For, 1861–1865*. Baton Rouge: Louisiana State University Press, 1994.

Meade, Robert D. *Judah P. Benjamin and the American Civil War*. New York: Oxford University Press, 1943.

Merli, Frank J. *The Alabama, British Neutrality, and the American Civil War*. Edited by David M. Fahey. Bloomington: Indiana University Press, 2004.

———. *Great Britain and the Confederate Navy, 1861–1865*. 1970. Reprint with new introduction by Howard Jones, Bloomington: Indiana University Press, 2004.

———, ed. *Journal of Confederate History: Special Commemorative Naval Issue on CSS Alabama*. Brentwood, Tenn.: Southern Heritage Press, 1989.

Milton, David H. *Lincoln's Spymaster: Thomas Haines Dudley and the Liverpool Network*. Mechanicsburg, Pa.: Stackpole Books, 2003.

Mitford, Nancy, ed. *The Stanleys of Alderley*. London: Chapman and Hall, 1939. Reprint, London: Hamish Hamilton, 1968.

Monaghan, Jay. *Abraham Lincoln Deals with Foreign Affairs: A Diplomat in Carpet Slippers*. Introduction by Howard Jones. Lincoln: University of Nebraska Press, 1997. (Originally published as *Diplomat in Carpet Slippers: Abraham Lincoln Deals with Foreign Affairs*. Indianapolis: Bobbs-Merrill, 1945.)

Morley, John. *The Life of William Ewart Gladstone*. 3 vols. London: Macmillan, 1903.

Murfin, James V. *The Gleam of Bayonets: The Battle of Antietam and the Maryland Campaign of 1862*. New York: Thomas Yoseloff, 1965.

Myers, Phillip E. *Caution and Cooperation: The American Civil War in British-American Relations*. Kent, Ohio: Kent State University Press, 2008.

Nevins, Allan. *War Becomes Revolution*. Vol. 2 of *The War for the Union*. New York: Scribner, 1960.

Newton, Lord. *Lord Lyons: A Record of British Diplomacy*. 2 vols. London: Edward Arnold, 1913.

Niven, John. *Gideon Welles: Lincoln's Secretary of the Navy*. New York: Oxford University Press, 1973.

Oates, Stephen B. *With Malice toward None: The Life of Abraham Lincoln*. New York: Harper and Row, 1977.

Owsley, Frank L. *King Cotton Diplomacy: Foreign Relations of the Confederate States of America*. Rev. by Harriet C. Owsley. Chicago: University of Chicago Press, 1959. Reprint with new introduction by Howard Jones. Tuscaloosa: University of Alabama Press, 2009.

Owsley, Frank L., Jr. *The C.S.S. Florida: Her Building and Operations*. Philadelphia: University of Pennsylvania Press, 1965. Reprint, University of Alabama Press, 1987.

Paludan, Phillip S. *"A People's Contest": The Union and Civil War, 1861–1865*. Lawrence: University Press of Kansas, 1988. 2nd ed., 1996.

———. *The Presidency of Abraham Lincoln*. Lawrence: University Press of Kansas, 1994.

Parish, Peter J. *The American Civil War*. New York: Holmes and Meier, 1975.

Perkins, Dexter. *The Monroe Doctrine, 1826–1867*. Baltimore: Johns Hopkins Press, 1933.

Prest, John M. *Lord John Russell*. London: Macmillan, 1972.

Rable, George C. *Fredericksburg! Fredericksburg!* Chapel Hill: University of North Carolina Press, 2002.

Randall, James G. *Constitutional Problems under Lincoln*. Rev. ed. Urbana: University of Illinois Press, 1951.

———. *Lincoln the President*. 4 vols. New York: Dodd, Mead, 1945–55.

Randall, James G., and David H. Donald. *The Civil War and Reconstruction*. 2nd ed. Lexington, Mass.: D. C. Heath, 1969.

Rawley, James A. *Abraham Lincoln and a Nation Worth Fighting For*. Wheeling, Ill.: Harlan Davidson, 1996.

———. *Turning Points of the Civil War*. Lincoln: University of Nebraska Press, 1966.

Reid, T. Wemyss. *Life of the Right Honourable William Edward Forster*. 2 vols. London: Chapman and Hall, 1888.

Ridley, Jasper. *Lord Palmerston*. New York: E. P. Dutton, 1971.

———. *Maximilian and Juárez*. London: Constable and Co., 1993.

Robinson, Charles M. *Shark of the Confederacy: The Story of the CSS Alabama*. Annapolis, Md.: Naval Institute Press, 1995.

Rose, Anne C. *Victorian America and the Civil War*. New York: Cambridge University Press, 1992.

Saul, Norman E. *Distant Friends: The United States and Russia, 1763–1867*. Lawrence: University Press of Kansas, 1991.

Schantz, Mark S. *Awaiting the Heavenly Country: The Civil War and America's Culture of Death*. Ithaca, N.Y.: Cornell University Press, 2008.

Schoonover, Thomas D. *Dollars over Dominion: The Triumph of Liberalism in Mexican-United States Relations, 1861–1867*. Baton Rouge: Louisiana State University Press, 1978.

Sears, Louis M. *John Slidell*. Durham: Duke University Press, 1925.

Sears, Stephen W. *Landscape Turned Red: The Battle of Antietam*. New York: Ticknor and Fields, 1983.

———. *To the Gates of Richmond: The Peninsula Campaign*. New York: Ticknor and Fields, 1992.

Sexton, Jay. *Debtor Diplomacy: Finance and American Foreign Relations in the Civil War Era, 1837–1873*. Oxford, England: Clarendon Press, 2005.

Smith, Elbert B. *Francis Preston Blair*. New York: Free Press, 1980.

Smith, Goldwin. *The Treaty of Washington, 1871*. Ithaca, N.Y.: Cornell University Press, 1941.

Spencer, Warren F. *The Confederate Navy in Europe*. University, Ala.: University of Alabama Press, 1983.

Sprout, Harold, and Margaret Sprout. *The Rise of American Naval Power, 1776–1918*. Princeton: Princeton University Press, 1946.

Stevens, Kenneth R. *Border Diplomacy: The Caroline and McLeod Affairs in Anglo-American Relations, 1837–1842*. Tuscaloosa: University of Alabama Press, 1989.

Still, William N., Jr. *Confederate Shipbuilding*. Athens: University of Georgia Press, 1969.

Striner, Richard. *Father Abraham: Lincoln's Relentless Struggle to End Slavery*. New York: Oxford University Press, 2006.

Summersell, Charles G. *CSS Alabama: Builder, Captain, and Plans*. University, Ala.: University of Alabama Press, 1985.

Taylor, John M. *Confederate Raider: Raphael Semmes of the Alabama*. Washington, D.C.: Brassey's, 1994.

Thomas, Benjamin P. *Abraham Lincoln: A Biography*. New York: Alfred A. Knopf, 1952.
———. *Russo-American Relations, 1815–1867*. Baltimore, Md.: Johns Hopkins Press, 1930.

Thomas, Benjamin P., and Harold M. Hyman. *Stanton: The Life and Times of Lincoln's Secretary of War*. New York: Alfred A. Knopf, 1962.

Thomas, Emory M. *The Confederate Nation, 1861–1865*. New York: Harper and Row, 1979.

Thompson, Samuel B. *Confederate Purchasing Operations Abroad*. Chapel Hill: University of North Carolina Press, 1935.

Tilby, A. Wyatt. *Lord John Russell: A Study in Civil and Religious Liberty*. London: Cassell, 1930.

Todd, Richard C. *Confederate Finance*. Athens: University of Georgia Press, 1954.

Trevelyan, George M. *The Life of John Bright*. Boston: Houghton Mifflin, 1913.

Tucker, Spenser C. *Blue and Gray Navies: The Civil War Afloat*. Annapolis, Md.: Naval Institute Press, 2006.

Tyrner-Tyrnauer, A. R. *Lincoln and the Emperors*. New York: Harcourt, Brace, and World, 1962.

Vanauken, Sheldon. *The Glittering Illusion: English Sympathy for the Southern Confederacy*. Worthing, England: Churchman, 1988.

Van Deusen, Glyndon G. *William Henry Seward*. New York: Oxford University Press, 1967.

Varon, Elizabeth R. *Disunion: The Coming of the American Civil War, 1789–1859*. Chapel Hill: University of North Carolina Press, 2008.

Walpole, Spencer. *The Life of Lord John Russell*. 2 vols. London: Longmans, Green, 1889.

Walther, Eric H. *William Lowndes Yancey and the Coming of the Civil War*. Chapel Hill: University of North Carolina Press, 2006.

Warren, Gordon H. *Fountain of Discontent: The Trent Affair and Freedom of the Seas*. Boston: Northeastern University Press, 1981.

Wells, Tom H. *The Confederate Navy: A Study in Organization.* University, Ala.:
University of Alabama Press, 1971.

West, Richard S., Jr. *Gideon Welles: Lincoln's Navy Department.* Indianapolis: Bobbs-
Merrill, 1943.

West, W. Reed. *Contemporary French Opinion on the American Civil War.* Baltimore:
Johns Hopkins Press, 1924.

Wills, Garry. *Lincoln at Gettysburg: The Words That Remade America.* New York:
Simon and Schuster, 1992.

Willson, Beckles. *John Slidell and the Confederates in Paris (1862–65).* New York:
Minton, Balch, 1932.

Winks, Robin W. *Canada and the United States: The Civil War Years.* Baltimore: Johns
Hopkins Press, 1960.

Wise, Stephen R. *Lifeline of the Confederacy: Blockade Running during the Civil War.*
Columbia: University of South Carolina Press, 1988.

Woldman, Albert A. *Lincoln and the Russians.* Cleveland: World, 1952.

Woodham-Smith, Cecil. *Queen Victoria: From Her Birth to the Death of the Prince
Consort.* New York: Alfred A. Knopf, 1972.

Woodman, Harold D. *King Cotton and His Retainers: Financing and Marketing the
Cotton Crop of the South, 1800–1925.* Lexington: University of Kentucky Press, 1968.

Young, Robert W. *Senator James Murray Mason: Defender of the Old South.* Knoxville:
University of Tennessee Press, 1998.

Articles, Essays, Papers

A. M. G. "The Pride of Mr. Laird." *Blackwood's Edinburgh Magazine* 294 (1963): 213–23.

Adamov, E. A. "Russia and the United States at the Time of the Civil War." *Journal of
Modern History* 2 (December 1930): 586–602.

Adams, Brooks. "The Seizure of the Laird Rams." *Massachusetts Historical Society
Proceedings* 45 (1911–12): 243–333.

———. "The British Proclamation of May, 1861." *Massachusetts Historical Society
Proceedings* 48 (1915): 190–241.

———. "The Crisis of Foreign Intervention in the War of Secession, 1862." Paper for
Massachusetts Historical Society (April 1914): 2–54.

———. "The Crisis of Foreign Intervention in the War of Secession, September–
November 1862." *Massachusetts Historical Society Proceedings* 47 (1914): 372–424.

———. "The Negotiations of 1861 Relating to the Declaration of Paris of 1856."
Massachusetts Historical Society Proceedings 46 (1912): 23–84.

———. "The *Trent* Affair." *American Historical Review* 17 (April 1912): 540–62.

———. "The *Trent* Affair." *Massachusetts Historical Society Proceedings* 45 (November
1911): 35–148.

Adams, Henry. "Why Did Not England Recognize the Confederacy?" *Massachusetts
Historical Society Proceedings* 66 (1942): 204–22.

Anderson, Stuart. "1861: Blockade vs. Closing the Confederate Ports." *Military Affairs*
41 (December 1977): 190–94.

Barker, Nancy N. "France, Austria, and the Mexican Venture, 1861–1864." *French
Historical Studies* 3 (Fall 1963): 224–45.

———. "The French Legation in Mexico: Nexus of Interventionists." *French Historical Studies* 8 (Spring 1974): 409–26.

———. "Monarchy in Mexico: Harebrained Scheme or Well-considered Prospect?" *Journal of Modern History* 48 (March 1976): 51–68.

Bauer, Craig A. "The Last Effort: The Secret Mission of the Confederate Diplomat, Duncan F. Kenner." *Louisiana History* 22 (Winter 1981): 67–95.

Baxter, James P. "The British Government and Neutral Rights, 1861–1865." *American Historical Review* 34 (October 1928): 9–29.

———. "Some British Opinions as to Neutral Rights, 1861–1865." *American Journal of International Law* 23 (July 1929): 517–37.

Bellows, Donald. "A Study of British Conservative Reaction to the American Civil War." *Journal of Southern History* 51 (1985): 505–26.

Beloff, Max. "Historical Revision No. CXVIII: Great Britain and the American Civil War." *History* 37 (February 1952): 40–48.

Bernath, Stuart L. "British Neutrality and the Civil War Prize Cases." *Civil War History* 15 (December 1969): 320–31.

———. "Squall across the Atlantic: The *Peterhoff* Episode." *Journal of Southern History* 34 (August 1968): 382–401.

Berwanger, Eugene H. "Union and Confederate Reaction to French Threats against Texas." *Journal of Confederate History* 7 (1991): 97–111.

Blackett, R. J. M. "Pressures from Without: African Americans, British Public Opinion, and Civil War Diplomacy." In *The Union, the Confederacy, and the Atlantic Rim*, edited by Robert E. May, 69–100. West Lafayette, Ind.: Purdue University Press, 1995.

Blair, William A. "The Seven Days and the Radical Persuasion: Convincing Moderates in the North of the Need for a Hard War." In *The Richmond Campaign of 1862: The Peninsula and the Seven Days*, edited by Gary W. Gallagher, 153–80. Chapel Hill: University of North Carolina Press, 2000.

Blaug, Mark. "The Productivity of Capital in the Lancashire Cotton Industry during the Nineteenth Century." *Economic History Review*, 2nd series, 13 (1961): 358–81.

Blumenthal, Henry. "Confederate Diplomacy: Popular Notions and International Realities." *Journal of Southern History* 32 (May 1966): 151–71.

Bonham, Milledge L., Jr. "The French Consuls in the Confederate States." In *Studies in Southern History and Politics: Inscribed to William Archibald Dunning, PH.D., LL.D., Lieber Professor of History and Political Philosophy in Columbia University, by His Former Pupils, the Authors*, 83–104. New York: Columbia University Press, 1914.

Booth, Alan R. "Alabama at the Cape, 1863." *American Neptune* 26 (April 1966): 96–108.

Bourne, Kenneth. "British Preparations for War with the North, 1861–1862." *English Historical Review* 76 (October 1961): 600–632.

Brady, Eugene A. "A Reconsideration of the Lancashire 'Cotton Famine.'" *Agricultural History* 37 (July 1963): 156–62.

Brauer, Kinley J. "British Mediation and the American Civil War: A Reconsideration." *Journal of Southern History* 38 (February 1972): 49–64.

———. "Seward's 'Foreign War Panacea': An Interpretation." *New York History* 55 (April 1974): 133–57.

————. "The Slavery Problem in the Diplomacy of the American Civil War." *Pacific Historical Review* 46 (August 1977): 439–69.

Broadbridge, Stanley. "The Lancashire Cotton 'Famine,' 1861–1865." In *The Luddites, and Other Essays*, edited by Lionel M. Munby, 143–60. London: Michael Katanka, Ltd., 1971.

Brook, Michael. "Confederate Sympathies in North-East Lancashire, 1862–1864." *Lancashire and Cheshire Antiquarian Society* 75–76 (1977): 211–17.

Callahan, James M. "Diplomatic Relations of the Confederate States with England, 1861–1865." In *The Annual Report of the American Historical Association for the Year 1898*, 267–83. Washington, D.C.: Government Printing Office, 1899.

Carpenter, John A. "The New York International Relief Committee: A Chapter in the Diplomatic History of the Civil War." *New-York Historical Society Quarterly* 56 (July 1972): 239–52.

Claussen, Martin P. "Peace Factors in Anglo-American Relations, 1861–1865." *Mississippi Valley Historical Review* 26 (March 1940): 511–22.

Coddington, Edwin B. "The Civil War Blockade Reconsidered." In *Essays in History and International Relations, in Honor of George Hubbard Blakeslee*, edited by Dwight H. Lee and George E. McReynolds, 284–305. Worcester, Mass.: Clark University Press, 1949.

Cohen, Victor H. "Charles Sumner and the *Trent* Affair." *Journal of Southern History* 22 (May 1956): 205–19.

Coletta, Paolo E. "Recognition Policy." In *Encyclopedia of American Foreign Policy: Studies of the Principal Movements and Ideas*, 3:882–92. 3 vols. New York: Scribner, 1978.

Cortada, James W. "Florida's Relations with Cuba during the Civil War." *Florida Historical Quarterly* 59 (July 1980): 42–52.

Crawford, Martin. "William Howard Russell and the Confederacy." *Journal of American Studies* 15 (August 1981): 191–210.

Crook, Carland E. "Benjamin Théron and the French Designs in Texas during the Civil War." *Southwestern Historical Quarterly* 68 (April 1965): 432–54.

Crook, David P. "Portents of War: English Opinion on Secession." *Journal of American Studies* 4 (February 1971): 163–79.

DeConde, Alexander, ed. *Encyclopedia of American Foreign Policy: Studies of the Principal Movements and Ideas.* 3 vols. New York: Scribner, 1978.

Earle, Edward M. "Egyptian Cotton and the American Civil War." *Political Science Quarterly* 41 (December 1926): 520–45.

Ellsworth, Edward W. "Anglo-American Affairs in October of 1862." *Lincoln Herald* 66 (Summer 1964): 89–96.

Fehrenbacher, Don E. "Only His Stepchildren: Lincoln and the Negro." *Civil War History* 20 (December 1974): 293–310.

Ferris, Norman B. "Diplomacy." In *Civil War Books: A Critical Bibliography*, edited by Allan Nevins, James I. Robertson Jr., and Bell I. Wiley, 1:241–78. 2 vols. Baton Rouge: Louisiana State University Press, 1967. Reprint, Wilmington, N.C.: Broadfoot Publishing Co., 1996.

———. "The Prince Consort, *The Times*, and the *Trent* Affair." *Civil War History* 6 (June 1960): 152–56.

———. "Transatlantic Misunderstanding: William Henry Seward and the Declaration of Paris Negotiation, 1861." In *Rank and File: Civil War Essays in Honor of Bell Irvin Wiley*, edited by James I. Robertson Jr. and Richard M. McMurry, 55–78. San Rafael, Calif.: Presidio Press, 1976.

———. "William H. Seward and the Faith of a Nation." In *Traditions and Values: American Diplomacy, 1790–1865*, edited by Norman A. Graebner, 153–77. Lanham, Md.: University Press of America, 1985.

Fredrickson, George M. "A Man but Not a Brother: Abraham Lincoln and Racial Equality." *Journal of Southern History* 41 (February 1975): 39–58.

Gallagher, Gary W. "A Civil War Watershed: The Richmond Campaign in Perspective." In *The Richmond Campaign of 1862: The Peninsula and the Seven Days*, edited by Gary W. Gallagher, 3–27. Chapel Hill: University of North Carolina Press, 2000.

Gavronsky, Serge. "American Slavery and the French Liberals: An Interpretation of the Role of Slavery in French Politics during the Second Empire." *Journal of Negro History* 51 (January 1966): 36–52.

Gentry, Judith F. "A Confederate Success in Europe: The Erlanger Loan." *Journal of Southern History* 36 (May 1970): 157–88.

Ginzberg, Eli. "The Economics of British Neutrality during the American Civil War." *Agricultural History* 10 (October 1936): 147–56.

Golder, Frank A. "The American Civil War through the Eyes of a Russian Diplomat." *American Historical Review* 26 (April 1921): 454–63.

———. "The Russian Fleet and the Civil War." *American Historical Review* 20 (July 1915): 801–12.

Graebner, Norman A. "European Interventionism and the Crisis of 1862." *Journal of the Illinois State Historical Society* 69 (February 1976): 35–45.

———. "Northern Diplomacy and European Neutrality." In *Why the North Won the Civil War*, edited by David Donald, 55–78. New York: Collier, 1962. (Reprint of original published in 1960.)

Greenleaf, Richard. "British Labor against American Slavery." *Science and Society* 17 (Winter 1953): 42–58.

Gwin, Stanford P. "Slavery and English Polarity: The Persuasive Campaign of John Bright against English Recognition of the Confederate States of America." *Southern Speech Communication Journal* 49 (Summer 1984): 406–19.

Hanna, Kathryn A. "Incidents of the Confederate Blockade." *Journal of Southern History* 11 (May 1945): 214–29.

———. "The Roles of the South in the French Intervention in Mexico." *Journal of Southern History* 20 (February 1954): 3–21.

Harrison, Lowell H. "The CSS *Shenandoah*." *Civil War Times Illustrated* 15 (1976): 4–9, 44–47.

Harrison, Royden. "British Labor and American Slavery." *Science and Society* 25 (December 1961): 291–319.

———. "British Labour and the Confederacy: A Note on the Southern Sympathies of Some British Working Class Journals and Leaders during the American Civil War." *International Review of Social History* 2 (1957): 78–105.

Heckman, Richard A. "British Press Reaction to the Emancipation Proclamation." *Lincoln Herald* 71 (Winter 1969): 150–53.

Henderson, Conway W. "The Anglo-American Treaty of 1862 in Civil War Diplomacy." *Civil War History* 15 (December 1969): 308–19.

Hernon, Joseph M., Jr. "British Sympathies in the American Civil War: A Reconsideration." *Journal of Southern History* 33 (August 1967): 356–67.

Higham, Robin. "The Russian Fleet on the Eastern Seaboard, 1863–1864: A Maritime Chronology." *American Neptune* 20 (January 1960): 49–61.

Hoslett, Schuyler Dean. "Southern Expectations of British Intervention in the Civil War." *Tylers Quarterly Historical and Genealogical Magazine* 22 (January 1941): 76–82.

Jarvis, Rupert C. "The *Alabama* and the Law." *Transactions of the Historical Society of Lancashire and Cheshire* 111 (1959): 181–98.

Jenkins, Brian. "Frank Lawley and the Confederacy." *Civil War History* 23 (June 1977): 144–60.

———. "William Gregory: Champion of the Confederacy." *History Today* 28 (May 1978): 322–30.

Jentleson, Bruce W., and Thomas G. Paterson, eds. *Encyclopedia of U.S. Foreign Relations.* 4 vols. New York: Oxford University Press, 1997.

Johnson, Ludwell H. "Lincoln's Solution to the Problem of Peace Terms, 1864–1865." *Journal of Southern History* 34 (November 1968): 576–86.

Johnson, Robert E. "Investment by Sea: The Civil War Blockade." *American Neptune* 32 (January 1972): 45–57.

Jones, Howard. "History and Mythology: The Crisis over British Intervention in the Civil War." In *The Union, the Confederacy, and the Atlantic Rim*, edited by Robert E. May, 29–67. West Lafayette, Ind.: Purdue University Press, 1995.

———. "To Preserve a Nation: Abraham Lincoln and Franklin D. Roosevelt as Wartime Diplomatists." In *War Comes Again: Comparative Vistas on the Civil War and World War II*, edited by Gabor Boritt, 167–95. New York: Oxford University Press, 1995.

———. "Toward a More Perfect Union: Lincoln and the Death of Slavery." In *Presidents, Diplomats, and Other Mortals: Essays Honoring Robert H. Ferrell*, edited by J. Garry Clifford and Theodore A. Wilson, 15–28. Columbia: University of Missouri Press, 2007.

Jones, Robert H. "Anglo-American Relations, 1861–1865, Reconsidered." *Mid-America* 45 (January 1963): 36–49.

———. "Long Live the King?" *Agricultural History* 37 (July 1963): 166–69.

Jones, Wilbur D. "The British Conservatives and the American Civil War." *American Historical Review* 58 (April 1953): 527–43.

Kennett, Lee. "The Strange Career of the '*Stonewall*.'" *United States Naval Institute Proceedings* 94 (February 1968): 74–85.

Khasigian, Amos. "Economic Factors and British Neutrality, 1861–1865." *Historian* 25 (August 1963): 451–65.

Krein, David F. "Russell's Decision to Detain the Laird Rams." *Civil War History* 22 (June 1976): 158–63.

Kushner, Howard I. "The Russian Fleet and the American Civil War: Another View." *Historian* 34 (August 1972): 633–49.

Kutolowski, John. "The Effect of the Polish Insurrection of 1863 on American Civil War Diplomacy." *Historian* 27 (August 1965): 560–77.

Laas, Virginia J. "'Sleepless Sentinels': The North Atlantic Blockading Squadron, 1862–1864." *Civil War History* 31 (March 1985): 24–38.

Landry, Harral L. "Slavery and the Slave Trade in Atlantic Diplomacy, 1850–1861." *Journal of Southern History* 27 (May 1961): 184–207.

Leary, William M., Jr. "The *Alabama* vs. the *Kearsarge*: A Diplomatic View." *American Neptune* 29 (August 1969): 167–73.

Lebergott, Stanley. "Through the Blockade: The Profitability and Extent of Cotton Smuggling, 1861–1865." *Journal of Economic History* 41 (December 1981): 867–88.

———. "Why the South Lost: Commercial Purpose in the Confederacy, 1861–1865." *Journal of American History* 70 (June 1983): 58–74.

Lester, Richard I. "An Aspect of Confederate Finance during the American Civil War: The Erlanger Loan and the Plan of 1864." *Business History* 16 (July 1974): 130–44.

Logan, Frenise A. "Activities of the *Alabama* in Asian Waters." *Pacific Historical Review* 31 (May 1962): 143–50.

———. "India—Britain's Substitute for American Cotton, 1861–1865." *Journal of Southern History* 24 (November 1958): 472–80.

Logan, Kevin J. "The *Bee-Hive* Newspaper and British Working Class Attitudes toward the American Civil War." *Civil War History* 22 (December 1976): 337–48.

Long, John S. "Glory-Hunting off Havana: Wilkes and the *Trent* Affair." *Civil War History* 9 (June 1963): 133–44.

Lorimer, Douglas A. "The Role of Anti-Slavery Sentiment in English Reactions to the American Civil War." *Historical Journal* 19 (June 1976): 405–20.

Lutz, Ralph Haswell. "Rudolph Schleiden and the Visit to Richmond, April 25, 1861." *Annual Report of the American Historical Association for 1915*. Washington, D.C.: Government Printing Office, 1890.

MacChesney, Brunson. "The *Alabama* and the Queen's Advocate—A Mystery of History." *Northwestern University Law Review* 62 (September–October 1967): 568–85.

Maynard, Douglas H. "The Escape of the *Florida*." *Pennsylvania Magazine of History and Biography* 77 (April 1953): 181–97

———. "Plotting the Escape of the *Alabama*." *Journal of Southern History* 20 (May 1954): 197–209.

———. "Union Efforts to Prevent the Escape of the *Alabama*." *Mississippi Valley Historical Review* 41 (June 1954): 41–60.

McConnell, Roland C. "From Preliminary to Final Emancipation Proclamation: The First Hundred Days." *Journal of Negro History* 48 (October 1963): 260–76.

McPherson, James M. "'The Whole Family of Man': Lincoln and the Last Best Hope Abroad." In *The Union, the Confederacy, and the Atlantic Rim*, edited by Robert E. May, 131–58. West Lafayette, Ind.: Purdue University Press, 1995.

Meade, Robert D. "The Relations between Judah P. Benjamin and Jefferson Davis:

Some New Light on the Working of the Confederate Machine." *Journal of Southern History* 5 (November 1939): 468–78.

Merli, Frank J. "The American War with Blockades: Reflections on the Union Blockade of the South." Paper delivered before Tenth Naval History Symposium, U.S. Naval Academy, Annapolis, Md., September 1991.

———. "The Confederate Navy, 1861–1865." In *Peace and War: Interpretations of American Naval History, 1775–1978*, edited by Kenneth J. Hagan, 126–44. Westport, Conn.: Greenwood, 1978.

———. "Crown versus Cruiser: The Curious Case of the *Alexandra*." *Civil War History* 9 (June 1963): 167–77.

Merli, Frank J., and Theodore A. Wilson. "The British Cabinet and the Confederacy." *Maryland Historical Magazine* 65 (Fall 1970): 239–62.

Milne, A. Taylor. "The Lyons-Seward Treaty of 1862." *American Historical Review* 38 (April 1933): 511–25.

Morgan, James M. "The Confederate Cruiser *Florida*." *United States Naval Institute Proceedings* 42 (September–October 1916).

Nagengast, William E. "The Visit of the Russian Fleet to the United States: Were Americans Deceived?" *Russian Review* 8 (January 1949): 46–55.

Neely, Mark E., Jr. "The Perils of Running the Blockade: The Influence of International Law in an Era of Total War." *Civil War History* 32 (June 1986): 101–18.

Oates, Stephen B. "Henry Hotze: Confederate Agent Abroad." *Historian* 27 (February 1965): 131–54.

———. "'The Man of Our Redemption': Abraham Lincoln and the Emancipation of the Slaves," *Presidential Studies Quarterly* 9 (Winter 1979): 15–25.

O'Rourke, Alice. "The Law Officers of the Crown and the *Trent* Affair." *Mid-America* 54 (July 1972): 157–71.

Orzell, Laurence J. "A 'Favorable Interval': The Polish Insurrection in Civil War Diplomacy, 1863." *Civil War History* 24 (December 1978): 332–50.

Owsley, Frank L. "Ambrose Dudley Mann." *Dictionary of American Biography*, 12:239–40.

Park, Joseph H. "The English Workingmen and the American Civil War." *Political Science Quarterly* 39 (September 1924): 432–57.

Pomeroy, Earl S. "French Substitutes for American Cotton, 1861–1865." *Journal of Southern History* 9 (November 1943): 555–60.

———. "The Myth after the Russian Fleet, 1863." *New York History* 31 (April 1950): 169–76.

Potter, J. "Atlantic Economy, 1815–1860: The U.S.A. and the Industrial Revolution in Britain." In *Essays in American Economic History*, edited by A. W. Coats and Ross M. Robertson, 14–48. New York: Barnes and Noble, 1969.

Rakestraw, Donald A. "Foreign Relations: The Civil War." In *Encyclopedia of the United States in the Nineteenth Century*, edited by Paul Finkelman, 1:508–12. 3 vols. New York: Scribner, 2001.

Roberts, William P. "James Dunwoody Bulloch and the Confederate Navy." *North Carolina Historical Review* 24 (1947): 315–66.

Scherer, Paul H. "Partner or Puppet? Lord John Russell at the Foreign Office, 1859–1862." *Albion* 19 (Fall 1987): 347–71.

Schmidt, Louis B. "The Influence of Wheat and Cotton on Anglo-American Relations during the Civil War." *Iowa Journal of History and Politics* 16 (July 1918): 400–439.

Schoonover, Thomas. "Napoleon Is Coming! Maximilian Is Coming? The International History of the Civil War in the Caribbean Basin." In *The Union, the Confederacy, and the Atlantic Rim*, edited by Robert E. May, 101–30. West Lafayette, Ind.: Purdue University Press, 1995.

Sears, Louis M. "A Confederate Diplomat at the Court of Napoleon III." *American Historical Review* 26 (January 1921): 255–81.

Smith, Geoffrey S. "Charles Wilkes and the Growth of American Naval Diplomacy." In *Makers of American Diplomacy*, edited by Frank J. Merli and Theodore A. Wilson, 1:135–63. 2 vols. New York: Scribner, 1974.

Sowle, Patrick. "A Reappraisal of Seward's Memorandum of April 1, 1861, to Lincoln." *Journal of Southern History* 33 (May 1967): 234–39.

Spencer, Warren F. "The Jewett-Greeley Affair: A Private Scheme for French Mediation in the American Civil War." *New York History* 51 (April 1970): 238–68.

St. Clair, Sadie D. "Slavery as a Diplomatic Factor in Anglo-American Relations during the Civil War." *Journal of Negro History* 30 (July 1945): 260–75.

Strong, Edwin, Thomas H. Buckley, and Annetta St. Clair. "The Odyssey of the CSS *Stonewall.*" *Civil War History* 30 (December 1984): 306–23.

Warren, Gordon H. "The King Cotton Theory." In *Encyclopedia of American Foreign Policy: Studies of the Principal Movements and Ideas*, edited by Alexander DeConde, 2:515–20. 3 vols. New York: Scribner, 1978.

Whitridge, Arnold. "The *Alabama*, 1862–1864: A Crisis in Anglo-American Relations." *History Today* 5 (March 1955): 174–75.

———."British Liberals and the American Civil War." *History Today* 12 (October 1962): 688–95.

Wright, D. G. "Bradford and the American Civil War." *Journal of British Studies* 8 (May 1969): 69–85.

Zorn, Roman J. "John Bright and the British Attitude to the American Civil War." *Mid-America* 38 (July 1956): 131–45.

Dissertations, Theses, and Unpublished Manuscripts

Gallas, Stanley. "Lord Lyons and the Civil War, 1859–1864: A British Perspective." Ph.D. dissertation, University of Illinois at Chicago Circle, 1982.

Vanauken, Sheldon. "English Sympathy for the South: The Glittering Illusion." B.Litt. thesis, Oxford University, 1957.

Walker, Tillie. "The Confederate Steamer *Alabama.*" M.A. thesis, University of Alabama, 1938.

Wilkinson, Martha Allan. "The Public Career of James Dunwoody Bulloch." M.A. thesis, University of Alabama, 1940.

Index

Adams, Charles Francis, 30, 215, 351–52
(n. 54); Antietam and, 224, 228; battlefield
victories and, 115, 143, 144, 152, 154; British
neutrality and, 44, 49–50, 51, 53, 70, 145,
245, 274, 333 (n. 2); British shipbuilding
for Confederate navy and, 125, 191–94,
195, 196, 199–200; Bull Run, First, and,
64, 162; Bull Run, Second, and, 211; Civil
War intervention by French and, 273–74,
275; Civil War mediation consideration
by British and, 146, 147–49, 150–51, 162,
173, 201–2, 203, 204, 206; Confederate
diplomatic commission to Europe and,
37, 38, 50, 53; cotton embargo by Confederacy and, 120; emancipation and, 121,
122, 125, 162, 280; European intervention
in Mexico and, 75, 127; recognition of
Confederacy as belligerent and, 44, 50,
70, 132, 145; recognition of Confederacy
by British and, 37, 39, 50, 52–53, 64, 66,
118–19, 120, 163, 170, 173, 237, 240; slavery
and, 60, 146, 173; *Trent* affair and, 94,
102–3, 106–7, 111; Union blockade and, 53,
58, 103, 126; as Union diplomat to Great
Britain, 31, 32, 80, 330 (n. 43); war possibility during *Trent* affair and, 94, 102–3;
war possibility with European intervention in Civil War and, 58, 59, 60, 200, 201
Adams, Charles Francis, Jr., 44, 86, 87, 102
Adams, Henry, 94, 102, 109, 298; battlefield
victories and, 149, 161, 171, 173; British

lack of support for Union and, 80, 170;
cotton and, 103, 208; recognition of
Confederacy and, 118, 300; slavery and,
60, 211
Adams, John, 31
Adams, John Quincy, 6, 31
Alabama, CSS, 69, 196, 198–99, 200–201,
290, 353 (n. 24), 354 (n. 40), 355 (n. 49).
See also *Enrica*; "No. 290"
Albert, Prince, 98, 109
Alexander (tsar), 100, 205, 293
Alexandra (warship), 290
American Colonization Society, 161
American Revolution, 28, 55, 282
American Union, The (Spence), 202, 292
Andrew, John, 93
Antietam, 220, 226, 229, 251; aftermath,
220–21, 230, 264; British reaction to,
221–25, 239, 249, 358 (n. 15), 360–61
(n. 42); Civil War mediation consider-
ation by British after, 225, 228, 233, 234,
235, 239–41, 247, 249, 282, 358 (n. 17)
Anti-Slavery Society, 125
Appomattox, 319, 373 (n. 80)
Argyll, Duke of, 202, 224; Civil War media-
tion and, 204, 210–11, 225, 236, 238; cotton
and, 207–8, 210; emancipation and, 33,
207, 241–42, 279; slavery and, 36, 210, 251,
283; *Trent* affair and, 95, 107
Army of the Cumberland, 281
Army of the Potomac, 61, 264

Atherton, William, 194, 197, 198
Atlanta, 317, 319
Austin, John, 268, 365–66 (n. 36)
Austria, 332 (n. 76), 365–66 (n. 36); Civil
War mediation and, 191, 203, 217, 247, 248,
265, 269; Mexico and, 76, 77–78, 126, 129,
287, 294, 310, 311, 312; war with France,
259–60, 364 (n. 17)

Bagehot, Walter, 32, 170
Bahama (steamer), 198
Baja California, 76, 310
Banks, Nathaniel, 311
Baring Brothers, 292
Baroche, Jules, 131
Bates, Edward, 30, 184, 211
Bazaine, Achille François, 311
Bee-Hive, 99, 232
Belgium, 11, 101, 133, 162, 236, 255–56, 265.
   See also Leopold
Belmont, August, 61–62, 185
Benjamin, Judah P., 19, 93, 208, 342–43
   (n. 5); Antietam and, 221; Confederate
   secretary of state appointment, 115–17, 343
   (n. 6); emancipation and, 177, 318; Euro-
   pean financial loans and, 292; European
   intervention in Civil War and, 141–42,
   153, 177, 258, 260–61, 364 (n. 11); Napoleon
   III and, 256, 294, 314, 316; recognition
   of Confederacy and, 145, 175, 221, 318;
   358 (n. 14); recognition of Confederacy
   by British and, 126, 170, 261, 365 (n. 34);
   Union blockade and, 152–53, 260, 261,
   295, 348–49 (n. 18)
Bennett, James G., 288, 289
Bermuda (Confederate ship), 68
Bigelow, John, 200
Birkenhead Ironworks, 193
Blackwood's Edinburgh Magazine, 232
Blair, Francis P., 317
Blair, Montgomery, 184, 317
Bonaparte, Prince Napoleon Jerome.
   See Napoleon, Prince
Border States, 16, 28, 39, 155, 167, 176, 243,
   250; emancipation and, 121–22, 123, 161,
   182, 185, 203, 230, 231, 232, 240, 278
Boston Courier, 103

Brady, Mathew, 3, 220
Bright, John, 32, 96, 105, 167, 210, 300; Civil
War intervention and, 204, 237; Civil War
neutrality and, 208; cotton and, 62, 103;
slavery and, 33, 251, 279, 283
British Foreign Enlistment Act of 1819, 40,
44, 52, 125, 192, 193, 194, 196, 197, 200,
290–91
British recognition of Confederacy, 29, 34,
125–26, 165, 326 (n. 2), 366 (n. 37); battlefield victories and, 6, 115, 117, 216–17, 285;
as belligerent, 43, 44–45, 47–50, 51, 58, 61,
69, 70, 93, 114, 145, 150, 154, 155, 284, 311;
Bull Run, First, and, 62, 63, 64, 84; Civil
War armistice proposal and, 248–49, 257,
261–62, 272, 273–74, 276; Civil War intervention and, 4–5, 50, 253–54; Civil War
mediation and, 3, 189–91, 201–2, 205–6,
209–12, 216, 217, 218–19, 221, 233–34,
235–36, 246, 247, 323; cotton and, 162, 295;
cotton embargo threat to force, 14, 17–19;
cotton unofficial embargo to force, 49,
119–20, 130, 157, 173, 183; De Leon meeting
with Palmerston and, 152–60, 178, 319,
349 (n. 19); emancipation and, 121, 122,
223, 318, 319, 373–74 (n. 88); end of hopes
for, 307, 321–22; with France, 131, 134–35,
136–37, 167, 175, 248, 250–51, 265–67,
295–97, 298–99, 300–301, 302–3, 304,
305–6; Gladstone's speech for, 236–39,
240, 241, 244, 249, 257, 270, 361 (nn. 45,
51); international law and, 5–6, 248,
267–70, 365 (n. 34), 365–66 (n. 36); "King
Cotton Diplomacy" and, 2–3, 11–12, 13,
14, 20, 31–32, 48–49, 307, 322; motion in
Parliament by Gregory for, 31, 32, 36, 53,
118; motion in Parliament by Lindsay
for, 148–50, 155, 159, 162–63, 164, 167, 168,
169, 170–74, 181; motion in Parliament
by Roebuck for, 295, 296, 300–302; Mure
papers and, 65–68; Russell refusal to
guarantee against, to Union, 35–36, 39;
slave rebellions and race war and, 120–21,
122; *Trent* affair and, 93, 94, 103, 109–10,
111; Union blockade and, 25, 27, 39, 57,
83, 99, 104, 225–26, 243, 265–66; Union
dread of, 21, 24, 37, 42, 108, 212

255–56, 259, 273, 276–77, 291, 295–96, 297, 299, 307, 308–16; Napoleon III and, 165–66, 255–56, 277, 285, 290, 291, 292, 294–97, 306–16, 318, 369–70 (n. 22); navy of, 38, 44, 52, 63, 125, 191–201, 355 (n. 49); peace talks and, 316–18; playing down issue of slavery, 3, 14–15, 63, 120, 124, 134, 160, 283; as Republic started anew, 1–2, 7, 9–10, 28, 47–48, 187–88, 282; slavery and, 10, 38, 39, 60, 80–81, 84–85, 142, 155, 166, 176, 186–88, 276–77, 279, 318, 358 (n. 14); *Trent* affair and, 83, 88–89, 93, 94, 99, 100, 102, 103, 104, 106, 108–9, 110, 111, 152, 159, 338 (nn. 10–11); Union blockade and, 41, 43, 44, 100, 115, 119–20, 130–31, 141, 142, 152–53, 155, 161, 260–61, 265–66, 295, 304, 331 (n. 69), 343 (n. 10), 347 (n. 69); Western Theater defeats, 115, 117, 139, 143, 151–52, 153, 188–89, 219, 281, 303, 346–47 (n. 66), 347 (n. 3). *See also* Benjamin, Judah P.; British recognition of Confederacy; Cotton; Davis, Jefferson; France; French recognition of Confederacy; Great Britain; Russia

Constitutionnel, 55, 170, 316

Corinth, Miss., 151, 152, 188

Corn Laws (Great Britain, 1846), 14

Cortes, Hernando, 58

Corwin, Thomas, 76

Cotton: British textile workers and support of Union and, 208–9, 227–28, 280, 322, 328 (n. 13), 348 (n. 13), 351 (n. 45), 356–57 (n. 65); Confederacy attempts to bribe France with, 152–53, 167, 292, 350 (n. 32); Confederacy destruction of, 143, 147, 161, 304; Confederacy official proposal to embargo, 14, 17–19; as Confederate basis for financial loans, 3, 14, 117, 292–93, 304, 322; Confederate unofficial embargo of, 49, 119–20, 130, 157, 173, 183; European economic distress from lack of, 137, 258, 266, 272–73, 287, 350 (nn. 28–29); from India, 12–13, 131, 208, 210, 350 (n. 28), 356 (n. 64); "King Cotton Diplomacy," 2–3, 9, 11–14, 15–16, 20, 31–32, 49, 84, 307, 322; lack of, as reason for Civil War intervention, 134–36, 150–51, 163, 168, 171, 191,

209, 234, 238, 239, 272–73, 300, 327–28 (n. 10), 350 (n. 32); Union blockade and, 56, 73–74, 76, 77, 100, 110, 118, 119–20, 130, 134, 136, 152–53, 157, 161, 208, 268, 304, 343 (n. 10), 348–49 (n. 18), 350 (nn. 28, 32). *See also* British recognition of Confederacy; France; French recognition of Confederacy; Great Britain

Cowley, Lord, 58, 100, 101, 129, 219, 241, 244, 246, 261; European intervention in Civil War and, 256, 258; recognition of Confederacy by France and, 133, 134, 135, 136, 138, 258, 295; Union blockade and, 134, 135

Crimean War, 25, 72, 96, 100, 169, 196, 205, 208, 217, 293

Crook, David P., 6

Cuba, 83–84, 87, 88, 299, 307, 309, 332–33 (n. 77), 337 (n. 1), 370 (n. 27)

Cushing, Caleb, 9, 44

Cutting, Francis B., 184

Dallas, George, 42

Dana, Richard Henry, Jr., 92

Davis, Jefferson, 19, 351 (n. 50); Benjamin secretary of state appointment and, 115–17; Bull Run, First, and, 61, 84; Confederacy as Republic started anew and, 1–2, 7, 9, 10; Confederacy recognition and, 10, 15–16, 84, 117, 152, 153, 278, 307, 321–22; Confederacy recognition and emancipation and, 318, 373–74 (n. 88); Confederacy recognition by France and, 277, 314, 315; Confederate commission to Europe and, 16–17, 84, 322, 331–32 (n. 73); Confederate navy and, 38, 63; Emancipation Proclamation and, 278; European financial loans to Confederacy and, 292–93; European intervention in Civil War and, 10–11, 177, 277, 291; Inaugural Address, vi, 9; "King Cotton Diplomacy" and, 13, 14, 15–16, 322; Mexico and, 277, 291, 313, 314, 315; Napoleon III and, 277, 291, 314; peace talks and, 317–18; slavery and, 223, 278, 318, 358 (n. 14); *Trent* affair and, 93, 108–9; Union blockade and, 161, 350 (n. 32); Union victories in Western Theater and, 115

Dayton, William L., 139, 151, 212, 244, 362
(n. 63); battlefield victories and, 285; Civil
War neutrality and, 54–55, 58; emancipation and, 122, 234; European intervention
in Civil War and, 77, 110, 255, 273, 275,
286–87, 302, 331 (n. 70); European intervention in Mexico and, 75–76, 77, 79, 126,
127; French intervention in Mexico and,
126, 128, 129, 299, 308, 312, 313, 315–16;
recognition of Confederacy as belligerent and, 131–32, 145, 167, 350 (n. 34);
recognition of Confederacy by France
and, 138, 250–51, 299, 304; recognition of
Confederacy by France and Britain and,
302, 303, 305; *Trent* affair and, 99, 105, 340
(n. 42); Union blockade and, 75, 110; as
Union diplomat to Paris, 54, 59, 285
De Bow's Review, 13
Declaration of Independence, 10, 52, 123,
186, 187–88, 279
Declaration of Paris (1856), 41, 43, 44, 65,
66, 68, 94, 133, 161, 260
De Leon, Edwin, 273, 348–49 (n. 18), 350
(n. 32); British recognition of Confederacy and, 152–60, 168, 170, 178, 319,
349 (n. 19); French recognition of
Confederacy and, 176–78, 349 (n. 19),
351 (n. 50)
Democratic Party, 16, 189, 259; Civil War
mediation and, 126, 210, 219, 254, 262,
264, 265, 288, 295, 316; congressional
election defeats of Republicans and, 166,
210, 219, 254, 263, 288; defeat in 1864
Presidential election, 317
Derby, Lord, 135, 136, 167, 238, 243, 374
(n. 91)
Diplomacy during the American Civil War
(Crook), 6, 375
Disraeli, Benjamin, 135, 136, 137, 163, 170
Donoughmore, Earl of, 319, 322, 374 (n. 91)
Dred Scott decision, 16
Drouyn de Lhuys, Edouard, 244, 368 (n. 5);
Civil War intervention and, 255, 256, 265,
274, 286–87, 363–64 (n. 9); Mexico and,
308, 310–11, 312, 313, 314, 316; Poland and,
293; recognition of Confederacy and, 256,
297, 298, 299, 302–3, 305, 306

Du Bellet, Paul Pecquet, 15, 328 (n. 19)
Dudley, Thomas Haines, 192–95, 196, 197,
198, 199

Economist, 12–14, 15, 32, 60, 62, 163, 169–70,
292, 302
Edwards, Samuel Price, 194, 195, 198
Emancipation: black enlistment in army
and, 281, 368 (n. 68); British views on,
30–31, 33, 38, 80–81, 99, 227; British workers' support for, 227–28, 280; Civil War
intervention and, 213, 228, 235, 241–42,
246–47, 277, 280, 282, 290, 322, 332–33
(n. 77); colonization and, 123, 161, 185,
231; Confederacy and, 28, 80–81, 99, 177,
222–23, 310; Confederacy recognition
and, 121, 122, 223, 318–19, 373–74 (n. 88);
confiscation and, 121, 123, 124, 151, 163,
182, 185; fear of slave rebellions and race
war with, 122, 123, 146, 185, 186, 229,
230–32, 235, 240, 243, 283; gradual, with
compensation, 121–22, 123, 124, 161, 163,
185, 222–23, 231, 237, 310; Union determination for, 100, 121–22, 151, 184–89, 206–7,
213, 282, 343 (n. 16), 349 (n. 25). *See also*
Border States
Emancipation Proclamation, 205, 249, 318;
British reaction to, 231–32, 278–80, 283,
304, 322, 359 (n. 27); Confederacy and,
230, 231, 277, 278, 282; Democratic Party
opposition to, 288, 289; first reading of
draft of, 184–85; French reaction to, 290,
291, 320, 360 (n. 36); Lincoln preparing to
declare, 228, 231, 248, 250, 251; as military
tool, 234, 235, 268, 281–82, 360–61 (n. 42),
362 (n. 61); preliminary, 228, 229–31, 279,
360 (n. 34)
Émile Erlanger and Company, 264, 291, 292,
304
Engels, Friedrich, 278
Enrica, 197–98. See also *Alabama*, CSS; "No.
290"
Erlanger loan, 2, 264, 291, 292–93, 295,
304–5, 369 (n. 17), 371 (n. 49), 375
Eugénie (empress), 78, 177
European Trading Company, 304
Everett, Edward, 69, 70–71, 92, 294

Fairfax, Donald, 89, 338 (n. 11)

Field, Cyrus, 276, 367 (n. 55)

Fifth Amendment of the Bill of Rights, 187

Flahault, Count, 129, 137–38, 175, 244

Florida, CSS, 69, 125, 193, 199

Forey, Elie Frédéric, 164

Forster, William E., 32, 33, 53, 118, 172, 237, 301

Fort Donelson, 115, 117, 118, 119, 139, 151, 153

Fort Henry, 115, 117, 139, 151, 153

Fort Sumter, 32, 38, 39, 48, 55

Fould, Achille, 131

France: Anglo-French relations at beginning of War and, 24–26, 27, 57, 58, 59–60, 72–73, 96, 100, 101; Civil War continuing neutrality and, 143, 323–24, 353 (n. 21); Civil War declaration of neutrality, 45, 54–55, 58, 332–33 (n. 77); Civil War intervention and, 55, 78, 79, 144, 153, 178, 265, 266, 270–77, 284, 285–88, 290, 291, 295–97, 349 (n. 19); Civil War mediation and, 170, 182, 207, 209–10, 212–13, 217, 218, 225, 241, 244, 249, 254, 255, 262; Confederacy attempts to bribe, with cotton, 152–53, 167, 292, 350 (n. 32); Confederate independence considered inevitable by, 54–55, 76, 130, 175; cotton and, 12, 16, 100, 105, 322, 336 (n. 51); cotton and Civil War intervention and, 72–74, 76–77, 99, 130–31, 133, 134, 135–36, 145–46, 168, 209, 272–73, 285, 287, 327–28 (n. 10); economic distress from lack of cotton, 161, 163, 272–73, 287, 350 (n. 29); economy of, 161, 170, 209, 285, 350 (n. 29); emancipation and, 231, 232, 290, 291, 320, 360 (n. 36); Mexico and, 3, 4, 75–76, 126, 127–30, 146, 165, 167–68, 175, 259, 299, 317, 318, 340 (n. 46), 345 (n. 36); navy of, 132, 133, 310; Poland and, 293; shipbuilding for Confederate navy and, 258–59, 260, 315, 353 (n. 21), 373 (n. 80); slavery opposition, 15, 55, 130, 134, 163, 176, 255, 323; *Trent* affair and, 94, 96, 99–101, 105, 110, 137; Union blockade and, 55, 110, 133, 134, 135, 138, 265, 295, 350 (n. 32); war with Austria, 259–60, 364 (n. 17). *See also* French recognition of Confederacy; Napoleon III

Frank Leslie's Illustrated Newspaper, 3

Fraser, Trenholm and Company, 192

Fredericksburg, 143, 281, 286

French recognition of Confederacy, 3, 6, 331 (n. 70), 331–32 (n. 73); battlefield victories and, 139, 140–41, 143, 144, 207, 285, 305; as belligerent, 55, 58, 59, 131–33, 145, 155, 167, 311, 350 (n. 34); Civil War armistice proposal and, 253, 257–60, 265–66, 277; Civil War intervention and, 253–54, 286; Civil War mediation and, 207, 209–10, 211–12, 288; cotton and, 16, 133, 163, 209, 255–56, 291–93, 295; De Leon and, 153, 176–78, 349 (n. 19), 351 (n. 50); emancipation and, 121, 223, 310, 318; with Great Britain, 131, 134–35, 136–37, 167, 175, 248, 250–51, 265–67, 295–97, 298–99, 300–301, 302–3, 304, 305–6; Lindsay meetings with Napoleon and, 133–38, 139, 295, 296, 297, 298–99, 300, 301–2, 305, 306–7; Mexico and, 76, 79, 80, 128, 164, 276–77, 290, 297, 299, 308, 309–10, 313, 314, 315, 316, 323; motion in British Parliament by Lindsay and, 148–50, 155, 159, 162–63, 164, 167, 168, 169, 170–74, 181; motion in British Parliament by Roebuck and, 295, 296, 300–302; Slidell meetings with Napoleon and, 164–69, 174–75, 176, 207, 256–60, 295–96, 298, 350 (n. 33), 370 (n. 27); Union blockade and, 73–74, 77, 83, 99, 104, 130–31, 142, 346 (n. 64); Union dread of, 42, 108, 212

Fugitive Slave Act of 1850, 85, 123

Garnett, James, 119, 226, 359 (n. 24)

Gasparin, Count Agénor-Etienne de, 189

Geoffroy, Louis de, 140

Gettysburg, 199, 285, 303, 304, 305, 313, 319

Gettysburg Address, 320

Gibraltar, 105

Gibson, Thomas Milner, 159

Gladstone, William E., 67, 68, 98, 132, 159, 330 (n. 52), 362 (n. 61); atrocities of Civil War and, 191, 202, 253, 276; battlefield victories and, 219–20, 224, 249; Civil War intervention and, 35, 210–11; Civil War intervention with French and, 271, 272, 276; Civil War mediation and, 162, 182, 191, 202, 204, 208, 218, 219–20, 225,

235–36, 247; Civil War neutrality and, 160, 238; speech supporting recognition of Confederacy by, 236–39, 240, 241, 244, 249, 257, 270, 361 (nn. 45, 51)

Globe, 315

Gorchakov, Prince Alexander, 100, 169, 234, 253, 255

Grand Design for the Americas, 164, 260, 294–96, 298, 308–12, 320, 369–70 (n. 22), 372 (n. 66)

Grant, Ulysses S., 115, 188–89, 303, 319, 346–47 (n. 66)

Granville, Earl, 98, 204, 225–26, 236, 249, 355 (n. 56), 359 (n. 21)

Great Britain: Anglo-French relations at beginning of War and, 24–26, 27, 57, 58, 59–60, 72–73, 96, 100, 101; Antietam and, 221–25, 239, 249, 358 (n. 15), 360–61 (n. 42); Bull Run, First, and, 61, 63–64, 67, 113, 162, 207; Bull Run, Second, and, 212, 215–16, 249, 319, 323, 357 (n. 2); Civil War continuing neutrality and, 114, 125–26, 144, 178, 191, 273–74, 307, 314, 316, 323–24, 353 (n. 21); Civil War declaration of neutrality, 42, 44–46, 47–51, 53–54, 55–57, 60, 61, 93, 332–33 (n. 77); Civil War intervention and, 23–24, 26–27, 31–33, 35–39, 42–44, 50–51, 53, 62–63, 70, 110, 119, 144, 153, 284, 290, 307; Civil War intervention and emancipation and, 228, 235, 241–42, 246–47, 280, 282, 322; Civil War mediation and, 146, 169–70, 173, 178, 181–82, 191, 201–2, 204, 207–8, 209–10, 223–24, 225–26, 235–36, 257–58, 358 (n. 17), 359 (n. 21), 360–61 (n. 42); Confederate independence considered inevitable by, 33, 38, 52, 60, 61, 62, 64, 69, 109, 113, 149, 181, 182; cotton and Civil War intervention and, 150–51, 171, 234, 238, 239–41, 268, 276, 327–28 (n. 10); cotton dependence, 12–14, 27, 29, 31, 33, 59, 74, 77, 103, 120, 210, 327 (n. 6); cotton surplus in, 13–14, 18–19, 48, 49, 57, 74, 119, 146, 160, 163, 226, 227; economic distress from lack of cotton, 33, 103, 137, 160–61, 162, 163, 171, 181–82, 208, 226–27, 234, 350 (n. 28), 356 (n. 64), 359 (n. 24); emancipation and, 207, 213,

231–32, 278–80, 283, 304, 359 (n. 27); European intervention in Mexico and, 128, 130, 163; fear of slave rebellions and race wars and, 120–21, 122–23, 182–83, 185, 235; lack of support for Confederacy, 174, 302, 322, 351 (n. 45); navy of, 95, 96, 99, 101, 105, 200, 355 (n. 47); New Orleans capture by Union and, 143–44, 145, 146, 173; Poland and, 293; self-interest of, 39, 42, 45, 52, 68, 80, 332–33 (n. 77), 353 (n. 21); shipbuilding for Confederate navy and, 44, 68–69, 125, 191–201, 290–91, 353 (n. 21), 354 (n. 40), 355 (n. 47); slavery opposition, 11, 14–15, 23, 29, 30–31, 33, 36, 51, 70, 99, 118, 125, 172, 204, 210–11, 227–28, 279–80, 322, 323, 330 (n. 45), 337 (n. 67); textile industry of, 12–14, 59, 119–20, 143, 150, 163, 327 (n. 6), 350 (n. 28), 356 (n. 64); textile industry of, support for Union, 208–9, 227–28, 280, 322, 328 (n. 13), 348 (n. 13), 351 (n. 45), 356–57 (n. 65); *Trent* affair and, 83, 88–91, 94–104, 110, 118, 170; Union antipathy, 80, 152, 170, 329–30 (n. 38); Union blockade and, 42–43, 51, 53, 56–57, 103–4, 109, 110, 111, 113, 117–18, 134, 136, 146, 159, 161, 268, 271, 290, 343 (n. 10); war possibility during *Trent* affair, 92, 93, 94–95, 96–97, 98–99, 101, 102–3, 104, 105, 110, 113, 340 (n. 38); war possibility with Civil War intervention, 36, 58, 59, 66–67, 71, 173–74, 183, 201–2, 233–34, 236, 243, 301, 323. *See also* British recognition of Confederacy; Canada; Palmerston, Lord; Russell, Lord John

Greeley, Horace, 91–92, 206, 222; Civil War mediation and, 288–89, 317

Gregory, William H., 114–15, 173, 280–81; motion in Parliament to recognize Confederacy and, 31, 32, 36, 53, 118; Union blockade and, 117–19

Grey, George, 236, 245, 248, 263

Gros, Baron, 298, 302–3, 305, 306

Grote, George, 96

Gurowski, Adam, 92, 97, 108, 278

Haiti, 120, 161, 336 (n. 51)

Hamel, Felix, 194, 195, 199

Hammond, Edmund, 170, 191, 195, 205, 207, 224, 231, 239
Hammond, James H., 9, 11–12
Harcourt, William Vernon, 107, 267, 275, 365 (n. 34)
Harding, John, 197, 198
Harper's Weekly, 3
Hay, John, 30, 72, 317
Hercules, HMS, 197
Hill, A. P., 221
Historicus. *See* Harcourt, William Vernon
Holcombe, James P., 317
Hotze, Henry, 111, 122, 137, 351 (n. 50), 365 (n. 34); British textile workers and, 208, 209; *Index* publication and, 68, 153, 176, 335–36 (n. 42); recognition of Confederacy and, 118, 297, 301
Hunter, Robert M. T., 93, 115, 142, 317, 318
Hurlbert, William Henry, 309
Huse, Caleb, 44, 332 (n. 76)

Illustrated London News, 238, 302
Index, 68, 153, 176, 275, 335–36 (n. 42)
International law: civil wars and, 4, 40, 45, 51, 60–61, 70–72; European intervention in Mexico and, 79; neutrality and, 5–6, 40, 45, 48, 51–54, 61, 69, 114; nonbelligerent nations halting war and, 6, 70–72, 218, 253, 262, 267–70; recognition of independence of rebellious states and, 5–6, 248, 267–70, 365 (n. 34), 365–66 (n. 36); self-interest and, 10–11, 322; *Trent* affair and, 83, 88, 89, 91–94, 95, 97–101, 106–8, 338 (n. 9), 340 (n. 42), 341–42 (n. 66), 342 (n. 68); Union blockade and, 25, 26–27, 39–41, 44, 45, 48, 54, 55–57, 69, 104, 130–31, 333 (n. 10), 334 (n. 17), 343 (n. 10)
Isabel II (queen of Spain), 126
Italy, 40, 129, 153, 167, 212, 244, 254, 256, 258, 294, 362 (n. 63), 364 (n. 17)

Jackson, Stonewall, 221
Jewett, William Cornell, 288
Johnson, Andrew, 281, 319
Johnson, Reverdy, 162, 349 (n. 26)
Journal of St. Petersburg, 274
Juárez, Benito, 75, 165, 167, 313, 320

Kansas-Nebraska Act of 1854, 85
Kearsarge, USS, 200–201
Kenner, Duncan F., 318–19, 373–74 (n. 88)
Kent, James, 88
King Cotton Diplomacy: Foreign Relations of the Confederate States of America (Owsley), 6–7, 375

La France, 244, 299
La France, le Mexique et les États-Confédérés, 308–9
Laird, John, 193, 194
Laird Brothers of Liverpool, 192, 193, 194, 195, 196, 199, 201
Lawley, Francis, 236, 275, 361 (n. 45)
Layard, Austen Henry, 199, 239, 307
Lee, Robert E., 142, 151, 216, 217; Antietam and, 220–21, 224, 226, 228, 229, 230, 239, 264; Appomattox and, 319, 373 (n. 80); Bull Run, Second, and, 221, 319, 323; Chancellorsville and, 291; Gettysburg and, 285, 303
Le Mexique, ancien et moderne (Chevalier), 309, 310
Leopold (king of Belgium), 126, 203, 258, 262–63, 276, 355 (n. 54), 373 (n. 76)
Lewis, George Cornewall, 68, 107, 125, 224, 357 (n. 2), 362 (n. 62); Civil War intervention and, 160, 242–44, 245, 247, 248–50, 267–70, 275, 282, 324, 362 (n. 60), 365 (n. 34), 368 (n. 70); Civil War intervention with French and, 267, 271–72, 366 (n. 42); Civil War mediation and, 205, 233, 236, 269–70; Civil War neutrality and, 267–68, 269; cotton and, 33, 114, 226; emancipation and, 243, 268, 362 (n. 61); Mexico and, 78–79; recognition of Confederacy and, 159, 248, 267–70, 365 (nn. 34–35), 365–66 (n. 36), 366 (nn. 37–38); *Trent* affair and, 95, 96, 97, 98–99
Liberia, 161
Lincoln, Abraham, 253; Antietam and, 220–21, 222–23, 228, 230; assassination, 319; battlefield victories and, 143–44, 151, 303; British neutrality and, 45, 47–48, 49, 50, 53–54, 60, 219; Civil War reconciliation plan by French and, 286, 288,

289–90; Declaration of Independence and, 187–88; as diplomat, 21, 322; emancipation and, 151, 162, 182–83, 184–89, 203, 206–7, 213, 227, 235, 239–42, 276–77, 343 (n. 16), 349 (n. 25); Emancipation Proclamation, 184–85, 205, 250, 251, 268, 277–80, 281–82, 283, 290, 304, 320, 360–61 (n. 42); Emancipation Proclamation, preliminary, 228, 229–32, 234, 248, 279; European intervention in Civil War and, 10–11, 27–28, 36–38, 146–48, 178–79, 189, 190, 203, 209–10, 216, 261, 274, 306; European intervention in Mexico and, 127, 128, 129–30, 167–68, 350 (n. 34); foreign affairs inexperience, 20–22, 322; gradual emancipation with compensation and, 121–22, 123, 124, 161, 163, 185; Inaugural Address, vii, 10, 29, 123–24, 186, 344 (n. 24); McClellan, removal of from command and, 264, 265, 365 (n. 31); Mexico and, 308, 311, 312, 313, 314–16; Mure papers and, 66, 68; Napoleon III and, 289, 294, 313; peace talks and, 316–18; personal qualities, 20–21, 22; playing down issue of slavery, 28, 29, 55, 63, 69, 71, 124, 182–83, 322; religion and, 186–87; Russia and, 169, 205, 234, 293–94, 367 (n. 51), 369 (n. 19); Seward and, 21, 22, 27–28, 36–38, 281, 290, 329 (n. 36); slavery, elevation of issue and, 120, 121–22, 123, 161–62, 182, 183, 185–88, 208–9, 222, 228–30, 234, 276–77, 283; slavery and, 100, 172, 189, 203, 206–7, 211, 344 (n. 19), 353 (n. 15); *Trent* affair and, 91, 92–93, 97, 98, 101, 102, 104–6, 107, 109, 341 (n. 57); Union army and, 54, 164, 189, 211, 281, 368 (n. 68); Union blockade and, 39–41, 45, 48, 53–54, 56–58, 64, 261; Union preservation and, 1, 4, 7, 10, 20, 21, 28, 69, 70, 71, 123–24, 143, 162, 182, 186, 206–7, 277, 289, 316; war possibility with Civil War intervention and, 66–67, 323. *See also* Union

Lindsay, William S., 99, 259, 292; meetings with Napoleon for Confederacy recognition, 133–38, 139, 295, 296, 297, 298–99, 300, 301–2, 305, 306–7; motions in British Parliament for Confederacy recognition,

148–50, 155, 159, 162–63, 164, 167, 168, 169, 170–74, 181
Locke, John, 187
Logan Act of 1799, 289
London Emancipation Society, 172
Louisiana, 168, 291, 294, 296
Lowell, James Russell, 107
Lyons, Richard B., 36, 37, 63, 64, 81, 113, 125, 145; British neutrality and, 58, 59, 132; Civil War intervention by British and, 23–24, 25–27, 266, 280, 365 (n. 31); Civil War mediation and, 175, 191, 225, 244, 261, 264, 266, 288; cotton and, 191, 208; European intervention in Civil War and, 73–74, 77, 100, 139–40, 143, 146–47, 151, 265–66, 272, 274; on leave in Great Britain, 147, 149, 162, 349 (n. 26), 360 (n. 34), 363 (n. 2), 365 (n. 31); Mure papers and, 65, 67, 68; slavery and, 23, 320; slave trade and, 122–23, 163, 344 (n. 19); *Trent* affair and, 83, 94, 98, 99, 100, 103, 104, 106, 109, 341 (n. 57); Union blockade and, 27, 40, 41, 42, 57, 114, 137

Madison, James, 106, 107
Magenta, battle of, 259–60, 364 (n. 17)
Maguire, Matthew, 196
Mallory, Stephen R., 19, 93
Malta, 105, 365–66 (n. 36)
Mann, Ambrose D., 17, 94, 162, 236; Napoleon III and, 256, 294, 313, 373 (n. 76)
Marx, Karl, 209, 278
Mason, James M.: battlefield victories and, 115, 118; British recognition of Confederacy and, 84, 134, 148, 162, 167, 170, 171, 173, 174, 175, 189–91, 295, 296, 301, 366 (n. 37); Civil War mediation and, 163, 182, 260, 276, 280, 364 (n. 11); as Confederate diplomat, 83–84, 87, 114–15, 136–37, 138, 152, 153, 159, 221, 292–93; cotton and, 130, 161, 162, 293; emancipation and, 318, 319, 322, 373–74 (n. 88); mission of, 83–84, 87, 88, 92, 97, 108, 307; personal qualities, 84–86; recognition of Confederacy and, 121, 346 (n. 64), 346–47 (n. 66); release of during *Trent* affair, 105–7, 109, 110; *Trent* affair and, 83–84, 88–89, 91–99, 101–2, 105–10,

337 (n. 1), 338 (nn. 9–11), 341–42 (n. 66); Union blockade and, 117, 161, 261

Maximilian Joseph, Archduke Ferdinand: Mexico and, 77–78, 126, 129–30, 294, 308, 310, 311, 312–16, 320, 323, 344 (n. 29), 345 (n. 36); recognition of Confederacy and, 308, 310, 312–16

McClellan, George B., 101, 217; Antietam and, 220–21, 222–23, 224, 230, 264; Bull Run, Second, and, 211, 221; as Democratic Presidential candidate, 317; emancipation and, 230; Peninsula campaign and, 141, 143, 149, 151, 152, 162, 170, 173, 184, 203, 205, 230; propaganda about in Great Britain, 171, 172, 173; relieved of command, 264, 265, 365 (n. 31)

McLeod, Alexander, 22, 33, 329 (n. 27)

Memminger, Christopher G., 19, 292

Mercier, Henri, 26, 76, 105, 113, 132, 293; Civil War armistice proposal and, 225, 234, 264–65, 302; Civil War mediation and, 152, 175, 176, 182, 203, 209–10, 212–13; Civil War reconciliation plan by French and, 287, 288, 289; European intervention in Civil War and, 58, 59, 73–74, 77, 100, 146, 254, 256, 263, 266, 274, 363–64 (n. 9); French recognition of Confederacy and, 16, 73–74, 147, 175, 305; Mexico and, 127, 128, 314, 315, 316; peace mission to Confederacy and, 139–43, 346 (n. 64), 346–47 (n. 66)

Merrimack. See Virginia, CSS

Messrs. Fawcett, Preston and Company, 192–93

Metternich, Prince Richard, 77

Mexican War, 15, 86, 256

Mexico, 39, 370 (n. 27); European intervention and, 3, 4, 27, 69, 75–80, 101, 126–30, 163, 262, 340 (n. 46); French intervention and, 3, 4, 75–76, 126, 127–30, 146, 165, 167–68, 175, 259, 299, 317, 318, 340 (n. 46), 345 (n. 36), 350 (n. 34); monarchical government in, 164, 309–10, 311, 312–13, 316, 320, 323, 344 (n. 29); Napoleon III and Confederate recognition, 276–77, 290, 294–96, 297, 299, 307, 308–16, 323, 372 (nn. 63, 66); Napoleon III and impe-

rial interest in, 255–56, 266–67, 273, 285, 286–87, 291, 293, 306, 319–20; War of the Reform, 69

Militia Act, 151

Miller, Thomas, 197–98

Milne, Alexander, 95, 98, 99

Milner-Gibson, Thomas, 204, 236

Mississippi River, 115, 144, 221, 311

Mocquard, Jean François, 177

Moir, James, 89

Moniteur, 273, 302, 308, 316, 358 (n. 15)

Monitor, USS, 125

Monroe, James, 6, 106, 107

Monroe Doctrine, 75, 154, 315

Moran, Benjamin, 94, 125, 199, 348 (n. 6), 356 (n. 59); battlefield victories and, 115, 143, 149, 152, 224, 358 (n. 15); British recognition of Confederacy and, 171–72, 173, 240; Civil War intervention with French and, 274; Civil War mediation and, 149, 206

Morgan, Edward, 194

Morning Herald (London), 215

Morning Post (London), 32, 33, 95, 203, 215

Morning Star (London), 279

Morny, Duke of, 131, 177

Morrill Tariff, 18, 31, 62

Motley, John Lothrop, 311

Mure, Robert, 64, 65–68

Murfreesboro, 281

Napoleon (prince), 73, 177

Napoleon I, 72, 221

Napoleon III (emperor), 16, 362 (n. 63); Civil War armistice proposal and, 257, 258, 273, 275, 276, 286, 287–88, 289, 296, 298, 302, 306, 307; Civil War intervention and, 55, 72–74, 131–38, 145, 146, 164–69, 177, 244, 253, 285–86, 346–47 (n. 66); Civil War intervention with Great Britain and, 178, 207, 257, 258, 262–63, 272, 295, 298, 300–302, 306; Civil War mediation and, 182, 203, 209, 254, 255–62, 270–72, 363 (n. 1), 364 (n. 22); Civil War military intervention and, 257, 258, 259, 261, 266–67, 269, 276, 306, 363–64 (n. 9); Civil War reconciliation plan and, 286–88,

Trent, HMS, 83, 88–89, 90, 91, 92, 107, 341–42 (n. 66)

Tropic Wind (British schooner), 57

Twisleton, Edward, 96, 97, 108

Two Years before the Mast (Dana), 92

Uncle Tom's Cabin (Stowe), 15

Union: Antietam and, 220–21, 224, 228, 229, 230, 233, 234, 239, 249, 251; Appomattox and, 319; battlefield victories and, 185, 186, 189, 191, 213, 304, 305, 313, 317, 319, 323; British shipbuilding for Confederate navy and, 125, 191–201, 353 (n. 21), 354 (n. 40); British textile workers' support of, 227–28, 280, 322, 351 (n. 45), 356–57 (n. 65); Bull Run, First, and, 61–64, 73, 74, 80, 92, 93, 162, 212, 219; Bull Run, Second, and, 211, 212, 215, 216, 219, 224; Chancellorsville, 291, 295, 300; Civil War mediation and, 165–66, 169, 205, 217–18, 224, 233–36, 246; congressional elections of 1862 and, 166, 209, 210, 219, 243, 254, 263, 265, 288; Declaration of Independence and, 4, 10, 123, 186–88; European financial loans and, 2, 61–62, 292; Fort Sumter and, 32, 38, 39, 48, 55; Fredericksburg and, 143, 281, 286; Gettysburg and, 199, 285, 303, 304, 305, 313, 319, 320; Mexico and, 69, 75–80, 126–30, 146, 167–68, 273, 297, 299, 306, 307, 308, 311–19; *Monitor* victory and, 125; Morrill Tariff and, 18, 31, 62; navy of, 1, 40, 41, 56, 58, 95, 118, 174; New Orleans capture by, 143–44, 145, 146, 147, 148, 149, 153, 154, 173, 349 (n. 26); peace talks and, 316–18; Peninsula campaign and, 141, 143, 149, 151, 152, 162, 164, 170, 173, 184, 203, 205, 207, 230; playing down issue of slavery, 3, 28, 29, 55, 62, 63, 69, 71, 120, 182–83, 283, 322; preservation of, as only outcome of Civil War, 1, 7, 10, 60, 70, 71, 123–24, 143, 186, 191, 206–7, 243, 245, 246, 289, 316, 318, 329–30 (n. 38); Russia and, 169, 206, 254–55, 257, 274, 293–94, 307, 367 (n. 51), 369 (n. 19); Vicksburg, 199, 295, 301, 303, 304, 305, 313, 319; war possibility during *Trent* affair, 92, 93, 94, 95, 96, 101–3, 104, 105, 109, 113; war possibility with European intervention in Civil War, 36, 58, 59, 66–67, 71, 173–74, 183, 201–2, 233–34, 236, 243, 301, 323; Western Theater victories, 115, 117, 139, 143, 151–52, 153, 188–89, 219, 281, 303, 346–47 (n. 66), 347 (n. 3); wheat exports, 14, 48, 50, 178, 238, 327–28 (n. 10), 351–52 (n. 54); Yorktown and, 141, 143, 347 (n. 3). *See also* British recognition of Confederacy; Cotton; Emancipation; French recognition of Confederacy; Lincoln, Abraham; Seward, William H.

Union blockade, 115, 126, 155, 257; armistice proposal and, 271; blockade-running and, 69, 94, 118, 200, 208, 291, 304; British neutrality and, 53–54, 55–57, 99, 100, 114, 132, 133; effectiveness of, 141, 142, 154, 156, 295, 343 (n. 10), 347 (n. 69); European challenges and, 75, 103–4, 110, 111, 117–19, 135, 136–37, 138, 146, 159, 161, 165, 243, 346 (n. 64); Lincoln proclaiming, 39–43, 44–45, 48; port closures before official, 25, 26–27, 56–58, 64, 260–61; recognition of Confederacy and, 225–26, 243, 265–66; *Trent* affair and, 83–91, 113. *See also* Cotton; France; Great Britain; International law

U.S. Constitution, 5, 54, 56, 344 (n. 24); abolition of slavery and, 4, 10, 122, 123, 187–88, 277; Confederate and Union interpretation of, 10, 47–48, 187–88; Declaration of Independence and, 186–88; Thirteenth Amendment, 320

U.S. Senate Foreign Relations Committee, 93, 207

U.S. Supreme Court, 45, 89, 334 (n. 17)

Vallandigham, Clement, 288

Vane-Tempest, Lord Adolphus, 172

Vattel, Emmerich de, 40, 51, 71, 88, 91, 106, 107, 108, 218

Vicksburg, 199, 295, 301, 303, 304, 305, 313, 319

Victoria (queen), 38, 44, 95, 96, 98, 203, 204, 217, 258, 355 (n. 54)

Villiers, Charles P., 204, 226, 236

Virginia, CSS, 125